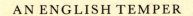

AN ENGLISH TEMPER

By the same Author

Only Connect – On Culture and Communication
The BBC Reith Lectures 1971

Speaking to Each Other:
Vol 1 About Society
Vol 2 About Literature

The Uses of Literacy

Auden: An Introductory Essay

An Idea and Its Servants:
UNESCO from Within

AN ENGLISH TEMPER

ESSAYS ON EDUCATION, CULTURE AND COMMUNICATIONS

RICHARD HOGGART

1982
CHATTO & WINDUS
LONDON

Published by
Chatto & Windus Ltd
40 William IV Street
London WC2N 4DF

*

Clarke, Irwin & Co Ltd
Toronto

BRITISH LIBRARY
CATALOGUING IN PUBLICATION DATA
Hoggart, Richard
An English temper.
1. Education — Great Britain
2. Culture
I. Title
370′.941   LA632

ISBN 0-7011-2581-0

Printed in Great Britain by
Ebenezer Baylis & Son Limited
The Trinity Press, Worcester, and London

CONTENTS

ACKNOWLEDGMENTS

Virtually all these essays have been published before, though not usually in these versions nor always with the same titles. I acknowledge the following sources of earlier publication or presentation. The place of publication was London unless otherwise stated.

'The Role of the Teacher', in *Teaching On Equal Terms,* ed. J. Rogers, BBC, 1969.

'Higher Education and Personal Life':
- For the Quail Roost Seminar, North Carolina, December 1968.
- In *Higher Education: Demand and Response,* ed. W.R. Niblett, Tavistock Publications, 1969.

'The Uncertain Criteria of Deprivation':
- For a conference on literacy at the University of Edmonton, Alberta, October 1976.
- In *Education for Uncertainty,* ed. E.J. King, 1979.
- In *Curriculum Context,* ed. A.V. Kelly, 1980.

'Class Bias in British Education', in *The Observer,* 13th January 1980.

'The Student Movement and its Effects':
- For the SRHE Annual Conference, December 1978.
- In *Proceedings* of the Conference, 1979.
- In *Political Quarterly,* Vol. 50 No. 2, April – June, 1979.

'After Expansion – the Case for Diversity':
- For the Annual Conference, American Association for Higher Education, Chicago, March 1978.
- *Occasional Paper, No. 1,* Advisory Council for Adult and Continuing Education, Leicester, 1978.

'Leisure and Education in the Eighties': lecture on BBC-TV 2 in the series 'Work and Leisure', Royal Institution, February 1980.

'The Importance of Literacy':
- For a conference on Literacy at City College, CUNY, New York, April 1980.

Acknowledgments

'Leisure and the Eighties':
- In *Journal of Basic Writing*, CUNY, New York, 1981.
- 'Matthew Arnold, HMI':
- For BBC Radio Three, 22 March 1980.
- Small extract in *The Listener*, 27 March 1980.

'On Language and Literacy Today':
- For a workshop on language and literacy in Canada, for SSHRC of Canada, Toronto, October 1979.
- In Report of the Conference Proceedings, 1980.
- In *The Literary Review*, 9 February 1980, Edinburgh.

'The Autobiography of Henry Adams':
- For BBC Radio Three: 'What Books I Please', 4 November 1980.
- In *New Universities Quarterly*, Vol. 35 No. 3, Summer 1981.

'George Orwell and the Art of Biography':
- For BBC Radio Three, 23 November 1980.
- In *The Listener*, 27 November 1980.

'Allen Lane and Penguins':
- For the memorial service to Allen Lane, August 1970.
- Privately printed as a pamphlet, 1970, Cambridge.

'Humanistic Studies and Mass Culture':
- For a conference at Bellagio, 1969, on 'Theory in Humanistic Studies', organised by *Daedalus*.
- In *Daedalus*, Journal of the American Academy of Arts and Sciences, Vol. 99, No. 2, Spring 1970, Boston, Mass.

'Fashionable Conformity or Cultural Development':
- For a Council of Europe symposium on 'The Future of the Performing Arts', Athens, March 1976.
- In *New Universities Quarterly*, Vol 31, No. 1, Winter 1976 – 77.

'Excellence and Access':
- For a Gulbenkian Conference of Secretaries-General of Commonwealth Arts Councils, University of Kent, April 1979.
- In *New Universities Quarterly*, Vol 33, No. 4, Autumn 1979.

'The Future of Broadcasting':
- For a VPRO symposium on the future of the Dutch broadcasting system, Hilversum, April 1979.
- In *De Toekomst van de Nederlandse Omroep*, 1979.

'The Mass Media and One-Way Flow':
- 8th Annual STC Communications Lecture, London, May 1978.
- Published by STC (Standard Telephone & Cables Ltd) as a pamphlet, 1978.

'Culture and its Ministers': in *Art, Politics and Will*, essays in honour of Lionel Trilling, ed. Q. Anderson, S. Donadio and S. Marcus. Basic Books, New York, 1977.

Acknowledgments

I also acknowledge with thanks permission to quote as follows:

T. S. Eliot: excerpt from 'Little Gidding', *Four Quartets,* Faber and Faber and Harcourt Brace Jovanovitch (New York); in 'The Autobiography of Henry Adams'; excerpt from *Notes towards the Definition of Culture,* Faber and Faber and Harcourt Brace Jovanovitch, (New York); in 'Humanistic Studies and Mass Culture'.

Edwin Muir: excerpt from 'The Good Town', Faber and Faber and Oxford University Press, New York; in 'Humanistic Studies and Mass Culture'.

Su Braden: excerpt from *Artists and People,* Routledge & Kegan Paul; in 'Excellence and Access'.

Tariq Ali: excerpts from 'Culture, the Media and Workers' Democracy', in *Media, Politics and Culture,* Macmillan; in 'The Student Movement and its Effects' and in 'Excellence and Access'.

E. P. Thompson and *Stand* (Newcastle) for excerpts from *Stand,* Vol. 20, No. 2; in 'Excellence and Access'.

FOR CATHARINE CARVER

*A fine editor and
a fine friend*

PREFACE

These essays represent about a third of my published work in, chiefly, the second half of the Seventies. Naturally, they tend to be the larger pieces. To be more exact, four date from the end of the Sixties and just missed being in an earlier collection.

That there are no essays from 1970 – 75 is easily explained. I was in that half-decade far too busy trying to be an international civil servant (in cultural and intellectual affairs). But it will be plain that material in some of the essays was gathered during those five years. More important and more pervasive: the experiences I had with UNESCO have affected my whole approach in most things I've subsequently written. So these pieces can fairly be said to emerge from the decade as a whole.

Roughly speaking, the essays in the first section – on Education – are trying to come to grips once again with British education, especially higher education, and trying to indicate where it's stuck and how it might go forward again. The essays in the second section – Culture and Communications – start with a small group on individuals who were, through print or in person, important to my own cultural understanding and who are in different ways remarkable indicators of the cultural stresses of their times.

Those are followed by essays on the arts and modern societies and on the mass media. These groups have both national and international frames of reference. All the essays have been edited for this book, some heavily.

I now realise that I've now been practising the long essay, which sometimes starts life as a formal lecture, for almost a quarter of a century. It's a teasing form and more demanding than is generally recognised. I like some of its disciplines. But it is also constricting and constraining. My next book will start at page 1 and go right on to the end.

As always, I owe a great deal to a number of people. I particularly want to thank the members of the Reprographic Unit at Goldsmiths' College, Catharine Carver, Ruth Scott, Roy Shaw and my wife, Mary.

R.H.
1981

EDUCATION

THE ROLE
OF THE TEACHER

I believe, from thinking about my own temptations, that the main occupational risk for an adult education teacher is intellectual flabbiness. You are not sufficiently often challenged. Your colleagues are likely to be scattered far and wide, or on different shifts. You don't meet them in regular seminars or simply over coffee from day to day, or argue with them at staff meetings about the point of the examination questions you propose setting or the shape of a syllabus or a reading-list. Many public examinations are hard to defend and liberal adult education is the better for being without them. But one thing they may provide for the tutor himself: a simple, practical check on the coherence, level and progress of his teaching.

The situation is made trickier because students in adult education tend to be deferential. They look up to the tutor too readily and this tempts some of us into over-easy relationships, relationships not firm enough for good teaching. In adult education conferences, one can often recognise tutors of long standing. They look nice but a bit unchallenged, a bit too relaxed in their friendliness. They tend to suck pipes ruminatively, to wear shapeless pepper-and-salt tweeds, to have pleasant crinkly smiles. They are not aggressive or overstrained, they don't puff nervously on cigarettes, they don't look as though they have been trained in public relations. They look very decent and helpful. You can visualise them sitting on the edge of the table in front of an adult class, swinging their legs, genuinely friendly, not at all pushing, saying: 'It all depends what you mean by . . .' or 'That's a very good point, Mrs Johnson, but I wonder whether you've considered . . .'. Even more than most teaching, adult education invites its tutors to a range of attractive self-deceptions, forms of role-playing. The worst forms are the nicest because they encourage attitudes towards the students and their abilities which, though well-

3

intentioned, are forms of patronage. They don't lead you to test the students or yourself to the top of their or your bent. The price you pay, over the years, for this too-easily adopted role of kindly sage, this endless fence-sitting, is intellectual slackness.

Inevitably, there are many variants. The most obvious is the man who is over-fond of his own voice, who too obviously 'likes to hear himself speak'. A smile appears on his face as he talks, as though he is actually tasting the sound of his own rolling periods; or you can recognise the element in yourself by the feeling of almost physical pleasure when you are led into that kind of rhetoric. It's like finding you can fly, for a few yards. Those of us who were brought up in the Nonconformist chapel tradition are especially at risk here – the combination of rhetoric, earnestness and the urge towards charismatic relationships is heady. Welshmen – chapel, plus song, plus rich deep voices – are the worst risks of all. The Danes, with their Grundtvigian background – the Folk, the Land and the Word – are high risks too. Welshmen in Danish adult education summer schools are formidably rhetorical personalities.

The urge towards a generalised charismatic relationship, that way of showing-off one's personality which ends in the rhetoric of a lay preacher, is the strongest of all temptations. You have to learn to suspect those evenings when you feel a throb come into your voice, your eye seems bright and eager, and the students look up at you with a touch of wondering admiration. Two types of teacher – in any kind of education, but adult education is an especially dangerous area in these ways – should particularly be suspected: the charismatic, an imaginative pied piper of Hamelin; and the systems-builder, an intellectual pied piper of Hamelin, who offers a complete guide and system to experience. Men who are a combination of both – some types of Marxist are like that – are the most dubious. Any teacher who begins to acquire fans, disciples, followers, ought to suspect himself until he has examined as honestly as he can the nature of these relationships. He may well be getting between the students and their own hold on the subject. We should be glad to be judged by the degree to which our students stand on their own feet, out of our shadows. Which means we have to try to make sure they retain their freedom to be critical of us. Or, if that sounds too grand, ironic about us and towards us.

Because we are so little tested from outside, by day-to-day contact with colleagues, we have to try to frame our lives so that we are faced with challenges, not over-worryingly but steadily. The most obvious way to ensure this is to contribute to one's subject itself (to the subject, not simply to the teaching of the subject), so that we are in contact, even though at long distance or longish intervals, with very good minds in that subject. Or we may be able to attend regular staff seminars at the nearest university. Much more important is the challenge that can come from within the class itself, from really looking at and listening to the class members. Once we have taken the measure of the temptation to get swollen-headed in teaching adult education classes and begun really to look at and listen to our students, we discover that in any class there are several people who are in some ways actually or potentially better equipped than we are. Which comes back to the point above, about not getting between them and the experience. We have to do what we can to give them the chance to develop in their own best way – though we can know very little about what that best way may be for any one student, and our particular contribution to it will be and ought to be relatively minor.

Again, this comes back to making the atmosphere in the class consistently critically alert, rather than pally or admiring. We have to break the slightly smothering caul of respect for the tutor, so that students can criticise our work honestly and openly. I don't mean aggressively, though I would rather have some aggression than pussy-footing. It is hard enough for a student to be articulate in class-discussion without having one hand tied behind his back by the wrong kind of respect or friendliness towards the tutor. I was given a chance to learn this particular lesson early, since in my very first class-meeting, a young woman – experienced in the classes of a good older tutor – stood up when the 'discussion period' began and frankly criticised the way I had conducted the first hour. I had read a prepared lecture, out of nervousness.

We and they need to be involved, testing each other all the time, not working from stock materials or stock positions and doings, without being in the last resort personally involved on either side, without having our sense of self-identity bound up with the class. There are many ways in which that kind of unhealthy relationship can develop, for both students and tutors. We have to give the students room, so far as we are able to help here, to steer clear of the wrong relationships, so that they can find their own intellectual identities better. Then the kinds of class-and-tutor or individual-and-tutor relationships which *can* be healthy and useful may also emerge.

5

They will only emerge from this more direct and honest base, not from being encouraged as ends in themselves, or vaguely regarded as the necessary foundations for good teaching and learning. Brought in too soon or too directly, they are false foundations.

It is as well to realise, first, how *little* one can do in any one class meeting or one session. This wonderfully disposes the mind towards working-out what best one can do and how to do it. It also inhibits that sort of breast-feeding, that over-maternalism characteristic of enthusiastic but vague or nervous teachers. We all know about the pointlessness of cramming students with facts. We recognise less the dangers of smothering them with our own attitudes and responses. Some English teaching, for instance, is so backward that it does attempt to cram data into students. The more characteristic defect of English Literature teaching is an unthinking or selfish attempt to transmit attitudes, prescribed opinions. There should be no received opinions or attitudes. Every book studied is a new book, being read for the first time. More in English Literature than in other subjects the old saw applies: you are not giving something; you are trying to make something happen. What you can help to happen, in any one class-meeting of two hours, may seem little but can be important – a new way of looking, a new insight, a better grasp on ordering and so on – or the beginnings of such qualities; they may only be retained, and made part of the student's frame of mind, after several weeks or months.

If we work on these lines, we find that most of our regular students can take as much as we can give, so long as we avoid those devices, those ways of making the subject a mystique, which are really ways of hiding behind it, of refusing to come out into the open for fear of being challenged. If we bend our minds to them, most things can in the end be said fairly simply, at least the kind of things most of us are trying to say. Most things we have to say can be stripped down to understandable elements without loss. In adult teaching, most technical languages can be dispensed with; or, where they are necessary, they can be slowly built up and justified throughout a session. Virtually all knowing allusions or name-dropping of references can be relegated to the syllabus or the book-lists. There is never any justification for starting a sentence: 'As Chomsky says, of course ...'. or 'We recall, naturally, that Wittgenstein argued ...'. We don't recall any such thing, neither the students nor us. *They* didn't know it before; and it probably didn't come to *us* lightly, from our well-stocked minds – we noticed it when we were working with our books at our desks. Once stripped down in this way, many of our points begin to seem obvious or tautologous – which is a gain. It is a gain for us as intellectuals and as teachers, and a gain for the students. It makes the odds in the classroom more even, between us and them; and it makes the odds between different kinds of students, graduate and non-graduate, more even too. This procedure stretches both us and the students. But if we do lose any students by it, they are as likely as not to be graduates who treasure their degrees and tend to feel superior to, say, a motor mechanic or a secondary-modern-school housewife in the class; and who find by this method, though their degree has given them the ability to move among received opinions, that out in the open where mind and feelings come freshly to a text, they have no special ability and may even find the work harder than those not shaped by study for a degree.

Obviously, to work like this requires careful preparation. Adult education teaching is not a soft option, fag-end work we can tuck in somehow, no matter how tired we may be. As much if not more than other forms of teaching, it demands energy if it is to be done well. It is a delicate balancing act, and if we are tired we will simply fall off. I am always surprised to discover that roughly the same sort of material with roughly the same sort of group can go either very well or very badly – according to my own grip on any particular evening, my own tiredness or freshness.

Throughout, I am thinking chiefly of the problems of teachers in the arts and humanities. Probably teachers of languages and crafts are less tempted to these kinds of attitudes and intellectual postures. From such experience as I have had, though, I would risk this generalisation: that if the main temptation of the humanities tutor is over-stylishness, that of the teacher of more straightforwardly content-bound subjects is an *inadequacy* of style. There is an over-tight sticking to 'the book', to what has to be 'got through.' Here, the main complaint among students is of just plain dullness; and it probably stems from both a lack of confidence and a failure to realise – a failure not at all helped by the general climate – that the teaching of even the most 'routine' subjects need not be at all routine, is an exciting field for experiment, and at the moment a wide-open field. So what can we do? Take risks. Take time off for a few half-hours each week to ask ourselves why we think our subject is interesting, no matter what the world outside says about it. (If we can't find convincing reasons, perhaps that's a fair warning that we would be happier elsewhere.) Ask ourselves – it is intrinsically a very interesting question – how the subject hangs together in our own minds, what is the structure or pattern or shape of our grasp of it; and then ask ourselves where the students are at the moment, intellectually and imaginatively, in their relation to the subject's possibilities. Finally, how can they be brought to have at least the sort of grasp on the subject that we have? At this point we are ready to take big risks; and there is not likely to be any more a feeling of dullness or repetition.

In planning each evening the object is to keep the class taut, varied and full. But not hectic either; which means that there will be varieties of pace and tone – and spaces between. I am not suggesting that all this can be deliberately planned in advance. But that, roughly, is how it is likely to come out, though much of it will be decided on the spot, taken as it comes, with *ad hoc* decisions being made all along the way. I suppose hardly anyone nowadays uses the old division of an adult class meeting into one-hour-talk and one-hour-discussion. Just how best the two hours should be broken up will vary with the subject or the needs of a particular aspect of a subject, or of a particular evening. Even if there is some quite sustained presentation by the tutor early in the evening, or at intervals throughout, it won't normally be material read in consecutive sentences and paragraphs for a considerable length of time. But even this is not an absolute rule; almost any type of teaching can have a point with some subjects, some tutors, some students and some stages in learning. One can present an argument which seems important for that evening in several different ways and from several angles. One is trying to measure all the while the extent to which the point is being understood, how far the students are able to engage critically with it. As far as possible, one makes it concrete; or, alternatively, translates the concrete into the abstract so that the students have the chance to grasp a new – even if small – intellectual pattern or movement. And so on, in many varieties of approach and stress, staying with what seems a useful point until, so far as one can bring it about, each member of the class has seen the point, is in a position to begin to 'make it his own'. This steady going backwards-and-forwards with a group requires a good deal of honest-trading in relationships, and a low degree of embarrassment about speaking publicly by the class members. One is, to repeat a point made earlier since what I've just said has been filling it out, not so much giving as 'putting in the way of'.

None of this can be done properly without a thoroughly-planned syllabus, one thought out tactically and strategically. Neither the tutor nor the student should be in doubt about the overall aims of the course and its larger pattern of working over the session; nor about the place of each week in that pattern; nor about the shape of any one week in itself. The syllabus should be as clear a guide as we can make it, and so should its partner – the reading-list. A reading-list is not a bibliography, a more or less impressive list of whole books. It is a tool which will include whole books, probably grouped in several lists according to their importance to the particular course; it will just as valuably include parts of books, advice on specific chapters, on magazine articles, on cheap editions and so on.

It follows that part of each weekly session will need to be devoted to establishing where you are in the syllabus and where you hope to go next, to helping fill out the sense of a coherent journey. Similarly, each week, something will need to be said about the reading which is to follow, both short-term reading for the next meeting and long-term, background or preparatory reading for the next main phase of the course. If the course is to achieve anything like what it sets out to do, not only the tutor but also the students must prepare in advance regularly and for both short- and long-term goals. They must prepare, week by week, by reading and writing. It is a joint matter, but one in which the tutor has primary responsibility for keeping the lines braced.

There may not be a long, set 'discussion period' but there will be a lot of discussion, sometimes for substantial periods at a time. 'Socratic procedures', we usually say, and this is right. But we need to define more thoroughly what we mean by 'Socratic'. We shouldn't mean baiting or elaborate dangling or elegant fence-sitting. We should mean helping the students to think and feel for themselves by carefully-phrased questions – serious, relevant but not proselytising questions – designed to set them off in enquiry on their own and in their own ways. We should mean raising alternatives, making contrasts, so that they are stimulated into making the right jumps themselves. To work in this way is difficult, the hardest discipline of all for the tutor. It is so much easier just to *tell* them, or lead them straight to an open door. The right procedure is much more like, to borrow an image from I. A. Richards, providing hand-holds or pointing to

cracks in the rocks, to which they must stretch and then hoist themselves over to the next level. The point is the muscular development,
not the height reached.

For some of us, the greatest difficulty of all is to control *ourselves,* to
listen without intervening. Knowing when to shut up has all sorts of
aspects: it means knowing that it may be best to keep silent even
though there is a pause, because that may allow a student who has
been thinking quietly to contribute, perhaps in a way one wouldn't
have suspected; it means resisting the temptation to short-circuit the
whole procedure by giving too many little lubricating lecturettes –
clever, perhaps, and even illuminating, but still not as useful as the
students' finding their own way in their own time. It means, most of
all, shutting up so as to listen better until we hear what is really being
said behind often clumsily-chosen words. When we do that, it is
surprising how often what is being said is intelligent and sensitive,
more intelligent and sensitive than our training and assumptions
might have led us to guess. We are, for the nth time, trying to provide
a ground on which they find things out for themselves. Though, of
course, we also have to try to learn to recognise when it will be useful
if we do intervene, when there is a prospect not of fruitful silence but
of sagging emptiness. We have to try to learn which students will gain
by being encouraged to contribute in discussion, and for which of
them that direct invitation might at the present time be a setback and
personally painful. It isn't always right to assume one can or should
get all the silent ones to speak in the group as soon as ever possible.

We need to have a fair idea of possible lines for the discussion, of
several main points which seem, in advance – given the subject at
this point, and the state of a particular class – likely to be most useful
to pursue. With alternatives, so far as one can see. But this is not a
programme for discussion. It is available as one possibility. We have to
be ready to scrap the whole or parts of it, to shift direction, divert for
a while, according to the needs of the actual situation. Sometimes an
unexpected difficulty will keep the class stuck near what we thought
would be the first of several points, and one of the easiest. Sometimes
someone, or the group as a whole, will throw up an approach better
than any we had thought of in advance, and we must then follow that
line. All of which means being as alert and responsive and open and
unjealous as we can; and making decisions on the run.

So far I have said more about the group as a whole than about the
individual students. When a good adult class is working well, it is a

10

community of a special and unusual kind and very valuable for all its members including the tutor. The activity of the group as a whole, in a good discussion session, pushes on for all, is an integral part of, the education offered. Still, the more important question in the end is what happens to the individual students, to each separate member of the class. To the tutor's understanding of what is being achieved by each member, and in what ways he can help any one person, the best single guide is the student's written work. This is why justifications for not asking for written work, or for only asking for it irregularly or in an undemanding way – justifications which are quite common nowadays – do not wash. They are anti-educational. Written work is immensely the best guide we have to the needs of each individual; nothing else, not even the most apparently rewarding group discussions or private talks, can take its place.

Written work has, so far as possible, to be tailored to the needs of each individual, to be seen as part of a larger relationship – of letters exchanged between class-meetings, short private discussions before or after class, individual guidance on reading. In this way, we are less likely to fail to know each student as a distinctive individual, with distinctive problems and possibilities. Since most adult classes are small, this doesn't seem too much to ask. It follows that the marking has to be particularly close and detailed. It may run from pedestrian matters of grammar to a quite elaborate taking-up of issues; but always it should aim to be practically and positively helpful. Good marking is time-consuming and demands close attention; a set of ticks in the margins, a few hieroglyphics and 'Thank you very much. Keep it up' at the end are just not sufficient.

For what is the point of 'marking' in adult education? By what criteria does one assess the work? By its comparison with, say, internal university essays? Or by the distance of each particular individual from the point at which he started out, or reached in his last essay? These are not mutually exclusive; yet there can be no real doubt about the general direction an answer ought to take. It has two aspects. We, the teachers, should aim at as high a standard as our own minds are capable of reaching. It can't be higher or better, but shouldn't be worse. Because, again, properly guided most students will also be able to reach it. That standard will be established not by overt statements or mark-schemes, but in all sorts of implicit ways.

The second aspect is the establishing of standards for the students; and they will differ with each individual. Here, our objective is to help each one as far as we can to reach his or her own next best standard at each stage of the class. With these two elements in play – the tutor's objectives and the standards defined by those, and each student's possibilities and the standards defined by them – we can avoid the rigidity of fixed external standards which ignore the different needs of each student; and we can avoid that sloppy relativism which doesn't stretch *any* student because 'they are all, in their own ways, doing wonderfully'. We can avoid, too, competition between students because that is irrelevant and damaging in adult classes.

The only people who are being judged from outside are us, the tutors; and that by the demands of the subject, which we have to respect. So we can't define standards for the students until we have defined for ourselves the objectives of our teaching, and the standards these therefore demand from us. The standards possible for each student will then take time to emerge. We have to build up, steadily but as soon as we can, a graph of each student's needs, possibilities, failings. This means not only writing a great deal on their essays – which is for our benefit as much as for theirs, since it clears our minds to write our reactions down – but keeping notes on each student. We may think we have good memories and can retain a clear sense of what each student was like at the start, where their essays began to pick up and in what way, what main weaknesses remain and so on. But if we do keep notes, and use them to check on the accuracy of our memories over several months, we will probably get a shock. Eventually, with these notes, we will have quite a good map of each student's progress. If we still feel a little rudderless and wonder whether we are losing our sense of what had better be called 'public' standards, we can always show a range of essays to an interested colleague and ask him for a frank opinion on them and on our marking.

All these may well seem like counsels of perfection. But each has been followed by some tutors, and the best tutors I have seen have done all these things and more for much of the time. But some of us do hardly any of these things any of the time — because, in Britain, it is regarded as unnecessary or 'square' to think about the practice of good teaching. Our characteristic amateurism here is inexcusable.

1969

HIGHER EDUCATION
AND PERSONAL LIFE

═══════

We have been seeing clearly in recent years a major change in the relations between students, universities, and society. This change is the culmination of two slower developments spanning the last two decades. The first was a change in the role of universities, when they became much more institutionally tied to the needs of the country. In this phase – though many more students were admitted to universities and in Britain were given reasonable grants – some of the more important needs of students were relatively neglected. In the second phase, which began in the early Sixties, students (and some staff, especially junior staff) judged the nature of the changes in the universities and found them on the whole unacceptable. The major authorities within universities and in society were then being asked to justify themselves by the people they were training to serve that society; in particular, they were being asked to justify the gap between public moral assertions about the nature of the university and the reality; and these are fair questions.

The literature on the subject is voluminous. There is material on the sociological, social-psychological, and individual psychological backgrounds of the more revolutionary students, on the correlation between subjects studied and the propensity to rebel, on the comparative historical development of student activism in different countries, on the links between administrative structures within different universities and student dissidence, and so on. Much of it is useful, but none of it is or can be decisive. The phenomenon is too complex to be caught within the language of one discipline or by a massive aggregation of different disciplines. It engages our assumptions about society and the individual at levels we are not fully aware of, but which affect our inquiries no matter how 'objective' we try to make

13

them. The subject needs the controlled, subjective insight of a good novelist. In the nature of things, what it gets almost always is either intelligent partial 'objectivity' or intelligent impressionistic guesswork. I am not trained to be 'objective' in the social scientist's sense and do not claim the insight of a creative writer. But the best contribution I can make lies on the subjective-literary side rather than elsewhere. So I will try to describe the changes in British university life during the last few decades (in particular, in the relations between students and staff) in a local and personal way. Perhaps it might seem also a parochial and provincial way. But we abstract and generalise enough. It is just as important to try to interpret the feel of our own experiences day by day and as year has succeeded year, to recall as accurately as we can what it felt like to live through these changes. We will never know 'the whole truth'; but this way may recall some aspects of 'the truth' which tend to be neglected. And so they may find an echo in the experience of people thousands of miles away in societies which look, at first, very different indeed.

I attended, as an undergraduate in the middle Thirties, one of the larger of our provincial universities, Leeds – large for Britain and those days – about one thousand five hundred strong. I had been born and educated in the town. Most of us were provincials, Northerners; from our type of area hardly anyone went to Oxbridge. Not that the university as a whole was full of working-class scholarship boys. The medical students, the engineers, the chemists were mostly middle class – but Northern professional or mercantile middle class, probably many of them educated at Northern public schools which had smoothed but not removed their Yorkshire voices, sent along to the university by their fathers with a good allowance and a sports car, to be well trained and go back into the business. This was in the sciences; but in the arts faculty the students were overwhelmingly working-class to lower-middle-class. Students whose parents were teachers were in our upper social grade. Most of us were the first members of our families ever to go to university.

What did we expect? We expected to have an enjoyable, even an exciting time in some respects. We had read Evelyn Waugh and though we did not expect to behave like his characters, and didn't particularly want to, we looked forward to some moments of suitably irresponsible student fun. We expected to be helped to 'get on', professionally. Some of us expected to be introduced to the intellectual life. Though some of us had strong political interests, a critique of the university as such and of its role in society didn't usually figure in them. If you belonged, as I did, to the Socialist Club you looked outwards; you did not discuss university. The list I've given shows that we expected quite a lot from the university: but in a crucial sense we expected less from it – less of social and individual meaning – than students came to expect after the late Sixties.

What did we find? We found a remarkably ordered and, on the whole, satisfied society. We found a society willing, if we were prepared to make the effort, to introduce us to the intellectual life; and a society pretty well assured about the nature, scope, and relevance of the intellectual life. The number of potential intellectuals among the students was small and so was the number of staff willing to introduce them to the life of the mind. This was not only a provincial characteristic. I believe it applied to Oxbridge too, though to hear some people in Britain talk about the small proportion of 'genuine intellectuals' in universities today, as compared with their time at Oxbridge in the Thirties, you would think that eighty per cent or ninety per cent of Oxbridge undergraduates at that time were committed to intellectual life. I simply do not believe it. The evidence suggests that only a small minority were of that kind, and this is not surprising in view of Oxbridge's social role at that period.

The staff at Redbrick universities in the Thirties knew that most of us were destined to become school teachers, that only a minute minority would ever work in universities or become intellectual journalists, and that even fewer would become what used to be called 'civilised businessmen' or 'cultivated professionals', that only a very few would be actual contributors to intellectual life or well-heeled supporters of it. But they assumed, vaguely but amiably, that something was gained by a period there, that a glimpse of the intellectual life was never quite pointless.

Socially, the university community had a similar assurance about what it could and should offer. It was, in a phrase I often heard, though usually accidentally, 'rubbing some of the rough edges' off us. It was introducing us to the social style with which British intellectual life was then worn. This was presented as, by implication, a universal intellectual style but was, as one can see now, a very special style, one definable in historical and social terms. It was not the style of Hardy or Lawrence or Burns, or even of the LSE, but the style of Oxbridge from which most of our teachers came (and to which many of them hoped eventually to return), and it was predominantly professional

15

middle-class and southern in its origin.

Quite a lot of the staff, including the senior members, lived out their assumptions about their social role in ways which it is easy – and sometimes justified – to laugh at, and I have often done that myself. Those of us who became professors tell ourselves that we are kept far busier than our predecessors with routine work, and this is probably true. But they had books to write, and anyway selfish men can always find excuses for filling their day with other things than entertaining students. So they had to make a special effort to entertain us to sherry and other touches of gracious living in their homes, and I've no doubt they often wished they could simply not bother. But they did bother. Their social lights may have been curiously tinted but a surprising number tried to live up to them, and lived up to them well.

In the halls of residence, university senates tended to install as wardens gracious widowed ladies or dignified elderly gentlemen. They carpeted and curtained them at remarkable expense. The expensive fittings were partly justified on the ground that the best is cheapest in the long run. But they served a larger purpose. The whole enterprise of hall provision was felt to be an integral part of the civilising aspect of university education. And it expressed itself in a very English way – slightly comically, like something out of an early issue of *Punch*; but also humanely – it wasn't mean or hard or mechanised. You could, as I did, resent the faint overhanging air of patronage, but you didn't feel like a 'thing', a 'number', just an item in the computer of the multiversity. The tone was taken, without much stopping to think, from a particular socio-cultural group; and it shared the limits of that group's outlook. It also had some of its virtues, the virtues of the liberal-minded, intellectual English middle-class – a very special kind of integrity, a patient tolerance, a remarkable directness, and an overriding concern about people.

But we, especially those of us who came from the poorest kind of homes, had to make our own sense out of the profound clash. We were invited, especially if we were bright or in other ways particularly acceptable, to become part of that decent, civilised middle class. Hardly anyone recognised what contradictions psychologically this posed for us. Most of the staff were themselves from professional middle-class backgrounds and those who had worked their way up had usually taken the tone of the group they had joined. They might retain a working-class burr or a relish for salty jokes, but that was a form of role-playing within their new class and so served their membership of it. By default, if not more explicitly, the assumption was that we were growing away from our background and, if not positively rejecting it, at least quietly letting it go, finding it increasingly dull and un-nourishing. In many ways this was true, especially when viewed from their position. But, though we might reject much in our background, we also found a lot in it which pulled us, even though we couldn't say what it was and no one helped us to say. There was a gap between our emotional evidence and our intellectual evidence which could be painful, but which had to be bridged if our emotional and intellectual growth were to continue. The problem couldn't be solved – though some of us tried this way – by digging a deep ditch between our professional and intellectual life and our personal and emotional life. That way you got all sorts of 'sports' – the socially bitter research chemist or the professor who managed to be both sentimental about his humble origins and snobbish about his present elevation.

Overall, we knew that jobs were hard to get, movement limited, opportunities abroad not common (nor often desirable, in the fag-end of the Empire) and that practically all of us taking courses in the faculty of arts would go into the state teaching system. In fact, most arts students had scholarships or grants, e.g. many were supported by their local education authorities (city authorities), sometimes having promised to teach for a stated number of years after graduation. Some local authorities made loans, not grants. I don't think this intimidated many, but it did draw invisible boundaries round possibilities, temper the atmosphere, cause some submerged anxiety and playing safe.

So the universities did reflect the nature of a dominant part of their society, of its trained and 'civilised' middle-class; they had remarkably little close knowledge of the body of working-class people outside, or of the potentialities of more than the minute proportion of the working classes whom they saw in their classrooms. In this sense, they were sustainers of a certain view of society. In another sense they stood apart from society. They didn't draw much money from industry and commerce for services directly rendered; they were jealous of their freedom from government intervention, and they had an idiosyncratic, amateur independence of style. Even though most of the funds of the civic universities came from the UGC you had the feeling that that body was composed of gentlemen, all of whom

17

belonged to the Athenaeum – that the vice-chancellor certainly did and that most provincial professors did too. Most of the universities were pyramidal in their structure of authority and the professoriate was at the top of the pyramid. The professors soon reminded their vice-chancellors if they got uppish that they were only *primus inter pares.* One might not be willing to accept the professors' particular social forms or assumptions, but one could learn a great deal from their independence of public power and authority. They really did see themselves, and act, as people who believed they had special rights and freedoms and capacities. This made a few self-willed and self-indulgent in their professional conduct. But hardly any were public relations men or government's men.

Jump thirty or forty years on and most of this has changed. Society itself, the universities, the students, the universities' relations to society, the students' expectations from university – all have changed. Like most countries, Britain has become more technological, more managerial, more professionalised. So her universities have expanded; not as much as in most countries but still a good deal, enough to have shocked some people and made them talk about opening the doors to the unintellectual multitude. As far as I know there is no evidence that university standards have gone down and some things suggest they may have gone up. It is still relatively difficult to get into British universities. The pressure from the sixth forms, from people with very good A-level certificates, seems to build up all the time. Of course, the A-level examination may have been made progressively easier, but that doesn't seem likely.

So jobs became easier to get, even for arts graduates. You didn't have to go into schoolteaching, though many still did. You could think of management training in industry or of interesting new openings in a range of institutions of higher education, or of the mass media or of a year or so abroad, in North America or one of the newly independent countries; again, many do. On a close look and especially in the early Eighties, some of these openings prove to be less numerous or less attractive than they seemed on the Appointments Board notices. But still, undergraduates have less of a feeling that they are going straight down a single line, blinkered.

The feeling of inhabiting a firmly three-tiered pyramidal society has been weakened, but we are less sure of exactly who is speaking to whom and from within what relationships. The sense that there was a smallish group who did know the relations and due tones, who had authority and style, a tight, confident, prescribing group (of which the university world was a small offshoot with some saving variations) – this sense has all but gone. Or should have. Naturally, there are some people who haven't noticed and act as though nothing has changed. In such a situation you can convince others as well as yourself for a time, and it then does seem as though nothing *has* changed. There are people like this in politics, in the higher levels of administration and in senior common rooms. But that tells something about the tenacity of personality, not about changes in British society.

The universities have more and more become servicing agencies for this increasingly complex and centralised society. They have geared themselves to, more and more taken money for, its purposes; they have trained the experts it needs for the middle ranges of its work upwards. Their professors have become 'department heads' and their vice-chancellors managing directors of multimillion-pound institutions, under pressure to talk about 'plant' and 'cost efficiency', rather than about 'The Idea of a University'. One of the odder paradoxes is that some large provincial universities managed to become cellularly bureaucratic while still retaining their old pyramidal structures of power – a remarkable physical phenomenon. No wonder it became fashionable to say that the secondary beneficiaries of the students' demand for participation would be the non-professorial staff.

But here comes in the biggest paradox of all. I have argued that the universities have more and more become, on the one hand, servicing agencies of large-scale centralising forces in society. On the other hand, the British universities, to a degree that we have not on the whole recognised, have also been over the last dozen years the proving-grounds for immense changes of attitudes among young people generally. The causes of these changes are not to be found in the universities; they lie outside in society and they have a long history. But they came to full expression in the universities; it was the students' role to try to cause the wave which has built up within society finally to break. They are more intelligent and emotionally articulate than most; they are for the moment free of continuing professional, financial and domestic responsibilities. More than anyone else they are able to stand, as it were, apart from society and ask what it's all in aid of. They have been acting out a phase in what could be one of the most important secular changes in attitudes of the last two or three hundred years. We could be seeing the beginning of the end of the protestant ethic in its two main forms of expression: in its

19

attitudes to competitive work and to the sexual life. Both have come under very powerful challenge.

It may seem strange that all this has been going on in universities while at the same time they have continued publicly to claim a pastoral function. But universities have become the arenas for this change in a fit of absence of mind, almost unconsciously. By and large, they haven't really known what was happening, what contradictory forces were at work within themselves. One result has been that, in most places, they have steadily relaxed their *in loco parentis* rules to an extent that would still startle conventional opinion in the country if it were widely known. At provincial universities in the early Sixties there would be a shocked response if it were discovered that (say) contraceptives were on sale in the Students' Union building; today that would be old hat. In most universities there has been a steady loosening of the rules in halls of residence, of the conditions on which students may go into flats, and so on. Virtually all members of staff know that a great many students live together.

Or one may get a hint of these changes through the difference in students' attitudes when they discuss with a member of staff a problem which involves sexual behaviour. As, for example, when an unmarried girl asks for two or three weeks off so as to have a baby. Up to the middle Sixties such a girl was likely to be at least slightly embarrassed. Nowadays, it isn't so. A girl may be either upset about the mess she has got into or composed because she has sorted out the difficulties. But she does not feel that she is telling you something with which you are morally concerned. I am not saying that students today are promiscuous. I am suggesting that in their attitudes towards sex they seem to have made two important changes: they do not give the moral weight we were taught to give to the idea of premarital virginity or of confining sexual relations to one member of the opposite sex, the one you eventually marry; second, and this follows from the first, they do not think their university teachers have a role as moral mentors in matters such as these.

It would be wrong to put the main stress on changes in attitudes to sexual life. More important, and trickier to describe, is what looks like a change in attitudes towards ambition and competitiveness. Many intelligent students today are deeply suspicious of internecine strife, of 'getting on'. They have decided to be unpushing. I have known them decide to settle for a Second Class degree rather than a

First, not so as to 'have a good time' in the old way but, as they argued, so as to stay with their group – because that is more 'real' than the kind of ladder-climbing isolation the degree structure invites. The stress is on the small-scale, particular, personal, non-materialistic. Or think of the student case against examinations: it is not at bottom a reformist case – that examination methods need to be improved. It is a revolutionary case – that they must be done away with. This is part of the wider rejection of quantitative competitiveness, the insistence on the importance of communality and on the superior reality of the personal and particular. The ideal is of a world much more fluid than ours, much less pyramidal.

How do the students view the universities themselves? Again, there is an apparent paradox. In one sense they expect less than we often assume; in another sense they expect more, more than we ourselves always expect and more than we expected when we were students. They expect to be able to go to a university if they are bright, almost as a right. But they do not want to be introduced to a style of life which goes with the professional training. They want neither the cultivated bourgeois style of before the war, nor the meritocratic life-style which some university departments now implicitly offer. They may believe in 'style' but not as something passed on from us to them. Style is their own 'thing', not ours.

The search for style is part of the self-defining search of their generation; part of their independence from and as against the world of adults. So here they don't want much from the university.

But they also expect a great deal from the university. They admire the Idea of the University. They want the university to stand for that Idea, for the integrity and courage of the intellectual life. And they are disappointed. They find most of us interested in our 'subject', not in the life of the mind. They find most teaching simply dull rather than a dialogue.

They want the universities to stand in a critical relation to society. With the detached clarity of their time of life they regard society as a mess if not an affront. To them, the overarching realities of the situation – East/West tensions and the profit system – make decent human relations almost impossible (again, the stress on the real and personal); and they are not at all amused to be told that this is the impatient idealism of youth. They justifiably feel patronised when that is said to them by people who seem to have hedged their bets all the way as university teachers. They think themselves involved in a politics of mistrust, of deep mistrust.

Yet their basic attitudes are not at all distrustful. Listen to their vocabulary, to the recurrent words, such as 'real', 'real event', 'genuine happening', 'participant', 'significant participation', and so on. They are rejecting the split life implicitly offered to them by the universities for the future: first, that they shall be trained to serve society, quite lucratively; second, that they will then be allowed a limited degree of freedom as individuals, so long as that freedom doesn't lead them to any sort of active larger commitment, to taking action against the overall thrust of society, its drive towards what they see as empty, authoritarian materialism. They are angry because they dream of a university as a moral community and they find that most members of staff, though they may say this themselves on platforms, do not live it out.

Of course, it is easy to find reasons for discounting what the more active students are saying. One can argue, quite rightly, that there are only a few of them and that most students seem to want just to get on quietly with working for their degrees. But this has always been so with any movements for reform. The important thing is that the few may be in touch with, and implicitly speaking for, a great many others. Or one can say, as is often said, that there is some correlation between being a leader in student revolt and having personal psychic difficulties. Perhaps many of the catalysts were prompted by some inner need in themselves. But it's at least as important for us to ask why they were able to become catalysts, what that reveals about the culture. Or some people say that most student rebels come from the arts and social science faculties and go on to suggest that that indicates that students are not expected to work in those faculties and have no proper 'motivation'. It would be rather surprising, in fact, if a large proportion of student leaders did *not* come from the faculties which should be concerned with thinking speculatively about society. So any such correlation is fairly obvious as a fact and scandalous as an attempted rebuttal.

To all this the reaction of staff has been very mixed and rather slow. On the largest, single, clear challenge we have had over the last thirty years – expansion – the record was good. The universities expanded quickly and, on the whole, well. They did so not simply to serve more effectively a technological society but because a great number of people within universities as well as outside were convinced that we had been mean in the provision of higher education and that there was a human duty to provide far more. So we admitted several times more university students than there were before the war and, on the whole, kept up standards well. We were slow in devising changes in teaching and examination methods to meet this expansion, but all in all the expansion was carried out humanely. Almost everywhere, university people fought to keep the close tutorial system, even though it meant that their own teaching-loads went up steadily right through two decades. And we refused to accept the kind of harsh wastage which can so easily come with rapid expansion, as it came in France and several other countries.

We have been less adequate on the two trickier challenges: on the need to look again at the structure of power and responsibility within the universities themselves; and on the changed relationships of the universities to society. So that when both these challenges have been put, often aggressively, by students we have been in difficulties. It is never pleasant to have thoughts which you should have had years ago prompted for you, least of all by people you are supposed to be leading intellectually. Academics can be as resentful as other people, and where their professional pride is touched are quick to react. Then their combination of high drive, introversion, articulateness and self-justification goes into action; and it is fierce. In the circumstances, I was surprised by the number who, after the first jolt, recovered themselves and were flexible and open. They didn't want to be paternalistic, though they might enjoy being fatherly where they could; but they were ready to change the modes if that seemed needed and right. They couldn't, as they say, 'go all the way with the more extreme advocates of change', whether among students or younger members of staff; but they went a long way in re-educating themselves. On the other side of the range were members of senates who felt deeply resentful. They were hurt because their paternalism was part of their self-respect; they thought the existing system by and large the best; they were sure they knew every student in their departments, and so on and so on; and now they felt rejected. So they looked for forms of words which would allow them to express their sense of outrage without actually using what they recognised as the tainted words of paternalism. For instance, they often used false analogies to justify their mild authoritarianism. A common one, in response to the student demand for participation, is to say that no one in his senses would let a first-year medical student attempt a heart transplant; he has to learn and be under authority for a time. But a first-year medical student ought to be involved in some sort of dialogue, at the right points, about the social assumptions behind the medical training he is being given.

Another response by those who are hurt is to fall back on a pure, detached, narrowly academic definition of the purpose of a university, as in these extracts:

The university staff are appointed to research and to teach certain disciplines and for no other purpose...

A university should not be loosely compared to a democracy. Its purpose is to establish that some citizens are more gifted and intelligent than others, and to give them extra opportunities (to continue with research, to take up posts in higher education, to accept the best openings in industry)...

Examinations are the best possible way of grading students in any highly competitive area of society...*

All of which had a fine confidence but hardly seems to have risen to the height of this great argument. In fact, it is another form of the professionalised, un-Socratic conception of the university as a production belt for computerised intelligences.

This kind of thing shows the gap at its most dramatic. The active students saw themselves as standing for a platonic conception of the university, engaged with bringing a fresh stream of thought to bear on its society. To them it seemed that, with a few exceptions, the staff took up one of two positions, neither acceptable. Either they believed that the universities are generally educative, cultural and intellectual bodies, but interpreted this as the presentation of a style of life which seemed to the students increasingly out of touch. Or the staff said that to think that universities have any such 'civilising' function is to be wholly mistaken. To them universities are the institutions in which are trained the higher intelligences of a society, for its uses. They can say this in a variety of tones. Some of them say it in a tone of weary, unexpectant cynicism; they know that's the way the world wags and always will wag. Others are rather more unpleasant, since they seem never to have worried enough even to feel disillusioned. To them it is a nuisance for anyone, whether staff or students, to talk about the 'civilising' purposes of a university. One gets on with the job in medicine or engineering or what you will and leaves all such questions to the journalists. The first group – the old-style, civilised bourgeois – are, of course, disappearing, though, as I've said, a number are still to be found in arts faculties. The second group – the

* 'Comment', *Critical Survey*, Summer 1968, pp. 190-91.

neutral technocrats – are increasingly powerful, especially in faculties of science and technology. They are hard-nosed reductionists. This was bound to be so; it is in the nature of the situation. But it is a dangerous situation and one that cannot be settled by neat tactical arrangements. It requires us not just to look at the universities but to look at society far more than we have been used to doing, and then at the relations which have grown up between the two; and then to make the most searching value-judgments we can.

We have each to make sense of the picture as best we can and to decide where we stand. I will try to sum up my own position.

I think a lot *is* still wrong with our universities and that we have been too slow to think about anything other than practical answers to pressing problems. The structure of power within universities, syllabuses, the methods of teaching, and the systems of examination, all need serious critical examination. They received it in the planning of some of the new universities, but in some of the older universities this kind of scrutiny only began (where it did begin) as a result of student pressure.

I think, too, that a lot is wrong with our society, that in becoming centralised and technologised it is in danger of losing its own sense of individual human beings, of creating feelings of alienation (and that it has done this in many instances); and that, in particular, it is making us less able to feel that we can be committed to relationships outside our face-to-face acquaintances; and that the media of mass communications on the whole reinforce this sense of being no more than voyeurs at an interesting but non-significant succession of events. Tragedy and comedy become aesthetic objects mediated through technology and of roughly the same weight – or weightlessness, since they are not connected to any decision by us.

But I also think that there are many things which are valuable within British universities and British society, and that these things are cavalierly slid over by most student and staff radicals. Whatever the international links and parallels, we shall go wrong if we do not start with the peculiar virtues (as well as vices) of the British situation. This is not in the slightest degree chauvinistic, but a recognition of what it is fashionable to call 'existential' reality.

British universities are in some ways creatures of the state, of the society which pays for them. But not altogether. They are not in the position of German universities before the war, or Russian universities now; they do not have the kind of problems with local authorities or trustees which some American universities have. To say, as Mr David Triesman of Essex said: 'Universities are linked to a set of productivity norms which, in order to be met, need a system as authoritarian as any other factory'* – to say this is to over-extend a sound point, to abstract it from the cultural setting which qualifies it and gives it meaning, and to express it in a rhetoric just as unreal, abstract, and technologised as the world it sets out to attack. British universities are not wholly or simply subservient to State or government, or to local businessmen. They have a lot of freedom and on the whole it is *real* freedom, freedom to say and do a great deal. Of course, if an academic is persistently awkward, some other people are likely to try to silence him, and their methods are not always fair. But this is human nature and has to be fought, and fought openly. It is still a long way from organised witch-hunts. There is room for free controversy and more than lip-service is paid to integrity in speaking out. Naturally, those who exercise this right of critical controversy do not attract big private grants for their departments. But what do we expect?

One can say much the same about the atmosphere within the universities. There are a great many rigidities and snobberies; and since snobbery has many disguises, its forms are often not recognised even by the most snobbish members of staff themselves. But there are also a great many decencies. The same professor who resists any suggestion of even partially opening the senior common room to students (usually on the ground that it is the equivalent of his 'club' on the campus) or who stands up for the principle of double discipline for students caught breaking the law (on the ground that the university as a whole is a sort of 'club'), that same professor may spend a large part of his weekend trying to sort out fairly and humanely a problem to do with one particular student in his department. On the whole, staff are not remote from students, nothing like as remote as they are in most other countries; in most departments in most British universities, every student is known quite well by at least one member of staff, and often by more than one. You need only attend a final examiners' meeting, especially when borderline students are being discussed, to have this brought home.

This mongrel mixture of attitudes within the universities reflects a similar mixture in society at large. The extreme student radicals argue that society is thoroughly corrupted and at bottom authori-

* Scanner 1, *New Left Review*, No. 50, 1968, pp. 59-71

tarian; that the amiable part-yielding which it (like the universities) seems capable of is worse than frank opposition because, in the end, it gets you nowhere but meanwhile blunts your cutting edge. So-called free speech is only a five per cent permitted deviation, permitted only so long as it doesn't cause anything to change importantly. If it seems to promise to do that, then it is either withdrawn or subverted. The much talked-about patience of the police is only a façade. If anyone really tries to push things to the point at which they challenge the structure, then the mask is dropped and the police become ruthless, exposed as the agents of naked power. On this reading, the circle is complete. There can be no way out through the channels and styles of thought of society today. Rational challenges to the rationalistic, goal-conscious, closely structured societies of the late twentieth century are dead ends, tricks of the system.

It is plain that any approach to internal reform must go along with an effort to redefine the universities' relations to society. The students, remember, are saying that a university which trains people in highly skilled disciplines should also make them critically aware of how those disciplines are used, what values they are made to serve in society at large. They are acting from the belief that universities should not be simply or primarily the passers-on of acceptable styles among the controllers and sub-controllers of society, but places where those values are continually questioned. They are asking for a special kind of commitment and engagement. It is easy to accuse them of being ridden with the wrong kind of social concern, to argue – as in one sense it is right to argue – that a university *should* be a kind of ivory tower into which we go to learn *before* engaging with society, in which we learn to think disinterestedly, to get a perspective in time, to entertain other imaginative and intellectual experiences than those of the immediate, the expedient, the time-bound, the pragmatic, the contemporary.

That is fine in so far as it rebukes the call for the cruder kind of socially committed courses which a few of the revolutionary students have made; and in so far as it rejects the claim that a university should be specifically 'a pressure group on major social issues'. The links are not as simply one-to-one as that.

Such qualifications apart, the claim that universities should be 'outside' society is based on a misapprehension. Universities are not and cannot be uncommitted, unengaged. They are socially engaged in a thousand ways and at various levels, some complicated, some

27

simple. They are engaged when they decide to take on this research rather than that. I do not mean simply when they take on a certain kind of research because funds are offered for it from outside. I mean something more in the bone than that; that the nature of the culture suggests some lines and not others, and that only the rarest people will be free from that kind of atmospheric pressure. We are engaged as individual teachers in the very way we regard degrees and career prospects, in our assumptions about where the university, our subject, and our students 'fit' into society. We all have such a picture, no matter how unexamined it may be. We are engaged in the way we live out a certain relationship to the value-judgments of our culture, and this affects our whole personal and professional styles. Hence we are engaged in the way we treat other members of staff and in our manner towards our students as we pass them in the corridors. It is in the air of departments, in their grain, no matter how little some of us may have thought of it. We are all members of this society, in some sort of dialectical relationship to its assumptions; and as university teachers we are professionally involved in institutions which are closely and paradoxically related to that society – institutions which underwrite much of its main thrust and also are arenas for criticising it. There can be no such thing as 'unengaged' university work and teaching. There is no such thing as an 'unengaged' university teacher; we are all, in a way, promoting styles. This is true of all subjects. It follows that it should be impossible for students in some of the major professional departments – in engineering, medicine, law – to have their training without also being made to articulate and question critically within their departments' courses themselves, the relationship of those professionalisms to society. I remember one university teacher saying, 'We mustn't spoil them for the world of work'; but we may have to risk just that, so that they will improve that work and that world.

All this has been about the larger relations of universities to society. But, just as real participation between students and staff as members of a common body must start in departments, so the rethinking of relationships between the university and society ought to begin in local action. Most British cities hardly know they have a university. There are some public connections through court and council; there is Rag Day and its mixture of resentment and amusement; there are a few cultural offerings from gown to town. But not much else; and most academic staff live in the favourite enclaves and go round each other's parties. It is a very *in*organic relationship.

I have, for what seemed good reasons, talked chiefly about the active, articulate minority and especially about the politically active minority. But there are many other kinds of student and towards them all we have to decide where our responsibility lies. What about those who are unexpectant and silent disapprovers, apparently? Or those who drop out? Or what about the quiet girls from sheltered homes who are bewildered rather than stimulated by the huge breakers of the new permissive group life? 'I wish I'd been born in Jane Austen's time. I'd have known what the rules were,' one said to me. What sort of meaning can that hoary old phrase 'pastoral care' have today?

Speaking for myself, I would at any time have been uneasy about assuming a pastoral role in the way that used to be defined. It implied two attitudes, neither of which I possess: acceptance of certain fixed social norms and a certain sense of personal completeness. As to the first I am, to put things as briefly as possible, republican, agnostic, and socialist. I don't promote these positions in my teaching. But I have no doubt that, in a deep-seated way, they permeate my style, as do the attitudes of those of my colleagues who are royalist, religious and right-wing. One has to try to make sure that students are not tempted into imitation by charisma, and that they have as good a chance as possible to keep separate what you are saying from what you are. I do not think they can expect more, or we do more, than that.

The doubt about the second pastoral assumption – 'a certain sense of personal completeness' – is more fundamental. Like most fairly self-critical people anywhere, I expect, I feel most of the time and in most important things quite *un*finished, *un*assured, not like one who can give students an example of 'balance, maturity, wholeness'. Those who are most confident here, confident of their ability to advise, are not usually best fitted to do so, except in minor matters.

I believe my most important act of pastoral duty towards my students is to try to help them to respect the intellect and imagination used with integrity. Can I go further than that? I argued earlier that students today do not want us to be fathers or uncles, to assume that we are in *in loco parentis*. The hold of their peer-group is stronger than any pull we have. But some students do get into serious difficulties and then may want someone to talk to. Again, often their own colleagues can help best. But sometimes an older person *can* help.

29

Here a university tutor might be more useful than a parent, just because he has some emotional distance; this can clear his mind and reassure students too, since they are wary of emotional involvements which might damage their independence. But I would not call this kind of thing 'giving advice'. It is more like listening, talking together, thinking aloud and commenting 'in parallel', as it were. It is a strange situation, but that is where I would start if I were trying, having rejected the old definition of 'pastoral care', to describe the sense in which I do still feel that I have a responsibility other than the academic to my students.   1968

THE UNCERTAIN CRITERIA
OF DEPRIVATION

During the last twenty years there has taken place, in both the United Kingdom and North America, a continuous debate about 'cultural deprivation' and its implications for education. By the 'cultural deprivation' theory at its purest children from some kinds of home (those of the poor, blacks, Indians, immigrants) are regarded as cut off from certain essential social and linguistic experiences and so as at an educational disadvantage. They are 'trapped in the 'cycle of deprivation' and are at best 'empty vessels' when they enter the classroom, at worst locked into restricting forms of behaviour and expression. It is difficult to pick up a British book from the Sixties concerned with education and society which does not, directly or implicitly, take up a position about this very large theory. One of the most outstanding among British names is that of Basil Bernstein. What was chiefly taken from him during the Sixties, and applied in different ways, was the notion of 'restricted' and 'elaborated' codes of discourse.

A restricted code is seen as confining its user to the concrete, the immediate, the metaphorical speech of the here and now; whereas an elaborated code gives access to rationality, shows language in use as the bearer of the grounds of meaning. Bernstein himself says that these early concepts have been misunderstood and misused. They certainly fed the debate in ways he seems not to have intended. Some people took him as suggesting that the duty of schools was to persuade children to deny the language of their background and learn the elaborated code of – and here we come to the inevitable social-class element in British debate – the middle-class. Such people tended to equate the use of a restricted code with the condition of being culturally deprived.

It follows from the 'cultural deprivation' theory that compensatory action should be taken on behalf of children so situated, that there should be 'positive discrimination' in their favour, that whereas the financing of schools in areas of deprivation tends at present to be lower than that of the schools which train those about to enter university, the balance should be shifted; the state should intervene to give such deprived children some of the advantages enjoyed by children from stable, comfortable and literate homes.

The reactions against the purer forms of cultural deprivation theory were political, social and educational. Central to the political reaction is the argument that what any particular society at any particular time calls 'knowledge' is what the dominant 'estates' of that society choose to call knowledge. It follows that what are called the 'fundamental educational values' by which the disadvantaged are tested and found to be wanting are not fundamental or objective at all but rather the culturally determined values of the dominant sectors of a society, and in the British case of the dominant middle-class. They play back their own answers to their own questions; their tests are circular and self-validating (as some old style IQ tests, we now see, so blatantly were). The educational process is therefore shaped so as to enforce the consensus values of our particular type of capitalist society; and the mass media, perhaps even more insistently than the education system, reinforce the sense that this world is immutable, objectively out there, rather than a historical and contingent, man-made structure. Hence, it is 'The Hidden Curriculum' of the schools rather than the explicit list of subjects taught which one should analyse more thoroughly. The hidden curriculum is that pattern of assumptions which is carried, day in day out, by the sanctions of the school, by these actions and attitudes which are encouraged and praised and those which are discouraged and frowned on; it is recognisable as much by what it omits as by its positive acts, it is as much implicit as explicit; and it is carried at least as much by tones of voice in the teacher as by statements.

On this view – and it provides a salutary shift of balance – the 'cultural deprivation' theory, if it is too simply conceived, blames on the shortcomings of the home ills which arise much more from both the short-sightedness of the teachers themselves and from the whole drive of society, its uses and misuses of the educational system. Whenever I read this part of the debate I am reminded of the traditional role of the British '1902 Act' grammar schools. I mean the schools set up by the local municipality to cater for the brighter children from homes where there was no money to pay for a grammar school education. As one of the 'scholarship winners' from a very poor district, I went to such a school along with others – though not many; only two or three classes were taken in each year from a catchment area of a good few thousand – from either similarly poor backgrounds or, at the highest, from genteel skilled-craftsmen backgrounds. I owe a lot to that school and in particular to a couple of individual teachers, a master and a mistress, who thought they detected talent which should be specially encouraged. But there was no doubt that the school saw itself as called to make us into minor, lower-middle-class professionals. Which meant in most cases that the brighter among us were expected to become teachers and the very brightest perhaps to go to university for our teacher training rather than to a mere teachers' training college. There was an insistent pressure, no less strong from being only partly conscious in the minds of the teachers, to cut us off from the culture of the streets to which we returned each night and to offer us the prospect of suburban living on the other side of town.

It was an extraordinary all-embracing atmosphere. It has been described in more than one novel but David Storey's novel *Saville* captures as well as any book I have read the spirit of such schools, on their good sides as well as their bad. That spirit is by no means dead. I know of a girl who, not all that long ago, was transplanted from Yorkshire to the Midlands. She was twelve years old and therefore had to change grammar schools. Reading aloud in class during her early weeks there she said 'bath' with the short Yorkshire 'a'. She was stopped and told that that wasn't a 'proper' pronunciation, that the proper pronunciation had a long 'a', 'bath'. The objection to this sort of thing is not so much that the correction was ill-founded, though certainly few who have given any thought to linguistic practice in the last ten years or so think any longer that there is a 'proper' pronunciation in such cases. The objection is much more that, to the young girl concerned (and in Britain we learn to read such signs from a very early age), the rebuke was a snobbish one; she was being rebuked for not employing the accepted genteel southern forms of pronunciation encouraged in that Midlands city grammar school.

So, though one can certainly learn the bases of the intellectual life and be well-trained in certain ways at any reasonably good British grammar school, and though one may well – if one is bright – be taken up and pushed along by one's teacher, I think it fair to say that

33

all in all the British local authority grammar schools did an inadequate job in assessing and responding to their own socio-cultural positions and therefore to their best possible roles. This is one reason among several why I welcome the movement towards comprehensive education in Britain.

The reaction against the simpler forms of cultural deprivation theory also takes a social and cultural form. Here, it is argued that what are called deprived groups can be, if we know how to listen to them, culturally as rich and complex as the dominant, defining middle-class. In Britain three books, all of which appeared towards the beginning of the Sixties, probably did much to reinforce this response even though no one of them was specifically a contribution to educational thinking. I have in mind Raymond Williams's *Culture and Society* (1958) together with what is really a companion volume, *The Long Revolution* (1961), E. P. Thompson's *The Making of the English Working Class* (1963) and my own *The Uses of Literacy* (1957). It is worth noticing, incidentally, for a small instance of the way a change in opinion gathers force from several directions at once, that though we all three knew each other and knew we were writing sizeable books, though we all spent the heart of the Fifties in writing them, though we were all in the same field of work (evening classes for adults sponsored by the universities which employed us, and given up to a hundred miles from base); yet we did not discuss the books before they appeared and so had no prior knowledge of the similarities in the impulses behind them, of the complementarities or the differences.

Raymond Williams gave greater depth to the concept of 'the working classes' in itself. In this connection, I always think first of the way in which he argued that the imaginative creativity of working-class people expressed itself not in the practice of the high arts (what access did they have?) as in the creation of institutions (the co-ops, the unions, the friendly societies and clubs, etc., etc.) which themselves embodied and practised a subtle and humane conception of the relations between people. Edward Thompson's book is a magisterial account of the struggles and achievements of the English working class over the immense and painful transition from an agricultural to an industrial economy. Since, even at grammar schools, we tended to be offered a view of English history which stressed the imperial achievement by 'great men' and left 'the workers' in the wings – the people of England who have not spoken yet, but are presumed ready to come forward and die in battle if suitably officered – Edward

Thompson's and Raymond Williams's writings were powerful correctives for those teachers and others who wished to face them. My own book was neither an essay in cultural analysis nor an historical study; but its efforts to describe, from within as it were, the texture of urban working-class life in the Thirties added to what was offered by the other two.

From books such as the above and rather similar later work in England came the argument that working-class culture and working-class language were more complex than we had been used to assume. In the United States this position has been carried very much further in the remarkable work of Labov. I suppose it is an indication of both the greater resources and the greater commitment to long-term and intensive fieldwork among American scholars that, to the best of my knowledge, no one in Britain has produced anything approaching Labov's work in its scope and sustained application. Bernstein's work is now considerable in size but its empirical base does not compare with Labov's: it is much more theoretic and abstract. Labov and his team did long studies of the speech habits of their chosen subjects. His analysis, done in great detail from recordings, of the speech of urban black youths does more than any other single work I know to destroy the argument that social deprivation inevitably connotes also verbal deprivation. It is not simply that Labov is showing that the speech of such people may be strong in, for example, concrete metaphors. That would fit some English views, where it is readily agreed that working-class speech may be racy, down to earth, and full of vivid images, but where it is also assumed that that speech lacks the capacity to handle abstractions. What Labov shows is that this urban black speech, once we have learned how to interpret it (by not trying to read it as though it were an aberrant form of grammatically exact middle-class or 'educated' speech), can handle complex concepts very effectively indeed – especially about relationships and roles and the world outside their own local area, as seen by those youths.

Coming in from yet another angle, some people have argued that discussions which stress the verbal deprivation of socially deprived people often have behind them the unspoken assumption that more favoured social groups normally have a capacity for live discourse which is to be emulated, or even that most middle-class homes are centres for conversations which habitually deploy complex arguments. But in fact – they continue – the speech of such people, whether in Britain or North America, is often bland and blunted, and shows no sign of becoming less so. The number of those who can handle language publicly in a lively way whilst also managing the exposition of ideas is limited, and no single class or profession seems to have a special hold on the capacity ... especially not national trade union leaders, who often seem – as they climb to the top – to believe they have to make their language more and more polysyllabically redundant and periphrastic; nor especially politicians who between them exhibit far more kinds of bad rhetoric than of good speech.

I always remember in this connection two experiences of my own. One was a reply I had from the Public Relations department of a big American airline, in answer to a well-merited complaint couched in economical and unambiguous terms. It began: 'We are privileged to have shared your thoughts on the customer-efficacy of our service ...' The other occasion was in a remote Scottish village grocer's. A travelling salesman from Glasgow poured out for quite a while to the shopkeeper a well-rehearsed sales talk about special offers and reductions, all in the boneless persuasive language of the advertising and promotions business. In the end the elderly grocer cut him short and said simply: 'Young man, give me no more of your inducements. Show me your list of goods and I will tell you what I will buy.' There is only one word of more than one syllable in that utterance, and that word rings of Biblical morality.

All this kind of analysis is clearly useful so long as teachers take heed of it and of its implications for their own practice. Teachers *should* have a better understanding of the relations between current assumptions about education, about modes of teaching and about their society's dominant drives. They should aim for a more inward knowledge of the lives and cultures of their pupils. They would thus have a fuller knowledge of their own positions as mediators between society and the family, between young people in deprived situations and the larger society outside. They should have tried to think through all this web of issues much more than most teachers have done so far. I am arguing throughout that an important and interesting debate about fundamental educational purposes has been going on in Britain and in North America over the last fifteen years or so, that the main lines of that debate can be followed for the expenditure, in Britain, of a few pounds a year on paperbacks, but that the majority of teachers, or for that matter the majority of senior civil servants or of politicians, hardly know that the debate has been and is still taking place.

I have so far sketched in, very briefly, the basic case for cultural and linguistic deprivation; and I have also briefly put the objections to the simpler forms of that view, objections which may be political or cultural or linguistic. Those objections have done something to discourage a simplistic attitude in those who hold too unqualified a version of the idea of cultural deprivation. People may not be 'as daft as they look' to an outsider who cannot interpret the inwardness of their habits and language. If we pull away from the pit of an over-simplified neo-paternalism we had better take care not to drop into the pit of reductive identification with what we see as a rich working-class culture. That is its own kind of romanticism.

Working-class people, even the most deprived, can be verbally more skilful than we have been used to thinking; their ways may be as dignified and humane as those of the genteel. Nevertheless, there are many people from deprived homes whose language shows no trace of traditional vigour, who are indeed locked into restricting forms of speech, who have virtually no command of language for activities outside the home or neighbourhood, of those types of speech which will allow them to move with reasonable effectiveness through the public situations – elections, applications for public assistance, medical needs, educational questions, shopping itself day by day – which complex societies increasingly present to all of us. They are not used to handling concepts even in their own kinds of speech; they are neither numerate nor really literate. Their lives do not give them the opportunity or the habit of planning forward, of making long-term choices between options. Their children seem therefore destined to become the new hinds of late twentieth-century industrial society.

Since those societies are massively committed to keeping most people quiet, consumers of its palliatives, these people are at the tail end of a continuous process. They can scarcely read – except for that simplified stuff which is meant to make them buy and buy; they do not discuss, in any recognisable sense of the word; instead, they face an almost nonstop stream of simplified opinionation designed to fix them in certain prejudices. These are the people at the very bottom of the social body and they need all the help that can be given them, all the informed help; or they will remain trapped in the cycle of their deprivation.

I put this so strongly because some of those who have reacted against the purer forms of cultural deprivation theory and have insisted on the possible richness of working-class culture are in danger of themselves falling into a new myth. The wastage of human beings in our society is still great. We are right to think that the aim of education should not be to destroy working-class culture and substitute for it a universal lower-middle-class culture. But these are not the only options. People do have a right to be offered, to the tops of their bents, what all those of us who engage in educational debates have and value, a grasp of the public use of language which is the essential tool for understanding our own situations and the nature of our society better, and for deciding what we can do to improve matters. To wish less for people is implicitly to hand them over even more firmly to the new social controllers, the low-level mass-persuaders.

Between those who plan their educational aims in the light of a strongly held theory of cultural deprivation, and those who oppose that position on political grounds or in defence of continuing working-class values there is a third educational position; or, rather, two different kinds of third position. The first begins by arguing that the conclusions which can be legitimately drawn from discussions about culture and class in relation to education, interesting and important though they may be, are essentially tactical rather than strategic. An understanding of the strengths of working-class culture and of the powers and limits of its available language may well affect the way teachers set about their work, help to define starting points, suggest qualities to connect with and build upon; and all that can be useful. But such knowledge does not in itself define what is to be done, does not provide basic educational aims; it provides rather the frame within which non-contingent educational aims are to be pursued. This is, again, a very bare version of a complex position and misses much of its intricacy; but it does not seriously distort it.

People with this point of view are likely to go on to argue that a primary attention to cultural considerations produces the risk of 'levelling down' in educational aims, of asking less from children than, differently approached, they are capable of giving. One interesting offshoot of this position is to be seen in the London 'Right to Learn' group who are concerned with the fact that, in their view, the current debate has induced in many teachers in poor areas an unduly low expectation of what their pupils are capable of, and hence unjustifiably low educational aspirations for them.

At its most central point, this position argues that there are still basic educational aims which are not altered by the social conditions of pupils, that these basic aims are to introduce pupils to a common core of intellectual and imaginative values beyond those of a particular historical consensus. There are variants of this general idea. Hardly anyone is more serious about basic educational aims than G. H. Bantock; but he does make specific aims largely dependent on his social judgments about the educability of different groups within society, and from this posits different educational purposes for each, according to their presumed levels of intelligence.

Those who hold to the idea of a common core of intellectual and imaginative values, no doubt affected by but not determined by particular circumstances, are not, it is important to say, necessarily arguing that there is a 'body of knowledge' out there, a sort of bundle of mental baggage which every child should take with him on his journey through school. That is an inert approach. The current debate in the United Kingdom about the pros and cons of a 'core curriculum' is bound to throw up this set of arguments. A recurring British educational nightmare is that some government will try to impose a system in which all children of a certain age are said at a certain time of day to be studying the same set books, acquiring the same items of information. I do not think the more thoughtful of the proponents of a 'core curriculum' are suggesting this at all. They are much more nearly arguing for an education which aims to offer all children the opportunity to develop certain valuable intellectual and imaginative *capacities*; and they recognise that – depending upon a child's social and cultural background, and much else – there is more than one route to acquiring those capacities. I imagine that this is what Raymond Williams has in mind when he argues for a common culture, but one which can best be acquired by starting from strong and differentiated social experiences.

It is important to stress again the value of starting and indeed the absolute need to start from *where people are*. This is always a double process; it is partly an understanding of what pupils or students are really saying and so of the texture of their lives, the better to understand the connections which can be made and developed from; it is partly a process of self-examination by the teacher, and this is quite a difficult process in which we strip ourselves of the protection given by those academic or pedagogic styles which give us the edge over members of the class. I mean styles in language, in presentation of material and in virtually all aspects of our own comportment. If we do undertake that process we will be constantly surprised by how far people can go in perception; people who, faced with the more usual methods of teaching, appear stupid, silent or morose.

My own first thirteen professional years were spent teaching adults, few of whom had any academic background, in the evenings. I started by in effect giving these groups, of a dozen or so, hour-long lectures of the sort I had myself been given at university; then, in the second hour, I told them we would have 'the discussion'. Of course, the discussions were dead and I had to do most of the talking. I had given them no purchase on the material, no way of bringing to bear their emerging interests and abilities; I had set up the whole business in safe terms, safe for me but not for them since they could not play that game without learning the rules and conventions within which I had decided it would operate. Naturally, that procedure was discarded very quickly, once I began to see how important it was for the students to be able to use their own languages, to set their own paces, to move outwards from their own experiences and their own modes of coping with their experience into the world of, say, a great novel. I deliberately say 'great' because an erroneous way of 'starting where the students are' is to offer to adult classes simplified texts, second-line literature with an obvious social commitment, or to be so consistently encouraging that any comment by any member of a class – no matter how mistaken it may really be – is greeted as a most interesting insight. Once again, we owe it to other people to let them be challenged by great literature in the way we always claim we ourselves are. The tutor is not only trying to see further into people's potential capacities; he is also the representative of intellectual standards and must therefore, if necessary by a rigorous approach, try to encourage his students to face what they may not want to face, slowly to start to disembarrass themselves of prejudices, sentimentality and the rest.

The other form of this third position is more radical than the one I have just described and finds the first form too narrowly intellectual, if not downright academic. It too, however, begins by rejecting as inadequate a major concentration of interest on social-class differences in educational thinking. It regards such a concentration as over rigid, two-dimensional. It starts from the major problems of the present day and from the view that these problems affect us all, whatever our social class or level of prosperity. It argues, therefore, that education must aim above all to introduce us not just to intellectual values but to *human* values and to the massive contemporary challenges to those values – challenges often made in the name of the intellect, of rationality, of 'common sense'.

On this view most school procedures and syllabuses are out of date, academic in the limiting sense, *subject-bound*. These people too would start from the concrete, from situations in the 'real' lives of pupils. They would shape teaching around issues which bear upon their pupils day by day, but which they at present see only in an immediate, on-the-pulses way, without having the tools with which to make larger sense of what is happening to them. Thus teaching would be 'theme' not 'subject' centred, and would try to keep in place all the time both intellectual and imaginative issues; it would be centred on the whole individual and his life experiences, not on an abstract idea of the 'trained mind' in a narrower sense. It would deal with issues in the environment – the pressures of urban life on the individual and the family, the role of the mass media, racism, the increasing gap between the developed and the underdeveloped world (I say 'under-developed' and would in some instances say 'undeveloped' rather than using the United Nations' preferred word 'developing' – which is a verbal cosmetic). All this can lead to some exciting and inspiring new teaching. But, like all new modes, it can be unwisely used. Some teaching in Britain which is inspired by this outlook is sloppy; there is still a case for teaching the major intellectual disciplines as we have habitually known them.

The debate I have been describing has had some considerable achievements. Above all, it has offered teachers and others the opportunity to take a more open and diverse view of class/culture differences and so of children's possibilities. It offers a more pluralistic and richer set of approaches than were assumed in, for example, those local grammar schools I described much earlier. It discourages us from seeking to iron out, in the name of 'proper' educational and social standards, social and cultural differences which are still important, not necessarily divisive, and together contribute to the still quite rich fabric of British social life. The recognition of these varied values, not only in educational terms, but in all aspects of culture, is one of the better products of the debates since the early Sixties.

I do not think the most radical holders of views on the relations between educational systems and authority will see anything like the changes they want. This is partly because they will not be likely to carry with them more than a minority even of the left wing in politics, partly because on the whole open societies do not take such giant radical leaps (neither of these characteristics is necessarily or wholly a matter of selfishness among the powerful), and partly because their case is not wholly sustainable; it has a lot of truth in it, but is not completely true.

Meanwhile, there are some rules of thumb which need holding on to firmly. One I have already more than hinted at: that, in spite of all the pros and cons of the debate about where the blame for educational insufficiency lies, there are some children who need special extra provision and care. Another is that, whatever the limitations of some old-established educational attitudes towards class, manners and language, not all middle-class attitudes are bad nor even the bad ones unique to the middle classes; conversely, and even when we have recognised the hitherto insufficiently recognised virtues of working-class life, not all working-class habits are good nor are even the good ones unique to working-class people. These are simple enough assertions but sometimes they need to be made.

If this seems doubtful, let me give you only one example from many. A contemporary book on education and class in Britain discusses the advice given by a headmaster, that his pupils donate some of their pocket money to good causes and take up voluntary work on behalf of needy members of the community. Having quoted the headmaster, the author says:

It is possible to read this passage as giving some substance to (the view) that schools attempt to foist dubious middle-class values on the poor.

Let us adopt the careful insurance policy phrasing and comment:

It is possible to read this passage as an expression of the headmaster's belief that whatever your social class and whatever your opportunities in life it is good to help the poor, the sick and the old.

We are not told where the author stands, and presumably he does not actually know where the headmaster stands. Maybe the headmaster had thought through the matter of values and socially-conditioned behaviour further than the book's author seems to assume.

Even more complicated is the wide, undifferentiated sea of total relativism, the reluctance to recognise that some values, attitudes, habits may be morally preferable to others. Here is a distinguished writer on modern educational theory putting one toe into the shallower waters of that sea: he is grappling with the matter of value judgments:

It is at least possible that some kinds of knowledge are superior in some meaningful way to other kinds of knowledge.

Note the similarly cautious phrasing of this passage with that quoted just above. But if, and in spite of all the pitfalls, people engaged in education do not think that some kinds of knowledge *are* superior in some meaningful way to others then on what criteria can they devise a syllabus in any subject?

I suppose the far end of this line is the position taken by some teachers, on their being convinced that there is no point in making their pupils – from deprived homes – merely marginally numerate and literate (which is all that present conditions sometimes seem to make possible) since they seem then more securely trained to be the obedient helots of a corrupt society. Better to let them be as they are, since they will inevitably spend their days on the worst kind of routine work, work which demands nothing seriously numerate or literate from them. Why should they be only partially trained, trained only so far as to bind them more securely?

There is something in the basic analysis, but the conclusions from it are deeply mistaken. It *is* wrong for teachers to be satisfied to train children to be just sufficiently literate as to accept, but not literate enough to challenge, some of the dominant values of open commercial democracies. But the teacher's response should be to increase the pressure on all sides to get them through to a fuller literacy and numeracy, to help them stand up better on their own feet as articulate, critical, judging human beings. To do that, drawing on all we know of their background and all we know of the values of intellectual life, is the best single aim any of us could set ourselves. To do less than that is a sort of betrayal of them as humans, and of the intellectual life itself. With such an aim at its heart, the debate about culture, class, language and education could begin to find its proper focus.   1976

CLASS BIAS
IN BRITISH EDUCATION

A few years ago I took part in a television programme about the depiction of class on television. The research for the programme gave reasonably clear indications that the correlations between family, class, school, college, and access to some of the main professions were probably still as strong as thirty years before. The BBC seemed to find the film embarrassing and it had no second showing. I was told by three senior officials that I was in error; Britain was now a classless society; to insist otherwise was a leftist illusion.

More recently I gave a lecture to a group of foreign professionals attending a conference about British society today. I said that both the sense and the reality of class were still very strong. The first questioner, a Latin American, asked why I argued thus, since they'd been very confidently assured by a previous speaker that 'class' no longer existed in Britain.

And so it goes on. The more articulately defensive heads of public schools pooh-pooh, in just the right accents and inflections, the idea that privilege still reigns in this country, and in particular that there are excessively strong links between social class and educational and professional opportunities. They claim that their schools are now democratic and open; and then go on to talk about British society and the role of such schools within it in a way which makes you awe-struck at the cultural cocoon in which they have been wrapped all their lives.

At the turn into the Eighties, two important studies* make it harder for anyone of goodwill to continue talking in that way. In spite of all the intended reforms of recent decades, no significant reduction in class inequalities has in fact been achieved. We are not

*_Origins and Destinations: Family, Class and Education in Modern Britain,_ by Halsey, Heath, Ridge; _Social Mobility and Class Structure in Modern Britain_ by John H. Goldthorpe.

becoming much more open, socially *or* educationally.

Even the meritocracy, about whose human thinness and unforgivingness T. S. Eliot and Michael Young warned us, is not emerging. The new service class, which is similar to what used to be called the 'meritocracy', and which does to some extent recruit from the working class – some bright fish jump the rapids – looks after its own in much the old manner. The social-educational links remain massively firm.

Put it another way. The 'to-him-that-hath' law still runs strong in this country. Create a new social benefit because it is badly needed, especially by the working classes, and 'the service class' will take best advantage of it. Such reforms usually mean 'increased subsidies to the affluent.' They will fill the Arts Council subsidised theatres; they will take better advantage of the National Health Service because they know how to make their wants articulate and will not be easily bullied or ignored; they will get most from the billions of extra money poured into education, and especially into higher education, in the last twenty years.

Taken all in all, the educational reforms of those years have nevertheless shown that the pool of educable talent is larger than has been conventionally assumed and asserted. But the connections between social class and opportunity remain so tenacious that there is still virtually no more chance for working class people than there was thirty-five years ago.

Here is a litany for repeating each evening: in the late 1970s the burghers of Sheffield decided to set up their own 'independent' day grammar school; so much for the 1944 Act and the idea of equal opportunity. In 1979, a British Government, in the face of all the evidence of need elsewhere, set up the Assisted Places scheme. We do not have an educational system: we have an education-and-class system, and that's very different. We are still, at the least, two nations: and the crevasses between the main groups are hardly less deep than they were when Disraeli wrote.

What a brave Secretary of State for Education must first tackle is the excessively privileged status of the public schools. He can start by taking away their fiscal advantages by which the taxpayers, most of whom will never see inside such a school, subsidise them. Integration will and must follow. These schools are wasteful of resources and talent needed elsewhere; they reduce the articulate critical pressure needed within the State system; they are socially disastrous because they are monstrously separatist. We need to be diverse but not

45

divided, least of all in this way.

Consider, for instance, the lawyers who go from the cloisters of Eton or Winchester to those of New College or King's, and then to those of Gray's Inn – and then spend their lives straightening the jackets of the rest of us. They do not *know* this society; and no amount of *bonhomie* with the man they buy their fags from in High Holborn will make up for that lack. This is the fiftieth year since D. H. Lawrence died and the twentieth year since the Lady Chatterley trial. I still remember the appalling impression created at that time by the style and manner of some representatives of the English legal system resisting what they thought was in effect a breach of the bastion; and little has since changed.

Where such tight links exist, the freedom to buy education for your children is not like the freedom to smoke or not, to drink or not, to have expensive holidays or not. Access to good education should be as much a universal social right as access to pure water; and we don't buy better water than the people down the hill.

So what is to be done? A further virtue of these two books is that they both, after deploying their considerable evidence as objectively as they can, make explicit value judgments and proposals. Goldthorpe raises the question of why resentment by working-class people to this process has not been more evident, and concludes that it has probably been muffled by the increasing prosperity enjoyed by all classes, at least until recently. I would myself also point to the role of the admen and the mass media as opiate manufacturers for the consumer society.

Goldthorpe doubts whether *fragmentary* reforms via the politics of consensus can substantially alter things; the built-in resistances are too great. Yet he is not looking for blood in the streets. He sees the increasing collective aggressiveness of the unions as a reaction against the whole process he has described, but wants that collective force to be put behind demands for more than simply wage increases, behind a wide and radical range of movements towards a more open and just society.

Halsey's is the more specifically educational theme. He doesn't expect the millennium, but does see some grounds for hope, particularly now that the 'service class's' educational demands seem to have been substantially met. Still, the current climate certainly doesn't encourage the hope that funds will be transferred to working-class needs.

Against such perspectives we should give overwhelming priority to three areas. First, the comprehensive schools. We must get those right, and in our own best way, which means getting nearer solving a lot of other related social problems. But there can be movement and progress against all the odds, as Rutter's *15,000 Hours* showed. And comprehensive schools already often do better than most of the press leads us to believe.

Second, we have to put much more into providing for those 16- to 19-year-olds – more than half of the age group – for whom education has been such a failure that after they leave school at sixteen they never go back to any sort of educational provision.

Third, we have to recognise the crucial importance of making much more provision for continuing education, as the means of providing better for those of us who realise belatedly, and at different stages in life, that education can have something to say to our condition, professional, social, recreational or spiritual.

We should do all this, not just for economic reasons – because we hope it will help the economy to revive – but for the good of our souls. As long as our educational system is as class-based as these studies confirm, we will be a poorer society in every way: but above all morally. We should be deeply ashamed at the way such bias persists in the national life. It is virtually a case for the European Commission on Human Rights!   1980

THE STUDENT MOVEMENT
AND ITS EFFECTS

===

We all see, in changes which surprise us, what we want to see; and hindsight usually only hardens the pattern we first see by further simplifying it. But it is not false hindsight to remember why some of us, on balance, welcomed the increased student activity in the late 1960s. We thought the students were at bottom asking the right questions, raising the right issues. They were saying, for instance, that universities were not the homes of sweetness and light or of severe inquiry they had been led or had led themselves to expect. Rather they were places where people pursued their advanced researches cut off from the wider society and the uses it made of their work. The best researchers might be very good but were too hermetic. The educated professional was less in evidence than the academic entrepreneur. Universities showed an ill-thought-through disposition not to question society but to accept it and serve it, whether in industry or commerce or the social sciences or the training of teachers. All this is part of the process by which the universities had ceased to be training centres for an elite and become training centres for the much larger numbers needed to serve a more and more complex society. They had lost a traditional role and assumed an uncritical function.

So students came to criticise their universities the more, because they had expected more of them and been by and large disappointed. It follows that some of those out in the front of these disputes were among the best of their generation, intellectually and imaginatively. I agree with Colin Crouch that the deeper impulses behind student activism were idealistic rather than simply politically activist, and that the most powerful search was often for a greater sense of community. He makes the interesting suggestion that, though these students may have rejected 'the community of scholars' as it was offered to them, thinking it something of a sham, they did often find a sense of community in the sit-ins and demonstrations, a sense of community their predominantly middle-class homes had not given them. Bernard Crick is interesting and unusual, too, in his suggestion that the sense of a need for communication was even stronger than that for participation. Participation has been much more of a fashionable word, but communication – as a to and fro process – points deeper; hence, one supposes, the power of the word 'dialogue' throughout the debates.

In short and at bottom the student movement – at its best – was asserting that there should be ideals, principles, values, a constant critical questioning within society and pre-eminently within the universities, rather than an acceptance, a getting on the industrial, commercial or social bandwagon. This always needs saying and not only by the young. Some much older people have borne the heat of this battle for decades – and some young people in each generation appear in this respect to have been born middle-aged. So at best the students reminded us of perspectives, ideals, we easily forget – not necessarily out of sinfulness or conspiracy but because life goes on and one gets tired or in a routine, caught up with the day-by-day.

So how does one begin to draw up a first profit and loss account? The student movement did, I believe, contribute to some useful changes within higher education. Some people would argue that these changes were part of secular movements under way before the student movement found its voice in the late 1960s. We all have our favourite images for these changes. Here is one of mine. Soon after I joined Birmingham University in the early 1960s, the campus hairdresser was turned out of the grounds for offering French letters for sale. I felt sorry for the hairdresser. Hairdressers seem to have been selling French letters – discreetly stuck behind the edges of the mirrors – since Chaucer's day. Only a few years later, in the late 1960s, the pill was easily available through the university doctor. Student activism may have helped on that process; but the change towards greater sexual openness throughout the 1960s was the pre-eminent agent. I noticed also that the new openness often bore harder on the girls than on the men. Greater choices, greater anxiety; some of them were exploited. In all these matters the student movement, if it did not initiate, helped to promote and define.

In looking at universities in general the students were right to claim that the 'authorities' – essentially the professoriate – had too much centralised power, and were smug with it. One of the results of the disputes of the last decade has been the widening of the line of authority to include not only students but also members of staff other than the professoriate. But again one feels the need to fill out the picture. I remember over many years not only the smug professors but the hardworking and the honest. British universities largely run themselves; they do not have a full-time 'Administration' with superior powers; and the cost is high, especially to those members of staff who are willing to work long and hard on all the unavoidable detailed work. During the 1960s, when the great expansion came after Robbins, the best of those people, whether in organising expansion in established places or in setting up the new universities, nearly destroyed themselves physically with overwork, and certainly put off publications which could have reinforced their scholarly reputations. By their lights they were doing a very good job indeed. So now we have students in the governments of universities and polytechnics, to a greater or less extent. That in principle is a gain. So is the greater general openness and greater tendency towards consultation in most places.

Yet the gain, the *sense* of gain, is – perhaps inevitably – less than had been hoped; and there seem to be two main reasons. First, that in largely self-governing societies the committee process is inescapably slow and time-consuming, requiring the spending of lots of time on detail, on all the apparatus of necessary bureaucracy. I agree with David Riesman that bureaucracy should not be a dirty word. It is the inevitable result of trying to see that justice is done in large, inescapably complicated, administrative organisms. So students who, unless they are full-time sabbatical officers, have much else to do – such as study – find committee attendance often a great nuisance, even if they are willing in principle to help by working on them. A further result of the new style is that committees have increased in number, and paperwork increased, too. This, too, is inevitable, but should be acknowledged as a cost. More important and difficult is the fact that the range of joint committees, some of them with spending powers, have blurred rather than removed or redefined the powers of the still existing structures of responsibility, e.g. of deans, heads of departments, etc. This problem has not been resolved yet and should not be kept under the carpet much longer.

The other and naturally more troublesome aspect of the working of the new committees, with their changed compositions and constitutions, comes not from the students who are *willing* within the time available to make them work but from those who regard them, and have probably always regarded them, as mere tokenism, shams, the sort of phenomena by which 'the authorities' will always manage to get what they want; or even regard them, more absolutely, as instances of precisely those formal managerial structures to which they are wholly opposed in favour of a vastly more democratic, open, participatory, a qualitatively different way of proceeding. They will therefore seek to instruct their representatives on joint committees to take an immovable mandate from, say, the union executive; or they will themselves provoke contestation from within a committee exactly so as to disturb the system, to gum up the works.

This can lead to interesting tangles as when, for example, the demand is for some facility which costs a lot of money and whose financing is categorically prohibited as a legitimate public expense by one's paymasters – the DES, the local authority or the UGC. Even a weak or accommodating vice-chancellor or principal, unless he has a bottomless private chest or is prepared to try to make dubious virements between financial heads and hope to deceive the auditors, has hardly any room for manoeuvre. It may seem to him the clearest common sense that all should sit down as a *joint* committee and discuss ways of getting the furthest one can. But if the student members refuse to engage in such a dialogue so as to maintain their long-range main principle – that this facility *should* be provided free by the funding agencies – then the short-term result is not necessarily stalemate. Rather, 'the authorities' have had the power, because of the urgent need to decide on the issue, handed back to them unilaterally.

It is true that from one angle the old guard of most senior people do have the cards stacked on their side. But they do not always win. And they will have to listen even more if the committees are allowed to have their democratic due time in finding the best ways to work. But if you do not believe that this process can *ever* produce sufficiently radical change, you will do your best to ensure that the system does not work, even in its newly modified forms. The student movement helped along but did not initiate – the new universities did most here, of any single group of contributors – a fresh look at the map of learning, an attempt to redefine subjects, to break what had often

51

become self-justifying definitions; and to encourage a better scrutiny of syllabuses, some of which were very tired and old; and to look anew at the curriculum and especially at their hidden thrusts and assumptions; and to look at the need for more varied methods of assessment. They also encouraged a greater interest in teaching itself, about which universities in particular had been unjustifiably careless. Remembering all this, we should remember also that, in general, the characteristic virtues of British higher education were retained throughout this difficult expansive period. By contrast I think the calls for *relevance* in the curriculum, though hot and strong, went round in circles, and got hardly anywhere. But I shall return to that subject later.

Nor was the exact nature and justification of the claimed pastoral role of university teachers faced squarely. It seemed sufficient to damn it out of hand as paternalism. Hence, many university teachers gave up that role in embarrassment. One of the ironies is that today's full-time sabbatical student officers, who seem much more numerous than their predecessors, often find themselves carrying out what is – though they would not call it that – pastoral work of a most intensive kind, and being very sharply criticised by their own members if their attention to these issues is not available for unconscionably long hours.

Lastly, in these changes and gains, the students' movement as a whole is now recognised as a contributor to any national debate about higher education. It has, the opponents of the changes so far would say, been absorbed into the system and muted. It has, its supporters would say, made some limited but real gains; nothing revolutionary, certainly, but more gain than loss. But others would say that the student movement led to a decline in the general public standing of the universities.

And if those gains seem little and *with the grain,* set against all the effort and radical fervour which went to bring them about, to what can the relative modesty of the gains and the relative quietness of institutions of higher education today be ascribed?

Why did the impulse fade? The overwhelmingly first reason is international and secular. The energy left the student movement all over the world as the 1970s advanced; and we do not know for certain why. We say it was partly because the Vietnam war ended. We say with more confidence that in the very much bleaker climate of the 1970s, when jobs are at a premium, it is – though the number of active, radical students may be not at all or only a little smaller – it is harder to persuade any large number of other students to risk a revolutionary act. I know several student leaders of the late 1960s who are now teaching in higher education, and have lost none of their edge. I know some others who are in market research or commercial television and have no such edge any longer, or have had to put their ideals to the margins of their lives. Their juniors, coming out ten years later, have neither of those types of glittering prize or option to be at all sure of.

In Britain itself the modified nature of the gains is also partly to be explained by the well-known and inescapable British inertia, that slow frictional refusal to be rushed, of which the senior people in authority in higher education display only one occupational form (though a well-honed one). This is the means by which the British capacity to absorb dissent works at its most effective. Some students and staff are deeply suspicious of it and wish to alter the system root and branch. As will be clear now, I belong (have always belonged) to those who believe that, faced with an offer which looks fair but *may* turn out to be a sham, it is not all discreditable to *start* by trying to make it work in the genuine way it proposes.

Much more important, in this first sketch of considerations on why things did not go much further, faster: the perspective of those most in the front was too narrowly political, it therefore did not lead them to do full justice to the force of the emotions on which they could draw in the larger student body. There were several reasons for this, beginning with the fact that they were too much given to foreign models, foreign practice, foreign approaches and foreign modes of discourse. Whether they should or should not, British workers do not and are not likely in any nearly foreseeable future to march side by side in the streets with British students as they did in France. The idea does unimaginative violence to the realities of the texture of British social life. Nor are British students as, for example, are the law students of Latin America, traditionally seen as the next wave of real political force and likely leadership. Again, that situation will not come about in the foreseeable future here, even if we were to think it desirable.

Tariq Ali, not a native Englishman, put his finger on this error as it is made by many on the far Left:

Their conceptions are totally unrelated to the society in which they are working and the political consciousness of the working class ... We are not going to win the working-class in Western Europe away from bourgeois democracy unless they are convinced that the system they are fighting for is going to be more democratic, not less democratic, than that they have already. Who can blame them?*

The British student movement in the late 1960s was, in short, not sufficiently rooted in the soil of British experience. It was not only intellectually but also imaginatively too derivative, and this made it less able to recognise both the actual constraints and limits before it and, just as important, the best possibilities for movement, growth and change. How often, whether in praise or, more likely, in criticism, did the names of Newman, Arnold, Eliot, Orwell or Leavis occur in the student literature of the time? One would think that the political model being drawn upon had been found somewhere over the mid-Atlantic or mid-Channel, without the intervention of any British history. I take it that this is much of what is behind Colin Crouch's approach to the subject. He adds that in a deeper manner the British student movement, even at its most lively, was nevertheless English to the core in another sense, in that with some exceptions it showed a gentleness rarely found elsewhere. For whatever reasons, the basic system was not overturned. I cannot regret that, since I believe that what would have come from such a radical overturn would almost certainly have been worse than what it superseded and because I believe that with all their faults – and I have spent a lot of time criticising them over the years – the British universities as at present constituted, and now the polytechnics, provide a better base for reform than anything else likely to be created from whole cloth. Much of what was hoped for by the student – and let us remember the staff – movement has still to be brought about. But something has been done and the *base* for improvement is still there.

So what might be the next move forwards? It is not for me to tell today's students what their own corporate bodies should do. I shall instead reflect on what I think I should go for if I were myself once again a student. It will naturally all start from the position I have outlined, that I am myself a social democrat, a reformer rather than a believer in revolutionary change. That being said, here are some main issues which a reformer, willing to work hard, and willing to see the institutions as more than the servants of existing society, and willing to try to ask basic questions about the present state and the

* Tariq Ali: 'Culture, the Media and Workers' Democracy', in *Media, Politics and Culture, A Socialist View,* ed. Carl Gardner, 1979.

future of this and other societies, might stress.

As to reforms inside the institutions of higher education, first, I will mention only two things which still need doing; but they are important. 'Relevance' should be defined better across all disciplines. Too often it means something simply tagged on – whether by an impatient professor who is adding it to his specialised curriculum only because he is being pushed from outside, or by a politically conscious student who has no more thought it through than the professor. Relevance is nothing if it is not organic to a subject and its inner importance; so it is not easily defined. Similarly, relevance is a confidence trick if it is bought at the expense of our right – the right of all of us – to grapple with the hardest.

Second, we need to push forward further the implications of varied assessment. The increase in variety is a gain, both a human and a pedagogical gain. But its claims have now been pushed so far, not just by students but by many staff, that some students are being denied the right to be tested, to test themselves, by the best intellectual standards. I know, from trying to write, what a difference there is between what one can *say* and what one *writes down*. Only writing – alone with a piece of paper – shows you where you are muddled, where you are cutting corners, where you are self-indulgent or plain ignorant and so on. No group activity, useful though it may be in other ways, can be a substitute for this. Staff or students who deny themselves or others the opportunity to be thus personally stretched are doing wrong to the free and honest intellectual life, which is after all one of the best things these societies have pointed towards: that is, their admittedly patchy but crucial commitment to the search for objectivity and honesty and its free circulation. Without that hard commitment to the difficulty – and contingency – of life, bridges will fall down if we are engineers, and metaphorical bridges of all kinds – but no less important bridges – will collapse if we come from disciplines where the consequences of muddle and inadequacy are less spectacular.

Few things are more elegant and beautiful than the sight of a solitary human being putting himself to the test through language. Which is why, though most forms of political extremism do not greatly distress me, the misuse of language for propaganda or rhetoric, whether from the Right or the Left and by people of any age, does.

Imagine three kinds of higher education institution. First, that which is *institution centred,* committed very much to keeping itself in being in its present shape. That outlook has rightly taken a bad knock in these latter years. Secondly, the idea of such institutions as *student-centred*. This was the battering-ram used to break up the first notion. It still has a lot of life. It is more than a useful corrective. It expresses a truth: that the needs of the individual are greater and more important than those of the institution as such, and that the institution should always be ready to change to meet them so far as ever possible.

There is the rub or qualification. 'So far as ever possible.' What could qualify such a claim? Only the claims of the search for truth. This is where we come to the third kind of institution. In higher education, of all places, the individual has no right to demand that truth be mitigated or adulterated because he cannot meet the hard demands of a search for it. He has to accept that in some things he may have second-rate equipment or inadequate staying power. This is the hardest challenge of all.

So much for possible lines of action *internal* to institutions of higher education. Let us look wider now, to British society in general.

First, it would be wrong to undervalue the place from which we start: British society has many faults and sins. Yet it is still one of the more comfortable, humane societies of the world. You have only to go across the globe today, or look back in time to working-class life here only fifty years ago, to recognise the truth and the force of this statement. That must be where we begin.

On the other hand, Britain is still a badly one-sided society. So many social reforms, meant particularly to help the needy, end by being chiefly a further aid to those who already know what they want and how to make best use of publicly provided facilities. In this context, the greater provision in higher education of the last two decades has been a benefit chiefly to the aspirant lower-middle-class and upwards. In the next decade, we must look in particular at the needs of those sixteen-nineteen-year-olds who leave school with no particular skill or prospects even of a basic job. This field broadens into questions about part-time work, city colleges (rather than the present emphasis on full-time education for eighteen-year-olds on large campuses), paid educational leave and the rest. Behind it all is the by now inescapable knowledge that the links between certain schools, universities, social groups and entry to some of the main positions of power or influence in this society are still far too close for comfort. There is a lot to do. This challenge has to do, above all, with that old and too much discredited phrase 'the quality of life'.

Externally, that is, outside the United Kingdom, there are two overwhelming issues. The first is about the needs of the Third or undeveloped world. As to this, the developed world sits by-and-large unheeding, comfortable, parochial, short-sighted. Its response to the call from the undeveloped world for a New International Economic Order is proof enough of that.

Above all, on the world level, elsewhere and also here, the major issue before all of us for the next twenty years, and whatever our ages, is human rights, the right to think and to speak freely and the right not to be spied upon. It would be egregious to suggest that the problem here is of the same order as that in most other countries. It would be blind to think it does not exist here.

To conclude: the student movement embodied and stressed the importance of ideals beyond the immediate present. Such a call had not, has not been greatly heard in Britain since the late 1940s. No doubt it aroused all the more resentment in some people because it suggested that what they called their 'realism' was more an unjustified complacency (about South African investments, for instance). But wholly linked to such a sense of purpose there should always be – these are simple things to say but they need saying precisely because the idealism was so generous – a recognition of the need, the importance, not to patronise people, nor to be unjust to them, nor to oversimplify problems. This is the minimum perspective we should all at any time start from, students or staff.   1978

AFTER EXPANSION,
THE CASE FOR DIVERSITY

It is becoming clear that, for higher education in developed open societies, the early Eighties will be a watershed at least as important as the early Sixties.

The early Sixties set in motion a process which continued for a decade in most such countries: an unparalleled expansion in university and other higher education. The United States led the way; but the more slow-to-respond British system surprised itself. Today we have about 13 per cent of the 18-21 age-group in full-time higher education. That may seem small by US standards; but it represents almost a threefold increase since 1960.

What a strange period that now appears. One of the most firm of our many assumptions now seems rather like a dream from which we are being bidden to wake. What made us decide that two hundred acres, two or three miles out of town (towns which were preferably somewhat historic), with halls of residence scattered pleasantly through them, should be the general mode? What element in the *Zeitgeist* made almost all of us conclude this at about the same time? Was it simply that opportunities for big spending produce their own rationalisations, as surely as water finds its own level? Universities rationalise as well as any other institutions. I remember my first vice-chancellor ruminating, when we were 900, that about 1,500 was the ideal size for a university, on grounds which encompassed the needs to have a 'good spread' of subjects and the argument that democratic relations between different members of 'the university community' similar to those of an Athenian city-state emerged at about that size. I remember that that figure crept upwards through the late Fifties and into the Sixties to 3,000 and 4,000 and beyond. And we finally saw a new university, one with a somewhat specialist bias, planned for 10,000.

58

But to come back to space and accommodation. I was as much rapt by the two-hundred-acres-plus-residences concept of the Sixties as were most others who took part in those debates. I suppose one of my own main impulses was the feeling that the post-war maintenance grants had done a good deal to widen the horizons of poor students, those who formerly had had little opportunity to look further than their home-town universities, and thus were committed to a more or less nine-to-five student day, given the routines of many homes. That pattern seemed well worth loosening. Others, from different backgrounds, thought more of the new universities as seeking to create, in Basil Spence New Town complexes, civilising, human and moral relationships similar to those they had themselves enjoyed at Balliol or King's. Neither was a mean aim; though the latter especially seems a bit narrowly comical now. But it is dead. It is as dead as the dream of high-rise housing. Indeed the campus dream is, come to think of it, the equivalent, in higher educational and predominantly middle-class terms, of what the high-rise concept was for working-class people. Both tried to think about what was best for *other* people. Neither was in itself an unworthy dream. Both went too far and went on too long; and they were inadequately rooted, socially and psychologically. We do well to escape from them.

The British expansion within the universities had three main characteristics: it attended above all to the full-time needs of those aged eighteen or thereabouts; it grew linearly, by doubling and trebling entrants to existing courses; and it was conceived as essentially a servicing operation. That is, expansion developed the sciences and technologies for the perceived needs of society, and also increased admissions to the humanities with the umbrella justification that, though smaller proportions than hitherto would become scholars or high level teachers, these disciplines in themselves give a humane training suitable for a wide range of generalist or executive or managerial professions.

As a result higher education did well by a range of people, running from the full-time Oxbridge student to the sandwich-course student at a northern polytechnic. The differences between those on each end of that line are still considerable, but in one sense they belong to a continuous and at least partly-coherent whole. They have done well not only because they have been able, if minded and fitted, to contribute to the advancement of knowledge but on two other grounds. They have been given professional training to a level which

59

pulls them some way out of the ruck; and they have been offered a generally liberating and liberalising education if they were willing to acquire it.

Meanwhile, a great body of other people are arguably further away from education as either a professional or a civilising force than they should be or we care to recognise. Still, it might be as well to list the main virtues of British universities. As Shirley Williams used to show with some splendid charts when she was Education Secretary, we are still among the world leaders in producing men and women who make imaginative breakthroughs at the frontiers of knowledge, and major technological breakthroughs also. That we don't do very well at applying those inventions to industrial and commercial purposes and then selling the products is another and well-known story; at that point the Japanese pass us, going the other way.

We are economical in our manner of producing graduates. Our degree courses are shorter than those of most countries, and wastage is remarkably low. Given that to fail in the middle of a university course is more of a social slur here than in most countries, this is a doubly good thing. But it is also a result of something we should not undervalue, the relatively high degree of care we give to individual students.

The great achievement of the universities (existing and new), the polytechnics and the colleges, during the expansionist Sixties, lay precisely here: that they proved that more needn't mean worse in staff or students. It is true that some people acquired academic posts then who wouldn't have got them in the Fifties, and certainly wouldn't if they had applied in the Seventies. But, in most subjects, the dilution was not serious.

There are many qualifications to the three main thrusts noted above. Some, concerned that simple expansion which opened the doors to more and more of the eighteen-plus cohort begged a great many questions about differences of opportunity and development, made special arrangements to admit older students and students without the usual minimum entrance requirements. Some teachers – especially in the technologies (most teachers of the humanities seem to me to have been merely carried along by events; or perhaps I am more critical of them because it seems right to expect more in such a matter) – insisted that their course should require their students, *within* the course structures themselves, to face issues outside the technological or narrowly academic.

Even today most teachers in higher education are massively ignorant of or massively unconcerned about some of the major problems before us, and especially before any one who cares about the links between the social structure and educational opportunity. How much have the universities contributed in their own best ways – as the homes of many of the finest minds of the day – to understanding the huge problem of illiteracy and its eradication, or to that of the great numbers who leave school at sixteen, barely literate and numerate and with few further prospects? Precious little. Instead they have in the main gone on satisfiedly processing the eighteen-year-olds of socio-economic groups A to C, with a few upstarts from D.

But though the majority of teachers did not ask many questions about whom they should teach, or about the adequacy of their assumptions as to their subjects, and so about those subjects' relations to society, they nevertheless shouldered – as the Sixties passed – heavier teaching loads and sometimes excessive administrative work. There are three fundamental principles of British university staffs: the overriding need for first-rate scholarship, the importance of face-to-face small group teaching (though its cost in time is high) and the importance of self-government by the teachers themselves, rather than by a 'faceless administration'. These are powerful and valuable principles and on the whole they were not diluted in the Sixties. To maintain them in the face of such a rapid and large expansion was a major achievement.

Yet we should also remember the other great structural change in higher education in the last couple of decades; the binary system. I thought the division wrong at the time it was created; those doubts have been amply borne out. However much people in universities may protest at the statement, in general the polytechnics are quietly assumed to be lower forms of higher education. The interchange between the two sectors is almost incredibly underdeveloped (yes, faults on both sides have contributed to this lack of co-operation); and the fear of transbinary work in the *one* institution verges on the neurotic – (fear of comparisons, fear of different systems of validation and monitoring, or of funding). The Chinese Wall is strong and high. Meanwhile, it is plain that more transbinary work in large institutions would be helpful and invigorating as well as logical.

Let us accept also – and be generous about – the fact that, as anyone knows who taught in universities throughout the period, for a substantial number a good part of those three years was spent somewhat 'aimlessly', that it was a period of 'finding one's feet', 'finding oneself', that many 'drifted' into higher education because it was available and 'put off the day of decision' (the grants may never have seemed adequate to the recipients, but they are by international standards surprisingly good), that 'one seemed to go on to university as a matter of course', especially if one came from a middle-class home. Those quotations are from my own students of the Sixties. If we lived in an endlessly expanding financial world, fine; we could go on doing *more* of just that. It has been splendid for *our* children and those of our kind.

It has not been so good for others. That £2,500 a year or more which each full-time student cost in, say, the late Seventies would go a long way towards improving matters for more than one 16 to 19-year-old, or towards helping to keep down fees for mature and part-time students who are by now being increasingly priced out. Increased demand would follow supply if the doors were more welcoming. And so one could go on. The non-system, which is really a very successful system, leaves a lot of potentially bright children by the wayside (it is a very specially-shaped filter).

It seems to me now that the failure of universities to think more fundamentally about expansion may help to explain one aspect of the student disturbances of the Sixties. Obviously the impulses behind those events were more than simply a reaction against the role then being played within society by the universities; they questioned some basic drives of our kinds of society. The universities were most directly affected by those challenges because they are the homes of some of the most intelligent in their generation, at a most sensitive time in their lives. But the particular anger with which the students often turned upon the universities themselves was fed by the sense that they should have stood for a searching criticism of the nature of these societies but had instead – devotedly, painstakingly and with lots of goodwill – settled into providing more and more for the already agreed needs of such societies.

But now we are at a turning point. The phase of continuous substantial growth is over; at the best we have seen, during the last few years, a levelling-out; at the worst, there has been some contraction. Not even the wealthiest country could have maintained the Sixties' and early Seventies' rate of growth. It would, sooner rather than later, have distorted the pattern of public or private spending. Even now, with capital grants for building virtually unavailable in most countries, many of the existing buildings and plant are being only marginally maintained. More important, in Britain – and we may not be alone in this – the demographic information is unmistakable. From 1982/3 until at least 1990/1 the number of eighteen-year-olds will decline progressively and markedly. But until 1982/3 their numbers will increase. Suppose staff, buildings and resources were provided to do as well for these numbers as for today's smaller number of 'able and willing' eighteen-year-olds (and that would seem just, though costly, and perhaps politically unpopular). What should happen to the staff, the buildings, the resources, after 1982/3? Should they be cut back so that the released public resources may be used elsewhere – on the National Health Service, or on the needs of those numerous and deprived 16- to 19-year-olds who are not likely to enter full-time higher education, or on public housing, or on the old and poor? These questions are not easily answered.

Undoubtedly, the Eighties should be seen by universities as a time for thinking about their roles much more than they did in the Sixties. In times of gross expansion we can get along without asking too many questions about priorities. I am not now arguing that the prospect of hanging concentrates the mind wonderfully, that the universities should think about changes in their roles simply because they may otherwise find themselves with fewer staff and buildings. I am saying that the universities should now take the opportunity, more thoroughly than they did in the Sixties and Seventies, to enquire into their own best functions.

There are two main areas for attention. The first concerns the students. The universities will need to think more about their links with age groups other than the eighteen-plus. It is commonplace, but so far not much acted upon, that as we become technologically more sophisticated many more people will need further training at different stages in their lives. The universities are only one part of the educational provisions needed to cope with these changes. But they are a crucial part, both for what they can directly provide, and because they are at the peak of intellectual enquiry and should be developing the analysis of needs generally.

So the area at present loosely called 'continuing education' has a good claim to become the main point of growth within higher education in the Eighties. The universities are being invited to ask themselves how far their concentration on full-time, eighteen-plus students, taking continuous three- to four-year courses for first degrees and then, some of them, immediate 'end on' higher degrees (all of it good in its own terms) matches the range of needs. The increasing speed of change in the professions and sciences and technologies demands that greater stress be put on more varied forms of study, on refresher courses, in-service courses, paid educational leave, part-time study by home-based students, credit transfers and much else of those kinds. There are risks in such changes but fewer than is often assumed, and the gains could be great. It follows also that better provision needs to be made for the delayed needs of those who at eighteen do not wish to continue in full-time education, and better options for those who at present simply drift into full-time higher education because alternative routes are not easily available. It should not be immensely difficult to provide better for late entry several years after eighteen, when work or travel have shown some people that full-time higher education is what they really want, or for even older people who, for one reason or another, fall off the educational conveyor belt, but discover at twenty-five, thirty, or thirty-five, that they do wish for a university training. The provision for such people is still quite inadequate, and though their urge to learn is usually strong, they are looked at dubiously by some university teachers. Will they fit in? Can they cope with essay writing, steady intellectual work on their own, etc? In my experience, their urge to learn can carry them through well, so long as steps are taken to reduce adventitious handicaps. (Still, unless they are lucky, they are likely to find that some employers look at them askance; at their age they are expensive to employ.) In short, the universities should be looking much more at second chance entries.

All this concerns people who at some point in their lives realise what they are missing. But in Great Britain one half of those who leave school at sixteen never set foot in an educational establishment for the rest of their lives. Society's needs call for more than this, and society should require better than this if it is to be politically, socially and for its individual members more nearly adequate. So much in the culture turns most people away from the idea that education has anything to offer after the compulsory years end.

The expansion of higher education in Great Britain has produced much the same result as the great expansion in public funding for the arts over the last twenty or so years. Better provision is being made for those who already know what they like and want. The predominantly middle- or lower-middle-class acceptance of better provision for higher education was to be expected and should not be in itself regretted. But the universities should not regard this state of affairs as a fact of nature. It is always easy to accept someone else's writing down of his own worth and expectations. A strong demand does not at present exist among children and parents from that 50 per cent who go no further after sixteen. But it is not good enough simply to take for granted what Lessing called 'the *wantlessness* of the poor'. That today we are talking about not necessarily the poor in financial terms but, often, about the children of quite prosperous working-class people who are nevertheless poor in intellectual and imaginative expectations does not reduce the problem.

From all such changes in approach, there should emerge closer links between universities and other parts of the education system. Local education authorities, technical and further educational institutes, the schools at all levels would gain from feeling themselves part of a seamless fabric of educational provision for all ages; they should be aware of their local universities, respect them as the intellectual apex of the system, and draw on them regularly at different times in response to different needs and interests. British universities are rarely so regarded today.

Yet even all this does not go far enough. Most of what I have said so far has been about 'continuing education' in a predominantly practical sense. I want also to suggest that universities are called to do even more.

Most university systems in the developed Western world make some kind of provision for those outside their walls, a provision not only of studies towards forms of validation or authentication but of studies for their own sakes. The universities regard themselves therefore as to some extent committed to making their disciplines available beyond their precincts. It is felt that such provisions are owed to the community, may strengthen democratic practices and assist individual development; that they have, in a broad sense of the words, a moral purpose and justification. In Britain this impulse was born in both Oxford and Cambridge in the mid-nineteenth century, and its achievements have been notable. It has numbered among its 'tutors' some of the best university teachers of their generations (who confirmed that a commitment to teaching can reinforce original scholarship); it has helped – because adult classes are nothing if not dialogues – to define or redefine some subjects (especially in the social and political sciences and in the humanities); it has improved the understanding of the value of high-level face-to-face teaching (in adult education a class will evaporate if the subject is not made interesting; but a teacher will fall out of love with himself if he tries to hold students at the expense of his subject's demands). British university extra-mural education has, above all, produced its own teaching form – the three-year tutorial class, which requires close, guided reading and regular written work.

That tradition is still alive. Most British universities have an extra-mural department. Many are good and some are exceptionally good; and they usually have some friends and supporters within the internal staffs. But overall they are regarded as marginal to the 'real' life of the universities, as something which comes near the bottom of the queue when resources are being argued over (if they were not able to draw 75 per cent of their costs by direct grant from the Department of Education and Science, they would receive even shorter shrift in some places). Senior university people will naturally say the right respectful things about their extra-mural tradition and commitment, and some will fully live up to their words. But figures and inadvertent comments tell; for most people extra-mural work is peripheral. It can have the crumbs after the eighteen-year-olds have been fed.

If the universities were right to feel called to help those outside the walls in the mid-nineteenth century, the need is even more marked today. A hundred years ago the most evident general need was for basic education in literacy below the normal university level. Today we have a population which is almost wholly literate, virtually none of whom have had less than nine to eleven years' full-time schooling and many much longer. Yet the general level of social, personal and political literacy is below that which a modern society should be content to accept. Thus, the figures for television viewing are so massive as to indicate an uncritical soporific use of the medium by millions; our mass circulation daily newspapers set you searching for a new phrase – say, 'aborted literacy'; and there is much similar evidence. Shorter hours, earlier retirement and the rest will exaggerate the situation unless universities take their share, along with other parts of the educational system, in helping to develop a better use of leisure. Given that societies become more and more centralised and complex, and that democracy's claims to adequate citizens' participation are still largely unrealised, the universities are already overdue in defining their own best late-twentieth century intervention. It should match the great leap outside the walls of the mid-nineteenth century.

All this will call for rethinking by members of staff. There seems no reason why some university teachers should not have contracts which involve full-time, day teaching to eighteen-year-olds studying for traditional first degrees, together with evening teaching – perhaps on the far side of town – to part-time students of different ages, some working for degrees, some doing so for love. When I hear objections to such ideas (and they are on first hearing strong) I recall that, especially in their early professional years, a substantial number of internal teachers do conduct extra-mural classes in the evenings, though for extra payment. The mixture is not novel.

It is not difficult to imagine a typical university arts department as it might be if it took stock on the lines I've sketched. It would take stock, first of all, of the hitherto often sacrosanct 'definition of the subject'. To that process, the increased numbers of mature students would contribute.

Its students would still be, to a majority, 18 to 21-year-olds, of course. Its mature students would be recruited in several different and more flexible ways than at present and would come for different reasons, personal or professional. Some would be on paid educational leave, some on refresher or retraining schemes. There would also be a good number of part-time students by day and in the evening.

Some would be taking degree courses, others shorter courses to bring their subject-competence up to date. That is, such courses would be seen as an integral part of the provision made within the 'straight' subject department, not something left to the people over in the Education Block. There would be a good range of weekend courses and conferences and at least one annual departmental summer school.

The academic staff of the department would have terms of service which required them to teach by day or in the evening (not doing any more teaching than they do under day-time only arrangements, but spreading it between the day-time students and those part-time students who come in the evening). Staff might also, one can easily imagine, be required to take part-time degree courses in centres up to ten miles or so away. It is easier for one person to travel than for ten.

Such a department should naturally have a sizeable postgraduate commitment. It is worth stressing here that nothing I have said so far poses a threat to the maintaining of the highest academic standards. International reputations will still be able to be made – and not only by those who choose to opt out of the new style. There will be postgraduate students, full-time, working in some quite traditional parts of the discipline; there will be a lot more part-time postgraduate students; and the way to postgraduate work which crosses disciplines will have been made much easier. It can be done; it is being done in a few places and with success.

It follows that the adult or extra-mural or continuing education departments of the universities should, in the Eighties, become much more central within their institutions. Through them, as through that provision of more functional continuing education which I described earlier, and through the fuller assumption of their role as the foremost intellectual centres within their areas, the universities could enter an era in which their sense of belonging to their local communities was better fulfilled. I believe this is possible without weakening their membership in the national and international intellectual and scientific communities.

I am not at all advocating easy routes to something which might be designated as university provision but would in reality fall short of it. That danger has not always been avoided. Sometimes one gets the impression that it is the very people who most assert that universities must maintain their high standards who will, when pushed, agree to a form of provision for others which, though officially described as of university level, is from its inception quietly assumed to be second-class. Some of the degrees made available through Institutes of Education were approved after relatively cursory inspection and would hardly have passed the normal internal scrutinising bodies. I suggest that some were allowed to go through, by the severer upholders of 'university standards', because these people were only mildly interested in them and knew in their bones that they would be from the start a form of second-class citizens' degree.

What I have said so far seems to throw light on a phrase often used today in talk about continuing education: that it should be 'student-centred not institution-centred'. So far I have tended to suspect the phrase, thinking it might be a chip off that fashionable, clumsy block which argues that students know precisely from the age of eighteen what is intellectually right for them and how to define their own programmes. I now see that, in the context I have been outlining, the phrase 'student- not institution-centred' can have an exact meaning. It can mean that universities and other institutions of higher education should recognise that there are many people of different ages who can make proper calls upon them – far more than they have been used to thinking; and that they should try to meet these needs better. The universities could face, and I hope they will welcome it, a much more varied and open life than they have been used to.

Most of what I have said so far about the roles of universities has been concerned, inevitably, with the students' perceived, or not-yet-perceived but none the less justifiable needs. It has been about a kind of provision by response. It is not therefore different in kind from provision in response to, say, the felt needs of *society*. It is an aspect of that provision. Either the student says: I want to be an engineer, or a teacher of English, because that will give me a comfortable job, or because it will meet some other of my needs as I at present conceive them. Or 'society' says: we need more engineers/teachers of English; please supply them to the highest specification.

Yet universities should be more than responders to the felt needs of students or the known needs of society as it is at present constituted. I said at the start that the universities' response to major expansion throughout the Sixties had three main characteristics: the concentration on increasing the number of eighteen-year-olds admitted, linear expansion in already defined 'subjects,' and an acceptance of the demands of society for growth in this way or that, and to this end or that, as society itself already defined its needs. Those two latter characteristics are inter-related.

I have claimed that university expansion too much took for granted the existing definitions of subjects, and so missed an opportunity to question the justification for some of those boundaries. The Sixties should have prompted the question: even if this training is right for the next generation of university teachers and for some who will teach in the grammar schools, is it right for the greatly increased new numbers? I would in some instances have gone further and asked: is it right even for those who will become university teachers? Or are the boundaries to some extent artificially drawn? I took a first and a higher degree in 'straight' English studies and respect what I got from them: a sense of what it is to work in depth in an area, under the supervision of people who are themselves committed to that discipline. But such an opportunity need not be mutually exclusive of others which could also be very valuable. Most 'straight' English Literature courses are so English Literature-centred that they are in the end – when all credit has been given to the practice of working in depth – repetitive and narrow. When they go outside the literary discipline, as they must sooner or later if they are to talk seriously

69

about good literature, they are damagingly under-equipped.

Similarly, the universities do not sufficiently examine the demands society makes on them. The universities are asked not only to do more than this but to be more than this, to criticise society directly (and I do not mean only to criticise adversely; I mean to be critically aware). It is commonplace to hear people internationally respected in their fields – literary scholars or medical experts or what you will – delivering themselves of social or cultural judgments of such unconsideredness that one wonders how it is possible for people to arrive at those eminences with no greater degree of self-questioning. Universities are highly intelligent institutions; but they are insufficiently speculative and intellectual outside their known disciplines.

At such moments one remembers R. H. Tawney's triple prescription for a university's purposes. First, to advance knowledge. Nothing I have said would weaken that aim. They have also, he went on, to train clever young people to pursue the same end. True, also. But we do not need universities to fulfil these two purposes. Subject-centred, research institutes, each staffed by the best men in their fields and with the brightest of the new generation attached to them, a hermetic set of knowledge-advancing and transmitting institutions, would suffice. Tawney's third point makes the difficult jump. Universities are also, he claimed, places in which people are made aware of the moral situation of their disciplines, are led to question the terms of life offered by their societies and those they have so far proposed for themselves. Universities are in the hardest sense classless; they must be open to all who can and will make the effort to meet their very difficult demands. Their gods are the search for objective knowledge and its free circulation once gained. I do not see how a university worthy of the name can evade this third criterion; but many universities today find themselves too busy with the first and second criteria to pay much attention to the third.

So we arrive at the limits of the idea of 'student-centred education'. Earlier, I defended that notion against that of 'institution-centred education'. Now I want to set another idea *against* it. In the best analysis, university education is not student-centred. It is subject-, or discipline-, or truth-centred. Teachers and students together pay their dues to the demands of the search for truth.

It follows from all I have said that any subject – medicine or engineering or English Literature or Philosophy – should be so approached that its personal and social meanings can be seen as integral with the 'subject' itself. Attempts to tack on social implications as an afterthought are generally misguided. So is much of the talk about 'relevance', since it often leads to diluting the difficulties of a discipline on behalf of the idea of contemporaneity. Advanced training in any discipline which does not face that discipline's organic links with values is merely a training of people to fit the needs of whatever society a university happens to be in, whether that society be totalitarian or fascist or marxist or social democratic. If the training of students within universities across the globe were to be in any one discipline in all respects the same the idea of the university itself would have suffered a mortal blow, above all in 'open' societies such as ours. It is time to recall the idea of the university as a place of free, objective enquiry into the nature of our lives.

So an important debate has opened before the universities. One must hope that it will not be based chiefly on the wish of university authorities to retain at all costs the staff and resources which they built up in the years of great expansion. It is not enough to reiterate fidelity to the main recommendation of the Robbins Committee: that university places should be available to all those qualified and willing to accept them. It was and is a good principle. But it is not axiomatically enough to meet the demands of the next fifteen or twenty years. I hope the universities will go further and, through encouraging new thinking and new experimental practices, prompt the task of redefinition. What is needed is not only a redefinition of the role of the universities towards society and towards individuals but a reassertion of the responsibilities of intellectual life itself, within democratic societies.   1978

NOTE.   I have deliberately not mentioned the Open University, since there would have been room for no more than a brief reference. Its importance to the approach I have called for seems to me very great indeed, and very obvious. Still, those who do not yet appreciate this will not be convinced by a paragraph or two.

LEISURE AND EDUCATION
IN THE EIGHTIES

It is becoming clear that the Eighties should see continuing education placed in the front of our thinking – for both the good of the economy and for the best use of our new leisure. Just what should be meant by the phrase 'continuing education' (it's at present a sort of portmanteau) is only now beginning to be defined. Essentially, it will require us to draw a new map of the educational process, to have a different model in our heads. And that will mean big changes in structure and, if not in the overall level of expenditure, then in the way that expenditure is apportioned.

We will need to get out of thinking of education as an 'end-on' process whereby everybody has a largish single block of initial education up to sixteen and then some groups, getting smaller as we move up the age-range, have further and yet further blocks added to the original block. We have rather to think of education as a continuous and continuously available resource, for our different needs at different parts of our lives ... professional, technical, recreative, remedial, spiritual.

And we have to come to regard all kinds of educational institutions as integrally, organically, parts of their communities. The scope of those communities will vary. A primary school will be tied in to a relatively small local area. A university will be tied into its city, its region and so out to the nation and to the international community. But all will be taking part in the same general process towards greater openness and flexibility in responding to needs other than those for which they may have been originally and more narrowly conceived and shaped.

This is going to call for a lot of changes in attitudes from everyone: the jealous headmaster, the resentful caretaker, the restrictive union official, the suspicious professor, the bureaucratic Registrar. Above all, it will be a challenge to that dreadfully characteristic British assumption that there is only a limited amount of good stuff of any kind – in this case, education – and that if you spread it more widely you inevitably spread it thin. It is interesting, and inevitable, that those who say this have usually done very well out of the system themselves. Pull up the drawbridge. But it's a mistaken assumption. We are still an under-educated nation, and education made more widely available need not be thinner education. It can grow by what it feeds on.

So much for the overall approach. Ah, but this is bound to cost a very great deal, is the immediate response of many. But I am arguing first for a redistribution of available funds. Halsey and others claim, in *Origins and Destinations,* that the professional classes have by now been provided to the limit with the kinds of education at all levels their offspring need; and that the time is ripe to move some of these resources over to relatively neglected areas and social groups. Even that will require a great deal of re-thinking, many changes of heart and some political courage. But we do make that sort of jump sometimes. Look at the Open University, which would never have been created if some people had not had imagination and determination.

It may be useful to divide the claims for continuing education into four rough piles, and to look at some much more closely than at others. First, the practical or economic case. It rests on the often repeated assertion that many more of us will need refreshing and retraining at more than one stage in our working lives. This has been said so often in the last few years that people are begining to react against it, as though they can hardly bear one more reference to the microchip revolution. Fair enough. Still, put things at their simplest. Very very many more people are going to need in-service training, transfer training and the like as the professions and skills in which they were trained change, become more sophisticated or disappear all together. The more alert industrialists have seen this and are beginning to make provision; many in the polytechnics and some in the universities have taken the message also. It seems almost against nature to find much of good cheer in the educational cuts. But we can already see that, among the more energetic in higher education, the threat of reduced funds have sharpened their minds towards greater provision of up-dating education for professionals outside, provision which can be economically self-supporting or even provide some surplus towards the needs of subjects which can never be self-sufficient but are academically essential.

In practical terms, this aspect of the changes opens up a great many areas for development – such as much better provision for part-time students within higher education; a more serious examination of the idea of 'educational credits' (credit transfer is already on the move) and much more attention to the concept of Paid Educational Leave. France has that already, conceived as largely vocational, and by law funded by industry. They are moving into stage two, where the pressure is for PEL to be fully available also for education which is not necessarily vocational. We are relatively far behind many European countries here. I agree with John Goldthorpe, in *Social Mobility and Class Structure in Modern Britain,* that the unions above all should diversify their interests, recognise that wage gains alone won't make up for the other disadvantages experienced by many of their members, and begin to be much more active on the educational and other social fronts. PEL could be one good early cause.

There is a more immediate matter, one which calls for more compensatory or remedial educational provision. If the first part of the case for continuing education arises from the changing needs of an increasingly sophisticated society, this part is about those who have fallen through the cracks, about the illiterate or only near-literate. Not just gypsies or canal people but many others, going about in normal occupations. For me, the typical image (because I knew such men as a boy) is a forty-odd-year-old bachelor, living alone in one room or with his married sister and her family, and secretly, so far at least as the outside world is concerned, unable to read or write. There are many many others of both sexes in this plight; in fact, between one and a half and two million illiterates. Far too many. All praise to those who brought this to our attention and insisted on the need for a crash job. And crash it was, via the main adult education agencies and the BBC. But short-term and underfunded. We shouldn't have to argue so much for reasonably adequate funding for such a plain need, or have wholly to suspect the enthusiasm for volunteers in LEAs. It's all too small. And when central government passed the main responsibility over to the LEAs some simply ignored it. They are hard-pressed, but adult literacy should be as protected an area as initial schooling or mandatory grants for university and polytechnic students. All the illiterates won't present themselves, but those who do should be provided for; and much more should be done to help the others see what they are missing. I don't feel guilty as a professional that my own children were able to take good advantage of what's on offer educationally. I do think we should recognise that our own capacity to take easy advantage of increased provision carries with it the duty to put even more effort into helping the deprived and unaware. We should not therefore rest easy without an adequate and continuing literacy programme.

There is a necessary follow on. To be illiterate does not mean simply to be unable to read and write. It means existing in a twilight world where all sorts of aids to growth are not available to you. Maybe illiterate peasants could be wise as, working in the fields, they watched the year turn. But wise old shepherds are out nowadays. We live in a society which can make no sense to you unless you have some of the tools for making an order, a liveable mental space, within it. And that starts with words, spoken, written and read.

Even if people are made literate that is not in itself enough, as UNESCO discovered years ago. Simple literacy, with nothing consistently to feed on, drains away. The *practice* of literacy is part of the growth of our whole being and of our involvement with others, at all times of our lives. It informs conversations at work or at home; through reading it extends and challenges; through writing it tests most severely of all. It may be said that many people who are officially literate aren't at such a level of development yet; and that would be true. But for the moment let us concentrate on these most obviously in need.

For outside the nearly two million who need help to become literate there is a large penumbra of others who are only near-literate and so have not been able to develop their grasp to a point which makes them able to cope with the quite complex demands of society; who can't adequately handle, for instance, the increasing number of printed forms which have to be completed by a working adult. So, to put things at their lowest level, they are likely to be consistently conned. Experts reckon that the total of illiterates and near-literates is more than three million. I suppose that means roughly seven per cent of the adult population – far more than we can afford or should be willing to accept. They need adult basic education, social, political, professional, personal. Again, by no means all of them will easily come. But provision should be there for those who are ready and willing; and much more effort should be put into understanding how to encourage the others to overcome their shyness, even their

75

shame, and to steer round all those cultural forces which suggest to them that any sort of education is old-hat, do-gooding, not for the likes of them who, it is implied, are already living a full rich life what with the betting shop, the telly and the boozer! Some efforts are being made here, good ones; but far fewer than we need.

To provide properly will cost money; but relatively little in comparison with the need and the results or compared with, say, the cost of financing fulltime higher education. The rewards will be there in a more economically effective society. But the case is overwhelming in its own terms. We owe it to these others.

So far I have been making the case for continuing education in what are at bottom practical terms: because of the needs of a changing economy or because of the needs of the illiterate and near-literate. Catching up or being remedial. But I don't regard that side as what best points to the future of continuing education or as that which best links with the greatest achievements of our past in adult education. We can do, have done and are doing more and richer things than that.

Adult education takes only about half per cent of the total education budget at present. But for that half per cent the voluntary needs of about two million adults are catered for through an almost bewildering range of provision. The United Kingdom, for a century and a half at least, has been a leading nation in this kind of provision, usually organised at local level, provided by both public and voluntary agencies, addressing itself to all kinds of personal and social needs, not necessarily seeking public credits – degrees, diplomas or the like – but done 'for its own sake'; which really means for the inner needs of the individuals who seek it. We can divide this provision into two main streams.

First, the recreational. I am deliberately using the latest grand word. This whole area is often scoffed at, regarded as a 'frill', felt to be the first candidate for cuts. 'Flower arranging and all that sort of stuff', middle-aged, middle-class ladies throwing pots or doing Music-and-Movement or contorting themselves in yoga positions. That sort of snideness comes from the obscure recesses of our national anti-intellectualism and, even more, of our anti-art traditions. It is fed by most of the persuasive engines of modern consumer society – where you do nothing in a sustained or serious way but simply, week after week, toy – like an overfed child – with what the organs of mass taste dish up for you. Such sneers do us no credit at all. There is something fine in the thought of all those people, of all ages, all over the country, setting off night after night to sit in often not very comfortable classrooms to work at something for love alone, not for job improvement – leaving behind the fire and the television and passing straight by the Bingo hall.This kind of thing has as much right to public support as have libraries and public baths and allotments. I'm not suggesting it should all be free. But pricing policy can be either a butcher's cleaver or a very sensitive educational instrument in its own right. What I am saying is that we are well past the point at which any educational official, full-time or elected, has the right to treat us as odd or importunate because we expect that kind of provision to be regarded as as normal a part of the educational services as anything else. Who can doubt that, as leisure increases, the demand for this kind of activity will grow enormously? And once again very special efforts are needed to widen the range, to reach those who don't yet know what they are missing.

The fourth element of the case for continuing education is the critical one: in two senses. First, because it is often the hardest part of the argument for many people, especially public officials and politicians, to accept; and second, because it has to do with the Arnoldian idea that societies need a constant stream of critical thought flowing across their institutions and processes.

All open, consumer societies tend to flaccidity, to leading people into 'letting *Them* do it', to handing things over increasingly to professionals even in areas where the professionals need watching like hawks, to making the home and local amusements paramount and public and national duties a bore, to the private occupations which the consumer and communications industries want us to have because they are best for profits and for a quiet life all round. So these societies, though they rightly praise their own commitments to freedom of speech and debate, seem progressively to lose the will to engage in those processes, to lose their yeast, their irritants, their interventionists. The corporate state in its political, administrative and industrial-commercial aspects more and more goes its way insufficiently challenged. All the signs are that, as the balance between work and leisure shifts, this tendency will increase. It follows that very much more weight has to be put on our right and need to know and to act as free individuals. Most of us agree with that sort of remark. We are not so willing to measure its implications. Indeed, much in our world – including our educational world – is antagonistic to such a measuring. For to act well as a democrat in the way I've sketched doesn't come by accident, or by repeating the cant phrases of collectivism and solidarity, or by passing resolutions in a group. Two million card-carrying members passing one resolution can be as purblind as one individual. Here adult education is about the responsibility of the individual *before* that of the collective. Here it can help the individual cast a more critical eye on the terms of life offered by all parts of society – the educational system itself, the job, the profession, the mass media. Here each individual, though work in a class or group may sustain and support him, is finally alone, reading, thinking, writing, trying to 'make his own mind up'. It cannot be easy; there are no short cuts and no collective cheap tickets. We often forget this to our cost today, educationists included; it is part of a more general failure of nerve among teachers. We are uneasy before the demands of intellectual training, fearful of seeming snobs. Examples abound. Here is the most relevant one for my theme. Consider how a jewel of the whole British adult education system in this century, the element which other countries recognise as a major invention – the three-year tutorial class for adults with sustained reading, writing and discussion – has over the last thirty years been run down by almost every university extra-mural department. The rationalisations are familiar: that the people for whom it was designed – workers not reached by earlier inadequate public education – have now all been brought out of the shadows; that people are too busy today and that with modern, technical aids we can teach them more quickly and painlessly. (This is as if to say that it's old-hat to take nine months to produce a baby); that the tutorial class is old-fashioned and unglamorous; or that it is élitist, the remnant of a bookish, bourgeois culture which we should not try to sell to our students. This is dreadful, thin stuff, a whole set of treasons of the clerks, of sinnings against the light.   1980

THE IMPORTANCE
OF LITERACY

There is in Britain now quite a steady flow of right-wing protestations that our educational system has come to ruin. For those of us on the Left the situation is difficult. We may not want to accept the equally strident but contrary claims of some colleagues on our own wing. We may well feel, as I do, that beneath some of the often over-stated assertions of what we call 'Black Paper' writers there lie some justified doubts about what is happening to our educational system. It is well past the time at which the Left should itself loosen its over-rigid hold on the pieties and slogans of progressivism in education and look soberly at those issues which right-wing writers have so far largely preempted but not in general illuminated.

Were I not chiefly concerned here with the literacy of books, I could have found some encouragement in the record of British broadcasting at its best over the last thirty years or so. I have in mind especially the achievements in current affairs coverage by both our television systems, a record which has shown that far more people are capable of following and willing to follow serious programmes on important issues than you would ever have imagined from reading our popular press. That press, as the pressures of competition for advertising increase, has narrowed and narrowed its focus, like a soft-porn photographer over-addicted to the zoom lens; so that now the number of bare nipples, sometimes in colour, on any one day in some of the newspapers exceeds the number of items about, say, world political issues. We'd best regard these as no longer newspapers. They do not tell us as much about the existing or potential range of interests of their readers as the television current affairs programmes do. They tell us that, if newspapers narrow their focus to more and more pin-ups and sports gossip, they will feed our appetite for those things (but we do not necessarily confuse them with *new*spapers). For news and comments we go elsewhere, especially to broadcasts. That would be a more promising approach to the understanding of our present popular newspapers and their relations to broadcasting than one which regards them as the fallen daughters of C.P. Scott of The Guardian.

One other achievement of television which has also shown that the potential, imaginative and intellectual, of many of us is far greater than a glance at the news-stands would suggest is the television play. It is suffering somewhat now, chiefly because of the twin pressures of competition and rising prices. But it can still do magnificent things, and its record over twenty years or so is superb and illuminating. It has attracted some of the best young dramatists, and for two reasons. They have seen television as a new kind of drama, not as an adaptation of theatre dramas to a small screen. They have recognised and developed the special possibilities of the medium itself and have made creative use even of its clear limitations. They have been excited also by the idea of a 'theatre' which has no fixed location or fixed type of audience, which is labelled neither West End nor 'for the carriage trade'. They know that their plays will go into living rooms where sit people who would otherwise never in their lives see a play, who would not dream, for complicated socio-cultural reasons, of 'setting foot' in a theatre, but who nevertheless can show responses, can be captured by experiences, which one might never have suspected if television hadn't come along. We are still learning this. It has long been current wisdom that the troubles in Northern Ireland are 'switch-off' subjects for television viewers. Yet a BBC *Play for Today,* not directly about Northern Ireland but informed and affected by it, had an audience of thirteen and a half million, which is almost a quarter of the whole population of Britain.

So, if this were a wide-ranging or would-be comprehensive survey of 'British Literacy' there would be such good elements, and others, to point to. But my range is narrower. I really want to talk about respect for the intellectual life – or the lack of respect, rather – which one finds in Britain today. I have a slightly unusual angle on entry to the subject since I have spent twenty-four years in British higher education (roughly half as a university tutor outside the walls, giving classes to volunteer adults at night, anything up to sixty miles away from the university itself; and most of the other half as an internal university teacher of English – with a year teaching in the States roughly sandwiched between those two large slices). After all this, I went off to Paris in 1970 and there spent five and a quarter years at UNESCO Headquarters. That experience taught me above all how fragile is the hold on Human Rights and the principle of free speech across most parts of the globe.

There is commonly in British education today a reluctance to impose intellectual effort, coupled with a mistrust of the more sophisticated forms of verbal expression, written and oral – though not of technical languages, technical jargon, or that kind of circumlocutory speech which appears to put ordinary acts into a self-sustaining and self-justifying technological world.

A typical example of this latter came over on BBC Radio not long ago. A man was being asked whether some new electronic gadget was cheap enough to be bought for the home. His reply came out of the linguistic world of complex forward planning. Behind it one could almost hear talk about the 'scenario' of 'options' for 'space probes'. He replied: 'It would fit very well into the realm of conceivability for the average person'. You and I could afford it.

Last, in this brief list of attitudes at different levels in British education, something about the schools. The battle about comprehensive education is going on at least as strongly in Britain today as it was twenty years ago. We are not making much progress with it. One aspect, recently put forcibly in a book, shows the hooks on which we hang ourselves. The writer argues that the needs of the great majority of people, those who form the bulk of pupils at any large comprehensive school, are so over-riding on democratic and egalitarian grounds that the loss of adequate academic training for the gifted pupils (often shown by the inadequacy of pre-university teaching at some comprehensives, or more pervasively in the generally anti-intellectual and anti-academic atmosphere of some such schools) that this loss is a price we should be willing to pay so that the great bulk of people can be at least reasonably educated. But this is a false antithesis, and at the bottom not only profoundly mistaken but also profoundly illiberal, a dead-end rejection of much of the best in the Western tradition.

There is, it hardly needs saying, an elaborated ideology behind that and much similar educational writing today, and its common elements are fairly easily identified. It is usually put forward by people who are themselves quite highly-educated. They are commonly, to use their own language, 'anti-bourgeois and the whole bourgeois tradition'. They reject what they see as an implicit invitation by the educational system at all levels to, in the French term, 'embourgeoisify' pupils and

81

students by introducing them – on the false grounds that these are part of a universal and objective tradition out there – to bourgeois forms of speech and bourgeois literature and history.

They argue that, for example, working-class urban teenagers do not need to be introduced to the 'elaborated codes' necessary for public competence. They argue instead that the common speech of urban teenagers who have left school at the minimum leaving age, sixteen, ungrammatical and limited in vocabulary though it may be, can nevertheless be a sophisticated instrument of communication. (Since I too admire the work of Labov, their main source, I understand what they are saying and to a limited extent accept it.) They go on to argue that to offer people entry into the world of more publicly-accessible and acceptable speech is to do them no favour but is rather by stealth to mould them into the values and attitudes which that form of converse carries – into becoming a supporting sub-branch of the ruling bourgeois world.

I think them substantially mistaken. The usual public forms of speech and writing are needed by as many of us as possible so that we shall manage better – socially, personally, politically, at work. At the lowest level, they are needed to help us prevent ourselves from being cheated by the armies of admen and door-to-door salesmen and fast talkers in which our kinds of society abound. Noble savages are no longer likely to emerge, least of all from big city society; if they did, they would soon be picked clean. Nor need our attempts to give this kind of command to our students mean we are also selling them a whole hidden bourgeois ideology (or an ideology of any other kind). That is precisely the chief educational challenge before us. To meet it requires us to get below the levels of both unexamined socio-cultural assumptions in ourselves and the simpler forms of rejection of those assumptions – which often have the shrill tones of people who have just discovered original sin.

I think, too, of much of the language of the proponents of what are known as 'Community Arts' in Great Britain. The definition of art has been enormously widened recently and I do not myself in principle regret that. But thereafter the problems begin. Some of those who work in the Community Arts reject the relevance of *all* the traditional forms of art, since they see them as merely historically-conditioned bourgeois products. They believe the giving of funds to such activities is a late-capitalist device to maintain the forms and powers of this kind of society. They call themselves 'Community

Artists' and their activities 'Community Arts' because they usually work in the more deprived urban areas, and their main effort is to involve the surrounding community as such rather than to find 'promising' individuals and educate them out of their communities. I do not doubt the sincerity of their intentions, nor the personal sacrifices they often make; and some of their work is inventive, remedial, imaginative and sometimes genuinely funny, too. My worry about it is different. It is that it has appropriated an OK word – 'community' – and that its single-minded grip on that word shows its failure to recognise the importance, in lasting intellectual and imaginative literacy, of individual – indeed lonely – effort. Individualism it is likely to dismiss as a product of the ambitious, self-seeking, bourgeois mentality. It also rejects, again as a bourgeois myth, the idea of different standards of effort, of achievement and, finally, of 'gifts'. I support the Arts Council's giving of funds to these activities – though not beyond measure, in comparison with the funds going to the more traditional arts. I know that, because in their nature these arts are trying to grow in places where the land has not before been tilled, much of what they spend may be wasted. That is the price for helping good work to be done and good things to happen (I should add that community artists stress the *process* of making art as more important than the end result, than what is made or can be imaginatively exchanged with other individuals; again, that can be a tenable point of view). I can even envisage that eventually this kind of activity in some of the least-provided areas of Britain may produce new art forms which might never have emerged without all their experiments. But in the end judgments have to be made, not judgments from a blinkered set of preconceptions about what are acceptable artistic forms and what not, but judgments about honesty before the material and respect for the materials, and about that combination of natural gifts and unremitting efforts which is needed for almost any considerable achievement. I will not, to take an actual case, agree that a short story by a London taxi-driver encouraged by his local Community Arts organisation is good *simply* because it has come out of a community context and is by a taxi-driver who has before not written a line. I won't call it 'remarkable' if I find it self-indulgent, unexamined and ungifted. That does no justice to him, or to what he might eventually produce, or to the idea of art itself.

We cannot leave people in corners, having to our own satisfaction redefined those corners as nicer than the outside, more public world.

We are talking about something different from training people to acquire bourgeois speech and assumptions. Nor are we asking them to learn to express themselves like advertising executives, PR people or many union officials. We are talking about having that respect for them which requires us to help them gain greater, more articulate and more self-conscious, access to their own personal and social lives. We are asking for this kind of provision and this kind of effort not just so that people can manage their public situations better – though that is useful, since so many words uttered publicly today are out only to persuade us or make us conform – but so that they can stand up better in all sorts of deeply personal ways. If that sounds as though I think that, say, an acquaintance with the best that has been thought and said automatically makes you a better person, I do not. But that experience can make us *see* better, and so can illuminate our moral choices. The rest, as always, is up to each one of us and our moral wills.

We all need literacy, imaginative and intellectual literacy, because it is an essential part of our movement towards greater critical self-awareness brought to bear on our own lives and on what society offers us as the desirable life. We all need the continued nourishment which can be given by contact with other, finer, minds. 'The unexamined life is not worth living'. It may be that 'all art aspires to the condition of music'; it may be that music, the visual arts, dance, all work on our consciousness at levels well below those of literature. But literature is the most open, explicit, self-aware, contentious, muddy, involved, of all the arts. It tries actually to *say* things as they are and beyond a shadow of doubt; so it is always laying itself on the line, inviting contradiction. In the process it lays its authors on the line, too, and so is – both in its creating and in the response to what is created – the most exposed and taxing of the arts. It demands a discipline of the mind and heart, and the result is always up to be challenged and often is as shaking to the writer as to the reader; perhaps more shaking. Let me venture one personal example. Writing parts of my book, *The Uses of Literacy,* I found I was holding some of my own more submerged characteristics – which I had not before suspected, and often did not find particularly admirable – to a scrutiny I did not greatly enjoy. That came out of the actual writing of those parts. Some of my very elderly relatives found parts of the book embarrassing, not because they discovered anything particularly shocking in the skeletons revealed in the family cupboard, but because the whole idea of a public self-analysis was alien to them and deeply disturbing. Some things ought not to be thought of, after that fashion. People whose backgrounds have locked them into such a response have been denied one of the more valuable exercises of the human heart and mind.

I was, not all that long ago, in a public baths, built *circa* the turn of the century, lavatorially-tiled, smelling of chlorine, very bleak-looking, very shabby. I had been there often, so was beginning to be known. This particular morning the attendant on duty was a man of, I suppose, just over twenty. He was far too heavy for the good of his health. He sat in the dreary cabin provided at the side of the pool for the use of the attendants, smoking a good deal, brewing a succession of cups of tea and leafing through the day's issue of one of the popular newspapers. On the face of it he looked typecast as what our right-wing press likes to call a 'yobbo' or 'layabout'. That day, as I was getting dressed and we were alone in the place (it was about 8.30 in the morning) he walked over to me, looked up at the great glass roof held up by its Edwardian wrought ironwork and asked: (I will not try to reproduce his speech): 'Have you ever noticed all that iron stuff? It's pretty, isn't it? The other day I found in a cupboard at the back a lot of them old kind of photos – you know, all browns. But they were really pretty.' His vocabulary was massively inadequate to what he was trying to say. His conscious sense of the amazing thing that was happening inside him was almost non-existent, and I guess he may soon pass the point at which he can be moved to utter such obscure intimations to a near-stranger (though perhaps it was easier because I *am* a near-stranger, and because he's guessed that I am connected with an artistic institution, the College up the road).

I end with that true story, finally, because it underlines once again that we must resist the constant pressure to undervalue others, especially those who do not inhabit our own publicly-articulate world; and also because it underlines our duty not to romanticise the situations such people are in, but to help them, whilst not doing wrong to whatever may be good in their present worlds, to help them in the right ways, to – and I choose the verb deliberately – *surmount* that world.   1980

MATTHEW ARNOLD, HMI

─────

. . . though I am a schoolmaster's son . . . school teaching or school inspecting is not the line of life I should naturally have chosen. I adopted it in order to marry a lady who is here tonight and who feels the kindness as warmly and as gratefully as I do. (Cheers.) My wife and I had a wandering life of it at first. There were but three inspectors for all England. My district went right across from Pembroke Dock to Great Yarmouth. We had no home; one of our children was born in lodgings at Derby with a workhouse, if I recollect right, behind and a penitentiary in front. (Laughter.) But the irksomeness of my new duties was what I felt most, and during the first year or so this was sometimes almost insupportable. But I met daily in the schools with men and women discharging duties akin to mine, duties as irksome as mine, duties less well paid than mine, and I asked myself, Are they on roses? Would they not by nature prefer, many of them, to go where they liked and do what they liked instead of being shut up in school? I saw them making the best of it; I saw the cheerfulness and efficiency with which they did their work, and I asked myself again, How do they do it? Gradually it grew into a habit with me to put myself into their place, to try to enter into their feelings, to represent to myself their life, and I assure you I got many lessons from them.

Matthew Arnold: speaking at a banquet given him on his retirement from being one of Her Majesty's Inspectors of Schools, in 1886. When he had started in that work, just before he was thirty, he had no idea that it would be his whole career. But it was. He served thirty-five years.

And served magnificently. I doubt whether, in all the parade of devoted HMIs since Arnold, there has been a better one. He saw so much and so well. He argued over decades for 'a more deliberate and systematically reasoned action on the part of the State in dealing with education in this country'; so, among much else, he stressed the central importance of compulsory popular education, the case for infant schools, the case against payment by results – and even about the care and cleanliness of buildings. Coming back in particular to the annual reports he made on the elementary schools, many years after I first read them on the fringes of my work in preparation for a degree in English literature, I am enormously impressed all over again by their richness and also – something less expected – their great present pertinence. Stylistically, they do not have the bounce of *Culture and Anarchy:* they are sober and telling. They throw a very severe light on aspects of our approaches to education today.

It's a heroic personal story and ought to make those of us who have moved into educational administration grumble less about the little time we have left for 'our own work'. Arnold's other role – as a creative writer – was fulfilled on the margins. He wrote many of his essays and poems in boarding houses and hotels, far from home and usually alone, after a hard day's inspecting. Always he respected the teachers:

although I thus press for the most unvarnished and literal report on their schools, I can assure the teachers of them, that it is from no harshness or want of sympathy towards them that I do so. No one feels more than I do how laborious is their work, how trying at times to the health and spirits, how full of difficulty even for the best: how much fuller for those, whom I too often see attempting the work of a schoolmaster – men of weak health and purely studious habits, who betake themselves to this profession, as affording the means to continue their favourite pursuits: not knowing alas, that for all but men of the most singular and exceptional vigour and energy, there are no pursuits more irreconcilable than those of the student and of the schoolmaster. Still, the quantity of work actually done at present by teachers is immense: the sincerity and devotedness of much of it is even affecting. They themselves will be the greatest gainers by a system of reporting which clearly states what they do and what they fail to do; not one which drowns alike success and failure, the able and the inefficient, in a common flood of vague approbation.

Arnold's own education had hardly prepared him for seeing deeply into the elementary schools. Rugby, where his father was headmaster, prepared upper middle and professional-class boys to succeed in the same styles of life as their parents, often via Oxford and Cambridge. Against that background, Arnold could envisage without great difficulty a new and more important role for the day *grammar* schools, because they had at least some characteristics in common with the great public schools; they gave an academic training. But the role of the elementary schools – those for 'the great masses' – was much harder to see, except in a very long perspective. But he kept on trying.

To two kinds of issue Arnold frequently returns. Both are still germane today. On one I think him substantially right. On the other, which is culturally particularly complex, time has disproved him: but his approach is still more suggestive and challenging than the great bulk of educational writing today, or at any time. And his prose is better. There's not a 'learning situation', 'teaching situation', 'supportive situation', 'caring situation', or 'ongoing, viable classroom situation' in the whole opus.

Here is Arnold on the importance of being introduced to our own literary heritage, as an indispensable part of what it is now fashionable to call 'the core curriculum', and as a former of character so long as it is not watered down:

It is not enough remembered in how many cases his reading-book forms the whole literature, except his Bible, of the child attending a primary school. If then, instead of literature, his reading-book, as is too often the case, presents him with a jejune encyclopaedia of positive information, the result is that he has, except his Bible, no literature, no *humanising* instruction at all. If, again, his reading-book, as is also too often the case, presents him with bad literature instead of good – with the writing of second or third-rate authors, feeble, incorrect, and colourless – he has not, as the rich have, the corrective of an abundance of good literature to counteract the bad effect of trivial and ill-written school-books; the second or third-rate literature of his school-book remains for him his sole, or, at least, his principal literary standard. Dry scientific disquisitions, and literary compositions of an inferior order, are indeed the worst possible instruments for teaching children to read well. But besides the fault of not fulfilling this, their essential function, the ill-compiled reading-books I speak of have, I say, for the poor scholar, the graver fault of actually doing what they can to spoil his taste, when they are nearly his only means for forming it.

The recent arguments about a 'core curriculum' (one can't really dignify them with the title of debates) got bogged down in absurd and predictable anti-centralist arguments, references to educational totalitarianism, and the usual snide references to the dangers of ours becoming like the French system. Arnold, incidentally, who greatly admired much in French education, was very sharp about that routine reaction when he met it.

But who today, observing many intelligent university students in the humanities, could do other than say to Arnold's shade: You were right, but it's gone further now. Even those who go to the universities – those institutions you so much prized – often arrive ignorant of the most fundamental elements of 'the best that has been thought and said'. Students now taking Honours degrees in English literature at British universities are, I assume, as intelligent and imaginative as their predecessors. But you have to be careful about making in class what seem useful comparisons between authors because students are as like as not to say 'Oh, Keats? Sorry. We didn't *do* him at school.' And if you try to move out from a hidden quotation in Eliot or Auden or Greene to talk about the associations and contrasts it sets up, you may find that the quotation strikes no chord at all; there is often hardly any comparative literary stock in the mind.

Arnold links, again rightly, the need for a hold on the common literary heritage with the value of learning things by heart. In the report for 1863 he was able to say:

No more useful change has in my opinion ever been introduced into the programme of the pupil-teachers' studies than that which has lately added to it the learning by heart of passages from some standard author. How difficult it seems to do anything for their taste and culture I have often said. I have said how much easier it seems to get entrance to their minds and to awaken them by means of music or of physical science than by means of literature; still if it can be done by literature at all, it has the best chance of being done by the way now proposed. The culture both of the pupil-teacher and of the elementary school-master with us seems to me to resist the efforts made to improve it and to remain unprogressive, more than that of the corresponding class on the Continent.

By 1882 he was still fighting (what has since proved a losing battle):

People talk contemptuously of 'learning lines by heart'; but if a child is brought, as he easily can be brought, to *throw himself into* a piece of poetry, an exercise of creative activity has been set up in him quite different from the effort of learning a list of words to spell, or a list of flesh-making and heat-giving foods, or a list of capes and bays, or a list of reigns and battles, and capable of greatly relieving the strain from learning these and of affording a lively pleasure.

We all know today the engaging educational justifications for never helping children to learn anything by heart: they must come to things in their own good time (when will that be? it hardly ever seems to happen after adolescence); they must not be required to learn things by rote, must not have things stuffed down their throats, (the language is being screwed up so that the case can be more easily dismissed) and so on. Yet when we are young we memorise easily, and often with pleasure. I am forever grateful to those teachers who 'stuffed' my head with large parts of Shakespeare, Pope, Keats, Wordsworth, Tennyson and the rest. After that, and on my own, it seemed easier to pick up lots of Yeats and Hardy and Eliot and Auden. Without that mental baggage, I'd feel half-naked.

It might be tempting to assume from what I've said so far that Arnold sought to give each pupil a sort of posh, culture-vulture finish. Not at all. He saw through that, as this splendid comparison of letters, with which he ended his report for the year 1867, shows:

... I will conclude by placing in juxtaposition a letter written in school by an ordinary scholar in a public elementary school in my district, a girl of eleven years old, with one written by a boy in a private middle-class school, and furnished to one of the Assistant Commissioners of the Schools Inquiry Commission. The girl's letter I give first:

DEAR FANNY, – I am afraid I shall not pass in my examination; Miss C says she thinks I shall. I shall be glad when the Serpentine is frozen over, for we shall have such fun. I wish you did not live so far away, then you could come and share in the game. Father cannot spare Willie, so I have as much as I can do to teach him to cipher nicely. I am now sitting by the school fire, so I assure you I am very warm. . . .

From your affectionate friend,
M—

And now I give the boy's:

MY DEAR PARENTS, – The anticipation of our Christmas vacation abounds in peculiar delights. Not only that its 'festivities', its social gatherings, and its lively amusements crown the old year with happiness and mirth, but that I come a guest commended to your hospitable love by the performance of all you bade me remember when I left you in the glad season of sun and flowers. And time has sped fleetly since reluctant my departing step crossed the threshold of that home whose indulgences and endearments their temporary loss has taught me to value more and more . . .

We break up on Thursday, the 11th of December instant, and my impatience of the short delay will assure my dear parents of the filial sentiments of

Theirs very sincerely
N—

Arnold concludes:

To those who ask what is the difference between a public and a private school I answer, *It is this.*

The most difficult and important cultural themes which run through Arnold's reports are part of his gallant attempt to grapple with questions about the role of each of the main classes in society, and so of each kind of school for the training of those classes. 'The education of each class in society has, or ought to have, its ideal, determined by the wants of that class, and by its destination', he proposed. To use his own labels from *Culture and Anarchy,* he recognised that 'the barbarians', the aristocracy, could no longer be expected to give a responsible lead to the country. ('Whence, I say, does this slackness, this sleep of the mind, come, except from a torpor of intellectual life, a dearth of ideas, an indifference to true culture?', he asked apropos the aristocracy.) Then who would give a lead? For in his view there had to be a guiding élite. It is easier to laugh at this idea than to answer it properly. Today we are likely to begin an answer by saying that élites are out, and that in time and by due democratic process right decisions may be expected to emerge from the great body of us, so long as we are informed and free. We can all hope so. But tell that to those who make their fortunes out of our steadily worsening popular press, or to teachers in what we used to call 'elementary' schools, who often feel they are being implicitly expected to do more than provide fodder for that press and all it represents. Ah, comes the reply, but that is because the structures of communication are wrong; if the structures were right, people would ineluctably come to choose well. That depends. If the structure is 'right' in today's Communist countries it has so far failed to produce any intellectual resurgence – except *in resistance to* the régimes. In the commercial West, the only structures which were even marginally right were those of early public-service radio and television. And they were with some justice laughed out of countenance because they were so much the happy hunting ground of one special sort of élite. A narrow élite – they all seemed to have been to Oxbridge – but certainly a terribly responsible élite.

So Arnold wasn't silly or merely wrong-headed or old-fashioned in asking us to face better the need for some kind of what he liked to call a 'clerisy' in any society. More modern words such as 'gatekeeper' or 'opinion former' simply *look* neutral, and so beg all the questions; but that is just what we congenitally do today as part of our overall rejection of élitism.

No: Arnold's greatest weakness was not in raising the idea of a clerisy. It was simply that he did not see how things would develop in the decades after him and so came to the wrong conclusions in the matter; and we may all hope to be forgiven for such a failing in prognosis. He saw hope of a lead from the middle class:

A liberal culture, a fullness of intellectual life, in the middle class, is a far more important matter, a far more efficacious stimulant to national progress, than the same powers in an aristocratic class.

He talked of 'placing in the great middle-class the fullest, freest and worthiest development of the individual's activity'. That was their 'destination', to use his word. So he came to regard the grammar schools as the trainers of a new clerisy. Rugby and water? No – that would be unfair. But today the idea that the day grammar schools or public schools could or should provide such an intellectual or imaginative lead sounds like a preposterous joke.

Nevertheless, he did say again and again that in the long run the future lay in the elementary schools. Here he is, writing to his wife, in his very first year as an Inspector, 1851, from Oldham Road Lancastrian School, Manchester:

I think I shall get interested in the schools after a little time; their effects on the children are so immense, and their future effects in civilising the next generation of the lower classes, who, as things are going, will have most of the political power of the country in their hands, may be so important . . .

And here, in the report for 1871 he makes a point which is quite precisely – indeed appallingly – apt to this very day:

. . . the whole use that the Government, now that its connection with religious instruction is abandoned, makes of the mighty engines of literature in the education of the working classes, amounts to little more, even when most successful, than the giving them the power to read the newspapers.

But he never gave up in his hopes for the future of 'the lower classes'. His Victorian public rhetoric enshrined a very clear insight:

This obscure embryo, only just beginning to move, travelling in labour and darkness, so much left out of account . . . will have . . . a point towards which it may hopefully work.

I suggest that, were he alive today, Arnold might say that the crucial test of both the educational and the social health of this country will be its success or failure with comprehensive schools. Getting them right is overwhelmingly the most important educational issue of the day. And beyond those schools lies the whole range of further and higher education, part and full-time. Arnold greatly admired good evening schools, especially when they drew on the whole community. This prompts one final word about clerisies. If we are going to reject the idea that any particular social group or level of education has or gives *rights* to leadership – as I believe we must – then we must also surely put increasing hope in the concept of voluntary continuing education for all who want it, whatever their background. This kind of provision, easily available throughout life, offers (as its great progenitors such as Mansbridge, Temple and Tawney knew) unique and freely-willing opportunities for the individual to take a better critical grasp on issues within society and within the self. And that, at bottom, is what Arnold was always talking about.   1980

ON LANGUAGE
AND LITERACY TODAY

Literacy studies in Great Britain have made some gains, especially over the last fifteen or so years. The main advance is that we have become much more receptive to the variety of ways in which sophisticated communication can take place. We now know that many forms of speech which were previously dismissed as illiterate, ungrammatical or ungenteel can carry a complex range of meanings. We don't even have to say any longer that oral communication among people who hardly ever put pen to paper is interesting and alive *only* because it is concrete and metaphorical rather than abstract and conceptual. We know that apparently disconnected and uneducated speech can keep in play very elaborate structures of assumptions. We know a good deal more about non-verbal communications. We are more open to a great range of linguistic inventiveness; we almost all now welcome linguistic diversity. All that is a gain – and has become something of a fashion.

So what am I bothered about? I suppose by what can happen to almost any intellectual fashion: that it can temporarily blind its adherents to the limits of its usefulness. Take, for example, linguistic and literacy studies about children. Work of this kind is almost universally marked by a care and concern, a range of generous impulses, which only a curmudgeon would fail to recognise. But good intentions are never enough; generous impulses are never enough; sooner rather than later they are likely to get in the way of the fuller development of the very children these people do genuinely care about.

One often finds in this work a romanticism which expresses itself in that soft-centred phrase: 'The artist is not a special kind of a man; every man is a special kind of artist'. Of course, I see what is meant and in my time I've drawn aid from the declaration. But it's been so over-used and over-extended today that it's become a justification for levelling, a denial of the existence of gifts in some which the rest of us don't have, and of efforts by some which the rest of us won't make. So it should now be buried, since it has become the servant of an easy populism. It is related to the single-minded enthusiasm of some people for 'grass roots broadcasting' (for which I hope a good future). But the same people do not normally want to discuss the problems of how to structure and finance broadcasting on the national level, and those must be solved if broadcasting is to be a strong fifth estate, casting a critical eye on governments and parties and unions and corporations.

Similarly, work of this kind is often lopsidedly over-protective towards children. It is more fearful of submitting them to intellectual effort than of their straining muscles in, say, folk-dancing. Above all, it is afraid of anything which might be interpreted as a moral judgment. The following typical passage is from a recent English book on literacy and the school child. It is about a class in which a pupil had been rebuked for what the teacher thought was 'lazy' speech. It seems to me that, if the incident is accurately reported, the child *had* used a lazy form. But the author of this book cannot quite bear that thought. He says:

When language is seriously studied in its own right, it becomes clear just how awesomely complex is the socio-linguistic competence of *all* speakers. [True: that is what I remarked on earlier. But we do not have to assume that every form of 'vulgar' or non-'correct' speech has now to be hailed as an instance of a fluid, diverse, linguistic inventiveness. It might just be lazy, as the teacher said, unless that word has left the vocabulary. The author of this book on literacy continues] And when such a position is reached, it becomes impossible to maintain a position of linguistic prejudice or intolerance.

It is easy to see the linguistic slide here into hurrah and boo words. A teacher has committed the contemporary error of suggesting that some of us sometimes may be linguistically lazy (a sin I for one often commit). The author of this study responds, first, with the not altogether relevant reply that we now know that much hitherto unregarded speech is complex. He then goes on to throw in some pejorative words such as 'prejudice' and 'intolerance' so as to imply that anyone who doesn't accept every single form of speech as an instance of wholly acceptable linguistic diversity (instead of labelling some with naughty words such as 'lazy') is 'prejudiced' and 'intolerant'. It's not a very respectable way of arguing; but it avoids the risk of introducing 'moral judgments' into teaching.

What a strange mental world this suggests: what an odd psychological landscape teachers are being asked to evoke for their pupils. It recalls that beautiful poem of Auden's, 'In Praise of Limestone' in which, as so often, he evokes landscapes as the symbols of human attitudes. The great bare, raw plains are for the boss-men who want to rule others by drilling them; the harsh peaks are for the saints who want above all to rule their own passions, alone. But most of us like to stay in the comfortable, rolling, suburban, wrap-around, pliable, gregarious, limestone landscapes, where we demand little of others and they do the same by us. The passage I quoted above, and many others like it, are the educational-writers' equivalents of this near-horizontal, limestone-landscape world. The attitude has spread far, and to all levels. The common response by specialists in modern English to virtually any linguistic shift is: 'people seem to want to use the word/phrase/part of speech that way; therefore we accept and incorporate it; there are no other criteria'. So the new form spreads like the collared dove.

All these elements, as I am sure you have already recognised, are part of a very much wider process which runs through education of all kinds, through debates about the arts, through all the areas in which in the end we have to come up against questions of values and standards. In open societies where the liberal democratic spirit is still said to be honoured, that spirit, as Isaiah Berlin has discussed in an elegant and almost elegiac essay*, is so much on the defensive as to be largely disabled – especially to attacks from the Far Left, which are nowadays much more common and just as violent as those from the Right. Berlin notes that it is particularly embarrassing to resist the Far Left since liberals fear to be caught sinning against the light. So there is a powerful and widespread drag towards finding challenge-free and value-free approaches to all parts of education and indeed all areas of intellectual life; and since language is the most value-laden and value-significant of all our activities, the drag is especially strong there. It is this sense of a trap which must be evaded which gives the main impetus to the spread of such offerings in higher education as 'communication skills' courses. If we put all our effort into the mechanics, into *how* we can communicate with that person or group over there, into the machinery of the process, than we may avoid facing the substance, the *what* that is to be communicated – for that may be unpleasant or taxing or quite unacceptable to our hearers.

* *Fathers and Children, Turgenev and the Liberal Predicament: The Romanes Lecture, 1970.*

'To communicate all is to forgive all' is the modern version of an old bromide. Reinhold Niebuhr pointed out thirty years ago that fuller communications and greater understanding of each others' natures might, on the contrary, increase suspicion and hatred. I once had to recommend that a fairly senior UNESCO officer should not have his contract renewed, since his work was well below an acceptable level. The officer pushed aside all specific, itemised failings and summed up the situation as he saw it thus: 'The difficulty between me and Mr Hoggart is a failure in communication'. Had we communicated fully, presumably, all the hard evidence of administrative incompetences would have been flushed away in a warm bath of communicative togetherness. I remembered then a story about Attlee as Prime Minister who did not waste time. A Minister he was replacing asked for an interview so as to discuss the reason for his dismissal. 'You have to go', said Attlee, 'because you don't measure up to the job.'

In America, Mina Shaughnessy's work* reaches humane, imaginative levels in the approach to the teaching of basic-writing which the vast bulk of work in 'communications skills' gives no inkling of. In Britain one can begin mounting a precise criticism of such courses by saying that they virtually all ignore, seem not to have noticed, that a central element in communication or non-communication in our country lies in the handling of tone, written or spoken. Almost any English speaker of English is responsive to and able to employ a range of tones of considerable complexity. To look closely at those is to learn a great deal about the power of the sense of class in British life even today, and about its relations to geography, to certain schools and colleges, to a few professions and much else. To the long-established range of tones must now be added some which have emerged during the last few decades, especially in the populist press and the more populist reaches of broadcasting. By now most English popular broadcasters have given up feeling they have to adopt trans- or mid-Atlantic tones so as to avoid the minefields of tone-and-class. We now have our own populist tones – oddly enough, most of them light and high-pitched (for example, Jimmy Young on Radio 2). But, except for a few specialists, we do not examine all this. If we did, we would be led very much further than most courses in 'communications' have begun to imagine.

* *Errors and Expectations, a guide for the teacher of basic writing,* by Mina Shaughnessy, 1977.

To come back to the main thread, which is that an adequate definition of literacy invites us, forces us, to recognise that if we try to take short cuts, if we put up with lazy or evasive linguistic practices, we will sell our subjects and our students short. A great many of us have been doing that in the past few decades. As a result, what began as a democratic impulse has become undemocratic, because it has eroded the students' chances of reaching towards the best and hardest.

One cause of this state of affairs, I am arguing, is that many of us who work in education have been guided by ill-thought-out prescriptions. Seeing how badly-educated many of our pupils then prove to be, some of us excuse ourselves by saying that they were ineducable anyway, and that is why they are now only near-literate adults; and that can be a self-justifying fiction.

Take another common practice, by which some of us excuse a failure to require students to gain at least something of a sense of history, and a disinclination to bore them with what at first might seem dry learning. The way in is via the word 'relevance'. That word has been much misused recently so as to justify a great many bad habits, and we should declare a ten-year moratorium on its employment. A 'relevant' course is one which may be assumed to be instantly exciting to the students: a 'non-relevant' course is one which the students may be reluctant to start, since it will be assumed to be out of date or old-fashioned, and hence boring.

Not long ago I was speaking to a group of university extra-mural tutors and said something about the need, if you are a tutor in literature, to help adult students read the great texts in English since Chaucer. I added that sometimes today such classes had been dropped in favour of courses in 'communication skills' or in the socio-cultural analysis of mass communications. A man stood up and said he didn't at all agree; he didn't see why adult students should be forced to study what I – with a traditional English literature background – wanted to foist on them as the Great Tradition, and that it was more important to offer them subjects 'relevant' to their condition. (Is there anything more relevant to their condition than much of Shakespeare?) such as, he added, precisely those studies in mass communications which you have yourself done much to foster over the years. 'That is not what I meant at all. That is not it, at all,' I felt like murmuring with Prufrock.

On the far Left, a similar attitude takes the form of rejecting almost all the usual literary tradition as so much 'bourgeois crap', quite irrelevant to the needs of the emerging workers' culture. Insofar as such cultural forms may be emerging, good. But there is no sufficient reason why they should be set *against* an ill-conceived, reductive definition of 'high art'. But this is what, for example, the clamorous demands that the Arts Council should substantially cut off aid to building-based theatres and the classic repertoire in favour of new, alternative dramatic initiatives display. Yet, as we have seen, liberal democrats in Britain find it hard to take up a position on the middle ground, for fear of being lumped with the contributors to the Black Papers – people who have seen some of these problems, but tend to respond to them in a spirit of alarmed educational small-mindedness.

So it is more than time to take stock, especially of the full demands of certain disciplines, and of what might be seen as essential parts of our common heritage, and hence of what should then follow as practice.

First, we have to insist again, and consistently, that words – all aspects of the use of words – matter, and have to be respected. We should therefore, at whatever level we are teaching, require regular writing, and should mark it in detail, thus gradually showing in practice that to write, whether a letter to the local educational authority or a full-length novel, is a considerable discipline, and that probably no other activity so well tests us all round. This is also an essential grounding for the fuller appreciation of creative writing itself, as practised by those who make it their life's work.

So we come to the literary and linguistic heritage. Matthew Arnold, in his old-fashioned way, used to talk about 'touch-stones' and 'the best that has been thought and said', as essential parts of the intellectual baggage of educated people. Such phrases usually raise a small smile in educational circles today. I don't think we should be much put off by such routine reactions. In talking about the literary and linguistic heritage no one, so far as I know, is suggesting that we should draw up a list of 'the hundred best books which all students . . .' and so on and so on. Still, most of *us* who are middle-aged and in educational work do in fact have a good, common literary background, and few of us would like to think of our minds as lacking that rich seam. It has become part of the way we respond to our own experiences; it sharpens and focuses and criticises and sometimes helps to put in order our responses. It reveals how other people have made better sense of similar experiences by catching them in forms of language which thereafter stick in our consciousnesses like burrs.

Why should we deny anyone willing, or capable of being led to be willing, access to that store? – which is more than a store, since a store is a static repository, and these things become a living part of our engagement with our own lives.

When I began work as a university extra-mural teacher of literature thirty years ago there were some in that profession who argued that we did wrong to introduce mature working-class students to Shakespeare and other classic writers. We had to give them – yes – 'relevant' literature; and relevant literature was *The Ragged Trousered Philanthropists* and Gissing and Shaw and Wells. Here is the false setting of things against each other again, and the elision of differences of level. Today their successors are likely to say, again out of well-intentioned democratic impulses, that courses for such people should be not book-based but centred on tape-recorded oral records ... a coal miner's memories of the 'Thirties, a Union meeting in a big factory, a tape-recorded 'dramatised documentary' about the lives of working wives.

One thing my five years with the UN – at UNESCO – did was reinforce my sense of the great beauty and power of the effort by any individual to face his or her experiences and try to capture them in words, without face-saving or hiding from the self and without trying to woo or coo at anybody else. The fineness of that effort, the demands it makes on us and, sadly, its increasing rarity, I would say – these were all brought home to me with a weight I shall never now shrug off or would wish to shrug off. The conviction came chiefly from visits to the Eastern Bloc because there, although acts of public communication are going on all the time – on radio and television, in the press, on the hoardings, in a flood of public statements, there was hardly ever the sound of a disinterested, lonely, absorbed, brooding voice.

The voices were above all interested, manipulative, cautious, guarded, operational; they had aims but no purposes. But if that realisation began to tempt me to feel in any way self-congratulatory about the West it didn't take long to remember that such voices are today having a harder time in the West too, precisely because the liberal democratic spirit is, as I've said, so torn within itself; and also because, and *therefore* because, the voices which are increasingly riding high in our societies are also the persuasive and manipulative – not so much from centralised government authorities but from a variety of sources, from political parties and unions and above all from many aspects of the market-place. The experience of reading disinterested writing may not make us better people. It may nevertheless lead us to see moral dilemmas in a clearer light; and that could be the beginning of wisdom. Hence, the weakening of these kinds of voice all over the world is a major human loss.

It begins to look as if later generations will have less and less opportunity to make contact with the past, as though we are steadily losing a language and a literature together. Who will reverse the flow? Not much help can be expected from most people in most university departments of literature, in North America or Britain. For those departments have in the last twenty years or so expanded enormously, and at the same time become more and more 'strictly professional' in their general outlooks. At what they decide to do, they are often extremely competent. It is their restricted definition of what they should do which gives cause for concern.

'English Literature' is not at all 'out there' and objectively to be defined, but is an artificial construct, determined by battles long ago, continuing professional interests and, above all, a whole range of implicit but none the less powerful social and political assumptions. There is therefore no strictly definable field to be called 'English Literature'. There have been, over the centuries, books of many sorts coming out of a vast range of contexts, artistic, social, psychological and political. The field is hence in one sense quite limitless and undefinable. Yet, yes, it has to be defined. But any definition has to begin by recognising both the enormous variety of materials which need to be addressed and also the error of approaching them in a relative void, free of the constant attempt, the integral attempt, to come to grips with them as part of a continuous and continuing historical process. In not recognising this, I think many university English departments have failed to meet the main intellectual challenge before them.

We are moving more and more into the area where plastic language carries no more than plastic thoughts and exchanges. But the process is about more than language; it is about no less than the definition of democracy, and its survival. It is about the submerging of such movement as there is towards the growth of genuine democracy in an institutionally-centralised populism. The lapse, by intelligent liberal democrats, into an amiable or dry or disillusioned relativism is at such a time a main contribution to the process.

Well, it's a slow business, is the very least one can say. The appearance of a democratically effective and articulate working-class is still a long way off, and a great many forces work against its emergence.

Meanwhile we remain both divided and headless; and democracy is more under challenge from within than it has ever been.

These threats, I have been arguing, are highlighted by our weakened sense of the importance of language. We usually forget this because we live in the blind and lucky West. The Soviet and East European dissidents do not forget it because they are fighting for basic human rights, and because they know that in this fight 'words alone are certain good', that only in and through the struggle with language will the real radical criticisms be made, and the real possible alternatives be explored – through poetry and the novel, above all. They have been *forced* to choose and to fight, or to think themselves less than human; and a few of the very brave have sat, in difficult and dangerous conditions, and written their testaments; and been duly punished. Meanwhile, we stand by and let our own values bleed to death.   1979

CULTURE AND COMMUNICATIONS

THE AUTOBIOGRAPHY
OF HENRY ADAMS

Some books choose us, rather than we them. They have a powerful effect on us because we are, somehow, called to them at just the right moment. No doubt they have to be in some ways 'good' books, but they aren't necessarily as important to the world at large as their effect on us might suggest. We usually find them in late adolescence; they speak to an emerging but not yet fully understood interest, and one which may stay with us all our lives.

The field of interest first rather foggily focused for me when I read *The Education of Henry Adams* at the age of nineteen has remained dominant. I hardly remember how I came to the book, though I suspect my eclectically generous professor, Bonamy Dobrée, tossed out the title one day. That was part of his cunning as a teacher, to derail us off the traditional tracks. Certainly Adams and this particular book might well seem a bit recherché, even today. My experience suggests that only a small number of people have read it – this autobiography (though some critics won't allow its right to that title) of a New England Brahmin, the descendant of two American Presidents, who – inevitably – went to Harvard. About that, he had a characteristically ambivalent attitude:

In effect, the school created a type but not a will. Four years of Harvard College, if not successful, resulted in an autobiographical blank, a mind on which only a water-mark had been stamped.

The stamp, as such things went, was a good one. The chief wonder of education is that it does not ruin everybody concerned in it, teachers and taught. Sometimes in after life, Adams debated whether in fact it had not ruined him and most of his companions, but, disappointment apart, Harvard College was probably less hurtful than any other university then in existence. It taught little, and that little ill, but it left the mind open, free from bias, ignorant of facts, but docile. The graduate had few strong prejudices. He knew little, but his mind remained supple, ready to receive knowledge.

Then, again inevitably, came an educational topping off in Germany, a good few years in diplomacy and thereafter a career as a historian – a good historian, though he felt himself a failure overall. He had been born in 1838 and died in 1918; and felt he had spanned whole centuries. *The Education* was privately printed in 1906, his sixty-eighth year, and not publicly issued till the year of his death. An odd, withdrawn, pursed-up sort of book, it nevertheless worked on me – I now see – at quite deep levels and in three main ways. Its themes – the stresses of cultural change – spoke to my own as yet inchoate interests; its wrestlings with the problems of form in this kind of writing – how best to handle the interplay of personal experience and public meanings – helped set me off on a similar search; its stances and tones before life – a narrow but subtle range of voices – were notes from the New World which chimed in with some in such native writers as Arnold and Hardy to whom I'd already become attached.

Adams' overriding theme is that of confronting the chaos of the modern world. That world was seen as diverse, multiple – 'multiverse', he called it – broken-apart, relativist, thrusting; he was not at home there. We had gone from unity to diversity in seven centuries, he decided; from the stability of mediaeval culture, the art and architecture of the twelfth century, to this disorder. And his almost colonial New England background did not help:

What could become of such a child of the seventeenth and eighteenth centuries, when he should wake up to find himself required to play the game of the twentieth? . . . As it happened, he never got to the point of playing the game at all; he lost himself in the study of it, watching the errors of the players.

Wherever he was, he was not truly at home. New England had prepared him for a sharply defined form of life; a plain living, high-thinking and almost certainly political life: 'one lived in the atmosphere of the Stamp Act, the Tea Tax, and the Boston Massacre. Within Boston, a boy was first an eighteenth century politician, and afterwards only a possibility; beyond Boston the first step led only further into politics'.

But into what politics? For the massive energy and diversity of the new America was producing new men, new types of men; and Henry Adams was neither at ease with them nor liked them, these thrusting New York bankers who'd emerged since the 1840s, or the new breed

106

of politicians who inhabited Washington during the Sixties. Here as in many other places in the book he gives us vignettes of the political life of the time – notably in London and Washington – without which our sense of those times is poorer. But he was out of place and could become waspish: 'America had no use for Adams because he was eighteenth century, and yet it worshipped Grant because he was archaic and should have lived in a cave and worn skins'. The dynamo at the Chicago Fair of 1893 seemed to offer a new kind of unity; but wasn't it the unity of common spiritual disintegration? When he and his father landed in America after roughly a decade in Europe they felt wholly displaced:

Had they been Tyrian traders of the year 1,000 BC landing from a galley fresh from Gibraltar, they could hardly have been stranger on the shore of a world, so changed from what it had been ten years before.

In the last few pages of this very long book he comes back again to these new, vigorous and unscrupulous powers as he saw them:

They were revolutionary, troubling all the old conventions and values, as the screws of ocean steamers must trouble a school of herring. They tore society to pieces and trampled it under foot. As one of their earliest victims, a citizen of Quincy, born in 1838, had learned submission and silence.

The ambivalent attitude to America itself was mirrored even more boldly in his ambivalence towards Europe, and especially towards England. He spent seven years in London as private secretary to his father, who was the Minister of the United States to the Court of St James. One might have expected him to feel immensely at home in Europe and in some ways he did, as have many later displaced American intellectuals. For almost all of them the relationship contained both love and hate. For Henry Adams, especially in his attitude to Britain, the dislike is much more evident. 'The British mind is the slowest of all minds', he said, and talked about the 'thick cortex of fixed ideas' in the brain of a typical Englishman of the establishment. He gives us some remarkable pictures of English intellectual life in the Sixties as seen by a highly discriminating foreigner, one with a far finer consciousness, and conscience, than the British public schools normally produced. He describes in detail the complex British politicising during the American Civil War, the endless cunning of Palmerston and, worse, the behaviour of Gladstone. 'Never in the history of political turpitude,' he says of him, 'had any brigand of modern civilisation offered a worse example.' He was more at home with Monckton Milnes at Monk

Fryston, where he met Swinburne and other artists and intellectuals most of whom did not frequent the London political scene. But still he was always on the outside looking in. And he would not hunt, race, shoot or gamble or be a womaniser.

Wherever he was, in fact, he was always between two worlds. Matthew Arnold's 'Dover Beach' and parts of 'The Grande Chartreuse' sum up perfectly one whole part of Adams' character 'Wandering between two worlds, one dead, the other powerless to be born'. He knew this, and herein lies much of his attraction – a chilling attraction, sometimes: and usually epigrammatic, which I suppose is why he appears so often in so many books of quotations:

Society is immoral and immortal; it can afford to commit any kind of folly, and indulge in any sort of vice; it cannot be killed, and the fragments that survive can always laugh at the dead.

Or again:

All State education is a sort of dynamo machine for polarizing the popular mind; for turning and holding its lines of force in the direction supposed to be most effective for State purposes.

He was quite unable to accept the present. He had a sharply critical mind, but yet one suffused with a baffled mystical yearning. He knew he was foolish to seek 'a moral standard for judging politicians' and to long for 'a world that sensitive and timid natures could regard without a shudder'. But so it was. Whilst re-reading Henry Adams, I was also reading Bertrand Russell's autobiography. By contrast, Russell – for all his dialectical brilliance – seemed brittle.

Adams was intensely self-conscious, anti-heroic, undramatic. Yet he did feel he had something to say, and something very important. Here is where his problems of form lay. How could he best suggest his own overriding sense of being, though a small and in the end a non-significant figure, one to whom nevertheless things happened which did have a wider than usual significance? He did it first of all by seeking symbols, especially symbols of dialectical opposites – the Virgin and the Dynamo, outstandingly, for the great medieval/modern dichotomy. He teased at those types of symbolic opposites for page after page till they began to carry quite considerable weight. It was those and a range of other devices of style which allowed him to present his life as both in itself insignificant yet as in some ways illustrating great movements of cultural change. He was one of the earliest writers to see that technologies change not only our outer styles of life but the inner rhythms of our minds and hearts.

His most important formal device was to eschew the 'I' and speak of himself only in the third person singular. That might avoid many of the dangers of seeming to pose and become emotionally self-indulgent; it might give distance and avoid direct intimacies. It often produces an odd effect, even when he is being rather pawkily comical towards himself: 'At past fifty, Adams solemnly and painfully learned to ride the bicycle'. But in general it helps. It keeps him buttoned-down in the best Boston manner, and yet allows him to be quite open about his own deficiencies, though still without coming too close. Oddly enough, we end by feeling almost as though he is looking at himself and talking to himself rather than directly addressing us; we are eavesdroppers, licensed to do so for our possible greater under-standing of the interplay between social change and the individual conscience.

Adams' play of dominant tones matches well this approach to society-and-the-individual and this distancing form. He is, before all else, unexpectant, resigned, elegiac and elegant – yet still ironic towards himself. He is fastidious – without a belly-laugh in all the 500 pages; he never appeals to the *homme moyen sensuel*. Like T. S. Eliot, he is the sort of man of whom others are tempted to say that he seemed to have been born middle-aged. He is wounded, grave, concerned and at bottom very sad. There were particular reasons as well as those of basic temperament. His wife had committed suicide in 1885. They had married in 1872. The autobiography omits reference to Adams's life from 1872-92. He had seen his sister die of tetanus in Italy in 1870:

The last lesson – the sum and term of education – began then . . . Flung suddenly in his face, with the harsh brutality of chance, the terror of the blow stayed by him thenceforth for life. . . . He found his sister, a woman of forty, as gay and brilliant in the terror of lockjaw as she had been in the careless fun of 1859, lying in bed in consequence of a miserable cab-accident that had bruised her foot. Hour by hour the muscles grew rigid, while the mind remained bright, until after ten days of fiendish torture she died in convulsions.

One had heard and read a great deal about death, and even seen a little of it, and knew by heart the thousand commonplaces of religion and poetry which seemed to deaden one's senses and veil the horror. Society being immortal, could put on immortality at will. Adams being mortal, felt only the mortality.

So the painful honesty before the self marches on, self-critical to a degree that sometimes seems almost masochistic and reminds us yet again of Eliot, in so many ways a fellow spirit:

> ... the shame
> Of motives late revealed, and the awareness
> Of things ill done and done to others' harm
> Which once we took for exercise of virtue.
> Then fools' approval stings, and honour stains.

And yet – in case this has not already become clear – this was also a very clever personality indeed, and a very tough one in the pursuit of truth; much tougher than the personalities of most of the aggressive New Men he so mistrusted.

I am drawn to *The Education of Henry Adams* for all these large reasons. And, I now realise, also for more local reasons – because he was a teacher in the humanities who never ceased to question himself on the awful challenges of that demanding profession:

The historian must not try to know what is truth, if he values his honesty: for, if he cares for his truths, he is certain to falsify his facts ... The mind resorts to reason for want of training ... Nothing is more tiresome than a super-annuated pedagogue ... (but) A teacher affects eternity; he can never tell where his influence stops.

For whom was he writing? For 'the survivors', he characteristically said. If so, those survivors still exist and are reborn in each generation; and somewhere along the road they will, if they are lucky, meet Henry Adams.   1980

GEORGE ORWELL
AND THE ART OF BIOGRAPHY

Like W. H. Auden, George Orwell asked that no biography of him be written. Though they were very dissimilar writers, their reasons for the injunction were much the same: each – the one pawkily, the other fiercely – wanted to be remembered for their works and saw their lives as intensely private. Neither has had his wish in death. Inevitably. There's no law against writing a man's biography: all his executors can usually do is prevent access to papers. Even so, as in Orwell's case, researchers as persistent as Stansky and Abrahams – in *The Unknown Orwell* and *Orwell: The Transformation* – can get a good long way by interviewing everyone who is willing to talk. A great many were and are. I imagine that it was this circumstance which led the late Mrs Orwell to suggest that Professor Bernard Crick write a life; not an 'official biography' but a study based for the first time on unrestricted access to the papers she still controlled.*

That she asked Bernard Crick to do the work – he had already done some very interesting writing about Orwell – nevertheless raised a few eyebrows in more purely literary circles. How could a political scientist get at the inwardness of Orwell as a writer? Still, some people added eventually, he might at least be able to make more sense than a literary critic would of Orwell's politics. So Professor Crick, one might say, was not so much dismissed with, as accepted with, a caution.

In fact, he has written a quite different sort of biography than either a strictly literary or a strictly political scholar would have produced. The literary judgments within his book are everywhere competent and often better than that; and his political knowledge shows to good effect. But neither of those qualities points to the unusual nature of this work, or explains the character of its success.

George Orwell: A Life, by Bernard Crick.

111

That is overwhelmingly due to the *distancing* which the author practises towards his subject; he simply refuses to come in close personally. This is a quite deliberate strategy, as he makes clear in his long and fascinating introduction (itself worth inclusion in any collection of essays on the problems of biography). He has thought very hard about the nature of that form and come to some firm conclusions. Above all, he has decided to reject what he calls the British tradition in biography, inward and interpretative, weaving between the subject's private life and the changes in his art, making a succession of main movements and changes seem an organic whole, and, above all, trying to relate the inward life (and, this being England, the childhood) to the strains and stresses of the writer:

All too often the literary virtues of the English biographical tradition give rise to characteristic vices: smoothing out or silently resolving contradictions in the evidence and bridging gaps by empathy and intuition (our famous English 'good judgment of character' which, compared to the French stress on formal criteria, lets us down so often): and this all done so elegantly that neither contradictions nor gaps in the evidence are apparent to any but scholarly eyes ...

It is Lytton Strachey and *Eminent Victorians,* and all those after him, from whom Professor Crick deliberately turns. It can also be an American style as may be seen in Stansky and Abrahams, since their studies are nothing if not thematic and extensively interpretative. Towards them, incidentally, Professor Crick is polite if sometimes corrective; I guess he respects how far they got *without* access to the papers. So: 'distanced' is the first word which comes to mind for his manner. Here is a typical sample:

On 27 October 1922, Blair sailed for the East on SS *Herefordshire,* from Birkenhead to Rangoon. New arrivals and departures are the set pieces of biographies, but so often it has all to be made up; there is no way of knowing what frame of mind he was in or quite what burden, if any, he thought he was carrying, this difficult, interesting, independent-minded, self-contained nineteen-year-old, committed only to scepticism towards authority and a love of literature but hardly of learning.

The choice is, as I've said, deliberate. Professor Crick refers to 'the externality of my method' and is fully aware of the costs of such a self-effacing, undramatic, un-'clever', unassertive approach. 'An honest biographer must be more dull than he could be,' he says. One wishes that lots of twentieth-century biographers before him had thought about the task so far as to be able to say that; and autobiographers too. He will not put his thumb on the scale, or parade himself; he is dispassionate, almost laconic, dry, removed, disciplined, careful, separated, impersonal but not detached, always concerned about keeping his distance, never Olympian or godlike – it is, after all, too easy to sound superior to a dead subject of whom you would have been in awe in life. He never claims too much or obtrudes, to the point that sometimes one *could* do with a word or two more about where he himself stands. He is neither 'knocking' nor knowing; nor is he reverent.

Let me give one specific case. He is deeply, and rightly, sceptical about the reliability of memory. We all select and embroider, especially in our memories of famous persons we have known. So, 'hindsight' is one of his favourite critical words. He does not deceive himself into thinking that he can, in some magisterial way, choose between plainly conflicting accounts of the same incident. He lets each side speak for itself, contenting himself with adding a few open questions on the nature of the disagreement and on the *possibly* correct explanation.

He is also sceptical, it follows, about some of Orwell's own accounts of events in his life, and about Orwell's casualness as to facts if to be casual suited his dramatic and fictional needs. He circles around that essay about Orwell's prep school days, 'Such, Such Were the Joys', like a self-conscious cat before a booby-trapped mouse. It follows also that he can only accept such pieces as 'How the poor Die', 'A Hanging' and 'Shooting an Elephant' once he has pinned them as 'documentary short stories', neither wholly fact nor wholly fiction. This is a clarifying cautiousness.

There are at least two good reasons why such an approach is valuable, one general, the other particular. The general one is that, as Professor Crick says, British biography gets away with murder, psychological murder; it could do with a stiff dose of dispassion. The particular reason concerns Orwell. Orwell is a writer whom many of us, for different reasons (not all of them connected with his writing), feel driven to make into a culture-hero. There may be good, not at all discreditable reasons for this. He's someone whose work we find hard to separate from his personality. We do not often feel 'negative capability' in him; we meet an exceptional personality, whose life and art were one and who, we feel, *lived out* his beliefs. But there is a danger here which Professor Crick – who does greatly admire Orwell – is out to avoid himself and will not encourage in others: the danger of

113

myth-making.

It isn't that he does not wish Orwell's talents to be recognised and admired. He does, and his book reminds us again and again why so many of us find Orwell so attractive. He was English in the grain (not, Professor Crick notes, British – the word would seem, and is, wrong, a public word). Many quotations and incidents here reinforce this, and especially the extracts (which are generous) from some of the lesser-known works. For myself and among much else, I remembered again the precision of Orwell's hatred of the Establishment: 'because they tried to monopolise patriotism'. That places and judges generations of bad teaching in prep schools and public schools, and subserviently imitative grammar schools for that matter.

Bernard Crick describes another aspect of Orwell in this way: 'He assumed the indivisibility of citizenship and culture.' That explains some of Orwell's freshness, indicates how he cut at fashionably solipsist intellectualism and reasserted the need to recognise ordinary roots. I have myself written a few lines about the importance of the sense of smell in Orwell's writings. But I hadn't made the precise connection which is made here, that Orwell was haunted by smell because 'he associated smell with oppression'. The natives in Burma smelled and so did the poor in England. As he says in *The Road to Wigan Pier,* of the slum interiors:

It is a kind of duty to see and smell such places now and again, especially smell them, lest you should forget that they exist.

One could go on and on. One more very typical quotation only:

If liberty means anything at all, it means the right to tell people what they do not want to hear.

Such a spare, hard style had had to be fought for; but it was well earned.

We see more clearly from this book – though Stansky and Abrahams, too, brought it out – how very slow and at first how conventional a start Orwell made. What comes over movingly also is that, though we now are often tempted to see his early death as inevitable, to be expected, part of his life's pattern, to Orwell those last few weeks in University College Hospital, London, were meant to be a getting better, a preparation for all the work which lay ahead. Professor Crick's method ensures, as I guess I've sufficiently shown, that he is not concerned, is specifically against, any writing for effect. But his passage about *1984,* coming at the very end of Orwell's life, as it proved, has, by its terseness and the terseness of what has preceded it, great force:

The book was fully compatible with what he had written before and much of its inspiration arose from what he had done before. It does not summarise his life's work, however, it is not his *summa,* and it is not even a political last testament, or a last testament of any kind. It was, once again, the last great book *he happened to write before he happened to die.* (**My italics.**) He would have written about other things, great and small.

We are not presented with an easy hero or simple saint. Orwell's sex life, for example, was not above reproach. More than once Professor Crick gives instances of a touch of sadism – as in his severe beating of Rayner Heppenstall when Heppenstall came in very drunk to their shared flat; or the gleeful energy with which he took an adder apart. He was in many ways a hard man as well as a very gentle one; hardest of all to himself, as his first wife Eileen very well knew. She told a friend that her brother would have come from the ends of the earth if she had needed him, and added: 'George would not do that. For him his work comes before anybody.' The friend added, and I believe Eileen would have agreed: 'For Orwell, his work was more important than any personal relationships, and I believe that he cared for himself only in his capacity as a writer.' It is a chillingly impressive but fundamentally correct judgment. In pursuit of these contrasts within Orwell and within his writing, Professor Crick makes towards the end a simple but useful distinction:

He loved the land and he loved England and he loved the language of the liturgies of the English Church. 'Orwell-like' conveys all these things; 'Orwellian' other things (1984 and all that). He should be remembered for both.

The point of Professor Crick's persistently unromantic approach is that, to borrow a fashionable phrase from another discipline, it 'demythologises' Orwell. It makes it more difficult for his admirers to idealise him, to see too simple a fit between the works and the man, to make too emblematic the journey from Eton and what it represented to that stance of his as the voice of bare, ascetic, English democratic socialism. Orwell's *was* that voice and we are right to be grateful for it: he was also in some respects an old Etonian to the end of his life, at some depths he had not plumbed.

There is a further point, a further gain, from an approach such as this. It doesn't get between us, the readers, and the author's works. It doesn't try to present us with a total frame within which to see, interpret, 'make sense of' the writings. It presents us with a great deal of careful evidence – not simply such records as the awful treatment of the manuscript of *Animal Farm* by publishers, but more important issues. Yet almost everywhere it then moves on to the next date in the calendar. In some ways this is a pity, since Professor Crick might have said many more useful things about the nature of Orwell's writing than he has allowed himself. But, as I've said so often, his restraint is formidable.

Let me give just one example of how this restraint operates since it is also an instance of how, because Professor Crick puts so much material before us, the reader is set off into letting his own knowledge of the work interact with what is now offered by way of evidence, so that new understandings emerge. The example is relatively small, but nevertheless quite cogent.

It concerns Orwell's prose style. About that Professor Crick makes, on the whole, only glancing comments, though they can be telling: 'He made common words sharp, made them come to life again until under his spell one thinks twice before one uses any polysyllables, still less neologisms.' True, but Professor Crick does not push on any further. Similarly, 100 pages further on, he quotes from an early essay in which Orwell writes of the need for a very cheap newspaper, ending: 'Even if it does no other good whatever, at any rate the poor devils of the public will at last feel that they are getting the correct value for their money.' Professor Crick comments: 'The pithy use of ordinary phrases like ''fair means or foul'', ''ugly bump'' and ''poor devils'', the irony of the last sentence; and even the pseudo-precision of ''*doubtless* some of the circulations have come down'', these are all devices found frequently in his famous essays.' True again. But there are other reverberations from, in particular, that special use of 'poor devils' which cry out for more probing, something to do with the cultural and class and status echoes the phrase sets off and which are themselves, Orwell's use of such words, at the very heart of his more powerful prose.

I wrote something myself a few years ago about Orwell's use of bluntly idiomatic expressions so as to prevent his readers from feeling that they were having a 'literary' experience, so as to hit them across the face. He *demonstrates* through his recurrent 'this, this and this' and 'one of those'; so he *indicts*. I knew at the time that I was no more than scratching the surface, especially in reading a passage such as this from the opening of *The Road to Wigan Pier:*

There were generally four of us in the bedroom, and a beastly place it was, with that defiled impermanent look of places that are not serving their rightful purpose.

It's easy to see what one is responding to in the second half of the sentence: the sense of displacement you get when a sitting-room is made into a bedroom, and the two very precise epithets. But it's the word 'beastly' which hits you and echoes. It has great force, but *where* does that force come from? What *world* does the phrase itself invoke? It is not a word which was used in my own original social class (far more than we recognise, our epithets of love and hate are set early in childhood by the class from which we start). I could never have used 'beastly' any more than 'super', until I reached the point of feeling confident to do so through understanding their socio-linguistic relations better, or in ironic inverted commas. Orwell helped liberate 'beastly' for general use. But where did *he* get it from? I'd assumed – in general correctly – that it came from his social group; and I could hear Mrs Blair saying: 'That's rather a beastly thing to do, Eric!' But its origins are altogether clearer and its force greater once we've read, in this study, some of Orwell's letters home from his prep school, St Cyprian's, at the age of eight.

I am very glad Colonel Hall has given me some stamps, he said he would last year but I thought he had forgotten. It's a beastly wet day today all rain and cold. I am very sorry to hear we had those beastly freaks of smelly white mice back. I hope these aren't smelly ones. If they aren't I shall like them.

Orwell's essay on the horrors of St Cyprian's takes its title – 'Such, Such Were the Joys' – from one of Blake's *Songs of Innocence,* 'The Echoing Green', and Professor Crick does some good work in showing how the material of those experiences is used throughout Orwell's life but is also distorted, as all echoes distort. Listening to the extraordinary, emotive force of the repeated 'beastly' in that letter, and hearing it a quarter of a century later in *Wigan Pier,* we realise that for Orwell (as for all of us) the 'echoes' we take from our childhood have, and continue to have, at least as much to do with tone as with incidents. Our language reveals us more than almost any other of our ways of expression. To understand this is to understand ourselves and all writers better and, above all, to understand how gifted and committed writers, such as Orwell, take and transmute words and phrases and movements which have been too long locked in their class situations.

I have said more than once that I for one could have wished that Professor Crick had relaxed his self-imposed discipline a little so as to give us more political-cum-literary analysis of his own. But he has been determined not to write that kind of book, and one respects that, as well as the result it gained. Had he mixed the categories, he would probably have spoiled the main achievement. It is a considerable achievement. By a patient, unspectacular, unflourishing marshalling of the evidence, much of which we have not had before, he has built up a personality – seen, yes, resolutely from 'outside', but still close up – so that two things happen. We are given much more evidence, as nearly as possible 'objective', to set against our own knowledge of the works and so to readjust that knowledge; and, probably more important, there is created a picture – again, at a due and chosen distance – warts and all, of this driven, gentle, cruel, ascetic but also creaturely man which other, more interpretative or internal, methods could not give so convincingly (though I still believe such studies have their place). We see Orwell slowly move to his belated fame, and then suddenly die. As we do so, our respect is certainly qualified but not weakened by our new knowledge.   1980

ALLEN LANE
AND PENGUINS

By now there are many thousands of Penguin graduates all over the world. Some of us saw the first handful of titles reach the shops, and from then on began to buy new books for ourselves. The war years strengthened the links; in that time the kitbags of intelligent laymen usually carried a Penguin or Pelican or two. That was the earliest generation. By today the members of Penguins' citizens' university cover several successive generations; they are in their sixties, their fifties, their forties, their thirties, and their twenties. For us all – in our efforts to train and nourish our minds – Penguins have a special place.

To create something new like this at any time you have to keep three elements in play. You are reacting away from a certain set of circumstances; you have to avoid falling, by the force of your reaction, into new pitfalls; and balancing between these two, you have to build a new position, a new place to stand.

What Allen Lane's initiative reacted from was something bedded very deep in British society, for all that people denied it then and today deny it even more. Penguins, by their very appearance in that form, by their availability, their flexibility and their variety, made an implicit attack on the assumption that there are fairly well-defined and determined links and layerings between intelligence and class and formal education. Therefore, right from the start, they struck at some of the more hidden and powerful forms of snobbery and of establishment – at the conventional snobberies and establishments of the mind. They struck, as all such initiatives must do if they are to be effective, at a precise and particular point – at the status quo within both the publishing world and the bookselling world. For in the world of those close relatives as it was then, and in spite of their undoubted other virtues, the common man seeking for knowledge did not feel particularly at home. He knew 'Them' when he saw them.

But in an operation such as this, success is at least as much a matter of knowing – once you have broken away from the old positions – what not to do as of knowing what you positively want to do. Penguins could have embodied and institutionalised new attitudes even less adequate than the old ones, because more self-conscious. Sometimes they *have* made mistakes like that, but not consistently. They could have seemed over-earnest and talked down. Of course, they were out to do us good. But they had to avoid those morally superior attitudes and tones – and there is a rich range of them – which so easily go with the intention to do good to men's minds, whether in Britain or elsewhere. Equally, they had to avoid falling into another compendious trap, the trap which contains the merely arty and fashionable, the culture-vulture and the intellectual smart-alec; though at the same time they had to keep up with, and take risks in judging, the main intellectual and imaginative trends, or they would have been little more than a paperback reprint house, riding on the wave of other men's gambles.

This is the way you gradually create, and begin to recognise yourself, a distinctive new style. In Penguins it was, to put it at its simplest, a certain disposition towards knowledge and towards people. That disposition is, again to be quite basic, 'democratic' – if the word retains any of its old good meanings. I will try to revive some of those meanings as I go along. It means, first, an unusual kind of openness; it means assuming, as if it is a fact of nature, that access to intellectual life is the right of all men. This attitude belongs to a long-standing and honourable tradition in Britain. Think, especially, of the rich nineteenth-century achievement in many kinds of education for adults and workers, and of many forms of cheap publishing from that time on. In some ways, Penguins continue that line. But their style and tone are different. If we understood better the peculiar kind of 'openness', the peculiar 'classlessness', of Penguins we would understand better also the distinctive feel of mid-twentieth-century cultural change in Britain. I can think of three achievements of this type. All three made a first move which looks simple but is really very bold – they trusted a far wider range of people than had commonly been trusted before in their areas of activity, trusted them to choose the better when they saw it.

'Openness' and 'an open mind' can be polite ways of describing intellectual promiscuity. Penguins' intellectual openness was reinforced by a political and, more important, a moral conscience. The political conscience was most powerfully expressed in the range of pre-war Penguin Specials. It still survives, necessarily less dramatically but still powerfully. So does the more general moral sense. This is why we have always felt that Penguins 'stood for something', that there were not only some things it would not do (it's pretty easy for anyone to claim that), but that Penguins have decided there are some things that should be done, even at considerable cost; and that it is up to Penguins to do them.

What I called Penguins' basic attitudes towards the life of the mind underpins their attitude towards their readers. They made assumptions about possible relationships which to some people are beginning to seem old-fashioned, touching maybe but probably mistaken. They assumed that you can make contact with others by trying to speak straight to them, and that it matters to try to connect, is not just a deluded speaking into the void. Again, this tradition in Britain is long and has a special flavour. Remember that extraordinarily characteristic range of discursive voices which we hear all the way up through the nineteenth century, and in this century hear again strikingly, in Forster and Lawrence and Orwell. Their tones differ a great deal but at their best have common roots. They are in touch with the palpable detail of that day-to-day life they share with their readers; they are out of step with the big battalions; and they care very much about making contact with individuals. But – and this is the acid test – they care more about what they are trying to communicate than about the act of communication in itself. They know in their bones that when care for communicating takes precedence over care about content, then the activity becomes mindless – 'togetherness' with intellectual pretensions. One has to care first about what one is saying, care also about sharing it with others, recognise how difficult that sharing is, but be willing at times to break the connections rather than lose hold of the truth ... and then you may indeed 'communicate' well.

Something of this particular concern Penguins have managed to show. A sense of caring about the mind and its disciplines; a sense, too, of caring that people should *know* which implies a respect for people in themselves, whatever their backgrounds; a respect for what they might aim to become if they were shown other perspectives. In all this, Penguins have stood for the idea that our potentialities are greater than the pressures of our time and place and circumstances might have led us to assume.

Some newspapers and journals have from time to time got near this position. But on the whole their connections with certain social classes more than with others, or their underlying party-political allegiances, or the implicit pressures of advertising (not sinister pressures – the pressure of being aware, underneath, of the relationships between class and consumption and taste are enough) – these have prevented newspapers and periodicals from consistently striking that tricky balance which Penguins have managed to hold most of the time.

Of course, Penguins are in business and aim at a profit. But you do not usually feel that 'It's your money they're after'; that choices are made solely, or even pre-eminently, on commercial grounds; that you yourself are in the end, and whatever the public-relations trimmings, seen as just a consumer and a customer. You feel, rather, a sort of equality, a shared sense that certain things matter, and that when Penguin editors have said 'That's not quite a Penguin manu-script' they were usually referring to some values more important than those of the sales chart.

I said a while back that some people have come to think this belief in being able to make contact mistaken. They find themselves deciding that in the end we do not make contact; that when we think we are communicating straight, and about 'real' things, we are doubly deceiving ourselves; we hear only the echo of what we want to hear, so that our closed personalities may remain closed and undisturbed. If this is so, then Penguins will go down as one of the last expressions of the liberal dream, the dream which made men think that if they tried to speak honestly and clearly they might indeed reach one another.

Hence the working approach of Penguins. The basic seriousness of the enterprise shows most relevantly in its editing of commissioned non-fiction. From the start, Penguins took firm hold on an important truth which is rarely grasped: good popularisation is not a watering-down, and so is very difficult to achieve. In fact, we ought to find another word for this tough process.

To write well for 'the intelligent layman' you have to share with him a particular set of working-values – assumptions about the role of intelligence and of intellectuals, and about possible relationships within the wider life of society. This set of circumstances does not exist everywhere. So, again, Penguins' achievement is by implication telling something to our credit. Not that we always know this ourselves. Most teachers in adult education know (and no doubt the influence of W. E. Williams, who had been trained in that hard school, was crucial with Allen Lane and with Penguins for many years). But many academics, if they came to paperback publishing (and after a while most of them hoped they would, because it had been made so respectable), came at first as though they were doing somebody – Penguins themselves, or 'the common man' as they often liked to say – a favour by writing for them. So they tended to write slackly, and tried to let irrelevant verbal bonhomie do duty for the disciplined care which clarity demands. Penguins' editors told them they were mistaken, that to write clearly, as clearly as your subject's complexity allowed, was not to oversimplify or to personalise unnecessarily; that Jude and Leonard Bast and Paul Morel and Gordon Comstock and all the many thousands for which they stand are worth writing for to the top of one's bent. This was the critical moment for many academics. At that point, having pruned your subject of its unnecessary terms of art and internal conventions, you were faced with what you really had to say; and sometimes saw clearly, for the first time, that you had nothing new or important to say at all. One of the best tributes to recent British academic life is that many academics did face that moment squarely.

All these qualities combine to produce the character we recognise as Penguins at their best. Of course, Penguins have not always lived up to their own best self. Sometimes they have had their eyes on the main chance; occasionally they have come near to abusing their trust (that large capital of readers' goodwill on which they can now draw). But on the whole the balance has been held. I have tried to show that this balance is derived from a set of interlocked assumptions and implicit assertions – about knowledge and the mind, about class and education and opportunity, about speaking to each other, about responsibility and freedom. The Penguin enterprise ranks as a remarkable expression of important aspects of our recent cultural history, and an important contributor to the process of cultural change.

So we come back to the word 'democracy', which seemed too loose and ill-defined to use confidently earlier. The British shy away from definitions. When asked for them, they tend to bridle at first, then to look superior, and finally to say. 'Look, I wouldn't want to try to define it ... ["the democratic outlook", "good journalism", "responsible broadcasting"] ... but [and here comes the characteristic British phrase] you know it when you meet it in action.' When you look at the whole Penguin achievement you know that it constitutes, in action, one of the more democratic successes of our recent social history.

I did not know Allen Lane very well, but when we did meet we seemed to have a natural *rapport,* which bridged a great many obvious differences. And he was very kind to me, in practical as well as less palpable ways. Shyness, boyishness, impulsiveness, shrewdness, toughness; they were obviously all there. So was the lonely courage of a man caught up with an idea. He had shown that courage all his life, and his end called for it in the fullest degree.

It was inevitable that Allen Lane should come to live for the Penguin idea, that it should become bound up with his sense of his own personality. It does not greatly matter that, as is usually said, he was not an intellectual in the accepted sense (nor was he an intellectual *entrepreneur* in the usual, slightly belittling, sense either). A man such as this does not need consciously to know all the meanings of what he creates. We are sometimes lived in by powers we are ourselves not able to assess fully. What such a man does need is 'nous', a sense of something wrong or missing in his field, and a dream of something better, of some better possibility way out there. He needs enormous and unremitting application, a flair for recognising those choices which will help realise his dream, and firmness in rejecting those which will not, the ability to play an emerging conception like a holy fish, the courage to take large risks and not look back if they fail. He needs the capacity to gather around him and to hold for long periods of time, men – some of them more intelligent or imaginative than he is – who can give the idea flesh and blood; and who give him loyalty because they see that the idea is bigger than either they or he. It is – the Penguin enterprise – a remarkable achievement, the combined achievement of a succession of very talented men. But overall it is the achievement, the creation, of one man.   1970

HUMANISTIC STUDIES
AND MASS CULTURE

I intend to look at two problems: at the relation of the mass media to humanistic studies, and at how the sociology of literature and art might bear on such studies. My focus is less on theory within the humanities than on what we might learn from the theoretical work of certain other disciplines. Learning something about procedures in these other disciplines may lead us to become more effectively theoretical ourselves; or it may make us more determinedly concrete.

It seems best to talk not about 'the humanities' in general, but about a particular field: literature, literary criticism, and the study and teaching of literature, especially within universities. This can be justified on more than personal grounds, for in these areas we have a great many assumptions and even prejudices, but hardly any agreed theory. I am inclined to argue that we do not need an agreed theory; in this I tend to be on the side of F. R. Leavis in the famous exchange between him and René Wellek. But we should not give our unconsidered assumptions the status of a firm and coherent philosophy. Nor should we sit so comfortably sure of the wholeness and rightness of our 'subject'.

Sometimes I think there is no recognisable discipline of 'English', no genuine whole, but only a set of contrived frontiers and selected approaches which, for complicated historical and cultural reasons, have come to be known as 'a subject'. Thousands are living within this frame of reference: it is part of the self-justifying, self-perpetuating, closed world of 'English studies'; and it has its counterparts among the other humanities.

There are, it is true, a few outriders, a few inorganic additions: sometimes the History of Ideas, sometimes courses in Literature, Life and Thought, sometimes sixteenth or seventeenth or eighteenth or nineteenth century Background, sometimes even the Sociology of

125

Literature. None of these, however, has effectively prompted a rethinking or redefinition of the subject itself; they have been made to serve it in a subordinate way. They are used within a set of assumptions that do duty for sustained thought about relationships. These assumptions are the more powerful for not being brought to the surface, to the point where they might be challenged. They are assumptions about art and its socio-cultural relationships, about culture in general (especially about mass culture and mass art), about audiences and levels and élites and minorities and masses, and about the effects – good and bad – of literature and the arts. Too many people in schools of literature, and indeed in the humanities in general, work from such fixed patterns of socio-cultural assumptions, patterns almost wholly decided by their cultural conditioning and imitative role-playing. Apart from the inadequacy of this outlook, when we make social judgments outside literature or when we comment on mass art, it limits our reading of those documents of high culture whose proponents we claim to be.

The study of mass communications and mass arts leads to more general questions about mass culture, and thus to the social sciences, where theoretically-guided work on mass society has been done. One begins to move into what are sometimes called the human or cultural sciences. It was from here that I began to believe that English studies have to be redefined.

What challenges to our common assumptions are caused by a study of mass culture? First, a close look at the mass media and at other elements in mass culture not only helps broaden our understanding of mass society, but affects our views on traditional culture as well. Mass art proves to be complex, both in itself and in its relations to its audiences, and its cultural meanings, therefore, cannot be easily inferred. It cannot be adequately assessed by the usual dualisms and dichotomies (though some of them are useful if handled carefully): machine-tooled versus spontaneous, brutal versus genteel, low versus high, processed versus live, evasive versus honest, conventional versus challenging, falsely-resolving versus truly-exploring, symptomatic versus representative, and exploitative versus disinterested. From this investigation one may also learn something about 'high art', as it is conventionally classified: that, for example, its 'complexity' is sometimes only an appearance, only an ability to operate within the intellectual and artistic fashions of its day.

Second, work in the mass media can make our approach to traditional art forms more flexible. It becomes harder for us to assume that the big three – plays for the theatre, the novel, and poetry – are a natural and sufficient triumvirate. Our difficulties here have some-times been comical. I am thinking, for example, of some early intellec-tual encounters with film – from accepting only the art film, to admiring *genre* for its own sake (as in Westerns), to enthusiastic slumming (as for 'bad' 1930s 'B' films), to *auteur* theory, or to applied structuralism. In addition, there is that accepted wisdom about the radio feature as 'an art form' which makes people in Britain repeat the same three of four names in every discussion, beginning with Dylan Thomas' *Under Milk Wood* and Louis MacNeice's *The Dark Tower*. It is all a considerable muddle.

As long as we learn to respond to their particular characteristics and qualities, the new media can sharpen our sense of the possibilities and the limits of traditional forms. One result of this double process will probably be that traditional forms will become more fluid and multi-dimensional, as we can already see in some theatrical work.

Third, from looking at mass culture we can learn something about audiences. We can learn, above all, that responses may be more various and capacities greater than our simplified models suggest. To judge mass art intentionally, to see it as wholly and effectively exploita-tive, is not good enough. The mass media may alert us to the danger of such oversimplifications. Although they may indicate and underline our confusion, they cannot in themselves reduce it. One of our common clichés runs like this: Sentimental art is for sentimental people and reinforces their sentimentality, thus making them even cruder emotionally than they were before. But we know very little about what we do as individuals – whether we are intellectuals or not – with the emotions we experience from the arts, high, middle, or low. Perhaps some kind of 'bad' art can inspire 'good' feelings, and vice versa.

The important distinctions here may be between the effectively phony and manipulative and other kinds of unsophisticated art. Those questions in particular need a lot more attention than they have had so far.

Similarly, the size and composition of the audiences for a few British television programmes (some satirical, some comical, but none of them officially classified as 'cultural') bring into question many of our assumptions about the relations between 'sophisticated' responses and level of education (let alone level of social class). None of these discoveries need make us stop being critical of many, and probably of most, features of mass culture. They will sharpen that criticism; and they will also make us less likely to react from a high-brow disdain to its mirror image: mass-culture-slumming for fun.

Fourth, a closer look at some parts of mass culture, especially at parts of what is known as 'pop culture' or of teenage culture (the two overlap to some extent), may occasionally reveal an unsuspected energy, an implicit criticism of the terms of mass society and of mass culture, a thrust back from the grass roots, and a kind of imaginative inventiveness that nothing in our assumptions gave us reason to expect. To recognise such things is to begin to understand better both the pressures of mass society as a whole and possible resistances to it.

From here it is only a short step, but one more of us will have to take, towards trying to understand by this kind of inward experience other expressive phenomena of mass society which do not belong to even our newly-widened categories of artistic forms, such as changes in styles of dress or of public speech or of gesture. We know about language as gesture; this is gesture as language. Of course we do not have to go so far as this. Those who feel drawn in this direction however, will not break the line of inquiry, but will continue it naturally.

All this undoubtedly worries some people. Life is too short, they will say, to spend much time on any but the best work. Surely, to go along this route is to risk having all our standards dissolve in a mush of relativity, a fashionable selling-out of all intellectual standards. Surely, not even the most upright of us can avoid being tainted; who would be bold enough to claim that strength?

> We have seen
> Good men made evil wrangling with the evil,
> Straight minds grown crooked fighting crooked minds.*

The study of mass culture need not weaken our distinctions and standards; it may give them a stronger hold, although it may certainly reduce our pride. The closer study of mass society may make us have sad hearts at the supermarket, but at the same time it may produce an enhanced and tempered sense of humanity and humility, instead of the sense of superiority and separateness that our traditional training is likely to have encouraged. Since we are continuing a characteristic feature of the best social criticism of English writers, we are led to ask insistent questions about the quality of life our society offers, questions about its imaginative range and truth. It is tempting and sometimes justifiable (especially since we

* Edwin Muir: 'The Good Town'.

tend to use it sloppily) to laugh at that phrase 'quality of life'. But I am more and more disposed to keep it, to ask of all the arts and styles of a society what qualities of life rather than levels of brow they express. This is neither a new nor an *outré* idea. You will remember Eliot's essay on Marie Lloyd of 1923 or his *Notes Towards the Definition of Culture* of 1948:

The reader must remind himself as the author has constantly to do, of how much is here embraced by the term *culture*. It includes all the characteristic activities and interests of a people: Derby Day, Henley Regatta, Cowes, the 12th August, a cup final, the dog races, the pin table, the dart board, Wensleydale cheese, boiled cabbage cut into sections, beetroot in vinegar, nineteenth-century Gothic churches and the music of Elgar. The reader can make his own list.

If, working within mass culture, we then turn back to 'good art' as it is traditionally defined, we can bring an increased sense of the relations between art and integrity – the search for self-knowledge, the self-forgetful contemplation of experience and of dimensions outside ourselves and our society – as well as of a heightened awareness of the relations between art and culture. Without this kind of immersion and this acquaintance with the details of mass culture and art, we cannot speak properly even about the relations between high art and contemporary culture because we have falsified the context. Of course, we do not have to speak about these relations; we can stay within the world of English studies in themselves. But most of us, while claiming to do no more than that, also make unsubstantiated forays into cultural criticism, not necessarily casually, but in the course of our teaching. We should at least try to be consistent.

In the study of mass arts, there is need for more connections than have commonly been made between humanistic disciplines as traditionally defined and the 'human studies' within the social sciences. I have in mind, for example, the impressively theoretical European tradition in the study of 'culture and society' during the nineteenth century, as well as large parts of American social-scientific work in this century. Think of the relevance to a student of literature of studies in anomie and alienation (especially since this work has counterparts and challenges within the cultural criticism made by the literary tradition). Or think of possible relationships and conflicts between such concepts as *'verstehen'*, 'empathic understanding', and 'participant observation' in sociology and the 'creative imagination', 'impersonality', and 'negative capability' in literary criticism. There is a rich and provocative field to be explored in the interplay between ideas on character, relationships, setting and the nature of the dramatic within literary criticism, and sociological literature on symbolic interaction, role-playing, and the definition of the situation.

On a more practical level, there are the differences between sociological content-analysis and close critical reading, each side tending to undervalue the other. Both can be subtle and sometimes they seem close to each other, but the differences in general approach are crucial. In addition, the argument about effects has a substantial literature in the social sciences; and about effects literary people for centuries have spoken with assurance. These are only a few obvious areas in which literary criticism and sociology can be usefully studied together.

There are, it is plain, opportunities for making more connections between literary work on myth and symbol and work in areas of anthropology, particularly structural anthropology. Structural analysis of this kind (for example, Lévi-Strauss on myths) also suggests useful work in the study of mass art or older forms of conventional art, since in such productions one is more likely to find common patterns of signs or agreed codes than in individual imaginative explorations. From this point, one is led to more recent developments in structuralism and semiology.

All these are perfectly reasonable aspects of the study of literature, more fully conceived than it is at present. There are also, of course, the traditional humanistic subjects, and with these, too, our links need developing. There are more crucial and relevant ways of starting to make connections than we usually assume. Thus, with history, one can focus directly on these two related questions: the exact ways in which good literature may be 'evidence' for the historian, and the need for a close, full, 'literary-critical' reading by the historian of many of the documents (not just accepted literary documents) he uses.

Two issues – or clusters of issues – seem to be especially interesting among those which arise if one tries to work in the borderland between literature and the social sciences. They both concern 'values,' although, strictly speaking, that word is being used differently in each case.

The first has to do with the claims we make for a good writer. We praise his capacity for 'representative selection', his grasp of 'significant detail', the 'revealing moment', and the 'epiphany' in many phrases that are common currency in literary criticism. And we say that although 'low art' is only 'symptomatic' – like boils on the body cultural – 'high art' is 'representative', sees further, and is more 'true.' It reveals its truth precisely by obeying the internal rules of its kind of art, not by being a set of explanatory statements. But these claims are harder to substantiate than we seem to think and are not made any more true by mere reassertion.

Actually, I doubt that they can ever be proved; I doubt whether they are that kind of knowledge. But they can be teased out further than they usually are, to the benefit of all concerned. If the status of this kind of intuition were examined more fully by literary critics, then what they said might not only bear out literary claims; such study might also bear on the social sciences, in which area also creative power is seen as mysterious, and the language generally used to discuss procedures and processes (say, in making hypotheses) sounds remarkably like that used by literary critics to describe creativity in the arts.

The second cluster of problems is that whole area concerned with how we analyse the 'values' of a culture, whether through its expressive arts or through any other activity. Most literary people assume that the literature of a society is engaged with its patterns of values (dominant or otherwise), which can be interpreted fairly easily. But these are very difficult matters, and we can learn a lot about them from the argument about values and value-interpretation going on within the social sciences (as well as from that more obviously relevant general area, the sociology of knowledge). In both literary and social scientific studies, there are people who deeply distrust discussion of values. Since the debate is not alive in their field, students of literature tend to become distrustful formalists of one sort or another. The social scientists are often ready to argue, and they argue powerfully. I do not myself, it hardly needs saying, share their views; but I do not think we should dismiss them with remarks about unimaginative reductionists. In *The Human Sciences and Philosophy*, Lucien Goldmann correctly relates attitudes like these to the a-philosophical and a-historical drift in some contemporary social sciences. At one point Lévi-Strauss draws his fire and inspires his neatest formulation. I quote it because of its precision and relevance to the general discussion of the social sciences rather than for any judgment on the work of Lévi-Strauss. Goldmann speaks of a 'formalistic system that tend to eliminate in a radical way all interest in history and the problem of meaning'. Even here, many different kinds of people might hold what at first glance look like similar views.

The people themselves, however, range from those who adjust fairly easily to the dominant rationality of their day to those of great integrity and intelligence who challenge our value judgments and the criteria on which they are based as, in the end, relative, culturally conditioned, and impressionistic. If we refer to 'the common reader' or 'the common pursuit of true judgment,' they ask why the codes of a particular Western European society at a particular point of time should be given absolute validity. They invite us to justify the claim that a 'good writer' informs us about society, is in some way in touch with 'truth,' against the view that he is simply an interesting and engaging storyteller. In short, the debate over values among social scientists can challenge the humanist to clarify some of his vague assumptions, especially in areas concerned with the moral meanings, moral insights, and moral functions of art.

In this perspective our usual literary studies seem claustrophobic. But what is the likely outcome of extensions of the kind I have described? We may come to a clearer understanding of the nature and power of literature itself: above all, of the ways the study of literature can help us know a culture. Literary-critical reading may be ingrown: but it is also highly developed and more subtle than most social scientists realise. An emphasis must now be placed on skill in cultural reading – for the sake both of literature and of the human studies within the social sciences. The close reading of forms of mass art may seem too elaborate a process to be worth the effort. The sociologist might offer, instead, the useful alternative of asking people what mass amusements mean to them. This suggestion, however, does not provide an adequate substitute for experiencing things in themselves, since we cannot know what we respond to until we have explored both the objects and our responses to them. For example, effects-analysis could be more sharply focused if inquirers began with a well-developed sense of the 'thing – the programme, the film, the story – in itself'.

Although these are comparatively minor practicalities, there is a larger case for the humanities here. The value of literary studies to the social scientist – whether the student of mass communications, of more traditional art forms, or of culture as a whole – lies in the ability to make his models or assumptions more adequate to the full human implications of his subject. In an examination of communication in the arts, literary-cultural studies can direct the social scientist away from various instrumental approaches to more expressive ways;

from the conception of the artist as propagandist or message-maker, consciously manipulating artistic expression to evoke a particular response, to an appreciation of more oblique approaches – of symbolism and myth, of art as gratuitous play, celebration, or contemplation, and of art for art's sake, 'being' in itself rather than existing as a channel to some other event or end. In the attempt to understand the cultural significance of any work of art, for the humanist a full reading, in and for itself, is the equivalent of participant observation to the sociologist. But one remembers that there is disagreement within the social sciences about the justifications for participant observation.

Literature at all levels has the unique capacity to increase our understanding of a culture. It may create or expand our awareness of a whole order of existence – what another life was like, how individuals faced experience within a dominant frame, what 'truth' appeared to be for a different society, or what it felt like to strain against this pattern. By making us know what love and hate and freedom and tyranny feel like, literature helps define or redefine the meanings of those words in other times. It can also reveal what the major tensions, overt or hidden, seem to have been and what they felt like on the pulses. The arts can penetrate what it is fashionable to call the deep structures of society, the underlying play of tensions and assurances, of stresses and releases. This is also true of art that is determinedly antisocial, against its own society or any assumed orders. For all its loosenesses and lack of analytical rigour, the English tradition in literary-cultural criticism has always been concerned with making a deeply human critique. It has kept a firm focus on individuals, on what happens to people. This tradition can best inform our cultural reading of any of the arts, 'high' or 'mass'. Here, literary-cultural reading need not just stand at the side of the social sciences. It can challenge them and seek to modify their vision – but only if we approach the arts for themselves, not as sardine tins to be opened for their insights into culture; only if we approach them as things in their own right, not as message-bearers or information-carriers. This brings us to the most important and difficult aspect of all, that of the 'autonomy' of art.

I do not believe such an 'autonomy' exists, except as a way of speaking that directs our attention to an important truth. I do not believe there is such a thing as art 'in itself'. Nor do I believe that art is socially determined, because it cannot be adequately explained in social or cultural terms, even though it is culturally conditioned. Unless one accepts and responds to art as a form of free artifice, one will not enjoy it or appreciate it or understand either its individual psychological meanings or its cultural and social significances. The medium is the message, and only in that sense can one speak of a 'message'. Form is part of content, and content is defined by form. The choice of available forms is conditioned – not entirely, but for most practical purposes – by the culture. Yet, although one responds to these forms as if in and for themselves, this is not to say that they are 'autonomous.' Nor is it to say that one can find their origins in some social need or ritual. Those origins may lie deeply in some basic movement of the psyche or in some metaphysical condition, independent of all cultural influences. The pursuit of these questions is not relevant to this particular essay. But to raise them is relevant, since they may help define the limits of even the fullest cultural reading.

In this discussion, we have come full circle to a nice paradox. Students of the humanities, especially literary people, are commonly accused of being too concrete, too wedded to the particular, and are told they must grapple more with theory. I agree that we ought to engage more in theoretical questioning; if we do, we will and should alter the definitions and boundaries of our subjects. But the paradox is this: at the far end of that encounter with theory, we again seem to reach a confirmed sense of the importance, the overriding importance, of concreteness. To quote a social scientist, J. D. Douglas: 'We must work from the clearly observable, concrete phenomena upward to abstractions about meanings in any culture'.* The expressive arts should be approached as concrete phenomena, as concrete as social habits, rituals, or gestures, but with even more subtlety, since they are richer, more complex, and in touch with more dimensions of our being than are most overt social 'facts'.

We must start with 'the thing in itself', and only from there can we begin our investigations. We may and should go on to genre-reading and to all kinds of wider relations between approaches. In practice we may be doing several different kinds of things at roughly the same time – reading for Tone, reading for Value, and reading for Meaning. But we will not get far unless we start with close literary-cultural reading, one we can apply to all the expressive arts, not just literature, and at all levels.

We read 'for values' or 'for meanings' not to judge the 'literary

* In *The Social Meanings of Suicide*.

value' of the work, but to understand better the values assumed within it, against which it braces itself, or to which it reacts. Talcott Parsons once described values as 'elements of a shared symbolic system serving as a criterion or standard of selection'. For the purposes of 'reading for values', this definition must be widened to include reactions against or positions ignoring such shared values. Literary-cultural reading responds first to the language and the form, rather than to the message or substance. Language is one way to seize a particular kind of reality; language and forms are patterns of rhetoric before experience. Less widely, the tone of voice is the most obvious carrier of cultural meanings. The way of talking to people – in *this* society at *this* time – reveals a great deal about a culture. Similarly, character, scene, dramatic moments, pauses, silences, images, stresses or lacks of stress, and the relationships we assume or would never think of assuming (omissions being just as important as commissions) – all these can tell us something about frames of assumptions, about the assumed orders that underpin a work. These may change under stress, but the work may be a part of that change.

Finally, we come full circle in yet another sense. We originally moved from the traditional humanistic concern with the high arts into the dangerously chaotic world of mass culture. Now we come back to reassert the power and overriding importance of the high arts for the student of culture. In fact, engagements with mass culture and with social-scientific theory can strengthen the high claims made for high art – but not easily or quickly. We usually make our high claims too quickly and easily, but the engagement with mass culture and with social-scientific analysis purges them before it reinforces them.

Explorations like these can strengthen our belief (they do not 'prove' it) that by working skilfully, inventively, and 'disinterestedly' within his medium, an artist can arrive at representative selection, significant order, crucial insights, and revelations, whether in particular local detail or in more extensive movements. Such an artist is, above all, true to the twin demands to look at life and to serve art. In addition, he is more likely than other artists to challenge the dominant culture (since all cultures in the end will cut moral corners to keep their orders steady). In these senses the engagements I have described can support the claim we now too often make as a matter of unexamined habit: that good literature contains, represents, or crystallises 'the maximum possibilities of consciousness at its time', and that that is its truth.

In returning to the claims made for literature as a way of exploring values, we come back with renewed force to all the old, rather stale, but moving phrases, to all the enormous, splendid, but not sufficiently scrutinised assertions: about literature as a criticism of life, about its reverence for life, and about the way it may enlarge our sympathies and redirect the flow of our sympathetic consciousness. We come back to our claim that literature is uniquely concerned with the total human response, with 'the quality of life,' in the fullest senses we are able to imagine.   1969

FASHIONABLE CONFORMITY
OR CULTURAL DEVELOPMENT?

My theme is the means of popularising the established 'performing arts', with some reference to communal cultural activity. I will begin with two deliberately provocative points. The first is about some of today's community or participant arts.

Sometimes the people who offer this kind of activity seem to assume that a form of community culture, perhaps based on a memory of an earlier oral or folk-culture, can be easily evoked. Certainly we do not have much of a community culture today insofar as the arts are concerned, and it is a very long time indeed since we did have one; it is not going to be easy, even if we agree that it is desirable to get back to that condition. Centuries of class divisions, spreading their effects through all aspects of life, massive industrialisation and urbanisation, the stress on individualism (especially in relation to the creation of and response to art), a healthy scepticism about hortatory or rhetorical calls to group solidarity (more pragmatic forms of grouping are accepted, as in the trade unions or in working-class neighbourliness) – all this has militated and militates against the easy acceptance of communal arts.

Those who seek to create that kind of art today should give more thought to historical changes in the sense of community and to the nature of popular art itself. A friend of mine was very interested in street theatre and travelled around to see it. His most striking experience was in a Lancashire mill-town where, on Saturday afternoons, there is still an open-air market well patronised by local housewives. A street theatre group had come along, set up their gear and started to perform. What they did, he said, seemed to be based on the assumption that Northern working-class people are still directly in touch with a nineteenth-century, earthy, music-hall tradition, with the Northern equivalent of the 'Knees up, Mother Brown' tradition

137

of London Cockneys. There is not space to go into all the historical-cultural misunderstandings behind that approach. At its best, it evokes a relatively harmless kind of nostalgia. But if it is that sort of nostalgia you are after then the most modern of modern media, television, supplies that regularly, through glossy Old-Tyme-Music-Hall programmes in specially renovated theatres or through long-running serials such as Coronation Street (which is so full of old-time warmth, agony, humour that it is as if embalmed in a romanticised past). My friend added that the most 'cultured' act he saw on that occasion was the behaviour of the local housewives, who gave the show a glance and then went quietly about their shopping as though they were too polite to laugh at it.

Goodwill does not make up for an inadequate thinking-through of just what it is you are trying to do, before you put up your flag, nor for a lack of talent. Art is a hard and unsentimental taskmaster. Without such self-examination we are likely to be guilty of both self-deceit and patronage of others. You cannot strike up a rapport with Northern or any other housewives by evoking some thinly-apprehended stereotype from the recent or any other past.

What are usually called 'the high arts' are certainly class-based, but the best examples of them are not class-bound. They rise clear of their historical limits to become examples and illuminations of human courage, perception, respect for the complexity and dignity of others and respect also for the materials from which art is made. Again, no amount of good intentions or earnest searching for community feeling can make up for the failure to recognise those disciplines. Nor is community feeling a good quality in itself; it is second-order, good only to the extent that the values the community recognises and acts out are themselves admirable. It is a great error to be willing to put aside the values, the core values behind European culture (in the arts, in education, in social thinking) in the name of an anti-bourgeois populism.

I would criticise also some of the donors to this kind of activity, the government departments, the arts councils and the like who are now giving much more to community arts than they would have done a few years ago. From one angle this is certainly a valuable move away from the position in which such bodies were happy to support only the traditional, recognised conventional 'high arts'. But this patronage often looks like an over-hasty conversion, a falling-over-backwards to be fashionable, a fear of being any longer open to the charge of being 'highbrow', a disinclination to face the vital question: it seems reasonable to give money to this kind of initiative but, since there are far more examples of it than can conceivably receive a subvention, how does one *distinguish* between different initiatives? How does one distinguish the genuine and promising from the self-deceiving and untalented? Vague cultural guilt produces mental indigestion; it has a bad effect on the capacity to choose. Without such choices, help to this kind of work will be like pouring cupfuls of water into randomly-chosen parts of a large sandy beach. Not to try to think this kind of situation through is, again, not to respect either art or people enough. There is an apt sentence in Lionel Trilling's remarkable final book, *Sincerity and Authenticity.* *

It is characteristic of the intellectual life of our culture that it fosters a form of assent which does not involve actual credence.

I have been rather heavy about the doubts one can have about some of this community art especially since, as I said at the start, I am interested in it. But it is important to provide some cold water in this area; the warmth of uncritical approval is becoming self-defeating.

My second deliberately provocative statement is that the increased official interest in cultural development, which is now characteristic of virtually every government in the world, ought to make us in the first place deeply suspicious. Much as we may want culture to be more widely available and participated in, we should approach governmental involvement in the process with a long spoon. From an international perspective we can see that this burgeoning official interest falls into three main clusters of attitudes. **

First is the interest among the new nations of the developing world. For them, cultural development is one aid towards achieving cultural identity and cultural unity; it is not difficult to see the challenges and the pitfalls in that approach. Second, there is the communist interest in cultural development, by which culture is seen as essentially a mirror and supporter of the status quo, the received ideology; and this covers both the artists and their audiences.

The third main group of related approaches includes most Western European states plus North America and those Anglo-Saxon nations who are on the other side of the globe. Naturally, there are differences in their approaches; but they all share a sufficient number of characteristics to be distinguishable as a coherent group. This third group

* *Sincerity and Authenticity,* 1972, p. 171.
** For a fuller description of these three approaches, see 'Culture and its Ministers' in this collection.

sees cultural development as above all a matter of personal enrichment, and work for cultural development as the effort to ensure that great numbers of people outside what one Western European minister called 'the charmed circle' of the cultivated are given access to what those lucky ones already enjoy.

This set of assumptions concerns not only the individual but also the group: the individual, because the idea of a *process* is invoked, a process which results in the emergence of a 'cultivated person'; the group because there is also an appeal, explicit or implicit, to the idea of the emergence of a community, a cultivated comity, a club of civilised people. It is as though the nineteenth-century statement, apropos the arrival of the vote – 'We must educate our masters' – has now been amended to 'We must civilise our masters' as working-class people, through transistors, motor bikes, motor cars, cheap air travel, become more noisy and sometimes more violently evident in the cities, on the beaches, everywhere.

So, well-meant though his attitude usually is, it is also usually patronising to a greater or less degree. It tends to see culture as a certain set of art-forms, and cultural development as the greater appreciation of them, the cultivation of attitudes towards them and, subsequently, towards 'life itself'; that is what 'cultivation' is. It pays much less attention to the historic contingency of these particular forms, their rooting in particular social circumstances. Its model for cultural development is simple. It sees those art-forms over there which are felt to be 'good for you'; it sees that audience – or those new possible audiences – of workers over there who so far have not appreciated those art-forms; it addresses itself to thinking out means or channels for passing the one to the other. Otherwise, chaos may come again and is indeed often felt to be only just around the corner:

Today what sort of culture can survive if it is confined to a self-regarding élite? The pressures of universal suffrage and the daily dose of television are taking control. Once every boy and girl, at the age of eighteen, whether their heads are empty or full, has a vote and can get near a television screen, it cannot be long before a culture which has been reserved to ten or fifteen per cent of the population is under attack.*

That is at least clear and unmistakable; but not encouraging. Attitudes such as those are hardly likely to promote 'access to culture' in the right ways, and their effect on the creative life could be baleful. At this point one feels close to Croce who argued, about twenty-five

* A Western European Minister of Culture at a UNESCO conference.

years ago, that in the interests of Western intellectual and artistic life, it would be better if UNESCO (then only four years old) be dissolved – UNESCO, whose mandate includes encouraging cultural development throughout the whole world. Croce had decided that official governmental assistance would kill the free air within which alone art can thrive:

> If (UNESCO) is dissolved by returning its mandate in spontaneous homage to that world of liberty whose needs it was intended to interpret, then its death will be a voluntary and a fine one, an example which will remain. It will therefore give proof that our Western world of liberty knows how to correct its errors.*

A statement like that is always tonic and should be met directly. So: what is the case *for* governments being active in the promotion of culture? The case for governments being involved in promoting literature is very much harder to make than that for ballet, music or the visual arts in general. There are two main reasons. First, most literature is a cottage industry and so does not positively need massive financial support before it can be created; second, literature is the most explicit of the arts – it uses words, and so can easily be accused of deviance and invite censorship or direction. A symphony, a ballet, a painting can usually – if meanings must be ascribed to them – be given a number of quite different 'meanings'; but on the whole a book says what it says – there is much less room for wholly variant readings.

Any discussion about the promotion of art must rest on the basis of some shared values, aesthetic and moral. I suggest that the Western tradition has rested on the twin assumptions that art has to do with the free exploration of artistic means and forms in themselves and with the free exploration of human experience in itself. It rests on the notion of honesty before the tools and before life; it therefore presupposes freedom for such explorations and the free exchange of them. It is before all else, therefore, an individual process, one which starts in the single personality. It does not begin as a group affair or with direct communal aims. But what it helps to bring about in the individual may be a basis – one of the best bases – for a communal life which is both freer and more honest. Behind such a view, it follows, is the idea of the artist as an independent, objective, critical (and so sometimes dissenting) person. The artist is a separate estate of

* Benedetto Croce, quoted in 'Should UNESCO Die?', *Manchester Guardian*, 19 July, 1950.

the realm, not a reflector of the one approved estate, that of the authorities.

One isn't saying that to appreciate in this full sense *The Magic Flute* or *King Lear* is therefore to be a better person. It is to say that one thereafter has a fuller sense of the possibilities – the depths, the heights, the complexities, the ambiguities, the disorder, the striving for order – within human life. One has had an analogical or symbolic exploration, in itself absorbing and beautiful but also pointing beyond itself, one which challenges our tendency always to narrow life to the predictable, repeatable and contingent. Something like this is at the heart of the artistic achievement and of artistic experience at their highest.

One has to begin with such an effort at finding a common intellectual base before one can reasonably get down to the more bread-and-butter aspects of governmental aid to the performing arts. If, on that base, one can agree that those arts are worth saving and developing further, then one can look more closely at the case for governmental aid to them. The initial case for official aid is then this: that to mount them on a fully international or even national level is extremely costly, that the private patron has virtually disappeared and that governments therefore have to pick up the bill for at least the basic infrastructure costs. This includes building, subsidies to major productions, bursaries for on-the-spot training of many kinds, the support of the different training schools and colleges needed and much else. These are extremely labour-intensive professions and so very costly; they are likely to remain so.

This being agreed, what are the main hindrances to the more widespread appreciation of these arts? They are all, in different ways, socio-cultural in origin. Thus, a physical concentration of provision for the high arts within capital cities and a comparative under-provision elsewhere can be found in most countries. It is now receiving a good deal of attention and so I shall say no more about it. It is, in any event, a relatively uncomplex issue. More important is the need for much closer attention to the whole ambience of such institutions. They should not put out signals which are unnecessarily offputting to the very people they are hoping to attract, nor should they attract them for the wrong reasons.

The point behind all this is that assistance to cultural development should be based on a well-considered effort to break down fortuitous historical barriers, to democratise without vulgarising (without passing on more a type of received gentility than the opportunity to appreciate the arts in themselves). Such aid must also be concerned to widen the range of the accepted in all parts of society, among the already 'cultivated' as elsewhere. The traditional performing arts should not be set in cultural aspic but should be seen as in a state of constant change; this implies new ways of mounting them, setting them against new work (as well as experiments with new forms of audience). Such changes are bound to produce cries of 'gimmickry' (and sometimes those accusations will be justified); but it is better to risk a few gimmicks than to lose life.

In such circumstances government will be wise to set up buffer bodies – frequently renewed buffer-bodies – to disburse funds for it. It is usually advisable for the state to keep itself – and to be kept – at one remove from the actual practice of the arts; or, better, at two removes. The fact that it is providing the money gives it fewer rights than officials often assume. The claim 'I am responsible for the right use of public funds and therefore I must be satisfied that this, that or the other is the case' has been more often used to tut-tut warningly about what might be the shock caused to the constitution of that hypothetical man on the Clapham omnibus of seeing a daring new play than simply to ensure that public money is not impractically spent.

Very much more money is being spent on the arts in most Western European countries today than was spent a couple of decades ago, notably by governments, some of whom have increased their grants several-fold. Industry and commerce are also becoming patrons on quite a large scale. Broadcasting authorities, both public and commercial, are inherently considerable customers for the performing arts and, recognising this fact of their lives, many also give direct grants for furthering the arts (as distinct from simply paying for the preparation of particular broadcast programmes).

For all that, the doubts persist. They persist both about what exactly is happening to artists, and about the relation – or lack of relation – of this increased public attention to the arts to the texture of the daily lives of most of us. In some respects, artists are more cherished than they have ever been ('For a society which has everything, an artistic halo is the next thing to be desired'), and yet artists are at risk. They are at risk not so much from political pressures as from commercial. The societies of Western Europe gain their very high standards of living partly from the concentration of production

143

and so of sales; you can make good cars more cheaply if you reduce the number of different makes. The same process is at work in the arts. You can sell certain kinds of paperbacks, well-produced and not all simply soporifics, remarkably cheaply if you issue them in scores of thousands. But concomitantly your possibilities of breaking-even on slim volumes of poetry are reduced and so is your interest in taking the risk. A successful artist may well be as prosperous as his celebrated Victorian antecedents. But he will have to face the risk of being invited to 'concentrate' his own output and so talent, to go on producing the kinds of thing which are already expected of him, to continue meeting the fashion which he helped create, to over-expose his own personality and that of his art, to turn his skin outwards as it were.

Or look more widely, at the contexts of the daily lives of most of us. Like most other Western European countries the United Kingdom has over the last twenty years or so given far more from public funds towards increasing the appreciation of the arts than would have seemed conceivable before the war. In the same period, immense damage has been done to a great many of the urban environments scattered around these islands. The pressures of trade and commerce have been allowed to justify the destruction of literally hundreds of fine buildings and ensembles. The centres of some of our older cities have had more damage done to them in the name of trade than Hitler could manage. Uniformly conceived shopping centres, malls, precincts have been put up on cleared central ground in cities and towns all over the country. They seem all to have been planned on drawing-boards in London, and hardly any pay respect or regard to differences in physical settings or in vernacular building tradition. This commercial concentration ensures that the old traders can hardly ever afford to re-enter the redeveloped areas; the rents and rates are too high. So the second-hand-book-sellers, the small craftsmen and the owner-run small bakeries stop trading or go somewhere on the outskirts. The new centres are taken over by chain-stores, shops catering for what they conceive to be mass taste in the cheapest possible way – chain shoe-shops, the cheaper supermarkets, chain dress-shops, chain electric-goods stores, chain snack-bars. By now you have a shopping area which proclaims from every tatty corner (and they go tatty overnight): 'We have been set up in obedience to someone's idea of mass-taste, to their drive to make the quickest and largest possible profit from that taste, no matter what the quality of the goods may be' (there are some shining exceptions, even among the big chains, I should in fairness add; but the general picture is as I have drawn it). So you have once again someone else's idea of what the body of people like and are presumed to be going to go on liking. You know then beyond a shadow of doubt where the great majority of the population has been consigned, this time not by comfortably-off professionals but by tough, computer-programming, chain-store executives. 'To Hell with Culture' indeed, to hell with all increased grants for the arts, if that presumed concern for 'the quality of our lives' doesn't also include, doesn't start with, doesn't give a pre-eminent place to, precisely the texture, the quality, of our daily environment, of the day-by-day lives of us all.

Most discussions about 'television and the arts' by 'the great and the good' – the cultivated top few per cent of the population – show this split in an advance form. They assume a divided society. They thus allow the television moguls to regard television's attention to art as a sort of buying-off or bail. Television companies – and I will concentrate on commercial companies supported by advertising revenue, since they show the split in its most advanced form – are willing to make some direct subsidies to the arts and to put some art programmes on their channels (occasionally at peak-times even, if pushed). They would not wish such programmes to interfere with the *bulk* of peak-time programmes, those which bring in massive audiences and so most revenue. Such companies have a built-in disinclination to experiment, to take a chance on what people *might* find interesting; they are naturally inclined to settle for what they *know* most people already find amusing. Nor could they be expected to be happy with the argument that the clear rift between the 'culture' programmes they sponsor and the abysmal level of some of their 'popular' programmes is a very bad thing indeed for any society, that one is an insurance policy for the other against too many attacks from the establishment, that therefore their support for official culture is of no importance compared with the prime place they give to the emotionally shoddy, the psychologically meretricious, the vulgarly greedy, that any talk of 'moving on from' the shoddy to the better programmes in that context is at best deceptive and at worst bogus.

But the top few per cent of the cultivated are not likely to present television's own top men with such nasty choices. They are more likely themselves to see matters in similarly split or separated terms; or at best in terms of a 'pyramid' with the 'charmed circle' at the top and the rest of us assumed to be 'aspiring upwards' to greater levels of cultivation. Their model of the role of television sees it as a channel down which seed-packets of known cultural goods are sent so that they may strike root in the almost barren soil of the masses (those whom one French analyst has called 'the non-audience'):

For me, the mass media offer many more possibilities for cultural development than they create obstacles. I believe, in fact, that if we only had books, even inexpensive editions, we could not aspire to the democratisation of culture or effectively enforce the cultural right which each of us possesses. The use of the mass media is absolutely necessary for us to attain this goal. But it is also evident that the mass media are simply a means, simply instruments. Everything depends on the use we make of them. And if you (a questioner) were referring to the necessity of ensuring that these media are put to good use, in other words, are used to facilitate the introduction of the masses into the universe of authentic culture, and not the degradation of that culture, then, of course, I am in perfect agreement with you.*

That is by a Western European, but in the actual formulations there is hardly anything with which an Eastern European minister would disagree. When public statements go on at that level of generality-with-banality it is no wonder that ministerial level conferences produce agreed resolutions of a considerable flatulence and wrong-headedness. Such a resolution was that at a UNESCO conference in the Seventies, on cultural development and the mass-media, which envisaged East and West shoving their best cultural packages – the Bolshoi, the Comédie Francaise, the La Scala Company, the Royal Shakespeare Theatre Company, the Moscow State Circus – across frontiers so that they might be stuffed down each other's television channels for the greater enlightenment of 'the masses' on each side and for the greater self-congratulation of all the officials concerned. By this means you can keep your eyes shut to two much more important considerations: that real cultural exchanges start in free dialogue and that television is not simply a 'means' but is a way of making art in its own right, new forms of art, new kinds of relationship with new patterns and mixtures of audiences. Without that, there's not much exploration and not much challenge.

If you do have such an unconsidered view of television and of its relationships to society then you are the more susceptible to the assaults of 'the puritan backlash', to the pressures of those who want television to restrict itself to what they consider material suitable to be

---

* A high level International Civil Servant.

beamed into 'decent households', those who define the 'undesirable' as that which has some sexual reference and the 'desirable' as that which explicitly upholds the cracker-motto domestic values which they think are as easy to act out as to utter. Hence, people such as this will complain vehemently about a television play which faces the fact that some people commit adultery, but will regard as 'very wholesome' a cosy, domestic programme such as *This is Your Life*, that prefabricated bath of maudlin sentimentality. If people are unable to see that here the desirable/undesirable labels need switching, then they can understand practically nothing about the way the arts work. One cannot expect more from people who actually set up national movements to censor television; one should be able to expect more from 'the great and the good'. Instead, they are likely to shuffle uneasily before the onslaught of the new censors, to admit that they themselves don't find some of the stuff on television today very much to their taste – and then to make a few gestures towards freedom of speech. Most politicians are likely to find a position between these two groups – between the new censors and the charmed circle; they are likely to say that, though they are of course against censorship, they think we can all of us recognise obscenity when we see it . . .

The overwhelming reason why societies should put a lot more money into cultural development is that all societies deform; and that commercially-oriented, open societies such as those in most of Western Europe, deform in their own special ways; not by a politics of scarcity but by the pressures of sustained persuasion towards fashionable conformities. They seek to turn us all into consumers, and art itself into a form of consumption – a marginal form which can be afforded after the soap powders, the cars, the drinks. It follows that, no matter how much such societies do to encourage the development of the arts, they have a prior duty towards people. That task is to encourage critical movements in society, movements which work against the society's own dominant trends. They have to help strengthen that criss-crossing set of forces which give a society its texture, its timbre, its oxygen, its yeast. It follows that very much more must be done in schools to help on the emergence of this critical and creative consciousness, in particular schools in those areas where the recognition of the intellectual and the imaginative life is hardest. It follows also that much more stress must be put on adult education. It means also that the broadcasting authorities must look more closely at their own relationships to society and so work out programmes which are 'cultural' in that wider and freer and more lively sense which has lain behind this essay.

In some respects, it is true, things have moved on in the last two or three decades. The large audiences for good music, the queues of people of all ages and from all social classes for important art exhibitions (which are helped on by personality-cult publicity) are signs of that movement. When I was a boy, growing up in a poor district of a large industrial town in Northern England, my great airhole to a wider imaginative world was the local public library. Luckily, some people more than half a century before had believed that there was more hidden ability in those huddled back-streets than was commonly assumed. Today it is fashionable and no doubt comforting to assume that those hidden audiences no longer exist, that all such people have been winkled out of 'the masses' by better educational opportunities, that therefore what the great bulk of those who remain behind are given (peak-time television shows, chain stores) is what they naturally and ineluctably want, that there is no more scope for 'missionary' work. I don't believe in missionary work. I do believe that there are abilities in many people which are still largely untapped, that our educational system at all levels is still tapping them inadequately and that the whole structure of our society – its predominant drives and their effects on our means of communication and on our provision for leisure – positively sets back what some of the more imaginative schools set in motion; that it is all too often a one-step-forward-two-steps-backwards business; that therefore societies owe it to the people of whom they are composed to gamble on undiscovered potentialities – that the greatest sin is to settle for that picture of people which societies foist on themselves at the highest level, and also try to foist on the body of people as their real portrait.

To be cultivated does not mean to be elegantly mannered. Nor, as I said much earlier, is it synonymous with being virtuous. Neither the making of nor the responding to art can in themselves make us one whit better; if they could, the problem of the wilfulness of man would be a great deal easier to resolve. But art can widen the sense of possibilities, gives hints of greater depths and other orders; it stands ready to assist us to make better choices if we so will; and in doing so it creates experiences – artistic experiences – which are beautiful and moving. I think this is what Matthew Arnold meant when he said:

148

Good poetry does undoubtedly tend to form the soul and character; it tends to beget a love of beauty and of truth in alliance together; it suggests . . . high and noble principles of action, and it inspires the emotions so helpful in making principles operative. Hence, its extreme importance to all of us.

The life of the mind is one of continual exploration. It is therefore, in the final analysis, a political activity. That kind of activity is neither cherished nor encouraged in most regions of the world. Its traditional home is Western Europe and one of its traditional expressions was, and to some extent is still, to be found in the high forms of the performing arts. To see these connections better – to help people make these connections better – is the heart of the matter.   1976

EXCELLENCE AND ACCESS

It seems that a thorough understanding of these issues by artists is necessary before any progress can be made towards making the arts *really* socially relevant in the complex society of the late 1970s. Before we can even talk about 'community arts' or 'artists in residence', it must be understood that the so-called cultural *heritage* which made Europe great – the Bachs and Beethovens, the Shakespeares and Dantes, the Constables and Titians – is no longer communicating anything to the vast majority of Europe's population. That the relevance of even artistic forms which were widely popular at the time of their creation are now only easily accessible to those already convinced that such culture is *their* heritage. It is not that these cultural forms are 'above people's heads' but that it is a bourgeois culture and therefore only immediately meaningful to that group. The great artistic deception of the twentieth century has been to insist to *all* people that this was *their* culture. The Arts Council of Great Britain was established on this premise. And it is on the basis of the concept that if you educate people by constantly placing the art you wish them to 'appreciate' in front of them, that ballet, symphony orchestras, theatre and paintings have been toured around towns and villages throughout the country. Yet such a premise implies others, and to me crucially important ones. First, it implies that those who do not appreciate these particular art forms fail to do so because they are 'uneducated' or possibly not sufficiently intellectual; not simply that they find the particular forms of expression irrelevant; and second, that other cultural pursuits enjoyed by such people are inferior and therefore not worthy of the same degree of funding and promotion. Yet over and over again, the Arts Council's policy has been seen to be of real value only to those people who find such expression relevant – the vast majority stay away.*

I begin with this long quotation from a book on the community arts because it incorporates many of today's arguments – from that field of work – about excellence and access. Ms Braden's book is different

*Artists and People, Su Braden, 1978, pp. 153-4.

150

from much discussion of this kind, it should be said, however, in that it is not aggressive. It is, indeed, very earnestly quiet in its tone. There is no doubt of Ms Braden's care and commitment. Nevertheless, as the above passage shows clearly, she makes what looks like a whole case out of a mixture of genuine facts (such as that Arts Council funded activities often reach a narrow and predictable range of people), faulty history and mistaken a priori conceptions. She practises an unnecessary but, in this field, common setting of different things *against* each other. On this argument, 'the vast majority' should not be offered the chance to enjoy Shakespeare or Beethoven on the grounds that the works of such artists are not 'socially relevant', are remnants of 'a bourgeois culture' and part of 'a great artistic deception'. Why must we have, as one of my tutors used to say, this 'ratpit of false comparisons', these partial truths which, asserted as whole truths and set together in an artificially coherent pattern, end in anti-imaginative and anti-intellectual restrictionist prescriptions for other people?

From the way the words 'excellence' and 'access' are commonly used today in debates about the arts, one would think they were irreconcilable. In one corner is the remaining band of professed 'élitists,' people who believe that in the arts as in education any substantial widening of access means popularisation, and that popularisation means dilution, watering down. In the other corner, and by now extremely talkative, are some of the proponents and practitioners of community arts, fringe arts and related forms. For them much wider access, participation, grass-roots activity is the over-riding aim. If that means a loss of some traditional 'excellences', then the price (they claim) is low. Indeed, at the extreme some community artists will argue that such excellence must and should be lost, since it is a false excellence, a model of and a defining of quality in art which is fatally limited and limiting, a bourgeois device foisted on people which prevents them from discovering their own, popular, workers', provincial art forms.

The Arts Council of Great Britain, its posture often seeming like that of an unathletic man trying to do the splits, stands straddling these two positions. Much of its money goes to the recognised 'high arts'; but not enough, the recipients never fail to say. Much also goes to community arts and its relations, such as fringe theatre. But not at all enough, as its proponents claim. The battles are incessant, insistent and bitter but repetitive and muddled. In politics, I am of the Left. But in what follows I shall inevitably criticise the far Left in the community arts more than the defenders of traditional forms and more than the Right. Not surprisingly, since there is hardly a sign of Right-wing community or fringe arts activity. This is a pity in some ways, since it prevents us from seeing how the Arts Council would react to professedly non-libertarian claims.

The initial worry about the statements of many who speak for community arts is that they both narrow and at the same time over-widen the definition of art. They narrow it by overwhelmingly stressing art as a *communal* process. If this were chiefly a deliberate counterbalance to the solipsist stress of much in bourgeois art it would be less questionable. But it works rather by asserting the primacy of communal artistic activity as *against* individual activity. Conversely, the definition of art is over-widened to the point that the very word 'artist' has itself become devalued. Any man or woman assumes a right to the title because that is their wish, or because they associate it with the desire to change people (both of them poor prescriptions for the making of art). In this mood, they are not likely to be talking about art. They are talking about directly affecting society politically, through a committed propaganda. Or they are talking about a sort of social work (which may well be necessary), and which they seek to make art explicitly serve. In both instances, art cannot do its own best work in its own best way.

The looseness of thought is matched by a looseness of expression, at least among those who join the committees and issue the manifestos; I know that hundreds of others in community arts work quietly and, by their lights, effectively. One community arts officer, and the phrasing is typical of a certain group, refers to 'the present corporate state, benign-type fascism'. It is hard to respect intellectually someone who can fudge the realities by that kind of blanket language. Nor are the favoured words used in ways which command more confidence. It isn't that the words are in themselves all bad; they can point to important ideas. But they are devalued by being used ritualistically, by rote, totemically. I mean the repetitious use of words such as: 'involvement', 'community', 'participation', 'meaningful action'; and, of course, passages like 'community arts can be preparation for community action'; 'social action through culture'; 'community art is an art used by working class communities to better themselves' – all of which blur difficult issues.

The intellectual habits of some of the spokesmen for community arts are often not much better. They confuse good intentions with the creation of art and artistic experiences. They assume that because their emotions are generous, that because they feel great sympathy with immigrants or coal miners, and because they really want to help people, those aspirations in themselves make them artists; so that whatever they turn their hands to, no matter how intellectually muddled or formally inept it may be, is art. As an Arts Council report noted: 'On occasions we have seen activities which appeared to amount to no more than admirable social activity, not justifying an Arts Council grant'.* The implicit syndrome runs: I have strong views. They show my heart is in the right place. Therefore anything I do in pursuit of the causes for which I care is both morally right and artistically unassailable; and anyone who says otherwise is motivated by political intentions or the desire to censure, is Right-wing and probably near Fascist.

This attitude produces two widely different results. On the one hand, it creates a backlash not only from the extreme Right but also from the worried and traditional and unpermissive, who see the arts being taken over by the Visigoths and complain in their newspapers or in the House of Lords. So the claims of the Left-wing community artists become self-validating. They are confirmed both in their view of the situation and in the lack of need to listen to *any* critic, since all are seen as 'censors'. The second result is that people who are by no means Right-wing and do not belong to the censorship lobby become, unless they are very tough, inhibited from criticising any community or fringe art for fear of being called fascist. If you can't retain the right to argue that, whilst you will defend X's right to say what he wants, you nevertheless think him on the evidence before you noisily unendowed, you have indeed been put in a totalitarian situation.

So one could go on. It needs to be said again and again that we don't acquire 'a sense of community' by willing or wishing it; that because an activity is provincial and small-scale those qualities don't in themselves give it one per cent more of virtue; and the fact that something is from the metropolis and belongs to the 'high arts' doesn't disqualify it or make it an automatic target for abuse. I use strongish words such as 'abuse' because the style of many proponents of community arts is extremely aggressive. It's a cops and robbers world most participants posit. Many of them are not talking about art

* *Community Arts*, A Report prepared by the Community Arts Evaluation Working Group, A.C.G.B., February 1977, para 443.

in any recognisable sense. They are talking about politics, confrontation, the bringing about of social change. What they call art is often propaganda which implicitly belittles the people they are working among. They are pointing to a dead end. To insist, as they do, that 'agitprop' is definitely what they are about does not improve matters. You can't by sheer force of assertion pick up that discredited word and make it legitimate. To do so is to cheapen craft, to distort experience and to be both contemptuous and – oddly enough – patronising towards your presumed audiences. Too many people at present engaged in community arts have not well enough thought through what it is they are about, have made the issues crude and simplistic, and themselves reveal a strong strain of anti-intellectualism.

Arrogance and sentimentality often combine to make up a form of emotional self-indulgence. That the people who are behaving in this way towards working-class people are themselves often from middle-class backgrounds is no surprise. There is a certain kind of vulgarity whose base is somewhere in the mid-middle-class and which is not often found in working class people. One had become used to the arrogance of élitists and used to discounting it; in any case, it is now muted. It is more distressing to meet the arrogance of the far left when one is oneself of the Left:

The revolutionary movement in the West today tends to have a very vulgar and philistine attitude to culture and the arts and a very narrow concept of what politics is. This is not uniformly the case, but in general it applies certainly in the Anglo-Saxon countries.*

The writer is Tariq Ali.

Perhaps the most weighty charge against many community arts positions is that they have no adequate historical base and so are often unEnglish in a disabling way. Unaware of, or inadequately in possession of, an understanding of the roots of British working-class culture, they talk about their audiences as though they were seventeenth-century peasants or a twentieth-century lumpen-proletariat. It is all in the head, and based on thin ideological models. They rarely give the impression of having read, say *The Road to Wigan Pier,* let alone *Sons and Lovers.* One hasn't much doubt about how short a shrift both Orwell and Lawrence would have given their professions and manner of utterance. Both of those were nonsense-detectors, as were Hardy and Gissing.

What is missing in this activity is a whole range of traditional

* In *Media, Politics and Culture,* op. cit. p. 159.

English working-class attitudes; the earnest desire for understanding, a respect for the life of the mind and of the imagination. As a result, both intellectual life and the arts themselves are belittled. The tradition of tolerance and charity and human warmth goes too. This is at bottom an ungenerous world, and in its habits often nearer to the fascism it attacks than to the British working-class tradition itself. If that sounds too much like the complaint of a social democrat, let me invoke someone whose Left-wing credentials are usually regarded as impeccable. I mean E. P. Thompson:

I can't assume . . . that intellectual violence and élitism are only to be found on the Right . . . There are some on the 'Left' who flirt with conceits of violence and aggression in a way which suggests a disorder of the imagination, a mere bravura of opinions . . . Within the vocabulary of this kind of 'Left' there are many 'dainty terms for fratricide'.*

Elsewhere in the same essay Edward Thompson makes the direct connection with the arts and their relevance:

If the message of the Left is to be *bang! bang!* then I wish they would get themselves poets to imagine this, to join feeling and attach form to the bangs . . . Somewhere (if poets did their work) another cluster of values would be defining themselves. These might be a little quieter, less invigilatory and dominative, less strident and more compassionate than those recently to be noted on the Left.

I have been sharply critical because I believe that is needed. But to avoid unnecessary misunderstanding let me add that I am as sympathetic as the most enthusiastic to the better aims and the better achievements of community arts, such as their revealing of artistic talent in people who, without them, would never have known of their own gifts. There is much to be said also on the achievements of fringe theatre (though the audiences for that kind of theatre are still predominantly middle-class). The fringe has been and is the nursery of new dramatic talent on a large and exciting scale. Here, though, as so often, the worst can be the enemy of the best and shout it down.

In the last few years the Arts Council has gone out on a great many limbs so as to be as hospitable as possible to new forms, no matter how outré they may be. As a result it is very often and bitterly attacked by the Right. The Left never acknowledges this taking of what are clear risks, regarding them as merely what the Arts Council should be about anyway (without recognising the social and cultural minefields which have to be breached when a publicly-funded body

* *Stand,* Vol. 20 No. 2.

acts like that in an area such as this). But let the Arts Council just once – even if only marginally and because of advice about possible libel – decide that one or perhaps two pictures out of a great many which they have bought should not be shown, let it withdraw those two and it will rouse a hornet's nest, stirred by the artists' own accusations that what you have here is Right-wing, near Fascist, censorship of the most outrageous kind, and stirred again by journalists who prefer to deal in such melodramatic and rhetorical models rather than in the more complicated, less dramatic, but more interesting truth.

I suppose the Arts Council could in such a situation do as the BBC used to do and claim that, since Left and Right attack, it must have got the balance about right. That doesn't at all necessarily follow. The fact that both sides attack a public body may mean that it has not got a clearly worked-out policy, that it leans intermittently to Left and Right and, lacking respect, gets clobbered by each according to the direction of lean. Indeed, I would say that the biggest single weakness of the Arts Council today lies just here; that it is doing what I called at the start the intellectual splits. The Council has not thought through the claims of the community arts any more than it has those of the 'high arts' when social class trappings have been removed from them. It has continued to give money to, say, (the most striking example) Covent Garden – considerable amounts of money – without thinking beyond the simple belief: opera must be kept up to international level. On the other hand, the audiences really are a small élite. It must therefore follow, here as in similar cases, that the Council's duty (by the terms of the Charter, it should be said) is not only to keep up the particular art but to spread further the appreciation of it.

On the other hand, the Council has given increasing amounts to community arts (far less than they need, its practitioners say; but every form of art could say that, and community arts grants have gone up very rapidly in the last few years). Yet the Council has been consistently unwilling to make real *choices* between community arts, to set up criteria. So it goes on funding a bewildering variety of activities. The variety show ... with clowns, inflatables, face-painting and play-schemes of one sort or another. All of which, whether it is strictly art or not, may be amusing and helpful to children in densely-populated areas. But the Marxists among the community artists attack the Arts Council for giving grants to such activities which are, they say, no more than 'populist rubbish'. Then the Council shies even further away. It doesn't want to be embroiled in such internecine strife; it smiles and swears interest in all sides. It hopes it is more nearly meeting its commitment to making the arts more available to new audiences by agreeing to fund as much community arts activity as it can possibly squeeze from the budget. As a result – as a result, that is, of neglecting to think about the question of excellence and its relation to access – it does well by neither side. It blurs its relations to grand opera and to community arts alike. It has become confusedly overstretched, without shape or form, expressing not a rich creative disorder in its giving but a worried darting from side to side, seeking a good repute by trying to be all things to all men and letting the questions of both access and excellence remain murky.

The Council has therefore encouraged by default a false dichotomy or conflict between access and excellence. It has encouraged those on either side who, seeing indecision, become more importunate and move in for the kill. The élitist reacts against the sillier manifestations of community art, repeats with great satisfaction that more really does mean worse, and says with total *self*-satisfaction: 'As for me, I am an unashamed élitist'. No one who is an élitist in a good sense (a lover for its own sake, and for the illumination it can give, of the best that has been thought and said) would express himself in that way. That really is snob's talk, élitism in the social sense.

On the other hand, the opponents of the 'high arts' become more strident and call for the cancellation of subsidies to 'all that bourgeois crap', being by now surer than ever in their belief that grants are being given, very large grants, to provide cheaper seats and better opera for a small, a very small, group. It is difficult not to recognise a substantial element of truth in this, if you look round the foyer or crush bar at Covent Garden on virtually any night.

So it is necessary to repeat one or two quite simple things. One is that though 'high art' should not be regarded as some sort of icing on top of the social cake, and though many people's attitudes to it are inextricably bound up with class snobberies, and though it is certainly affected by the social soil in which it is produced, nevertheless it is not wholly class-determined or defined. It can break out from the temporal soil in which it was made so as to speak to us all and at all times, if we have the opportunity and are willing. So we are mistaken to deny those with whom we come into professional contact, as teachers or community workers of whatever sort, the right of access to the high arts. In literature classes for the WEA thirty years ago, there was sometimes a tendency to suggest that the tutors should seek out 'workers' literature' or literature of political struggle. Shaw and Wells were all right but surely Forster and Woolf were irrelevant, the fag end of an effete culture? That spirit survives today in some groups who address themselves only to workers' literature, or perhaps only to oral literature. Such literature may be interesting, valuable and illuminating. But it is wrong to set that kind of thing *against* the great works of literature and to dismiss those latter as irrelevant. Working people have as much right to grapple with good art as have people of any other social group. To deny them that right, to claim that good art is an irrelevance from the past, is an instance of the higher unimaginative lunacy. But it is often said.

To stress again, since it is relevant at this point, something I hinted at earlier. The stress on the community nature of art is now so strong among people in that field that it is easy to forget that art, in both its making and its appreciation, is very often and at bottom an intensely and necessarily solitary thing. To say this need not be an instance of the power of the bourgeois solipsist view of art. Great novels, great symphonies, great plays are not written by groups. And the appreciation of these things, though it may be helped on by work in a group, is finally personal, something we must each take to ourselves. There is something one can respect in the community arts' effort to reach towards, to help create, a new sense of community, the reaction against anonymity and fragmentation, the revolt from the individual, self-serving, thrusting, consciousness and conscience. But it has over-simplified an inescapable and endless dilemma, that between the individual personality and the sense of community.

As a result, this attitude devalues all artistic activity. Art does not come more easily because one makes the right protestations. Even if we are only slightly gifted, art is a hard taskmaster to us as she is to the greatly gifted. She demands, from both the makers and the audiences, respect for the experiences we are trying to shape, respect for the artistic tools we have chosen so as to do that, and respect for those by whom we hope our work will be heard. At their best the community arts have in some ways widened access. Just as often, they have widened access by a sort of selling out, a rejection of the best in our common social and cultural and artistic traditions at all levels.

Behind much in their attitudes is an unrecognised patronising and even an implicit belittling of the very working people they hope to be affecting. Even if one does not deny their good faith, and even if one recognises their devotion and hard work, one is left with the feeling that they are offering working people a form of snobbery no better than that they attack; a reverse snobbery which says – that kind of thing (opera, Shakespeare, ballet, symphonic music) is not for you. Here is *your* kind of thing, a nice bit of bold, communitarian, simplified *agitprop* activity.

Nor, as we have seen, has the Arts Council addressed itself seriously so far to the question of limited access. We know from their own researches that many of the traditional arts funded by the Arts Council go to those social groups who already appreciate them; that is, predominantly, socio-economic groups A and B, with some from C. This division, and it shows no sign of weakening, mirrors that increasingly sharp split in the press between the readers of the 'serious' papers and those of – now – the *Daily Star* and the other 'populars'; or split in broadcasting – in which, though we all know many good programmes are made, people tend to identify themselves by channel loyalty and to stick with their channel, so that for many millions of people the idea of, say, switching to BBC 1, let alone BBC 2, would seem to be against nature.

The moral of all this is plain. Whilst thinking further and better about the proper claims of community arts the Arts Council should, so far as the 'high arts' are concerned, put much greater emphasis on ways to widen access. It would not be difficult to set up several experimental schemes. More important, and more a continuing matter, the Council should address itself very very much more to making links with educational agencies at all levels, but particularly with agencies which work with people aged from sixteen to twenty; and these agencies will not all be formally within the field of education. It is surprising that no less than thirty years after it was founded the Arts Council appointed its first full-time officer concerned with education, diplomatically called the 'Educational Liaison Officer'. It is, however, not at all surprising that that initiative should have been resented by some of the Council and some of the Council's officers. Some feared 'vulgarisation' as a result of the effort to broaden access. After all, the arts are sui generis and any attempt at explaining them or making them accessible outside the charmed circle of the cognoscenti might result in taking the fine in-group sheen off them, mightn't it? How much more comfortable for us to enjoy the more advanced

159

forms of modern art without bothering about mediation, whilst also and at the same time giving easy aid to the more 'exciting' forms of community arts. Come to think of it, the two apparently opposed attitudes marry here; but the relation of each to the texture of British life and its people is minimal.

One of the disappointments in all this activity about community arts is what I earlier called its lack of a sense of history. It seems neither to have nor to recognise any past, except perhaps an ill-sustained notion of a distant folk past on which today's community arts are presumed to be able to draw. There is a surer and nearer example. The tradition of British adult education over the last century and a half has been in some respects a model to the world. Among its many great qualities are several which are very relevant here – such as the belief that people should be able to stand up and reach for the best and the most demanding; that, given that opportunity (not watered down), a surprising number will so reach, and that when they do their grasp will reveal that they and many others have far more abilities than either a closed élitism or an ill-thought-through communitarianism had realised. So they have the right to the best; no less.   1979

THE FUTURE
OF BROADCASTING

————————

Future-gazing in matters which concern public taste (or, especially, likely changes in taste as technologies develop) is notoriously difficult. In Britain we have only to recall that a very carefully measured assessment, two or three decades ago, of the likely increase in the numbers of television sets proved very quickly to be many times in error in both scale and timing. Yet even that area is less cloudy than the assessment of underlying attitudes, and changes in attitudes, in response to television or the other mass media. It is one thing to come to the impressionistic conclusion that television is encouraging a short span of attention or making us less sensitive to situations which should call out our compassion (both of these charges have been made). They can not be conclusively proved. But neither can they be disproved. So they may in the end be true; but by then we may not know it. I propose therefore not to predict but rather to describe what I think are likely to be the main paradoxical choices about broadcasting which are likely to be in play in the coming decade. I did not seek to see them as paradoxes; but that is how they emerge.

The first paradox is that between the possibilities for small-scale production and individual programming offered by the new technologies on the one hand and the pressure of national and indeed multinational, or international, interests on the other. Behind this contrast there lie problems of great subtlety; about, for example, the different responses of open and closed societies, about 'consensus' societies or politically highly unified societies and more explicitly fragmented and diverse societies.

A great many people are placing a good deal of hope in the possibilities of small-scale broadcasting. 'Small is beautiful'. Some see it as a way of escaping from the tyranny of the informationally or even politically centralised state. Some see it, whether they are viewers and listeners or programme-makers themselves, as a way of acquiring much freer and tailor-made programming. Some are just fed up with the complications of the big-scale and want to work on a more human level. Some want to get away from the pressures of the massive advertisers. So the hopes invested in the prospects for small-scale broadcasting can cover the whole political spectrum from left to right.

We are told that small-scale television can take our viewing out of 'real time'; we can control what we see and when we see it.* We can break the tyranny of the national programmes. We can select our own programmes and the time we see them (by storage and retrieval). Two elements are, in fact, running together here and roughly in the same direction: small-scale work which can be very local, and small-scale work which can be fitted to individual and even specialist tastes. In the one, we can see certain things because we are citizens of a small geographic entity, a town or rural community. In the other, we can see certain things because – with others spread across a country of 'X' million people – we have interests of special kinds, political, economic, artistic, social, intellectual or what have you. In the one case, television can play a part similar to that of the local newspapers; in the other, its part is that of the specialised or 'hobby' or professional journals. We could call them the horizontal and the vertical dimensions.

One need have little doubt that something of that sort will be possible. As economic break-even points are lowered, so more small-scale fragmentation by audiences becomes possible. That being agreed, the problems begin – as, again Dr Townsend fully recognises. In such a situation, he says, the viewer 'will not necessarily see more television – and it is quite likely that he will choose to see worse television'. These are striking assertions, though not spelled out in Dr Townsend's paper. We are nowhere told what 'worse' means in television terms, though it is plain that Dr Townsend does not mean technologically worse. Let me say what I, I guess being in tune with him, would mean by the expression. I would not mean that small-scale, self-programming television would be 'worse' because it would take away the capacity of some of us to decide what other people ought to have in a paternal way. That never was a good approach to television's best possibilities. In the last two

* See 'Tomorrow's Broadcasting – Chance or Design?', Boris Townsend, a paper given to a conference of Dutch broadcasters, Hilversum, 1979. This paper of mine followed Dr Townsend's and is in part a response to it.

decades there have been great advances in 'good' television programmes. Programmes on subjects which few thought they would be interested in, which few had even heard about, have proved to be immensely popular, to be appreciated and understood. Those programmes have been made not because someone making programmes felt that he wanted to 'do good to the masses' but for much subtler reasons. General television, television which can go into almost every home in the land, presents an extraordinary challenge to those who work in it.

If they believe that some subjects are in themselves immensely exciting, and if they think that television – by its inherent qualities – offers a unique opportunity to explore the character of these subjects, then they will be set on a remarkable course. This is how television has done its best work over the past two decades, where new interests have taken us by surprise. This is what will cease to be a stimulus if television becomes so fragmented in its production practices, because of technical advances, that we can all 'programme' in advance what it is we want to see. Since we are almost all inherently lazy and conservative, we will tend to 'programme' what we already know we like, what will reinforce our existing tastes. The set-up will no longer be such as occasionally to capture us, because the divine discontent in the heart of some programme maker has set him on a certain track. I think this kind of consideration may be behind Dr Townsend's reflection that we are likely to see 'worse' programmes under a fragmented system. The new system may destroy something of the best we now occasionally have.

At least as big a question, in the era of small-scale possibilities, will remain precisely how to cope with the larger scale. It will not go away simply because we have found out how to work on the smaller scale, and this for two reasons. One is financial, the other political; and the two are inter-linked. Financial considerations will be likely to ensure that, whatever the small-scale possibilities, companies will push to make large-scale programmes. Indeed, Dr Townsend's vision here is very deliberately sombre. He foresees not merely national or international programmes (buying in) such as we have now but transnational, intercontinental, multinational programmes. Those projected international operations which he envisages, from a satellite somewhere above Uganda, reaching about half a billion people with their all-embracing spectaculars and their multinational advertisements are a very far cry from the proposed small-scale programmes

163

for you and your kind only, or indeed from the best national programmes of today.

For, whatever the technical possibilities, the use made of those possibilities will be decided in most cases by a combination of financial
opportunities and political considerations. We may wish it were otherwise but at present, in the kinds of society most of us inhabit, so it is.
Politicians, large-scale business, powerful pressure groups of one sort
or another (but not small, 'worthy', pressure groups) will make most of
the running. They will, unless we change the way these things are
handled, basically decide on the use we make of the new technologies;
or the misuse; or the refusal to use. Does this need proof? Take two con-
trasting examples from today. One of the most common if not the most
common and popular application of Eurovision in what we call the free
and open societies is *Jeux Sans Frontières*. Was it worth all that technological inventiveness to arrive there? Some people, when that question is
asked, accuse the enquirer of élitism. I accuse them of easy contempt for
others. And if we turn to a non-free, a managed, society, we find that
the new technologies are just as much either misused or ignored.
Eastern Europe and in particular the Soviet Union are deeply
concerned about the possibilities of satellite broadcasting. That is
harder to jam than normal sound or television. They may well be
concerned that the West can beam politically undesirable material into
the East. But they usually argue that they wish simply to keep out
'undesirable and depraving material' in a moral sense. They are
probably right to be concerned about casual entertainment from the
West being beamed East; it might break up the psychological concrete
of Soviet authoritarianism more effectively than direct political
propaganda.

Thirdly, there is the developing world's relation to all these changes.
They are now accusing the developed world of neo-colonialism via
communications. The West, not on the whole out of political Machia-
vellianism but in its pursuit of cash, has almost swamped the emergence
of a full range of home communications in the developing world.

The critics in the developing world do have a point. So does the West
in its response to the new call, from the developing world, not just for
the free circulation of ideas but for a free 'and balanced' circulation. In
these matters, 'balance' can be the negation of freedom.

So, to sum up the main issue in the relation between small-scale or
individual and large-scale and (usually) national technologies: I have
argued that national television of one sort or another is not likely to be

easily forgone by politicians or governments of any persuasion. Few governments in larger states which like to think of themselves as having one voice would seriously contemplate even the Netherlands system. Television in particular is the most naturally 'massive' of all mass media. Whatever the technical possibilities of moving away from that characteristic, too many people – and I do not mean governments only but also the commercial producers of goods and the advertisers who serve them – have a very powerful interest in seeing that characteristic survive and strengthen.

There may be, however, something which looks like a disposition by politicians (though not by advertisers) to encourage the development of local broadcasting by both radio and television. In some countries where there is national broadcasting there is constant friction between the broadcasters, especially those in news and current affairs, whose professional attitudes lead them towards seeking to be part of the Fourth Estate, free to comment on political and governmental matters – friction between them and the government itself. Governments often, and the major political parties in general, find it difficult to think of broadcasters (often financed by public funds) criticising the government or 'getting between' the party system as a whole and the people. In such a mood, politicians may well think that the emergence of a network of local broadcasting, in which people more and more tend to occupy themselves with the affairs of their own backyards, may take their attention off national broadcasting so that they are less likely to form a phalanx in defence of the broadcasters' right to tell them what they think to be the truth about the way the country is going. This is a modern, technologically-assisted form of the principle of 'divide and rule'.

So, though I am as interested as most people in local or individual systems, I would think it a pity to forgo the better possibilities which a national and nationally-listened to or viewed system can offer. It seems to me right that nations which, in spite of regional differences, often have a moving *national* history; or nations whose unity may conceal a great many tensions, some of them always threatening to tear them apart, should sometimes debate as one. So long as they are all *nations,* speaking as one in international councils, regarded as one by those forces which influence the flow of trade, faced therefore not only with regional problems but with national problems of security or of economic change – so long as this is the case there will be grounds for saying that the broadcasters should be allowed to try to help a true national voice emerge from time to time, or a set of overlapping voices which together make up a sort of *genuine* effort at consensus (though one constantly changing); or better, that they should be able to envisage broadcasting as the orchestration of a society's conversations, dialogues, quarrels with itself. I deliberately put in that 'genuine' as a saving epithet. Even though I do not develop here the meanings of the word, it puts up a flag to warn the traveller that there is boggy ground ahead. It is never easy to find the right elements of a national consensus. In a country such as Great Britain, we too easily assume that such a consensus exists or can be easily discovered and evoked, especially at moments of great national crisis, joyful or sad. It has been one of the more important assumptions of the BBC that such a consensus does exist, so much so that they have sometimes seemed to be walking on the water. Asa Briggs' fourth volume of his *History of the BBC* describes vividly, chiefly through the forest of memoranda which circulated within the BBC at that time, how the coronation of Queen Elizabeth II almost three decades ago was one of the points at which television came of age. It went into a hitherto unparalleled number of homes with a beautifully-presented moving picture of what the top people at the BBC regarded as one of the greatest of all national communicative moments. It spoke to 'the people' as one; it was, one top official said afterwards, 'a miracle'. I have shared that feeling myself from time to time, perhaps most strongly on the televising of Churchill's funeral where the commentators, who naturally have special tones of voice for such occasions, voices drained so far as possible of regional or local or class connotations, evoked the suggestion of speaking to the whole people; and the superb photography, especially as the great horses drawing the gun carriage breasted the hill to St Paul's, embodied the same idea visually. It could be argued that the World Cup (if Britain is doing at all well) or the annual Cup Final, or even the Boat Race (which holds a special place in the national imagination, or perhaps chiefly in the imaginations of television producers who have been to either Oxford or Cambridge) or some other such events, are also meaningful expressions of national unity. But they are much thinner symbols than a Coronation or a death which interests everyone. The outstanding continuing attempt to express a sense of national unity here in Britain is the Queen's Speech to the nation on Christmas Day.

Recently it was designed to enshrine even more than ever the notion of the Monarchy as committed to all the best domestic values, with the Queen sitting on a settee with her daughter and baby grandson, the corgi dogs scrabbling around, the chintz covers, the splendid vases of flowers. But this annual rite is a wasting asset; more and more people, if they watch it at all, watch it as a peculiar and rather amusing socio-cultural phenomenon. Each country – I obviously avoid the word 'nation' at this moment – must have its own arguments about what is a 'genuine' consensus for it, and about when that consensus seems to be unnecessarily weak or when its growth needs to be resisted; and so of when the efforts of broadcasters to achieve a consensus are also to be resisted. In the United Kingdom, I think many of our assumptions about the firm ground for consensus are not well-based, that we are a more plural and pluralistic society than you might imagine from the pattern and the tones of much in our broadcasting, and that it is more than time to encourage broadcasters to understand this better and act on it more. This does not mean that we will fall apart; it means that we will need to understand better what it is that best expresses a sense of national history and so unity, across regions and classes and beyond the historic mere rites whose practice allows too many of us precisely *not* to think further. In television terms a beginning of that understanding may be found not in royal or suchlike occasions but in, say, some of our zanier comedy shows (which do in their own terms 'unite' the nation in a common, surrealist sense of humour right across age or sex or locality or party or belief or social class differences). There are other such hints of the way television, often unconsciously so far as the top planners are concerned, can point towards the elements of what I would call a 'genuine' consensus, which lies dormant much of the time as we go about our multi-faceted other businesses, but which can emerge from time to time in response to a variety of calls inspired by a variety of talents.

All such questions, and how interesting they are and substantially how uncharted, point to the more fundamental issues about the future of broadcasting as of much else in mass media. What we have had in the debate of the last few years (but how much they tell us about the next ten years I am not sure) are elements such as these; a tendency for governments and major parties to be more than ever suspicious of broadcasters and – in Britain – especially BBC, and so a related tendency to try to bring the Corporation to heel by controlling even more tightly its finances; by, e.g., giving essential licence increases little and late and for a short period only, so that longer term planning is inhibited. We have seen also a Seventies reaction against what we tend to call Sixties permissiveness. This is the Puritan backlash. It thrives on the selective use of evidence about the effects of television. But its opponents are not averse to the use of selective evidence on their own behalf either. In most countries, including Great Britain, the missing element is a serious debate about the relations between broadcasting and the main estates of the realm – parties, industry, unions; and a thorough debate about the relations between broadcasting and the individual, its impact on him or her. In such circumstances, broadcasting tends to drift towards an undifferentiated middle ground without sharp contours. With us the main result of this is that both the BBC and the commercial network – the latter set up, so we were told, to provide *hard competition* in good broadcasting for the BBC – are more and more coming together in this merged ground.

In Britain, we have now had more than twenty years of competition in television, between a publicly-funded corporation (BBC – by licence fee) and a privately-funded body (ITA, now IBA – by advertisement revenue). Those who called for this sort of competition in the early Fifties based their case above all on the argument – assertion, rather – that diversity is good in itself and that competition would make for more choice and so better broadcasting. The results do not exactly bear out those claims.

The BBC was shaken, and to some extent this had a tonic effect on it. At least equally, the effect on the BBC was not for the good. They sometimes take their eyes off the pursuit of good broadcasting in favour of the pursuit of mass audiences (since they fear being driven into a minority corner).

In the first years the commercial companies rode high. They were certainly not, most of them, competing in good broadcasting. They were after large audiences which put up their advertising rates. So much so, that the Pilkington Committee on Broadcasting which sat for two years and reported to the government in 1962 very severely criticised commercial television. One result was that, when new commercial television licences were issued, the regulations enforced by the supervisory body ITA were very much tighter. So it has remained. If you set up a system whereby profit is determined by the number of viewers delivered to the advertisers you have set up a system inherently in contradiction with the free search for good broadcasting. Good broadcasting means a wide range of different programmes, ample provision for minorities, the taking of gambles on potential tastes, risking ill-will or a loss of viewers in the effort to fulfil the medium's widest and best possibilities on behalf of your audiences. To increase advertising revenue you do not take risks, gamble on potential, or care for minorities – you tickle existing tastes; that must be your inherent nature.

If by now quite a number of good and varied programmes do emanate from the commercial channel, this is chiefly because progressively tighter regulations have ensured that, even against their nature, the commercial companies have been forced to provide working space, room, opportunity for the people who can and wish to make such programmes. It is like putting braces on recalcitrant teeth.

One result is that both networks – the one being pulled away from its purer public-service position towards more popular programming; the other being by force pulled from its commercialism towards more public-service programming – are more and more tending to meet and merge in a central, bland area. But there is still a big difference in the overall feel or texture of each channel. And audiences – especially the ITV audience – tend to be polarised and stick with the same channel.

The years since Pilkington reported have therefore abundantly confirmed the rightness of his main – and rejected – recommendation: that if you really want competition in *good* broadcasting you must make sure that the channels are competing for one and the same thing; to wit, good broadcasting! And that the way to ensure this is, in a channel funded by advertising revenue, to separate the programme-making job from the advertisement-revenue-receiving function. The receiver of advertising revenue must be able to dispose that revenue to the best ends of good broadcasting, not for profit. If you keep advertising profit and programme disposition in the same hands, the desire to 'maximise audiences' for as much of the time as possible will fight with the search for good broadcasting in the public interest as a whole.

It is clear that we should, if we care for more than our comfort, press for a secure place for broadcasting as part of the Fourth Estate, nationally; that we should, whilst recognising the value of small-scale work, try to get right the national (and the international) pattern and prospects. In Britain this might mean, for example, pressing for ways of editorialising more in broadcasting. Without such kinds of demands, we are likely to lose ground. 'We' is always a tricky word: I don't mean broadcasters by it, since I am not a broadcasting official:

I suppose I mean all those who care for the best future, the radical improvement, of democracy and of broadcasting.

So we come to another paradox about the future of broadcasting. It concerns the argument about whether broadcasting will eventually make morons of us all (the effects debate) or whether we will learn to 'put broadcasting in its place'. The upshot of the work done in different countries on the effects of television is that (a) it may have direct effects on some people who are particularly prone to be so affected; e.g. towards violence; and that for the rest of us (b) it may produce an insensitivity towards violence, may progressively desensitise us so that, though we may not be likely to commit acts of violence ourselves, we may become slowly less horrified by them around us, whether on the screen or in real life. That, put as simply as possible, seems to be the gist of existing research work (though by now these findings are becoming dated). The conclusions are tentative enough to allow some people to ignore them or even deny them altogether. And some others have inflated them and called for censorship. But if they do have any truth they must surely apply as much to the whole message put over by television – its total picture of the world – as to its representations of violence. If so, then one should be concerned not only about the emergence of a society insensitive to casual violence but also about one which is bathed in the bland light of a rapt consumers' world. In that case, the fact that throughout the mass media advertising is becoming glossier – in a stagnant economy – is only the latest irony.

Against that evidence, which might seem to point to the progressive dominance of television's structuring of our reality, one looks for more hopeful signs. There is some evidence from the United States that teenagers today are learning to put television in its place, that they turn it on when they want it and for very selective programmes only, do not think of sitting down before it just on the assumption that something will turn up or because they can think of nothing better to do than that, and generally use it like tap water – always available but not something you get hooked on.* One remembers that teenagers have generally been less avid television viewers than their parents: while mother and father are sitting before the box they get out of the house. Such hopes are not new. Sir William Haley, once Director General of the BBC and

---

* 'Television and Art: The Circle and the Triangle', by Douglas Davies. Prix Italia Seminar papers, Milan, 1978. Mr Davies cites, inter alia, *The Unseeing Eye: The Myth of Television Power in National Elections,* by Patterson and McClure.

the author of some of the very best observations on the nature of broadcasting, was arguing thirty years ago that good broadcasters sought through their programmes to show that the world was a wider and more interesting place than their viewers had assumed, and so aimed to put themselves out of business by encouraging viewers to seek other, more rewarding pursuits. Strange language to hear in the late Seventies! If that tendency emerged, what a circle we would have completed in our attitudes towards the effects of television viewing. We would have gone from the days when viewers were approached as *tabulae rasae* on whom the screen wrote its good or bad messages, to the period of Uses and Gratifications studies when viewers were thought to adopt television as an important element in their whole pattern of recreation, to the final stage of opting out, when they approached television only intermittently and for strictly limited and defined purposes. It's a progression one can hope for: but much is committed to seeing that it doesn't seriously come about. It is in the interests of so many people to ensure that it doesn't actually happen – politicians, commerce, advertisers, broadcasters themselves, and their unions.

Actually, I am rather more hopeful than that last sentence suggests. Whatever the errors of and misuse of television in the last couple of decades, one of the gains has been the emergence of a group of professionals committed to more than making programmes which suit the immediate needs of their masters, whoever they may be. It is largely to their credit, rather than to that of the orders they were given, that programmes have been made which are better than one might have expected, better than the various inside and outside pressures encouraged. The last paradox, then, is that such people – the best people in the business – should now be asked progressively to aim to put themselves out of business. At least, that is what I am offering them as a long-term aim. If they don't think more in that way few others will.

In the shorter term, we have seen that one of the chief results of the new technologies could be that national controls of broadcasting weakened. We would all be able to seek programmes which reflect the views we *already* hold. We are coming to the end of the worthy, regulated years.

That sounds fine, at first blush; very democratic and free. But it will have three results:

(a) we will not be tempted to widen our existing tastes, will not be taken by surprise. There will be less scope for inventing new kinds of 'good'

171

programme.

(b) we will not be asked to reconsider our existing opinions. National broadcasting has often aimed ahead of majority opinion on such issues as e.g. racism, capital punishment, the general rights of the citizen.

(c) parts of society which need help, and which broadcasting has so far helped enormously, are likely to suffer (the educationally disadvantaged, the blind, the deaf, deserted wives, solitary husbands, ethnic minorities, the old, the unemployed, etc. – none of these packs much political or commercial clout).

So we have to take the measure of the fact that free, multi-channel, tailor-made broadcasting means the weakening, if not the end, not only of national 'controls', 'paternalism' and the like, but of that thinking about the best uses of broadcasting (admittedly born out of the fact that broadcasting channels have so far been scarce resources) which caused the general broadcasting pattern to be somewhat better than most of us are, worthier, more aware of the lame and the halt, less chauvinistic or narrow-minded or self-protective or punitive.

Whatever the future possibilities for multiple broadcasting, the democracies must make provision for this kind of programming. It is one of the finer products of the first fifty years (the controlled years) of broadcasting.

The crucial ideas behind good broadcasting are always the same and all lead in the same direction, whatever our technological gear. They are:

1. That we should seek deliberately to widen taste, if only because, if that positive tendency is not built in, we will be likely insensibly to narrow it; and that

2. we must therefore gamble on the potential in all of us, our ability to respond to areas of life which a simple identikit of present taste (say, one drawn from looking at the recurrent pattern of interests represented in the British popular press), would lead us to expect; and that there is good evidence that a great number of people will respond to such an approach; and so

3. broadcasters should fight, and be supported in fighting, to retain substantial freedom to experiment in the ways outlined above rather than being required to deliver, slickly, goods tailored to preconceptions about the mean average of existing tastes.

This is the only worthwhile structure to fight for as we move up the Eighties. All other structures are about the promotion of something other than broadcasting, probably the interests of big business and the advertisers or those of politicians wishing to keep broadcasting as a harmless pastime and reflector, rather than as an important part of the Fourth Estate and of the dialogue within and between ourselves.   1979

THE MASS MEDIA
AND ONE-WAY FLOW

In the 1970s the UN system began to move into the full flood of a major debate on the mass media. Its epicentre is UNESCO, since within the UN system UNESCO has direct responsibility for most of the political and cultural aspects of communications issues. The UN is congenitally an inventor of grand labels, so we are now being told that the debate is about the search for a New World Information Order, and hence that it is a branch of the larger search for a New International Economic Order. That is fair. The New International Economic Order has been described as at bottom a claim, by the developing countries on the developed, for greater distributive justice; certainly that claim lies behind the wide spread concern about the present use of the mass media.

On the other hand, the communications debate started before the New International Economic Order was posited and so exists in its own right; in my own experience it is more than a decade old, especially in its more political forms. In these forms the argument is an aspect of both Eastern bloc/Western powers' political contentions and of the new developing nations' search for identity and coherence, and so of their emerging nationalism.

The central concern is with the one-way flow of communications. The late Professor Cherry preferred to call this 'dissemination', arguing that 'communication' should by definition be two-way. Whatever it is called, this is the process which ensures that most films seen throughout the world have been made in the USA, that most publishing flows from the major developed countries, that most news material prepared for all the main mass media emanates from American or British agencies; and, above all, that most television material seen on screens throughout the world is made in those same countries, with the USA overwhelmingly the major provider.

UNESCO's study *Television Traffic – A One-Way Street* (1974) found that between 100 and 200 thousand programme hours per year of US material went to television networks elsewhere (at very low prices, since production costs have usually been met by home sales). Among the major agents of the flow are Reuters, Visnews, EMI, Paramount, BBC, ITV and PA.

Developing countries buy the basic equipment but do not usually have cash enough to supply themselves with home-made material in the quantity required. It is tempting to argue that most highly-developed countries, including ourselves, are not essentially in a different position here, vis-à-vis the USA, than the poorer developing countries; we all put massive amounts of American material on to our screens. But the scale of the one-way flow as it affects developing nations is so much greater than what we experience that to claim we are all in the same boat would be flippant.

A further twist in the argument points out how very difficult it is not to more nearly balance the flow – that would be superhuman – but to get anything except the barest minimum of material, and that fitting the developed world's pre-conceptions, flowing in the other direction.

Further, the material we originate about the developing world is, it is claimed, partial and distorted:

The problems of the developing nations are seen with the eyes of journalists and producers from the developed regions; moreover, the materials they produce are aimed primarily at audiences of those regions. As a result, not only is the image of the developing nations often a false and distorted one, but that very image is reflected back to the developing countries themselves.

There are, though, qualifications such as the existence of some regional, 'gatekeeper and transformer', countries who are both enormous importers of Western material and also exporters to their own regions: for instance, India towards much of Asia through her film industry, Egypt towards other Arab states and Mexico towards much of Latin America. Yet these are minor qualifications in comparison with the main direction and force of flow. It would, incidentally, be interesting to know more about not only the similarities between countries in the TV material each selects for showing, but also the differences as shown by the differing programming patterns they create.

Those patterns depend above all on the structures provided for each television system (state controlled, commercial or mixed) which will in turn indicate the pressures under which the systems work. My own favourite pilot study would be a comparison of the programming patterns of two developed countries, Australia and New Zealand.

We need to appreciate better the force of the resentment in the developing world at the developed world's predominance in mass media production. As early as 1973 President Kekkonen of Finland, speaking on behalf of those developing nations at a congress on television exchanges, argued that 'freedom of speech has in practice become the freedom of the well-to-do'. More recently, the Director General of UNESCO (himself a native of Senegal), made the same point: 'freedom is perverted if there is only one-way communication and if the participants are not on an equal footing. May not freedom of information, however, if it is the privilege of those alone who are the most powerful, the most rich and the best equipped, lead to an effect of domination'. He went on to note 'a growing determination on the part of those who are currently at a disadvantage in the communications process to liberate themselves from their state of dependence', and called on the exporting nations to exercise better their responsibilities towards the rights of other nations.

It is claimed that this mass of material coming in from outside is both erasing traditional cultures and inhibiting the emergence of authentic cultural changes (for instance, in newly-created States). There is no clear proof that this is in fact happening, nor indeed any proof that it is not. The new nations go further and argue that the more powerful nations provide total ways of seeing the world, present through their news-gathering machines and with the claim that that news is objective and ideology-free, a view of the nature, order and significance of events which is in reality determined by Western assumptions as to what constitutes news, and what doesn't. This recalls the debate now in progress within Great Britain about the 'structuring of reality' by our own internal news processes. The two arguments are indeed closely related, but that by the developing world is more comprehensive.

Such objections are heard, first, from leaders in the developing countries, particularly on the grounds that their search for national identity and unity (essential and pressing in many cases, if their fragile entities are to survive) is being hampered by the overwhelming flood of material from the West, that the West is using the principle of the free flow of information selfishly, to smother emerging competition. It is, of course, an irony that the people who say this often have a very firm hold indeed on all aspects of communications within their own domains and, even if they do in principle believe in free speech (few do), are likely to say that it cannot as yet be afforded at home. Given the volatility of many of their régimes, they have a point. Jeremy Tunstall, in *The Media Are American,* goes further and claims that, whatever they may say for public consumption, some of these leaders like the easy and cheap availability of soporific and distracting television programmes on the grounds that they keep people quiet, unaware of the political realities or of the more challenging uses to which television can be put. If, as is almost always the case, the government's hold on news and current affairs remains firm, the resulting combination – loaded political information plus soporific general programming – is the nearest to *1984* so far reached.

But many intellectuals in these countries, usually younger men and not necessarily in official positions, are also deeply disturbed by the one-way flow. Our world is being distorted, they argue; even we, who have been trained in the West and who therefore have been intellectually Westernised, are nevertheless Africans or Asians or Latin Americans, with roots also in different ways of responding to experience. We do not wish to see these two visions as mutually exclusive. Nor can we happily accept the submerging of our existing local cultures by often thinner Western forms.

They go on to argue that the new media are not only predominantly *used* by the West but that what they are in themselves is determined by the West. So that what a popular newspaper *is* is likely to be predetermined by what Fleet Street has defined as a popular newspaper. Similarly, what television can do, what it *is* as a medium, has been so predefined by the developed powers that it is difficult for an African or Asian or Arab to approach the medium's possibilities with his own different eyes or to persuade programme planners in his own country to accept new ways of seeing television's possibilities.

So, from both politicians in power and from intellectuals not in power, the same cry goes up: this is neo-imperialist aggression; this is cultural imperialism. The West is still dominating and colonising us. They provide the machines (often not compatible as between the developed nations); they provide the programmes to fill the machines; they shape our realities day by day. The 1972 General Conference of UNESCO called on the major communicating countries to recognise their international responsibilities, on the grounds that otherwise the mass media could become vehicles for 'the domination of world public opinion or a source of moral and cultural pollution.' It went on to argue that the one-way flow from only a few virtually monopolistic countries might seriously harm 'the cultural values of most of the remaining countries', and called for a code of ethics for communication. Almost a year later, the Heads of State of the Non-Aligned countries, meeting in Algiers, asserted: 'Developing countries should take concerted action in the field of mass communications in order to promote a greater interchange of ideas among themselves . . . [and called for] . . . reorganisation of existing communication channels which are the legacy of the colonial past and which have hampered free, direct and fast communications between them.' They went on to argue that 'cultural alienation and imported civilisation, imposed by imperialism and colonialism, should be countered by re-personalisation and by a constant and determined recourse to the social and cultural values of the population which define them as a sovereign people'. That seems to contain most of the objections. The Ministries of Information of the Non-Aligned countries expressed similar concern at a New Delhi Conference in 1976.

All this is in the language of international governmental conferences and we rightly tend to suspect or smile at it. It slides over many of the more difficult complexities. There is, certainly, a state of dependency by many nations on only a few others in providing for the needs of the mass media. But on the whole this is not due to a conspiracy of the sort invoked by phrases such as 'cultural colonialism' (though there are elements of that). Much more importantly, this flooding is the result of world marketing's natural impulses; it will push its material into any crack or cranny where a dollar can be made, no matter how marginally. That is the nature of the animal. But it cannot do so by force or even bribery; not on this scale. The world buys, say, American television programmes not only because they are cheap but because they accurately gauge what will amuse most people in the world today, sad though that fact may sometimes seem. I have little doubt that, even after sixty years of earnest and culturally pure communications within the USSR, American soap operas would have massive majorities among Soviet viewers within a week if restrictions were lifted.

There are, though, clear remnants of former colonial links in the shape and flow of communication channels and in the patterns of dependence in communications. The physical networks of telecommunications have inevitably been built to service the advanced countries, and communication lines between developing countries –

e.g., within Africa – are still comparatively rudimentary. States which were formerly British colonies tend to rely heavily on British agencies; former French territories are tightly bound to Paris. There is a linguistic element here also. In territories newly forged into one, where there may be several local languages and no one fully dominant, and where the educated classes have almost all been trained in the former colonising countries, the languages of these countries – overwhelmingly English or French – become the common public languages.

Nor does the West do itself reasonable justice in exploiting this one-way flow. If this is neo-colonialism, it is often of a kind which desperately sells short the coloniser. In this game – where the thrust of the market often works against what one might call a 'balanced' presentation of the nature of the exporting country – the USA by all odds wins. She both feeds the market more than any other country, and shows herself in the worst light. There are two main reasons for this, one commercial, the other ideological. The pressures of commerce ensure that it is the more vapid or violent portrayals of 'American life' which are exported rather than the worthier but dull representations. Second, as an open democracy the USA makes an exceptional practice of washing her dirty linen in public (a quality which some other countries find quite impossible to understand and so take as a true picture of American life).

To anyone watching the relentless flow of American material through the mass media in, say, South East Asia, the USA seems inhabited chiefly by the corrupt, violent or bird-brained. One of the most striking of all contrasts in communications is between that picture and the one created by, say, reading an American local newspaper for a couple of weeks. They might inhabit different worlds.

Still, the massive one-way flow, with all its cultural implications, does exist and it is not likely that the developing countries will be content any longer simply to accept it. If the West shrugs the problems aside they will look elsewhere for support, to other powers who have their own, rather different, reasons for being concerned about Western dominance in mass media technology. Indeed, they have already looked elsewhere, notably to the Soviet Union; and they have been enthusiastically received.

Year after year in the past decade, the Soviet Union has put down resolutions at all the relevant UN conferences about the dangers of 'uncontrolled' growth in mass media activity. The formulation is usually that, in view of the great power of these media, it is the duty of sovereign States to ensure that they are not used for 'corrupting' ends; and, in particular, that States should agree not to transmit 'undesirable material' across each other's frontiers. It is of no use to point out that in open societies governments do not usually exercise this type of control of the mass media; the resolutions continue, with the phrasing only marginally altered.

Self-evidently, this is an aspect of the general Soviet fear of the free expression and circulation of opinion. In this instance, it takes on a special edge precisely because Soviet officials are shrewd enough to recognise that the Western powers are exceptionally effective in using the mass media in attractive, ingratiating, attention-catching ways.

This fear has been sharpened by the arrival of satellites. Mr Gromyko has spoken strongly on the theme at the UN General Assembly in New York; and the Soviets were even more than usually active in the drafting of an international instrument on satellite use, in particular seeking provisions to ensure that they are not used to carry 'degrading' commercial material, and that no State direct satellite broadcasts into another State's territory except with its agreement. The resultant *Declaration of Guiding Principles for the Use of Satellite Broadcasting for the Free Flow of Information, the Extension of Education and the Development of Cultural Exchanges* (1972) asserted:

Satellite broadcasting shall respect the sovereignty and equality of all States ... The objective of satellite broadcasting for the free flow of information is to ensure the widest possible dissemination, among the peoples of the world, of news of all countries, developed and developing alike ... Cultural programmes, while promoting the enrichment of all cultures, should respect the distinctive character, the value and the dignity of each, and the right of all countries and peoples to preserve their cultures as part of the common heritage of mankind.

That deeply self-contradictory formulation (it speaks for free-but-controlled communication) is, it will be seen at once, likely to sound recognisable chords of disquiet – and will seem also to seek to allay them – in the breasts of those who govern developing countries. Thus, the Soviet Union once again allied herself with anti-imperialism, against the former colonial powers, on behalf of the integrity of individual cultures. Which seems even more than usually odd when one sets it against the controls on national political self-consciousness within the satellite and absorbed countries, or, indeed, against the restrictions on comment with which Finland lives as a condition of her independence. On the other hand, the developed countries should recognise more that satellite development has been and is being far too much defined by profit-making rather than by public considerations and needs.

During my time at UNESCO (from the beginning of 1970 to the spring of 1975) and subsequently, such resolutions have marched with varying success through conference after conference, whether or not those conferences were specifically about communications. I met my first at the first-ever world conference of Ministers of Culture, in Venice during August 1970. A debate on communications initiated by Eastern Europe and critically engaged in by the West finally produced a battily paradoxical resolution which ran:

Whilst respecting the freedom of artists, States will ensure that the media of mass communication are not employed to propagate material which is subversive of agreed values . . .

UNESCO's biennial General Conference, which fell in autumn of that same year, for the first time took up – with India in the lead – the theme of imbalance in the flow of information and its presumed effect on cultural identity ('the rights of less privileged nations to preserve their own cultures'). The 1972 Helsinki Conference on Cultural Policies for European Ministers took up the same theme. The line of such meetings goes on – the latest was held at Yaounde in the summer of 1980. It made the usual criticisms of imbalance and neo-colonialism.

Meanwhile, activities more directly concerned with communication matters were continuing, notably in the preparation of a *Draft Declaration on Fundamental Principles governing the use of the mass media in strengthening peace and international understanding and in combating war propaganda, racialism and apartheid*. A draft proposing stringent limitations on the free flow of information went before the 19th General Conference of UNESCO at Nairobi in autumn 1976. By then a good many people had realised that things were on a collision course and the offending draft declaration was not adopted. Instead the Director General was charged with preparing a new draft, one which could meet with the largest possible measure of agreement, for submission to the twentieth General Conference at Paris in autumn 1978. (There, the Declaration, much amended, was duly passed.)

Another just possible ray of hope came with the establishment of the MacBride Commission. To give it its full name, the International Commission for the Study of Communication Problems was established by the Director General after the Nairobi General Conference.

181

The Chairman was Sean MacBride, a Nobel and Lenin prizewinner and, among much else, a founder of Amnesty International. There were fifteen other members, all, it was claimed, 'serving as individuals'. This was the usual humbug. Some acted indisputably *in propria persona:* some were just as indisputably high-level government officials, and acted as such.

In its early days, the Commission seemed to ally itself with the argument that the 'free flow' principle needs redefinition, and began to promote its extension into 'free and balanced flow'. This was too close for comfort to Orwell's extension of 'All men are equal'. In the West, our almost automatic response is that a free flow is not likely to be inherently balanced and a thoroughly balanced flow by definition is not likely to be free. Still, one would feel happier if some of our professional organisations did not so much content themselves with the cry that *all* talk of better balance implies stifling freedom. Some people's freedom is already being stifled precisely because of lack of balance.

In the event, the MacBride Report proved to be better than one had begun to fear during the first year of its two-year life. Inevitably, it compromised and more or less smothered incipient radicalism in international verbiage. But it said some useful things. One sign that it had not associated itself too closely with any one political bloc may be seen in the fact that the developing countries thought it didn't go far enough in defining a programme of actions towards a new world communications order, the Soviet bloc thought it too Western in approach and the Western countries thought it gave too much weight to State intervention in communication matters.

The subsequent resolution on the Report arrived at a better formulation than 'free and balanced flow', in supporting 'the removal of internal and external obstacles to a free flow and wider and better balanced dissemination of information and ideas'.

This debate will go on. So what can the West itself do? A passage in a document issued quite early by the MacBride Commission puts the main contrast succinctly:

On the one hand people stress the continued existence of barriers to the freedom of expression and information, together with the violation – whether overt or concealed – of the conditions necessary to the free flow of news, ideas and people;

On the other hand, it is held that the concept of the free flow of information, as it has existed for the past thirty years and as it still exists at the present time, is a doctrine that serves the interests of the most powerful countries helping them to secure their cultural domination under cover of liberal, and not unattractive, ideas.

It is surprising how many people working in communications in countries such as ours (though there are some good exceptions) hardly know of the existence of this debate and of its present critical stage. When they do learn of it, they are usually inclined to argue at first that nothing can be done to improve matters, to imply that international market mechanisms have the force of acts of God or to bring out the routine assertions about the principle of free circulation, as though the consequences of the interplay between that principle and market mechanisms are not even to be examined.

This is not good enough. More can be done than we are usually disposed to think, and should be done. Not just because to continue shrugging off the very existence of a problem plays straight into the hands of the dictators in some developing countries, and it is their own people who then suffer even greater deprivation; nor just because, unless we do show more understanding, regressive measures will be taken by developing countries to cut back the import of Western material and we may not be happy with what goes and what stays. We have to do more, above all, because not to do so is lazy and selfish to an inexcusable degree. But we all too often act like that, overtly or by default. Not too long ago I discussed, with a senior European diplomatic official, the wish in the developing world for a Law of the Sea which would prevent the technologically-advanced nations from colonising the sea bed for its minerals, and hence inspired the proposal that the sea bed outside territorial waters should come under UN jurisdiction. He regarded that as a Utopianism quite outside the bounds of discussion. 'Let them stop moaning,' he said, 'we are the only ones who have the *capacity* to exploit the sea bed and we have plenty to do in settling who does what between ourselves; we'll sort it out.' No wonder the Arabs began to use their oil as a political weapon; no wonder the world's primary producers are trying to act together effectively.

First, then, we should try to take the measure of the problem much better, to recognise the justice of other nations' fears, to be genuinely concerned and to show that we are concerned, not simply disguised latter-day imperialists. The West is justly under criticism. Some of the material we flood over the world is rotten by any standards, and we are rightly rebuked for simply letting it flow. That it flows within our own countries too does not reduce the problem; it brings it back where it belongs. The homogenised culture we are helping to bring about is not particularly attractive, either internationally or nationally.

If we do face the problem thus directly I believe, since I have faith in human inventiveness, that substantial improvements could emerge. The essence is to resolve the paradox: that our freedom must be maintained whilst not being allowed to become a way of restricting freedom for others.

Initiatives which are positive rather than restrictive are needed, initiatives towards which the West could show itself interested and ready to help in any way sought; for instance, in helping to set up indigenous regional or Third World news agencies and networks (such as Inter-Press Service). Some of our main agencies are helping in this way already, but more is needed.

These news agencies could hardly oust the existing ones; they could very usefully complement each other. Similarly, in the face of suggestions that there be rigid import quotas against Western material, the West should be ready to discuss some interim voluntary limitations and also to help with positive steps towards the emergence of more indigenous material. Even harder: the West should think more about the picture of the Third World it promotes in its own countries or exports to the Third World itself. I suspect these distortions are only a little worse than those in the pictures of their own countries which some news media promote; so, in tackling this aspect we would once again be helping to reduce both an external and an internal problem. But these are only hints; many more similarly practical steps could be thought of without too much difficulty.

By such steps and by much else the West would be reasserting its commitment to the idea of free thought and free circulation, those ideas which the West itself put at the heart of UNESCO's constitution. These kinds of principle – the rule of law, freedom for the individual, the democratic process, free exchanges, so many aspects of the whole field of human rights – these, rather than sophisticated technology, are the West's great gift to the world. The West itself does not always live up to those principles, externally or internally. In the matter of communications the crucial point, we have seen, is that she tends instead to use the idea of freedom as justification for the unfettered operation of market forces which distort and inhibit the freedoms of other people. We should not yield the importance of the principle of freedom, but should recognise its price and show that we are willing to try – in this matter at least – to ensure that all of us can have things both ways. We still have considerable moral capital among many intellectuals in the developing world since many of them, trained in the West, learned there to respect the freedoms of the West. They need support against those in their own countries who can all too easily argue that the West's insistence on freedom seems chiefly to be used to protect the freedom of the over-developed nations to rule the roost over the developing.   1978

CULTURE
AND ITS MINISTERS

For hundreds of years the cultural heritage of mankind was passed on, like a property, to a few heirs. Only slowly did the idea grow that culture, regardless of how it may be defined, is the property of no one. (Minister of Culture, France)

Socialist multinational art performs a new social function differing from that of former ages in content and aim. (Minister of Culture, USSR)

Culture defines the originality of the people in terms of its historic roots, and its readiness to face the future. Our culture is thus our identity card in the community of nations. (Minister of Culture of a New African State)

Among the governments of the world, and virtually right across the world, the last decade has seen an increased and unprecedented interest in 'culture' and in the role of the state in 'promoting cultural development.'

In 1970, when UNESCO held a world conference of Ministers of Culture – the first ever held – it found itself host to more ministers and their high officials than it had imagined in even the most optimistic forecasts. True, there were very few artists; but the conference was, in the terms by which ministerial conferences are assessed, exceptionally successful – chiefly, I think, because it allowed all these people (who by and large did not know one another) to take stock of common, new problems.

By now it would be difficult to find a sovereign state which does not have a Minister of Culture or someone with a similar position, whatever his title. The British still balk at the title 'Minister of Culture', but for years now they have had a 'Minister with Special Responsibility for the Arts,' or something similar. Inevitably, they are self-conscious about it: at the Venice Conference the then Minister confided to the assembled Plenary session: 'I will let you into a secret – in my country we have no clear idea what culture means.' Which baffled most of his hearers, until they decided it was 'typical British humour and understatement.' He was right, however, if patronising; and many of his listeners were in the same boat without always knowing.

Like Britain, the United States doesn't have a Minister of Culture; but it has arrangements for supporting the arts on a scale hardly thinkable ten or fifteen years ago. Among the nations which don't balk at the title, one thinks first of France and Malraux; and then of all the new nations which, no matter how poor they may be, appointed a Minister of Culture very quickly after their formal incorporation as sovereign states; or of the Eastern European countries where the Minister of Culture is likely to rank high in the supreme governing body.

If you go on to ask why 'culture' has become such a magic word to so many governments you are led into a thicket of contradictions, contradictions not only between countries but within the same Ministry or even the same Minister. Obviously, any unravelling of the main strands will do less than justice to the complexities and inter-weavings. Still, some main lines are predominant in some countries, some in others.

There is, first, the idea of culture as the acquiring of individual virtue. This is, among official attitudes, by far the most disinterested strain, marked by a benevolent, a missionary or a paternalistic spirit. After democratisation, the vote, literacy, there is culture; and that too must be spread; culture is a sort of silver-plating.

There are some less attractive variants of this first group of official attitudes. These lack benevolence, are mainly defensive and have developed in reaction to a feeling of threat. Their holders feel threatened by what they regard as masses of disaffected, rootless workers with their insistent transistors and insistent bodies, peeling on beaches.

Yet again, it is felt by some that 'cultivation' and the more and more sophisticated techniques of modern industry are related and support each other. The need to 'spread culture' is, in this view, a necessary concomitant of prosperous modern life. The Minister of Culture of one of the very few wealthy Asian nations can say: 'Long considered a luxury, culture is (today) generally understood as being essential for social and economic development . . .'

The second main group of official attitudes sees culture as an ideological underpinning, a support to the prevailing ideology. To people who hold this view culture, properly interpreted, leads inevit-

187

ably to their state's present form. Therefore, the role of the artist is to reflect, embody, celebrate, and justify that interpretation:

The art of socialist realism truthfully reflects in its various forms the exploits of the people in building the new society, disseminates among the people the noble ideas of revolutionary humanism and internationalism, calls upon them to struggle actively for peace and friendship among peoples, and educates in them a feeling of patriotism and a deep sense of civic duty.*

This implies set arts and fixed roles for artists. Art forms are pre-eminently channels for known truths, not answers provisionally arrived at after experiment. The assurance is considerable, because the categories are fixed:

Alongside the development of painting, graphic art, sculpture, and decorative-applied art, monumental art glorifying historical exploits of our people has, owing to the care lavished on it by the state, made particularly spectacular progress in recent years.*

The artist works in known forms and utters known truths. The notion of an artist as both inside and outside his society at the same time – personally engaged with his culture as he experiences it, not as it is interpreted to him by others, and therefore led also to try to stand outside that culture and all ready-made interpretations of it – this notion is, in a strict sense, almost inconceivable. People from other societies may talk about the 'subordination' and 'castration' of the artist in these circumstances, and in their own terms that makes sense. The Communist official will reply in his own terms too, and dismiss such talk as individualistic, bourgeois nonsense. Before that stage is reached, it is useful for Westerners to have realised the total alienness of their attitude to Communist thinking.

It is important at this stage not to confuse methods with principles. The methods of censorship at all levels in Communist countries may be and often are brutal and horrifying; but the principles which are being protected by those measures are regarded as self-evident and indisputable. In this view, the artist does not have a privileged relation to the truth. He is the spokesman or celebrant, through a particular set of forms, of ineluctable truths decided elsewhere and by other processes. His individual views, therefore, are of no particular importance or interest.

I remember one occasion when a Western European artist, shocked by a nasty instance of intellectual censorship by an Eastern European Government, cancelled an agreement to perform in that

* Minister of Culture, USSR.

country. It seemed his one sanction. Perhaps he thought that he might shock the Ministry of Culture into seeing the error of its ways. If so, he misread the situation. The Vice-Minister for Culture, who handled the matter, was much more shocked than the Western European artist. He was furious that some self-important peacock of an individual had thought he had any grounds, right, or status to put his nose into what were, manifestly and only, matters of governmental decision: someone, battling for a compromise, tried to explain to him that Western artists like to see their artistic and moral integrity as one, and therefore would not happily practise their arts in a situation in which they felt their consciences compromised. The Vice-Minister was outraged. He raised his voice very high and shouted with total conviction, 'So much shit!' And there the matter ended.

Whatever the calls for détente, this attitude is not likely to change substantially during our lifetimes. Here, the ideological barriers to change are as strong as those against, say, abortion in a very devout, traditionally Roman Catholic country. Add to that the internal political dangers of a relaxation of government controls over art, and you realise that any changes which might encourage the idea of the right and freedom of individuals to speak and write on major matters according to their consciences will be insignificant. Such changes will usually be the result of some particular political need of the moment – and so ad hoc, and liable to be withdrawn when the need changes – rather than part of an alteration in the basic position. A profound change in policy is highly unlikely.

The third main strand in official attitudes is based on the idea of culture as national identity. This is the strongest drive of all; cultural development is assumed here to be politically crucial. So a Minister of Culture of a new nation can typically say (it is a basic theme): 'We can never hope to build a nation if we are not united by a common culture.'

Naturally, this drive is especially strong in Africa and Asia. It is even stronger among those nations which feel that their sense of identity as peoples was subverted or destroyed by Western colonialisation. The aim is to get back to what they once were, or think they were, to get back over the deep ditch cut by colonialism, to reconnect with their roots so that the good sap flows again:

In a country which has successively seen seven languages and seven different cultures, and in which a score of political regimes have done their utmost to reduce the natives to the rank of second-class inhabitants and destroy even the memory of their predecessors, 'national culture' is scarcely an adequate term to use.*

The complications here are enormous – especially since so many of the ruling groups in the new nations have only a vestigial or nostalgic memory of their own cultures. They are products of the Sorbonne or the London School of Economics or, the younger ones, of Cal. Tech. or Harvard Law School. The tension between their acquired Western culture and their original, native culture can be great.

When we come to speak of our own values, we find ourselves following patterns derived from our imported cultural requirements. Thus we are always, or almost always, somewhat apart from the mass of our people, since nothing in our intellectual and cultural background predisposes us to have an insight into their concerns or to understand their deep-seated aspirations.

It is therefore time for us to turn to the people to hear the message of our cultures, handed down by word of mouth from generation to generation, so that we can adapt them to our present-day life without allowing ourselves to be disconcerted by their diversity. What we have to do instead is to lay hold on the similarities – a sustained effort to adapt and to return to the fountain-head – since we, the intellectual élites, have been nurtured by foreign cultures rather than by the realities of our native African soil.**

But, and it is a very big *but,* the rulers themselves, the present rulers – be they Normaliens or alumni of MIT or ex-lance-corporals – want to stay in power. Yet they rule over newly created societies, many of which have never before been unified. Some of these new nations were formed by the departing colonial powers, drawing straight lines on a map or carving intricate, or politically and economically significant, new boundaries. They include people who have been historically divided on tribal lines and have sometimes been hostile towards one another, people who may well speak quite different languages which may not yet have orthographies.

Thus we come to the real rub. The search is not only for national identity. It is also, and even more strongly, for national unity. The Minister of the new African state spoke of the need not to be 'disconcerted by (the) diversity of cultures' in each new nation, and of the need to 'lay hold on the similarities'. That is the heart of the matter. There has to be a centre round which the similarities can be made to accrete. Which culture, which language shall be chosen as the official culture and language of the new nation? The answer is

* Minister of Culture, Tunisia.
** Minister of Culture, new African State.

usually pragmatic: the culture and language of the ruling group, of the president and his henchmen.

And what history will the nation have? There may very well be no national history but only the histories of different tribes – and those probably oral – (there are few written histories, and those are often produced by offbeat colonisers and their missionaries). In the years immediately preceding liberation, the beginnings of a national self-consciousness may have been forged through the act of kicking out the colonisers. Usually, however, the 'national' history is a selective compound of events and figures, set into a frame which tends to justify the present set up and the present ruling group. As with the Communist states, all things move ineluctably to the present happy state of affairs, to a people who love the president and the one party.

It then becomes the duty of the Minister of Culture to illustrate, spread, and reinforce that history. In that effort songs, stories, verses, dances, the full range of oral and craft traditions are given an increased and all-embracing symbolic significance. So the Minister of Culture has a key role. In all this (and no matter how vivid one's interest in the differences between cultures) the spirit begins to flag under the barrage of claims that this or that culture has a mystical hold on the truth, a beauty to which no other culture – least of all those of the technological, corrupted West – can aspire. The simplest of local apothegms are held to capture deep truths with all the power of Shakespeare. Sometimes one feels like making a case for the holy perfection of Yorkshire culture and the imaginative power of its idiomatic sayings.

I have described this pattern only in terms of new nations. But a variant of it can be found in some old but relatively small nations which are now caught in the hegemonic embrace of a super power. With them the rediscovery of the *exact* nature of their traditional national culture – in these cases, there really has been a long-standing *national* culture – is part of their assertion of their own identity against Big Brother outside. I think of Ceauşescu's Rumania or of the immense Polish interest in 'national cultural values' which is expressed regularly in resolutions presented by that country to the UN General Assembly and the UNESCO General Conference.

All three strands of the huge, new, official interest in culture I have described share these qualities: they assume the responsibility of the state for more than material matters; they express a search for some kind of cohesion or harmony in societies, in a period when religious cohesion is regarded as no longer possible or not desirable; and they imply that 'culture' is at bottom a very serious and probably a directly political matter.

It may be useful now to approach the subject from a different angle. In non-governmental discussions, the word 'culture' is commonly used with a wide range of meanings. We may say that these meanings cluster round two main poles, the aesthetic and the anthropological: the one conceives culture as having to do primarily with art forms, their creation and appreciation; the other defines culture as 'the whole way of life' of a people (a way of life of which art objects are admittedly a significant part). Similarly, one can often recognise two main impulses behind the widespread contemporary drive to 'spread' culture, to make it available. These are, respectively, the 'handing-on' or 'transmission-belt' approach and the 'process' or 'inner change' approach. With the first, it is assumed that one is giving something, with the second that one is helping to make something happen. The first tends to put very great importance on access to 'the high arts' and their wider appreciation by those who have previously been denied that opportunity; the second seeks above all a certain kind of change in the individual consciousness, the arriving at a certain temper of mind, a certain 'fineness' of spirit (a fineness which may certainly have been acquired in the course of learning to respond to 'the high arts').

If we examine the three main official approaches to culture in the light of the preceding assumptions we see that both types of assumption are present in official thinking, though nowhere in a pure state. The simplest combination might seem to be the aesthetic plus the transmission-belt views: that is, 'culture' equals the high arts; and 'cultural development' equals transmitting them. But no one holds that combination of views in quite so neat a form.

The combinations are, instead, roughly like this. One group of nations – let us call them the developed, mixed-economy, free-enterprise, open group – certainly tend to see 'culture' as having primarily to do with artistic forms and objects. Their approach to the business of spreading culture often looks, at first glance, like a fairly pure transmission-belt form. One sees this in particular, for example, when they discuss 'the role of the mass media in cultural development'. Television is not seen as a new kind of communication which can create new forms and new relationships with audiences. It is seen as a channel through which we send existing good things. But the

192

attitudes of this group are rarely as simple as that. Listen a little longer and you almost always discover that, behind the apparently simple pattern 'known good goods → channel of transmission,' there lies – though not always consciously – the idea of culture as *process,* the enormous, awe-inspiring idea that in the last resort the aim of culture is to refine, elevate, and *free* the individual and his independent consciousness.

The attitudes of a second group of nations – who may be called the developed socialist group – combine some of the elements above and leave one element very severely alone. They talk predominantly about culture as certain art forms and styles, almost entirely inherited from the pre-Communist period and on the whole fixed and hardly subject to modification. But they also talk about the beauty and distinctiveness of their respective cultures and cultural values in a clearly anthropological way; and they want 'their peoples' to appreciate those values (though they are then talking about the appreciation of attitudes identified by authority, not of a continuous process or a becoming). They therefore overwhelmingly see the attempt to spread culture in its transmission-belt form. One is passing something on, not causing something to happen, least of all to the individual.

The new nations, by contrast with both the other groups, put the main emphasis in their definitions of culture on the anthropological aspect. They naturally give very great weight to their artistic traditions, but to those traditions seen as significant expressions of the idea of culture as a 'whole way of life'. It is the whole way of life of 'our people' which gets the main attention. The spreading of culture is less a matter of individual self-fulfilment as an immersion in, a dyeing in the vat of one's traditional culture. There is no suggestion of a movement towards an independent critical self-awareness (or towards the free play of informed opinion which the existence of such individuals can set off). It is rather as though people were expected, separately or – preferably – in known groups (family, village, sub-tribe, etc.), to become linked umbilically to the one great mother.

All of this makes the planning of large-scale cultural conferences particularly interesting. Two years after the Venice World Conference which I mentioned at the beginning, UNESCO arranged a similar conference for European ministers of culture only. Its most important theme was 'access and participation,' how one makes it possible for more people to approach the arts and also actively to take

193

part in them. This is very much a 'developed area' approach, though in its simpler forms (and we did not hear many subtle formulations at the European Ministers' Conference) a very out-of-date one. The more important theme of *freedom* to create and to appreciate was not seriously discussed.

But when, later, a similar conference was prepared for Asia, 'access and participation' played a lesser role, seemed not quite relevant. The assumption was that you couldn't propose to give or increase access to an element in which most people were assumed to be still immersed anyway, from which they had never been separated.

One heard, instead, much about the existence of diverse, living, local, oral cultural traditions and of the importance of using the new mass media in such a way that they linked on to those traditions and strengthened them instead of swamping and destroying them. The chaos of life in the huge new cities of the developing world lay like a nightmare reality or an even worse portent behind these debates. And of course one heard much about cultural identity and unity but very little about upon what particular historical bases – in any one nation – that identity and unity should be established.

In its turn, the Conference of African Ministers in late 1975 put enormous emphasis on the African cultural personality as a whole and (even more than the Asian Conference) on the search for cultural unity within each particular new state. The generals and their lieutenants have learned that language in some sophisticated forms.

In the face of all these more or less impure elements in the official interest in culture, one is bound to wonder why those of us who live in developed, open, non-paternalistic, non-centralised, non-authoritarian societies should welcome official support for cultural development at all. Aren't the officials bound to get things wrong, both the definitions and the consequent actions? Isn't *any* difficulty or shortage for artists preferable to *any* state intervention, no matter how hedged in with saving clauses or how apparently well-intentioned it might be? Wouldn't it be better for governments to put their money into indisputably useful activities such as cancer research or practical development aid?

This is a good, strong argument. Sometimes, especially after seeing at close hand a particularly gross or silly example of state intervention, I have felt like settling for that position; and all the time one side of me would *prefer* to be able to settle for it.

But still, I usually end by thinking there are certain things apropos culture which 'public authorities' – I prefer to say 'public authorities' rather than 'governments' because public authorities can be non-governmental, and help to culture is usually better given in that way – can usefully do. But before we discuss these possibilities we really have to ask what definition of 'culture' we are working under. What exactly might an open, developed society justifiably mean by 'cultural development'?

It is tempting but hardly adequate to take refuge in that favourite English formulation: 'We don't like definitions or abstractions. So we won't try to define culture, art, etc. But we can recognise them when we see them, and that's the important thing.'

Of the three different general definitions of culture assumed by officialdom which I described above, the third – culture as state-formation – clearly doesn't fit the kind of society I am now talking about. It is too centralist, too authoritarian, too closed, too anthropological, and too collective. In developed open societies the high level of education and of communication, the existence of multiple cross-currents of opinion, the stress placed (no matter how much it may be subverted by the great power-blocs in a society) on the freedom of the individual to make up his own mind – all put such societies well past the point at which they could or would promote a unitary, traditional, national culture.

The middle definition – culture as ideological underpinning – is even more obviously inapplicable and against the nature of open societies. Yet one can argue that, at another level, such societies (and indeed all societies, no matter how 'advanced' they may be) do promote a more or less generally acceptable version of both the national culture and the national ideology. The whole mythology of the 'American way of life' as put forth by schools and the media is a good instance of that.

Still, the official definition of cultural development in these societies tends to be, as we saw much earlier, more aesthetic than anthropological, more or less Arnoldian, to stress rather heavily certain particular forms of 'high culture' but also to pay implicit due to the idea of cultural development as a process within the individual and within society, a refining and 'uplifting' process.

In short, this approach has habitually given a dominant role to certain fixed forms (the high arts) in stimulating and validating a desired process. Clearly, no definition of the cultures of these societies which omitted their achievements in music, literature and the visual arts would be adequate. Yet the role of those arts in the whole matter of cultural development has been regarded in too fixed a way by official thinking. They have been seen as constituting a pantheon to which a much larger-than-usual audience is now to be admitted, for their own greater good.

There are changes under way here. It has been easy for cultural analysts over the last twenty years or so to show the inadequacy of the above assumptions about culture, their unconsidered or ill-considered, social-class foundations (the high arts of the high bourgeoisie); and generally and rightly to argue for a greater pluralism in forms, styles and sources.

The result is that today you would have difficulty in finding anyone in the field – a 'cultural administrator' or 'cultural entrepreneur' or 'cultural animator' – who did not try to practise considerable pluralism, who was as ready to give funds to street theatre as to opera, to the newest pop group (so long as he had been convinced that it was at one musical frontier or another) as to a symphony orchestra, or to a study of the strip cartoon as to one of poetry.

All of which is a far cry from the neatly interlocking set of artistic and social assumptions which guided most such disbursers of public funds a couple of decades ago. The difficulty about changing these assumptions, however, is that as often as not the baby has gone out with the bath water. There are, to change the metaphor, deep ditches on both sides of the road towards cultural development – and by now a great many people, having climbed out of the highbrow right-hand ditch with cries of release and salvation, have fallen just as heavily into the populist left-hand. So now they insist that everything is as valuable as everything else, that only cultural snobs and culture vultures would try to 'make distinctions' or introduce, into any discussion of aims for the use of the public funds available, the dread word 'standards'.

Someone will in turn react against that position, and probably soon; a reaction is by now overdue if we are going to understand better what we really might justifiably mean by support for cultural development in open societies. But for the present, if you like a vigorous but unpopular argument, you need only go to one of those frequent conferences of cultural planners and criticise cultural egalitarianism and populist levelling.

If I think of the art I know best, which is literature, it seems to me that this art asks for two kinds of disposition in its readers.

The first is a readiness to learn to respond to the medium itself.

This begins as a love free of ulterior purposes – the sort of fascination, with words and all the intricate objects into which they can be shaped, which makes someone a poet rather than a politician. Without this love of language itself one isn't, though one might be engaged in all sorts of useful and interesting things, engaged with literature, with the art, at all.

The second disposition is a readiness to be, so far as is possible, disinterestedly involved in the exploration of human experience. I mean willing to be introduced to experiences outside those which merely confirm our own ways of seeing things. This disposition is much less valued or encouraged throughout the world than we in the West like to assume. It means trying to stand outside ourselves and our societies and entertaining possibilities we would probably, for our peace of mind, rather not entertain. It means feeling unsupported by the rigid and firm 'truths' of any group at all. It requires from the reader some of those qualities which should be required from the writer himself in the face of the experiences he is trying to capture. I know of no fully adequate words for these qualities but I will call them here radicalism and honesty. Without 'the gift of language' no one is likely to write well. But the gift can be wasted and frittered away. Without radicalism and honesty towards the total business of exploring-experience-through-language, no one is likely to produce a work of literature.

The authentic marks of literature, the signs that we are in the presence of creative art, rather than of some other activity such as instruction, exposition, domination, persuasion, flattery or amusement, is the presence of those two quite inseparable qualities. The search for radicalism and honesty towards experience compels the same attitudes towards language. But it may – and perhaps more often does – work the other way round; a love of language demands the effort at radicalism and honesty in the use of language; and from that moment you are concerned not only with the words in themselves but with the experience the words are seeking to capture. Dishonest words show a dishonest handling of experience; the attempt to be honest towards experience drives one to remake the language and the forms.

By now we are fully involved with the matter of standards, with making distinctions (even if we do not actually lay them out point by point, but rather express them by closing a particular book at page three, or by recognising that a certain poem has nothing to give us).

We are a long way past the point at which categories such as 'high art' and 'low art' can seem useful, since we can by now recognise that what sometimes professes, by its forms and tones, to be high art may be dead toward language and experience, inauthentic, unconvinced and unconvincing. And we may find, in work conventionally assigned to other levels of 'brow,' signs of just that authenticity. At this point we are beginning to stand up in the middle of the road; we have crawled out of both the right- and the left-hand ditches.

The most important aspect of those qualities essential to the creation of art, those qualities which are therefore essential to a well-founded justification for encouraging 'cultural development,' is one many of us simply take for granted. Yet over large areas of the world it is not only *not* taken for granted, it is not even recognised or admitted. Nor are there indications that readiness to admit it is growing. This is the assumption that the effort to arrive at an open, discriminating, individual consciousness (whether in an artist or in those who respect his work) is a good thing in itself, that the indivi-dual has nothing more important to address himself to than this kind of effort. For this assumption means that the arts, though they need not directly concern themselves with 'moral striving' and though they do not in themselves necessarily make any one of us, artists and audiences, one whit better morally, are nevertheless the purest of all human activities, the freest expression of the human interest in the meaning of experience, in trying to see life fully and straight by capturing and ordering it in language or some other medium. If that almost impenetrable phrase, 'beauty is truth, truth beauty' means anything, it means something like this.

On this view one is overwhelmingly assuming, in any talk about 'cultural development,' the worthwhileness of an internal process, one which begins with the person and assumes that a worthwhile sense of community can only be reached by moving out from that secured base in the individual consciousness. At this point one is saying something extraordinarily demanding; and one has reached the only indispensable foundation for the encouragement of cultural development. The rest is propaganda or entertainment.

But still, in what we like to call 'free' societies, shouldn't people be left to find out such truths for themselves? Yes, ideally. But in fact no societies are free; all societies deform. The authoritarian society deforms as an act of policy. It is not therefore likely to provide antibodies to its own planned deformations. Open societies deform because of their inherent drives; but they can sometimes be persuaded to encourage activities which try to counteract those drives.

Open societies, by their built-in technological thrust, by their reduction of most aspects of life to forms of consumption, by the way their systems of communication – from education through newspapers to television – support these characteristics, such societies concentrate choices, seek to narrow and homogenise taste in goods, styles, attitudes, in art forms and in responses to experience as much as in motor cars or soft drinks. All this affects company directors as much as truck drivers. We are not talking about a dispossessed working class.

One *can*, however, introduce a social-class point. In such societies, for all their 'freedom' and 'openness,' there is still less opportunity for many people to become imaginatively and intellectually aware than there is for others. I do not mean – though it is true, but is a result rather than a cause – that many people, and especially young people, cannot afford to go to the opera or theatre. I mean rather that a great many forces ensure that it is harder for a working-class child to break out of the centralising and narrowing spiral of choice than it is for one who has been brought up in a home with books, one where television is sometimes switched off, or one who has been to a school where the weight of predominant attitudes did not dismiss the idea of a drama group or a voluntary painting class or a discussion group, or one who can reasonably expect to go on to university.

On the basis of all this – on the argument for the *possible* liberating power of the arts, and on the fact that all societies, if left to their own devices, tend to limit rather than liberate – one can found the case for public intervention in favour of cultural development. The basic assumption must be that most of us have more promise than we, whether we are looking at others or considering ourselves, are led to believe. So public authorities must contribute, not so as to provide a glazed sugar-coating over 'the masses', but so as to help break up the very concept of 'masses' itself; they must gamble on the inherent possibilities of all people, and work towards opening up, widening, increasing, choices. Well-conceived initiatives of this sort almost invariably show that most of us have more imaginative and intellectual energies than a market-research, consumers' profile would suggest or could even begin to admit. Such profiles or prophecies, in the nature of the setup, tend to be self-fulfilling. Like sleepwalkers, we tend to go where we are led in the half-light.

199

But, to rephrase an old chestnut, how can we know what we like to do till we see what it is possible to do? This is a far more adequate motto for public officials than that even hoarier expression of a 'dilemma', about whether one should 'give the people what they want' or 'give them what they ought to have'. This false contradiction has served the marketeers of taste immensely well; and it has scared away, or made tongue-tied, many public authorities who wished to use public money to help broaden opportunities. After all – the opponents of public intervention say – isn't it obvious that, respect the arts as we all may, the major instruments of communication do precisely 'give people what they want'. Don't the viewing and reading figures prove it? Isn't it just as obvious, they go on, that the very idea of giving people what they *ought* to have is an élitist, patronising, paternalistic, do-gooding relic of authoritarianism and not to be indulged in at any cost?

That false dilemma still has horns strong enough to impale a lot of people. The providers do not 'give people what they want' in anything other than a very simple and limiting sense. They do certainly seek out those things which amuse more of us more of the time than others, and then concentrate on providing them. They are not concerned with other things which we, if we were from time to time regarded as belonging to other groupings than that of a great solidified mass, might want and want more intensely and actively. In short, their definition of 'want' is based on the assumption that you provide well if you find the least controversial common denominator of current taste; it therefore reinforces the current spectrum of taste and the system which produces it. In the deepest possible sense, it works against change.

Similarly, the formulation 'giving people what they *ought* to have' is a falsely reductive one, an instance of cultural slogan warfare. But translate it into something like: helping to make available more and different things than the centralising and narrowing drive of the market allows; assume that most of us (again, not a 'benighted working class' only) can enjoy, respond to, a far greater range of intellectual and imaginative experiences than the present achievements of our educational and communication systems would lead anyone to believe. You are then in an altogether different gallery. One very powerful English 'communicator' once said that no one who has not run a huge communications instrument – in this instance, a popular newspaper – has any idea just how low and limited the taste of 'the masses' really is. Did he really think that either the reality or the potentialities of his readers – in their day-to-day home lives or working lives – were adequately caught, defined, illustrated in the particular frame of assumed attitudes found daily in the great mass instrument he was responsible for? Apparently he did. He too, incidentally, was generally regarded as a 'very cultivated' man.

The range of things we might appreciate is far wider than he, or any other of the highly placed operators of modern society, can allow themselves to believe. If they did come to accept this premise, they would then be hung up on the appalling question of *choice*. If 'potentials' are the starting-point, if one cannot decide what to make available from a simple feedback of numbers, by the gross test of the existing common denominators of taste, how on earth *can* one decide *what* to offer? At this point we are at last facing a real but useful dilemma. Most successful experience in this area confirms that a good rule of thumb, one which works from the assumption that most other people are inherently no less sensitive than we are, is to choose between possibilities not out of some cultural-pyramid theory ('leading people onwards and upwards from brow to brow') but on the basis of how far things excite and challenge and move those particular people who for the moment have to decide. They may sometimes fall on their faces, and should be able to recognise when they are being self-deceptive or self-indulgent. But serious enthusiasm is a better general guide than either patronage or cynicism.

All of which leads to the argument that public authorities should make experiments of a sort and to a degree which commercial authorities cannot dare to make – experiments with ways of increasing 'access and participation', and experiments with no-strings ways of helping artists. Add the public authorities' role in supporting performances of those arts (opera, ballet, symphony orchestras, etc.) which require a larger capital outlay and larger recurrent expenditure than audience receipts are likely to bring in, and there is basically little more the public authorities should do; except thereafter to keep well off the grass. I would, however, be inclined to add this qualification: that if the public authorities had to choose between either encouraging artists directly or trying to promote greater appreciation of the arts generally, I believe they should choose the latter. It is safer for all concerned. Almost inevitably, direct official support for artists causes artists themselves insensibly to acquire inhibitions against being *too* shocking, too way-out. Better to help

audiences grow, so that artists get their support obliquely, from sufficiently large, free, critical and responsive publics.

Still — to double back at the close – some public authorities do try
to help experimentation.

I wonder if those in authority are wise and brave enough to encourage the
showing of experimental art and new interpretations of the classical tradition.
All really great art disturbs our thoughts and feelings and shows one something of the truth of the human condition. There are those who see a political
risk here. But governments must take this risk if men are to be free to become
confident, creative and responsible citizens!

It was a British Minister speaking. The rhetoric is certainly plummy
and the generalisations rather facile, but the occasion was a large
ministerial conference, and in them one does not expect close
analysis. And when one thinks of what is *usually* said on such
occasions and of what is *actually* done in many countries in the cause
of 'cultural development', a statement like that – and the fact that it
is to some slight extent practised in a few countries – is a refreshingly
good fact in an almost overwhelmingly naughty world.   1977

INDEX

THE DEVELOPMENT
OF THE INFANT
AND YOUNG CHILD

NORMAL AND ABNORMAL

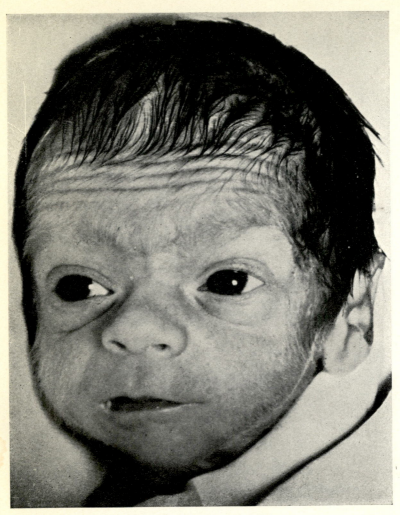

"What does the future hold?"
(A normal premature baby.)

to face title page

THE DEVELOPMENT
OF THE INFANT
AND YOUNG CHILD
NORMAL AND ABNORMAL

BY

R. S. ILLINGWORTH
M.D. LEEDS, F.R.C.P., D.P.H., D.C.H.

Professor of Child Health, The University of Sheffield.
Paediatrician, The Children's Hospital, Sheffield, and the
Jessop Hospital for Women, Sheffield.

FOURTH EDITION

E. & S. LIVINGSTONE LTD.
EDINBURGH AND LONDON

1970

First Edition 1960
Second Edition . . . 1963
Third Edition 1966
Reprinted 1967
Fourth Edition . . . 1970

SBN 443 00677 6

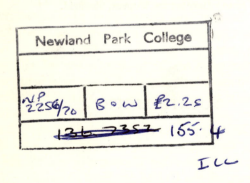
Printed in Great Britain

PREFACE TO THE FOURTH EDITION

FOR the purpose of this new edition every word of the previous edition was read and checked. As a result a large number of alterations have been made, including the addition of over 120 new references, and the removal of some old out-dated ones. Many chapters have been completely rearranged and largely rewritten. I have added an important new section entitled "What we can and cannot do in developmental assessment", because I think that it is most important that everyone concerned with children should know the possibilities and limitations of our assessment methods. In all several hundred additions and alterations have been made in order to bring this book thoroughly up to date. Nine new illustrations have been added.

I have tried to make the chapters on the developmental history and examination more practical, by naming the minimum essential features of the history and examination as distinct from the optimum and more comprehensive examination which is necessary in more difficult cases.

In view of comments made by a reviewer of the previous addition, I wish to make it clear again that this book is not intended to cover psychological development and variations, such as the basis of behaviour problems. I have covered these elsewhere – in The Normal Child (1968, 4th Edition, London, Churchill).

Plates No. 65, 68, 70, 95, 96, 99, 101, 102, 103, 104, 105, 106, 113 are by myself; all the other photographs are by the Photographic Department of the United Sheffield Hospitals.

SHEFFIELD, 1970.   R.S.I.

PREFACE

A THOROUGH knowledge and understanding of the normal development of the infant and young child is just as fundamental to anyone
concerned with the care of children, especially paediatricians, as
is anatomy to the surgeon. Family doctor, paediatricians and
others must know the normal, and the variations from the normal,
before they attempt to diagnose the abnormal. I doubt whether a
paediatrician will complete any out-patient clinic without having
had to make at least one developmental assessment. Without
such an assessment he is unable to make a proper diagnosis, to
arrange proper treatment, and to help the parents or family
doctor or school medical officer as much as he should.

The doctor inevitably has to assess the development of every
baby which he sees in a well baby clinic, for otherwise he is not
doing his job properly; he could not hope to diagnose the abnormal,
to detect the early signs of cerebral palsy or of mental subnormality,
of a hearing or visual defect, of subluxation of the hip, or of
hydrocephalus, unless he were first conversant with the normal
and then looked for the variations from the normal. In the hospital
ward one does not carry out a developmental examination on an
ill child with bronchopneumonia, and in a private house one does
not assess the development of every young child with asthma;
but in both places there are innumerable circumstances in which
a developmental examination is essential, and without it the
examination is seriously incomplete.

It is because I regard developmental assessment as an essential
part of everyday practice that I wrote this book, in order to
describe just what can be learnt about a child's development with
a minimum of equipment in an ordinary mixed clinic, and not in
a special room, at a special time, with special complicated equipment. Everyone dealing with children needs this knowledge. It is
not just the province of an expert who does nothing else.

Because I am convinced that the best assessment must be based
on a full consideration of prenatal, perinatal and environmental
factors which affect development, and on a careful developmental
history, I have written separate chapters on these matters. I
have placed particular emphasis on the normal variations which
occur in all fields of development, and on the reasons for these

variations. I have repeatedly emphasised the difficulties in developmental assessment, and the reasons why assessments in infancy can never have a high correlation with intelligence tests in older children, and still less with success in later life. I have discussed in detail the reasons for the limitations in developmental testing. Perhaps the most important chapter is the last one – on the pitfalls in developmental assessment.

The limitations and fallacies must be known and understood. There is a rapidly increasing interest in the physiology and pathology of pregnancy in relation to the foetus, and attempts to correlate events in pregnancy with the development of the infant are liable to give entirely fallacious results unless the difficulties of developmental testing, its possibilities and its limitations, are fully understood. As in other kinds of research, one must avoid the mistake of making accurate analyses of inaccurate data.

This book does not attempt to discuss the normal physical and emotional development of the child. I have confined the book to the study of the infant and preschool child.

I wish to express my gratitude to Arnold Gesell and Catherine Amatruda, above all others, for giving me the privilege to work under them and for teaching me the fundamentals of child development, so that I could then continue to learn for the rest of my working life.

R.S.I.

CONTENTS

CHAPTER 1

THE NEED FOR KNOWLEDGE OF CHILD DEVELOPMENT

All those with responsibility for the care of children, whether child welfare doctors, general practitioners, paediatricians or others, require a thorough knowledge of the normal, and of variations from it, in order that they can recognise the abnormal —and in particular mental and physical handicaps. They will need this knowledge on almost every day of their work.

Every parent feels a natural curiosity about the development of his children, and if with a previous pregnancy there had been an unfortunate experience, such as a miscarriage or stillbirth, or if the child born alive proved to be mentally or physically handicapped, there is all the more reason why he should be concerned about the wellbeing of subsequent children. Sometimes there is a potentially noxious factor during pregnancy, such as an infection, injury or illness, or there is a difficult delivery, and the child is ill at birth or shortly after, so that the parents are anxious to know whether he is developing normally or not. There may be a family history of mental deficiency, epilepsy, or other handicap, which heightens their anxiety. The family doctor, and others who are responsible for children, need to be in a position to reassure them with a fair degree of confidence, based on the necessary knowledge.

A husband and wife, who are unable to have children of their own, may decide to adopt. They should be able to rely on a doctor to give a sound opinion as to whether the child offered to them for adoption is mentally normal or not. In my opinion the decision is of such momentous importance for the happiness of the parents and child, that the paediatrician should be the one to examine such babies. A thorough knowledge of child development, and in particular of all the factors which may have affected his development in the past and which may affect it in the future, is essential for a reasonable opinion to be possible. It is a double tragedy for a husband and wife, who have been unable after several years of marriage to satisfy their normal desire to have children of their own, to adopt a child who subsequently proves to be mentally defective.

It is a worse tragedy if a child who is in fact normal is said to be mentally defective or spastic and therefore unsuitable for adoption. Such a mistake is likely to cause serious psychological trauma and emotional deprivation, and may affect his whole life. At the time of writing this I saw a four year old who was in a foster home because a doctor had said three and a half years previously that the child was spastic and unsuitable for adoption. He was not, therefore, adopted. In fact the child was absolutely normal. The result of the mistake was that the boy had to change homes and 'parents' when four years old, in order to be adopted. All too often babies are passed as suitable for adoption without any developmental examination at all, merely on clinical impression, and rejected without any expert examination or assessment.

On innumerable other occasions the doctor needs to call on his knowledge of child development. He is confronted with a child with an odd-looking face, or a skull of unusual shape or size and he wants to assess his attainments and the outlook for him. The baby may have a mild degree of hydrocephalus or craniostenosis, and the physician is asked by the surgeon for advice as to whether he should operate or not. The physician will be guided by the present attainments of the child in relation to the previous rate of development, and by the subsequently observed rate of progress.

The physician is anxious to know whether a child who was born many weeks prematurely, or with a severe degree of asphyxia, or who had cyanotic attacks or convulsions in the newborn period, or a subdural haematoma, is progressing satisfactorily. He is constantly confronted with the problem of convulsions, whether due to epilepsy or other causes, and knows the frequent relationship between convulsions and physical and mental handicaps. He sees children with congenital anomalies, such as cleft palate or congenital heart disease, and wonders whether there is additional mental retardation. He wants to follow up children born with haemolytic disease of the newborn. He wants to observe the rate of mental development of children with hypothyroidism under his care, as one of the checks on the adequacy of his treatment. He is anxious to know whether a head injury, or an attack of pyogenic meningitis, or of virus encephalitis, has left any permanent mental sequelae. He is repeatedly faced with the problem of children with cerebral palsy, and wants to assess their mental development, with particular regard to the type of education most suitable for them.

He is often asked to advise about babies and young children whose behaviour is bad, or who are backward in one or several fields of development. He is concerned about the young baby with severe feeding difficulties, such as difficulty in swallowing and excessive regurgitation. In all these he needs to eliminate mental and physical defects by his developmental examination.

The physician is constantly confronted with the child who is backward in all fields of development, and in whom mental deficiency is suspected. An incorrect diagnosis of mental deficiency is a tragedy, and the diagnosis must never be even hinted at until one is sure of one's ground. Early diagnosis, however, is important for many reasons. It may provide the pointer to curable conditions, such as developing hypothyroidism, or to certain other metabolic conditions, such as phenylketonuria, which are amenable to treatment; and it is desirable that the parents should be told about the position, so that they can face and plan the future. I have asked innumerable mothers how soon they think that parents should be informed that their child is backward. Without exception they have answered that they should be told as soon as possible, so that they are not left to find out for themselves after months or even years of lingering doubts, often after visits to one doctor after another, in the effort to find someone who will tell them the truth. The diagnosis, however, must be based on really sound evidence, for it is a shocking tragedy if parents are told that their child is mentally defective, when in fact he is normal.

It is important to distinguish backwardness of environmental origin from backwardness due to a low innate level of intelligence. In the former case a great deal can be done to help, and to raise the child's performance to a higher level. In the latter case the correct diagnosis should lead, amongst other things, to the avoidance of overprotection by the parents, and of efforts to push him beyond his capabilities.

In addition, having decided that a child is mentally backward, one will try to give the parents the prognosis with regard to the likelihood of his learning to walk, talk, go to school and earn his living.

I should have thought that the rôle of developmental diagnosis was obvious and I may seem to have laboured the point by citing the above examples. Several writers, however, have belittled its value, and criticised any attempts to assess a child's development. Many of these doubts are related to the firm conviction possessed by many that developmental tests in infancy have no predictive value.

CHAPTER 2

THE PREDICTIVE VALUE OF DEVELOPMENTAL ASSESSMENT

The Development of Mental Testing

I propose to give only a brief outline of the development of mental testing. For a more complete account the reader should refer to textbooks of Psychology.

STUDIES OF INDIVIDUAL CHILDREN

According to Goodenough[24] Tiedemann in Germany (1787) was the first to publish a detailed record of the development of one child, but it was not until Charles Darwin[13] in 1877 published a detailed account of the development of one of his own ten children that interest was aroused. Charles Darwin wrote: 'My first child was born on December 27th, 1839, and I at once commenced to make notes on the first dawn of the various experiences which he exhibited, for I felt convinced, even at this early period, that the most complex and fine shades of expression must all have had a gradual and natural origin'. He described the rooting reflex, hearing in the newborn period, the absence of tears in the first few weeks except when his coat sleeve accidentally caught his child's eye, the first co-ordinated movements of the hands at 6 weeks, the cephalocaudal sequence of development, the reciprocal kick, hand regard at 4 months, the first sign of anger (at 10 weeks), of humour (at 3 months), of fear, imitation and of enjoyment of the sound of the piano (at 4 months). He described the first association of a person with her name (at 7 months), the first signs of jealousy, love, curiosity, association of ideas, deceit, moral sense, inhibitions, laughter, shyness, sympathy, and handedness. He had already published his famous and fascinating book *The Expression of the Emotions in Man and Animals*,[12] which incorporated some of these and many other observations on crying, sobbing, laughter and other emotions.

In 1893 Shinn[40] published one of the most complete records of a young baby's development. In 1931 Shirley[41] wrote an extremely full account of 25 children in their first two years.

5

DEVELOPMENTAL TESTS

The history of developmental testing was mentioned by Bayley.[5] According to her, Binet's original aim was to identify children who were unlikely to benefit from regular school instruction. She wrote that in 1912 Stern and Kuhlman suggested that a child's relative status could be indicated by a ratio between his mental age and his chronological age—the intelligence quotient.

In the early part of this century Arnold Gesell, while studying mentally defective children, began to think about the early signs of mental deficiency and so set about the study of the normal infant. A large series of books followed, of which I consider the most valuable today are *Developmental Diagnosis*, *The First Five Years of Life*, and *Biographies of Child Development*. These established 'norms' of development, describing the development of infants and children from just after the newborn period, to the age of 5 years. The philosophy of development, the technique of developmental testing, and the interpretation of results, are all discussed in detail in his books.

I shall not attempt to review all the infant tests which have been described, but will refer to books by four authors—those of Charlotte Bühler,[7] Psyche Cattell,[9] Ruth Griffiths[25] and Haeussermann.[26] Bühler's tests are of interest and importance because of her attempt to cover all fields of development, and not merely sensorimotor skills. The tests are described in detail, and are easy to apply. Cattell's tests are modified from those of Gesell. Her book has the merit of providing simple instructions for the application of the tests, but like Bühler she does not describe the philosophy of developmental testing, or the importance of the history. This criticism applies still more forcibly to the book by Ruth Griffiths, whose tests are again modified from those of Gesell. No attention is paid to the history and environmental circumstances, the tests being entirely objective. I shall explain that in my view proper interpretation of development on this basis is impossible. In marked contrast to the above is the book by Haeussermann, which is concerned mainly with developmental testing in handicapped children. A full account of history taking and the interpretation of results makes this a most valuable book.

PREDICTIVE VALUE

The Gesell View on Developmental Testing

I have summarised elsewhere the rationale of Arnold Gesell's philosophy of development.[29] I wrote: 'It would seem reasonable to suppose that if careful detailed observation were made of the course of development of a sufficiently large number of babies, record being made of the age at which various skills were learned, it should be possible to establish some relationship between records so obtained and their subsequent progress through childhood. Though it is impossible to say what is "normal", there is no difficulty in defining the "average", and it should be easy to determine the sequence and rate of growth in the average child and to note the frequency with which deviations from the usual growth pattern occur as a result of known or unknown factors. Having determined the developmental pattern of average children, it should be possible to determine whether an individual child has developed as far as the average one of his age, taking into account all factors which might have affected his development. By making further examinations at intervals in order to assess his rate of development, and by taking into account all possible factors in the child and his environment which might affect the future course of his development, one ought to be able to make a reasonable prediction of his future progress provided that one knows the frequency of abnormal growth patterns. Arnold Gesell and his staff at the Yale Clinic of Child Development made such studies for 40 years or more, and they are convinced that such prediction is in fact possible'. By 1930 Gesell[19] estimated that he and his staff had examined more than 10,000 infants at numerous age periods. He wrote that 'attained growth is an indicator of past growth processes and a foreteller of growth yet to be achieved'. He emphasised the 'lawfulness of growth', and said that 'where there is lawfulness there is potential prediction'. He constantly called for caution in attempting to predict a child's future development, because of all the variables concerned. To use his words: 'Diagnostic prudence is required at every turn', and 'so utterly unforeseen are the vicissitudes of life that commonsense will deter one from attempting to forecast too precisely the developmental career of any child'. Gesell followed one group of 30 infants up to adolescence.[23] He wrote: 'In no instance did the course of growth prove whimsical or erratic. In only one case within the period of 10 years was there a marked alteration of trend, namely, from a low average to a high average level'. Elsewhere[21, 22] he wrote: 'By methods of developmental diagnosis supplemented with clinical experience, it is possible to diagnose in the first year of life nearly all cases of amentia, of cerebral injury, many sensory and motor defects, and severe personality deviations'.

Views of Others

There is a considerable body of opinion which strongly favours the view that developmental tests in the first few years have no predictive value.

In 1933 Bayley[4] described her well known study. She carried out 200 sensorimotor test items on 61 infants, and followed 49 of the children for 3 years. The longer the time interval between any two tests, the lower was the correlation. She concluded that behaviour in the early months had little predictive value with regard to future intelligence. She thought that the tests 'measure different functions rather than a unit function of intelligence'. She added: 'There was no evidence for a general factor of intelligence during the first three years, but the findings indicate instead a series of developing functions or group of functions, each growing out of but not necessarily correlated with previously matured behaviour patterns'.

Elsewhere[4] she wrote that 'in general, tests are of great value in judging and diagnosing a child's current status, but they are of very little use in predicting what the child's I.Q. will be a few years later. It seems evident that the very nature of intelligence in children under two or three years of age is such that the tests in these early ages will have little if any predictive value'.

A report from the Child Adoption Research Committee in New York[11] included the following comment: 'It is practically a truism that performance on a baby test alone is no accurate indication of the level of intellectual development of an individual in the future'. Correlations between Cattell scores and later tests were only ·2 to ·26. The mean age of the initial test was 15 months, and that of the subsequent Binet test was 63 months. No mentally defective children were included in the study, no infant having a test score below 90. Michaels and Brenner[38] examined 50 adopted children when they were four years or over, and concluded that 'The psychologists' findings suggest that the case worker's tendency to assume that infant tests provide a safe index of potential development is not warranted'. Bowlby[6], probably largely on the basis of evidence mentioned above, remarked confidently that: 'Mental tests have no predictive value in the first 18 months of life'. 'Probably the best guide to the intelligence of the child is the intelligence of the parents, though for many reasons this can be no more than a very rough guide'.

Kirman[32] wrote that: 'Few people are so bold as to claim to be able to measure intelligence in babies or to predict the future course of their mental development'. He added that: 'It is only very seldom that a child of less than two can safely be diagnosed as definitely mentally defective'. Kirman has had considerable experience of errors in diagnosis of mental deficiency in children sent to the Fountain Hospital, London, and it is probably on the basis of these errors that he made the above comments. Elsewhere[33] he again wrote of the difficulty of predicting mental deficiency in a young child, pointing out the low predictive value of tests under the age of 5 years. He declared that only the severest forms of mental defect could be diagnosed in the early years.

Eysenck[17] wrote that 'intelligence testing before the age of six, or five at the earliest, should be discouraged, because,' he said, 'testing before the age of two has no predictive accuracy at all for adult intelligence'. J. E. Anderson[1] wrote that: 'Infant tests as at present constituted, measure very little, if at all, the function which is called intelligence at later ages. Preschool intelligence tests, while they are instruments of some value and usefulness, measure only a portion of that function'. Apgar et al[2] spoke of the meagre value of Gesell ratings of adaptive behaviour at 2 years as compared with the Stanford-Binet score at 5.

Wittenborn[46] attempted to determine the value of the assessment of infants in Gesell's clinic for the purposes of adoption, by means of a follow-up examination with Binet tests at the age of 5 years or more. His conclusion is as follows: 'We find no means of refuting an hypothesis that the infant examination has no useful predictive validity. Although we cannot prove that the hypothesis of no predictive validity is true, it describes our data'.

Sontag et al.[43] examined 140 children yearly from 3 to 10 or 12 years, and concluded that 'the levels of I.Q. at preschool age have hardly any predictive value'. Reiman[39] discussed the dilemma in which the adoption societies are now placed because of the worthlessness of developmental tests, and blamed them for placing undue reliance on the tests. He raised the question of whether the child should be examined at all, but concluded that perhaps he should be examined and that the history might be taken.

It will be seen that there is considerable agreement amongst psychologists that developmental testing in infancy is of little value.

In contrast to the views cited above, other workers have been less definite in their condemnation of infant testing. Some of them found quite good correlations between early and later tests.

Cattell[9], in her chapter on the statistical basis of her tests, which were based on those of Gesell, found that tests at three months had relatively slight predictive value, particularly if the score were low: but if a child had a high score at three months there was an appreciably better than average chance of his having a high rating on the Stanford-Binet scale at 2 or 3 years. The ten children with a rating below 88 had scores varying between 76 and 150 at 3 years. Of the 10 infants receiving the highest rating at 3 months, only one fell below 100 in the 3 year follow-up period. Tests at 6, 9 and 12 months gave higher coefficients of ·88, ·86 and ·89 respectively.

Escalona[15] followed up 72 infants in whom the original assessment was thought to be a reasonably accurate figure, the child having 'done his best' at the time. She graded the results into 6 categories, retarded, borderline, low average, average, high average, and superior. On retesting, 68 per cent. were in the same range, 31 per cent. in the adjacent range, and none were in a lower range. She paid considerable attention to the child's behaviour and degree of activity and concentration, as well as to his background, as distinct from mere test scores. In a further study, Escalona and her colleagues[16] examined 58 infants between the age of 3 and 33 weeks using the Cattell and Gesell tests, and again at 6 to 9 years, using the Wechsler scale. For infants tested at 20 weeks and above, both Cattell and Gesell scores showed slightly positive relationships to the later intelligence range, but clinical appraisal as distinct from purely objective tests significantly predicted differences in later intelligence. When infant assessments were examined for their ability to distinguish between subjects who would later be of average or above average intelligence, clinical appraisal (but neither of the objective tests alone) achieved this discrimnation at a highly significant level (·002).

MacRae[37] tested 102 children under three years of age, dividing them into five categories—defective, below average, average, above average and superior, retesting them at a medium age of 9 years and two months. The Gesell tests were used for all but 12 of the initial examinations, and the Cattell tests for the remainder. The Wechsler intelligence scale was used at school age. Seventeen were initially tested in the first 6 months, 27 in the second 6 months, 38 between 13 and 24 months, and 20 between 25 and and 36 months. For three quarters the lapse of time between tests was 56 months or more. The correlations between the initial and final tests were significant beyond the 1 per cent. level. In 19 the infant rating was one category higher than the final rating, and in 13 it was one category less. MacRae concluded that: 'The predictive value of infant tests has been underestimated by investigators who have attempted to interpret infant test ratings in terms of specific scores of I.Qs'.

Drillien[14] demonstrated the predictive value of developmental tests (mainly Gesell) in her extensive follow up of premature babies. She found, as others have, that it is much easier to predict mental dullness in infancy then mental superiority. Of 16 children found at 5 years to be unsuitable for education at an ordinary school (I.Q. less than 70), 12 were given the same level at 6 months and at each subsequent examination. No child scored higher than very dull at any test at any age. Of 16 found to have an I.Q. of 70-79 at school age, 12 were rated at this level or lower from 6 months.

Simon and Bass[42] described a follow-up study of two groups of children, dividing them into three categories—above average, average and below average. The first consisted of 56 children who were examined twice before the first birthday (average age of initial examination 4 months) and re-examined at an average of 28 months. The second group consisted of 46 infants examined twice before the first birthday, and re-examined after the age of 5 by the Stanford-Binet or Wechsler tests.

Table I shows that there was a fairly high correlation between the initial and subsequent tests in each group. In all cases the clinical history and social factors were taken into account in making the initial

TABLE 1
(SIMON and BASS)[42]

Grading in Infancy		Retest grading						
	Number	Below Average	Average	Above Average	Coefficient of mean square contingency	Chi square	Probability
GROUP A							
Above average –	31	0	2	29 ⎫			
Average – –	20	1	9	10 ⎬	+·52	20·135	Smaller than ·001
Below average –	5	1	3	1 ⎭			
GROUP B							
Above average –	18	0	1	17 ⎫			
Average – –	21	1	7	13 ⎬	+·45	13 842	Between 0·1 & ·001
Below average –	7	5	1	1 ⎭			

assessment. It will be noted that the least predictable group was that classified as 'average'. Cavanaugh *et al.*[10] found poor correlation between Cattell tests at 6 months and Stanford-Binet tests at 4 years, but moderate correlations between tests at 1 year and 4 years.

In a comparison between test scores of 20 months and 10 years in 639 full term children,[46] the Cattell scores at 20 months gave r = ·49 at 10 years. A combination of Cattell scores, paediatricians' rating, social quotient, perinatal stress score, and parental socioeconomic status, yielded a multiple R of ·58 with the 10 year I.Q. score. For children with a Cattell score of below 80 at 20 months, a combination of infant test scores and paediatricians' ratings yielded a multiple R of ·80 with the score at 10 years. The majority of children with a low Cattell or paediatricians' rating at 20 months had serious school difficulties at the age of ten.

In a critical letter concerning the predictiveness of developmental tests, Knobloch[35] discussed the function of infant testing, and described follow-up studies by Pasamanick and his colleagues at John Hopkins Hospital, which indicated that in fact these tests, properly carried out, have considerable predictive value. In one study quoted by her, fifty negro children were examined in infancy and re-examined at 7 years of age by different examiners unaware of the initial findings. The correlation between the two examinations was ·5. Correlations of ·5 to ·75 were obtained in another study of 100 infants examined at several ages between 16 weeks and 18 months. She described another follow-up study of 300 infants examined at the Johns Hopkins Hospital at 14 weeks, with re-examination at 3 years by an examiner who had no knowledge of the findings at the initial examination; the correlation was ·5 in those without intellectual impairment, and ·75 in those with such impairment. Between 40 weeks and 3 years 50 per cent. of the 300 infants varied less than 10 points, and 75 per cent. less than 15 points.

Hindley[28] compared the Griffiths scores on 80 babies at six months and 18 months with Stanford Binet scores at three and five years; the intercorrelations varied from 0·32 between scores at six months and five years, and 0·78 between scores at three and five years. He suggested that later scores may reflect the cumulative effect of environment and the gradual emergence of inherited differences of ability.

Ausubel[3] summed up the position as follows: 'Developmental norms are valuable because they provide a standard or frame of reference for evaluating and interpreting the status or current behaviour of an individual. They can be abused if the range of variability is overlooked: if expectations for *all* children are geared to group averages: if substantial parallelism is expected between component rates of growth:

if they are unwarrantedly applied to individuals who could not be included in the sampling population: and if individual guidance is predicated upon normative comparisons alone to the exclusion of information regarding individual patterns. They are also abused if they are regarded as inevitable and immutable products of maturation or as necessarily desirable. But because an instrument is subject to abuse is no reason for declaring it valueless or urging its abolition as some over-zealous but misguided exponents of the "clinical" approach have suggested'.

Comments on the Literature

The evidence on which so many writers have proclaimed the lack of predictive value of developmental tests in the early years does not seem to be adequate, and there is plenty of evidence for the contrary view, namely that properly used, developmental tests are of the utmost value.

No one, of course, should expect developmental tests when repeated to give a constant value. The variability of I.Q. test results in older children is well known. Burt's[8] comments on I.Q. prediction are particularly apt. The following were his words: 'Since genetic constitution merely determines growth-tendencies, and since the child's observable progress and performance are the result of innumerable factors, both internal and external, we could never hope, even with the most precise specification of the newborn infants' equipment of genes, to make infallible predictions about his ultimate level. No competent psychologist has ever supposed that an I.Q. can be exactly ascertained, much less that it will remain immutable for each individual child'.

I suggest that following main reasons for the widely held views that developmental tests in infancy have no predictive value:

1. Reliance on purely objective tests

Psychologists, in an attempt to be really scientific, tend to use purely objective tests, and to pay little or no attention to physical findings, to the perinatal history, to the family history, to the socioeconomic position of the family, or to other factors which may affect a child's development. I am convinced that these efforts to be scientific and objective lead to inaccuracy. As Simon and Bass[42] wrote, 'they have limited their interest to the intelligence quotient, instead of forming a clinical judgment based on the child and his environment as a whole'. Similar sentiments were expressed by Macfarlane[36].

In some cases workers have used the Gesell tests. There is a great difference between using Gesell's tests and using Gesell's method. Before Gesell or his staff examined a child, a social worker had visited the child's home and gone into the social and family background in detail. A full developmental history was then taken in the clinic, the child being examined physically and developmentally, and then at the ensuing staff conference the whole child was discussed and a clinical assessment was reached, or else it was decided that further observation was required before a decision could be made.

Whatever tests are used, whether they are those of Gesell, or Gesell's tests modified, as by Cattell or Ruth Griffiths, purely objective testing can only reveal one part of the child's development. The tests have value, but their value is unnecessarily restricted. To give an example, a 6 months old baby should bear almost his full weight on his legs. If his mother has kept him off his legs because she was afraid that if he bore weight he would develop rickets or knock-knees, those who advocate purely objective testing would mark him down for his inability to bear weight, whereas this inability has no possible relationship to his developmental potential. It is not surprising that Hindley[27] writing about the Griffiths scale, wrote 'we must conclude that predictions based on existing infant tests within the first eighteen months are very uncertain.'

2. *Failure to record the quality of performance.*

The tests used by several workers were all or none tests. Either the child passes a test or he does not. The essence of Gesell's teaching is that development is a continuous process, and it is the task of the examiner to determine how far he has developed. For instance, it is not enough to give an all or none score for sitting without support at 7 months. He may be on the verge of achieving it, he may sit like an average child, for a few seconds only without support, or he may sit securely and be able to pivot like a child of 9 months. One has to decide how the child achieves the skill, not just *whether* he does.

3. *Reliance on sensorimotor tests.*

Many of the tests described do not throw light on the really important matter of how much interest and alertness the child shows, or on the degree of his responsiveness, interest and concentration. They do not show these details because they cannot be scored, and yet they are the most important of all, as was well recognised by Gesell. Bayley herself noted that these aspects of development were not covered by her tests.

4. *Failure to assess the rate of development*

Various testers have made no attempt to observe the *rate* of development in assessing a child. For this purpose a detailed developmental history is essential, in order to assess the previous rate of development, followed by repeated examination, in order to assess further progress.

Whenever one is in doubt about a child's development, as one should be if there were a preceding history of emotional deprivation, illness, or other factors which might have affected the child, it is essential to see the child again in order to observe the rate of development, before an assessment is made. Bayley and others did not do this. Their tests were impersonal, instead of being personal and individual.

5. *Errors of interpretation.*

In some papers the figures given do not quite correspond with the opinions expressed by the writers.

For instance, I have tried several times to understand Wittenborn's[47] figures, and hope that I have not misinterpreted them; but they do not seem to indicate quite such a low level of prediction as he claimed. Of 30 children who were placed for adoption after the developmental examination, 14 were given a developmental quotient below 100; 8 of these had a subsequent Binet score below 100. Of 16 infants given a D.Q. of 100 or more, 14 had a Binet score of 100 or more. In another study, he scored the educational and occupational status of the adopting parents of 30 children, and related them to the Binet score of the children. None of the infants placed in families with high educational and occupational scores had I.Q. results below 110, while more than half placed with families with low scores had I.Q. scores below that figure. This was exactly what Gesell's clinic tried to achieve. An attempt was made to match the infant's developmental potential with that of the adopting parents, and Wittenborn's figures, if they can be considered valid in view of the mode of selection, seem to indicate that the developmental assessment was in fact quite successful.

Wittenborn stated that his failure to prove the value of developmental tests in infancy corresponded exactly with the findings of Cattell. But Cattell's findings, to which reference has been made, indicated that in fact there was quite a good correlation between her tests in infancy and those carried out in later years.

Knobloch[35] discussing Wittenborn's findings, remarked that it is unsatisfactory to use adopted infants for the purpose of assessing the validity of infant tests because of the difficulties of the early environment, differences in foster homes, and sometimes because of the effect of institutional care. She added that Wittenborn failed to discuss the purpose of the developmental examination and had not indicated that any poor placements were made on the basis of failure to diagnose neurological or intellectual deficits.

6. *The absence of a physical and neurological examination.*

In the assessment of an infant's developmental potential the child must be considered as a whole. It is obvious that a full physical examination is essential in order to detect the presence of any sensory or mechanical defects which could affect his development.

7. *Exclusion of mentally retarded children.*

Finally, in many of the studies the babies were heavily 'selected'. For instance, the average I.Q. of Bayley's cases at the age of 9 years was 129. Mentally defective children were not included. Wittenborn's cases were so selected that it is difficult to know what attention should be paid to them. Defective children had already been excluded before they came to Gesell's clinic for assessment for suitability for adoption. Wittenborn noted this, but made the strange comment that 'one could suppose for the most part these children are identified without the aid of infant examination'! Wittenborn then selected a group of those already selected children, and added some highly selected infants of members of the staff of Yale University Clinic. It seems that only 114 of the group of 310 were assessed at the age of five or later, the remaining 196 not being examined. The reader is left to conclude (without evidence) that those not followed up would have fared the same as those who were followed. It is very difficult to provide evidence that those followed up are truly representative of the whole. One can imagine, for instance, that some parents may not be willing to bring their children because they are backward, or for other reasons which would mean that they were different from children of parents who were pleased to co-operate in the study.

The 'selection' of children for study is of great importance, for the various studies described, on which so many have based their conviction that developmental tests have no predictive value, have excluded the very children in whom a confident prognosis can be most readily given—the mentally defective ones. Terman and Merrill[44] remarked that the I.Q. of dull children is much more constant than it is in normal or supernormal children. Goodenough[24] wrote: 'Inasmuch as radical changes in the treatment of backward and feebleminded children are more likely to depend upon the results of mental tests than is the case with children of normal or superior intelligence, the greater dependability of the intelligence quotient at the lower levels, is a matter of considerable importance for those actively concerned with the welfare of children'. Gesell[22] wrote that 'Practically every case of mental deficiency can be diagnosed in the first year of life, excluding, of course, the small number of exceptional cases which occur from secondary causes in later infancy or early childhood'. Thomas[45] reviewed the difficulties of early developmental assessment and of evaluating studies of developmental prediction. He mentioned amongst other things the problems of sampling, of the population base rates and of clinical impressions.

Personal Studies

I cannot agree that it is only the severe cases of mental deficiency which can be diagnosed in infancy. In a recent study at Sheffield[30] we followed up 135 children who were considered at any time in the first two years of life to be mentally retarded, however slightly. Cases of mongolism, cretinism, hydrocephalus and anencephaly were excluded. In 10 of the children the mental retardation was of postnatal origin, and in the others it was of prenatal or natal origin. Apart from these exclusions, the cases were in no way selected, in that *all* children seen by me or by members of the department who were considered to be backward were included—even though one or two very shortly after the initial assessment were subsequently thought to be normal. The initial diagnosis was based on a clinical assessment in the Out-patient Department, using some of the Gesell tests, with full consideration of the developmental history and other data. All but 2 of the survivors were traced and re-examined, using for the most part Terman and Merrill tests at the age of 5 years or later. All but 5 of them were retarded. In 77 the initial diagnosis was made in the first year, and in 59 it was made in the second year. A total of 34 had died. In all 10 in whom autopsies were performed, gross anomalies of the brain were present.

Of the 101 survivors who were traced, 59 on follow-up examinations were seriously subnormal (I.Q. score below 50), 24 had an I.Q. score of 50 to 75, 13 had an I.Q. score of 76 to 94, and 5 had an I.Q. score of 100 or more. Of 67 who were thought to be severely retarded in infancy, 55 on follow-up examination were found to be ineducable. Of 20 who were regarded as only slightly retarded in infancy, only 2 on follow-up examination were found to be ineducable. I shall refer later to the 5 who were found to have an I.Q. score of 100 or more.

The figures indicate conclusively that mental retardation can be confidently diagnosed in the first two years, even apart from the obvious forms such as mongolism. For practical purposes this is the most important function of developmental tests. It does not matter much whether a baby has a developmental quotient of 110 or 130: but it matters a great deal for purposes of adoption if his developmental quotient, being 70 or less, gives a reasonably likely prediction that the child is going to be mentally retarded in later years.

At the Children's Hospital, Sheffield, infants have been examined every week for the purpose of assessment for suitability for adoption. They were seen in their first year, usually at the age of six months. There was some degree of selection of babies for assessment, in that babies who were obviously defective, such as mongols, would not be sent to me. Severely defective infants would therefore be excluded. Those sent to me were thought to be within normal limits. The study is continuing and will do for some years. On the basis of tests described in this book they are graded as follows:

Grade 1 .. Possibly above average.
     2 .. Average.
     3 .. Possibly below average.
     4 .. Inferior.

When they reached school age, they were examined by School Medical Officers (who knew nothing of my grading), I.Q. test scores being made on the basis of Terman and Merrill and other methods. The following were the mean I.Q. scores at school age for each of the grades allotted in infancy. The total number of children so far tested at school age is 156.[31]

Grade allotted in infancy	Mean I.Q. at age 5-8
1	109·1
2	107·3
3	99·8
4	84·1

Only 2 of 110 children (1·8 per cent) thought in the first year to be average or possibly better proved to have an I.Q. score at school of below 80, and 3 of 46 children thought to be doubtful or retarded had an I.Q. score of over 120.

It should be noted that in the earlier part of the investigation above, the assessment was rendered more difficult by the fact that the infants had been in an institution for the first six months or more of their life, and came direct from it, so that there was the factor of emotional deprivation which would have retarded their development. It was not possible to decide how much retardation had been caused by this factor and how much of it would be reversible. The institution was subsequently closed, the infants being placed in foster homes at the age of 9 or 10 days.

The figures support the contention that mental inferiority can be diagnosed more easily than mental superiority. One is more likely to underestimate potential than to overestimate it.

I have no evidence from my own work so far that mental superiority can be diagnosed with reasonable confidence in infancy. Some of the workers quoted have adduced some evidence to that effect. But the fact that mental retardation can be diagnosed in infancy indicates that developmental tests, in this important practical matter at least, do have a definite predictive value.

Knobloch[34, 35] rightly pointed out that the principle function of developmental tests in infancy is the detection of abnormal neurological conditions and of subnormal developmental potential. She added that these tests are not intended to detect mental superiority or precise I.Q. scores later. Although a small percentage may be considered superior, the question of whether they remain so depends on their later experiences. She added that: 'As clinicians we would feel that an examination which would allow us to make the following statement is an eminently acceptable and useful tool. This infant has no neurologic impairment, and his potential is within the healthy range: depending on what his life experiences are between now and 6 years of age, he will at that time have a Stanford-Binet I.Q. above 90, unless qualitative changes in the central nervous system are caused by noxious agents, or gross changes in milieu alter major variables of function,' and: 'The studies that we have done indicate that when care is taken to eliminate bias and the infant examination is used as a clinical neurological tool by a physician adequately trained in its use, good correlations are obtained. These studies have not been challenged by the critics of infant evaluation: they have merely been ignored'.

In Chapter 18 I have put together the common errors in developmental diagnosis—errors made by many of us who attempt to assess the developmental status of infants and young children.

Conclusion

Developmental Prediction. What We Can and Cannot Do.

Everyone who attempts to assess the development of babies should be fully conversant with the limitations of developmental prediction. Below I have summarised what we can hope to do, and what we must not expect to be able to do.

What we can do (but not necessarily in the earliest weeks), is as follows:—

1. We can say how far a baby has developed in relation to his age, and we can therefore compare him with the average performance of others at that age; and we can say something about his rate of development. By so doing we can say something about his developmental potential.

2. We can diagnose moderate or severe mental subnormality.

3. We can diagnose moderate or severe cerebral palsy.

4. We can assess muscle tone.

5. We can diagnose moderate or severe deafness.

6. We can diagnose moderate or severe visual defects.

7. We can diagnose subluxation or dislocation of the hips.

8. We can diagnose neurological defects in infancy.

9. As a result of our developmental and neurological examination, we are in a better position to give genetic counselling.

What we cannot do is as follows:–

1. We cannot draw a dividing line between normal and abnormal. All that we can do is to say that the further away from the average the child is in anything, the more likely he is to be abnormal.

2. We cannot make accurate predictions of his future intelligence and achievements, because these will be profoundly affected by environmental and other factors in the future. There never will be a high correlation between developmental assessments in infancy and subsequent intellectual achievement.

3. We cannot eliminate the possibility that he will undergo mental deterioration in future months or years. Possible causes of this include severe emotional deprivation, personality defects, a bad home, bad education, lack of opportunity to achieve his best, psychoses, degenerative diseases of the nervous system, various effects of epilepsy, metabolic disease, hypoglycaemia, lead poisoning, meningitis, encephalitis or severe head injury.

4. If he has suffered severe emotional deprivation before we assess him, we cannot assess, at one examination, the extent of the damage which he has suffered, or its reversibility.

5. If he is backward, and does not show microcephaly, we cannot be sure that he is not a slow starter (delayed maturation).

6. If he was a low birth weight baby, and we do not know the duration of gestation, we cannot distinguish true prematurity from dysmaturity (as in the small for dates baby) in retrospect, except only in the newborn period. Hence if attempting to assess him, for example, at six months, we do not know whether to make any correction for prematurity. For instance, if he weighed 3 lbs. 8 oz. (1590g.) at birth, and was therefore possibly two months premature, we would not know whether to compare him with an average four month old baby or with a six month infant.

7. We cannot make a sensible prediction for a full term baby at birth, or in the first four weeks, unless there are grossly abnormal signs; and still less can we make any valid assessment of a prematurely born baby, until, after due correction for prematurity, he has reached at least four to six weeks of age. For instance, if he were born eight weeks prematurely, it would be rash indeed to assess him until at least 12 to 14 weeks after delivery.

8. We cannot rely on diagnosing mild cerebral palsy or mild mental subnormality in the early weeks.

9. If we find abnormal neurological signs in the first few weeks, we cannot be sure, unless they are gross, that they will not disappear; and if they disappear, we cannot be sure that when he is older, at school age, the finer tests of coordination then available will not show that there are in fact some residual signs, such as clumsiness. The older the infant, the less likely it is that abnormal signs will disappear, and after the first year it is unlikely that they will be anything but permanent.

10. We cannot eliminate in infancy the possibility that the child will subsequently display specific learning disorders, or difficulties of spatial appreciation.

11. We cannot translate into figures Gesell's "insurance factors"—the baby's alertness, interest in his surroundings, social responsiveness, determination and powers of concentration— features which are of much more predictive value than the readily scorable items, such as gross motor development, or sphincter control.

12. We cannot say what he will do with his talents, or with what we have termed his developmental potential. This will depend on a wide variety of factors, such as his personality, his determination, ambition, willingness to work hard, ability to profit from mistakes, the quality of his home and of his education, opportunity, the right choice of subject for study or of career, his creativity and originality.

13. We cannot prove, in any but the most exceptional cases, that a child's mental or neurological deficits are due to birth injury rather than to prenatal causes.

14. We cannot normally predict mental superiority.

Finally, it must be remembered that there are many aspects of ability (Vernon[45a]); they include verbal, numerical, spatial, perceptual, memorising, reasoning, mechanical and imaginative qualities. It would hardly be likely that tests in infancy would detect these with a high degree of reliability.

We should constantly bear in mind the purpose of developmental examination. It is not to predict the future intelligence or success of the child. The purpose is to determine whether the baby is developing normally for his age, and whether he has any mental, physical, neurological or sensory handicaps, so that if possible appropriate treatment can be given. When assessing a child for adoption, we want in particular to diagnose cerebral palsy or mental deficiency. All these we can do; but we do not want to be able to say whether in later years his I.Q. will be 110 or 120; this we cannot do.

Summary

Correlations between developmental tests in infancy and subsequent intelligence test scores and future achievements cannot be high, and never will be, largely because the child's intelligence and future performance will be profoundly affected by environmental and other factors.

We can say how far the child has developed in relation to his age and to the average performance of others at that age.

We can diagnose moderate or severe mental subnormality, cerebral palsy, visual or auditory defects, and neurological abnormalities, in the early weeks; but we cannot diagnose the mildest cases of mental backwardness or cerebral palsy, or of hearing or visual defects. We cannot eliminate the possibility of mental deterioration. We cannot usually be sure that abnormal neurological signs in early infancy will not disappear. We cannot score some of the most important features of a baby's performance. We cannot say what a child will do with his talents.

REFERENCES

1. ANDERSON, J. E., in MARTIN, W. E., STENDLER, C. B. (1954) *Readings in Child Development.* New York: Harcourt Bruce.
2. APGAR, V., GIRDANY, B. R., McINTOSH, R., TAYLOR, H. C. (1955) Neonatal Anoxia. *Pediatrics,* **15,** 653.
3. AUSUBEL, D. P. (1958) *Theory and Problems of Child Development.* New York. Grune and Stratton.

4. BAYLEY, N. (1933) Mental Growth during the First Three Years. *Genet. Psychol. Monogr.*, **14,** 1.
5. BAYLEY, N. (1958) Value and Limitations of Infant Testing. *Children,* **5,** 129.
6. BOWLBY, J. (1951) Maternal Care and Mental Health. *Bull. Wld. Hlth. Org.*, **3,** 357.
7. BÜHLER, C. (1935) *From Birth to Maturity.* London. Kegan Paul.
8. BURT, C. (1959) General Ability and Special Aptitudes. *Educ. Res.*, **1,** 3.
9. CATTELL, P. (1947) *The Measurement of Intelligence of Infants and Young Children.* New York. The Psychological Corporation.
10. CAVANAUGH, M. C., COHEN, I., DUNPHY, D., RINGWALL, E. A., GOLDBERG, I. D. (1957) Prediction from the Cattell Infant Intelligence Scale. *J. cons. Psychol.*, **21,** 33.
11. Child Adoption Research Committee, New York (1951) A Follow up Study of Adoptive Families.
12. DARWIN, C. (1872) *The Expression of the Emotions in Man and Animals.* London. Murray.
13. DARWIN, C. (1877) A Biographical Sketch of an Infant. *Mind,* **2,** 285.
14. DRILLIEN, C. M. (1961) A Longitudinal Study of the Growth and Development of Prematurely and Maturely Born Children. *Arch. Dis. Childh.*, **36,** 233.
15. ESCALONA, S. (1950) The Use of Infant Tests for Predictive Purposes.
16. ESCALONA, S. K., MORIARTY, A. (1961) Prediction of Schoolage Intelligence from Infant Tests. *Child Development,* **32,** 597. *Bull. Menninger Clin.*, **14,** 117.
17. EYSENCK, H. J. (1953) *Uses and Abuses of Psychology.* London. Pelican.
18. GESELL, A. AMATRUDA, C. S., CASTNER, B. M., THOMPSON, H. (1930) *Biographies of Child Development.* London. Hamish Hamilton.
19. GESELL, A., THOMPSON, H. (1938) *The Psychology of Early Growth.* New York. Macmillan.
20. GESELL, A., HALVERSON, H. M., THOMPSON, H., ILG, F. L., CASTNER, B. M., AMES, L. B., AMATRUDA, C. S. (1940) *The First Five Years of Life.* New York. Harper.
21. GESELL, A., AMATRUDA, C. S. (1947) *Developmental Diagnosis.* New York. Hoeber.
22. GESELL, A. (1948) *Studies in Child Development.* New York. Harper.
23. GESELL, A. (1954) in *Carmichael's Manual of Child Psychology.* New York. Wiley.
24. GOODENOUGH, F. L. (1950) *Mental Testing.* London. Staples.
25. GRIFFITHS, R. (1954) *The Abilities of Babies.* London. University of London Press.
26. HAEUSSERMANN, E. (1958) *Developmental Potential of Preschool Children.* London. Grune and Stratton.
27. HINDLEY, C. B. (1960) The Griffiths Scale of Infant Development. *Child Psychology and Psychiatry* **1,** 99.
28. HINDLEY, C. B. (1965) Stability and change in abilities up to five years; group trends. *J. Child. Psychol. Psychiat.*, **6,** 85.

29. ILLINGWORTH, R. S. (1968) *The Normal Child*. London. Churchill.
30. ILLINGWORTH, R. S., BIRCH, L. B. (1959) The Diagnosis of Mental Retardation in Infancy. A Follow-up Study. *Arch. Dis. Childh.*, **34**, 269.
31. ILLINGWORTH, R. S. (1969) Assessment for adoption; a follow up study. *Acta Paediat. Scand.*, **58**, 33.
32. KIRMAN, B. H. (1953) The Backward Baby. *J. ment. Sci.*, **99**, 531.
33. KIRMAN, B. H. (1958) Early Disturbance of Behaviour in Relation to Mental Defect. *Brit. med. J.*, **2**, 1215.
34. KNOBLOCH, H. (1959) Pneumoencephalograms and Clinical Behaviour. *Pediatrics*, **23**, 175.
35. KNOBLOCH, H. PASAMANICK, B. (1963) Predicting Intellectual Potential in Infancy. *Amer. J. Dis. Child.*, **106**, 43.
36. MACFARLANE, J. W. (1953) The Uses and Predictive Limitations of Intelligence Tests in Infants and Young Children. *Bull. Wld. Hlth. Org.*, **9**, 409.
37. MACRAE, J. M. (1955) Retests of Children given Mental Tests as Infants. *J. genet. Psychol.*, **87**, 111.
38. MICHAELS, R., BRENNER, R. F. Child Adoption Committee of the Free Synagogue, New York. Unpublished, quoted by Bowlby, J. (1951).
39. REIMAN, M. G. (1958) Considerations about Mental Deficiency in Planning for Adoption. *Amer. J. ment. Defic.*, **63**, 469.
40. SHINN, M. W. (1893) *Notes on the Development of a Child*. California. Univ. of California Press.
41. SHIRLEY, M. M. (1931) *The First Two Years*. Minneapolis. University of Minnesota Press.
42. SIMON, A. J., BASS, L. G. (1956) Toward a Validation of Infant Testing. *Amer. J. Orthopsychiat.*, **26**, 340.
43. SONTAG, L. W., BAKER, C. T., NELSON, V. L. (1958) *Mental Growth and Personality Development, a Longitudinal Study*. Lafayette. Child Development Publications.
44. TERMAN, L. M., MERRILL, M. (1937) *Measuring Intelligence*. Boston: Houghton, Mifflin.
45. THOMAS, H. (1967) Some problems of studies concerned with evaluating the predictive validity of infant tests. *J. Child Psychol. Psychiat.*, **8**, 197.
45a. VERNON, P. E. (1969) *Intelligence and Cultural Environment*. London. Methuen.
46. WERNER, E. E., HONZIK, M. P., SMITH, R. S. (1968) Prediction of intelligence and achievement at 10 years from 20 months pediatric and psychologic examinations. *Child. Development*, **39**, 1063.
47. WITTENBORN, J. R. (1957) *The Placement of Adoptive Children.* Springfield. Thomas.

CHAPTER 3

PRENATAL AND PERINATAL FACTORS WHICH AFFECT MENTAL DEVELOPMENT

The number of prenatal factors known to be related to the child's mental and physical development is steadily increasing. Below is a summary of the present position. Unless they also affect the child's development, I have not mentioned those related purely to disease states or to congenital anomalies, such as the association of hydramnios with obstruction of the alimentary tract in the foetus.

Genetic Factors

Hereditary factors play a part in the tendency to multiple pregnancy and premature labour, in the occurrence of hereditary diseases and congenital malformations, such as hydrocephalus, and in the development of intelligence and personality. I shall return to the subject of hereditary diseases associated with mental retardation in Chapter 5.

While in some conditions, such as phenylketonuria, the genetic factor is well understood, in others the genetic or hereditary factor is far from clear. One difficulty lies in the fact that if a mother gives birth to two or even three abnormal children, the cause of the foetal defect is not necessarily genetic. It could well be an abnormality in the uterus or placenta which was operative in both or all the pregnancies. Another difficulty is the heterogeneous nature of the types of mental deficiency. Comparatively few definite types have been separated off from the main body, so that it is impossible in most cases to give a definite prognosis when a parent has a defect, or when a defective child has been born and advice is sought about the risk of another child being affected.

Heredity and Intelligence

This subject has been reviewed so often, that I propose to devote only a small amount of space to it. Sir Francis Galton in 1869[48] was one of the first to study the genetics of genius. He made the observation that 977 eminent men had 535 eminent relatives, as against a total of 4 eminent relatives among 977 ordinary men. It is certain, however, that environmental factors were also involved. Terman and Oden[140] followed up 1,528 children with an intelligence quotient of 140 or more. 348 of their children were found to have a mean I.Q. of 127·7. The number with an I.Q. of 150 or more was 28 times that of unselected persons.

The genetic factors in intelligence—'Intelligence A', as distinct from 'Intelligence B', which is Intelligence A modified by prenatal and postnatal factors—have been studied in another way—by comparing the intelligence of children placed in foster homes with that of their real and adopting parents. I shall refer to this in the following chapter which concerns the effect of environment on intelligence. Skodak and Skeels[127] studied 100 children who were placed in foster homes, and assessed their intelligence quotient at intervals from 6 months to the fourteenth year. They made the observation that there was no correlation between the child's I.Q. and that of the true mother at first, but there was an increasing correlation with increasing age. This was presumed to be due to the increasing effect of genetic factors.

Honzik[62] made comparable observations. She studied two groups of over 100 children, testing them at intervals between 21 months and 16 years of age. Children in one group were brought up by their own parents, and in the other by foster parents. The parents were assessed by the number of years which they had spent in school, and the mothers were given intelligence tests. She, too, found that there was no correlation between the performance of the parents and children in the early tests, but that there was an increasing correlation as the children grew older. She remarked that even though in the study by Skodak and Skeels the true parents did not rear any of the children, the increasing parent-child resemblance in the two investigations suggests that the relationship is largely due to genetic factors which tend to become manifest during the later school years.

I shall refer later to the difficulties in the interpretation of these studies of children in foster homes.

Penrose[104, 105, 106] wrote a full discussion of the genetics of intelligence in his book *The Biology of Mental Defect*. He showed that the genetics of mild retardation are different from those of severe mental deficiency. In the first place, a severely defective person is considerably less likely to have a child than a mildly defective

parent. The intelligence of a mildly retarded child is more likely to approximate that of the parents than is that of a severely retarded one. When retardation is mild, the I.Q. of the children is likely to be somewhere near the mean of that of the parents, or between the I.Q. of the father and the mean of that of the population as a whole (100).[21]   For example, the mean I.Q. of unskilled labourers is 86·8, while that of their children is 92.

If normal parents have a child of low grade mental deficiency of non-specific type, the chance of another being affected is less than 3 per cent. If the child, however, has one of the known recessive types of mental deficiency, such as phenylketonuria, Tay-Sachs disease, or certain forms of familial deafmutism and mental deficiency, the likelihood of another being affected is 25 per cent. Sporadic forms of mental deficiency, such as tuberous sclerosis, carry a much smaller risk of involvement of siblings.

Mongolism is in part a genetic condition. The risk of a mongol being born to a mother of 25 years of age is 0·05 per cent. whereas that for a mother of 45 years is 2·5 per cent. The overall risk of a mongol being born is 0·15 per cent.[106]

Carter and Evans[24] studied the siblings of 642 index patients with mongolism. Among 312 siblings born after the index patient, 5 were mongols, while only one would be expected on the basis of the incidence in the general population. Among 927 siblings born before the index patients there were 4 mongols, while only 1·5 would be expected.

In mothers under 25[57] there is a higher risk of a chromosomal translocation than of a regular trisomy.   In mongols with a chromosomal translocation there is a great chance of one of the parents also having a chromosomal abnormality, and this in turn increases the risk of subsequent children being mongols.

Before giving genetic advice to a mother chromosomal studies are essential. If a mother under 25 has a chromosomal translocation there is a 2 out of 3 chance that her child will be a mongol or will carry the translocation.

It is not generally recognised that in the unusual case of a mongol becoming pregnant, there is an approximately 50 per cent likelihood that the child will be normal.[95]

Consanguinity is associated with an increased risk of the birth of a mentally defective child.[94]

The early surveys[19, 49, 52] gave a gloomy picture with regard to the children of mental defectives. One report[19] showed that among 3,650 children of mentally defective mothers, 24·8 per cent. were similarly defective, and another 18·4 per cent. were retarded. On the other hand Skodak[126] studied 16 children whose mothers were feeble-minded, with a mean I.Q. of 66·4 and found that the mean I.Q. of the children was 116·4. (Range 95–131).

Brandon[16] investigated 150 pregnancies of 73 certified mentally defective women. There were 41 deaths, including miscarriages and stillbirths. Seventy-four of the 109 survivors were tested and their mean I.Q. was 89·1. Of the 109, 12 had been certified, but 6 had been discharged, and 4 were in schools for educationally subnormal children. Only 4 had an I.Q. score below 65. In my own study of babies seen for adoption purposes, the mean I.Q. at school age of 21 children who had a mentally defective mother or father was 100·1[65]

Hereditary conditions related to development include gross anomalies of the central nervous system and epilepsy. According to Fraser[45] and others the risk of a child being born with a gross anomaly of the central nervous system when the parents are normal is 0·6 per cent. When the parents are normal the risk of their having a child with hydrocephalus alone is 1 in 1,000, and of having a child with hydrocephalus and spina bifida is 1 in 3,000. It has been found in Sheffield that the risk of a subsequent child being affected with hydrocephalus, spina bifida or anencephaly is about 1 in 15. If two affected infants are born, the risk is even greater.[83] The risk of a normal parent having an epileptic child is 0·4 per cent.; if one is affected, the risk of another being abnormal is 2·4 per cent. The risk of an affected parent having an affected child is 2·5 to 5·0 per cent. About 3·2 per cent. of parents, siblings or children of epileptic patients have fits.

Hereditary factors are also concerned with the child's personality, though the inherited characteristics are profoundly affected by his environment.

Haemolytic Disease and Kernicterus

Kernicterus is due to a variety of conditions, of which the chief is haemolytic disease of the newborn. It may also occur in premature babies without haemolytic disease if the serum bilirubin is allowed to rise too high before a replacement transfusion is carried out.[29] The serum bilirubin level in premature babies may reach dangerously high levels if large doses of vitamin K are administered in the newborn period, or given to the mother during labour.[85] Sulphonamides may also cause a rise in the serum bilirubin.

There are differences of opinion as to the level of intelligence to be expected in kernicterus. Gerrard[50] found that of 19 children with kernicterus, only 6 had an I.Q. test score of 85 or more. Two of these were described as 'average', and 2 had an I.Q. of 100. Byers, Paine and Crothers[22] carried out I.Q. tests on 19 children with kernicterus. The I.Q. test score ranged from 90 to 110 in 7, from 70 to 90 in 4, and from 50 to 70 in 3. It was below 50 in 1, and in 4 the test was unsatisfactory.

The level of intelligence to be expected in infants who had haemolytic disease is probably related to the depth of jaundice allowed to develop. Gerver and Day[51] found that the mean I.Q. of 68 children who had haemolytic disease of the newborn was 11·8 points below the average. Camp[23] followed up 51 children aged 3 to 15 who had had neonatal jaundice without evident neurological damage, and compared them with 49 controls who had not had visible jaundice in the newborn period. The controls had a significantly higher mean intelligence quotient. Camp argued, with good reason, that it is most unlikely that hyperbilirubinaemia has an all or none effect—either causing frank kernicterus or nothing at all. It is much more likely that there is either no effect at all, or all grades of damage from the most trivial intellectual impairment to the fully developed picture of kernicterus.

It might well be that the reduction of the serum bilirubin level (and elevation of the serum glucose) by the immediate feeding of premature babies, as advocated by Smallpiece and Davies,[128] will be of advantage to the development of these babies.

Day and Haines[32] studied 68 babies who had had a replacement transfusion. The degree of jaundice was significantly related to the level of intelligence. Eleven children who were rated severely ill with jaundice and anaemia, had an I.Q. averaging 23·1 points below that of their siblings. Their figures, though not statistically significant, suggested that the intelligence quotient has improved following the introduction of replacement transfusions.

It is difficult to obtain a clear picture of the level of intelligence to be expected after haemolytic disease of the newborn because of the number of variables involved. Factors of importance are the indications used for carrying out a replacement transfusion, the degree of completeness of the replacement, the level which the serum bilirubin was allowed to reach before a further replacement was performed, the degree of prematurity, and the duration of time during which the serum bilirubin was allowed to remain at dangerous levels.

In the assessment of results it should be remembered that some practice induction of labour in selected cases of haemolytic disease, and that this premature delivery might have a bearing on the child's future development.

Social Factors

It is obvious that a wide variety of social factors operating before the child is born will affect his future development.

PARENTAL POVERTY AND DEFECTIVE MATERNAL NUTRITION are associated with a higher than average incidence of maternal toxaemia, anaemia, premature delivery, and infant and child morbidity. Poverty is associated with overcrowding, which has an indirect effect on the child. It is well known that whereas the incidence of severe mental deficiency is the same in all social classes, the incidence of slight subnormality is much more common in the poor than in the well to do.

One investigation[58] showed that the mean I.Q. of 3 or 4 years old children of 612 women who had received vitamin supplements in pregnancy was significantly greater than that of controls. It is known that protein and vitamin supplements reduce the incidence of toxaemia and premature separation of the placenta.

It was found in Aberdeen[3] that primigravidae in a poor social class had a higher risk of foetal deaths due to malformations of the central nervous system than did other mothers.

Other studies in Aberdeen showed the important bearing which social factors have on obstetrical complications, and on the mode of delivery. They indicated the need for caution in ascribing abnormalities in the infant to birth injury unless due consideration is given to underlying social class differences in their relation to the events of pregnancy. The Aberdeen workers confirmed the work of others to the effect that slight mental retardation is much more common in the lower social classes, but that serious mental subnormality shows no social gradient.

O'Connor[99] in this country wrote that both high and low grade defectives are significantly more common among clerical and manual classes than in professional classes. In Syracuse City, in the United States, the rate of mental retardation per 1,000 population was 17 in classes 1 and 2, and 65·3 in class 6.

It has been suggested[75, 103] that more mentally defective children are born in the first three months of the year than at other times. The critical first three months of formative intrauterine life are therefore in the hot summer months. The highest number of defectives were born following particularly hot summers. The authors suggested that this might have been due to lower protein intake in hot months. It might, however, have been due to many other factors, such as the amount of exercise taken in the early weeks of pregnancy. There have been similar studies concerning time of birth and the incidence of anencephaly, spina bifida, cerebral palsy, congenital dislocation of hip, and other conditions. It should be noted that some of these studies refer to the date of birth, whereas it is obvious that the date of conception is more relevant. It is not easy to obtain this in retrospect with accuracy. A useful Australian study provided further evidence. Abnormalities were charted in terms of time of conception over a 16 year period. The abnormalities included hydrocephalus, anencephaly, spina bifida and mongolism. They showed a marked fairly regular periodicity, such as would be consistent with the waxing and waning of infectious disease epidemics. Mongolism showed a clustering with regard to time and place of conception.

Lander et al.[78] investigated the month of birth of 10,705 mental defectives, and found that significantly fewer were born in September than controls—mainly because fewer mongols were born in that month.

THE AGE OF THE MOTHER has a bearing on foetal development. The older the mother, the greater is the incidence of anomalies of the central nervous system and the greater the incidence of dizygotic twins. In addition older mothers, who have not previously had children, tend to over-protect them.

I have already mentioned the relationship of the age of the mother to the incidence of mongolism. Dayton and Truden[34] studied the relationship of the age of the mother to the incidence of mental retardation in 23,422 families. The older the mother the higher was the incidence of mental retardation.

Older mothers are more likely to have premature labour than young mothers, and are more likely to give birth to children with a ventricular septal defect.

THE RÔLE OF THE AGE OF THE FATHER is as yet uncertain, though it is known that achondroplasia and Aperts' syndrome (craniostenosis with syndactyly) are associated with advanced paternal age,[14] and both are often associated with mental deficiency. The paternal age does not seem to be of significance in regular mongols (trisomy 21) or 15:21 translocation mongols. In mongolism associated with fusion of chromosomes 21 and 22 advancing paternal age is highly significant.[107] Advanced paternal age is also associated with an increased incidence of malformations of the central nervous system and sense organs, of mental deficiency, osteogenesis imperfecta, and certain forms of congenital heart disease.[33, 96, 108]

The possibility that abnormalities of the spermatozoa may be related to perinatal disease was discussed by Spector.[136] It has been shown in Sweden that an excessive number of abnormal spermatozoa may be related to abortions, premature delivery and congenital malformations. The possibility that drugs taken by the father may affect the spermatozoa and so the foetus cannot be ignored.[17]

A comprehensive review of the experimental work concerning possible changes in the spermatozoa and ova resulting from delays in reproduction was provided by Lanman.[77]

There is an inverse relationship between the SIZE OF THE FAMILY and the intelligence of the child.[71] The size of the family may also affect the child's development in other ways. Along with the spacing of births, it will certainly affect his psychological development. Surveys have shown that in general the eldest, the youngest and the only children are more intelligent than intermediate ones.[86] This cannot be due to genetic factors, for obvious reasons, and is presumably due to environmental factors, such as the amount of contact which the child has with adults, and the amount of attention which his mother is able to give him. When two-child families are considered, the mean I.Q. score is higher when there is a longer interval between births. The relatively lower mean I.Q. scores in twins (to be discussed later) may be due to similar factors.

OTHER SOCIAL FACTORS which affect the child's development

include illegitimacy, the parental age and intelligence, and the mother's upbringing. Drillien[39] in a study of the relationship of social factors to premature births, found that the social class of the father was less important than that in which the mother had been brought up—with particular regard to the efficiency of the grandmother.

CIGARETTE SMOKING. There is said to be a relationship between cigarette smoking and premature births.[125] Data from 7,499 patients indicated that the incidence of premature births was approximately twice as great for smoking mothers as for non-smokers. When all variables have been taken into consideration, it is clear that smoking during pregnancy considerably increases the incidence of low birth weight babies.[123]

Premature Delivery and Small-for-Dates Babies

There have been numerous studies of the intellectual development of prematurely born babies.

Dann, Levine and New[31] studied 100 infants who weighed 1000 g. or less at birth. On follow-up examination the mean I.Q. was 94·8, as compared with a figure of 106·9 for their siblings; 59 per cent had eye defects.

McDonald[88] followed up 1066 children with a birth weight of 4 lbs. (1800 g.) or less assembled by the Medical Research Council between 1951 and 1953 while investigating the relationship of oxygen therapy to the development of retrolental fibroplasia. 13·6 per cent of the surviving singletons and 5·9 per cent of the twins or triplets had cerebral palsy, an I.Q. below 50, blindness or deafness. Many of the children who had died were known to have had defects. Of 206 children who weighed less than 3 lbs. at birth, 33 per cent had a defect.

In another study,[25] 51 children with undifferentiated mental deficiency had a significantly lower birth weight than 51 children who had an I.Q. of over 110, matched for sex, age, area of residence and social factors.

Heimer et al.[59] observed the incidence of neurological handicaps at the age of 30 months in 318 premature babies seen at King's County Hospital, Brooklyn. The incidence of neurological abnormalities was as follows:

	Total Babies	Percentage Handicapped
Less than 1,251 g.	39	39
1,251–1,750 g.	104	24
1,751–2,100 g.	175	13

The incidence of abnormalities was higher in the boys. The incidence of abnormalities was higher where there had been a low body temperature or an infection.

Drillien, in a series of publications later brought together into one volume,[39] described a detailed follow-up of prematurely born children in Edinburgh. The series included 110 children weighing 3 lbs. (1,360 g.) or less at birth: 72 were over five years of age. Over a third of those of school age were unsuitable for education in a normal school; over a third of those in an ordinary school were educationally retarded, and less than a third were doing work appropriate to their age. Seventy per cent. of those of school age showed restlessness, overactivity and other behaviour problems. Of 51 with siblings, 76 per cent. were inferior intellectually to their full term born siblings. The I.Q. score fell steadily with decreasing birth weight. Twins scored less than singletons. She suggested that neurological damage might have been caused by dehydration from starvation, hyperbilirubinaemia, or disturbance of the acid base balance. The possible effect of social grouping was described, because of the known increased incidence of premature births in the lower social classes; but she found that in all social groupings the small premature babies fared less well than their full term siblings or controls compared with full term babies. Twice as many with a birth weight below $4\frac{1}{2}$ lbs. were working below their intellectual capacity. She quoted the findings of the National Maternity Survey of 1946, in which it was found that 9·7 per cent. of premature babies secured grammar school places, as compared with 22·0 per cent. of full term controls. There was also a marked excess of disturbed behaviour in all birth weight groups when there was a history of severe complications of pregnancy, such as toxaemia or abnormal delivery.

In a study of 94 Colorado infants who weighed 1,500 g. or less at birth, 67 were evaluated at 10 years of age. Sixty-nine per cent were handicapped to some degree. Twenty-five had an I.Q. score of 89 or less. Eighteen had serious eye defects. They were below average in physical growth.[85]   Takkunen *et al*.[139] followed 110 infants weighing 1,750 g. or less at birth. Forty-one per cent. had neurological defects. The mean I.Q. score was 94·8. Forty-nine per cent. were assessed as 'immature for ordinary school'.

Douglas, in his extensive survey of children born in 1948, followed over 400 prematurely born children for 8 years and over 350 for 11 years.[37] In all respects the prematurely born babies fared less well than the controls. The teachers' comments concerning powers of concentration, attitude to work and discipline were unfavourable as compared with comments on controls. These differences were ascribed in part to adverse home conditions, lack of parental care and low educational aspirations.

Douglas[36] found that prematurely born children scored less than controls in tests of reading, vocabulary and intelligence than controls.   They were proportionately more handicapped in reading than in either vocabulary or picture in telligence. Douglas found that those prematurely born children in whom there had been no good obstetrical cause for the prematurity, and for whom the small size could not be explained by the size of their parents, scored outstandingly less than others who were born prematurely. This is not an unexpected finding.

Several workers have described psychological difficulties in prematurely born children.   Shirley[124] described a variety of features — short flitting attention, distractibility, irascibility, stubbornness, negativism, shyness, and overdependence on the mother.   They tended to be clumsy in manipulation and locomotion. Beskow,[12] in his study of 273 prematurely born children at the age of 9 to 15, found them mentally and physically infantile, late in development of ethical sense, with a primitive, unrestrained need for movement, emotional lability, poor concentration and excessive fatigability.

It is difficult to assess these reports because of the possibility of other factors.   Firstly, defective concentration, over-activity, and other features may be due in part to the lower mean level of intelligence of prematurely born children.   There is a higher incidence of prematurity in the lower social classes, and in these classes there is also a lower overall mean I.Q. than in the upper classes.   Baird,[7] in his study of 363 primiparae in Aberdeen, found a striking excess of low intelligence scores in women who gave birth to premature babies. It was only when the birth weight of a baby was $7\frac{1}{2}$ lbs. or more that there was an excess of mothers of superior I.Q. and a deficiency of those with a low I.Q. In those giving birth to premature babies there was also a striking excess of small women. The excess of women of sub-average I.Q. was greatest in small women. Secondly, knowing the association between prematurity and maternal illness, such as toxaemia, one wonders whether the mother's illness may have been responsible for the subsequent psychological features in the child. Severe maternal illness may lead to undesirable factors in the management of the child, such as overprotection. This, in turn, may be aggravated by anxiety occasioned by the greater incidence of infections in the prematurely born child in the first 2 years of his life.

It may well be that the outlook for a prematurely born child depends on the cause of the premature labour. This is pure conjecture, but one feels that the outlook might be better for a child born prematurely as a result of artificial induction of labour on account of dysproportion than it is for a baby born prematurely as a result of antepartum haemorrhage, toxaemia, or other conditions which might have caused anoxia or other damage to the foetus.

Most of the studies quoted, with the exception of those of Drillien[39] and McDonald[88] included 'small for dates' babies with the 'premature babies'. It is probable that the 'small for dates' babies are more at risk of mental and physical defects than the true premature ones.

In none of the follow-up studies of premature babies can one eliminate the possibility that some of the backwardness in the smaller premature babies was due to kernicterus, which might have been avoided if attention had been paid to the levels of serum bilirubin in the first 6 to 9 days of life. Freedman et al.[47] studied the development of 500 infants weighing less than 2,100 g. at birth. At 4 months the gross motor development of male infants (but not female infants) with a high serum bilirubin in the newborn period was significantly less than that of infants who had had a low serum bilirubin.

One may conclude by saying that the smaller the premature baby at birth, the greater the likelihood that he will have cerebral palsy or mental retardation, but the reason for this fact is not at all clear. There are many variables which make it difficult to be more precise about the intellectual potential of premature babies, and much more research on the subject is needed.

The Effects of Irradiation in Utero

Miller[93] examined 33 children born by mothers at Hiroshima at the time of the explosion of the atomic bomb. Fifteen were mentally retarded. The incidence of mental deficiency was related to the distance from the hypocentre and to the gestational age at the time of the explosion.

Plummer[110] found that 7 of 11 infants born by mothers close to the hypocentre of the atomic explosion at Hiroshima were microcephalic idiots. Yamazaki et al.[154] found that 4 of 16 infants similarly exposed at Nagasaki were mentally defective.

Courville and Edmondson[28] described a mentally defective child whose mother had been deliberately exposed to X-rays in an attempt to terminate pregnancy. At autopsy the child's brain was found to be abnormal. They referred to more than 60 cases in which mental deficiency was thought to have resulted from irradiation *in utero*. They wrote that the clinical picture is a constant one, namely microcephaly with severe mental deficiency, often associated with microphthalmos.

Maternal irradiation may lead to chromosomal abnormalities, including trisomies.[143]

Miscellaneous Prenatal Factors which Affect a Child's Development

1. *Infections during pregnancy.*

The association of rubella in the first 3 or 4 months of pregnancy with mental deficiency and other anomalies in the foetus is well known. The risk of mental deficiency occurring is less certain. Bradford Hill et al.[61] thought that the risk of a foetus being affected (by any of the recognised sequelae) was as high as 50 per cent. if the rubella were contracted in the first month of pregnancy, 25 per cent. if it occurred in the second month, and 17 per cent. if it occurred in the third month. Of 54 mothers who contracted rubella in the second and third trimesters it was probable that one had a child with related sequelae. Ingalls,[66] from his own figures and those of six other papers, found that 15·8 per cent. of 64 mothers who contracted rubella in the first trimester had an abnormal living foetus, as compared with 14·3 per cent. of 28 mothers in the second trimester. Jackson and Fisch[68] found that deafness (unilateral in a third), occurred in 30 per cent. of children born of mothers who had rubella in the first 16 weeks of pregnancy.

Toxoplasmosis and untreated syphilis are well known to be associated with mental deficiency in the child.

2. *Uterine anomalies.*

Hydramnios, apart from its well-known association with obstructive lesions of the foetal alimentary tract, is also associated with a somewhat higher incidence of achondroplasia, meningo-cele and mental deficiency, than that in the rest of the population. At the Jessop Hospital at Sheffield, it was found that of 287 births associated with hydramnios, 43 per cent of the babies were still-born or died in the newborn period. Congenital abnormalities were present in 41 per cent of the infants.[114]

An abnormal situation of the placenta (*e.g.* placenta praevia) and retroversion of the uterus are associated with a higher than average incidence of prematurity and foetal anomalies.

Bleeding during pregnancy is associated with a higher than average incidence of cerebral palsy, mongolism, and prematurity in the foetus.

The administration of anticoagulants during pregnancy carries with it the risk of cerebral haemorrhage in the foetus.

3. *Other foetal environmental factors including stress in pregnancy.*

Research by Sontag at the Fels Institute,[129,130] in the United States of America, has indicated that the mother's emotional state may affect the foetus. Sontag showed that emotional disturbance and fatigue in the mother increases foetal activity. He thought that prolonged nervous and emotional disturbance in the mother in the latter months of pregnancy may lead to hyperactivity, irri-tability and feeding difficulties in the baby, possibly through a chemical action. It would be difficult to prove, however, that the association between the mother's and the child's nervous system was not genetically related.

Stott[133, 134] adduced evidence that severe shock and emotion were significantly more frequent in pregnancies leading to mongoloid and other mentally defective children. He suggested that further research into these factors was necessary to determine

4

the significance of this observation. Sixty-six per cent. of 102 retarded children, as compared with 30 per cent. of 450 controls, had been born by mothers subjected to severe stress of emotion or illness during pregnancy. One might think that the incidence of stress in the controls is rather high. It has been suggested that parents of defective children might well try harder than others to find some causative factor in pregnancy. In any case, recent knowledge about the genetics of mongolism hardly give support to Stott's work.

Stott has subsequently reviewed the literature concerning the possibility that stressful experiences in pregnancy may affect the foetus. He considered that there is good evidence that psychological stress during pregnancy, such as that in wartime, is associated with an increased incidence of anomalies in the foetus.[136] He quoted Klebanov as finding that when women gave birth to children within a year or so of release from concentration camps, the incidence of malformations in the children and of mongols was four or five times greater than the normal incidence.

Thompson[141] engendered strong anxiety in rats by exposing them to the fear of electric shocks at the sound of a buzzer; they were able to escape through a door. The rats were then mated and became pregnant, and were then exposed to the same fear, but the door was blocked so that they could not escape. Their offspring showed striking differences from controls when examined at 30 to 40 days and 130 to 140 days. Their responses were more slow, and in various ways they showed more 'emotionality' all through their adult life.

Keeley[73] subjected pregnant albino mice to stress by over-crowding. When their litters encountered unfamiliar stimuli, they were less active than controls, they were slower to respond, and their reaction times were longer. The differences persisted at 30 and 100 days of age. These experiments appeared to indicate that prenatal stress had an effect on the performance in later life. Drillien and Wilkinson[40] provided confirmation of Stott's work. They studied the events during the pregnancies which had resulted in the birth of 227 mentally defective children, of whom a third were mongols. There was a significantly higher incidence of severe emotional stress in the pregnancy of mothers giving birth to mongols, than there was in the mother of non mongoloid defectives. This difference applied particularly when the mother was over forty.

Gunther[56] studied stress in pregnancy as a possible cause of premature labour, investigating 20 married mothers with no apparent physical cause for prematurity, and 20 controls. Mothers with many psychosomatic symptoms and domestic crises were more likely to have infants of low birth weight.

Taft and Goldfarb[138] carried out a retrospective study of 29 schizophrenic children of school age, 39 siblings of schizophrenic children, and 34 public school children. There was a much greater incidence of prenatal and perinatal complications in the case of the schizophrenic children, especially in boys. The complications include advanced maternal age, hyperemesis, antepartum haemorrhage, eclampsia and hypertension.

4. *The relationship of foetal activity to subsequent motor development.*

Richards and Newberry[118] recorded foetal activity in 12 infants by polygraph records for 5 to 6 hour periods at 1 to 2 week intervals in the last half of pregnancy, and compared the results with the motor development at the age of 6 months. There was a positive relationship, and 'rank difference coefficients in all cases were 4 times their probable errors'.

5. *The effect of drugs taken in pregnancy*

The thalidomide disaster has focused attention on the possible effect of drugs taken in the early weeks of pregnancy. The effect which thalidomide has had on the child's intelligence is so far unknown, because there has not been time to assess it. It is obvious that it would be exceedingly difficult to assess the development of a limbless infant, yet one has seen statements that 'thalidomide babies' are normal mentally. I saw one paper which purported to give the percentage of those babies who were mentally defective. As the figure given was considerably less than that of the population as a whole, the accuracy of the finding was questionable.

Other drugs taken by the mother may affect the child's development. Methotrexate may lead to deformities of the nervous system. Hypoglycaemic agents may have a damaging effect on the developing brain of the foetus. Drugs which increase the jaundice in a baby, particularly a prematurely born one, may damage the brain; they include promethazine, sparine and large doses of

Vitamin K. The occurrence of several cases of cerebral palsy on the shores of the Inland Sea in Japan was traced to the eating of fish contaminated by mercury which was discharged from a factory into the sea.[92]

Multiple Pregnancy

There is evidence that multiple pregnancy results in a slightly higher incidence of mental retardation and of cerebral palsy than do single pregnancies. The reasons are probably complex and interrelated. They include prematurity, abnormal delivery (especially in the case of the second twin), hypoglycaemia or anoxia (in the second twin), and possibly poor placental implantation. Looft[82] found a higher number of imbeciles in a group of 64 twins than one finds in the normal population. He also found that among siblings and parents of backward children there were more twins than among normal children. Rosanoff and Inman-Kane[122] studied 1,011 twins, one or other having mental disorders. There were 234 pairs of mentally defective twins. There was a greater incidence of mental defects in twins than in single births. They mentioned the occasional occurrence of markedly unequal intellectual development in monozygotic twins. Three out of 4 of 34 pairs of monozygotic twins had the same I.Q. or a difference of not more than 5 points, while only 1 out of every 6 of dizygotic twins were within that range. In 80 of the 87 pairs of monozygotic twins, both twins were mentally defective, while in 7 only 1 was affected. Of 147 dizygotic twins, both twins were defective, and in 91 pairs only one was affected.

McKinney et al.[89] found a lower mean test score in twins at 6 months and 4 to 5 years than in singletons. Drillien[39] in her follow-up of premature babies, found that twins scored less than singletons. Berg and Kirman[11] found that the incidence of twins in 230 mentally defective children at the Fountain Hospital was 6·1 per cent. They discussed possible reasons for the high incidence of abnormalities in twins. They suggested that twinning in humans is somewhat unusual, and that especially in monozygotic pairs it suggests a tendency on the part of the zygote to behave in an unorthodox manner. Twin pregnancy imposes additional burdens on the mother, so that any marginal defects in her capacity to nourish the embryo would be exaggerated. In addition twinning imposes a greater risk of birth injury and of prematurity. They thought that there was a greater likelihood that the second born twin would be defective. Graves *et al.*[54] however, found that the risk of birth injury was no greater in the second born than in the first born twin. It is known that the mean I.Q. of the smaller of twins tends to be lower than that of their larger cotwin. It has been suggested[116] that there is a tendency for the smaller of the twins, who in a way is a 'dysmature' infant, to have hypoglycaemia at birth. This could be related to subsequent intelligence.

In a Scottish survey, the mean I.Q. of twins was 4·83 points lower than for all non-twins.[135] In boys it was 5·55 points lower than for non-twins. Babson and colleagues[6] studied 20 pairs of surviving twins in which the smaller twin weighed less than 2,000 g. and weighed at least 25 per cent. less than the larger twin at birth. They studied 16 pairs at a median age of $8\frac{1}{2}$ years. The smaller twin fared significantly less well in height, head circumference, weight and I.Q. tests.

Alberman,[1] at Guy's Hospital, showed that there was a high perinatal mortality in the unaffected twins of a pregnancy in which one twin had cerebral palsy. This suggested that there had been an antenatal factor operating on both twins.

Newman[98] described peculiar examples of twins faring less well in intelligence tests when tested in different rooms than when tested in the same room. It seemed as if one child needed the presence of his twin sibling to achieve his maximum performance. Perhaps some of the above differences in uniovular twins are due to this phenomenon. He also wrote that mental retardation is commoner in uniovular than binovular twins, in girls than boys, in the first born than the second born, and in premature or markedly underweight twins.

Twins tend to be later in speaking than singletons.

In a study of prematurity and multiple pregnancy in relation to mental retardation and cerebral palsy, we found[64] that of 729 mentally retarded children without cerebral palsy, 20·9 per cent. were born prematurely and the incidence of twins was 3·8 per cent. In 651 children with cerebral palsy, the incidence of prematurity was 35·9 per cent. and that of twins was 8·4 per cent. By statistical analysis it was shown that the high incidence of twins in cerebral palsy was not related to the high incidence of prematurity, but that the high incidence of twins in the other group may well be due to the factor of prematurity. Zazzo's book[155] on the personality and development of twins should be read by all those interested in the subject. He pointed out that a genetic influence is not proved by the fact that there is greater concordance in monozygotic twins than in dizygotic ones. Monozygotic twins may well be treated by parents as more alike than dizygotic twins, and monozygotic twins tend to be more firmly attached to each other and therefore to develop similar attitudes.

Monozygotic twins tend to be smaller at birth, more prematurely born, to have a higher perinatal mortality, and to be more delicate than dizygotic twins. They are more unsociable, introverted and timid than dizygotic twins (or singletons). The average age of mothers of dizygotic twins is higher than that of mothers of monozygotic twins. All these factors have an obvious bearing on development, and they all indicate the complexity of the problem of the effect of nature and nurture on a child's personality and performance.

Abnormalities of Pregnancy and Birth

Stevenson[132], using the notes of psychologists, teachers, paediatricians, social workers and parents' comments, found that of 226 children at Boston, 73·9 per cent. were in good condition in the first two days of life; 19·2 per cent. of these were later 'maladjusted'. Of those in poor condition in the first two days, 39·0 per cent. were later maladjusted.

A series of papers from the Johns Hopkins Hospital[80, 81, 102, 121] has convincingly shown the relation between complications of pregnancy or delivery and the subsequent finding of epilepsy, mental deficiency, cerebral palsy and psychological disorders. In a study of 564 epileptic children in Baltimore, there was a significantly higher incidence of complications of pregnancy and delivery, and of abnormal neonatal conditions, than in a similar number of matched controls. (For controls the authors took the next registered birth, matched by race, place of birth and maternal age). The complications included conditions liable to lead to anoxia in the foetus, such as toxaemia, antepartum haemorrhage, placenta praevia, breech delivery and contracted pelvis, but not mechanical methods of delivery. Amongst white children, 17·2 per cent. had neonatal cyanotic attacks, fits or asphyxia, as compared with 5·7 per cent. of controls.

In a series of 561 mentally defective children, 34·4 per cent.

were born of mothers with complications of pregnancy, 25·8 per cent. were prematurely born, and 18·0 per cent. had neonatal abnormalities (as defined above): the corresponding figures for the controls were 25·2 per cent., 11 per cent. and 7·5 per cent. respectively.

In a series of 561 cases of cerebral palsy, 38 per cent. were born of mothers with complications of pregnancy, as compared with 21 per cent. of other children.

In another study they investigated 1,151 cases of behaviour disorders and matched them with 902 controls by class, location, race and sex. One of the problems commonly found was hyperkinesis. The range of I.Q. scores was 90 to 99. There was a significantly higher incidence of abnormalities in the prenatal and perinatal period than in the controls. This study is beyond reproach for the care with which all the variables were considered. One wonders, however, whether the greater incidence of maternal toxaemia and of antepartum haemorrhage in the behaviour disorder group, might have an indirect effect on the mother's management of her children and on the incidence of subsequent behaviour problems.

In an investigation[72] of the perinatal history of 372 children with reading disorders, matched with 205 controls, it was found that 16·6 per cent. had 2 or more of the above complications of pregnancy, especially preeclampsia, antepartum haemorrhage and hypertension, as compared with 1·5 per cent. of controls.

They found no correlation between abnormalities of pregnancy and speech disorders.[100] They studied the antecedents of 424 'non-defective and non-palsied children with speech disorders' and found no association between these disorders and complications of pregnancy.

In another study[101] they investigated the hospital records of 83 children with tics, and found a significantly greater incidence of complications of pregnancy than in a similar number of matched controls. They thought that there might be an association between tics and hyperkinesis, in that both are related to prenatal factors.

In discussing these effects they postulated 'a continuum of reproductive casualty', implying that whereas in the severest cases the result of these prenatal conditions is an abortion or stillbirth, in less severe ones there is organic disease, such as cerebral palsy, epilepsy or mental deficiency: while in the milder cases there are merely behaviour disorders and tics. Prechtl, working at Groningen, Holland,[112, 113] has carried out a unique follow-up study of full term babies into school age, comparing their later performance with various features of the new-born period. They found that undue excitability in the new-born period was apt to be followed by hyperactivity, short attention span, and learning difficulties in later years.

In this connection Macdonald[90] made an interesting observation in Glasgow concerning the predisposition to premature births. In a study of 515 mothers showing this tendency, he found that the incidence of abortions among the other pregnancies of the mothers of these premature children was unduly high. Drillien[39] also showed that in the pregnancy prior to the birth of a defective premature baby, there was a higher incidence of miscarriages or stillbirths than there was in the pregnancy preceding the birth of a normal premature baby.

Burke[20] studied the prognostic significance of convulsions in 46 newborn babies in Sheffield. Eighteen (37·5 per cent.) died. All the rest were followed up, rough Gesell tests being performed 6 months to $4\frac{1}{2}$ years later. One had hydrocephalus and spina bifida, 5 were severely mentally defective (1 with spastic quadriplegia), and 1 was blind in one eye.

In any further studies of this nature, it would be necessary to relate the condition at follow-up to the cause of the neonatal convulsions. It is likely that convulsions due to hypoglycaemia are much more harmful to the brain than those due to hypocalcaemia.

There is no doubt that there is an association between neurological abnormalities in the infant and abnormalities of pregnancy and delivery[42] but one study indicated that half of the infants suffering a birth hazard also suffered hazards in utero from events during pregnancy.[119] The interwoven social factors have already been mentioned. Postmaturity is now known to be dangerous not only to life, but to the well being of the infant if he survives, for it increases the risk of cerebral palsy.[144]

The antecedents of cerebral palsy are very similar to those of mental retardation, and both conditions are frequently present in the same child. I have summarised elsewhere[63] the known antecedents of cerebral palsy. Cerebral palsy is slightly more common in males, there is a genetic factor, it is more common in multiple pregnancies, there is a higher than average incidence of previous miscarriages and stillbirths, of antepartum haemorrhage and toxaemia, and of abnormal labour associated with anoxia rather than with mechanical trauma.

A popular concept today is that of the 'brain-injured child'. It is a term which I have always disliked, because it implies that the obstetrician or attendant has been in some way to blame for the child's difficulties.

Some workers, such as Strauss and Kephart[137] use the term in the wider sense, to include the effect of anoxia *in utero*, or of any other noxious factor after conception. Those interested should read their interesting two-volume book. Wortis[153] described the concept of brain injury as including children who are hyperactive, distractible, awkward, poorly integrated in motor performance, faulty in their perception, poorly organised, unpredictable in their behaviour, and who fall to pieces on relatively slight provocation. Whether the cause is infectious, traumatic, toxic or embryonic, the end result is supposed to be the same. Wortis was against generalisations on the brain-injured child, and felt that there is no one clear-cut picture of this condition. One book in a chapter on brain damaged children includes mongols, cretins and microcephalics.[43]

After reading various books and articles on 'brain-injured children', one is left with the feeling that it is difficult to prove by tests in later childhood that the features described are in fact due to 'brain-injury'[13, 115]. There is in fact no psychological test which is specific for such children, in that it does not give similar results in children without 'brain injury'.

One cannot be sure that some of the features described are not genetically determined, or due to environmental circumstances. I have referred elsewhere to the problems which the handicapped child has to face—the overprotection, and the lack of normal environmental stimulation. This, together with the delayed maturation seen in some handicapped children, may account for at least some of the manifestations ascribed by Strauss and Kephart and others to 'brain-injury'. The term 'minimal cerebral dysfunction', used in a symposium sponsored by the Spastics Society,[8] is preferable to the expression 'brain injury', in that it does not imply that the cause of the defect is known. Those interested should read the book.

The Prognosis of Neonatal Asphyxia

The literature on the prognosis of neonatal asphyxia is extensive and mostly difficult to evaluate. A critical discussion by Graham and her colleagues[53] should be read by all interested in the problem. They emphasised the need for more research, with the use of more accurate definition of the degree, duration and clinical features of asphyxia.

There has been a considerable amount of experimental work into the problem of asphyxia.

Windle and Becker[148] asphyxiated guinea pigs by clamping the uterine vessels of the mother or the umbilical cord of the foetus. All the piglets showed neurological signs and symptoms, including tremors, paralysis, spasticity, somnolence, and increased errors in the maze test. Two-thirds showed pathological changes in the nervous system, such as necrosis, oedema, chromatolysis and petechiae. Glial proliferation began at 5 days. In older specimens there was loss of nerve cells, atrophy of the brain and destruction of the pyramidal cells in the cortex.

In other papers Windle[149 150] described experiments on pregnant full term guinea-pigs delivered by Caesarian section. Some animals were subjected to asphyxia by occlusion of the placental circulation, while others were delivered normally as controls. Those animals in whom circulation was occluded for 8 minutes or more showed clinical and pathological changes similar to those described above.

Pathological evidence of the effect of anoxia has been provided by many workers, and in particular by Courville.[27] The lesions described by him include focal necrosis and scarring in the cerebral cortex, widespread diffuse or nodular cortical atrophy, focal or diffuse alterations in the corpus striatum, areas of cortical and subcortical softening incident to arterial occlusion, and demyelination and cyst formation.

That asphyxia in later life can produce neurological sequelae is well known. Nielson and Courville[98] told the story of a boy who was throttled by a sailor and who 6 months later developed athetosis. Plum et al.[109] followed 5 patients who had suffered severe anoxia as a result of carbon monoxide poisoning, anaesthesia or cardiac arrest. Autopsy examination was carried out in two. The predominant damage was cerebral hemisphere demyelination without significant neuronal damage. Clinically, deterioration tended to occur after the patients were discharged and they had resumed activity. The symptoms were irritability, apathy, confusion, clumsiness and extrapyramidal rigidity.

Experimental work in the newborn baby included that of Apgar *et al.*[4] They set out to determine whether there was any relationship between the foetal blood oxygen saturation at birth and the subsequent intellectual development. Gesell tests were used in the younger children and Stanford-Binet tests in the older ones. They could find no correlation at all.

Turkewitz, Moreau and Birch[142] studied three groups of infants in the first week of life, who differed in the Apgar score at birth. They applied 30 'lateralised somesthetic stimuli' to the perioral region of each infant, and measured the lateral direction of the first head turn. Normal infants with an Apgar score of 9 or 10 responded better to stimulation from the right than the left, and made more ipsilateral responses to stimulation from the right, while those with an Apgar score of 1 to 6 did not show these responses, being equally likely to respond predominantly to either side.

In a prospective study of 33 children who had an Apgar score of 5 or less, the performance at 30 months was no different from that of matched controls. In another study there was no correlation between a low Apgar rating and the quality of survivors at one year.[118]

An infant may appear to make a complete recovery after anoxia and other adverse perinatal conditions, such as abnormal hypotonia and decreased movements, while in later years he may prove to have neurological sequelae. Prechtl[111] of Gröningen has described what he terms the choreiform syndrome in school children who at birth had suffered anoxia, and had seemed to develop normally thereafter. The features included distractibility, poor performance at school, reading difficulties, clumsiness, poor concentration, and labile emotional behaviour, fluctuating between timidity and aggressive outbursts. They show distinct twitchings of the extremities, head and tongue, unlike true chorea, but nevertheless characteristic.

Ernhart *et al.*[44] who have previously carried out valuable studies on the sequelae of perinatal asphyxia, examined 355 children at the age of 3 years, in order to determine whether those who had anoxia at birth were in any way different from those whose condition at birth was satisfactory. 116 children constituted the anoxic group: 159 children were normal at birth, being full term, with an uneventful prenatal and neonatal course, with an easy delivery. In addition there was a complicated group of 80 children who had mixed difficulties such as prematurity, haemolytic disease, skull fracture and intracranial haemorrhage. The definition of anoxia was satisfactory. The follow-up examinations were carried out without knowledge of the newborn classification. The follow-up assessment consisted of a battery of psychological tests, and a neurological examination.

The only significant psychological differences concerned the 'cognitive' or 'intellectual' functions. There was a greater impairment in conceptional ability than in vocabulary skill in the anoxic children. In addition the I.Q. score was slightly less in the anoxic children than in the normal controls. There were more abnormal neurological findings in the anoxic group than in the controls. They comment that perinatal events contribute their portion to the crippling of human capacity.

The authors discuss the possibility that there may have been genetic factors which were associated with both the perinatal complications and the inferiority found at 3 years.

This is a carefully planned and controlled study, contributing useful information to our knowledge of the sequelae of perinatal asphyxia.

In an extensive Chicago study,[9] children were selected from over 40,000 births on account of several anoxia at birth. They were compared with their sibling controls and others who had been delivered spontaneously. The ages at follow up ranged from 3 to 19 years. It was a retrospective study. The incidence of feeblemindedness (as shown by intelligence tests) was 20 per cent. in the anoxic group and 2·5 per cent. in the controls. E.E.G. abnormalities were found in 36 per cent. of the anoxic group but in none of the control group. A battery of psychological tests, such as the Bender-Gestalt, figure completion, and other tests, showed no other differences.

The authors made the point that only isolated children in the anoxic group were abnormal; there were no material differences between the group as a whole. Many of the anoxic children were of superior intelligence.

A valuable long term study was carried out at Aberdeen[46] where legitimate full term singletons with moderate or severe asphyxia at birth, were followed up at the age of $7\frac{1}{2}$ to $11\frac{1}{2}$, by a full battery of psychological tests. Very few indeed showed either intellectual or neurological defects.

Conclusions

It is not easy to interpret the numerous studies on the effects of neonatal asphyxia. One major difficulty lies in the fact that neonatal asphyxia (and similarly neonatal convulsions or cyanotic attacks) are likely themselves to be due to some prenatal noxious influence acting in utero. One must look beyond the asphyxia, convulsions or cyanotic attacks to the causes of those conditions, and avoid the usual mistake of ascribing subsequent deficits in the child to something in the immediate postnatal period when in fact it was due to a prenatal factor.

When any prospective study is carried out, the follow-up must be nearly complete, for otherwise it will be difficult to interpret. For instance, if only two thirds of one's cases can be traced, one will have to convince the reader that the two thirds followed up were in all respects the same as the one third not followed—and that will be a matter of great difficulty.

We have to admit that we do not know how much developmental potential is being lost as a result of difficult deliveries. It is interesting to speculate how much the intelligence and performance of children in this country could be raised by improved obstetrical care, by the prevention of anoxia, and by improved paediatric care in the newborn period.

With this preamble, one can summarise the influence of pre natal and perinatal factors as follows:

1. Genetic factors have a great bearing on the child's development, but the majority of children of a mentally defective mother or father will be normal. Parents of superior intelligence are likely to have children of a superior intellectual level.

    Genetic factors operate in connection with many forms of mental deficiency, congenital anomalies, prematurity, and multiple pregnancy. They are also concerned with the child's basic personality.

2. Kernicterus is now virtually preventable, and if therefore kernicterus is excluded, there is no evidence that haemolytic disease of the newborn affects the child's development. It is not clear how much relationship there is between the height of the serum bilirubin reached in a premature baby and the subsequent intelligence unless there is kernicterus.

3. Social factors, such as poverty, nutritional status, age of mother, upbringing of the mother, and excessive smoking

during pregnancy, have some bearing on the infant's development, the latter owing to a small association with prematurity.
The older the mother, the greater the risk of mongolism
and certain other forms of mental retardation. Poverty
and malnutrition are associated with a lower than average
intellectual level in the child, and with a higher rate of
prematurity.

4. Though there is a difference of opinion, there is good evidence that the lower the birth weight the greater the incidence of cerebral palsy, epilepsy and mental retardation,
though the great majority of prematurely born children will
grow up to be entirely normal.

There is some evidence that certain emotional and education problems are somewhat commoner among prematurely
born children than among full term ones.

5. Heavy irradiation of the pregnant woman may lead to mental
retardation in the baby.

6. Certain abnormalities of pregnancy, such as antepartum
haemorrhage, maternal toxaemia and abnormalities of the
placenta, are associated with an incidence of prematurity,
mental deficiency, epilepsy, and cerebral palsy, which is
greater than that found when these abnormalities are
absent. In the case of rubella in the first 3 or 4 months,
the risk of a child being seriously affected is probably
in the order of 10 to 20 per cent. In the case of the other
abnormalities, no figures are known, but one can say that
the great majority of babies born of mothers who had
antepartum haemorrhage, maternal toxaemia or placenta
praevia will be normal, and these factors must not be exaggerated. The presence of any of these factors, for instance,
must not cause one automatically to declare that a child is
unsuitable for adoption.

Maternal syphilis, if properly treated, should not affect
the baby's development. Toxoplasmosis may be associated
with severe mental deficiency in the baby. Hydramnios is
frequently associated with defects in the foetus.

There is evidence that emotional stress in the mother in the
latter part of pregnancy may have an effect on the baby's
mental development.

7. Multiple pregnancies are associated with a higher than average incidence of cerebral palsy and mental retardation, though the great majority of children will be normal.

8. Severe asphyxia in the newborn period is associated with a higher than average incidence of cerebral palsy (especially athetosis) and mental retardation, and perhaps of certain behaviour problems, but the great majority of infants who suffer asphyxia at birth grow up to be normal.

Cyanotic attacks are associated with a high perinatal mortality. The relationship to subsequent development is as yet uncertain. Convulsions in the newborn period, apart from carrying a high immediate mortality, are associated with a significantly higher than average incidence of mental retardation, but most of the survivors will be normal.

It is apt to be fallacious to ascribe a child's physical, mental or psychological handicap to asphyxia neonatorum. The asphyxia may itself have been due to an underlying brain defect.

Defects in a foetus are rarely due to a single prenatal factor. Prenatal factors tend to act in combination, so that abnormalities in the foetus tend to be the product of multiple factors, genetic and environmental.

REFERENCES

1. ALBERMAN, E. D. (1964) Cerebral Palsy in Twins. Guy's Hosp. Rep., 113, 285.
2. ALM, I. (1953) The Long Term Prognosis for Prematurely Born Children. A Follow-up Study of 999 Premature Boys Born in Wedlock and of 1002 controls. *Acta Paediat. (Uppsala)*, Suppl. 94.
3. ANDERSON, W. J. R., BAIRD, D., THOMSON, A. M. (1958) Epidemiology of Stillbirth and Infant Deaths Due to Congenital Malformation. *Lancet*, 2, 1304.
4. APGAR, V., GIRDANY, B. R., McINTOSH, R., TAYLOR, H. C. (1955) Neonatal Anoxia. A Study of the Relation of Oxygenation at Birth to Intellectual Development. *Pediatrics*, 15, 653.
5. ASHER, C., FRASER ROBERTS, J. A. (1949) A Study of Birth Weight and Intelligence. *Brit. J. soc. Med.*, 3, 56.
6. BABSON, S. G., YOUNG, N., KANGOS, J., BRAMHALL, J. L. (1964). Growth and Development of Twins of Dissimilar Size at Birth. *Pediatrics*, 33, 327.
7. BAIRD, D. (1959) The contribution of Obstetrical Factors to Serious Physical and Mental Handicap in Children. *J. Obst. and Gyn. B.E.*, 66, 743.
8. BAX, M., MacKEITH, R. (1962). Minimal Cerebral Dysfunction. *Little Club Clinics in Developmental Medicine*. No. 10. London: Heinemann.

54   THE DEVELOPMENT OF THE INFANT AND YOUNG CHILD

9. BENARON, H. B. W., BOSHES, B., TUCKER, B. E., COHEN, J., ANDREWS, J. P., FROMM, E., YACORZYNSKI, G. K. (1960) Effect of Anoxia during Labour and Immediately after Birth on the Subsequent Development of the Child. *Amer. J. Obstet. Gynec.*, **80,** 1129.
10. BENTON, A. L. (1940) Mental Development of Prematurely Born Children. *Amer. J. Orthopsychiat.*, **10,** 719.
11. BERG, J. M., KIRMAN, B. H. (1960) The Mentally Defective Twin. *Brit. med. J.*, **1,** 1911.
12. BESKOW, B. (1949) Mental Disturbances in Premature Children at School Age. *Acta Paediat. (Uppsala)*, **37,** 125.
13. BIRCH, H. G. (1964) *Brain Damage in Children. The Biological and Social Aspects.* Baltimore. Williams Wilkins.
14. BLANK, C. E. (1959) The Genetics of Acrocephalsyndactyly. Ph.D. Thesis, Univ. of London.
15. BLEGEN, S. D. (1953) The Premature Child. *Acta Paediat. (Uppsala).* Suppl. 88.
16. BRANDON, M. W. G. (1957) The Intellectual and Social Status of Children of Mental Defectives. *J. ment. Sci.*, **103,** 710, 725.
17. BRITISH MEDICAL JOURNAL ANNOTATION (1964) The Drugged Sperml **1,** 1063.
18. BRIT. MED. J. (1969) Annotation. Starving the Premature, **1,** 459.
19. BROCK STERILISATION COMMITTEE (1934) Transmission of Mental Defect., quoted by *Brit. med. J.* (1958), **1,** 31.
20. BURKE, J. (1954) The Prognostic Significance of Neonatal Convulsions. *Arch. Dis. Childh.*, **29,** 342.
21. BURT, C. (1943) quoted by Penrose, L. S. (1956 b.)
22. BYERS, R. K., PAINE, R. S., CROTHERS, B. (1955) Extrapyramidal Cerebral Palsy with Hearing Loss Following Erythroblastosis. *Pediatrics*, **15,** 248.
23. CAMP, D. V. (1964) Psychological Evaluation of Children Who Had Neonatal Hyperbilirubinemia. *Amer. J. ment. Def.*, **68,** 803.
24. CARTER, C. O., EVANS, K. A. (1961) Risk of Parents who have had One Child with Down's Syndrome (Mongolism) having Another Child Similarly Affected. *Lancet*, **2,** 785.
25. CHURCHILL, J. A., NEFF, J. W., CALDWELL, D. F. (1966) Birth Weight and Intelligence. *Obstet. and Gynec.*, **28,** 425.
26. CORNER, B. (1952) Life for the Premature Baby. *Bristol med. chir. J.* **69,** 117.
27. COURVILLE, C. B. (1952) Ultimate Residual Lesions of Antenatal and Neonatal Asphyxia. Their Relation to Certain Degenerative Diseases of the Brain Appearing in Early Life. *Amer. J. Dis. Child.*, **84,** 64.
28. COURVILLE, C. B., EDMONDSON, H. A. (1958) Mental Deficiency from Intrauterine Exposure to Irradiation. *Bull. Los Angeles neurol. Soc.*, **23** 11.
29. CROSSE, V. M., MEYER, T. C., GERRARD, J. W. (1955) Kernicterus and Prematurity. *Arch. Dis. Childh.*, **30,** 501.
30. DANN, M., LEVINE, S. Z., NEW, E. V. (1958) The Development of Prematurely Born Children with Birth Weights or Minimal Postnata Weights of 1000 g. or less. *Pediatrics*, **22,** 1037.
31. DANN, M., LEVINE, S. Z., NEW, E. V. (1964) A Long Term Follow-up Study of Small Premature Infants. *Pediatrics*, **33,** 945.

32. DAY, R., HAINES, M. S. (1954) Intelligence Quotients of Children Recovered from Erythroblastosis Foetalis Since the Introduction of Exchange Transfusion. *Pediatrics*, **13**, 333.

33. DAY, R. L. (1967) Factors Influencing Offspring. *Am. J. Dis. Child.*, **113**, 179.

34. DAYTON, N. A., TRUDEN, D. (1940-41) Age of Mother at Birth of Child and Incidence of Mental Retardation in Children. *Amer. J. ment. Defic.*, **45**, 190.

35. DE HIRSCH, K., JANSKY, J., LANGFORD, W. S. (1966) Comparisons Between Prematurely and Maturely Born Children at Three Age Levels. *Am. J. Orthopsychiat.*, **36**, 616.

36. DOUGLAS, J. W. B. (1956) Mental Ability and School Achievement of Premature Children at 8 Years of Age. *Brit. med. J.*, **1**, 1210.

37. DOUGLAS, J. W. B. (1960) Premature Children at Primary Schools. *Brit. med. J.*, **1**, 1008.

38. DRILLIEN, C. M. (1957) The Social and Economic Factors Affecting the Incidence of Premature Births. *J. Obstet. Gynaec. Brit. Emp.*, **64**, 161.

39. DRILLIEN, C. M. (1963) *The Growth and Development of the Prematurely Born Infant*. Edinburgh: Livingstone.

40. DRILLIEN, C. M., WILKINSON, E. M. (1964) Emotional Stress and Mongoloid Births. *Develop. Med. child Neurol.*, **6**, 140.

41. DRILLIEN, C. M., in GAIRDNER, D. (1965) *Recent Advances in Paediatrics*. London: Churchill.

42 DRILLIEN, C. M. (1968) Studies in Mental Handicap. *Arch. Dis. Childh.*, **43**, 283.

43. DUNHAM, E. C. (1955) *Premature Infants*. 2nd. ed. London. Cassell.

44. ERNHART, C. B., GRAHAM, F. K., THURSTON, D. (1960) *Arch. Neurol. (Chic)*, **2**, 504.

45. FRASER, F. C. (1958) Genetic Counselling in Some Common Pediatric Diseases. *Pediat. Clin. N. Amer.*, May, *P.* 475.

46. FRASER, M. S., WILKS, J. (1959) The Residual Effects of Neonatal Asphyxia. *J. Obstet. Gynaec. (Brit. Emp.)*, **66**, 748.

47. FREEDMAN, A. M., BRAINE, M., HEIMER, C. B., HOWLESSAR, M., O'CONNOR, J. W., WORTIS, H., GOODMAN, B. (1960) The Relationship of Neonatal Hyperbilirubinaemia of the Premature to Retarded Development. London *Conference on the Scientific Study of Mental Deficiency*, p. 68.

48. GALTON, F. (1869) *Hereditary Genius. An Inquiry into Its Law and Consequences*. London: Macmillan.

49. GARRISON, K. C., FORCE, D. G. (1959) *The Psychology of Exceptional Children*. New York: Ronald Press.

50. GERRARD, J. (1952) Kernicterus. *Brain*, **75**, 526.

51. GERVER, J. M., DAY, R. (1950) Intelligence Quotient of Children Who Have Recovered from Erythroblastosis Foetalis. *J. Pediat.*, **36**, 342.

52. GODDARD, H. H. (1914) Transmission of Mental Defect., quoted by *Brit. med. J.* (1958), **1**, 31.

53. GRAHAM, F. K., CALDWELL, B. M., ERNHART, C. B., PENNOYER, M. M., HARTMANN, A. F. (1957) Anoxia as a Significant Perinatal Experience. *J. Pediat.*, **50**, 556.

54. GRAVES, L. R., ADAMS, J. Q., SCHREIER, P. C. (1962) The Fate of the Second Twin. *Obstet. and Gynec.*, **19**, 246.

55. GREWAR, D. A. I., MEDOVY, H., WYLIE, K. O. (1962) The Fate of the Ex-premature—Prognosis of Prematurity. *Canad. med. Ass. J.*, **86**, 1008.

56. GUNTHER, L. M. (1963) Psychopathology and Stress in the Life Experience of Mothers of Premature Infants. *Amer. J. Obstet. Gynaec.*, **86**, 333.

57. HAMERTON, J. L., BRIGGS, S. M., GIANELLI, F., CARTER, C. O. (1961) Chromosome Studies in the Selection of Parents with a High Risk of a Second Mongol Child. *Lancet*, **2**, 788.

58. HARRELL, R. F., GATES, A. I., WOODYARD, E. R. (1956) The Influence of Vitamin Supplementation of the Diets of Pregnant and Lactating Women on the Intelligence of Their Offspring. *Child Develpm. Abstr.*, **31**, No. 587.

59. HEIMER, C. B., CUTLER, R., FREEDMAN, A. M. (1964) Neurological Sequelae of Premature Birth. *Amer. J. Dis. Child.*, **108**, 122.

60. HESS, J. H. (1953) Experience Gained in a Thirty Year Study of Prematurely Born Infants. *Pediatrics*, **11**, 425.

61. HILL, A. B., DOLL, R., McL. GALLOWAY, T, HUGHES, J. P. W. (1958) Virus Diseases in Pregnancy and Congenital Defects. *Brit. J. prev. Soc. Med.*, **12**, 1.

62. HONZIK, M. P. (1957) Developmental Studies of Parent Child Resemblance in Intelligence. *Child Develpm.*, **28**, 215.

63. ILLINGWORTH, R. S. (1958) *Recent Advances in Cerebral Palsy*. London: Churchill.

64. ILLINGWORTH, R. S., WOODS, G. (1960) The Incidence of Twins in Cerebral Palsy and Mental Retardation. *Arch. Dis. Childh.*, **35**, 333.

65. ILLINGWORTH, R. S. (1969) Assessment for Adoption: A Follow Up Study. *Acta Paediat. Scand.*, **58**, 33.

66. INGALLS, T. H. (1957) German Measles and German Measles in Pregnancy. *Amer. J. Dis. Child.*, **93**, 555.

67. INGRAM, T. T. S. (1964) *Paediatric Aspects of Cerebral Palsy*. Edinburgh. Livingstone.

68. JACKSON, A. D. M., FISCH, L. (1958) Deafness Following Maternal Rubella. *Lancet*, **2**, 1241.

69. JACOBS, P. A., BROWN, W. M. C., BAIKIE, A. G., STRONG, J. A. (1959) The Somatic Chromosomes in Mongolism. *Lancet*, **1**, 710.

70. JANUS-KUKULSKA, A., LIS, S. (1966) Developmental Peculiarities of Prematurely Born Children. *Develop. Med. Child Neurol.*, **8**, 285.

71. JONES, H. E. (1933) in Murchison, C. *A Handbook of Child Psychology* Worcester: Clark Univ. Press.

72. KAWI, A. A., PASAMANICK, B. (1958) Association of Factors in Pregnancy with Reading Disorders in Childhood. *J. Amer. med. Ass.*, **166**, 1420.

73. KEELEY, K. (1962) Prenatal Influence on Behaviour of Offspring of Crowded Mice. *Science*, **135**, 44.

74. KNOBLOCH, H., RIDER, R., HARPER, P., PASAMANICK, B. (1956) Neuropsychiatric Sequelae of Prematurity. *J. Amer. med. Ass.*, **161**, 581.

75. KNOBLOCH, H., PASAMANICK, B. (1958) Seasonal Variations in the Births of the Mentally Deficient. *Amer. J. publ. Hlth.*, **48**, 1201.

76. KNOBLOCH, H. (1959) Syndrome of Minimal Cerebral Damage in Infancy. *J. Amer. med. Ass.*, **170**, 1384.

77. LANMAN, J. T. (1968) Delays During Reproduction and Their Effects on the Embryo and Foetus. *New Engl. J. Med.*, **278**, 993.

78. LANDER, E., FORSSMAN, H., AKESSON, H. O. (1964) Season of Birth and Mental Deficiency. *Acta genet. (Basel)*, **14**, 265.

79. LIDBETTER, E. J. (1933) Transmission of Mental Defect., quoted by *Brit. med. J.* (1958), **1**, 31.

80. LILIENFELD, A. M., PASAMANICK, B. (1954) Association of Maternal and Fetal Factors with the Development of Epilepsy. *J. Amer. med. Ass.*, **155**, 719.

81. LILIENFELD, A. M., PASAMANICK, B. (1955) The Association of Maternal and Fetal Factors with the Development of Cerebral Palsy and Epilepsy. *Amer. J. Obstet. Gynec.*, **70**, 93.

82. LOOFT, C. (1931) L'Évolution de L'Intelligence des Jumeaux. *Acta Paediat. (Uppsala)*, **12**, 41.

83. LORBER, J. (1965) Pediatrics **35**, 589.

84. LUBCHENCO, L. O., HORNER, F. A., HIX, I. E., METCALF, D., HASSEL, L., COHIG, R., ELLIOTT, H. (1961) Development of Premature Infants of Low Birth Weight; Evaluation at 10 Years of Age. *Amer. J. Dis. Child.*, **102**, 752.

85. LUCEY, J. F., DOLAN, R. G. (1958) Injections of a Vitamin K Compound in Mothers and Hyperbilirubinemia in the Newborn. *Pediatrics*, **22**, 605.

86. LYNN, R. (1959) Environmental Conditions Affecting Intelligence. *Educ. Res.*, **1**, 49.

87. McDONALD, A. D. (1962) Neurological and Ophthalmic Disorders in Children of Very Low Birth Weight. *Brit. med. J.*, **1**, 895.

88. McDONALD, A. (1967) Children of Very Low Birth Weight. MEIU Research Monograph No. 1. London. Spastics Society and Heinemann.

89. McKINNEY, L. NUNPHY, D., PESSIN, V. (1958) A Comparative Study of 26 Sets of Multiple Births. *Amer. J. Dis. Child.*, **96**, 624.

90. MACDONALD, I. S. (1959) Familial Predisposition to Prematurity. *Scot. med., J.*, **4**, 190.

91. MEIER, C. W., BUNCH, M. E. (1950) The Effects of Natal Anoxia upon Learning and Memory at Maturity *J. comp. Physiol. Psychol.*, **43**, 436.

92. MILLER, R. M. (1967) Prenatal Origins of Mental Retardation: Epidemiological Approach. *J. Pediat.*, **71**, 454.

93. MILLER, R. W. (1956) Delayed Effects Occurring within the First Decade after Exposure of Young Individuals to the Hiroshima Atomic Bomb. *Pediatrics*, **18**, 1.

94. MOTULSKY, A. G., GARTLER, S. M. (1959) Consanguinity and Marriage. *Practitioner*, **183**, 170.

95. MULLINS, D. H., ESTRADA, W. R., GREADY, T. G. (1960) Pregnancy in an Adult Mongoloid Female. *Obstet. and Gynec.*, **15**, 781.

96 NEWCOMBE, H. B., TAVENDALE, O. C. (1965) Effect of Father's Age on the Risk of Child Handicap or Death. *Am. J. Human Genetics*, **17**, 163.

97. NEWMAN, H. H. (1940) *Multiple Human Births*. New York. Doubleday, Doran.

98. NIELSEN, J. M., COURVILLE, C. B. (1951) Asphyxia. *Neurology*, **1**, 48·

99. O'CONNOR, N. (1958) in Clarke, A. M., Clarke, A. D. B., *Mental Deficiency, the Changing Outlook*. London: Methuen.

100. PASAMANICK, B., CONSTANTINOU, F. K., LILIENFELD, A. M. (1956) Pregnancy Experience and the Development of Childhood Speech Disorders. *Amer. J. Dis. Child.*, **91**, 113.

101. PASAMANICK, B., KAWI, A.   (1956)   A Study of the Association of Prenatal and Paranatal Factors with the Development of Tics in Children.
J. Pediat., **48,** 596.

102. PASAMANICK, B., LILIENFELD, A. M.   (1955)   Association of Maternal
and Fetal Factors with Development of Mental Deficiency.   *J. Amer.
med. Ass.*, **159,** 155.

103. PASAMANICK, B., KNOBLOCH, H.   (1958)   Seasonal Variation in Complications of Pregnancy. *Obstet. and Gynec.*, **12,** 110.

104. PENROSE, L. S.   (1938)   A Clinical and Genetic Study of 1280 Cases of
Mental Defect. *Spec., Rep. Ser. med. Res. Coun. (Lond)*, No. 229.

105. PENROSE, L. S.   (1941)   Inheritance of Mental Defect.   *Sci. monthly,*
52, 359.

106. PENROSE, L. S.   (1956)   Some Notes on Heredity Counselling.   *Acta
genet. (Basel.)*, **6,** 35.

107. PENROSE, L. S.   (1962)   Paternal Age in Mongolism. *Lancet*, **1,** 1101.

108. *Perinatal Problems* (1969)   The Second Report of the British Perinatal
Mortality Survey. Edinburgh. Livingstone.

109. PLUM, F., POSNER, J. B., HAIN, R. F.   (1962)   Delayed Neurological
Deterioration after Anoxia. *Arch. intern. Med.*, **110,** 18.

110. PLUMMER, G.   (1952)   Anomalies Occurring in Children Exposed in
Utero to the Atomic Bomb in Hiroshima. *Pediatrics*, **10,** 687.

111. PRECHTL, H. F. R., STEMMER, C. J.   (1962)   The Choreiform Syndrome
in Children. *Develop. Med. Child Neurol.*, **4,** 119.

112. PRECHTL, H.   (1963)   in Foss. *Determinants of Infant Behaviour*. London.
Methuen.

113. PRECHTL, H., BEINTEMA, D.   (1964).   The Neurological Examination of
the Full Term Newborn Infant. *Little Club Clinics in Developmental
Medicine*. No. 12. London: Heinemann.

114. RAHIMTULLA, K. A.   (1961)   Hydramnios in Relation to Foetal Mortality.
Arch. Dis. Childh., **36,** 418.

115 REGER, R. (1965) *School Psychology*. Springfield. Charles Thomas.

116. REISNER, S. H., FORBES, A. E., CORNBLATT, M.   (1965)   The Smaller of
Twins and Hypoglycaemia. *Lancet*, **1,** 524.

117. RICHARDS, T. W., NEWBERRY, H.   (1938)   Studies in Fetal Behaviour.
Can Performance on Test Items at 6 Months Postnatally be Predicted on
the Basis of Fetal Activity? *Child Develpm.*, **2,** 79.

118. RICHARDS, F. M., RICHARDS, I. D. G., ROBERTS, C. J.   The Influence of
Low Agar Rating on Infant Mortality and Development.   *Clinics in
Develop. Med.* No. 27, p. 84.

119. ROBERTS, C. J.   (1966)   The Functional Development of the Nervous
System in Infancy. M.D. Thesis. University of Birmingham.

120. ROBINSON, N. M., ROBINSON, H. B.   (1965)   A Follow-up Study of
Children of Low Birth Weight and Control Children at School Age.
Pediatrics, **35,** 425.

121. ROGERS, M. E., LILIENFELD, A. M., PASAMANICK, B.   (1955)   Prenatal
and Paranatal Factors in the Development of Childhood Behaviour Disorders. *Acta psychiat. scand.* Suppl., 102.

122. ROSANOFF, A. J., INMAN-KANE, C. V.   (1933)   Relation of Premature Birth
and Under-weight Condition at Birth to Mental Deficiency. *Amer. J.
Psychiat.*, **13,** 829.

123. RUSSELL, C. S., TAYLOR, R. (1968) Smoking in Pregnancy. *Brit. J. Prev. Soc. Med.*, **22,** 119.
124. SHIRLEY, M. (1939) A Behaviour Syndrome Characterising Prematurely Born Children. *Child. Develpm.*, **10,** 115.
125. SIMPSON, W. J., LINDA, L. (1957) A preliminary report on Cigarette Smoking and the Incidence of Prematurity. *Amer. J. Obstet. Gynec.*, **73,** 808.
126. SKODAK, M. (1938) Children of Feeble-Minded Mothers. *Child Develpm.*, **9,** 303.
127. SKODAK, M., SKEELS, H. M. (1949) A Final Follow-up Study of 100 Adopted Children. *J. genet. Psychol.*, **75,** 85.
128. SMALLPEICE, V., DAVIES, P. (1964) Immediate Feeding of Premature Infants with Undiluted Breast Milk. *Lancet*, **2,** 1349.
129. SONTAG, L. W. (1941) The Significance of Fetal Environmental Differences. *Amer. J. Obstet. Gynec.*, **42,** 996.
130. SONTAG, L. W. (1944) Differences in Modifiability of Fetal Behaviour and Physiology. *Psychosom. med.*, **6,** 151.
131. SPECTOR, R. (1964) Abnormal Spermatozoa and Perinatal Disease. *Develop. Med. child Neurol.*, **6,** 523.
132. STEVENSON, S. S. (1948) Paranatal Factors Affecting Adjustment in Childhood. *Pediatrics*, **2,** 154.
133. STOTT, D. H. (1957) Physical and Mental Handicaps Following a Disturbed Pregnancy. *Lancet*, **1,** 1006.
134. STOTT, D. H. (1958) Some Psychosomatic Aspects of Casualty in Reproduction. *J. psychosom. Res.*, **3,** 42.
135. STOTT, D. H. (1960) Interaction of Heredity and Environment in regard to Measured Intelligence. *Brit. J. educ. Psychol.*, **30,** 95.
136. STOTT, D. H. (1962) Abnormal Mothering as a Cause of Mental Abnormality. *J. Child Psychol.*, **3,** 79.
137. STRAUSS, A. A., KEPHART, N. C. (1955) *Psychopathology and Education of the Brain Injured Child.* New York: Grune and Stratton.
138. TAFT, L. T., GOLDFARB, W. (1964) *Develop. Med. child Neurol.*, **6,** 32.
139. TAKKUNEN, R. L., FRISK, M., HOLMSTRÖM, G. (1965) Follow-up Examination of 110 Small Prematures at the Age of 6-7 years. *Acta paediat. scand.* Suppl. 159, p. 70.
140. TERMAN, L. M., ODEN, M. H. (1947) *The Gifted Child Grows Up.* Stanford: Stanford Univ. Press.
141. THOMPSON, W. R. (1957) Influence of Prenatal Maternal Anxiety on Emotionality in Young Rats. *Science*, **125,** 698.
142. TURKEWITZ, G., MOREAU, T., BIRCH, H. G. (1968) Relation Between Birth Condition and Neurological Organisation of the Neonate. *Pediat. Research*, **2,** 243.
143. UCHIDA, I. A., HOLUNGA, R., LAWLER, C. (1968). Maternal Radiation and Chromosomal Aberrations. *Lancet*, **2,** 1045.
144 WAGNER, M. G., ARNDT, R., Postmaturity as an Etiological Facts in 124 Cases of Neurologically Handicapped Children. *Clinics in Develop. Med.* No. 27, P. 89.
145. WARKANY, J., MONROE, B. B., SUTHERLAND, B. S. (1961) Intrauterine Growth Retardation. *Amer. J. Dis. Child.*, **102,** 127.

146. WIENER, G., RIDER, R. V., OPPEL, W. C., HARPER, P. A. (1968) Prematures. Correlates of Low Birth Weight. Psychological Status at Eight to Ten Years of Age. *Ped. Research,* **2,** 110.

147. WILLERMAN, L., CHURCHILL, J. A. (1967) Intelligence and Birth Weight in Identical Twins. *Child Development,* **38,** 623.

148. WINDLE, W. F., BECKER, R. F. (1943) Asphyxia Neonatorum. An Experimental Study in the Guinea-pig. *Amer. J. Obstet. Gynec.,* **45,** 183.

149. WINDLE, W. F. (1944) Structural and Functional Alterations in the Brain Following Neonatal Asphyxia. *Psychosom. med.,* **6,** 155.

150. WINDLE, W. F. (1958) *Neurological and Psychological Deficits of Asphyxia Neonatorum.* Springfield: Charles Thomas.

152. WITTENBORN, J. R. (1957) *The Placement of Adoptive Children.* Springfield: Thomas.

153. WORTIS, J. (1956-7) A Note on the Concept of the Brain-Injured Child. *Amer. J. ment. Defic.,* **61,** 204.

154. YAMAZAKI, J. N., WRIGHT, S. W., WRIGHT, P. M. (1954) Outcome of Pregnancy in Women exposed to the Atomic Bomb in Nagasaki. *Amer. J. Dis. Child.,* **87,** 448.

155. ZAZZO, R. (1960) *Les Jumeaux, le Couple et la Personne.* Paris. Presses Universitaires de France.

CHAPTER 4

ENVIRONMENTAL FACTORS AND DEVELOPMENT

The Importance of Environment

Not many now would agree with the extreme view of the behaviourist school of some decades ago, exemplified by Watson's comment[90] which ran as follows: 'Give me a dozen healthy infants, well formed, and my own specified world to bring them up in, and I'll guarantee to take any at random and train him to become any type of specialist I might select—doctor, lawyer, artist, merchant, chief, and yes, even beggar-man and thief, regardless of his talents, peculiarities, tendencies, abilities, vocations and race of his ancestors. There is no such thing as an inheritance of capacity, talent, temperament, mental constitution and characteristics'.

The environment, particularly at home and at school, has a profound effect on a child's intellectual development and on his personality. To some extent the child's intelligence and personality are interwoven; but in the section to follow I shall discuss the effect of environment on the intellectual development only, mentioning the effect on personality when it has a more direct bearing on his intellectual development.

Experimental Work

Ethology, the study of the behaviour of animals, has much of relevance to the behaviour of the child. Those interested should read the books by Rheingold,[72] Cooke,[23] Hinde,[47] Foss[34] and others. Glaser and Eisenberg[40] reviewed the work on the deprivation of experience in animals. Weiss[91] and Garrison[36] discussed experimental work concerning the effect of practice on development.

Numerous experiments with rats, cats, dogs, goats, sheep and monkeys showed that separation of the animal from the mother at birth had a profound effect on the animal's development often for the rest of its life, even though it was returned to the mother within a matter of hours or days. The mother animal was likely to reject its young when returned to her, even though the separation had lasted only a matter of hours.

Other restrictive methods had a profound effect on the animal's development. Wolf[93] showed that rats deprived of vision in infancy experienced great difficulty in responding later to visual stimuli under the strain of adult competition. The same applied to those deprived of hearing in early life. They failed, in other words, when faced with stressful situations when older. Nissen *et al.*[63] limited the movement of the limbs of chimpanzees from 4 weeks to 31 months by encasing their limbs in cardboard cylinders. Abnormality of hand use persisted after release of the limbs. Hymovitch[48] described three experiments: (i) blinding rats in early life, keeping some in cages, and giving others free environment: the free ones were superior in problem solving at maturity; (ii) keeping some free and others in a cage. The free ones fared better; (iii) keeping some free early in life and putting them into cages later; keeping others in cages first and freeing them later. Those free early in life fared better than those freed later. Thompson and Heron[86] set about to examine the effects of restricting early experience in dogs on their exploratory activity later. Twelve Scottish terriers were restricted for the first 7 to 10 months, their 8 litter-mates, reared as pets, serving as controls.   The amount of exploratory activity later, and ability to perform complex tasks, was strongly correlated with the degree of restriction.

With regard to the effect of practice, Weiss[91] mentioned the example of the butterfly. The butterfly inside the pupal case is unable to move because of lack of space. After breaking the case it immediately frees itself by well co-ordinated movements, creeps out of its envelope, spreads its crumpled wings, and flies as soon as they have dried without ever having had a chance of learning and practising the various performances.

Carmichael[19] kept frog and salamander eggs until the head and tail buds appeared. At this time, one group was placed in a dish of plain water and the other group was placed in a weak solution of chloretone. This drug, while it does not interfere with growth, produces complete immobilisation. Practice for this group was made impossible. These tadpoles remained in this solution until those in the plain water were swimming in a normal manner. After this time, the drug was washed from the anaesthetised tadpoles and they were placed in plain water. The first movements then appeared within 6 to 20 minutes, and within half an hour both the frog and salamander tadpoles were swimming so well that they could not be distinguished from those that had been swimming normally in plain water for five days.

Concept of the Sensitive Period

There is abundant evidence that in many animals there is a

particular period of their development at which learning in response to the appropriate stimuli is easier than at other times. This is termed the sensitive period. Sometimes a stage of development comes beyond which learning is impossible: this is the so-called critical period. There are many examples of this in the books by Harriet Rheingold[72] entitled 'Maternal Behavior in Animals'. I have briefly with a colleague,[49] reviewed the literature concerning the sensitive period and adduced evidence that there is a sensitive period for learning in human beings. For instance, if a baby is not given solid foods when he can chew (usually at six or seven months) it becomes increasingly difficult to get him to take solids later. (Red squirrels, if not given nuts to crack by a certain age, never acquire the skill of cracking them later.)

If a child's congenital cataract is not removed by a certain age, the child will not be able to see. If a squint is not corrected in time, the child will become blind in the affected eye. If a cleft palate is not operated on by the age of two or three, it becomes increasingly difficult to obtain normal speech. The longer congenital deafness remains undiagnosed, the more difficult it becomes to teach the child to speak. Whereas young children may learn to speak a foreign language fluently with a good accent, adults settling in a country may never learn to speak the language of that country fluently, however intelligent they are.

There is much interest amongst educationalists in the application of the concept of the sensitive or critical period to the development of the preschool child. Maria Montessori[80] was one of the first to recognise the importance of these periods in the teaching of children. For instance, she found that children are more receptive for learning involving the sensory system, such as the learning of colour, shape, sound and texture, at the age of $2\frac{1}{2}$ years to 6 years than in later years. Kohberg[56a] wrote a detailed discussion of the role of early teaching of the pre-school child. It may be that the nursery school improves the performance of children from poor homes where the necessary stimulation at home is lacking.

In our book 'Lessons from Childhood'[51] we described many examples of children destined for fame who were given intensive teaching in the pre-school years and who displayed remarkable precocity in learning in later years. Well documented examples were those of John Stuart Mill, Karl Witte, Lord Kelvin and Blaise Pascal. Kellmer Pringle[71] showed that children starting at school early (4 years 6 months to 4 years 11 months) were considerably better at reading and arithmetic than late starters (5·0 years to 5 years 6 months). Elsewhere[70] she wrote that during the first five years of life, 'children learn more than during any other comparable period of time thereafter. What is more important, they learn how to learn, and whether learning is a pleasurable challenge or a disagreeable effort to be resisted as far as possible.

Evidence is accumulating to show that early failure to stimulate a child's desire to learn may result in a permanent impairment of learning ability or intelligence.

Learning to learn does not mean beginning to teach reading or arithmetic at the earliest possible time. It is far more basic and subtle and includes motivating the child to find pleasure in learning to develop his ability to pay attention to others, to engage in purposeful activity'.

Bloom[8] suggested that the whole pattern of learning is established before the child starts school. 'We are inclined to believe', he wrote, 'that this is the most important growing period for academic achievement'. He remarked that it is much easier to learn something new than it is to stamp out one set of learned behaviour and replace it by a new set. He wrote that the environment in the first years of life was vital for the child's subsequent learning, and laid down the pattern for the future. He suggested that failure to develop a good learning pattern in these years is likely to lead to continued failure later. He pointed out that the easiest time for a child to learn is when he is developmentally ready to learn, when he has no undesirable patterns to eliminate before he can learn new ones.

It may well be that the child's progress in certain subjects at school and later may be related to the age at which he was first taught them. If he is taught too soon, he will find it difficult and may develop such a dislike for them that he never learns them well: and if he is taught them too late, after he has lost interest in them, he may find it difficult to learn them later.

Nutrition and Development

There is suggestive evidence from various sources[82, 24, 68, 18] that malnutrition in infancy has a harmful effect on subsequent mental development. For instance, it was shown in South Africa that grossly malnourished Cape coloured infants, after correction of their malnutrition, fared less well mentally and had a smaller head circumference than controls matched for age and sex. Cravioto[24] found that recovery from malnutrition is accompanied by mental improvement except in children who had severe malnutrition before the age of six months. He remarked that the human brain is growing at its most rapid rate in the early weeks (gaining 1-2 mg. per minute in the perinatal period), and that damage at the period of maximum growth may be irremediable. There is some evidence[89a] that malnutrition affects the development of the human brain only when the malnutrition occurs in the prenatal period or in the first six months after birth.

Practice and Development

An essential factor in the achievement of new skills is the maturation of the nervous system. There is some histological evidence for this.[44, 88]

In children the effect of maturation of the nervous system has been illustrated by two groups of experiments and observation— the one involving restraint, and the other involving the effect of practice. The effect of restraint, such as swaddling, followed by release of the limbs, has been studied by various workers, and discussed by Greenacre[43] and others. Swaddling was practised by Jews, Greeks, and Romans before the time of Christ. It began to disappear in England in the eighteenth century. Swaddling is still widely practised in parts of Europe and Asia. In a visit to Leningrad in 1957, I found that swaddling was universally practised. All babies in hospital and brought up to hospital were swaddled. Swaddling in Albania was described by Greenacre as being particularly complete in the first year. The Columbia River Indians were said to bandage and fix the head so tightly that the head became flattened. In neither case was any intellectual impairment produced. Albanian children on release from swaddling accustom themselves to play material in the course of a few hours, and within that time go through the same series of steps for the completion of which our normal children require several months.

Dennis[27] described his drastic experiment in which he and his wife reared two infants from the beginning of the second to the end of the fourteenth month with no stimulation at all. No response was made to them. They were prevented from seeing other children or from playing with toys, and they were given no opportunity to practise any skills. Grasping, sitting and weight bearing were considerably retarded, but they rapidly caught up when given the chance.

Ausubel,[2] in a discussion of the theory of development, noted the importance of the principle of readiness to learn. Experimental evidence has shown, for instance, that if buzzards are caged for 10 weeks their flying ability is permanently impaired.

Efforts have been made to hasten the development of skills in babies by extra practice. Gesell[37] studied twin girls from 1 to 18 months. One twin was given daily training in climbing and cube manipulation from 6 to 46 weeks, while no extra training was given to the control twin. Gesell showed that practice and exercise did nothing to hasten the appearance of climbing and tower building, the time of appearance of these skills being determined by maturation. Dennis[28] found that additional practice had no effect on enabling children to walk early.

McGraw[59] determined the effect of toilet training on two sets of identical twins, one member of each pair being placed on the chamber hourly seven times each day after the first month. The other two were not allowed to sit on the chamber till 14 and 24 months respectively. In both cases the achievement in other ways was the same. There was no difference in the age at which sphincter control was acquired. She concluded that 'the results of this investigation indicate that early toilet training is, to say the least, futile'.

It would seem that an important cause of backwardness in children who are brought up in institutions is the lack of normal practice in acquiring new skills. A 6 months old baby, for instance, may be retarded in sitting, because he is not given the chance to sit propped up, like a child in a good home. He may be retarded in weight bearing on his legs, and in walking, because no one has time to play with him, to let him stand with support, and subsequently to walk with hands held. He may be retarded in speech, because the staff has not time to talk to him and read to him as a good mother can in her own home. He may be retarded in acquiring sphincter control, because he is not given the opportunity to use the chamber when he is beginning to ask for it.

Delay in sphincter control can be caused by mismanagement in the way of over-enthusiastic training, compelling the child to sit on the chamber when he is trying to get off it, or failing to give him the opportunity to empty his bladder or bowels, when he shows signs of wanting to do.

In conclusion, the acquisition of various skills is dependent on maturation of the nervous system. No amount of practice can make a child sit, walk, talk or acquire other skills until his nervous system is ready for it. On the other hand delay in the acquisition of skills may be caused by depriving the child of opportunity to practise them when sufficient maturation has occurred.

Emotional Deprivation in Young Children

The effect of emotional deprivation on mental and psychological development has been the subject of numerous papers, ably summarised in Bowlby's famous monograph.[10] This monograph is so complete that only a few earlier papers will be mentioned here. It seems to be agreed that emotional deprivation in the first three years is more harmful than similar deprivation later.

Lowrey[57] studied 28 children in an orphanage. All showed an inability to give or receive affection. Most of them showed aggressiveness, temper tantrums, speech defects, stubbornness, selfishness, finger sucking, and other behaviour problems. Their behaviour was unsocial and hostile. Lowrey found that when infants were placed in institutions after the age of two these symptoms did not develop.

Burlingham and Freud[14] found that babies placed in a residential nursery compared favourably in the first five months with those brought up at home, but thereafter they lacked liveliness and social responsiveness, and were less interested in their surroundings. They became backward in manipulation, and showed more autoerotic behaviour—thumb-sucking, rocking, and masturbation.

Goldfarb[41, 42] examined 15 children aged 10 to 14 who had entered an institution at a mean age of 4 to 5 months and remained there for an average period of 39 months before going to a foster home. He compared them with 15 children of the same age and sex who had entered foster homes at the mean age of 14 months. The intellectual attainment of those in the institution group was lower: their power of reasoning was poor: they showed a deficient ability to perceive relationships. The mean I.Q. of the institution group was 68, but 7 months after being placed in a foster home it was 75·8. The mean I.Q. of the foster home group was 101·5.

Spitz[78] described the decline in developmental quotient in children suffering from severe emotional deprivation in an institution.

Choremis and Baroutsou[20] studied 108 well nourished children aged 4 weeks to 3 years, comparing their scores on Gesell tests with 74 'dystrophic' infants of the same age, and 70 children deprived of family environment since birth. The 'dystrophic' infants were more retarded in motor development than in emotional and adaptive fields: the children who had been separated from their mother from birth were more delayed in motor, adaptive and personal social fields than in motor development.

Bowlby[10] in his review of the world literature, found a striking unanimity in the findings of workers in many parts of the world, though methods were different, and some studies lacked thoroughness, scientific reliability or precision. They all indicated that deprivation of maternal love in the first three years lead to physical, intellectual, and social retardation. Early signs were failure to smile, and reduced vocalisation—seen as early as 2 months of age. In older infants and children it was found that locomotion was less affected than other fields of development, while speech was the most affected, the ability to express being more retarded than the ability to understand. The longer the deprivation the lower the developmental quotient would fall. Bowlby found that the overall D.Q. fell from about 65 for those who have been in institutions for 2 to 6 months to about 50 for those who were in an institution for more than a year. Bowlby emphasised the fact that the first three years of life were the most important ones: separation from the mother in that period was of great significance to the child's future development. He pointed out that if one was uncertain about the suitability for adoption of a baby in an institution, one should not keep him there for observation of his progress, for he would regress further. He should be placed in a good foster home as soon as possible.

It is important to note that some of the early work on emotional deprivation has been the subject of considerable criticism. Goldfarb's children were clearly selected. For instance, 73 per cent. of the children placed in the institution were illegitimate, as compared with 33 per cent. of those placed in foster homes. For this and other reasons it appears that children with better promise for the future were chosen for foster home care. Spitz' work has been similarly criticised. Bowlby himself has admitted that in his earlier work he exaggerated the effect of emotional deprivation.[11]

A subsequent W.H.O. publication[94] contains a valuable series of articles which attempt to reassess Bowlby's work. It contains papers by Prugh and Harlow, Andry, Barbara Wootton, Mary Ainsworth, and others. The latter concluded that progressive retardation of general development resulting from severe deprivation may be arrested or reversed if relief is provided in the first two years, and especially in the first year: but that prolonged and severe deprivation beginning early in the first year and continuing for as long as 3 years usually leads to severely adverse effects, affecting the intellectual development and the personality—and these may resist reversal. Prolonged separation beginning in the third year may cause grave effects on the personality, but no permanent effect on general intelligence. Impairment in language, abstract thought, and capacity for strong and lasting interpersonal attachments, were less likely to be reversed than other effects.

It is clear that different children react differently to emotional deprivation. There may be genetic or constitutional factors which govern a child's response to his environment. Other factors are the quality of the parent-child relationship before the deprivation occurred, the age at which it occurred, the length of separation, the experiences during the period of separation, the completeness of the separation, and the attitude of the parents when the child is restored to them.

Emotional deprivation occurs not only in institutions, but in the home. Some parents are afraid of loving their children, and so are afraid of picking the baby up when he cries. Some mothers are unwilling to give up their work to look after their young children, and deprive them of their love just when they most need it. There are mothers who turn a deaf ear to the 12 months old baby who is left crying all day in a pram outside with nothing but a brick wall to see. Koupernik of Paris coined the phrase 'intrafamilial hospitalism' for this condition.

In recent years determined efforts have been made to reduce the risk of psychological trauma in young children, especially in those who have to be separated from their mothers in the first three years. For instance, many authorities now avoid placing illegitimate infants in institutions, but place them in foster homes within 2 or 3 weeks of birth. It was always difficult to assess the likelihood that a child would suffer psychologically from separation from his parents. In view of early placement in foster homes it seems likely that psychological trauma from emotional deprivation, such as that described by Bowlby, is now a great deal more rare than it used to be.

Many children have to be admitted to hospital in the first three years, but with the greater consciousness of the possibility of psychological trauma in such children, paediatricians and others have done a great deal to reduce or prevent emotional disturbance by such steps as the encouragement of daily visiting by the parents, admitting mothers with their children, and, in general, by the adoption of a more humane approach to the sick child.

Estimations of the Effect of Environment

The extent to which environment can affect intellectual development is uncertain. An extreme view is that of Bourne,[6] who suggested that severe mental defect can be caused by grossly perverted infant rearing, such as rearing by a psychopathic parent, or prolonged institutional care. Dr. Mildred Creak, in subsequent correspondence (p. 1,297), suggested that in such a child there would probably be underlying constitutional factors, or a psychosis. Stott,[85] in a good critical review of the effect of 'abnormal mothering', suggested that Bourne's work was fallacious for a variety of reasons. Amongst other reasons the children described by Bourne were placed in an institution because of their intolerable behaviour. They were therefore selected in the sense that they had caused maternal breakdown and had already shown severe behaviour disturbances.

Attempts to determine the relative parts played by environment and heredity in intelligence have been based on two groups of children. One group consists of children of identical heredity brought up in different environments (identical twins), and the other consists of children of different heredity brought up in the same environment (e.g. foster children).[16]

Skeels and others attempted to provide evidence of the latter type. Skeels [74] carried out mental tests on 73 children placed in foster homes under the age of 6 months. The tests were performed 12 to 60 months after placement. There was a 'zero correlation' between the true mother's I.Q. and that of the child. In a later study, however,[76] it was found that a correlation began to appear as the children grew older (see Chapter 3). Prior to that the children were 'consistently and unmistakeably superior to their natural parents—probably due to maximum security and rich intellectual stimulation' by the foster parents. The intellectual level remained consistently higher than would have been predicted from the intellectual, educational or socioeconomic level of the true parents.

Skodak[75] studied the children of 16 feeble-minded mothers, and found that when placed in an average or superior foster home at an early age, they were indistinguishable in mental development from children whose mothers were not feeble-minded. This observation, however, may be explained partly on genetic grounds, for it has been shown elsewhere (Ch. 3) that feeble-minded mothers are likely to give birth to children of higher intelligence than they have. Elsewhere Skodak[77] studied 98 families with at least one adopted child. Forty-six had 2 or more children, 35 had 2 or more unrelated adopted children, and 13 had adopted children as well as their own. Adopted children, unrelated to each other, but placed in a permanent home in infancy and brought up as siblings, were as similar in intelligence at comparable ages as natural siblings. In the small group of families in which there were adopted and their own children, the resemblance was less than in families with only adopted children. Wittenborn[92] found the same correlation between the adopting family and the adopted child.

Freeman[35] studied a group of 401 children placed in foster homes of higher socioeconomic level than their original homes, and showed that these children gained an average of 10 points in a 4 years period.

The Iowa studies by Skodak and others have been severely criticised by several educational psychologists. Lynn[58] suggested that the association between the I.Q. of the child and that of the foster parents could well be due to the efforts made by adoption societies to place a 'good child' in a 'good home'. In addition, intelligent foster parents may tend to have intelligent foster children because of personality qualities rather than intelligence as such. These will be discussed in a section to follow.

The follow up studies of Knobloch and Pasamanick throw considerable light on the problem. They studied the development of white and negro children and found that whereas motor development remained comparable in the two groups, those aspects of development most subject to social influences showed considerable differences with increasing age. The adaptive behaviour quotient rose from 105·4 to 110·9 for the white children and fell from 104·5 to 97·4 for the negroes. Language ability likewise improved in the white children and decreased in the negroes. There were corresponding changes in the overall I.Q. scores.[56] Drillien[30] made similar observations in the premature babies which she followed up at Edinburgh. The difference in performance between the babies in different social classes increased with increasing age.

Studies of twins have been few, on account of the difficulties involved in studying them under appropriate conditions.

Newman *et al.*[62] in a study of 19 pairs of monozygotic twins separated in early life and brought up in different environments, found an extreme range of variation of intelligence of 24 per cent. It has already been noted, however (Ch. 3) that variations in monogygotic twins occur under the same environmental conditions. Burt[17] traced 40 pairs of identical twins in London schools. The correlation between the education attainment of the twins who have been reared apart was only 0·62, as compared with 0·89 for twins brought up together. On the other hand, the correlations between the assessments for intelligence was as high as 0·88— almost identical with that of twins brought up together. There was therefore a high correlation between scores for identical twins even when reared apart.

In general, the figures given for the part contributed by environment vary from 13 per cent. (Burt[17]) to 50 per cent. (Penrose[67]), with those of Burks,[13] Vernon[89] and of Maddox[60] in between. Vernon gave evidence that environmental changes may cause I.Q. test score alterations of 10 to 20 points.

Clarke[22] in an excellent discussion of environmental factors in mental deficiency, concluded on the basis of measured recovery being equivalent to the degree of organic psychological damage, that cruelty and neglect may retard intellectual development by at least 16 points. In twin studies he calculated that the environment might have an even bigger effect on the I.Q. Stott[83] estimated that the I.Q. score of maladjusted children may increase by 20 to 30 points when the anxiety is allayed.

For full reviews of the nature-nurture problems the reader is referred to the papers by Maddox,[60] Lynn[58] and Burt.[17]

Stewart[81] found that the larger the family the less likely is a child to secure a place in a grammar school. She found that 38 per cent.

of only children entered a grammar school, as compared with only 6 per cent. of those with five or more siblings.

In conclusion, the extent to which environment can advance or retard intellectual development is uncertain. The general opinion, based mostly on studies of identical twins reared apart, seems to be that not more than 20 to 40 per cent. of an intelligence test score is likely to be the product of environment, the rest being the product of heredity. A more exact estimate cannot be given. There are difficulties in the two main methods of study—those of twins brought up in different environments, and of children brought up in foster homes. When identical twins are reared apart, one feels that some degree of selection of the environment is almost bound to occur, and that the environment selected is likely to be similar for each sibling. In the case of foster home studies, the main difficulty is the selection of the foster home and the attempt to match the infant's supposed mental qualities with those of foster parents.

The Duration of the Effect of Environment

The duration of the effect of environment, when the early harmful environment is changed, is a matter of opinion. It is generally agreed that when a child goes from an institution to a good foster home, he makes rapid steps forward and catches up to the average. Whether permanent intellectual harm is done is uncertain, but there is no evidence to that effect. Gesell's story of the Wolf child[38] is interesting in this connection, but it is uncertain how much credence can be paid to it. Gesell described a child who was brought up by wolves from 5 months to 7 years, and was then taken to a missionary station. When seen there he ran on all fours, cried like a wolf, especially at night, and lapped food like a dog. He showed his teeth and made harsh noises when children approached. Two and a half years elapsed before he was able to stand without help or say words. Five and a half years after reaching the missionary station he walked on two feet. By the age of 14 he would carry out simple errands. At 17 his mental age was $3\frac{1}{2}$. He was said to have developed normally until the age of 5 months.

The Qualities of the Home

The book by Pavenstedt entitled 'The Drifters',[65] a study of slum children, gives a valuable insight into the effect of a bad home.   It described the superior motor co-ordination of these children, combined with a lack of caution and self protective measures, resulting in frequent accidents, from which, however, they fail to learn.   Pain is rarely expressed.   The children tend to avoid difficult tasks instead of trying.   In their relationship to others they are need-oriented, distrustful and shallow, constantly fearing aggression, retaliation and blame.   They had no interest in books or stories, they were quite unable to take part in back and forth conversation, and their language development was poor, with a limited vocabulary.

A bad home is a major cause of backwardness in children. Cyril Burt[15] in his study of backward children, found that far fewer lived in better neighbourhoods of London, Hampstead, Lewisham and Dulwich, than in the poorer neighbourhoods, Lambeth, Hoxton and Poplar.   He suggested that the factors are impairment of health and general knowledge by poverty; inadequate sleep and overcrowding; employment out of school hours; domestic duties; absence of room for play; poor intellectual atmosphere at home and absence of books; non attendance at school—serious non attendance being three times commoner amongst the backward than among controls; and too slow or too quick promotion at school.   Jahoda and Warren[52] quoted work to the effect that there is no difference between the I.Q. of negro children in America and white children in the pre-school period; but that thereafter the negro children become separated from the white ones by an ever increasing gap.   The mean I.Q. of negro school children is 85.   It was postulated that this was due to the differences in the quality of the home, and socio-economic reasons.

The literature concerning the desirable qualities of a home is scanty.

Davis and Kent[25] mentioned some domestic factors which are relevant to a child's intellectual development—the importance of reward and punishment, the degree of stimulation, the degree of interest taken in the child's progress, and the standards of achievement expected.   Elsewhere[26] they discussed the effect of insecurity arising from parental over-ambition.   They described the ambitious parent as 'apt to make affection, acceptance and approval conditional upon satisfactory conduct and achievement. Instead of being the mainstay of the child's home environment, the threat of their withdrawal is a never-failing source of punishment'.

Bayley[5] included the following environmental features in a list of factors affecting a child's intelligence:

(1) Characteristics of the parents in respect to
   a) Understanding of the child's capacities and readiness for tasks of given difficulties.
   b) Willingness to grant the child autonomy relative to his capacities.
   c) Ability to offer stimulating experiences without exerting strong pressure to high achievement.
   d) Warm affectionate acceptance of child as an individual in his own right.
(2) Environmental opportunities geared to the child's stage of development; these include good teaching, varieties of experience, travel and discussion of ideas.

Elsewhere[6] she wrote of a slight tendency for mothers of higher socioeconomic status to be more warm, understanding and accepting, and for those of lower status to be more controlling, irritable and punitive. These differences were more evident in the mothers of boys than of girls.

Lynn[58] suggested that environment affected the intelligence test scores by two mechanisms. One was the direct learning from the environment and the copying of adults. The wider and more varied the intellectual stimulation, the greater his opportunity for learning and copying. The second one was a more complex matter, and involves the child's whole personality. He suggested that certain environmental factors have a permanent effect on the personality, and that this will in turn manifest itself in the way in which the child uses his ability. He suggested that the intelligence of parents may be a less important factor than the extent to which they attain middle class ideals, and that those produce character qualities such as persistence and ambition which affect learning. The higher mean intelligence of the only child may be due more to the mother affecting the child's personality, by giving him more time and attention than she could if she had several children, than to an effect on his intelligence as such. He suggested that over-protection and perhaps over-ambition might also act by giving the child the desire to achieve more, and even the anxiety that if he does not do well he will displease his parents.

Emotional deprivation may act in the opposite way, lack of stimulation and interest in the child's performance leading to a fall in the I.Q. test scores. Lynn suggested that Goldfarb's findings may be explained by the effect of deprivation on personality, rather than the mere lack of intellectual stimulation.

One of the most convincing studies of the effect of environment on a child's progress at school is that of Douglas,[29] in his follow-up study of 5,000 children born in the first week of March, 1946. He showed how children in lower social classes are apt to be sent to schools where the standard of work is lower than that of schools to which children of the middle or upper classes are sent. Those in lower social classes tend to be placed in a lower stream than those of the middle classes, and less is expected of them, so that they achieve less than others of the same level of intelligence. In addition, less is expected of children in poor homes, and they receive less stimulation at home—and so achieve less.

It is difficult to interpret Stott's observation[84] that children who had illnesses requiring hospital in-patient care for at least two weeks in infancy were significantly more retarded than controls, 7 to 11 years later, in reading and other abilities at school. He did not ascribe the subsequent poor performance to the illness, but rather to some prenatal factor which reduced the resistance to illness and also reduced the intellectual performance.

I have tried to summarise those qualities of the home which enable a pre-school child to achieve his best.[50]

Qualities suggested were:

Love and security; the constant avoidance of nagging, criticism, belittling, derogation, favouritism. Avoidance of prolonged separation from the parents.

Acceptance of the child, however meagre his performance; praise for effort rather than achievement.

Firm loving discipline, with a minimum of punishment. The teaching of behaviour acceptable to others. Giving him a chance to practice his new skills, e.g. to feed himself.

Encouragement to try to find out, to explore, to be curious; but it is unwise to allow him to fail. Success breeds success, and failure may lead to failure and refusal to try.

Encouragement, praise and reward rather than discouragement.

Encouragement of independence, and avoidance of over-protection. Calculated risks as distinct from thoughtlessness and carelessness.

Tolerance and understanding of the developing mind of the child, of his normal negativeness and aggressiveness.

Setting a good example—not only in behaviour, but in reading, television programmes, efforts to find out the causes of things.

Ambition for the child, but not over-ambition (expecting more of him than his endowment will permit). Expectation of success, of good behaviour.

Instillation of a sensible attitude to illness, without exaggeration of symptoms.

Instillation of a sensible attitude to sex.

Instillation of a tolerant attitude to others. Avoidance of criticism of others in his presence; instead teaching him to look for the good in people.

Provision of suitable play material—which will help him to use his hands, to think, to use his imagination, to construct, to determine how things work (e.g. interlocking bricks, bead threading, picture dominoes, jigsaws, constructional toys such as bildit—but not mechanical toys). Provision of suitable material which will help him to obtain the answer to questions which he has raised. Letting him develop his own play rather than telling him what to do. Encouragement of self initiated learning without providing all the ideas.

Encouragement of accuracy, thoroughness, self confidence, initiative, leadership.

Teaching curiosity, to wonder why, to explore.

Allowing him to learn from mistakes.

Teaching him to argue, to ask for the reason why, to ask questions, to think round a subject, to question what the parent says, what the radio says, to seek evidence.

Teaching persistence, creativity. It is thought that creativity is implanted in the home.

Giving opportunity to enlarge his vocabulary.

Reading to the child (e.g. from 12 months onwards).

Providing experiences outside the home—visiting the country-
side, seeing natural phenomena, visiting museums,
factories.

Environment and the Handicapped Child

The environment is important not only to the normal child,
but to the handicapped child.

There is abundant scope for research into the effect of environment in handicapped children. In one way or another the environment of the child with any but the mildest handicap is almost
bound to be different from that of normal children. He is apt to
be over-protected at home, so that his physical or sensory handicap is augmented by the factor of lack of practice and opportunity
to learn. He may be the subject of favouritism or rejection. He
may be the target of unkind criticisms or comments made by
neighbours in his presence. He may be deprived of normal tactile
and manipulative experience with toys and other materials. He
may be isolated from his fellows, and lack their companionship.
His activities outside school hours are restricted. He has to be
treated differently from normal children owing to his dependence
on others. He may have to be separated from his parents at an
early age in order that he can be trained in a residential school
suitable for his handicap, and the problem of emotional deprivation is added to the physical defect. Bender[7] remarked that
'children can tolerate a certain amount of inflammation and
structural damage to the brain if they have the emotional support
they need and are not isolated and deprived'.

Parmelee et al.[64] emphasised the great importance of distinguishing retardation in the blind child as a result of emotional
deprivation and absence of opportunity and experience, from true
mental retardation with a low I.Q. They wrote that 'the greatest
evil that can befall a blind child is to be judged mentally retarded
early in life and thereby be deprived of any opportunities for
intellectual development. Almost as serious for both the blind
child and his parents is the failure to recognise a child with serious
mental impairment early enough to spare both the torments of
trying to achieve impossible goals'.

A particularly valuable paper,[32] drew attention to the
pseudoretardation which may arise in blind children as a result
of deprivation of the normal sensory and motor stimuli. Delay

in giving solid foods may cause difficulty in chewing and eating: toilet training is apt to be delayed: they may be deprived of the opportunity to learn to dress themselves when developmentally ready to learn: they may lack the normal sensory stimuli because they are not given suitable toys: they may be stopped from placing objects in the mouth: the parents are liable to read to them less, so that their speech is retarded. They rightly emphasised that many blind children are classified as retarded or autistic, when the intelligence is not low, but they have merely lacked the necessary stimuli when they were developmentally ready to learn various new skills.

Much interest has been shown in recent years in the emotional problems of the mentally handicapped child. It is generally agreed that the mentally defective child is further retarded by being placed early in an institution.[33]

An interesting study by Kirk[54] showed how mentally retarded children can improve considerably with suitable education, in the preschool period or later, and how they can deteriorate as a result of emotional deprivation. He conducted a 5 year study of the effect of preschool teaching in mentally retarded children. Thirty of 43 children (70 per cent.) receiving preschool education showed an improvement of their intellectual status. He concluded that: 'It would appear that, although the upper limits of development for an individual are genetically or organically determined, the functional level or rate of development may be accelerated or depressed within the limits set by the organism. Somatopsychological factors and the cultural milieu (including schooling) are capable of influencing the functional level within these limits.'

Schlanger[73] studied the speech of 21 matched pairs of mentally retarded children, one group being brought up in an institution, another group being looked after at home. The speech of those brought up in the institution was much inferior to that of the other group.

It follows that as the environment is of such importance in the handicapped child, it must always be borne in mind in assessing his intellectual potential. It is easy to underestimate such a child's ability, because due attention has not been paid to the retarding effect of his environment. One might add that it is also possible to make too much allowance for his environmental difficulties.

The aim should always be to assess the mentally or physically handicapped child's maximum potential, and to help him to achieve it. When one first sees a handicapped child one must remember that owing to adverse environmental factors he may be functioning at an unnecessarily low level.

Handedness

The question of whether handedness is predominantly environmental or genetic in origin has not been decided. I have decided to include this subject here because of evidence that environmental factors play at least an important part in the establishment of handedness. The subject has been reviewed by Zangwill[95] Clark,[21] Barsley[4] and others.

Bakwin[2] wrote that archaeological studies of implements show that hand preference among aboriginal men was about equally divided, and that during the Bronze Age there was a shift to right handedness. He stated that the incidence of left handedness in female adults is 3·8 per cent., as compared with 6·6 per cent. in male adults. Morley[61] found that between 6 and 7 per cent. of the Newcastle-on-Tyne children in her survey were left handed. Brain[12] stated that between 5 and 10 per cent of school children are left handed. The incidence in uniovular twins is three times greater than that in the normal population.

It should be noted that left handedness is not just the opposite of right handedness. Those with right handedness are usually consistent in the use of the right hand, but most left handed persons are inconsistent in the use of the left hand.

Watson[90] wrote that 'handedness is not an instinct. It is socially conditioned'. Gesell and Ames[39] regarded handedness as developmental in origin. Hildreth[45] wrote that: 'Achieving handedness is essentially a learning process, involving habit formation, spontaneous reactions, postural adjustment, expression of choice, and responding in social situations'. He thought that the question of whether handedness is hereditary or environmentally conditioned has never been satisfactorily determined. Ausubel[2] remarked that 85 per cent. are predominantly right-handed by the end of the second year, but by the age of 6, 93 per cent. are right-handed. He regarded handedness as partly genetic and partly due to deliberate training measures and the cumulative impact of innumerable environmental cues. He added that cerebral dominance might be a consequence rather than a cause of handedness.

Clark[21] wrote as follows: 'The position may be summed up by saying that genetic studies have revealed that the development of handedness preference has a hereditary basis, in other words, that one's chances of being left-handed are greater if there are instances of left-handedness in the family. Few would deny, however, that factors other than genetic help to determine whether any particular individual will be right- or left-handed, the actual society in which he lives and its attitude to left-handedness. Other environmental factors, temperamental differences, and so on, all these play a part in determining whether latent left-handedness will be cultivated or suppressed. These factors will probably have their greatest effect on the intermediate, assuming left-handedness to be a quantitative trait'.

It is certainly one's experience that a high proportion of left-handed children have a left-handed parent, but that is not conclusive proof of a genetic factor.

Readers are referred to the comprehensive account of the genetic and neurological aspects of handedness written by Annette.[1]

While the cause of handedness is uncertain, the relationship to certain aspects of development is also undecided. It seems to be agreed by many that the training of a left-handed child to use the right hand does not in itself cause stuttering. It is felt that it is the way in which the child is taught which matters. If the training is a source of stress, stuttering may result. In this connection it should be remembered that in some cultures left-handedness is regarded as a stigma on the child, and this in itself might lead indirectly to insecurity and so to behaviour problems or stuttering. One wonders whether there is some such explanation for Pearce's findings in China.[66] Pearce investigated children in a boarding school, and found a much higher incidence of school difficulties in those with crossed laterality than in those without.

There seems to be some association between handedness and intelligence. Karlin and Strazzulla[53] discussed the literature concerning this, and indicated that there is a high incidence of left-handedness in mental defectives. Burt[15] found that left-handedness is half as common again in backward children as it is in the normal population, and twice as common among mental defectives, as it is in others.

This finding might be in some way due to delayed maturation in some mentally defective children, or to the fact that if there is ambidexterity, it is more difficult to train a retarded child to use one hand more than the other, or that less effort would be made to teach him to use the right hand in preference to the left.

Clark[21] concluded that there was no significant difference in the writing of left- and right-handed children. Elsewhere, however, she wrote that there is some truth in the suggestion that left-handers are bad writers. She wrote that 'it is a generalisation with only a certain amount of truth in it'. She felt that they suffer from more fatigue when subjected to prolonged periods of writing than those using the right hand. She wrote that 'there is an intimate connection between the development of speech and dominant handedness. There may be a connection between retarded speech and lack of dominance'. The rôle of crossed laterality was thought to be uncertain.

Hillman[46] wrote that 'all the evidence contained in the investigation of 1,847 children points to the fact that there is no connection between reading failures and handedness, eyedness or crossed laterality, or the lack of hemispherical dominance which may be associated with those characteristics. The papers show that the incidence of backwardness, normality and advanced reading is approximately the same in all the various groups of laterality characteristics'.

Spitzer et al.[79] investigated the incidence of mixed dominance in 103 children with reading disabilities, and 288 controls. There was no difference between the two groups.

Vernon[89] in her book on reading difficulties, summed up her views as follows: 'The relationship to reading disabilities of in-complete lateralisation and cerebral dominance is extremely obscure. It may, perhaps, be concluded that left-handedness need not in itself be a handicap to reading. But inevitably writing is harder for the left-handed child; and this may both make it more difficult for him to acquire an understanding of the correct order of letters in the word, but also set up a general dislike of linguistic pursuits, and anxiety over their performance. It is doubtful whether sightedness is of great importance: and lack of dominance of one visual cortical area over the other is still of doubtful significance. But ambidexterity and mixed handedness can only be associated with incomplete dominance of the major over the minor hemisphere, and this in turn produces general immaturity in motor and or linguistic functions, or in certain of these functions in particular.

'In some cases of reading disability incomplete lateralisation may be an important factor, especially when it is congenital. But it is doubtful whether this in itself is sufficient to cause permanent inability to read, unless reinforced by some additional factor'.

Eames[31] made the interesting observation that there was a 20 per cent. higher incidence of lateral dominance variations in 43 children aged 5 to 17 who had been prematurely born, than in 404 children of the same age who had been born at term.

In conclusion, there are many problems of handedness which remain unsolved. Handedness is in part genetic, and in part environmental in origin. The rôle of handedness in reading and writing difficulties has been exaggerated in the past, and it is probable that handedness is of little importance in these problems. Left-handedness is more common in mentally defective children, but the reason for this is not obvious.

Summary

The environment—the home, the neighbourhood, the school—has a profound effect on the child's development.

The concept of the sensitive or critical period described by ethologists may be applied to the developing child. Evidence is adduced to the effect that the child should be enabled to learn when he is first ready to learn.

The role of nutrition in the early years, of love and security, of the opportunity to practice and to develop independence, are all emphasised.

The qualities of a bad home and of a good home are discussed. I have listed some of the ways of helping a child to achieve his best.

The effect of environment on the handicapped child is discussed.

In conclusion, a child's I.Q. can be considerably raised or lowered by his environment. Nevertheless, genetic factors contribute a major part to the child's intelligence and ability; but the effects of nature and nurture are so intimately and intricately intermingled, that efforts to separate the effects of one from the effects of the other are doomed to failure, and are an unprofitable occupation.

REFERENCES

1. ANNETTE, M. (1968) Aspects of human lateral asymmetry and its bearing on intellectual development in childhood hemiplegia. Report to the Spastics Society. London.
2. AUSUBEL, D. P. (1958) *Theory and Problems of Child Development.* New York: Grune and Stratton.
3. BAKWIN, H. (1950) Lateral Dominance. *J. Pediat.,* **36,** 385.
4. BARSLEY, M. (1966) *The Left Handed Book.* London: Souvenir Press.
5. BAYLEY, N. (1956) A New Look at the Curve of Intelligence. *Proceedings of the* 1956 *Conference on Testing Problems of Testing Service.* p. 11-25.
6. BAYLEY, N., SCHAEFER, E. S. (1960) Relationships between Socio-economic Variables and the Behaviour of Mothers towards Young Children. *J. genet. Psychol.,* **96,** 61.
7. BENDER, L. (1958) Emerging Patterns in Child Psychiatry. *Bull. N.Y. Acad. Med.,* **34,** 794.
8. BLOOM, B. S. (1964) *Stability and Change in Human Characteristics.* New York: Wiley.
9. BOURNE, H. (1955) Protophrenia. A Study of Perverted Rearing and Mental Dwarfism. *Lancet,* **2,** 1156.
10. BOWLBY, J. (1951) Maternal Care and Mental Health. *Bull. Wld. Hlth. Org.,* **3,** 357.
11. BOWLBY, J., AINSWORTH, M., BOSTON, M., ROSENBLUTH, D. (1956) Effects of Mother—Child Separation: Follow-up Study. *Brit. J. med. Psychol.,* **29,** 211.
12. BRAIN, R. (1961) *Speech Disorders.* London: Butterworth.
13. BURKS, B. S. (1941) Heredity and Mental Traits. *Sci. monthly,* **52,** 462.
14. BURLINGHAM, D., FREUD, A. (1944) *Infants without Families.* London: Allen and Unwin.
15. BURT, C. (1950) *The Backward Child.* London: Univ. of London Press.
16. BURT, C. (1955) The Evidence for the Concept of Intelligence. *Brit. J. educ. Psychol.,* **25,** 158.
17. BURT, C. (1959) General Ability and Special Aptitudes. *Educ. Res.,* **1,** 3.
18. CABAK, V., NAJDANVIC, R. (1965) Effect of undernutrition in early life on physical and mental development. *Arch. Dis. Childh.,* **40,** 532.
19. CARMICHAEL, L. (1926) The Development of Behaviour in Vertebrates Experimentally Removed from the Influence of External Stimulation. *Psychol. Rev.,* **33,** 57.
20. CHOREMIS, C., BAROUTSOU, E. (1958) The Study of Psychomotor Development in Dystrophic Children and Children brought up in Foundling Homes. *Ann. pediat. (Basel),* **190,** 208.
21. CLARK, M. M. (1957) *Left Handedness.* London: Univ. of London Press.
22. CLARKE, A. M., CLARKE, A. D. B. (1958) *Mental Deficiency. The Changing Outlook.* London: Methuen.

23. COOKE, R. (1968) *The Biological Basis of Pediatric Practice*. New York: McGraw Hill.
24. CRAVIOTO, J. (1966) Malnutrition and behavioral development in the preschool child. *Courrier du Centre International de L'Enfance*, **16**, 117.
25. DAVIS, D. R., KENT, N. (1955) Psychological Factors in Educational Disability. *Proc. roy. Soc. Med.*, **48**, 993.
26. DAVIS, D. R., KENT, N. (1957) Discipline in the Home and Intellectual Development. *Brit. J. med. Psychol.*, **30**, 27.
27. DENNIS, W. (1941) Infant Development under Conditions of Restricted Practice and of Minimum Social Stimulation. *Genet. Psychol. Monogr.*, **23**, 143.
28. DENNIS, W. (1943) On the Possibility of Advancing and Retarding the Motor Development of Infants. *Psychol. Rev.*, **50**, 203.
29. DOUGLAS, J. W. B. (1964). *The Home and the School*. London: Macgibbon & Kee.
30. DRILLIEN, C. M. (1961) Longitudinal Study of Growth and Development of Prematurely and Maturely Born Children. Mental Development 2-5 Years. *Arch. Dis. Childh.*, **36**, 233.
31. EAMES, T. H. (1957) Frequency of Cerebral Lateral Dominance Variations among School Children of Premature and Full Term Birth. *J. Pediat.*, **51**, 300.
32. ELONEN, A. S., ZWARENSTEYN, S. B. (1964) Appraisal of Developmental Lag in Certain Blind Children. *J. Pediat.*, **65**, 599.
33. FARRELL, M. J. (1956) The Adverse Effects of Early Institutionalisation of Mentally Subnormal Children. *Amer. J. Dis. Child.*, **91**, 278.
34. FOSS, B. M. *Determinants of Infant Behaviour*. Vol. 1 (1961), Vol. 2 (1963), Vol. 3 (1965), Vol. 4 (1969). London: Methuen.
35. FREEMAN, F. N. (1928) quoted by Berko, M. J. (1955), The Measurement of Intelligence in Children with Cerebral Palsy. *J. Pediat.*, **47**, 253.
36. GARRISON, K. C. (1952) *Growth and Development*. New York: Longmans Green.
37. GESELL, A., THOMPSON, H. (1929) Learning and Growth in Identical Infant Twins. *Genet. Psychol. Monogr.*, **6**, 5.
38. GESELL, A. (1941) *Wolf Child and Human Child*. London: Methuen.
39. GESELL, A., AMES, L. B. (1947) The Development of Handedness. *J. genet. Psychol.*, **70**, 155.
40. GLASER, K., EISENBERG, L. (1956) Emotional Deprivation. *Pediatrics*, **18**, 626.
41. GOLDFARB, W. (1944) Effects of Early Institutional Care on Adolescent Personality. Rorschach data. *Amer. J. Orthopsychiat*, **14**, 441.
42. GOLDFARB, W. (1945) Effects of Psychological Deprivation in Infancy and Subsequent Stimulation. *Amer. J. Psychiat.*, **102**, 18.
43. GREENACRE, P. (1944) Infant Reactions to Restraint. *Amer. J. Orthopsychiat.*, **14**, 204.
44. HARDCASTLE, D. N. (1935) A Suggested Approach to the Problems of Neuropsychiatry. *J. ment. Sci.*, **81**, 317.
45. HILDRETH, G. (1949) The Development and Training of Hand Dominance. *J. genet. Psychol.*, **75**, 199.
46. HILLMAN, H. H. (1956) Abstract in *Child Develpm. Abstr.* (1957), **31**, No. 401.

47. HINDE, R. A. (1966) *Animal behaviour*. New York: McGraw Hill.
48. HYMOVITCH, B. (1952) The Effects of Experimental Variations on Problem Solving in the Rat. *J. comp. physiol. Psychol.*, **45**, 313.
49. ILLINGWORTH, R. S., Lister, J. (1964) The Critical or Sensitive Period, with Special Reference to Certain Feeding Problems in Infants and Children. *J. Pediat.*, **65**, 839.
50. ILLINGWORTH, R. S. (1968) How to help a child to achieve his best. *J. Pediat.*, **73**, 61.
51. ILLINGWORTH, R. S., ILLINGWORTH, C. M. (1966) *Lessons from childhood*. Edinburgh: Livingstone.
52. JAHODA, M., WARREN, N. (1968) Intelligence, nature and nurture. *New Scientist*, **39**, 188.
53. KARLIN, I. W., STRAZZULLA, M. (1952) Speech and Language Problems of Mentally Defective Children. *J. Speech Dis.*, **17**, 286.
54. KIRK, S. A. (1958) *Early Education of the Mentally Retarded*. Urbana: Univ. of Illinois Press.
55. KNOBLOCH, H. (1959) Pneumoencephalograms and Clinical Behaviour. *Pediatrics.*, **23**, 175.
56. KNOBLOCH, H., PASAMANICK, B. (1962) Mental Subnormality. *New Engl. J. med.*, **266**, 1092.
57. LOWREY, L. G. (1940) Personality Distortion and Early Institutional Care. *Amer. J. Orthopsychiat.*, **10**, 576.
58. LYNN, R. (1959) Environmental Conditions Affecting Intelligence. *Educ. Res.*, **1**, 49.
59. McGRAW, M. (1940) Neural Maturation as Exemplified by the Achievement of Bladder Control. *J. Pediat.*, **16**, 580.
60. MADDOX, H. (1957) Nature-Nurture Balance Sheets. *Brit. J. educ. Psychol.*, **27**, 166.
61. MORLEY, M. E. (1957) *The Development and Disorders of Speech in Childhood*. London: Livingstone.
62. NEWMAN, H. H., FREEMAN, F. N., HOLZINGER, K. J. (1937) *Twins. A Study of Heredity and Environment*. Chicago Univ. Press., quoted by Slater, E. T. O. (1938). *J. Neurol. Psychiat.*, **1**, 239.
63. NISSEN, H. W., CHOW, K. L., SEMMES, J. (1951) Effects of Restricted Opportunity for Tactile Kinaesthetic and Manipulative Experience on the Behaviour of a Chimpanzee. *Amer. J. Psychol.*, **64**, 485.
64. PARMELEE, A. H., FISKE, C. E., WRIGHT, R. H. (1959) The Development of Ten Children with Blindness as a Result of Retrolental Fibroplasia. *Amer. J. Dis. Child.*, **98**, 198.
65. PAVENSTEDT, E. (1967) *The Drifters*. Children of disorganised lower class families. London: Churchill.
66. PEARCE, R. A. H. (1953) Crossed Laterality. *Arch. Dis. Childh.*, **28**, 247.
67. PENROSE, L. S. (1956) *The Biology of Mental Defect*. London: Sidgwick and Jackson.
68. POULL, L. E. (1938) The Effect of Improvement in Nutrition in the Mental Capacity of Young Children. *Child Develpm.*, **9**, 123.
69. PRECHTL, H. in Foss. (1963) *Determinants of Infant Behaviour*. Vol. 2. London: Methuen.
70. PRINGLE, KELLMER, M. L. (1967) Speech, learning and child health. *Proc. Roy. Soc. Med.*, **60**, 885.
71. PRINGLE, KELLMER, M. L., BUTLER, N. R., DAVIES, R. (1966) 11,000 *Seven year olds*. London: Langham.

72. RHEINGOLD, H. L. (1963). *Maternal Behavior in Animals*. New York: Wiley.
73. SCHLANGER, B. B. (1954) Environmental Influences in the Verbal Output of Mentally Retarded Children. *J. Speech Dis.*, **19**, 339.
74. SKEELS, H. M. (1936) Mental Development of Children in Foster Homes. *J. genet. Psychol.*, **49**, 91.
75. SKODAK, M. (1938) The Mental Development of Adopted Children whose True Mothers are Feebleminded. *Child Develpm.*, **9**, 303.
76. SKODAK, M., SKEELS, H. M. (1949) A Final Follow-up Study of One Hundred Adopted Children. *J. genet. Psychol.*, **75**, 85.
77. SKODAK, M. (1950) Mental Growth of Adopted Children in the Same Family. *J. genet. Psychol.*, **77**, 3.
78. SPITZ, R. A. (1946) Anaclitic Depression. *Psychoanal. study Child*, **2**, 313.
79. SPITZER, R. L., RABKIN, R., KROMER, Y. (1959) The Relationship Between Mixed Dominance and Reading Disabilities. *J. Pediat.*, **54**, 76.
80. STANDING, E. M. (1957) *Maria Montessori*. London: Hollis and Carter.
81. STEWART, M. (1960) The Leisure Activities of School Children. London Workers Education Association.
82. STOTCH, M. B., SMYTHIE, P. M. (1967) The effect of undernutrition during infancy on subsequent brain growth and intellectual development. *South African Med. J.*, **41**, 1027.
83. STOTT, D. H. (1956) Unsettled Children and their Families. London: University of London Press.
84. STOTT, D. H. (1959) Infantile Illness and Subsequent Mental and Emotional Development. *J. genet. Psychol.*, **94**, 233.
85. STOTT, D. H. (1962) Abnormal Mothering as a Cause of Mental Subnormality. *J. Child Psychol.*, **3**, 79.
86. THOMPSON, W. R., HERON, W. (1954) The Effects of Early Restriction on Activity in Dogs. *J. comp. physiol. Psychol.*, **47**, 77.
87. THORPE, W. H., ZANGWILL, O. L. (1961) *Current problems in animal behaviour*. Cambridge: Cambridge Univ. Press.
88. TILNEY, F., CASAMAJOR, L. (1924) Myelogeny and Infant Behaviour. *Arch. Neurol. Psychiat.*, **12**, 1.
89. VERNON, M. D. (1957) *Backwardness in Reading*. Cambridge: Cambridge University Press.
89a VERNON, P. E. (1969) *Intelligence and Cultural Environment*. London: Methuen.
90. WATSON, J. B. (1931) *Behaviourism*. London: Kegan Paul.
91. WEISS, P. (1939) *Principles of Development*. New York: Henry Holt.
92. WITTENBORN, J. R. (1957) *The Placement of Adoptive Children*. Springfield: Thomas.
93. WOLF, A. (1943) The Dynamics of the Selective Inhibition of Specific Functions in Neurosis. *Psychosomat. med.*, **5**, 27.
94. WORLD HEALTH ORGANISATION. (1962) Definition of Maternal Care. A Reassessment of its Affects. Public Health Papers No. 14. Geneva.
95. ZANGWILL, O. (1960) *Cerebral dominance and its relation to psychological problems*. London: Oliver and Boyd.

CHAPTER 5

THE ASSOCIATION OF MENTAL SUBNORMALITY WITH PHYSICAL DEFECTS AND DISEASE

Congenital Defects

It is a general principle that any major congenital anomaly carries with it a risk of mental subnormality. Amongst major congenital anomalies I would include:

i) Defects of skeleton and skull—such as hypertelorism, the the first arch syndrome, achondroplasia, syndactyly, cleft palate.

ii) Congenital defects of the eyes and ears—such as optic atrophy, colobomata, congenital deafness.

iii) Congenital heart disease.

iv) Various congenital skin defects.

v) Diseases involving muscle.

vi) Endocrine defects—cretinism.

vii) Other metabolic conditions, such as those associated with abnormal aminoaciduria.

viii) Mixed genetic and chromosomal defects.

In a series of 1068 personally observed mentally subnormal children at Sheffield, excluding mongolism, cretinism, hydrocephalus and cerebral palsy, 312 had major congenital anomalies (29·3 per cent). They included 89 children with serious eye disease, of which 23 had optic atrophy, and the remainder had cataracts, colobomata, retinal changes, buphthalmos or anophthalmos: 43 children with congenital heart disease, and 13 with cleft palate.

This study was based on children seen in hospital, to which many children with severe congenital anomalies are sent, and it is not therefore completely unselected.

It is interesting to note that in a series of 702 personally observed children with cerebral palsy, only 53 had congenital anomalies (7·5 per cent).

I do not think that it would be profitable to discuss each of the numerous congenital defects separately: but I have picked out a few of the more important conditions associated with mental subnormality, including certain features of physical growth.

Physical Growth and Other Features

It is well recognised that mentally defective children tend to be small in stature.   Sexual development is often delayed and hypogenitalism in boys is common.   In some cases the stunting of growth is extreme.   A child under my care weighed 26 lbs. at the age of 11 years and was 37 inches in height, but no cause could be found after the fullest investigation. Jones and Murray[40] studied the heights and weights of 126 educationally subnormal children.   Seventy-three per cent. were below the average weight and 68 per cent. were below the average height.   There have been many other studies to the same effect.   I would say that when an infant fails to thrive and remains unusually small, when the food intake is adequate and the fullest investigation has failed to reveal a cause, the diagnosis of severe mental subnormality should always be considered and examined for by means of developmental testing.

Approximately 20 per cent. of the mentally subnormal children seen by me fell into the definition of prematurity, meaning that they weighed $5\frac{1}{2}$ lbs. (2,500 g.) or less at birth, whereas the incidence of prematurity in this country is between 6 and 7 per cent. Many of these, however, would be more correctly termed 'small for dates', meaning that they were unduly small for the duration of gestation.   It seemed that defective physical and defective mental growth had both commenced *in utero*.[93]

The age at which the *anterior fontanelle* closes is of little importance in the study of mental subnormality.   Though it may remain open unduly long in some mentally defective children without hydrocephalus, the intelligence is normal in the great majority of children in whom it has remained open longer than usual.   In microcephalic infants the anterior fontanelle closes unusually early, but it often closes unusually early in normal infants.

The teeth in mentally defective children are more liable to show caries than those of normal children. This may be due to poor nutrition, defective chewing or other factors. In a study of

319 mental defectives significant structural alterations were found
in the teeth of 84.[88] It was thought that the abnormalities were
of prenatal origin. The dental changes in association with kernicterus are well known.

Many workers have studied the *skin markings* on the hands of
mentally defective children. The frequency of whorls in the
palms of the feeble-minded and imbeciles is said to be less than
that in the general population.[23] Allen[2] pointed out that the distal
triradius, often thought to be characteristic of mongolism, occurs
in 10 per cent. of normal children and adults. It is said to be more
frequent in the relatives of mongols.

A single palmar crease is common in mongols and other mentally
defective children.[20] A single palmar crease was found in 3·7
per cent of 6,299 newborn babies. It was more common in boys
than girls, in premature babies, and in infants with congenital
anomalies. It is a useful pointer to a prenatal cause of a defect,
such as mental subnormality or cerebral palsy.

The incidence of the *female sex chromatin pattern* is higher in
mentally retarded males than it is in the normal population.[63]
Klinefelter's syndrome, which is commonly associated with mental
deficiency, is another example of chromosome abnormalities.

Mongolism

The subject of mongolism is so well known that I shall only
mention it briefly here, with particular reference to the level of
intelligence to be expected.

Mongols are developmentally at their best in the first few
months of life. Øster[66] remarked that a D.Q. of 75 in the first
year does not exclude the diagnosis. I have seen several mongols
who were able to sit without support on the floor at 7 or 8 months,
though the average age at which mongols learn to sit is 1 year.
Development then seems to slow down, so that they become
seriously mentally defective. I saw a full term mongol, for instance, who began to smile at 4 months, to grasp objects voluntarily at 7 months, to roll from prone to supine at 7 months, and
to sit without support at $7\frac{1}{2}$ months. When he was 8 months old,
however, I was interested to note his defective concentration and
the persistence of hand regard—a sure sign of retardation. He
walked without help at 34 months, and joined words to form sentences at 69 months. His I.Q. test score at 6 years was 28. Rela-

tively advanced development in early months should not, therefore, lead one to suppose that one is dealing with an unusually intelligent mongol. In one study Gesell tests in the first year did not correlate with subsequent development, but tests in the second year did.[83]

Perhaps because there is not much scatter in the eventual I.Q. score of mongols, it has proved difficult to predict their intelligence in the early months, and there is little published work on this. Two papers[24, 45] merely confirm Gesell's original observation, that mongols are developmentally at their best in the first months of life, and that thereafter their development slows down.

I feel unable myself to predict that a given mongol will prove to have a higher or lower I.Q. score than other mongols. I do not think that the relatively advanced motor development which one occasionally sees is indicative of a better than usual level of intelligence. I feel that one's estimate of the home environment, with the amount of love and stimulation which is likely to be given to the child, provides the only clue as to the possibility that an individual mongol will fare somewhat better than other mongols. Conversely, placement in an institution would suggest that he will fare less well than others more fortunately placed.

I know of no study in which the head circumference of infant mongols has been related to their eventual level of intelligence.

There have been many studies of the eventual intelligence quotient of mongols. Engler[22] tested 100 mongols. Twenty-seven per cent. were idiots, 71 per cent. were imbeciles, and 2 per cent. had an I.Q. over 50. (The I.Q. of idiots is roughly 0 to 24; of imbeciles 25 to 49; and of morons 50 to 69.)

Unless chromosome studies have been carried out, to exclude mosaicism, stories of mongols with a higher than usual I.Q. are of little significance.

Malzberg[60] in his study of 880 mongols in New York, found that 24·5 per cent. were idiots, 71·6 per cent. were imbeciles, and 5·8 per cent. were morons.

Øster[66] in his comprehensive study of 526 mongols, made the point that there is no relation between the degree of stigmata and facial appearance and the I.Q. He wrote that the majority are imbeciles, some are idiots, and a few are feeble-minded. He stated that the highest I.Q. recorded was 74.

Øster found that practically all mongols over 10 understand

when spoken to, and that most adult mongols speak intelligibly.
Speech, however, is retarded, with a husky voice and poor articulation. One or two had been known to learn to read and write,
but probably without understanding it. No mongol, he said, had
been found to be able to add sums. I have seen a 12-year-old
mongol who, as a result of prolonged and probably misguided
teaching, could read simple books (at the 5 to 6 years old level)
and make simple additions. On investigation, however, it was
found that she had no idea what she had read, and the figures
meant nothing to her. Her I.Q. test score was about 30.

Quaytman[76] tested 40 mongols between 2 years 8 months and
16 years of age attending a clinic. They were selected, in that
the worst mongols were more likely to have been placed in an
institution. Seventy-five per cent. had an I.Q. below 50, but 9
cases (22·5 per cent.) were said to have an I.Q. of 50 to 69 and
one was said to have an I.Q. of 70-79.

Wunsch[101] studied the I.Q. of 77 mongols, mostly aged 5 to 9
years in a state clinic for retarded children, and found that 10·9
per cent. had an I.Q. of 50 to 59, and 2·6 per cent. an I.Q.
of 60 to 69. Only 20 per cent. had an I.Q. below 30. Fifty-one
per cent. showed the docile behaviour usually attributed to them,
and 14·3 per cent. showed aggressive hostile behaviour. Blacketer-
Simmonds[8] had previously studied 140 mongols in a state colony
and compared them with 100 non-mongoloid defective controls.
He could find only three significant differences between the two
groups. Mongols appeared to be less docile, more mischievous
and more solitary than the others. Mongols showed the same
undesirable habits and tendencies as non-mongol defectives.
They showed no difference with regard to appreciation of music.

Benda[4] found that mongols were commonly stubborn,
aggressive and destructive. He found that there was a striking
difference between the I.Q. score of mongols brought up at home
and those brought up in an institution.

Tizard and Grad[91] could find no difference between the
personality of mongols and other retarded children of the same
age and intellectual level.

Brousseau[11] found that the I.Q. of 206 mongols was as follows:

I.Q.	Percentage
0—20	28·6
20·1—30	35·9

I.Q.	Percentage
30·1—40	28·6
40·1—50	5·8
50·1—66	1·0

The age at which 167 mongols learned to walk was as follows:

Age in months	Percentage
12—18	7·8
18—24	19·7
24—30	10·8
30—36	28·8
36—48	19·7
48—60	9·6
60—90	3·6

According to Gesell,[27] the average mongol learns to sit at 1 year, walk at 2 years, say single words at 3 years, feed himself at 4 years, acquire clean habits at 5 years, and to join words to make sentences at 6 years.

Engler[22] found that of 170 mongols, 11·2 per cent. learnt to talk by 2; 49·4 per cent. by 3; 61·7 per cent. by 4; and 81·2 per cent. by 5 years. Several mongols were unable to say any words by the age of 20 years.

Only 0·5 per cent. of 200 mongols were able to walk by 1 year, but 20 per cent. walked by 2 years, 60 per cent. by 3 years, and 83·5 per cent. by 4 years of age.

It is unfortunate that the number of mongols is tending to increase, probably because of improved surgical treatment of intestinal obstruction and Hirschsprung's disease in infancy, and of improved medical treatment of respiratory infections.

Carter[15] traced 698 of 725 mongols attending the Hospital for Sick Children, Great Ormond Street, London, between 1944 and 1955. Thirty per cent. had died within a month of birth, 53 per cent. within the first year, and 60 per cent. by the age of 10 years. The main causes of death were bronchopneumonia and congenital heart disease. He mentioned the higher incidence of leukaemia and of Hirschsprung's disease in mongols than in the normal population. In 1929 it was estimated that there were 0·24 mongols per 1,000 children aged 5 to 14 in several areas of England and Wales, while now there were 4 times as many—1·6 per 1,000.

In an Australian study, referred to by Kirman,[44] it was found that 25 per cent. had died by six months, and 50 per cent. by five years.

In conclusion, it is only rarely that a mongol has an I.Q. of over 50, though the developmental quotient in infancy may be much higher than that. A mongol may begin to sit unsupported at 7 or 8 months, but sitting is usually delayed until about a year. It is most exceptional for a mongol to walk unsupported at 1 year, the average age for walking being somewhere between 2 and 3 years. There is little truth in statements that mongols are different in behaviour from other mentally defective children of comparable intelligence. The survival rate of mongols is higher now than it was one or two decades ago.

Convulsions and Epilepsy

There is a strong association between epilepsy and mental deficiency, due to the frequent association between epilepsy and underlying brain disease. In any institution for mental defectives, convulsions are likely to be common. Kirman wrote that of 777 mental defectives in the Fountain Hospital in 1953, 185 (25 per cent.) had fits while in hospital. Of 218 mongols, only two had fits. In another study it was found that 41·3 per cent. of 254 mental defectives had fits.

In my series of 444 mentally retarded children without cerebral palsy, and excluding mongols, the overall incidence of convulsions was 31·3 per cent. In those slightly to moderately retarded the incidence was 16·3 per cent.; in those severely retarded the incidence was 46·8 per cent. None of 87 mongols had fits.

In 285 mentally retarded children with cerebral palsy, the incidence of fits was 37·5 per cent. In the slightly or moderately retarded ones the incidence was 22·8 per cent. as compared with a figure of 53·7 per cent. in the severely retarded ones. In all groups, cases of postnatal origin were excluded.

There is a strong relationship between the type of epilepsy and the level of intelligence. The so-called infantile spasms (akinetic seizures, 'salaam spasms, myoclonic jerks'), with the E.E.G. picture of hypsarrythmia are usually associated with severe mental deficiency. This kind of epilepsy is associated with a wide variety of diseases, including serious brain defects, phenylketonuria, neurodermatoses, sequelae of severe hypoglycaemia, toxoplasmosis and pyridoxin dependency. It may follow immunisation procedures. Jeavons and Bower, in their excellent review,[37] found that three per cent of their cases became mentally normal. Livingston et al.[53] described 622 cases, all followed for at least 3 years. A total of 142 were in an institution. Twenty-three had died. Only 11 of the remaining 457 had a normal I.Q. The others were retarded, the vast majority severely so. I have emphasised the striking fact that those children who appear to develop normally until five or six months, and then develop infantile spasms, become mentally defective immediately the fits begin, but do not undergo progressive deterioration. After a period of some weeks they commonly improve and may occasionally become normal. In view of the multiplicity of causes of infantile spasms, it is hardly likely that any particular treatment will have a significantly beneficial effect on the child's intelligence.

It seems that apart from the above type of epilepsy, repeated major convulsions cause some degree of mental retardation. Lennox[50] suggested that the reasons for deterioration in some epileptics lie in hereditary factors, psychological factors, including educational difficulties and behaviour problems, cerebral birth injury, the effect of drugs, and the effect of epilepsy itself—perhaps the result of multiple petechial haemorrhages or anoxia. To those might be added the effect of repeated head injuries.

Pond[73] discussed the various factors which affect the intelligence of epileptic patients. The factors were considered to be genetic, the effect of the brain lesion, the effect of drugs, the effect of fits, and psychosocial. Pond stated that petit mal did not lead to mental impairment, however frequent the fits are. Temporal lobe epilepsy led to the greatest degree of impairment.

The psychological difficulties of epileptic children are well known. Ounsted[67] described a syndrome of epilepsy with hyperkinesis, usually but not necessarily associated with a low I.Q. It was common in boys, and made them intolerable at school.

Hydrocephalus

Surprisingly little has been written about the intelligence quotient achieved by children with hydrocephalus. Now that operative procedures are commonly carried out on these children, it has become more important to know the natural history of untreated cases, in order that one can assess the results achieved by various surgical procedures. Laurence[49] followed up 179 of 182 unoperated cases seen in London. Eighty-nine (49 per cent.) had died. Nine remained progressive, and 3 were not traced. Eighty-one (47 per cent.) had become arrested, and of these 75 per cent. were in the educable range, 33 of them having an I.Q. of 85 or more, and 26 having an I.Q. of 50 to 84. Twenty-seven of the 81 had little or no physical disability. There was little relationship between the I.Q. and the circumference of the head or the thickness of the cortex as measured in the air encephalogram. A child with a cortical thickness of 0.5 cm. was found to have an I.Q. of 85, and another child with a similar measurement had an I.Q. of 100. Laurence's figures may be too optimistic. His case material consisted of children who were referred to a neurosurgeon who did not operate on children with hydrocephalus and therefore the patients referred were already to some extent selected. Even so, only about one-third of the survivors had an I.Q. of 85 or over at the time of the survey. Further prospective studies on an unselected series would be of value in order to determine the true prognosis of this condition. Such a study is in progress at Sheffield. Results[56] to date indicate that with a ventriculocaval shunt, the outcome is likely to be much better. It remains to be seen, however, what physical and emotional difficulties remain. It is known that children with arrested (untreated) hydrocephalus tend to be facile in behaviour, happy, pleasant and talkative, with a tendency to clumsiness and slight ataxia.

In a prospective study of an unselected series of 475 newborn babies born with spina bifida and hydrocephalus, and assessed by a Psychologist at the age of 5 to 9 years, the following were the I.Q. scores:–

	I.Q.	Hydro-cephalus with Spina Bifida	Spina Bifida Without Hydrocephalus	Hydrocephalus Without Spina Bifida	Total	Per-centage
Superior	120+	3	5	4	12	2·5
High Average	110-119	13	19	7	39	8·2
Average	90-109	73	54	35	162	34·1
Low Average	80-89	47	18	25	90	18·9
E.S.N.	51-79	83	14	18	115	24·2
50		21	3	33	57	1·2
		240	113	122	475	

In a review of 187 children with meningomyelocele in Melbourne[86] it was found that two-thirds died in the first year. Of 59, 25 were said to be subnormal mentally, but the evidence on which this statement was based was not mentioned. Forty-eight had locomotor disability.

Owing to the frequent association of hydrocephalus with meningomyelocele, one would expect that the mean I.Q. level of children with meningomyelocele would be rather low. In the absence of hydrocephalus, however, the mean I.Q. would probably be little below the average.

Out of 19 children who suffered from neonatal meningitis and survived with gross residual hydrocephalus, treatment by ventriculo-caval shunt resulted in prolonged survival in 14 children. Seven of these were of normal intelligence, but 7 others were retarded.

Megalencephaly

This term describes a generalised hypertrophy of the brain, with a cytological defect in the nerve cells. A full description of the condition was given by Kinnier Wilson.[95] According to Ford[26] it is commoner in males, and may be familial. The cranium is large, but the child lacks the facial appearance of hydrocephalus. The diagnosis is in part established by ventriculography, which demonstrates the absence of ventricular dilatation. There are varying degrees of mental deficiency.

Craniostenosis

The level of intelligence found in children with craniostenosis depends in part on the extent of the premature fusion of the sutures. In some of the mildest forms children appear to develop normally at first, but drop behind when it becomes impossible for the brain to enlarge further owing to the fusion of the sutures. In more severe ones, in which the skull is already severely deformed at birth, mental development seems to have been retarded before operation was possible.

I have the impression that the level of intelligence is lower when there are other associated congenital anomalies (as in Apert's syndrome).

Hypertelorism

MacGillivray[58] described the association of various anomalies with hypertelorism. They include shortening of the digits, amyotonia, and congenital heart disease. He stated that there is no correlation between the extent of skull deformity and the degree of mental deficiency. The intelligence may be normal, but it is usually defective.

Cleft Palate

As there was very little literature on the level of intelligence found in children with cleft palate,[33] we studied 112 consecutive cases of cleft palate with or without hare lip, taken from an alphabetical and entirely representative list. The mean I.Q. of 80 on whom we were able to carry out Stanford-Binet tests was 95·4; 47 had an I.Q. test score of less than 100, and 33 had an I.Q. over 100. School reports obtained on a further 17 gave comparable results. It appeared that the mean I.Q. was slightly lower than that of the population as a whole.

Achondroplasia

MacGillivray[58] found that 5 of 16 cases were mentally defective. He added that the mental defect in achondroplasia and Morquio's disease is static, while in gargoylism it is progressive. Jervis[39] wrote that 'a certain degree of mental impairment is often present'. Ford[26] stated that the I.Q. is in inverse relation to the size of the head. In three quarters the head is abnormally large. This is mainly due to megalencephaly, though in some there is dilation of the ventricles.

In contrast the intelligence is usually normal in DYSCHONDRO-PLASIA,[59] a condition which probably includes conditions termed multiple bony prominences, multiple exostoses, diaphyseal aclasia, chondrodysplasia, multiple congenital osteochondromata, Ollier's disease, and multiple enchondroses; and in PROGRESSIVE DIAPHY-SEAL DYSPLASIA (Englemann's Disease),[29] in which there is enlargement and cortical thickening in the diaphyses of long bones.

Neuromuscular Conditions

Mental retardation of slight degree is more often seen in children with muscular dystrophy than in other children. In a group of 30 children with progressive muscular dystrophy, the mean I.Q. was 82.[2]   In a study of 38 boys,[102] one third of the children had mental retardation.   It was suggested that there was a combined genetic and environmental factor.   In a group of 36 children, half had an I.Q. score of less than 90—an incidence three times greater than that of the normal population.[28] Worden and Vignos[99] found a mean I.Q. of 83 in 38 patients aged between 4 and 17 years.   There was no progressive deterioration.   It was suggested that children with muscular dystrophy tend to have special difficulties in reading and mathematics.   Dubowitz[21] has described intellectual impairment in children with muscular dystrophy before there were any signs of physical handicap.   He thought that there might be an associated sex linked genetic mechanism, causing intellectual impairment, or that some metabolite of degenerating muscle might damage the central nervous system.

A similar view was expressed by Cohen, Molnar and Taft.[17] They found mental subnormality in 20·9 per cent of 211 children with the Duchenne type of muscular dystrophy, but no increased incidence of subnormality in their siblings.   In 39 families with two or more affected children, there was complete concordance with respect to the I.Q. in 94·9 per cent.

Hypotonia may be due to a variety of pathological conditions, and many mentally subnormal infants, including all mongols, are hypotonic.   The intelligence in children with benign forms of hypotonia is likely to be normal.

Cerebral Palsy

I have reviewed the literature concerning the intelligence level in children with cerebral palsy elsewhere[34] and will summarise it below. Putting together 6 important papers on the subject, I calculated that the I.Q. of 55 per cent. of 2,480 children was less than 70. Twenty per cent. of the normal population have an I.Q. of 110 or more, as compared with 3 per cent. of 1,768 affected children described by four workers.

It seems to be the general opinion that the intelligence level of children with athetosis is little different from that of children with the spastic form of cerebral palsy.

With regard to the relation of the I.Q. to the distribution of spasticity in the spastic form, the I.Q. of those with spastic quadriplegia is likely to be the lowest, and of those with spastic diplegia to be the highest. The mean I.Q. of those with hemiplegia is about 77. There is probably no difference in the I.Q. of those with left and right hemiplegia, though there is a difference of opinion on this point.

The I.Q. of children with the rigid form of cerebral palsy is almost invariably extremely low. They are all in the ineducable class. The same applies to the I.Q. of those with the rare 'atonic' form of cerebral palsy.

I have no figures for the I.Q. of children with congenital ataxia. My clinical impression is that the mean I.Q. of these children would be considerably below 100.

It is generally agreed that the more severe the cerebral palsy, the lower is the I.Q. likely to be, though this does not necessarily apply to athetoid children. It is usually the case that the I.Q. tends to be less in children who have convulsions.

Neurodermatoses

1. *Sturge Weber Syndrome*

Greenwald and Koota[30] found mental changes varying from mild deficiency to profound idiocy in 60 per cent. of 50 cases of the Sturge Weber syndrome. Mental retardation, when it occurs, is more often mild than severe.

A good review of the subject is found in the paper by Peterman *et al.*[72] Thirty-one of 35 cases had convulsions. There was mental retardation in 19 (54 per cent.). Eye changes (glaucoma or buphthalmos) were found in 13. The essential part of the disease is a venous angioma of the leptomeninges over the cerebral cortex, which is usually associated with a portwine naevus, often in the area supplied by the trigeminal nerve. Circulatory changes resulting from the lesion of the leptomeninges subsequently lead to the other manifestations—hemiplegia, fits and mental retardation.

2. *Tuberous Sclerosis.*

Complete forms of this disease are rare. The manifestations include adenoma sebaceum, rhabdomyoma of the heart, hamartoma of the kidney, phakomata of the retina, epilepsy, periungual fibromata, and bone changes. Incomplete forms are much commoner. Mental retardation is usual, but not invariable.[82] Some show little defect in the early years, but deteriorate later.

3. *Neurofibromatosis.*

Mental retardation is a relatively infrequent manifestation of this disease. In one series of cases the mean I.Q. score was 85 to 90.[41]

Retrolental Fibroplasia and Blindness

Several authors investigated the connection between retrolental fibroplasia, other forms of blindness and mental retardation. Some came to the conclusion that retrolental fibroplasia was very frequently associated with mental defect. For example, Bjelk-hagen[7] attempted to trace every child who had retrolental fibroplasia and who was born in Sweden between 1945 and 1950. It appears that he succeeded in tracing almost all of them. Of the 38 so examined only 11 were considered to be normal; 14 were definitely retarded and the rest were described as 'uncertain'. The actual I.Q. scores of the children were not given. If we were to assume that all the children whose I.Q. was considered to be uncertain were normal the number of retarded cases would still be very high.

Potter,[75] and later Williams[94], studied those children who were resident in Sunshine Homes or Homes of the Royal National Institute for the Blind. Potter's study included 177 children with retrolental fibroplasia. 94 (53·1 per cent.) were said to have a normal I.Q.: 47 (26·6 per cent.) were retarded but 'probably educable', and 36 (20·3 per cent.) were mentally defective. Williams found that of 211 children with retrolental fibroplasia born between 1946 and 1952 and admitted to Sunshine Homes, 58 (27·4 per cent.) were ineducable. Of 294 children who were blind for other reasons, 54 (18·2 per cent.) were ineducable. These presumably included the cases already described by Potter.

Krause[47] reached a similar conclusion in his study of 107 children aged 4 to 17 with retrolental fibroplasia. The mentality was described as good in 71, poor in 20 and very low in 16. There were physical or neurological defects in 24.

Other authors found that blind children with retrolental fibroplasia were no more retarded than children blind for other reasons, or children of comparable birth weight.

Norris *et al.*[64] in a study of 295 children, of whom 209 had retrolental fibroplasia, found no evidence that the latter condition is associated with either a specific or generalised brain defect. They found that there was no evidence that the child with retrolental fibroplasia differs in intellectual level from other blind children. The authors misquoted the work of Arnold Gesell in several respects.

Dann, Levine and New,[19] in their study of 73 babies weighing 1,000 g. or less in the perinatal period, found 25 children with healed or permanent retrolental fibroplasia. The mean I.Q. test score was 91, with a range of 64 to 142. As the mean I.Q. of the whole series was 94, there was not a significant difference between the children with retrolental fibroplasia and the other babies of comparable birth weight.

Parmalee et al.[70] found that of 38 children with retrolental fibroplasia, 12 were retarded, with an I.Q. test score of less than 70. Of 22 children with blindness due to other causes, 9 were retarded. They found that there was a much higher incidence of mental retardation when blindness was due to optic atrophy than when it was due to other causes. They added that mental retardation in blind children could be caused by neglect, emotional deprivation or lack of stimulation.

It seems, therefore, that there is no doubt that the incidence of mental retardation in children with retrolental fibroplasia is much higher than that of the general population. It is uncertain, however, how much of this retardation is due to prematurity, to a specific effect on the brain, or to lack of emotional and intellectual experience.

Blindness and Other Serious Eye Defects

OTHER CAUSES OF BLINDNESS. Parmelee[69] studied the development of blind premature children, and found that they tended to be later than others in learning to sit and to walk. They were not later than other children, however, in beginning to smile, to take objects to the mouth, to pull themselves to the standing position, or to walk while holding on to furniture. Gesell and Amatruda[27] found that blind children were no different from others in their development except in visual pursuits.

On the other hand there is a frequent association between blindness and other defects with mental retardation. In my series of 1068 mentally retarded children seen in Sheffield, excluding hydrocephalus, cretinism, mongolism and postnatal cases, 89 (8·3 per cent.) had major eye defects, such as optic atrophy, choroidoretinitis or cataract. Hilliard[31] informed me that among 1,720 patients from all Units in the Fountain Hospital Group over a period of 11 years, 108 (6·3 per cent.) were known to have optic atrophy.

Sjogren and Larsson[85] studied 137 cases of microphthalmia or anophthalmos in Sweden. Fifty-eight were combined with oligophrenia. Twenty-eight per cent. of those with microphthalmia and oligophrenia had fits, and 71 per cent. had skeletal anomalies in the form of club foot or kyphosis. Five per cent. of the microphthalmic cases with oligophrenia had spastic quadriplegia, and 7 per cent. of the siblings were idiots. The condition was regarded as a dominant hereditary disease.

Deafness

A study of the intellectual level of deaf children was carried out by Kendall[85] in Professor Ewing's department at Manchester. He found that when children whose deafness resulted from the rubella syndrome, tuberculous meningitis or kernicterus were excluded, there was no significant difference in test score at any age level when the performance tests were administered to representative groups of deaf and ordinary children, balanced for socioeconomic status.

Foale and Paterson[25] found a higher incidence of hearing loss among the mentally defective boys at Lennox Castle, aged 10 to 19, than is known to be present in the school population of England, Wales and Scotland. The authors mentioned the importance of remembering that high frequency deafness causes symptoms resembling those of mental retardation, and that impaired hearing may be a factor in the low test scores in backward children.

Kodman et al.[46] tested 189 children and adults in institutions. Hearing loss was defined as one of 30 d b or more. The incidence of hearing loss in the group aged 7 to 19 years was 19 per cent. —almost four times that found in American public school children.

According to Lindenov[52] deaf mutism is only associated with amentia when there is retinitis pigmentosa.

Phenylketonuria

There is now a vast amount of literature on this subject. I have included the condition here, although Poser and Van Bogaert,[74] on the basis of neuropathological studies, suggested that this should be classified with the leucodystrophies— a metabolically determined disturbance of the glial cell-myelin sheath relationship.

Now that dietetic treatment is available, it is important to know the range of intelligence levels to be expected in phenylketonuria. There have been a few reports of affected children with normal or virtually normal intelligence. Low et al.[57] mentioned two cases with an I.Q. of 67 and 82. Coates et al.[16] described a child with a coexistent muscular dystrophy who had an I.Q. of 103. Cowie and Brandon[18] described a child with an I.Q. between 90 and 100.

Sutherland and Berry described a syndrome of phenylketonuria with normal intelligence but with behaviour disorders.[89] Allen et al.[3] described a 12 year old with an I.Q. score of 112.

Now that more is known about this condition, the diagnosis of phenylketonuria can no longer be accepted without full laboratory investigation. It is probable that some of the children said in the past to have phenylketonuria had a temporary high serum phenylalanine, or other condition which was not true phenylketonuria.

There is some correlation between the level of serum phenylalanine and the I.Q. score in atypical cases[32a] but not a close one. Among 43 children with borderline or normal intelligence, 19 had a serum phenylalanine of 20 mg./100 ml. or less, but 18 had a level of 21 mg./100 ml. or more. These atypical cases are not yet fully explained.

Wright and Tarjan[100] reviewed 362 cases from the literature. Sixty-three per cent. had an I.Q. of 1 to 20, 32 per cent. an I.Q. of 21 to 50, 4 per cent. an I.Q. of 51 to 70, and 1 had an I.Q. of over 71. Paine[68] reviewed 106 cases; 70 per cent. had an I.Q. of under 20, 84 per cent. an I.Q. below 30, 93 per cent. an I.Q. below 40, and 98·1 per cent. an I.Q. of under 50. The usual age for learning to sit was 12 to 15 months. Twenty-six per cent. had fits, and only a few were spastic, but 79 per cent. had abnormal electroencephalograms. Associated anomalies included congenital dislocation of hip, congenital heart disease and undescended testes.

Partington[71] found the following I.Q. scores in 75 patients aged two or more with untreated phenylketonuria.

I.Q. Score	Percentage
0—20	61.3
21—40	26.7
41—60	5.3
61—80	5.3
81+	1.3

These findings corresponded closely with those of Knox.[45a]

According to Hsia et al.[32] all that one can expect to achieve by dietary means is to preserve the status quo and to prevent deterioration. They based this opinion on 24 cases, 12 of which were treated, 12 serving as controls. The test period was one of 12 to

15 months. They emphasised the importance of keeping the serum phenylalanine down to normal levels. Berry et al.[6] in a discussion of 3 cases, found no notable improvement in intelligence, but there was an improvement in behaviour, motor ability, manual dexterity, and attention span with a reduction of tenseness and irritability. On the other hand Woolf et al.[98] in a study of 10 cases, described 'a sharp and significant rise in I.Q.' in almost every case. They said that the I.Q. continued to rise, the mental age plotted against chronological age showing a point of inflexion at the time the diet was started.

Berman et al.[5] compared eight treated cases with three untreated siblings and eleven unaffected ones. The intelligence quotient was significantly greater in the treated than the untreated cases, but less than that of the unaffected ones in spite of careful treatment. It should be noted, however, that there may be important features unrelated to the I.Q. In one study 13 children with phenylketonuria were matched for age, sex, I.Q. and race; affected children were more clumsy, talkative and hypersensitive.[84] Others have found overactivity and defective concentration in these children, not related to a low level of intelligence. It is clear that we need a fully psychological and psychosocial assessment of affected children.

It is obvious that many more cases need to be studied before a firm conclusion can be reached as to the improvement which can be expected from dietary treatment. The diet is expensive and unpopular with children, and if it is to be used properly, repeated time consuming laboratory tests have to be carried out, in order to maintain the serum phenyl alanine level at the normal figure.

The difficulty in assessing the effect of treatment lies in the increasing maturity of the child. It is difficult to know how much of the child's new skills and better behaviour are due to this factor. If one is to rely on the mother's story, one has to remember the great belief of many lay people in the magic of medicine, and the mother's opinion about improved behaviour and performance has to be taken with some scepticism. The occasional occurrence of normal I.Q. levels in untreated children makes it difficult to assess the value of early treatment.

If the child is already seriously retarded after the age of 2 or 3, it is doubtful at present whether one is justified in treating. Whether treatment is begun early or late, repeated developmental assessments must be made in order to decide whether continuation of treatment is justified.

For a full review of other metabolic causes of mental subnormality, the reader is referred to the book by O'Gorman.[65]

Congenital Heart Disease

Ross[80] described the association of congenital heart disease with mental retardation in 21 cases at the Johns Hopkins Hospital, Baltimore. She suggested that the intelligence quotient in congenital heart disease tends to be lower than the average. This corresponds with the findings of Bret and Kohler[10] in their study of 88 cases; but Landtmann et al.[48] found no significant lowering of the I.Q. in children with congenital heart disease.

In two studies of 98 children with cyanotic and 100 with acyanotic congenital heart disease, compared with 81 normal siblings and 40 normal children, the cyanotic children fared significantly less well than acyanotic or normal children.[51, 79] The factors responsible may be reduced manipulative and motor experience, less opportunity for exploration, overprotection and psychological problems arising from the handicap.

Mautner[61] found that 30-40 per cent. of mongols have congenital heart disease. He mentioned the well-known association of rubella during pregnancy with the subsequent finding of pulmonary stenosis and mental deficiency in the foetus. He suggested that anoxia in the cyanotic types might cause pathological changes in the brain.

Ireland et al.[36] found that the incidence of congenital heart disease in 723 mental defectives in institutions was 2·4 per cent. This is 7 times higher than that found in comparable ages in the general population. When mongols were excluded the figure was still much higher than in normal people. It is interesting that in my series of 1068 mentally retarded children (excluding mongols as before), 43 had congenital heart disease (4·0 per cent).

Thalidomide Babies

In a detailed study of 22 'thalidomide' babies[20a] it was found that the mean D.Q. was 90. The effect of institutional care was duly considered. In view of the known association between congenital anomalies and a lower than usual level of intelligence, this result was to be expected.

Cretinism

As good reviews of papers concerning the prognosis of hypothyroidism in infants and children were published by Bruch and
McCune[13] and Topper,[92] it would be superfluous to review the
literature again here. In general, one can say that previous papers
indicated that something like three-quarters or more of all treated
cases would have a lower than average intelligence quotient. The
paper by Radwin *et al.*[77] may be mentioned because of the useful
discussion of the problems involved in treatment. Of their 16
children, 10 had I.Q.s ranging from 82 to 107; 2 had an I.Q. of 77;
and 4 I.Q.s ranging from 42 to 70. The greatest amount of improvement occurred within the first year of therapy, but continued progress was noted for many years. They found that
skeletal maturation and the level of serum lipoids were not
reliable tests for adequacy of dosage of thyroxin.[78] They thought
that regression might result from overdosage. In later childhood
a characteristic picture was often found—slowness of speech and
movement, abnormal attitudes and manners, and greater pro-
ficiency in manual than in mental tests.

Topper[92] thought that the reason for inadequate intellectual
response to treatment might lie in primary amentia of prenatal
origin. He thought that the electroencephalogram might prove to
be of prognostic value. In 5 of the 7 cases (out of a total of 20)
who remained defective, the E.E.G. showed diffuse cerebral
dysfunction. Other factors were the amount of residual thyroid
tissue, and adequacy and promptness of institution of treatment.

Talbot *et al.*[90] wrote that 'only about 25 per cent. of the
patients who develop signs of thyroid deficiency before the age of
2 ever attain an intelligence quotient above 80'.

Smith, Blizzard and Wilkins,[87] in an important paper, reviewed
128 cases of hypothyroidism. Their results can be summarised
as follows: Ten of 22 with no thyroid function treated adequately
before 6 months of age, and 12 of 29 treated adequately before
12 months, attained an I.Q. greater than 90. In contrast none of
50 inadequately treated, or treated after 12 months, attained such
an intelligence quotient. Hypothyroidism acquired after 2 years
exerts little or no serious irreversible effect on mental development, as 13 of 17 cases achieved an I.Q. of 90 or more.

From a study of the literature and other reported cases, it was
concluded that the mean I.Q. of children treated early (in the

first three months) was around 90, and that this figure was significantly better than that of untreated children, whose mean I.Q. was around fifty.[97]

Head Injury

Permanent intellectual impairment is unusual after head injury, but slight impairment may occur.[81] It usually decreases as time goes by, and disappears by 3 months if recovery is to be complete.

Tuberculous Meningitis

Lorber[54] followed up 100 children who survived tuberculous meningitis, which had been treated at the Children's Hospital, Sheffield. Seventy-nine were followed for 5 years or more. Six had an I.Q. below 50; 14 had an I.Q. of 71 to 80; 24 had an I.Q. of 81 to 90; 25 had an I.Q. of 91 to 100; 16 had an I.Q. of 101 to 110; 6 had an I.Q. of 111 to 120; 3 had an I.Q. of 121 to 130; 2 had an I.Q. of 131 or more. It was guessed that the I.Q. of the 4 not tested ranged between 81 and 100. The importance of early treatment was emphasised. Those with a low I.Q. were all under 3 years of age at the onset, and all had come to hospital in a late stage, while those treated early fared well with regard to future intellectual level.

Sequelae of Meningitis and Encephalitis

Wolff[96] studied the intelligence of children who had had meningococcal meningitis two or more years previously. Out of a total of 179 cases occurring at Birmingham, 138 were followed up. The mean I.Q. of 26 who developed meningitis before 6 months of age was 76·3; 4 were idiots. The mean I.Q. of 27 who developed it between 6 and 12 months was 90·8; and the mean I.Q. of those developing it over 1 was 96·8.

Infection	Incidence of complications	Incidence of Sequelae in survivors of encephalitis Percentage
Measles	1 in 1,000	35
Chickenpox	?	20
Mumps	?	30
Rubella 1 in 5,000	1 in 5,000	2–5
Scarlet fever in 800	1 in 800	45
Whooping cough	?	35

Miller *et al.*[62] wrote a comprehensive review of post-infectious encephalomyelitis. In all cases coma and convulsions tended to carry a bad prognosis. The approximate incidence of neurological complications and the incidence of sequelae, is shown in above Table. In only a small proportion of these did the sequelae include mental defectiveness. In measles intellectual deficits occurred in children only. Intellectual sequelae were relatively more common in the case of whooping cough and scarlet fever.

Severe neurological sequelae, including mental retardation, have followed encephalitis in association with Roseola Infantum.[13] They may also follow post-immunisation encephalomyelitis.

Anoxia

Severe anoxia, such as that due to strangulation, carbon monoxide poisoning, or cardiac arrest due to anaesthesia, may cause mental deficiency and sometimes athetosis.

Lead Poisoning

Lead poisoning is known to lead to a reduction in a child's intelligence. Byers and Lord[14] followed 20 children who had been admitted to hospital in early childhood on account of lead poisoning, without much evidence of lead encephalopathy. Nineteen were subsequently retarded at school. Jenkins and Mellins[38] studied 46 Chicago children with pica, mostly from poor families. Thirteen died. Twenty-seven of 33 survivors were mentally defective, and in 20 this was ascribed to lead poisoning. Bradley and Baumgartner[9] compared the subsequent mental development of 9 children treated with B.A.L. and 9 treated with E.D.T.A., following them up for 2 to 5 years after their stay in hospital. Mental development was normal in all, but those treated with E.D.T.A. had fewer visuomotor sequelae.

Mentally subnormal children are likely to continue taking objects to the mouth long after normal children have stopped doing so, and they are more likely to eat dirt. Hence they are especially liable to suffer lead poisoning and further mental deterioration.

Summary and Conclusions

1. A wide variety of diseases and malformations, especially those involving the skull, eyes and skin, are associated with varying

degrees of mental retardation. Though certain anomalies, such as deformities of the ears, are often associated with mental retardation, these so-called stigmata of degeneration can never be used as an aid to diagnosis because they are much more often found in normal children. Nevertheless, the finding of severe congenital deformities of any kind should make one look particularly carefully at the level of mental development which the child has reached, and follow his developmental progress.

The anterior fontanelle is of little value for the assessment of a child's development. Physical growth is apt to be defective in retarded children.

More and more metabolic defects and abnormalities are being found in association with mental deficiency.

2. Though between a quarter and a third of all mentally retarded children have or have had convulsions, epilepsy *per se* is not usually associated with mental retardation. Mental retardation in epileptics is due to the underlying brain disease, or to the effect of frequent convulsions, to psychological causes in relation to epilepsy, or to some extent to the drugs used for treatment.

Infantile spasms are usually associated with severe mental deficiency.

3. Although mental retardation is found in varying degrees of frequency in the above conditions, each child has to be assessed individually, and never assumed to be mentally defective without a full developmental examination being performed. Nevertheless, the final assessment will be made against the background of the known facts concerning the intellectual level likely to be found in the various conditions described.

REFERENCES

1. ALLEN, G. (1958) Patterns of Discovery in the Genetics of Mental Deficiency. *Amer. J. ment. Defic.*, **62,** 840.
2. ALLEN, J. E., RODGIN, D. W. (1960) Mental Retardation in Association with Progressive Muscular Dystrophy. *Amer. J. Dis. Child,* **100,** 208.
3. ALLEN, R. J., GIBSON, R. M., SUTTON, H. E. (1960) Phenylketonuria with Normal Intelligence. *Amer. J. Dis. Child.,* **100,** 563.
4. BENDA, C. E. (1960) *The Child with Mongolism.* New York: Grune and Stratton.
5. BERMAN, P. W., GRAHAM, F. K., EICHMAN, P. L., WAISMAN, H. A. (1961) Psychologic and Neurological Status of Diet Treated Phenylketonuric Children and their Siblings. *Pediatrics,* **28,** 924.

6. BERRY, H. K., SUTHERLAND, B. S., GUEST, G. M., UMBARGER, B. (1958) Clinical Observations During Treatment of Children with Phenylketonuria. *Pediatrics*, **21**, 929.

7. BJELKHAGEN, I. (1952) Retrolental Fibroplasia in Sweden. *Acta Paediat. (Uppsala)*, **41**, 74.

8. BLACKETER-SIMMONDS, D. A. (1953) An Investigation into the Supposed Differences Existing between Mongols and other Mentally Defective Subjects with Regard to certain Psychological Traits. *J. ment. Sci.*, **99**, 702.

9. BRADLEY, J. E., BAUMGARTNER, R. J. (1958) Subsequent Mental Development of Children with Lead Encephalopathy, as Related to Type of Treatment. *J. Pediat.*, **53**, 311.

10. BRET, J., KOHLER, C. (1956) Incidences Neuropsychiatriques des Cardiopathies Congenitales chez L'Enfant. *Pediatrie*, **11**, 59.

11. BROUSSEAU, K. (1928) *Mongolism*. London: Baillière, Tindall and Cox.

12. BRUCH, H., McCUNE, D. J. (1944) Mental Development of Congenitally Hypothyroid Children. *Amer. J. Dis. Child*, **67**, 205.

13. BURNSTINE, R. C., PAINE, R. S. (1959) Residual Encephalopathy following Roseola Infantum. *Amer. J. Dis. Child.*, **98**, 144.

14. BYERS, R. K., LORD, E. E. (1943) Late Effects of Lead Poisoning and Mental Development. *Amer. J. Dis. Child.*, **66**, 471.

15. CARTER, C. O. (1958) A Life Table for Mongols with the Causes of Death. *J. ment. Defic. Res.*, **2**, 64.

16. COATES, S., NORMAN, A. P., WOOLF, L. I. (1957) Phenylketonuria with Normal Intelligence and Gower's Muscular Dystrophy. *Arch. Dis. Childh.*, **52**, 314.

17. COHEN, H. J., MOLNAR, G. E., TAFT, L. T. (1968) The genetic relationship of progressive muscular dystrophy (Duchenne type) and mental retardation. *Develop. Med. Child Neurol.*, **10**, 754.

18. COWIE, V., BRANDON, M. W. G. (1958) Follow-up Note on an Atypical Case of Phenylketonuria. *J. ment. Defic. Res.*, **2**, 55.

19. DANN, M., LEVINE, S. Z., NEW, E. V. (1958) The Development of Prematurely Born Children with Birth Weights or Minimal Postnatal Weights of 1000 g. or less. *Pediatrics*, **22**, 1037.

20. DAVIES, P. A. (1966) Sex and the single transverse palmar crease in newborn singletons. *Develop. Med. Child. Neurol.*, **8**, 729.

20a DECARIE, T. G. (1969) *A study of the Mental and Emotional Development of the Thalidomide Child.* In Foss, B. M., Determinants of Infant Behaviour. Vol. IV. London: Methuen.

21. DUBOWITZ, V. (1965) Intellectual Impairment in Muscular Dystrophy. *Arch. Dis. Childh.*, **40**, 296.

22. ENGLER, M. (1949) *Mongolism.* Bristol: Wright.

23. FANG, T. C. (1949) A Comparative Study of the A B Ridge Count in the Palm of Mental Defectives and the General Population. *J. ment. Sci.*, **95**, 945.

24. FISHLER, K., SHARE, J., KOCH, R. (1964) Adaptation of Gesell Developmental Scales for evaluation of development in Children with Down's syndrome (Mongolism). *Amer. J. ment. Defect.*, **68**, 642.

25. FOALE, M., PATERSON, J. W. (1954) The Hearing of Mental Defectives. *Amer. J. ment. Defi.*, **59**, 254.

26. FORD, F. R. (1952) *Diseases of the Nervous System in Infancy, Childhood and Adolescence.* Springfield: Thomas.

27. GESELL, A., AMATRUDA, C. S. (1947) *Developmental Diagnosis.* London: Hoeber.
28. GIBSON, J., JARVIS, J.M. (1961) Muscular Dystrophy. *Lancet*, **1**, 275.
29. GILLESPIE, J. B., MUSSEY, R. D. (1951) Progressive Diaphyseal Dysplasia. *J. Pediat.*, **38**, 55.
30. GREENWALD, H. M., KOOTA, J. (1936) Associated Facial and Intracranial Haemangiomas. *Amer. J. Dis. Child.*, **51**, 868.
31. HILLIARD, L. T. (1959) Personal Communication.
32. HSIA, D., KNOX, W. E., QUINN, K. V., PAINE, R. S. (1958) A One Year Controlled Study of the Effect of Low-Phenylalanine Diet on Phenylketonuria. *Pediatrics*, **21**, 178.
32a HSIA, DAVID YI-YUNG, O'FLYNN, M. E., BERMAN, J. L. (1968) Atypical phenylketonuria with borderline or normal intelligence. *Amer. J. Dis. Child.*, **116**, 143.
33. ILLINGWORTH, R. S., BIRCH, L. B. (1956) The Intelligence of Children with Cleft Palate. *Arch. Dis. Childh.*, **31**, 300.
34. ILLINGWORTH, R. S. (1958) *Recent Advances in Cerebral Palsy.* London: Churchill.
35. ILLINGWORTH, R. S. (1960) Convulsions in Cerebral Palsy and Mental Retardation. Their Frequency and Age Incidence. *J. ment. Defic. Res.* In Press.
36. IRELAND, C. R., WITHAM, A. C., HARPER, H. T. (1955) Congenital Heart Disease among Mental Defectives and an Assessment of Cardiac Survey Methods. *New Engl. J. Med.*, **252**, 117.
37. JEAVONS, P. M., BOWER, B. D. (1965) Infantile Spasms. *Clinics in Develop. Med.* No. 15. London: Heinemann.
38. JENKINS, C. D., MELLINS, R. B. (1957) Lead Poisoning in Children. *Arch. Neurol. Psychiat.*, **77**, 70.
39. JERVIS, G. A. (1952) Genetic Factors in Mental Deficiency. *Amer. J. hum. Genet.*, **4**, 260.
40. JONES, A. P., MURRAY, W. (1958) The Heights and Weights of Educationally Subnormal Children. *Lancet*, **1**, 905.
41. JONES, F. A. (1961) Clinical Aspects of Genetics. London: Pitman.
42. KENDALL, D. C. (1957) in Ewing, A. W. G. (1957) *Educational Guidance and the Deaf Child.* Manchester Univ. Press.
43. KIRMAN, B. H. (1957) Epilepsy and Mental Deficiency. *Communications des Invités Étrangers. Congres. National des Sciences Médicales.*
44. KIRMAN, B. H. (1964) The Patient with Down's Syndrome in the Community. *Lancet*, **2**, 705.
44a. KNOBLOCH, H., PASAMANICK, B. (1962) Mental Subnormality. *N. Engl. J. med.*, **266**, 1045.
45. KOCH, R., SHAVE, J., WEBB, A., GRALIKER, B. V. (1963) The Predictability of Gesell Developmental Scales in Mongolism. *J. Pediat.*, **62**, 93.
45a KNOX, W. E. (1960) An Evaluation of Treatment of Phenylketonuria with Diets Low in Phenylalanine. *Pediatrics*, **26**, 1.
46. KODMAN, F., POWERS, T. R., PHILIP, P. P., WELLER, G. M. (1958) An Investigation of Hearing Loss in Mentally Retarded Children and Adults. *Amer. J. ment. Defic.*, **63**, 460.
47. KRAUSE, A. C. (1955) Effect of Retrolental Fibroplasia in Children. *Arch. Ophthal.*, **53**, 522.
48. LANDTMAN, B., VALANNE, E., PENTTI, R., AUKEE, M. (1960) *Ann. Paediat. Fenn.*, **6**, Suppl., 15.

49. LAURENCE, K. M. (1958) The Natural History of Hydrocephalus. *Lancet*, **2**, 1152.
50. LENNOX, W. G. (1942) Brain Injury, Drugs and Environment as Causes of Mental Deficiency in Epilepsy. *Amer. J. Psychiat.*, **99**, 174.
51. LINDE, L. M., RASOF, B., DUNN, O. J. (1967) Mental development in congenital heart disease. *J. Pediat.*, **71**, 198.
52. LINDENOV, H. (1945) quoted by Gibson, R. (1956), The Widening Etiology of Mental Defect. *Canad. med. Ass. J.*, **75**, 685.
53. LIVINGSTON, S., EISNER, V., PAULI, L. (1958) Minor Motor Epilepsy. *Pediatrics*, **21**, 916.
54. LORBER, J. (1959) The Follow-up of Children with Tuberculous Meningitis with Special Reference to Psychiatric and Neurological Aspects. *Proc. roy. Soc. Med.*, **52**, 269.
55. LORBER, J., PICKERING, D. (1965) The Incidence and Treatment of Post meningitis Hydrocephalus in the Newborn. *Arch. Dis. Childh.* (In Press.)
56. LORBER, J. (1969) To be published.
57. LOW, N. L., ARMSTRONG, M. D., CARLISLE, J. W. (1956) Phenylketonuria. *Lancet*, **2**, 917.
58. MACGILLIVRAY, R. C. (1957) Hypertelorism with Unusual Associated Anomalies. *Amer. J. ment. Defic.*, **62**, 288.
59. MAHORNER, H. R. (1937) Dyschondroplasia. *J. Pediat.*, **10**, 1.
60. MALZBERG, B. (1950) Some Statistical Aspects of Mongolism. *Amer. J. ment. Defic.*, **54**, 266.
61. MAUTNER, H. (1950-1) Congenital Heart Disease in the Feebleminded. *Amer. J. ment. Defic.*, **55**, 546.
62. MILLER, H. G., STANTON, J. B. GIBBONS, J. L. (1956) Para-Infectious Encephalomyelitis and Related Syndromes. *Quart. J. Med.*, **25**, 427.
63. MOSIER, H. D., SCOTT, L. W. (1959) The Incidence of the Female Sex Chromatin Pattern in Mentally Defective Males. *Amer. J. Dis. Child.*, **98**, 447.
64. NORRIS, M., SPAULDING, P. J., BRODIE, F. H. (1957) *Blindness in Children.* Chicago: Univ. of Chicago Press.
65. O'GORMAN, G. (1968) *Modern trends in mental health and subnormality.* London: Butterworth.
66. ØSTER, J. (1953) *Mongolism.* Copenhagen: Munksgaard.
67. OUNSTED, C. (1955) The Hyperkinetic Syndrome in Epileptic Children. *Lancet*, **2**, 303.
68. PAINE, R. S. (1957) The Variability in Manifestations of Untreated Patients with Phenylketonuria. *Pediatrics*, **20**, 290.
69. PARMELEE, A. H. (1955) The Developmental Evaluation of the Blind Premature Infant. *Amer. J. Dis. Child.*, **90**, 135.
70. PARMELEE, A. H., FISKE, C. E., WRIGHT, A. H., CUTSFORTH, M. G. (1958) Mental Development of Children with Blindness due to Retrolental Fibroplasia. *Amer. J. Dis. Child.*, **96**, 614.
71. PARTINGTON, M. W. (1962) Variations in Intelligence in Phenylketonuria. *Canad. med. Ass. J.*, **86**, 736.
72. PETERMAN, A. F., HAYLES, A. B., DOCKERTY, M. B., LOVE, J. G. (1958) Encephalotrigeminalangiomatosis. *J. Amer. med. Ass.*, **167**, 2169.
73. POND, D. (1961) Psychiatric Aspects of Epileptic and Brain Damaged Children. *Brit. med. J.*, **2**, 1377 and 1454.
74. POSER, C. M., RADERMECKER, J. (1957) Subacute Sclerosing Leucoencephalitis. *J. Pediat.*, **50**, 408.

75. POTTER, C. T. (1954) The Problem of Blind Children and the Responsibility of the Paediatrician. *Proc. roy. Soc. Med.*, **47**, 715.

76. QUAYTMAN, W. (1953) The Psychological Capacities of Mongoloid Children in a Community Clinic. *Quart. Rev. Pediat.*, **8**, 253.

77. RADWIN, L. S., MICHELSON, J. P., BERMAN, A. B., KRAMER, B. (1949) End Results in Treatment of Congenital Hypothyroidism. *Amer. J. Dis. Child.*, **78**, 821.

78. RADWIN, L. S., MICHELSON, J. P., MELNICK, J., GOTTFRIED, S. (1940) Blood Partition in Hypothyroidism of Childhood. *Amer. J. Dis. Child.*, **60**, 1120.

79. RASOF, B., LINDE, L. M., DUNN, O. J. (1967) Intellectual development in children with congenital heart disease. *Child Development*, **38**, 1043.

80. ROSS, M. (1939) Mental Retardation Associated with Congenital Heart Disease. *J. Pediat.*, **14**, 21.

81. RUESCH, J. (1944) Intellectual Impairment in Head Injuries. *Amer. J. Psychiat.*, **100**, 480.

82. SCHEIG, R. L., BORNSTEIN, P. (1961) Tuberous Sclerosis. *Arch. intern. Med.*, **108**, 789.

83. SHARE, J., WEBB, A., KOCH, R. (1961) A Preliminary Investigation of the Early Developmental Status of Mongoloid Infants. *Amer. J. ment. Defic.*, **66**, 238.

84 SIEGEL, F. S., BALOW, B., FISCH, R. O., ANDERSON, V. E. (1968). School behaviour profile ratings of P.K.U. children. *Am. J. Ment. Def.*, **72**, 937.

85. SJÖGREN, T., LARSSON, T. (1949) Microphthalmos and Anophthalmos with or without Coincident Oligophrenia. *Acta psychiat. Scand.* Suppl. 56.

86. SMITH, A. J., STRANG, L. B. (1958) An Inborn Error of Metabolism With the Urinary Excretion of α Hydroxybutyric Acid and Phenylpyruvic Acid. *Arch. Dis. Childh.*, **33**, 109.

87. SMITH, D. W., BLIZZARD, R. M., WILKINS, L. (1957) The Mental Prognosis in Hypothyroidism of Infancy and Childhood. A review of 128 cases. *Pediatrics*, **19**, 1011.

88. SPITZER, R., MANN, I. (1950) Congenital Malformations in the Teeth and Eyes in Mental Defectives. *J. ment. Sci.*, **96**, 681.

89. SUTHERLAND, B. S., BERRY, H. K. (1960) A Syndrome of Phenylketonuria with Normal Intelligence and Behaviour Disorders. *J. Pediat.*, **57**, 521.

90. TALBOT, N. B., SOBEL, E. H., McARTHUR, J. W., CRAWFORD, J. D. (1952) *Functional Endocrinology from Birth through Adolescence.* Cambridge: Harvard Univ. Press.

91. TIZARD, J., GRAD, J. C. (1961) *The Mentally Handicapped and their Families.* London: Oxford University Press.

92. TOPPER, A. (1951) Mental Achievement of Congenitally Hypothyroid Children. *Amer. J. Dis. Child.*, **81**, 233.

93. WALTER, R. D., YEAGER, C. L., RUBIN, H. K. (1955) Mongolism and Convulsive Seizures. *Arch. Neurol. Psychiat.* **74**, 559.

94. WILLIAMS, C. E. (1958) Retrolental Fibroplasia Associated with Mental Defect. *Brit. J. Ophthal.*, **42**, 549.

95. WILSON, S. A. K. (1934) Megalencephaly. *J. Neurol. Psychopath.*, **14**, 193.

96. WOLFF, O. (1952) The Effects of Meningococcal Meningitis on the Intelligence and Hearing. *Arch. Dis. Childh.*, **27**, 302.

97. WOLFF, O. (1969) Personal Communication.
98. WOOLF, L. I., GRIFFITHS, R., MONCRIEFF, A., COATES, S., DILLISTONE, F. (1958) The Dietary Treatment of Phenylketonuria. *Arch. Dis. Childh.* **33,** 31.
99. WORDEN, D. K., VIGNOS, P. J. (1962) Intellectual Function in Childhood Progressive Muscular Dystrophy. *Pediatrics,* **29,** 968.
100. WRIGHT, S. W., TARJAN, G., LIPPMAN, R. W., PERRY, T. L. (1958) Etiologic Factors in Mental Deficiency. *Amer. J. Dis. Child.,* **95,** 541.
101. WUNSCH, W. L. (1957) Some Characteristics of Mongoloids Evaluated in a Clinic for Children with Retarded Mental Development. *Amer. J. ment. Defic.,* **62,** 122.
102. ZELLWEGER, H., HANSON, J. W. (1967) Psychometric studies in muscular dystrophy Type 3A (Duchenne). *Develop. Med. Child Neurol.,* **9,** 576.

CHAPTER 6

REFLEXES AND REACTIONS.

While a vast amount has been written about the development of the infant and young child, the neurological examination of the newborn baby has been remarkably neglected. The subject was barely mentioned by Arnold Gesell, whose developmental studies began with the child at 4 to 6 weeks of age. We owe our knowledge of the neurological and developmental examination of the newborn baby to a small body of workers, which includes especially Albrecht Peiper, André Thomas, Madame Saint Anne Dargassies and Heinz Prechtl. Their writings have been used extensively in the preparation of this section. Minkowski and Dargassies[15] have given me permission to quote their work at length.

Reflexes and Reactions in the Newborn Period

A considerable number of primitive reflexes have been described in the newborn period, but the value of many of them for developmental diagnosis has not been established. They may well repay further study, however, and because their status for the establishment of diagnosis and prognosis is as yet uncertain, felt that they should be described in some detail here. Most of these are shown in illustration, and I have not referred to the figure numbers in the text.

Much ingenuity has been used in attempting to describe new reflexes, holding, for instance, the baby's nose,[38] applying curtain clamps,[22] and even applying itching powder.[11] Dennis[5] reviewed many of these responses. The use of eponyms has lead to considerable confusion in attempting to understand them.

Oral Reflexes

Sucking and swallowing reflexes are present in full term babies and all but the smallest premature baby. Their absence in a full term baby would suggest a developmental defect. The sucking reflex is tested by introducing a finger or teat into the mouth, when vigorous sucking will occur.

The 'rooting' or 'search' reflex is present in normal full term babies. When the baby's cheek contacts the mother's breast or other part, he 'roots' for milk. It enables him to find the nipple without his being directed to it.

When the corner of the mouth is lightly touched, the bottom lip is lowered on the same side, and the tongue moved toward the point of stimulation. When the examiner's finger slides away from that point, the head turns to follow it.

When the centre of the upper lip is stimulated, the lip elevates, baring the gums, and the tongue moves towards the place stimulated. If the finger slides along the oronasal grove, the head extends.

When the centre of the bottom lip is stroked, the lip is lowered and the tongue is directed to the site of stimulation. If the finger moves towards the chin, the mandible is lowered and the head flexes. The above reflexes are termed 'the cardinal points reflexes' of the French writers.

We have found that these reflexes are difficult to elicit except when the child is near his feed time. They presumably correspond to the mouthing reflex described by Gesell.

Eye Reflexes

BLINK REFLEXES. Various stimuli will provoke blinking, even if the child is asleep, or tensing of the eyelids if the eyes are closed. For example, a sharp noise elicits the cochleo-palpebral reflex; a bright light elicits the visuo-palpebral or 'dazzle' reflex, in which there is blinking or closure of the eyes and a painful touch elicits the cutaneo-palpebral reflex. The naso-palpebral reflex consists of blinking in response to tapping the bridge of the nose. Peiper's optic reflex consists of opisthotonos when a bright light shines on the eyes. The ciliary reflex is blinking on stroking the eyelashes. McCarthy's reflex is homolateral blinking on tapping the supraorbital area. In abnormal babies the reflex is produced by stimulation at a distance from the supraorbital region—e.g. over the vertex of the skull. If it is difficult to elicit the reflex because the eyes are closed, stimulation of the circumoral region may cause the baby to open the eyes, so that the test can be more easily performed. The corneal reflex consists of blinking when the cornea is touched. The satisfactory demonstration of these reflexes shows that the stimulus, whether sound, light, or touch, has been received, that cerebral depression is unlikely, and that the appropriate muscles can contract in response.

THE DOLLS EYE RESPONSE. This is so named because there is a delay in the movement of the eyes after the head has been turned in any direction. If, therefore, the head is turned slowly to the right or left, the eyes do not normally move with the head. The reflex is always present in the first ten days, disappearing thereafter, as fixation develops. It would be asymmetrical in abducens paralysis. The reflex may persist beyond the first few days in abnormal babies.

RESPONSE TO ROTATION. The subject of rotational nystagmus in neonates was particularly well discussed by Peiper,[19] and recently Paine[18] showed its value in clinical work. The examiner holds the baby facing him and tilted forwards at about 30°. He then spins round two or three times. During rotation the eyes deviate in the direction of the movement; on stopping they deviate in the reverse direction and coarse nystagmus occurs. This test obviously depends on vestibular function, but it is particularly useful for demonstrating ocular palsies, as was shown by Benson.[1]

PUPIL REFLEXES. The pupil reacts to light, but in the premature baby and some full term babies the duration of exposure to the light may have to be prolonged to elicit the reflex. The light used should not be bright, for a bright light will cause closure of the eyes. Thomas remarked about the remarkable integration of reflexes which enables a newborn baby to turn his head towards the source of light.[31]

The photic sneeze reflex[1] consists of a sneeze when a bright light is shone into the eyes.

RESISTANCE TO PASSIVE OPENING OF THE EYES. This is present from birth.

André Thomas wrote that the baby only begins to respond to the rapid approach of objects to the eyes after 7 or 8 weeks or later.

Special Senses (see also Chapter 13)

The newborn baby can taste, smell, and hear. A sudden loud noise causes blinking of the eyes or the startle reflex, or a change in the respiration rate.

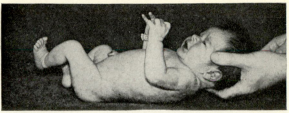

FIG. 1
Moro reflex, position for eliciting the reflex.

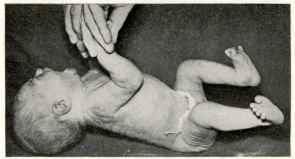

FIG. 2
Moro reflex, alternative position for eliciting the reflex.

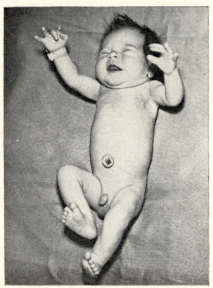

FIG. 3
Moro reflex, at height of abduction phase.

facing page 118

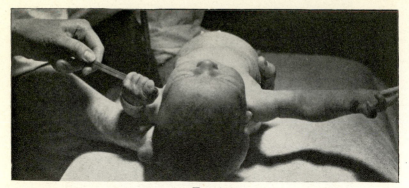

FIG. 4
Inhibition of Moro response in left hand because it is holding object.

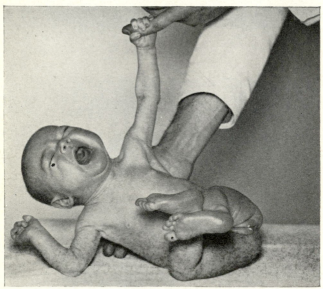

FIG. 5
Grasp reflex.

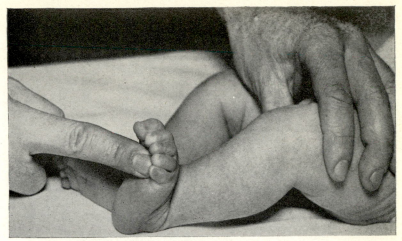

Fig. 6
Plantar grasp reflex.

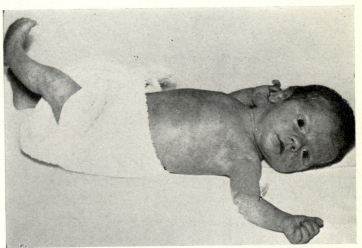

Fig. 7
The asymmetrical tonic neck reflex.

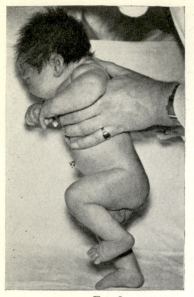

FIG. 8

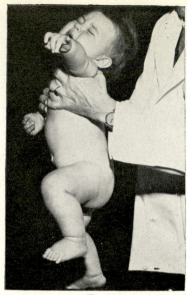

FIG. 9

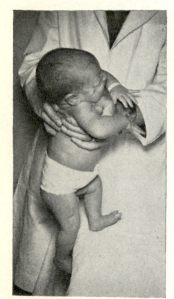

FIG. 10

FIG. 8
The walking reflex.

FIG. 9
Walking reflex in 5-month old baby
demonstrated by means of neck extension.

FIG. 10
Placing reaction of lower limbs. When the
front of the leg touches the edge of the
table, the baby steps over the edge.

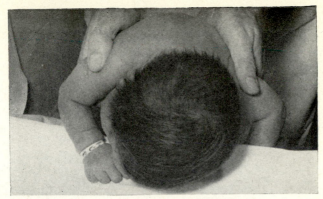

FIG. 11
Placing reaction of upper limbs.

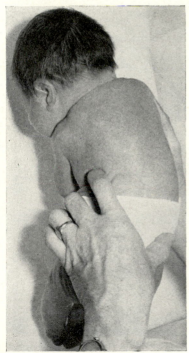

FIG. 12
Galant's reflex (trunk incurvation).

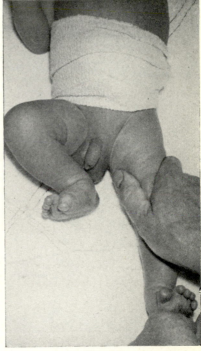

FIG. 13
Crossed extension reflex. First phase;
flexion of contralateral leg.

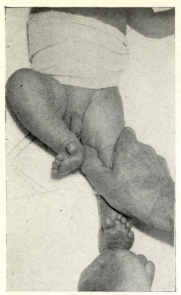

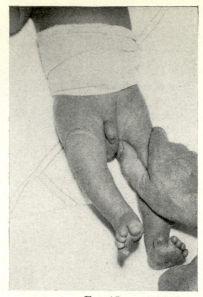

FIG. 14

Crossed extension reflex.
Second stage—Adduction.

FIG. 15

Crossed extension reflex.
Third stage—Extension.

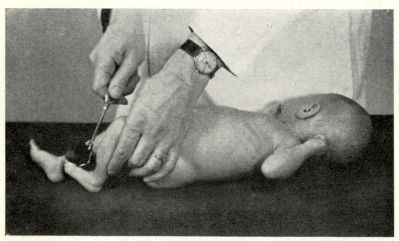

FIG. 16

Method of testing knee jerk. One begins by tapping over the dorsum of the
ankle and works up to the patellar tendon. The heel must be resting on the
couch, with the leg relaxed.

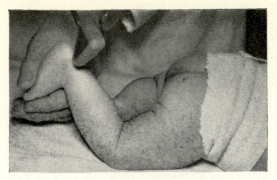

FIG. 17
Method of testing ankle jerk.

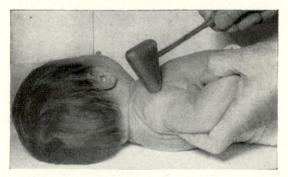

FIG. 18
Method of testing for biceps jerk—beginning over shoulder.

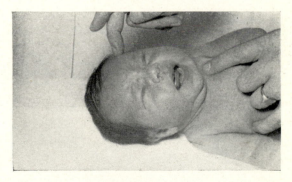

FIG. 19
Method of testing for McCarthy's reflex. (Baby crying, and therefore the response is not shown).

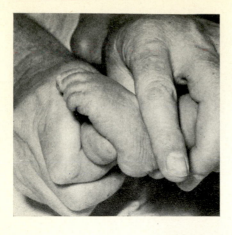

FIG. 20
Plantar response — incorrect method. Stimulation across sole of foot has elicited the grasp reflex.

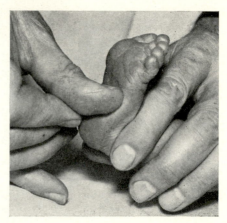

FIG. 21
Plantar response — correct method of eliciting it; stimulation of distal half of outside of foot.

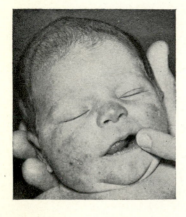

FIG. 22
Cardinal points reflex.

A sugar-coated finger in the mouth produces sucking and licking of the lips. The finger is followed when it is withdrawn.

A salt-coated finger causes a grimace, with little or no sucking movement. The finger is forced back with the tongue towards the lip, along with irregular head movements. The finger is not followed.

The olfactory sense of the neonate has been studied by several writers, with variable results.[25] Infants certainly grimace when an unpleasant odour is passed under their noses, and it would be surprising if the olfactory function were not developed in the neonate, for it is derived from the primitive brain.

Moro Reflex

This is a most important reflex. Much of what has been written about the reflex since its original description by Moro in 1918[26] was well reviewed by Mitchell.[16] It occurs spontaneously possibly as a result of some movement in 29·4 per cent. of newborn infants.[39]

The reflex can be elicited in two ways. The baby is placed supine and the back of the head is supported on the palm of the hand an inch or so above the table. Rapid release of the head initiates the reflex. The alternative method is to hold the hands and gently raise the baby a little way off the table (Fig. 1). Rapid release of the hands causes the sudden movement of the cervical region which initiates the reflex. A sharp bang on the table will produce the reflex, but this method is not as satisfactory as the previous two methods.

The reflex consists of abduction and extension of the arms. The hands open, but the fingers often remain curved. This is shown well in Fig. 3. This phase is followed by adduction of the arms as if in an embrace. (This descriptive term is appropriate, but the analogy should not be carried to the extent of suggesting that this is the purpose of the reflex. Pratt urged caution in this respect.[25]) André Thomas has termed it 'The arms of the Cross reflex'.

The reflex is also accompanied by crying, extension of the trunk and head, and movement of the legs (the nature of which depends upon their original position). The Moro reflex is present in premature babies, except the very small ones, but the arms tend to fall backwards on to the table during the adduction phase because the anti-gravity muscles are much weaker than in the full term baby. After a month or two the hand of the full term baby does not open as fully as that of the newborn child.

The Moro reflex has been assessed in various ways.

McGraw's[15] classification is based upon the maturity of the reflex, Stirnimann's[23] upon the type of the reflex, and Gordon's[6] upon the intensity. For clinical work we have found it useful to classify the reflex in the following way.

(a) Increased. The reflex is elicited easily, the movements are exaggerated and a tremor of the hands may occur.

(b) Decreased, due to hypertonus. The full movement of the arms is prevented by the increased muscle tone. Three grades of severity are seen. The mildest is failure to open the hands at the height of the reflex, next is incomplete movement of the arms, and most severe is the inability to elicit the reflex because the arms are so tightly flexed.

(c) Decreased, due to hypotonus. In cases with muscle weakness, for example, severe hypotonia, it is difficult to obtain the reflex.

(d) Decreased, due to cerebral damage.

(e) Asymmetrical. This type of response is usually seen with a peripheral injury, such as Erb's palsy or fracture of the clavicle or humerus, and in spastic hemiplegia. The response may be asymmetrical as a result of inhibition on one side if the hand is clenched or holding an object[5a]. It follows that when one is eliciting the response, the infant's head should be in the midline, and the hands should be open. It may not occur if the child is crying. It may be unobtainable in hypotonic or hypertonic babies, in severely shocked or otherwise abnormal infants, or in babies who are asleep, or heavily sedated by barbiturates. In hypertonic babies abduction is limited, and the hands may remain closed.

The reflex may be difficult to obtain in premature babies, but it is always present when they are awake and otherwise normal.

The Moro response is a vestibular reflex. It disappears by about 2 or 3 months of age.

The Startle Reflex

This is often confused with the Moro reflex. In the Startle Reflex, obtained by a sudden loud noise, or by tapping the sternum, the elbow is flexed (not extended, as in the Moro Reflex), and the hand remains closed.[18a]

The Grasp Reflex

This was termed by André Thomas the 'Tonic reflex of the finger flexors'. It consists of two parts, the grasp reflex, and the response to traction. The grasp reflex is elicited by introducing a finger or other suitable object into the palm from the ulnar side. (An empty thermometer case makes a useful stimulus and can be washed easily between examinations). When the palm is stimulated the fingers flex and grip the object. The head should be in the midline during this test. If it is not, it will be found that the grasp reflex is more easily elicited on the side to which the occiput is directed.[9] The dorsum of the hand should not be touched during the test because this excites the opposite reflex and the hand opens. This is one of the best examples of the conflict between reflexes, a phenomenon which is discussed in the writings of André Thomas and his colleagues.[32]

Once the grasp reflex is obtained the finger can be drawn gently upwards. As this is done in the full term baby the grip is reinforced and there is a progressive tensing of the muscles from the wrist to the shoulder, until the baby hangs from the finger momentarily. The record for this feat appears to be a grasping strength of 2·2 kg. as measured by a dynamometer.[36] It is facilitated by the initiation of sucking movements.

In the premature baby the arm can be drawn upwards, but when traction is applied the grip opens and there is much less tensing of the arm muscles.

A similar response can be demonstrated by gently stroking the sole of the foot behind the toes. With patience, the grasping response of both the hands and the feet can be obtained, so that the baby is made to hang suspended like an oppossum supported by his hands and feet.

The grasp reflex is much weaker by the age of 2 months and has disappeared in most normal babies by the age of 3 months. The grasp reflex is strongest at term.

The grasp reflex is assessed partly with regard to intensity, partly with regard to symmetry, and partly with regard to persistence after it should have disappeared. An exceptionally strong grasp reflex may be found in the spastic form of cerebral palsy and in kernicterus. It may be asymmetrical in hemiplegia and in cases of cerebral damage. It should have disappeared in 2 or 3 months and persistence may indicate the spastic form of cerebral palsy.

Foot Reflexes

The grasp reflex of the foot is mentioned above. The withdrawal reflex consists of a brisk flexion of the limb and occurs in response to a noxious stimulus such as a pin prick applied to the sole of the foot. It is commonly unobtainable in children with a meningomyelocele. It may be absent or weak in a baby born as a breech with extended legs.

The crossed extension reflex is obtained by holding one leg extended at the knee and applying firm pressure to or stroking the sole of the foot on the same side. The free leg flexes, adducts and then extends, giving the impression of attempting to push away the stimulating agent. It is not normally obtained after the first month. It may be obtained in the premature baby, but the adduction componement of the reflex does not appear until the thirty-seventh week of gestation.

André Thomas suggested that the plantar response is best obtained by holding the foot perpendicular to the ground and stimulating the anterior part of the first interosseous space. Asymmetry of response was regarded as of particular importance. He found that the typical Babinski response with fanning of the toes, as seen in the older child, is rarely seen when the outer side of the sole of the foot is stimulated. Stimulation of the sole of the foot does, however, cause movement of the ipsilateral limb away from the stimulus and movement of the contralateral limb towards it. Vajnorsky et al.[35] described a similar reflex. Passive dorsiflexion of the big toe causes flexion of the other toes. Ninety-eight per cent. of 632 mature, healthy infants showed this reflex in the early months. It disappeared by the age of 8 months.

Wilkinson and Brain[4] showed that in infants up to 8 days of age, the plantar response is almost always extensor. The response to pinpricks or cold can be obtained as high as the level of T3. It is usually ipsilateral.

From the age of 5 to 20 weeks a bilateral extensor response can be obtained by stimulation anywhere from the sole to the thigh. From the level of the abdomen and upwards the response is equally often flexor or extensor, and usually bilateral. After 21 weeks cold does not usually act as a stimulus of the response, and the receptor field shrinks from above downwards, presumably as a result of centripetal myelination of the pyramidal tracts. It is noted elsewhere (Ch. 16) that in disease of the pyramidal tracts in older infants and children the extensor plantar response may be obtained over a widely increased area. It can be obtained by stroking the tibia (Oppenheim's sign), by flexing the hip against resistance, and sometimes by stimulating the skin of the abdomen or thorax. I have several times demonstrated the plantar extensor response in a spastic child by stimulating the neck beneath the ear.

The responses to the application of various stimuli to the foot as described above, will repay careful study[4,12] and are important in the development of walking patterns later.[34]

Hip Reflexes

When one leg is flexed at the hip the other leg flexes.[14a] If strong pressure is applied to the femoral nerve in the inguinal canal the contralateral, and less often the homolateral leg extends.[7] A flexion reflex in response to strong inguinal pressure has been described as a sign of meningitis.[20]

Placing and Walking Reflexes[21]

The placing or limb placement reaction ([40, 41]) is elicited by bringing the anterior aspect of the tibia or ulna against the edge of a table. The child lifts the leg up to step onto the table, or elevates the arm to place the hand on the table. The reflex is constantly present at birth in full term babies weighing over 1,800 g., and after the first twenty-four hours in premature babies weighing over 1,700 g. Absence of the response suggests brain damage. Zapella *et al.* have suggested that it is absent in older mentally defective infants with a mental age of below three or four months.

The walking or stepping reflex is obtained by holding the baby upright over a table, so that the sole of the foot presses against the table. This initiates reciprocal flexion and extension of the legs, simulating walking. Owing to the action of the adductor muscles, one leg often gets caught behind the other. This must not be confused with adductor spasm. There is a wide gap between this automatic walking reflex and mature independant walking.[13] A walking reflex can be demonstrated in premature babies, but they differ from full term babies in walking on their toes.[28] The walking reflex disappears in normal children by the age of 3 or 4 weeks. The reflex can be demonstrated for several more weeks if the baby's head is extended when his foot is flat on the couch.[14]

Heel Reflex

Percussion of the heel or pressure on the sole of the foot causes extension of the limb.

Leg Straightening Reflex (A Righting Reflex)

When the sole of the foot is pressed on to the couch, the legs and body straighten. This presumably corresponds to the 'positive and negative supporting reactions' described by Bobath and Bobath.[3] They described the positive reaction as consisting of simultaneous contraction of extensors and flexors of the leg when the ball of the foot makes contact with the floor. The negative reaction occurs when the muscles relax as the foot is raised. The Bobaths also described the crossed extension reflex, which enables one leg to support the weight of the body when the other leg is lifted.

The Magnet Reflex

When the child is supine, the examiner's finger is pushed against the sole of the foot, and the knee and hip flex, and as the finger is withdrawn, the foot follows the finger.

Trunk Incurvation (Galant's reflex)

When the child is held in ventral suspension, or is placed in the prone position, stimulation of the back lateral to the spine, or of the lumbar region, causes flexion of the trunk towards the side of the stimulus (Fig. 12).

When the glutei are pricked on the outer side of the buttocks, the trunk flexes to the side stimulated.

Redressement Du Tronc

This is another reflex derived from the French workers. The baby is held with his back to the examiner. Firm stimulation of the soles of the feet causes extension at the hips and elevation of the trunk. The reflex appears at about 35 weeks' gestation, but extension of the spine does not begin until about 37 weeks.

The Tonic Neck Reflexes

These are asymmetrical and symmetrical. The asymmetrical one is the better known, and is always seen at intervals in young babies in the first two months. When the child is in the supine position and not crying, he may be seen to lie with the head turned to one side with the arm extended to the same side. The contralateral knee is often flexed. In normal babies passive rotation of the head causes some increase of tone of the upper limb on the side to which the rotation occurs, but one rarely sees full extension of the limb. The reflex normally disappears by the age of 2 or 3 months. In severe cerebral palsy the reflex persists and may increase. One may see obvious extension of the arm when the head is passively rotated. These reflexes are important in determining the posture of the neonate, and the asymmetrical one is seen frequently during the observation of babies.[8]

The reflex is much more marked in spastic babies, and persists much longer than in normal babies. The reflex is partly responsible for preventing the child rolling from prone to supine or vice versa in the early weeks. According to Bobath[3] the reflex prevents the spastic child from moving the arms forward and from bringing his hands together in the midline or bringing his hands to his mouth. It impairs hand eye co-ordination, preventing him from holding his head in the midline.

The symmetrical tonic neck reflex is evoked by flexion or extension of the neck.

On raising the head of a kneeling child, extensor tone increases in the arms, and flexor tone in the legs. If the reflex is strong, the child extends the arms and flexes the legs. Flexing the neck has the opposite effect. The influence of this reflex is seen in normal children when they raise the head and shoulders in the prone: it helps them to support themselves on the arms and to get on to hands and knees. The reflex disappears when they learn to crawl, a movement which demands independence of movements of the limbs from the position of the head.

In cerebral palsy the reflex is usually over-active. The child can only extend his arms in kneeling when the head is raised: the legs are then fixed in flexion. As long as the head is raised, the child is unable to extend his legs. If the head is lowered, the arms flex, the legs extend, and the child falls on his face. He is therefore unable to crawl.

Tonic Labyrinthine Reflexes

These reflexes affect all four limbs, and interact closely with the tonic neck reflexes. Their action in normal children is uncertain, but in children with cerebral palsy they cause marked changes in muscle tone. Their effect is most clearly seen on the head, shoulders, arms and trunk. While lying supine, the head of the child with cerebral palsy is pulled backwards, and passive flexion may be strongly resisted. In the prone position, flexion of the head, neck and spine occurs, and passive raising of the head is resisted.

When the normal child of 4 months or more is in the prone position, and the chin is passively raised, there is a protective extension of the arms, with the use of the hands for support. In the child with cerebral palsy, the response depends on the relative predominance of the tonic labyrinth and symmetrical tonic neck reflexes. If the former predominate, the child draws the arms up in flexion and remains in mid-air suspended by his head. He cannot support his body weight on his arms. He falls on his face when placed into the kneeling posture. He cannot get on to his hands and knees and cannot raise his head and extend the spine.

If the symmetrical tonic neck reflex predominates, there is tonic extension of the arms with flexion of the legs. If the head is flexed passively, the arms flex, the hips extend, and the child falls on his face. He cannot crawl, because the legs show strong flexor spasticity as long as the head is raised.

RIGHTING REFLEXES.

These make their appearance in a definite chronological order and are responsible for certain basic motor activities. They enable the child to roll from prone to supine and supine to prone.

They help him to get on to his hands and knees and to sit up. They are responsible for the ability to restore the normal position of the head in space and to maintain the normal postural relationship of the head, trunk and limbs during all activities. The reflexes include: (*a*) Neck righting reflex. This is present at birth, and is strongest at the age of 3 months. Turning of the head to one side is followed by movement of the body as a whole; (*b*) Labyrinth righting reflex acting on the head. This is present at 2 months of age, and strongest at 10 months. It enables the child to lift the head up in the prone position (when 1 to 2 months old) and later when in the supine position; (*c*) The body righting reflex, acting on the body. This appears at 7 to 12 months. It modifies the neck righting reflex, and plays an important rôle in the child's early attempts to sit and stand.

In severe cases of cerebral palsy the righting reflexes are absent. The child cannot turn to one side, as the neck righting reflex is inhibited by the tonic labyrinth reflex. The child cannot raise the head in the supine or prone position. The child has great difficulty in turning over and sitting up. In severe cases of cerebral palsy it will be found that when the examiner attempts to flex the child's head, holding the back of the head, there is strong resistance to flexion: the head will extend and the whole back may arch.

The Landau Reflex.

This consists of extension of the head, spine, and legs when the child is held in ventral suspension. If the head is passively flexed the whole body flexes. A subsidiary part of the response is partial extension of the lower limbs at the hip-joints. According to Mitchell [16a] the reaction is normally present from the age of three months, is present in most infants in the second six months, and becomes increasingly difficult to evoke after the age of one year. Absence of the reflex over the age of three months is seen in cases of motor weakness, cerebral palsy and mental deficiency. He regarded the reflex as a combined effect of labyrinthine, neck and visual reactions.

In most cases of cerebral palsy, the Landau reflex is absent, as the child cannot lift the head in this position, owing to the inhibition of the labyrinth righting reflex acting on the head by the tonic labyrinth reflex. With the head flexed, the child has too much flexor activity and is unable to extend the trunk and legs.

THE SPRUNGBEREITSCHAFT. (Protective extension of the arms).

This appears at the age of 6 months, and remains active throughout life. It consists of extension of the arms and hands as a protection from injury in falling. It is absent in cerebral palsy if the upper limbs are affected. The arms either remain flexed or show an asymmetrical tonic neck reflex altitude. In doubtful cases the test is of value to decide whether the upper extremities are involved or not.

The reflex is tested by holding the child round the waist in the air and lowering him head downwards towards the support. A normal child extends the arms and hands to reach for the support. In children with cerebral palsy the flexor spasticity in this position with the head hanging downwards is strong, and the arms are flexed and drawn back at the shoulders.

Tendon Reflexes

André Thomas paid surprisingly little attention to the knee jerks and other tendon jerks, and did not regard them as being important. I disagree with this attitude, because I consider that they provide information of considerable value in developmental assessment.

When the knee jerk is elicited in a newborn infant, there is commonly an associated adduction of the opposite leg. When the knee jerk is not obtained, the adduction of the opposite leg may occur alone. Exaggeration of the knee jerk, as indicated by a brisk response on tapping the anterior surface of the ankle, is confirmatory evidence of hypertonia. It suggests that one should observe the infant at intervals, in order to determine whether the exaggeration of the jerk persists or disappears. If it persists, it is suggestive of cerebral palsy of the spastic type. The same applies to the biceps jerk: if a brisk response is obtained by tapping at the shoulder, the child should be observed at intervals in order to assess the significance of the sign. A sustained ankle clonus is another sign which indicates the need for further observation. None of these signs by themselves signify abnormality.

Superficial Reflexes

Harlem and Lönnum[10a] have shown that the abdominal reflexes can always be obtained in the newborn baby. They studied two hundred full term infants, allowing the child to suck a pacifier if desired, and using a blunt needle as the stimulant. If the baby was crying they waited for him to quieten. They found that the reflex was reduced if there was abdominal distension. In that case they retested after the distension had disappeared. The reflex was difficult to obtain if the skin were dry, and in that case they oiled the skin.

In addition to the usual contraction of the abdominal muscles, as seen in adults, there is commonly a curving of the trunk to the affected side, with a tendency to contraction of the muscles on the opposite side. The response is more extensive than in adults, and the zone over which the reflex is obtained is wider. During or immediately after the response there is commonly flexion of the homolateral leg or of both legs. The reflex was not obtained in babies with serious cerebral lesions.

The Palmomental and Similar Reflexes

Babkin described a reflex consisting of opening of the mouth when the infant's palm is pressed. When the thenar or hypothenar eminences are stroked, there may be contraction of the chin muscles and uplifting of the leg.

When the child is asleep in the supine position, and the neck is touched, the hand strokes it while the head rotates. If the right ear is touched, the left hand strokes the neck. If the nose is tickled, both hands reach for the face.

Head Thrust Responses

The baby is held in the sitting position, with the body leaning slightly backwards. A hand placed against the back of the head thrusts the head forwards. The head opposes the movement.

When the baby is held in the sitting position, slightly leaning to one side, the head is flexed to that side. When the head is pushed to the other side, there is strong resistance by the lateral flexor muscles.

Thomas remarked that this response is marked even in premature babies, though there is a notable head wobble when the body is passively moved.

There is a less marked response when the head is thrust backwards when the child is held sitting with the body flexed.

The reaction to thrust increases as the child matures and the head wobble decreases.

The Jaw Jerk

Tapping the chin causes elevation of the mandible.

Other Responses

When the baby is held under the armpits and shaken, the head wobbles in all directions, but the limbs do not move. The opposite occurs in the older child.

Stimulation in the temporal region causes rotation of the head to the opposite side.

Vollmer[37] described a reflex consisting of a vigorous cry, flexion of extremities, lordosis of the spine and elevation of the head, when the infant, held in ventral suspension, is firmly stroked down the spine. It is said to be present in the first months, and it disappears by the age of three months.

André Thomas describes a reflex in the hand. Stimulation of the ulnar border of the closed hand causes extension of the digits, beginning with the little finger.

Rubbing the ear causes rotation of the head to the opposite side.

Kratschmer's reflex consists of respiratory arrest when the baby experiences a bad smell.

Infants exhibit a protective skin reflex after about ten days. They scratch the skin, if there is an itch. Peiper remarked that a child is seriously ill if he cannot keep flies off the face.

Summary

There are numerous reflex responses in the newborn. They are of considerable neurological interest. The value of many of these for clinical assessment is as yet in doubt.

For practical purposes the reflexes which provide important information for developmental assessment are mainly the following:–

> The Moro reflex.
> The grasp reflex.
> The tonic neck reflexes.
> The tendon reflexes.

REFERENCES

1. ANDERSON, R. B., ROSENBLITH, J. F. (1968) Photic Sneeze Reflex in the Human Newborn. *Develop. Psychobiology*, **1**, 65.
2. BENSON, P. F. (1962) Transient Unilateral External Rectus Muscle Palsy in newborn Infants. *Brit. med. J.*, **1**, 1054.
3. BOBATH, K., BOBATH, B. (1955) Tonic Reflexes and Righting Reflexes in the Diagnosis and Assessment of Cerebral Palsy. *Cerebr. Palsy Bull.*, **16**, No. 5.
3a BOBATH, K., BOBATH, B. (1956) The Diagnosis of Cerebral Palsy in Infancy. *Arch. Dis. Childh.*, **31**, 408.
4. BRAIN, R., WILKINSON, M. (1959) Observations on the Extensor Plantar Reflex and its Relationship to the Functions of the Pyramidal Tract. *Brain*, **82**, 297.
5. DENNIS, W. (1934) A Description and Classification of the Responses of the Newborn Infant. *Psychol. Bull.*, **31**, 5.
5a DUBOWITZ, V. (1965) Asymmetrical Moro Response in Neurologically Normal Infants. *Develop. Med. child. Neurol.*, **7**, 244.
6. FULDNER, R. V. (1962) The Tonic Neck Reflex. Letter. *Develop. Med. child Neurol.*, **4**, 94.
7. FULTON, J. F. (1949) *Physiology of the Nervous System*. 3rd ed. Oxford Univ. Press.
8. GESELL, A. (1938) The Tonic Neck Reflex in the Human Infant: its Morphogenetic and Clinical Significance. *J. Pediat.*, **13**, 455.
9. GESSELL, A. (1945) *The Embryology of Behaviour*. 2nd ed. New York: Harper.
9a GORDON, M. B. (1929) The Moro Embrace Reflex in Infancy: its Incidence and Significance. *Amer. J. Dis. Child.*, **38**, 26.
10. THE GRONINGEN MANUAL. (1960) Summer meeting of Little Club.
10a HARLEM, O. K., LÖNNUM, A. (1957) A Clinical Study of the Abdominal Skin Reflexes in Newborn Infants. *Arch. Dis. Childh.*, **32**, 127.
11. HARTMANN-KARPLUS, D. (1931) Untersuchungen über Juckempfinding, Knatzon und Pilomotorenreflex in Säuglingsalter. *Jb. Kinderheilk*, **132**, 140.
12. HOLT, K. S. (1962) The Plantar Response in Infants and Children. *Cerebr. Palsy Bull.*, **3**, 449.
13. McGRAW, M. B. (1932) From Reflex to Muscular Control in the Assumption of an Erect Posture and Ambulation in the Human Infant. *Child Developm.*, **3**, 291.
13a McGRAW, M. B. (1937). The Moro Reflex. *Amer. J. Dis. Child.*, **54**, 240.
14. MACKEITH, R. C. (1965) The Placing Response and Primary Walking. *Guy's Hosp. Gaz.*, **79**, 394.
14a MESINA, R. (1936) The Tonic Reactions of the Normal Child due to Position and Movement. *Rev. clin. Pediat.*, **34**, 510.
15. MINKOWSKI, A., SAINT-ANNE DARGASSIES, S. (1956) Le Retentissement de l'Anoxie Foetale sur le Systeme Nerveux Central. *Rev. franc. Etud. clin. biol.*, **1**, 531.
16. MITCHELL, R. G. (1960) The Moro Reflex. *Cerebr. Palsy Bull.*, **2**, 135.
16a MITCHELL, R. G. (1962) The Landau Reaction. *Develop. Med. Child Neurol.*, **4**, 65.
17. MORO, E. (1918) Das erste Tremenon. *Munch. med. Wschr.*, **65**, 1147.
18. PAINE, R. S. (1960) Neurologic Examination of Infants and Children. *Pediat. Clin. N. Amer.*, **7**, 471.

18a PARMELEE, A. H. (1964) Critical Evaluation of the Moro Reflex. *Pediatrics*, **33**, 773.
19. PEIPER, A. (1928) *Die Herntätigeit des Sauglings*. Berlin: Springer.
20. PEIPER, A. (1941) *Dtsch. med. Wschr.*, **67**, 541.
21. PEIPER, A. (1929) Die Schreitbewegungen der Neugeborenen, *Mschr. Kinderheilk*, **45**, 444.
22. PEIPER, A. (1936) Hautschutzreflexe. *Jb. Kinderheilk*, **146**, 233.
23. PEIPER, A. (1949) *Die Eigenart der Kindichen Hirntätigkeit*. Lepzig: Thieme.
24. PEIPER, A. (1956) *Die Eigenart der Kindichen Hirntätigkeit*. 2nd ed. Lepzig: Thieme.
24a PEIPER, A. (1963) *Cerebral Function in Infancy and Childhood*. London. Pitman.
25. PRATT, K. C. (1954) *Manual of Child Psychology*. Ed. L. Carmichael. 2nd ed. Chap. 4. London: Chapman & Hall.
26. PRECHTL, H. F. R. (1956) Die Eigenart und Entwicklung der frühkindlichen Motorik. *Klin Wschr.*, **34**, 281.
28. PRECHTL, H. F. R., Stemmer C. J. (1962) The Choreiform Syndrome in Children. *Develop. Med. child. Neurol.*, **4**, 119.
29. SAINT-ANNE DARGASSIES. (1962) Le Nouveau-né à Terme. Aspect Neurologique. *Biol. Neonat. (Basel)*, **4**, 174.
30. SAINT-ANNE DARGASSIES. (1954) Methode d'Examen Neurologique du Nouveau-né. *Étud. néo-natal*, **3**, 101.
30a STIRNIMANN, F. (1943) Ueber den Moroschen Umklammerungs-Reflex beim Neugeborenen. *Ann. Paediat. (Buseg)*, **160**, 1.
31. THOMAS, A. (1959) Integration in the infant. *Cerebr. Palsy Bull.*, **8**, 3.
32. THOMAS, A., CHESNI, Y., SAINT-ANNE DARGASSIES. (1960) The Neurological Examination of the Infant. *Little Club Clin. develop. Med.*, 1.
33. THOMAS, A., SAINT-ANNE DARGASSIES. (1952) *Études Neurologiques sue le Nouveau-né et le Jeune Nourrisson*. Paris: Masson.
34. TWITCHELL, T. E., EHRENREICH, D. L. (1962) The Plantar Response in Infantile Cerebral Palsy. *Develop. Med. child. Neurol.*, **4**, 602.
35. VAJNORSKY, J., BRACHFELD, K., STRAKOVA, M. (1958) A Contribution to the Reflexes of the Newborn Period. *Cs. Pediat.*, **13**, 277.
36. VALENTINE, W. L., WAGNER, I. (1934) Relative Arm Motility in the Newborn Infant. *Ohio St. Univ. Stud. No.* 12, 53.
37. VOLLMER, H. (1948) A New Reflex in Young Infants. *Amer. J. Dis. Child.*, **95**, 481.
38. WATSON, J. B. (1919) *Psychology from the Standpoint of the Behaviourist*. Philadelphia: Lippincott.
39. WILLEMSE, J. (1961) *De Motoriek van de Pasgeborene in de Eerste Levensuren*. Utrecht: Bisleveld.
40. ZAPELLA, M. (1963) Placing Reaction in Newborn. *Develop. Med. child. Neurol.*, **5**, 497.
41. ZAPELLA, M., FOLEY, J., COOKSON, M. (1964) The Placing and Supporting Reactions in Children with Mental Retardation. *J. ment. Defic. Res.*, **8**, 1.

CHAPTER 7

THE ASSESSMENT OF MATURITY

In the past, the term 'premature baby' was taken to include all babies who at birth weighed 5½ lbs. or less at birth (2500 g.), irrespective of the duration of gestation. This definition is no longer acceptable, because of the obvious fact that many babies weigh less than 2500 g. at birth though clearly born at term. Others, though born before term, are much smaller than the average for the duration of gestation. Low birth weight in relation to the duration of gestation may be due to malnutrition, abnormalities of the placenta, or hereditary or other factors. The behaviour of the 'small for dates' baby is quite different at birth from the truly premature baby of the same birth weight, and because the prognosis with regard to the development of hypoglycaemia in the newborn period and subsequent mental and physical development is different, it is of importance to recognise the distinguishing physical and neurological features.

It is obvious that a baby may be 'small for dates' and also born prematurely. For instance, a baby of 36 weeks gestation may weigh only 3 lbs. 8 ozs. (1590 g.). The average weight at birth in relation to the duration of gestation in England and Wales is as follows:

28 weeks	. .	2 lbs. 4 ozs.	. . 1023 g.
32 weeks	. .	3 lbs. 8 ozs.	. . 1590 g.
36 weeks	. .	5 lbs. 3 ozs.	. . 2358 g.
40 weeks	. .	7 lbs. 8 ozs.	. . 3410 g.

I am told that in Finland the mean weights are considerably higher than in England and Wales.

The distinction between the 'small for dates' and 'premature' baby is of more than academic interest. A mother's dates may not be accurate, and it is useful to be able to check her dates by an objective examination. In later weeks it may be important to assess a baby's development for the purposes of adoption. If one carries out such an examination at four months, and one does not know whether the 3 lbs. 8 ozs. baby was premature or born at term, one cannot assess his development. The behaviour to be expected of a four month old baby is very different from

133

that of a two month old baby (i.e. a four month old baby born two months prematurely). For this and many other reasons we need to know how to assess the maturity of a baby in the newborn period. For the knowledge of this subject we are indebted to the French workers ([13, 14]). The following are the main differences between a premature baby and a full term one (see Table 2, for summary). Wherever possible, I have included illustrations of the points described, but have not referred to the figure numbers in the text.*

1. *The Premature Baby sleeps for the most part of the day and night.* The full term baby may also sleep for a large part of the twenty-four hours, but not as much as the average premature baby.

2. *The Cry.* The premature baby cries infrequently; the cry is feeble, and not prolonged. The cry of the full term baby is more prolonged and more vigorous.

3. *Movements.* The premature baby shows faster, wilder and more bizarre movements of the limbs, with writhing of the trunk. The full term baby shows more frequent movements, which are more co-ordinated than those of the premature baby. The 28 to 32 week premature infant does not move one limb at a time, movement being generalised; the full term baby commonly moves one limb.

4. *Feeding Behaviour.* The premature baby cannot be relied upon to demand feeds, while the normal full term baby can. The premature baby may be unable to suck or swallow. He is particularly liable to regurgitate, and to inhale feeds, with resultant cyanotic attacks when being fed. Mouthing reflexes are difficult to elicit in the infant born before about 34 weeks of gestation: they are easily obtained in the full term baby.

5. *Muscle Tone.* The muscle tone of the premature baby is much less than that of the full term infant. Muscle tone increases first in the legs (by about seven and a half months of gestation) and later in the arms.

6. *Posture.* In the prone position the premature baby characteristically lies flat on the couch, with the pelvis low, and the knees at the side of the abdomen, the hips being acutely flexed.

---

* Most of the photographs of prematurity were photographs of an infant of 30 weeks gestation, two weeks after delivery.

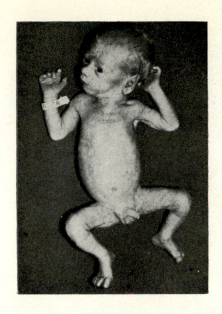

FIG. 23
Premature baby, supine.

FIG. 24
Full term baby, supine, flexed
position.

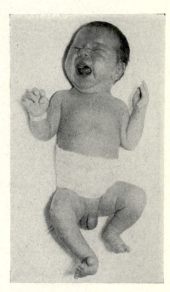

facing page 134

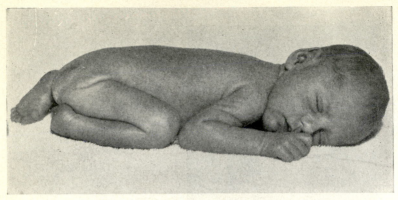

FIG. 25
For comparison with Fig. 26.
Prone position in premature baby. (At 9 weeks before term.)
Hips abducted, but flexed; pelvis less high than in full term baby.

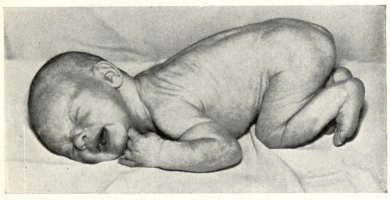

FIG. 26
Prone position, full term baby. (About 0-2 weeks of age.)
Pelvis high, knees drawn up under abdomen.

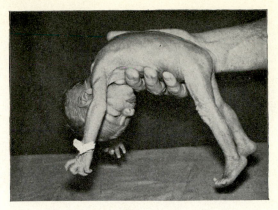

FIG. 27
Premature baby, ventral suspension.

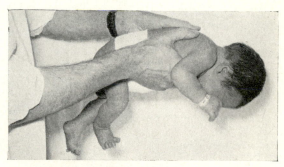

FIG. 28
Full term baby, ventral suspension.

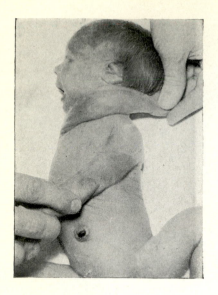

FIG. 29

Scarf sign. Premature baby. Note
position of elbow and hand.

FIG. 30

Scarf sign. Full term baby. Note
position of elbow and hand.

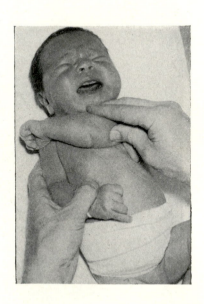

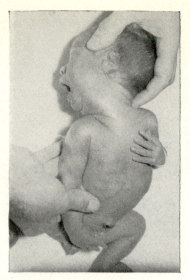

FIG. 31
Premature baby. Head rotation.

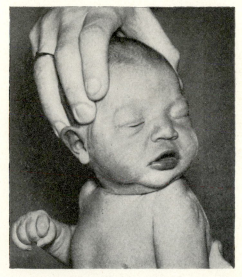

FIG. 32
Range of head rotation. Full term baby.
Chin on acromion.

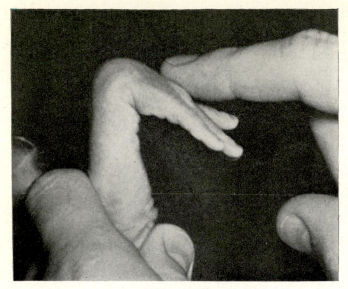

FIG. 33
Window sign, premature baby.

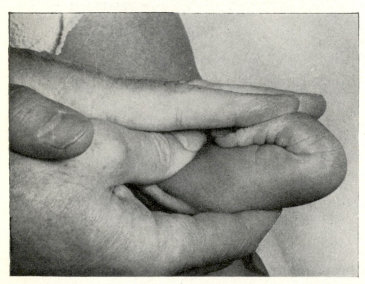

FIG. 34
Window sign, full term baby.

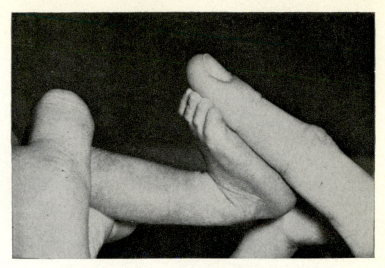

FIG. 35
Dorsiflexion of foot; premature baby.

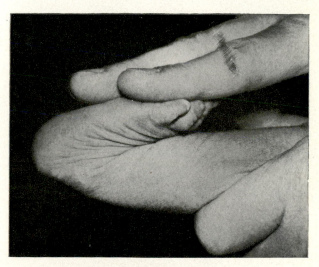

FIG. 36
Dorsiflexion of foot; full term baby.

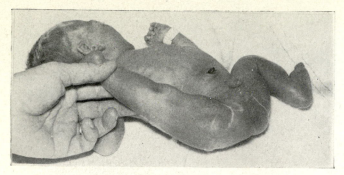

Fig. 37
Premature baby, hip flexed, full knee extension.

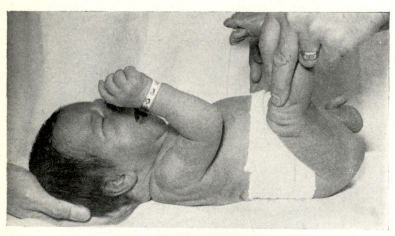

Fig. 38
Full term baby, hip flexed, limited knee extension.

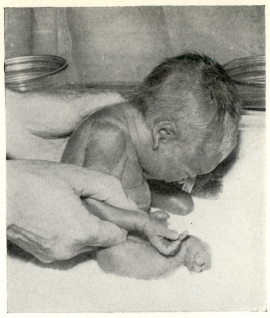

FIG. 39
Premature baby, sitting position.

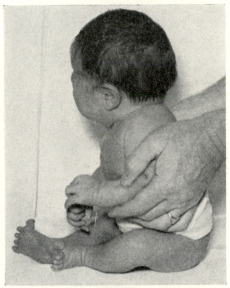

FIG. 40
Full term baby, sitting position.

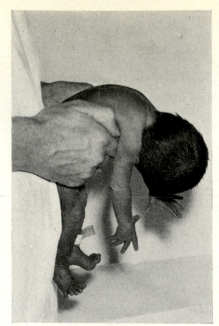

Fig. 41

Redressement du Tronc, premature baby. Unable
to straighten back.

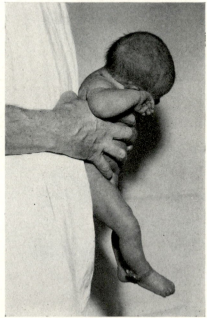

Fig. 42

Redressment du Tronc, full term baby. Straightens back.

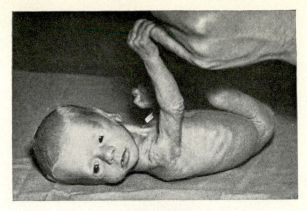

FIG. 43
Grasp response, premature baby.

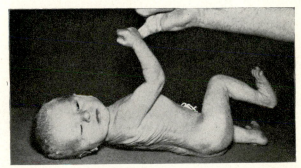

FIG. 44
Grasp response, full term baby.

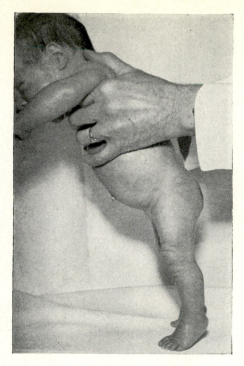

Fig. 45
Premature baby, 30 weeks
gestation, birth weight 3 lbs. 3 oz.
(1443g) 9 weeks after birth.

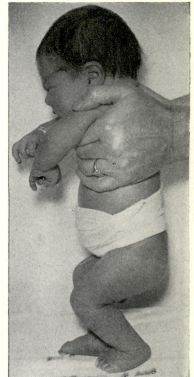

Fig. 46
Full term baby, sole of foot flat on
couch.

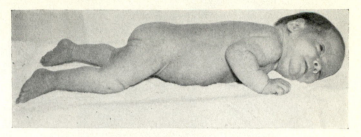

FIG. 47

Prone. Same baby as Figure 45. Compare full term, Figure 26, and
Premature baby Figure 25 and 6 weeks' baby Figure 63.

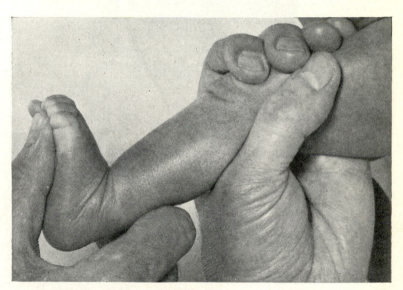

FIG. 48

Same baby as Figure 45.
Dorsiflexion of foot. Compare full term baby, Figure 36.

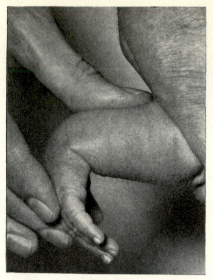

Fig. 49

Flexion of wrist. Same baby as Figure 45.
Compare full term baby. Figure 34.

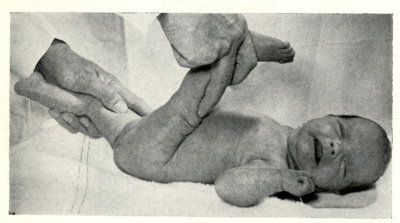

Fig. 50

Hip flexed, extension of knee. Same baby as Figure 45. Compare full
term baby. Figure 38.

The full term baby lies with the pelvis high, and the knees drawn up under the abdomen.

In the supine position, the twenty-eight week premature baby lies with the lower limbs extended and the hips abducted, so that the limbs are flat on the couch, in a 'froglike' attitude. The upper limbs lie in a similar position. The thirty-two week premature baby lies with the arms extended, but with the lower limbs flexed at the knee and abducted at the hip. The thirty-six week premature lies less froglike, mainly flexed. The full term infant lies with the limbs strongly flexed. The head in the twenty-eight to thirty-two week infant is turned to one side. The full term baby tends to keep the head aligned with the trunk.

7. *Head Rotation.* In the twenty-eight week premature baby the head can be rotated so far that the chin is well beyond the acromion: in the full term baby the chin can rotate only as far as the acromion.

8. *The Scarf Sign.* This depends on the deltoids, teres major and rhomboids. During the test the baby should be comfortable, in the supine position, with the head central. The hand is led across the chest to the opposite side of the neck. The hand of the twenty-eight week premature baby reaches well past the acromion: that of the full term baby does not go beyond the acromion. In the posterior scarf sign, which depends on the pectoralis major and latissimus dorsi, the hand is led behind the neck to the opposite side. There is a similar difference in the range achieved in the premature and full term baby.

9. *The Moro Reflex.* This is present in premature babies, except the very small ones, but the arms tend to fall backwards on to the table during the adduction phase because the antigravity muscles are weaker than in the full term baby.

10. *Wrist Flexion.* Flexion of the wrist of the 28 week premature baby is incomplete, so that a 'window' is formed between the hand and the forearm; that of the full term baby is complete, so that the hand is in contact with the forearm.

11. *The Grasp Reflex.* This is difficult to obtain in the twenty-eight week premature baby. There is no flexion of the elbow or contraction of muscles at the shoulder. In the full term baby the elbow and shoulder take an active part in the response.

The grasp reflex is at its strongest at forty weeks.

10

12. '*Redressement du Tronc*'—so called by the French writers.—When the infant is held with his back to one the young premature baby cannot extend the trunk. At thirty-five weeks' gestation the back begins to extend: at thirty-seven weeks the back extends and the child extends the neck, as in the case of the full term infant.

13. *Crossed Extension Reflex*. (Chapter 6). The reflex is incomplete in the young premature baby. In the case of the twenty-eight week premature baby, there is flexion of the opposite leg without extension or adduction. In the case of a thirty-two week baby some extension occurs after flexion: in the thirty-six week baby slight adduction follows the extension.

14. *Knee Extension*. When the hip is flexed so that the thigh is in contact with the side of the abdomen, the knee of the young premature baby can be fully extended. As maturity increases from twenty-eight weeks' gestation, less and less extension is obtained. In the full term baby extension is incomplete by about 20°.

15. *Dorsiflexion of the Foot*. In the twenty-eight week premature baby, dorsiflexion is incomplete, so that there is a fairly wide gap between the foot and the foreleg. In the full term baby the foot is brought into contact with the front of the leg.

16. *The Grasp Reflex in the Foot*. This is much weaker in the premature baby than in the full term one.

17. *The Walking Reflex*. This is very feeble in the twenty-eight week premature baby, but it is easily elicited in the thirty-six week baby and the full term one. The thirty-two week premature baby usually walks on the toes, whereas the full term baby walks with the foot flat on the couch.

18. *Ventral Suspension*. Held in ventral suspension, the young premature baby hangs limply, with no extension of the spine or neck, and with no flexion of the elbows, hips or knees. The full term baby has a straighter back, holds the head up a little, and flexes the elbows and knees and slightly extends the hips.

TABLE 2(a)

	6 months 28 weeks	6½ months 30 weeks	7 months 32 weeks	7½ months 34 weeks	8 months 36 weeks	8½ months 38 weeks	9 months 40 weeks
1. POSTURE	Completely hypotonic	Beginning of flexion of thigh at hip	Stronger flexion	Frog-like attitude	Flexion of the four limbs	Hypertonic	Very hypertonic
2. HEEL TO EAR MANOEUVRE							
3. POPLITEAL ANGLE	150°		110°	100°	100°	90°	80°
4. DORSI-FLEXION ANGLE OF FOOT			40–50°		40–50°	Premature reached 40 wk. 40° / Full term	
5. 'SCARF' SIGN	'Scarf' sign complete with no resistance		'Scarf' sign more limited		Elbow slightly passes midline		Elbow almost reaches midline
6. RETURN TO FLEXION OF FOREARM	Upper limbs very hypotonic lying in extension			Flexion of forearms begins to appear, but very weak	Strong 'return to flexion'. Flexion tone inhibited if forearm maintained 30 sec. in extension	Strong 'return to flexion' Forearm returns very promptly to flexion after being extended for 30 sec.	

TABLE 2(b)

	6 months 28 weeks	6½ months 30 weeks	7 months 32 weeks	7½ months 34 weeks	8 months 36 weeks	8½ months 38 weeks	9 months 40 weeks
1. LOWER EXTREMITY	—	Beginning of extension of lower leg on thigh upon stimulation of soles in lying position	Good support when standing up but very briefly (see illustration below)	Excellent righting reaction of leg ---> ---------> -------->			
2. TRUNK	—	—	—	± transitory	Good righting of trunk with infant held in vertical suspension (see illustration below)	Good righting of trunk with infant held in walking position (see illustration below)	
3. NECK EXTENSORS Baby pulled backward from sitting position	—		Head begins to right itself with great difficulty	Still difficult and incomplete	Good righting but cannot hold it	Begins to maintain head which doesn't fall back for few seconds	Keeps head in line with trunk for more than a few seconds
4. NECK FLEXORS Baby pulled to sitting position from supine	Head pendulant	Head pendulant	Contraction of muscles is visible but no movement of head	Head begins to right itself but still hanging back at end of movement	At first head is hanging back, then with sudden movement head goes forward onto chest	Head begins to follow trunk, keeps in line in upright position	Difference between Extensors and Flexors has diminished (see illustration below)
			Straightening of legs		Straightening of trunk / Stimulation	arm support	Straightening of head and trunk together

TABLE 2(c)

	6 months 28 weeks	6½ months 30 weeks	7 months 32 weeks	7½ months 34 weeks	8 months 36 weeks	8½ months 38 weeks	9 months 40 weeks
1. SUCKING REFLEX	Weak and not really synchronized with deglutition		Stronger and synchronized with deglutition	Perfect ---→	---------→	---------→	
2. ROOTING REFLEX	Long latency period. Response is slow and imperfect		Complete and more rapid. Hand-to-mouth attraction established	Brisk Complete --→ Durable	---------→	---------→	
3. GRASP REFLEX	Finger grasp is good and reaction spreads up whole upper limb but not strong enough to lift infant up off bed		Stronger	Stronger	The reaction of upper limb is strong enough to lift infant up off bed ---→	---------→	
4. MORO REFLEX	Weak, obtained just once, and not elicited every time		Complete reflex -→	-------→		---------→	---------→
5. CROSSED EXTENSION	Flexion and extension in a random pattern, purposeless reaction		Extension but no adduction	Still incomplete	Good response with:- 1. Extension ----→ 2. Adduction 3. Fanning of the toes	---------→	
6. AUTOMATIC WALKING	—	—	Begins tip-toeing with good support on sole and a righting reaction of legs for a few seconds		Pretty good Very fast Tip-toeing	● A premature who has reached 40 weeks. Walks in a toe-heel progression or tip-toes ● A full-term new born of 40 weeks. Walks in a heel-toe progression on whole sole of foot	

One of the French workers, Claudine Amiel-Tison,[1] has written a brief clear account of her method of assessing the maturity of the baby, basing the method largely on the assessment of tone.

Tables 2a, b, c summarise the method, which depends on:–

(a) *Passive Tone. Assessment of the Posture* (Table 2a)

Heel to ear manoeuvre—keep the child's pelvis flat, attempting to touch the baby's head with his feet.

Measurement of the popliteal angle when the pelvis is flat and the hip is fully flexed.

Measurement of the angle of dorsiflexion of the foot.

Scarf sign—carrying the arm in front of the baby's neck, observing how far the baby's hand goes beyond the tip of the shoulder.

Return of forearm to flexion; maintaining the arm in full extension for 30 seconds, and releasing it—observing the promptness of return to flexion. There is prompt return in the full term baby.

(b) *Active Tone*

Righting reaction of lower extremities and trunk, with the baby held standing; assessment of the support of the body and trunk righting.

Righting reaction of head; baby held sitting, head allowed

to fall slowly back; observation of extent of head raising. Also observation of head raising when the baby is pulled to the sitting position.

(c) *Reflexes*

Observation of the sucking, rooting, grasp, walking reflex, Moro reflex, crossed extension reflex.

Robinson[12] carried out 219 neurological examinations on 62 infants which had a gestation period varying from 25 to 42 weeks. He concluded that five tests were useful; below are the tests and the age at which the test becomes positive.

	Gestation in Weeks if Reflex is	
	Absent	*Present*
Reaction of pupil to light	Less than 31	29 or more
Traction from supine; flexing the neck when child is being pulled up.	Less than 36	33 or more
Glabellar tap reflex	Less than 34	32 or more
Neck righting (when examiner rotates the head, the trunk follows).	Less than 37	34 or more
Child turns head to diffuse light.	Doubtful	32 or more

Farr[8] used 10 signs in her attempt to estimate the gestational age; they were the degree of motor activity, reaction of the pupil to light, rate of sucking, closure of the mouth when sucking, stripping action of the tongue, passive resistance, forearm recoil, plantar grasp, the pitch and the intensity of the cry. We found that the reaction of the pupil to light is a difficult sign to elicit in the newborn baby.

Experience has shown that there is a significant degree of variation in the age at which these neurological signs appear. In consequence it seems reasonable to advocate that an assessment should never be made on the basis of single signs, but on a combination of signs. For instance, if ten signs are tested for, the mean maturational age for the total of the ten should be calculated.

In Table 3 we have attempted to summarise the main findings at four different gestational periods.

We believe that it is possible with experience to predict the neurological maturity to within two weeks, and as knowledge

TABLE 3

CRITERIA	MATURITY (WEEKS)			
	28	32	36	40
POSTURE (Supine)				
Arms	Limp abducted and extended	Extended abducted and flexed	Flexed but easily extended less 'frog-like'	Flexed strongly
Legs	Limp abducted and extended			Flexed strongly
Head	Lateral	Lateral	Move often in line with trunk	Aligned with trunk
POSTURE (Prone)				
	Pelvis flat on couch	Pelvis flat on couch		Pelvis high o couch
	Knees at side of abdomen	Knees at side of abdomen		Knees under abdomen
SPONTANEOUS ACTIVITY				
Generalised	Always	Always	Occasionally	Very Freque
Persist with other Activity	Yes	Occasionally	No	No
Individual Limbs	Never	No	Occasionally	Always
FEEDING BEHAVIOUR				
Ease of stimulating	Very difficult	Difficult	Fairly easy	Easy
Response	Feeble	Slow	Fairly brisk	Brisk
Persistence	None	Slight	Fairly good	Good
RANGE OF MOVEMENT				
Head rotation	Well past Acromion	Gradual	decrease	to acromion
Scarf sign	Well past Acromion	Gradual	decrease	to acromion
Wrist flexion	Wide angle	Gradual	decrease	acute angle
Foot dorsiflexion	Wide angle	Gradual	decrease	full flexion to front of l
Knee extension	Full	Gradual	decrease	limited
GRASP RESPONSE				
Grip	Difficult to obtain	Slow to obtain	Fairly easy to get	Brisk
Reinforcement	None	Little or none	Incomplete	Good
CROSSED EXTENSION				
Flexion phase	Weak	Present	Present	Present
Extension phase	Absent	Weak	Present	Present
Adduction phase	Absent	Absent	Absent	Present
WALKING REFLEX				
Ease of stimulating	Very feeble	Slow	Easy	Easy
Type of walk		On toes	May be on toes	Heel down

increases even greater accuracy may be possible. We suggest that the assessment, as in the case of physical characteristics, should be based not on single signs, which are variable, but on a combination of signs. Two extreme examples will serve to illustrate the value of the technique.

In the first case a severely toxaemic mother delivered a baby weighing only 2 lbs. 10 oz. The obstetrician refused to accept her claim that the duration of gestation was 39 weeks. Neurological examination, however, revealed a maturity of between 38 and 40 weeks.

The second baby was delivered at home. She weighed 6½ lbs., and was a good colour. The doctor could not understand why she deteriorated despite adequate attention. Examination on admission to hospital revealed that her maturity was only that of a 33 or 34 weeks foetus, and that she was, in fact a 'premature' baby of a pre-diabetic mother.

Other Distinguishing Features

Schulte *et al.* in Germany[15] and Dubowitz in Sheffield[5] simultaneously announced that there was a close correlation between motor nerve conduction velocity for ulnar and tibial nerves and the conceptional age. Small for dates infants had significantly higher conduction velocity values than preterm infants of comparable weight.

Engel and colleagues [6, 7] used photic and acoustic evoked responses in the electroencephalogram for the estimation of maturity. Photic latency was found to be inversely related to conceptional age. It was interesting to note that full term girls responded faster to light than full term boys. Several other attempts have been made to assess maturity by electroencephalographic means.[4, 11]

Bishop and Corson[3] estimated conceptional age by cytological examination of the amniotic fluid. They wrote that the cells of the amniotic fluid are primarily composed of desquamated foetal cells, squamous and sebaceous. The percentage of lipid containing cells reflects the progressive development of sebaceous glands with increasing gestational age. After a study of 350 specimens, it was found that when the count was less than two per cent, 85 per cent were premature; when the count was over 20 per cent, all were over 36 weeks gestation.

Several workers have studied the maturity of enzyme systems and of other biochemical features for the estimation of maturity. It is said[2] that the proportion of albumin and gamma globulin in the umbilical vein is less in premature babies than in full term ones.

Some have found that certain external characteristics of the baby correlate well with the duration of gestation.[9] They include the skin texture, skin colour, skin opacity, oedema, lanugo, skull hardness, ear form, ear firmness, the genitalia, the breast size, nipple formation, and the plantar skin creases. It is likely that none of these signs are reliable in themselves, but that the assessment of maturity should be based on a combination of signs.

Summary

For many reasons it is important to be able to assess the maturity or duration of gestation of the newborn baby.

The maturity can be assessed with considerable accuracy by a combination of neurological signs, but not by single signs; by a combination of physical features, but not by single features; and by the motor nerve conduction velocity. Other methods are still experimental.

The Prematurely Born Baby who has reached Term

When the prematurely born baby has reached term (e.g. a baby born at thirty weeks gestation, ten weeks after birth), there are certain differences from the full term baby. (Figures 45 to 50).

1. Held in the walking position, he tends to walk on his toes, while the full term baby walks with the foot flat on the couch. In the walking reflex, the rhythm of the stepping movements is less regular than that of a full term infant.

2. Muscle tone is less than in the full term baby.

3. Dorsiflexion of the foot and flexion of the wrist is less than in the full term infant, but extension of the knee with the hip flexed is more complete.

4. He tends to be more active than the full term infant.

5. In the prone position he kicks out more, holds the head up better, and tends to be more active than the full term baby. He lies flat, like a six week old full term baby. In the supine position the premature baby shows more varied and ample movement than the full term one.

REFERENCES

1. AMIEL-TISON, C. (1968). Neurological Evaluation of the Maturity of Newborn Infants. *Arch. Dis. Childh.*, **43**, 89.

2. BAZSO, J., ASZTALOS, M., KASSAI, L. (1966) Excerpta Med. Monogr. P. 585. Proc. of Symposium in Prague.

3. BISHOP, E. H., CORSON, S. (1968) Estimation of Fetal Maturity by Cytological Examination of Amniotic Fluid. *Am. J. Obst. Gyn.*, **102**, 654.

4. DREYFUS-BRISAC, C., MINKOWSKI, A. (1967) Electrocencephalographic Maturation and Low Birth Weight. To be published.

5. DUBOWITZ, V. (1968) Nerve Conduction Velocity—An Index of Neurological Maturity of the Newborn Infant. *Develop. Med. Child Neurol.*, **10**, 741.

6. ENGEL, R., CROWELL, D., NISHIJIMA, S. (1969) Visual and Auditory Response Latencies in Neonates. Festschrift in honour of C. C. de Silva. Colombo: Kularatne.

7. ENGEL, R., BENSON, R. C. (1968) Estimate of Conceptional Age by Evoked Response Activity. *Biol. Neonat.*, **12**, 201.

8. FARR, V. (1968). Estimation of Gestational Age by Neurological Assessment in First Week of Life. *Arch. Dis. Childh.*, **43**, 353.

9. FARR, V., KERRIDGE, D. F., MITCHELL, R. G. (1966) The Value of Some External Characteristics in the Assessment of Gestational Age at Birth. *Develop. Med. Child Neurol.*, **8**, 657.

10. NOLTE, R., SCHULTE, F. J., MICHAELIS, R., GRUSON, R. (1969) Bioelectric Brain Maturation in Small for Dates Babies. *Develop. Med. Child Neurol.*, **11**, 83.

11. PARMELEE, A. H., SCHULTE, F. J., AKIYAMA, Y., WENNER, W. H., SCHULTZ, M. A., STERN, E. (1968) Maturation of E.E.G. Activity During Sleep in Premature Infants. *Electroenceph. Clin. Neurophysiol.*, **24**, 319.

12. ROBINSON, R. J. (1966). Assessment of Gestational Age by Neurological Examination. *Arch. Dis. Childh.*, **41**, 437.

13. SAINT-ANNE DARGASSIES (1955) La Maturation Neurologique des Prématurés. *Études Neonatales*, **4**, 71.

14. SAINT-ANNE DARGASSIES (1962) Le Nouveau-Né à Terme. Aspect Neurologique. *Biol. Neonat. (Basel)*, **4**, 174.

15. SCHULTE, F. J., MICHAELIS, R., LINKE, I., NOLTE, R. (1968) Nerve Conduction in Newborns. *Pediatrics*, **42**, 17.

CHAPTER 8

ASSESSMENT OF THE NEWBORN BABY

The Value of the Neurological Examination

Hardly a day passes in a large Obstetrical Unit without a child being born who gives some anxiety with regard to his immediate survival, and if he survives, with regard to the ultimate developmental prognosis. Toxaemia, hypertension, antepartum haemorrhage, prematurity, foetal anoxia and difficult labours remain regrettably common, and all of them greatly predispose to foetal abnormalities. Cyanotic attacks and convulsions are frequently seen in the newborn baby, and both these conditions are associated with a much higher incidence of abnormality in the baby than that found in normal infants. Craig[6] found a strong correlation between cerebral irritability in the newborn period with abnormalities in later months. Prechtl and his co-workers in Groningen[10, 24, 25, 26] have found an important correlation between neonatal hyperexcitability (with overactivity, exaggerated Moro reflex, and a low frequency high amplitude tremor of the lower limb), with the development of the choreiform syndrome in later years. This syndrome, as mentioned in Chapter 4, includes overactivity, learning difficulties, short attention span, negativism, and jerky movements of the limbs, tongue and eyes.

The value of the neurological examination for the assessment of maturity is obvious. One is frequently faced with the problem of deciding how much allowance, if any, should be made for prematurity in a smaller than usual child thought by the mother to have been born at the expected date.

The neurological examination is important for the study of the effect of trauma and anoxia on the baby[12, 25] and this may have a bearing on future obstetrical management.

The Assessment at Birth

Apgar described an interesting method of evaluating the infant at birth, and in a subsequent paper she described further experience with it. The method is in regular use at the Jessop Maternity Hospital, Sheffield, and in other centres in the United Kingdom,

144

TABLE 4
*Evaluation of the Newborn Infant One Minute after Birth**
(APGAR)

Score	Heart Rate	Respiratory Effort	Reflex Irritability	Muscle Tone	Colour
2	100-140	Normal cry	Normal	Good	Pink
1	<100	Irregular and shallow	Moderately depressed	Fair	Fair
0	No beat obtained	Apnoea for more than 60 sec.	Absent	Flaccid	Cyanotic

*Each type of observation scored as indicated. Total scores: 8-10, good;
3-7, fair; 0-2, poor condition.

and in several countries outside the United States. The score is
established 60 seconds after birth, and at 4 or 5 minutes.

There is certainly a striking correlation between the Apgar
score and the mortality. With a score of 0 to 2 the mortality is
15 per cent.; with a score of 10, the mortality is 0·13 per cent.[4]
It remains to be seen how the scoring method will correlate with
subsequent development. It would seem probable that in the
low score group there will be a high incidence of children subsequently shown to be handicapped.

We have found it useful to make serial Apgar scores.[16] At the
Jessop Hospital, Sheffield, we studied 85 babies with an Apgar
score of 4 or less at one minute, and rescored them at minute
intervals for 15 minutes after birth. In most babies the score
began to rise in a minute or two, and gradually reached normal.
In 11 babies, all born by Caesarian section, the score fell in the
first few minutes and then rose. 40 per cent. of the 85 babies
had a score of 4 or less at 5 minutes and 15 per cent. at 10 minutes.
The longer the score remained low, the worse was the prognosis.

We suggest that in asphyxiated babies it is useful to assess the
Apgar score at least at one minute, three minutes and 10 minutes.

Graham *et al*.[12, 13, 14] have described a more complex method of
evaluating the newborn baby. They have attempted to distinguish
normal from 'traumatised' babies by assessing the pain threshold,
the maturation scale, eye fixation, irritability and muscle tone.
The pain threshold was measured by the strength of electric
shock necessary to elicit a specified response (movement of the

stimulated foot or leg). The maturation scale consisted of the assessment of the strength of the grasp reflex, the persistence and vigour of movements, the pushing out of the feet and kicking movements, the auditory reaction, the response to irritation by cotton or paper over the nose, and the head posture in the prone.

The visual reactions consisted of unco-ordinated eye movements, fixation, pursuit, and the ease of elicitation, the direction and distance through which the eyes move in response to a stimulus. The irritability was assessed by the sensitivity to stimuli which cause crying, the tone of the cry, and the ease with which the child is quietened. The muscle tone was assessed by the amount of spontaneous movement of limbs in the relaxed state, the frequency of trembling and the degree of head lag when the child was pulled to the sitting position.

They carried out the tests on 265 infants without perinatal complications, and compared them with 81 infants suffering from anoxia, neonatal birth injury or diseases or infections associated with brain damage. The scores were statistically significantly different in the 2 groups. Previous attempts by the authors to correlate blood oxygen levels with the effects of delivery had failed, because it was found that the oxygen levels were too transitory and changeable.

Desmond et al.[9] found that prolonged pulsation of the umbilical artery after birth was associated with foetal distress, and carried with it a high mortality. This can presumably be explained by the fact that anoxia causes relaxation of the umbilical artery, as opposed to constriction.

The Neurological Examination

The aim of the examination is the detection of abnormality of the nervous system due to maldevelopment, injury or infection; the assessment of the maturity of the nervous system; and the estimation of the child's developmental potential.

The examination, as always, is preceded by a careful history. In this case the history concerns those factors which may affect the integrity and development of the nervous system. They include genetic factors, infection, drugs taken during pregnancy and the obstetrical history.

Before the examination one must determine other factors which affect the condition of the baby. These include the time of the last feed, the nature of drugs given in the preceding 24 hours, and any symptoms which suggest an abnormality. These include particularly convulsions, vomiting, cyanotic attacks, irritability or drowsiness.

Conduct of the Examination

The conduct of the examination must be standardised because many of the signs are influenced by both internal and external factors.[20, 27] If only one examination is carried out this should be delayed until the third day or later because the signs are particularly variable earlier than this. One examination is insufficient, however, and Mdme. Saint Anne Dargassies wrote that one looks for criteria of normality in the first 5 days, for criteria of maturity between 6 and 9 days, and for criteria of progression of development from 10 to 15 days.[28]

About two hours after the last feed the baby is usually sufficiently alert to be responsive to the tests and yet is not too fretful. He should be placed on a table sufficiently large to allow rolling from side to side without any risk of falling. The room should be adequately warm and reasonably draught free. There should be a good diffuse light.

It is often advantageous to carry out the examination in front of the mother, who gains confidence from seeing her baby handled, and any points which arise can then be discussed at once.

For the purposes of research, or for the evaluation of minor signs, the standard practice must be adhered to, but in the busy daily care of the newborn this may not be possible, and the examiner must select the most useful parts of the examination, concentrate upon the babies at risk,[20] and develop experience to avoid drawing conclusions from signs influenced by external factors.

The examination is carried out in the following sequence: observation; estimation of alertness; estimation of muscle tone; elicitation of special reflexes; examination of cranial nerves and special senses; and the performance of special tests.

Observation

Careful observation amply repays the time spent upon it. The examiner must train his powers of observation to be aware of the many significant signs which can be seen from the moment the baby is first approached and not just when he is placed on the examination table.

The following features in particular must be noted.

The Posture

The normal full term baby lies on his side with arms and legs flexed. Placed on his back he rolls to one side or the other. Placed prone the head is turned to one side so that his breathing is unrestricted. His limbs are flexed and the pelvis is raised from the couch with the knees drawn high up under the abdomen. When he is supported in ventral suspension gravity is stronger than the extensor tone, and the head, arms and legs hang downwards, usually with some flexion of the elbow and knee and some extension of the hip. In contrast, when held in dorsal suspension the stronger flexor tone counteracts the effects of gravity and the baby lies in a position of incomplete extension.

When the baby is placed in the supine position, and the arm is extended and then released, the arm returns to the flexed position. If the arm is flexed and then released, it extends.

When held inverted by the ankles, the hips and knees are flexed; the arms are flexed and adducted across the chest.

Full extension of the legs would suggest increased muscle tone. The froglike appearance of the younger premature infant in the supine position would suggest hypotonia. It must be remembered, however, that if the infant were born as a breech with extended legs, the infant is likely to keep the legs fully extended in the newborn period.

Opisthotonos is usually abnormal: but after a face presentation, the head is commonly arched back, so that the baby gives the appearance of opisthotonos. Muscle tone, however, would be normal, whereas in true opisthotonos one would expect to find hypertonia.

It is important to note asymmetry of posture. This may result from asymmetry of muscle tone (as in spastic hemiplegia), or from fracture of the clavicle or humerus, or from a brachial plexus injury.

The Cry

A good nurse unfailingly recognises the high-pitched cry of an abnormal baby. The paediatrician readily recognises the hoarse cry of a cretin, or the 'crie du chat' of the rare chromosome abnormality. The cry may be absent altogether, or excessive and continuous. The former would be abnormal, and the latter may be so.

The Movements

Movements are spontaneous or provoked. Spontaneous movements include tremors, twitchings and sudden shock-like movements without any apparent stimulus. The Moro and startle reflexes are examples of provoked movement. It is particularly important to note symmetry or asymmetry of movement.

Prechtl[25] described the hyperexcitable child as showing low frequency, high amplitude tremors, exaggerated reflexes, and a low threshold Moro reflex. There is apt to be a marked startle reflex on gently tapping the sternum. The McCarthy reflex is obtained by tapping the skull some distance from the supraorbital region. Some such babies are hyperkinetic and cry excessively. He described the apathetic baby as having a high threshold for stimulation of reflexes, some responses being absent altogether. Such infants move less than normal babies, show a decreased resistance to passive movements, and are difficult to arouse. Twitching and rapid rhythmical movements are usually abnormal, though occasional tremors of the chin are normal Dijkstra [10, 24] paid attention to the occurrence of a limb tremor of low frequency (about five per second) which correlates with the later development of the choreiform syndrome.

Wakefulness and Sleep

Abnormal babies are apt to sleep for excessively long periods.

Other Features

A thumb across the palm in a clenched hand is usually abnormal.

It is useful to note the respiratory movements, because irregularity of respiration and apnoeic periods (cyanotic attacks) are often associated with cerebral damage.

The face repays careful study. The baby with kernicterus has a wide-eyed, anxious expression, and the baby with hydrocephalus has a prominent forehead, bulging fontanelle, distension of the scalp veins, and a down turning of the eyes so that a complete superior rim of sclera can be seen, giving a 'setting sun' sign.

There may be a roving inco-ordinated movement of the eyes. Facial palsy should be noted.

Other features which are noticed during the observation period include the presence of congenital malformations, the colour, the presence of skin pigmentation and of naevi.

Estimation of Alertness

It is so important to correlate the findings of the neurological examination with the general condition of the baby that we find the next most useful step in the examination is to make an assessment of the alertness of the baby.

The following are useful criteria for assessing this.

(a) General appearance and facial expression.

(b) Spontaneous activity.

(c) Respiration.

(d) The response to noxious stimuli, for example, pinching the lobe of the ear to cause the head to turn away, and pricking the sole of the foot to cause withdrawal.

(e) Elicitation of oral reflexes.

(f) Observation of feeding.

Items (e) and (f) are considered further. The seeking and obtaining of the nipple, and the whole process of feeding, is a complex mechanism which repays careful observation. It is well known that early feeding difficulties are frequently encountered with mentally retarded children. It is interesting that Turoskaya suggested that this is because the oral reflexes in these cases do not acquire their purposeful character which normally occurs about the second day of life.

The ease of elicitation of the oral reflexes is a good test of the alertness of the baby. Persistent absence of the reflexes is abnormal and carries a poor prognosis.

Ingram[19] considered that individual feeding reflexes give relatively little information about the state of maturation of the infant's nervous system. There are great variations in the ease with which the reflexes can be elicited, not only between one baby and another, and between one time and another, but with regard to the age at which the reflexes disappear.

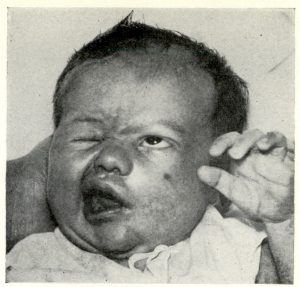

Fig. 51
Facial palsy.

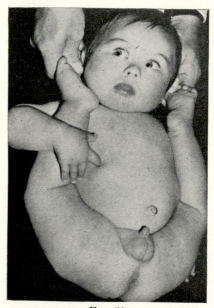

Fig. 52
Mongol, showing mark hypotonia.

facing page 150

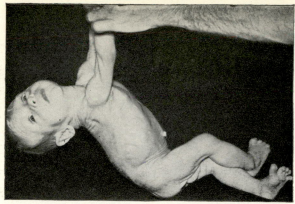

Fig. 53

Defective child with severe head lag, age 8 weeks.

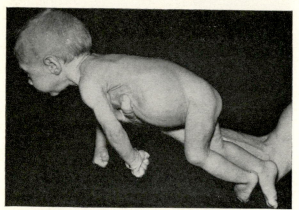

Fig. 54

Same child, with deceptive excessive extensor tone, giving impression of good head control in ventral suspension.

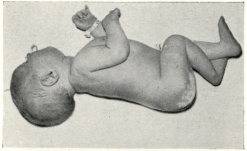

Fig. 55

Face presentation. Characteristic position, resembling opisthotonos, but muscle tone normal. Age 4 weeks.

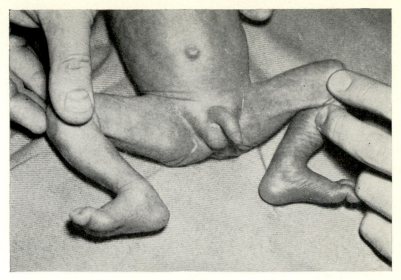

FIG. 56
Abduction of hip.

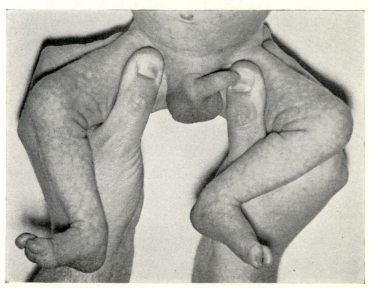

FIG. 57
Method of testing for subluxation of hips (Stage 1).

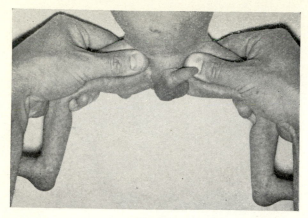

FIG. 58
Method of testing for subluxation of hips (Stage 2).

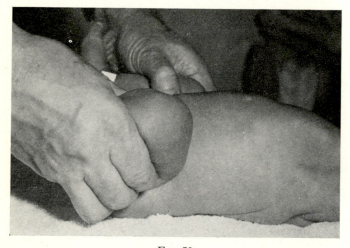

FIG. 59
Method of testing for subluxation of hips. The baby lies on his back
with the hips and knees flexed and the middle finger of each hand is
placed over each greater trochanter.

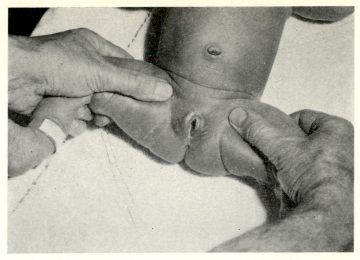

FIG. 60

Method of testing for subluxation of hips. The thumb of each hand is applied to the inner side of the thigh opposite the lesser trochanter.

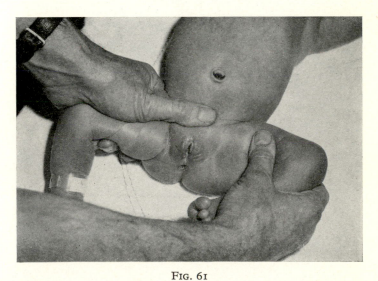

FIG. 61

Method of testing for subluxation of hips. In a doubtful case the pelvis may be steadied between a thumb over the pubis and fingers under the sacrum while the hip is tested with the other hand.

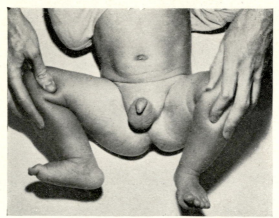

FIG. 62

Subluxated left hip, showing limited abduction.

Estimation of Muscle Tone

Muscle tone is difficult to define. It is that condition of the muscle, determined by physical, chemical, and nervous influences, which, although it is not an active contraction, determines the body posture, the range of movement at joints, and the feel of the muscle.[15] Tone is examined in the following way.

(a) Observation of posture. Posture is determined by the distribution of muscle tone, and already in observing the baby an impression will have been made as to whether flexor or extensor tone predominates.

(b) Consistency of the muscles. The muscles are gently squeezed between the finger and thumb, and the resistance is graded as normal, increased or decreased. If the consistency of the babies' muscle is always compared to the consistency of one's own muscle in the first interosseus space between the thumb and index finger, it is soon possible to use this as a standard for fairly accurate subjective judgements.

(c) Estimation of the range of movement. This is reduced in hypertonia and increased in hypotonia. Several of the manoeuvres used for assessing maturity are really methods of assessing muscle tone, which is less in a premature baby than in a full term one.

The range of movement should be estimated in the neck—by rotating the head, flexing it and extending it, and bending it sideways. When the child is held in the sitting position, the child should be able to raise the head a little; when he is half pulled to the sitting position, he should be able to raise it momentarily. The range in the shoulder muscles should be determined by eliciting the anterior and posterior scarf signs. The range in the elbows, wrists, hips, knees and ankles should be estimated in the usual way. In estimating the range of movement in the hip, it is advisable to use a constant method, e.g. flexing the hips to a right angle before abducting them. Normally the knees in a newborn infant should touch or almost touch the examination table. Abduction of the hip is restricted in hypertonia (and is almost invariably found in the spastic form of cerebral palsy), congenital subluxation of the hip, and occasionally in older children due to contracture of the adductor muscles.

It was stated that extension of the knees with the hips fully flexed is complete in premature babies, but not in full term ones, unless they were born as breech with extended legs.

11

Flexion of the knee in the prone position with the hip extended gives an indication of the tone of the quadriceps muscle.

Reduced dorsiflexion of the foot is almost invariable in the spastic form of cerebral palsy, and is therefore a most important sign to elicit.

The tone of the trunk muscles is estimated by flexing the hip on the thorax and by bending it sideways. It is also estimated by holding the baby in the supine position with one's hand under the back. In ventral suspension, excessive muscle tone may give the wrong impression of unusually good 'head control' (Fig. 54). The tone of the trunk muscles is also determined in the 'redressement du tronc' test (Ch. 7).

(d) The resistance to passive movement. In hypertonic infants, the excessive resistance to passive movement is readily determined.

(e) The recoil. The arms are extended, and then suddenly released. There should be a brisk flexion at the elbow. In hypotonic or apathetic babies, there may be no response at all.

(f) 'Flapping' the limb—the French 'Passivité'. The proximal part of the limb is shaken in order to produce rapid 'flapping' of the hand or foot. This test presumably measures the excitability and strength of the stretch reflexes, because normally the muscles tense and quickly arrest the flapping movements after a few beats. It is easy to detect hypotonia or hypertonia by this test.

A corresponding test is used in the older baby for testing head control. When he has been pulled to the sitting position, the body is wobbled from side to side in order to assess the degree of lateral movement of the head. By the age of six months this should be minimal. At four months the lateral movement is considerable.

(g) The tendon jerks and ankle clonus (Ch. 6). The briskness of the tendon reflexes, and the area over which the reflex can be obtained, give an indirect idea of the muscle tone in spastic children. A well-sustained ankle clonus is a good confirmatory sign of suspected spasticity—though the sign is by no means always significant, for it may disappear a few weeks after birth.

Whatever the method used, it is essential to note the symmetry of the muscle tone. Asymmetry is more important than increased but symmetrically increased tone.

Hypotonia is important because it has a vital bearing on the assessment of motor development. For a full review of the causes of hypotonia the reader is referred to the papers by Dubowitz.[11]

Hypotonia involving the lower limbs alone may be due to a meningomyelocele or diastematomyelia. It follows that the back of the child must be examined with these two conditions in mind. One also routinely examines the whole of the midline of the back for a congenital dermal sinus. A sinus in the cervical, dorsal or lumbar region, sometimes revealed by a tuft of hair or patch of pigmentation, may pass right through to the subarachnoid space, and cause recurrent meningitis or other neurological signs. There is a rare form of cerebral palsy in which in the early weeks there is hypotonia with signs of mental subnormality.

There are considerable variations in muscle tone in normal children. It must not be assumed that because muscle tone is greater than usual, organic disease is necessarily present.

The Hips

Up to the age of about two, the routine examination of any child includes examination of the hips, in order to exclude congenital dislocation. This is not strictly part of the developmental examination, but estimation of the range of abduction of the hips is part of the routine examination, and if the range is restricted, one has to distinguish the two commonest causes— hypertonia and dislocation.

Certain factors increase the risk that the child will have a dislocated hip. These are as follows:–

Family history of dislocated hip.

Geographical factors. (Dislocation is particularly common in Northern Italy.)

Breech delivery.

Severe hypotonia—as in meningomyelocele.

Severe spasticity.

Bilateral talipes in a girl.

Arthrogryposis.

Many articles have been written about the diagnosis of congenital dislocation of the hip in the newborn infant.

I feel confused by the description of the tests given in most of these papers, largely because of the use of the words backwards, forwards, upwards, and downwards. Hence I asked my orthopaedic colleague, J. Sharrard, F.R.C.S. to describe the principle tests in simple words which I could readily understand. Below is his wording:–

"1. *Ortolani's Test*. The child is laid on his back with the hips flexed to a right angle and the knees flexed. Starting with the knees together the hips are slowly abducted and if one is dislocated, somewhere in the 90 degrees arc of abduction the head of the femur slips back into the acetabulum with a visible and palpable click. This test can be done at any age but a click may not be produced in many babies particularly in the newborn period.

2. *Barlow's Test*. The baby is laid on his back. The hips are flexed to a right angle and the knees are fully flexed. The middle finger of each hand is placed over the greater trochanter and the thumb of each hand is applied to the inner side of the thigh close to but not quite in the groin. The hips are carried into abduction. With the hips in about 70 degrees of abduction the middle finger of each hand in turn exerts pressure away from the examining couch as if to push the trochanter towards the symphysis pubis. In a normal child no movement occurs. If the hip is dislocated, the greater trochanter and the head of the femur with it can be felt to move in the direction in which the pressure has been applied.

3. *Barlow's Test—Part 2*. With the hips in the same position as described in the last paragraph, the thumb, which is applied over the upper and inner part of the thigh, exerts pressure towards the examination couch. In a normal child no movement occurs. In a child with a dislocatable hip the head of the femur can be felt to slip out and to come back immediately the pressure is released".

After 4 or 5 weeks, the best single sign of subluxation or dislocation of the hip is limited abduction, with the hips flexed to a right angle.

The main causes of limited abduction of the hip are as follows:–

Normal variation. The hips of some normal babies abduct further than those of others. In part this is due to differences in muscle tone, but it also depends on the ligaments of the hip.

Increased muscle tone (in the adductors). As always, it is impossible to draw the line between the normal and the abnormal. Increased muscle tone is the most common reason

for unusually limited abduction of the hip in babies seen in
a well baby clinic.

Pathological hypertonia (cerebral palsy, usually of the spastic
type).

Subluxation of the hip.

Coxa Vara.

A variety of hip diseases.

Muscle contracture—mainly in hypotonic babies and children
who lie constantly in one position.

Examination of the Cranial Nerves

NERVES 2, 3, 4 and 6. The study of ocular movements in babies
is extremely difficult. Gross faults can usually be recognised,
using in particular the response to rotation (Ch. 6), and the Doll's
eye response. The reaction to light and the blink responses are
tested. Ophthalmoscopic examination of the eye is a necessary
part of the examination in a child suspected of being abnormal.

André Thomas used the following test for vision.[1, 2] The child is
held vertically, facing the dark part of the room. He is then
turned on his body axis to make him face the lighted part of the
room. The head and eyes turn more quickly to this part of the
room. The eye which is nearer to the window opens wider.
Finally the head and eyes are raised towards the sky. The child
is rotated further so that he turns away from the source of light.
His head and eyes do not follow the rest of the body as long as
the light is perceptible. They return to their original position as
soon as the light gives way to darkness.

Paine[23] used another rotation test. The baby is held facing
the examiner, who rotates two or three times (Fig. 152).
The baby opens his eyes. The eyes deviate in the direction of
movement as long as the rotation continues, and rotatory
nystagmus in the opposite direction occurs when the movement
stops. The responses are incomplete if there is weakness of the
ocular muscles or defective vision. Vision can also be tested by
the use of a revolving drum on which stripes have been
painted; the presence of nystagmus indicates that vision is present.

A good description of the methods used to test 7 day old babies
was given by Boston workers.[5] One to two hours after a feed
the infants were tested by a bright red two inch diameter ball
suspended by a rubber band 6-10 inches from the face. The ball

was moved slowly in different directions. One examiner handled the baby while two examiners observed the degree of horizontal and vertical deviation of the eyes, the duration of responsiveness and the associated head movements. Opticokinetic responses to a special moving drum were also recorded. The capacity to fix, follow and alert to the visual stimulus provided good evidence of an intact visual apparatus.

Newborn infants tend to keep the eyes closed when one tries to examine them, and any attempt to retract the eyelids makes the baby close the eyes all the more tightly. Babies may be induced to open the eyes by inducing sucking, or by swinging them round in one's hands.

Abnormalities which one may note in the neurological examination include fixation of the pupils, conjugate deviation of the eyes, slow lateral movements, or marked strabismus. Nystagmus (lateral, vertical or rotatory) is abnormal if it is sustained. The so-called 'setting sun sign', so commonly seen in the presence of hydrocephalus, may be entirely normal.

NERVE 5

The cardinal points reflex depends on the sensory tracts of this nerve.

NERVE 7

Facial weakness is detected when the baby is crying, feeding, or being tested for various facial and oral reflexes.

NERVE 8

Newborn babies respond to a loud sound by a startle reaction, a facial grimace, blinking, gross motor movements, quieting if crying, or crying if quiet, opening the eyes if they are closed, inhibiting their sucking responses, or by a catch in the respirations. There may be a change in the heart rate, as demonstrated by the cardiotachometer, and changes in the E.E.G.

NERVES 9, 10 and 12

A clue to lesions of these nerves will be obtained by noting abnormalities of the palate and tongue movements, the gag reflex and swallowing, and the cry.

NERVE 11

The strength of the sternomastoids and trapezii is usually apparent on inspection, and on rotation of the head.

The Primitive Reflexes

The most important reflexes to be tested are the asymmetrical tonic neck reflex, the Moro and grasp reflexes, the trunk incurvation reflex, and the crossed extension reflex. Others are examined in doubtful cases. Perhaps the main value of the asymmetrical tonic neck reflex is to be found after the newborn period, for its persistence after 2 or 3 months is abnormal, and found especially in cerebral palsy.

The trunk incurvation reflex is assessed with regard to symmetry.

Prechtl[26] has shown that in the case of a vertex delivery, stimulation of the foot by a pin causes flexion of the knee, hip and foot: in a breech with extended legs, it causes extension instead of flexion.

The Tendon Jerks

In our opinion the examination of tendon jerks is of considerable value. The most useful, and the easiest to test, are the biceps and supinator jerks, and the knee jerks. They may be absent in a severely shocked child, or in a child who has had brain injury. They are likely to be considerably exaggerated in the spastic form of cerebral palsy. In diseases of the pyramidal tracts the area over which the tendon jerks are obtained is greatly increased —just as in older children the area over which the plantar response is obtained is increased. Consequently one begins to test for the biceps jerk over the shoulder, and tap at intervals until the actual biceps tendon is reached. One begins to test for the knee jerk by tapping over the dorsum of the foot. One taps at intervals up the leg until the patellar tendon is reached. A brisk response over the shoulder may be the only indication that there is involvement of the upper limbs in a child previously thought to have a spastic paraplegia: a brisk response over the dorsum of the foot raises the suspicion of the spastic form of cerebral palsy. In all cases the symmetry of muscle tone or of tendon jerks is likely to indicate neurological damage.

Use can be made of the reflexes to make various muscle groups contract in order to detect muscle weakness.

In all cases one must remember that variation in a single reflex response is not necessarily abnormal. The response must be interpreted in association with the findings. One should determine how long a reflex remains abnormal. Apparent variations from the normal may be temporary only and must certainly not be taken to indicate permanent neurological disease.

Measurement of the Circumference of the Head

An essential part of the assessment of any baby is the measurement of the maximum circumference of the head (with the tape measure round the forehead and occiput). It is essential to use a non-elastic tape measure or one which does not stretch. Head measurement in this way should be part of the routine examination of every baby in a well-run baby clinic, general practice surgery, or hospital, just as much as examination of the hips for congenital subluxation or dislocation. When one is in doubt about its significance, one plots the figure obtained on a chart which shows the mean and the 10th and 90th percentile. If there is still doubt about the normality of the figure, serial measurements are essential, so that one can plot the rate of growth of the head. Figs. 63-66 show examples. In Figure 63 serial head measurements strongly suggest the development of microcephaly. Figure 64 shows the chart of a normal small sized infant with a correspondingly small head growing at a normal speed. Figure 65 shows the development of hydrocephalus.

The assessment of the head size cannot be made on the measurement of the maximum circumference alone. The head measurement must be related to the size of the baby as a whole. It is obvious that a large baby is likely to have a larger head than a small baby, and a small baby is likely to have a smaller head than a big baby. In a study of 1000 babies at the Jessop Hospital, Sheffield, seen at birth, 6 weeks, 6 months and ten months, we related the head circumference to the weight (Illingworth, 1965). It was shown that the average head circumference and weight was as follows:

	Males Head Circumference		Weight		Females Head Circumference		Weight	
	Inches	Cm.	lbs. and ozs.	Grammes	Inches	Cm.	lbs. and ozs.	Grammes
Birth	13·7	34·8	7·5	3180	13·8	35·0	7·5	3180
6 weeks	15·3	38·9	10·13	4860	14·9	37·8	10·0	4500
6 months	17·5	44·4	18·12	8520	17·0	43·2	17·7	7840
10 months	18·4	46·7	22·2	10,460	17·9	45·5	20·1	9380

It was then found, in studying the graphs in which head circumference was plotted against weight, that one could calculate the average head circumference for unusually small or large babies by subtracting or adding the following to or from the head circumference for each pound above or below the average weight:

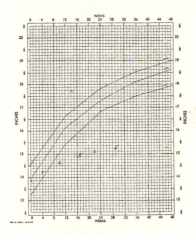

FIG. 63. Developing signs of microcephaly.

	Males		Females	
	Inches	Cm.	Inches	Cm.
Birth	$\frac{1}{3}$	0·8	$\frac{1}{4}$	0·6
6 weeks	$\frac{1}{4}$	0·6	$\frac{1}{4}$	0·6
6 months	$\frac{1}{8}$	0·3	$\frac{1}{8}$	0·3
10 months	$\frac{1}{10}$	0·3	$\frac{1}{10}$	0·3

Figure 66 shows a chart of a normal baby. At about the tenth week he began to grow rapidly in size (length and weight), and the head circumference grew at a corresponding rate. It would be easy, in such a case, to suspect the development of hydrocephalus.

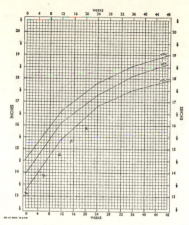

FIG. 64. Normal child with small head.

Dean[8] found that the relationship between the circumference of the head and that of the chest was useful for assessing children with severe malnutrition. Normally the circumference of the head is greater than that of the chest until the age of 6 months, and smaller thereafter. Dean found that in malnutrition the measurement least affected was the head circumference, and that the head is nearly always larger than usual in relation to the size of the infant as a whole.

The examination of the head includes not only the measurement of head circumference. One automatically palpates the anterior fontanelle and the degree of separation of the sutures.

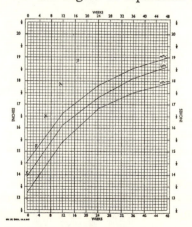

FIG. 65. Developing signs of hydrocephalus.

One also assesses the shape, remembering, however, that some degree of asymmetry is exceedingly common and entirely normal. Severe degrees, due to craniostenosis, hypertelorism and other conditions, are another matter. Although the maximum circumference is of great importance, it is not the only feature which matters. One pays more attention to the shape of the head. The head of a microcephalic child tapers off towards the vertex, and there is often a sloping forehead. Some children have what can only be called a badly-shaped head—the sort of head which one knows from experience is rather likely to be associated with poor mental development. This includes in particular the flat occiput.

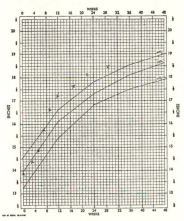

FIG. 66.   The chart at one stage suggested the development of hydrocephalus. In fact the rapid increase in the size of the head coincided with a rapid spurt in the growth of the baby as a whole.

A skull may be broad in the lateral direction, and narrow from back to front. In such a case the maximum circumference is greater than one would guess. I suspect that a head of this shape is more likely than more usual heads to be associated with mental subnormality.

The importance of the head measurement lies in the obvious fact that the head size depends largely on the growth in the size of the cranial contents, and therefore, on the size of the brain (unless there is another abnormality such as hydrocephalus). If the brain is not growing at a normal rate, the cranial circumference is likely to be small. It should be remembered, however, that some defective children have a large head (without hydrocephalus): they may have megalencephaly or hydranencephaly.

Microcephaly is usually found in children with fairly severe or severe mental deficiency when the defect dates from birth or

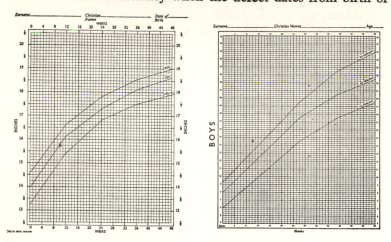

FIG. 67.   Head circumference chart, showing apparently 'normal' head circumference. In fact the child was a microcephalic. See Fig. 68.

FIG. 68. Weight chart, same child as Fig. 67. Child well above average weight. Head circumference small in relation to weight.

before birth. When a child develops normally for the first few months, and then develops mental deficiency as a result of some postnatal factor, the appearance of the head depends on the age of onset of the mental deficiency. The brain reaches half the adult size by the age of 9 months and three-quarters by the age of 2 years. If severe mental deficiency develops any time in the first year, microcephaly is likely to appear: if it develops after that, the head size is likely to remain normal.   This is an interesting differential feature between mental deficiency of early onset and that of later onset.

It must always be remembered that an unusually small head circumference by no means necessarily signifies mental deficiency. It may be a genetic trait. An open fontanelle in an older infant with a small head (*e.g.* in an infant of 9 to 12 months of age) is a useful indication that the child has not true microcephaly. Microcephaly must also be distinguished from craniostenosis by palpation and X-ray study of the sutures. In the same way an unusually large head may be merely a familial feature. One may summarise the causes of unusual head size in the following way:–

Small head:

Small size of the baby.
Familial feature.
Mental subnormality (microcephaly).
Craniostenosis.

Large head:

Large size of baby.
Familial feature.
Hydrocephalus.
Megalencephaly.
Hydranencephaly.

It is particularly important to note two other points. Firstly, the prematurely born baby has a relatively larger head than a full term baby; and secondly, an older infant with severe malnutrition (or the 'failure to thrive syndrome') has a relatively large head, because the brain (and therefore the skull size) suffers less from malnutrition than the rest of the body. I have several times seen wrong diagnoses of hydrocephalus made because one of these two points had been forgotten. The more usual mistakes are to fail to relate the head size to the size of the baby, or to fail to look at the mother and father for a familial explanation of a child's unusually small or large head.

Table 5 gives the mean head circumference at different ages

TABLE 5

Mean Head Circumference

(WESTROP AND BARBER[20])

Age	Boys Mean			Girls Mean		
	Inches	Cm.	σ	Inches	Cm.	σ
1 month	14·7	37·3	1·54	14·3	36·5	1·41
3 months	16·1	40·7	1·43	15·6	39·8	1·39
6 „	17·2	43·6	1·45	16·7	42·5	1·42
9 „	18·0	45·7	1·40	17·6	44·6	1·41
1 year	18·4	46·8	1·40	17·9	45·6	1·30
1½ years	18·9	47·9	1·40	18·5	47·0	1·32
2 „	19·4	49·1	1·47	18·8	48·0	1·35
3 „	19·8	50·4	1·35	19·6	49·5	1·45

The average skull circumference in premature babies was given by Crosse (1957).   Her figures are as follows:–

Duration of Gestation	Inches	Cm.
28	11	25
32	11·5	29
36	12·8	32
40	14·0	35

Table shows the mean head circumference from birth onwards.

MUSCLE TONE. Muscle Tone is estimated in the following way:

i) The muscle is palpated. The flabbiness of a hypotonic limb is obvious to the feel.

ii) The resistance to passive movement is estimated—in all four limbs, and in the neck muscles. Voluntary resistance to the movement has to be recognised.

iii) The range of movement is determined, especially in the knees, elbows, hips and ankles.

The range is usually increased in hypotonia and reduced in hypertonia.

The Minimum Examination

It is not always possible to carry out a full examination, either because the condition of the baby will not permit this, or more usually because of shortage of time.

The following is the minimum examination of the newborn baby from the neurological aspect:–

Observation of the face, eyes, quantity and symmetry of movements and the posture.

Palpation of the anterior fontanelle and cranial sutures.

Estimation of the muscle tone.

The Moro and grasp reflexes.

The knee jerks.

The measurement of the head circumference.

Examination of the hips.

Examination of the back for a congenital dermal sinus or other abnormality.

If there is doubt whether there is hydrocephalus or not, the examination will include transillumination of the skull.

Investigation, where relevant, include a subdural tap if an effusion is suspected, or rarely an E.E.G. or E.M.G.

The routine examination of any newborn baby includes screening for phenylketonuria by one of the methods of estimating the serum phenylalanine, and possibly other metabolic defects.

The Interpretation

The greater one's experience of developmental assessment, the more difficult it appears to become. This applies especially to the assessment in the newborn period.

The main difficulty is that abnormal neurological signs detected in the newborn period or in the early weeks may completely or almost completely disappear. For instance, the range of muscle tone varies widely in normal babies. All that one can say is that the further away from the average a child is in any feature, the less likely is he to be normal. Excessive tone may be a temporary phenomenon, and so may hypotonia, unless it is severe. One pays more attention to asymmetry of tone, but even quite marked degrees of asymmetry of tone, suggestive of a spastic hemiplegia, may disappear in a few weeks. Exaggerated knee jerks and even a well sustained ankle clonus by no means signifies a permanent physical defect. One pays a great deal more attention to a combination of abnormal signs than to a single one. I would pay no attention to exaggerated tendon jerks in an otherwise normal baby. I would regard a well sustained ankle clonus merely as an indication for examination at a later date, and I certainly would not even hint to the mother that there might be an abnormality. If, however, a baby in addition to displaying a well sustained ankle clonus had a small head circumference in relation to his weight, or showed delayed motor development, or had not begun to smile at his mother by six weeks (if full term), then I would certainly suspect an abnormality. I would also be influenced by a history of important 'risk factors' (page 325). For instance, if a baby showed exaggerated muscle tone, and had suffered hypoglycaemic convulsions, or had been a small premature baby, or was one of twins, I would be much more suspicious that the child was abnormal. On the other hand, one must remember that babies who suffered severe anoxia at birth are quite likely to be entirely normal in later months and years.

Amongst many impressive examples of recovery after displaying grossly abnormal signs in the newborn period are the following:–

(a) A baby with suprabulbar palsy whose mother had had hydramnios. He had signs of spastic quadriplegia, with well sustained ankle clonus, exaggerated tendon jerks, excessive muscle tone and tightly clenched hands. He had to be sucked out every 10 to 15 minutes for the first few weeks. By 12 weeks the sign of spasticity had largely disappeared. By 6 months the only residual sign was a slight abnormal hand approach to an object. At 10 years he was entirely normal, though there was a trivial tremor in the hands within normal limits. His progress at a normal school was average. In a paper on dysphagia I have described other examples of the complete disappearance of dysphagia due to bulbar palsy or inco-ordination of the swallowing mechanism.

(b) A child with typical signs of spastic hemiplegia in the first three months, one arm being notably stiff and relatively immobile. At the age of 12 years the only residual sign was a unilateral extensor plantar response, with no symptoms.

(c) Unilateral hypertonia in the early weeks. At school age no sign or symptom apart from slight general clumsiness.

As already stated, one can never be quite sure that when abnormal signs have disappeared a few weeks after birth, fine tests of manual or other motor dexterity will not in later years reveal some degree of abnormality.

If the child had neonatal convulsions, the outlook depends in large part on the cause of the convulsions. If they were due to hypoglycaemia, there is much more likely to be residual abnormality than if they were due to hypocalcaemia. Hypoglycaemia may itself be a manifestation of an underlying brain defect. Severe hyperbilirubinaemia should now no longer occur; but if it does, the child is at grave risk of being abnormal later.

Signs which are particularly liable to be followed by a permanent disability include the following:–

A shrill or high pitched cry.

A head circumference which is unusually small or large in relation to the size of the baby, when there is no relevant familial factor.

Excessive drowsiness or apathy.
Opisthotonos.
Excessive irritability.
Absence of the Moro reflex, oral reflexes, or blink reflexes.

Summary

The minimum neurological examination of the newborn baby has been described, together with details for more full examination. The minimum examination must include observation of the child's face, eyes, movements and posture, palpation of the anterior fontanelle, examination for the Moro, grasp reflexes, and the knee jerks; measurement of the maximum head circumference; examination of the hip movements and of the back for a congenital abnormality. It will include a test for phenylketonuria.

It is emphasised that abnormal neurological signs may disappear. One pays much more attention to a combination of abnormal signs than to a single one.

REFERENCES

1. ANDRÉ-THOMAS, SAINT-ANNE DARGASSIES (1952) *Études neurologiques sur le nouveau-né et le jeune nourisson.* Paris. Masson.
2. ANDRÉ-THOMAS, CHESNI, Y., SAINT-ANNE DARGASSIES (1960) The Neurological Examination of the Infant. *Little Club Clinics in Developmental Medicine.* No. 1. London. National Spastics Society.
3. APGAR, V. (1953) A Proposal for a New Method of Evaluation of the Newborn Infant. *Anaesth. Analg.*, **32**, 260.
4. APGAR, V., HOLADAY, D. A., JAMES, L. S., WEISBROT, I. M., BERRIEN, C. (1958) Evaluation of the Newborn Infant—Second Report. *J. Amer. med. Ass.*, **168**, 1985.
5. BRAZELTON, T. B., SCHOLL, M. L., ROBEY, J. S. (1966) Visual Responses in the Newborn. *Pediatrics*, **37**, 284.
6. CRAIG, W. S. (1950) Intracranial Irritation in the Newborn: Immediate and Long Term Prognosis. *Arch. Dis. Childh.*, **25**, 325.
7. CROSSE, V. M. (1957) *The Premature Baby.* London: Churchill.
8. DEAN, R. F. A. (1965) Effects of Malnutrition, Especially of Slight Degree, on the Growth of Young Children. *Courrier de Centre L'Enfance*, **15**, 73.
9. DESMOND, M. M., KAY, J. L., MEGARITY, A. L. (1959) The Phases of Transitional Distress Occurring in Neonates in Association with Prolonged Postnatal Umbilical Cord Pulsations. *J. Pediat.*, **55**, 131.
10. DIJKSTRA, J. (1960) *De Prognostische Cetekenis van Neurologische le Afwijkingen by Pasgeboren Kinderen Thesis.* Groningen.
11. Dubowitz, V. (1969) *The Floppy Infant. Clinics in Developmental Medicine.* London: Heinemann (In press).

12. GRAHAM, F. K., MATARAZZO, R. G., CALDWELL, B. M. (1956) Behavioural Differences between Normal and Traumatized Newborns. *Psychol. Monogr.* **70** Nos. 427, 428.

13. GRAHAM, F. K. (1956) Behavioural Difference between Normal and Traumatized Newborns. *Psychol. Monogr.*, **70**, 1, 17.

14. GRAHAM, F. K., PENNOYER, M. M., CALDWELL, B. M., GREENMAN, M., HARTMANN, A. F. (1957) Relation between Clinical Status and Behaviour Test Performance in a Newborn. Group with Histories suggesting Anoxia. *J. Pediat.*, **50**, 177, 556.

15. HOLT, K. S. (1963) The Measurement of Muscle Tone and Posture. To be published.

16. HOLT, K. S., GEEFHUYSEN, S. The Apgar Scoring System. *Develop. med. Child. Neurol.*, **4**, 343.

17. ILLINGWORTH, R. S., LUTZ, W. (1965) The Measurement of the Infants' Head Circumference and its Significance. *Arch. Dis. Childh.*, **40**, 672.

18. ILLINGWORTH, R. S. (1969) Sucking and Swallowing Problems in Infancy: The Diagnostic Problem of Dysphagia. *Arch. Dis. Childh.* (In press).

19. INGRAM, T. T. S. (1962) Clinical Significance of the Infantile Feeding Reflexes. *Develop. med. Child. Neurol.*, **4**, 159.

20. IRWIN, O. C. (1933) Motility in Young Infants, I Relation to Body Temperature, II Relation to Two Indices of Nutritional Status. *Amer. J. Dis. Childh.*, **45**, 531, 534.

21. LINDON, R. L. (1961) Risk Register. *Cerebr. Palsy Bull.*, **3**, 481.

22. MINKOWSKI, A., SAINT-ANNE DARGASSIES, S. (1956) Le Retentissement de l'Anoxie Foetale sur le Systeme Nerveux Central. *Rev. franc. Etud. clin. biol.*, **1**, 531.

23. PAINE, R. S. (1960) Neurological Examination of Infants and Children. *Ped. Clin. N. Am.*, **7**, 471.

24. PRECHTL, H. F. R., STEMMER, Ch. J. (1962) The Choreiform Syndrome in Children. *Develop. Med. child. Neurol.*, **4**, 119.

25. PRECHTL, H. F. R. (1961) *Little Club Clin. develop. med.*, No. 2.

26. PRECHTL, H. F. R. (1961) In Foss, B. M. *Determinants of Infant Behaviour.* London: Methuen.

27. RICHARDS, T. W. (1936) The Importance of Hunger in the Bodily Activity of the Neonate. *Psychol. Bull.*, **33**, 817.

28. SAINT-ANNE DARGASSIES (1962) Le Nouveau-né à Terme. *Aspect neurol. Biol. neo-natal.*, **4**, 174.

29. SHARRARD, J. W. J. (1969) Personal Communication.

30. TUROSKAYA, A. (1957) Nature of Sucking Movement in Babies. *Akad. Ped. Nauk. R.S.F.S.R.*, **2**, 105.

31. WESTROP, C. K., BARBER, C. R. (1956) Growth of the Skull in Young Children. *J. Neurol. Psychiat.*, **19**, 52.

CHAPTER 9

NORMAL DEVELOPMENT

THE PRINCIPLES OF DEVELOPMENT

These may be summarised as follows:

1. Development is a continuous process, from conception to maturity. This means that development occurs in utero, and birth is merely an event in the course of development, though it signals the beginning of extraneous environmental factors. As far as is known at present, a baby born, say 3 months prematurely, is developmentally the same 3 months after birth as a baby born at term.

2. The sequence of development is the same in all children, but the rate of development varies from child to child. For example, a child has to learn to sit before he can learn to walk, but the age at which children learn to sit and to walk varies considerably.

There is a sequence of development within each developmental field, but the development in one field does not necessarily run parallel with that in another. For instance, though the stages in the development in grasping and in locomotion (sitting and walking) are clearly delineated, development in one field may be far more rapid than in another. A child with cerebral palsy involving the lower limbs only will be late in learning to walk, but if his intelligence is normal the development of manipulation will be up to the average. I have termed this lack of parallelism between different fields of development 'Dissociation'[9].

3. Development is intimately related to the maturation of the nervous system. For instance, no amount of practice can cause a child to walk until his nervous system is ready for it.

4. Generalised mass activity is replaced by specific individual responses. For instance, whereas the young infant wildly moves his trunk, arms and legs, and pants with excitement when he sees something interesting which he wants, the older infant merely smiles and reaches for it.

5. Development is in the cephalocaudal direction. The first step towards walking is the development of head control—of strength in the neck muscles. The infant can do much with his hands before he can walk. He can crawl, pulling himself forward with his hands, before he can creep, using hands and knees.

6. Certain primitive reflexes, such as the grasp reflex and walking reflex, have to be lost before the corresponding voluntary movement is acquired.

THE SEQUENCE OF DEVELOPMENT

In the section to follow I shall outline the sequence of development in locomotion, manipulation, and other fields, basing it almost entirely on the work of Arnold Gesell.

In all cases the figures given are average ones. Most children will acquire the skills a little earlier or later than the dates given. They refer to full term babies: for prematurely born babies, an appropriate addition must be made to the ages mentioned in the sections to follow.

In order to avoid overlapping and confusion, I have combined a description of the normal course of development with the results of developmental tests. The equipment needed for these tests and the method of testing will be discussed in Chapter 13.

The Development of Locomotion

Every child goes through an orderly sequence of development, from the development of head control, to the stage of mature walking, running, and skipping. The development of locomotion can be observed when the infant is held in ventral suspension, when he is placed in the prone position, and when he is pulled to the sitting position. Subsequently it is seen in the sitting and upright posture. For a full discussion of the sequence of development in the prone position, the reader should refer to Gesell and Ames.[5]

VENTRAL SUSPENSION. When the newborn baby is held off the couch in the prone position with the hand under the abdomen, there is an almost complete lack of head control. By 6 weeks, however, he reaches an important and easily determined milestone, when he momentarily holds the head in the same plane as the rest of the body. By 8 weeks he can maintain this position, and by 12 weeks he can maintain the head well beyond the plane of the rest of the body. After this age the position of ventral suspension is not used for assessing head control in normal babies.

The position of the limbs in the young infant is of importance. By 4 weeks the elbows are largely flexed, and there is some extension of the hips with flexion of the knees.

Summary

Newborn	Head hangs completely down.
4 weeks	Head momentarily lifted up. Elbows flexed. Some extension of hips and flexion of knees.
6 weeks	Head held momentarily in same plane as rest of body.
8 weeks	Head maintained in same plane as rest of body: momentarily lifted beyond this.
12 weeks	Head maintained well beyond plane of rest of body.

PRONE. The newborn baby lies with his head turned to one side, the pelvis high and the knees drawn up under the abdomen. As he matures the pelvis becomes lower and the hip and knees extend. By 4 weeks he can momentarily lift the chin off the couch, and by 6 weeks he momentarily lifts the chin off so that the plane of the face is at an angle of 45 degrees to the couch. By 12 weeks he holds the chin and shoulders off the couch, with the legs fully extended. Soon he lifts the front part of his chest off the couch, so that the plane of the face is at 90 degrees to it, bearing his weight on the forearms. By 24 weeks he keeps the chest and upper part of the abdomen off the couch, maintaining his weight on the hands with extended elbows. He rolls from prone to supine, and a month later from supine to prone. He shows the 'frog' position, with the legs abducted, the soles of the feet coming together. By 28 weeks he can bear the weight on one hand. He can usually crawl by 9 months, though the first stage is accidental progression backwards. He pulls himself forward with the hands, the legs trailing behind. A month later he creeps, on hands and knees, with the abdomen off the couch. Subsequently he intermittently places one foot flat on the couch, and finally may creep like a bear on hands and feet, the last stage before walking.

Summary

Newborn	Head to one side, pelvis high, knees under abdomen.
6 weeks	Knees only intermittently under abdomen. Intermittent kicking out. Chin intermittently off couch.
8 weeks	Head mostly in midline. Lifts chin off couch so that plane of face is at angle of 45 degrees to couch.
12 weeks	Pelvis flat on couch. Plane of face reaches angle of 45 to 90 degrees to couch.
16 weeks	Chest off couch. Plane of face at angle of 90 degrees to couch. 'Swimming'—limbs stretched out in full extension, whole weight on abdomen.
20 weeks	Weight on forearms.
24 weeks	Weight on hands, with extended arms. Chest and upper part of abdomen off couch. Rolls, prone to supine.
28 weeks	May bear weight on one hand.
36 weeks	Progress backwards in attempt to crawl.
40 weeks	Crawls on abdomen.
44 weeks	Creeps, hands and knees.
48 weeks	Creeps, sole of foot intermittently on floor.
52 weeks	Walks like bear.
15 months	Creeps up stairs. Kneels without support.

SITTING. When the newborn baby is pulled to the sitting position, there is complete head lag. When half pulled up, however, he will raise his head. When in the sitting position, the back is uniformly rounded: he may lift the chin up momentarily. The head lag decreases with maturation, so that by 12 weeks it is only slight and by 20 weeks there is no lag at all. A month later he lifts the head off the couch when he is about to be pulled up, and at 28 weeks he raises it spontaneously and repeatedly. Meanwhile the back is straightening, so that by 24 weeks he can sit propped up in his pram with trunk erect. A month later he sits on the floor with his arms forward for support, and at 28 weeks without support for a few seconds. He learns to sit more and more steadily so that by 40 to 44 weeks he is really steady and can perform various movements, such as righting himself. By 15 months he can seat himself in a chair.

Summary

Newborn	Pulled to sit—complete head lag.
4 weeks	Held sitting—rounded back. Momentarily lifts the head up. Pulled to sit—almost complete head lag.
12 weeks	Head mostly held up when supported sitting, but it tends to bob forward.
16 weeks	Only slight head lag in beginning of movement when pulled to sitting position. In sitting position—head wobble when body is swayed. Back curved only in lumbar region.
20 weeks	No head lag when pulled up. No head wobble when body swayed by examiner. Back straight.
24 weeks	Sits supported in pram or high chair. When about to be pulled up, lifts head off couch.
28 weeks	Sits on floor with hands forward for support.
32 weeks	Sits momentarily on floor without support.
36 weeks	Sits steadily on floor for 10 minutes. Leans forward (but not sideways) and recovers balance.
40 weeks	Can go over into prone, and change from prone to sitting. Can pull self to sitting position.
48 weeks	Can twist round to pick up object.
15-18 mnths.	Seats self in chair.

STANDING AND WALKING. The walking reflex has already been described. It disappears by the age of 2 to 3 weeks. At 8 weeks the baby holds his head up momentarily when held in the standing position. In the early weeks the baby sags at the hip and knee, but by 24 weeks he can bear almost all his weight if his mother has given him a chance. At 36 weeks he stands holding on to furniture, and can pull himself up to the standing position, but cannot let himself down. At 44 weeks he is seen to lift one foot off the ground, and at 48 weeks he walks, holding on to the furniture. He walks without help at 13 months, with a broad base and steps of unequal direction and length, usually with the shoulder abducted and elbows flexed. At 15 months he creeps upstairs and can get into the standing position without help. At 18 months he can get up and down stairs without help, and pulls a doll or wheeled toy along the ground. At 2 years he can pick an object up without falling, can run, and walk backward. He goes up and down stairs with 2 feet per step. At 3 he can stand for a few seconds on one leg. He goes up stairs one foot per step, and down stairs, 2 feet per step. He can ride a tricycle. At 4 he goes down stairs one foot per step, and can skip on one foot. At 5 he can skip on both feet.

Summary

Newborn	Walking reflex (first 2-3 weeks).
8 weeks	Held in standing position, able to hold head up more than momentarily.
24 weeks	Bears almost all weight.
28 weeks	Held standing, bounces with pleasure.
36 weeks	Stands holding on to furniture. Pulls self to stand.
44 weeks	Standing, lifts foot.
48 weeks	Walks, holding on to furniture. Walks 2 hands held.
52 weeks	Walks, one hand held.
13 months	Walks, no help.
15 months	Creeps up stairs. Gets into standing position without help. Kneels without support. Can't go round corners or stop suddenly.
18 months	Can get up and down stairs without help. Pulls wheeled toy. Seats self on chair. Beginning to jump (both feet).
2 years	Up and down stairs alone, 2 feet per step. Walks backward in imitation. Picks up object from floor without falling. Runs. Kicks ball without overbalancing.
2½ years	Jumps with both feet. Can walk on tiptoes.
3 years	Jumps off bottom step. Goes up stairs, one foot per step; down, 2 feet per step. Stands on one foot for seconds. Rides tricycle.
4 years	Goes down stairs, one foot per step. Skips on one foot.
5 years	Skips on both feet.

Other Forms of Progression

Before babies learn to walk, they may learn to move from place to place by a variety of methods.

1. They may become proficient at getting about by rolling.

2. They may lie in the supine position, and elevate the buttocks and entire lower part of the body from the ground, progressing by a series of bumps on the buttocks.

3. They may hitch or shuffle—getting about on one hand and one buttock, or on both hands and both buttocks.

4. They may crawl backwards.

Other methods are also adopted.

Postures when Child is held in Inverted Position

McGraw[12] studied the postures in 77 children when held in the inverted position by the ankles. She described four phases.

1. The newborn or flexor phase, in which the knees and hips usually flex; the arms are flexed and adducted across the chest. After 4 to 6 weeks, there are fleeting extensor movements in the cervical spine.

2. The extensor phase, mostly between 4 and 6 months. There is full extension of the whole vertebral column. The arms are extended and abducted. There is less flexion of the knee and hip.

3. The righting phase. After a few more months there is flexion of the hips, neck and spine, with a deliberate effort to regain the upright posture.

4. The relaxed or mature phase. The arms hang loosely down. There is no pronounced flexion or extension of the spine or hips.

These patterns of posture are referred to again in the chapter on cerebral palsy.

Manipulation

The primitive grasp reflex of the first 2 or 3 months disappears before the voluntary grasp begins. At 4 weeks the hands are still predominantly closed, but by 12 weeks they are mostly open. One can see at this stage that the baby looks at an object as if he would like to grasp it. He will hold an object placed in the hand. At 16 weeks his hands come together as he plays, and he pulls his dress. He tries to reach for an object, but over-shoots the mark. At 20 weeks he can grasp an object voluntarily. He plays with his toes. Thereafter his grasp has to go through several stages[7, 8] from the ulnar grasp—with the cube in the palm of the hand on the ulnar side, to the radial grasp, and then to the finger-thumb grasp in the last 3 months of the first year. In the first 6 months the cube is grasped in the palm of the hand on the ulnar side: from 24 to 32 weeks it is held against the thenar eminence at the base of the thumb. From 32 to 40 weeks the index finger usually with the help of the ring and little finger, presses the cube against the lower part of the thumb; and between 40 and 60 weeks the cube is grasped between the volar pads of the finger tip and the distal volar pad of the thumb. The rapidity with which he drops the cube is a good index of the maturity of the grasp. If he repeatedly drops it in a matter of seconds, the grasp is unlikely to be a mature one. At first he is ataxic and over-shoots the mark, but soon he is able to reach for an object with precision. At 6 months he transfers objects from hand to hand, and as he can now chew, he can feed himself with a biscuit. He plays with his toes in the supine position. He loves to play with paper. Everything goes to the mouth. It is not till 40 weeks that he can pick up a small object of the size of a currant, bringing finger and thumb together. He goes for objects with his index finger. He can now deliberately let go of objects, but true casting—deliberately throwing bricks on to the floor, one after the other—usually reaches its height between 12 and 15 months. Before that he learns to hand a toy to the parent, at first refusing to let it go, but later releasing it. He spends long periods at 44 weeks and onwards putting objects in and out of a basket. He stops taking things to his mouth by about a year. By 13 months he can build a tower of 2 one-inch cubes, but he cannot build a tower of 10 until 3 years of age. By 15 months he can pick up a cup, drink from it and put it down without much spilling. At 18 months he turns 2 or 3 pages of a book at a time, but turns them over singly by the age of 2 years. By 2 years he can put his socks on, by 2½ he can thread beads, and by 3 he can fasten buttons, dressing and undressing himself. He can draw and paint.

Summary

Newborn	For first 2 or 3 months—grasp reflex.
4 weeks	Hands predominantly closed.
8 weeks	Hands often open. Only slight grasp reflex.
12 weeks	No grasp reflex. Plays with rattle placed in hand for several seconds. Pulls at his dress.
	Hands mostly open. Looks as if he would like to grasp object.
16 weeks	Hands come together as he plays. Pulls dress over face in play. Tries to reach object but overshoots. Plays with rattle placed in hand (and shakes it) for prolonged period.

20 weeks	Able to grasp object voluntarily.
	Ataxia, asynergia, dysmetria.
	Plays with toes.
	Objects to mouth.
	Bidextrous approach to objects.
24 weeks	Holds bottle. Grasps his feet.
	Palmar grasp of cubes. Drops one when another is given.
28 weeks	Transfers object from hand to hand.
	Unidextrous approach.
	Feeds self with biscuit.
	Bangs objects on table.
	Retains one cube when second is offered.
36–40 wks.	Finger-thumb apposition; can pick up currant between finger and thumb.
40 weeks	Index finger approach.
	Release beginning.
	Offers toy to examiner. Will not release it.
44 weeks	Puts one object after another into basket.
48 weeks	Gives toy to examiner.
1 year	Mouthing nearly stopped.
12–15 mnths.	Casting objects on to the floor.
15 months	Builds tower of 2 or 3 cubes (one inch).
	Holds 2 cubes in one hand.
18 months	Tower of 3 to 4 cubes.
2 years	Tower of 6 to 7 cubes.
	Turns door knob. Unscrews lids.
	Puts on shoes, socks, pants.
2½ years	Holds pencil in hand instead of fist. Begins to draw.
3 years	Tower of 9 to 10 cubes. Dresses and undresses fully.
	Manages buttons except back ones.
	Drawing—copies a circle.

For other tests after 1 year—see Chapter 13

The Use of the Eyes and Ears.

The reflex responses of the eye of the newborn baby have been described elsewhere (p. 117). The baby blinks at birth in response to sound, movement or touching of the cornea, but not on the approach of an object. When he is a few weeks older he displays a protective response to an object moving towards him.

The pupil responds to light after about the 29th week of gestation, and the baby begins to turn his head to diffuse light at about the 32nd or 36th week. The 26-30 week premature baby dislikes a bright light.

At birth he can barely fix with his eyes, and he can follow a moving object, such as a dangling ring, with difficulty in a range of about 45°. By 4 weeks he can follow in a range of 90° and by three months within a range of 180°. By three months he can fixate well on near objects. By 3 or 4 weeks he watches his mother intently as she speaks to him, fixating on her face, and by 4 to 6 weeks he begins to smile at her as she speaks to him. He will also smile at a face sized card with two eye dots—and still more at one with six dots. By three months or so he fixes his eyes well on his feeding bottle, and by four months he can fix his eyes on a half inch brick ('grasping with his eyes'). The newborn baby cannot integrate head and eye movements well; the eyes lag behind if his head is passively rotated to one side (Doll's eye reflex). The response disappears by two or three months.

The eyes of the newborn baby tend to move independently. Binocular vision begins at six weeks, and is fairly well established by four months. To achieve binocular vision, the visual fields must overlap so that corresponding parts of each retina have a common visual direction and form similar images. As binocular vision matures, the infant learns by trial and error to associate the visual fields and fusion becomes established. After six months lack of conjugate movements, a strabismus, means that treatment is required.

From 12-24 weeks he characteristically watches his hand (hand regard) as he lies on his back; but 'hand regard' can also occur in blind children, and so it is really a developmental pattern not requiring visual stimulation.

At five months he excites when his feed is being prepared, and at 6 months he adjusts his position to see objects—bending back or crouching to see what he is interested in. He cannot follow rapidly moving objects until he is nearly a year old.

According to Brown[2] the following is the visual acuity to be expected in the first five years:–

Age	4 months	6 months	1 year	18 months	2 years	5 years
Acuity	3/60	4/60	6/60	6/24	6/12	6/6

He may imitate sounds by 6 months, and by 7 months he may respond to his name. By the age of 9 to 12 months he knows the meaning of several words, including the names of members of his family.

There have been several studies relating to the ability of the foetus to hear in utero. [1, 15] Different tones were produced by a Jackson audio-frequency oscillator and amplified. Foetal heart wounds were picked up by a Bush microphone attached to the maternal abdomen, a gap of air space being maintained between the sound producing apparatus and the mother's abdomen. Each stimulus was preceded by a warning. The sudden foetal movements and acceleration of the foetal heart indicated that the foetus could hear.

Stirnimann[17] mentioned the case of a lady who had to stop attending orchestral concerts during the later months of pregnancy because the loud music made her baby so restless. The responses of the newborn baby to sound were discussed on page   .

At three or four months of age the baby begins to turn his head towards the source of sound.

Murphy[13, 14] described the sequence of development of sound localisation, making a sound approximately 18 inches from the ear. These are as follows:

1. The infant turns the head to the side at which the sound is heard (3 months).
2. The infant turns the head towards the sound and the eyes look in the same direction. (3 to 4 months).
3. He turns the head to one side and then downwards, if the sound is made below the ear. (5 to 6 months).
4. He turns the head to one side and then upwards, when the sound is made above the level of the ear. (at about 6 months). i.e. downward localisation occurs before upward localisation.
5. He turns the head in a curving arc towards the sound source. (About 6 to 8 months).
6. The head is turned diagonally and directly towards the sound. (About 8 to 10 months).

By the first year the ability to localise a sound source is almost as good as in the older child and adult.

From about 9 months the baby learns to control and adjust his responses to sounds. He may delay his response or inhibit it altogether. He may listen to hear the sound again and not attempt to make any localisation. This represents a further step in maturation towards understanding and controlling his environment.

Summary

4 weeks	Watches mother intently when she speaks to him. Opens and closes mouth. Bobs head up and down. Follows dangling object when brought to midline, less than 90 degrees. Quiets when bell is rung.
6 weeks	Smiles. Follows moving person. Supine—follows moving object from side to midline (90 degrees).
8 weeks	Fixation, convergence, focusing.
12 weeks	Turns head to sound. Hand regard. Follows moving toy from side to side (180 degrees).
20 weeks	Smiles at mirror image. No more hand regard after 24 weeks.
28 weeks	Pats image of self in mirror. Adjusts position to see objects. Imitates sounds.
40 weeks	Looks round corner for object.

General Understanding

The first sign of understanding can be seen any time from 1 to 4 weeks of age, when he begins to watch his mother when she speaks to him. He quiets, opens and closes his mouth, and bobs his head up and down. By 6 weeks he begins to smile, and 2 weeks later to vocalise. At 12 weeks he shows considerable interest in his surroundings, watching the movements of people in the room. He may refuse to be left outside alone, preferring the activity of the kitchen. He excites when a toy is presented to him. He recognises his mother and turns his head to sound. He may turn his head away when his nose is being cleaned by cotton wool. Between 12 and 16 weeks he anticipates when his bottle or the breast is offered, by opening his mouth when he sees it approach. At 20 weeks he smiles at his mirror image, and shortly after looks to see where a dropped toy has gone to. At 24 weeks when lying down he stretches his arms out when he sees that his mother is going to lift him up. He smiles and vocalises at his mirror image. At 6 months he imitates acts, such as tongue protrusion or a cough. He may try to establish contact by coughing. He enjoys peep-bo games. At 32 weeks he reacts to the cotton wool swab by grasping his mother's hand and pushing it away. He tries persistently to reach objects too far away. He responds to 'No.'

At 40 weeks he may pull the clothes of his mother to attract her attention. He imitates 'patacake' and 'bye-bye'. He repeats a performance laughed at. At 44 weeks he helps to dress, by holding his arm out for a coat, his foot out for a shoe, or transferring an object from one hand to another so that a hand can go through a sleeve. At 48 weeks he begins to anticipate movements in nursery rhymes. He begins to show interest in books, and understanding of words. At 11 to 12 months he may laugh when his mother puts an unusual object on her head. At 1 year he may understand a phrase such as 'where is your shoe?'

After the first birthday he shows his understanding in innumerable different ways. His increasing understanding is shown by his comprehension of what is said to him, by the execution of simple requests, by his increasing interest in toys and books, by his developing speech. His play becomes more and more complex and imaginative. He begins to appreciate form and colour, and by $2\frac{1}{2}$ years he can tackle simple jig-saws.

The main test objects used for observing his developing understanding are the pencil and paper, the picture book, the picture card with pictures of common objects, and formboards or cut-out forms.

Summary

4 weeks	Watches mother intently as she speaks to him.
6 weeks	Smiles.
8 weeks	Smiles and vocalises.
12 weeks	Much interest in surroundings.
	Excites when toy presented.
	Recognises mother.
	Turns head away when nose cleaned.
	Squeals of pleasure.
	'Talks' a great deal when spoken to.
16 weeks	Anticipates and excites when feed prepared.
	Shows interest in strange room. Laughs aloud.

20 weeks	Smiles at mirror image.
24 weeks	Displeasure at removal of toy. Holds arms out to be picked up. Likes and dislikes. Smiles and vocalises at mirror image. When he drops cube he looks to see where it has gone to. Excites on hearing steps. Beginning of imitation. Laughs when head is hidden in towel.
28 weeks	Expectation in response to repetition of stimulus. Imitates acts and noises. Tries to attract attention by cough. Enjoys peep-bo games. Responds to name. Keeps lips closed when offered food which he doesn't want.
32 weeks	Reacts to cotton wool swab by grasping his mother's hand and pushing it away. Reaches persistently for toys out of reach. Responds to 'No'. Imitates sounds.
36 weeks	Compares 2 cubes by bringing them together. Puts arms in front of face to avoid having it washed.
40 weeks	Pulls clothes of mother to attract attention. Waves bye-bye. Patacake. Repeats performance laughed at. Looks round corner for object. Responds to words, *e.g.* 'Where is daddy?' Holds object to examiner, but won't release it.
44 weeks	Drops object deliberately, to be picked up. He helps to dress.
48 weeks	Rolls ball to examiner. Will give toy to examiner. Anticipates body movements when nursery rhyme being said. Interest in picture book. Plays peep-bo, covering face. Plays game 'up, down'. Shakes head for 'No'.

For tests of general understanding after 1 year—see Chapter 13.

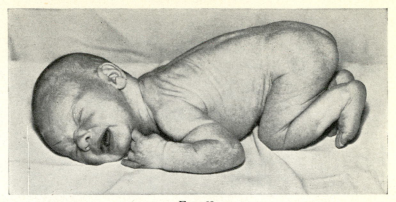

Fig. 69
About 0-2 weeks of age.
Pelvis high, knees drawn up under abdomen.

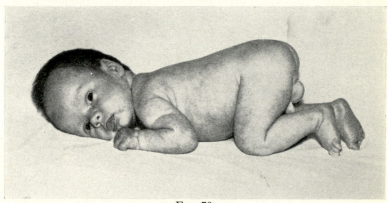

Fig. 70
About 3 or 4 weeks of age.
Pelvis high, but knees not under abdomen.

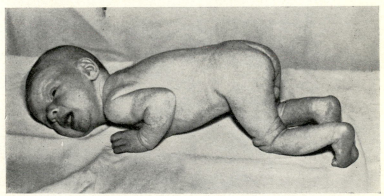

Fig. 71.—About 4 to 6 weeks of age. Pelvis still rather high.
Intermittent extension of hips.

facing page 182

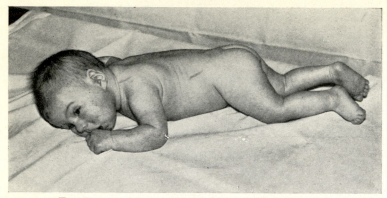

FIG. 72.—8 weeks or more. Pelvis flat. Hips extended.

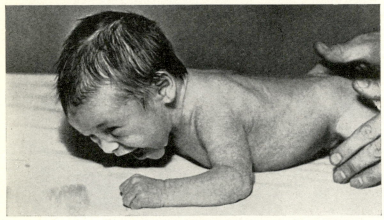

FIG. 73.—6 weeks. Chin held off couch intermittently, but plane of face not as much as angle of 45° to couch.

FIG. 74

10 to 12 weeks. Plane of face almost reaches angle of 45° to couch.

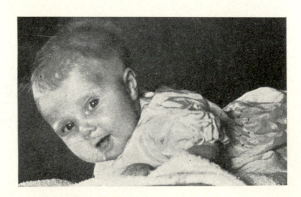

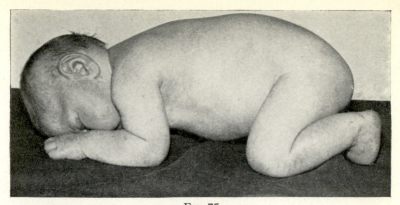

FIG. 75

Microcephalic mentally defective child, aged 9 weeks, showing prone position
similar to that of newborn boy.

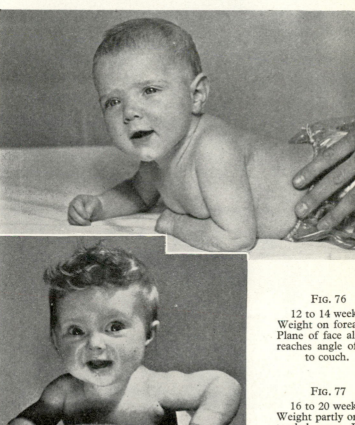

FIG. 76

12 to 14 weeks.
Weight on forearms.
Plane of face almost
reaches angle of 90°
to couch.

FIG. 77

16 to 20 weeks.
Weight partly on ex-
tended arms. Plane
of face reaches angle
of 90° to couch.

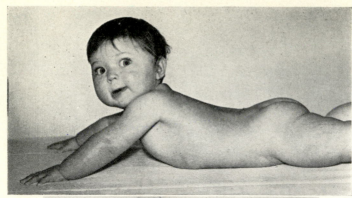

FIG. 78.—24 weeks. Weight on hands, with extended arms.
FIG. 79.—44 weeks. Creep position.
FIG. 80.—52 weeks. Walking like a bear.

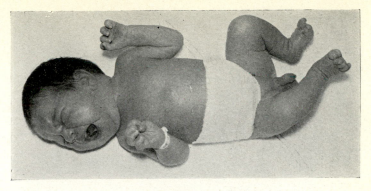

FIG. 81
Full term newborn baby, flexed position.

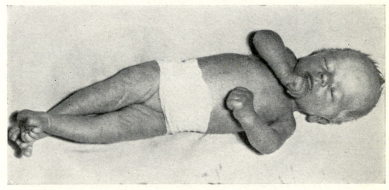

FIG. 82
Abnormal appearance of child aged 8 days. Hands very tightly closed.
The legs tend to cross and they are unusually extended. Knee jerks normal.
Cerebral haemorrhage. Severe convulsions age 3 days. (The development
was entirely average at 6 weeks.)

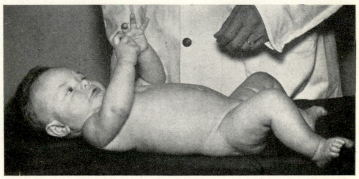

FIG. 83
11-20 weeks. Hand regard.

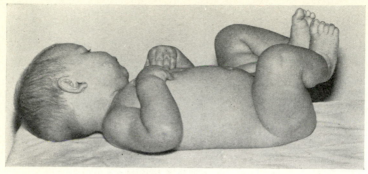

FIG. 84
12-16 weeks. Soles of feet come together.

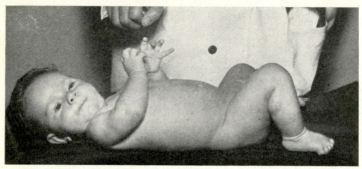

FIG. 85
16 weeks. Soles of feet on couch.

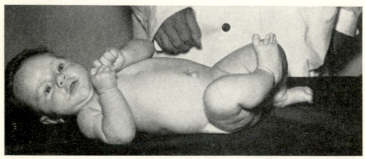

FIG. 86
16 weeks. Foot on opposite knee.

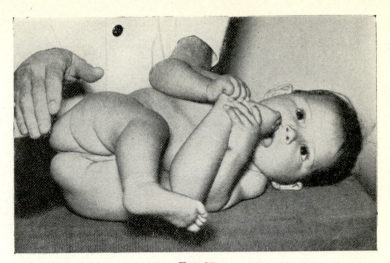

FIG. 87

20 weeks. Feet to mouth.

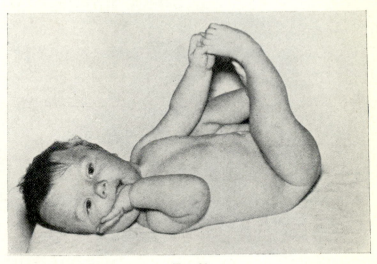

FIG. 88

20 weeks. Plays with feet.

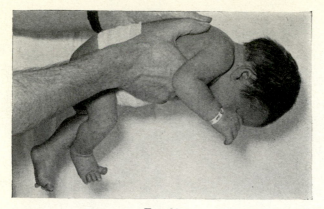

Fig. 89

Full term newborn baby, ventral suspension. Note flexion of elbows and knees, with some extension of hips.

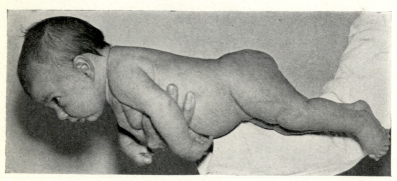

Fig. 90

Six weeks old baby, head held in same plane as rest of body.

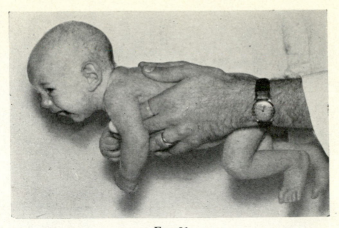

FIG. 91
Normal posture at 8 weeks.
Head held up well beyond plane of rest of body.

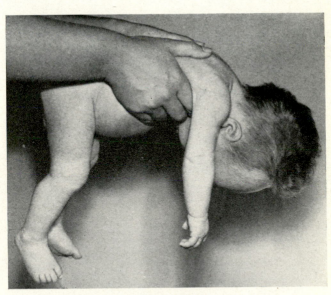

FIG. 92
Abnormal posture. Child of 6 weeks.
Head hangs down too much. Arms and legs extended. No
extension of hips.
(Child with cerebral palsy.)

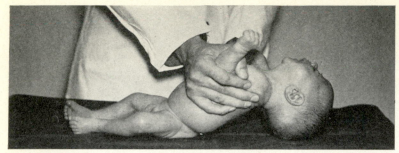

FIG. 93.—First 4 weeks or so. Complete head lag when being pulled
to the sitting position.

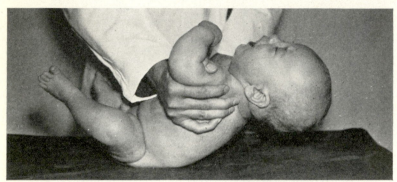

FIG. 94.—About 2 months. Considerable head lag when he is pulled to the
sitting position, but lag not complete.

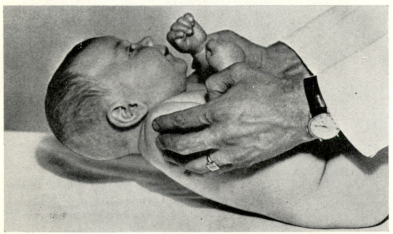

FIG. 95.—4 months. No head lag when pulled to the sitting position.

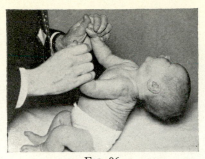

FIG. 96

Newborn baby, half pulled to
sitting position: head lag.

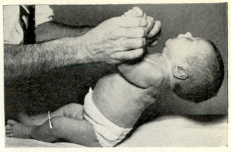

FIG. 97

Same, seconds later, lifting
head up slightly.

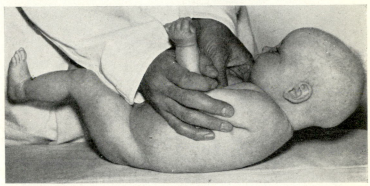

FIG. 98

5 months. Lifts head from supine when about to be pulled up.

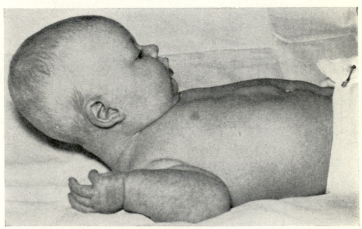

FIG. 99

6 months. Head lifted up spontaneously from supine position.

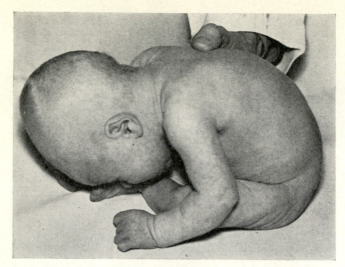

FIG. 100
First 4 weeks or so.
Completely rounded back.

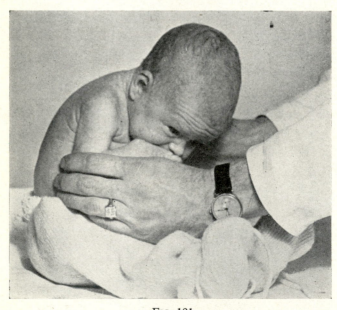

FIG. 101
4 to 6 weeks.
Rounded back. Head held up intermittently.

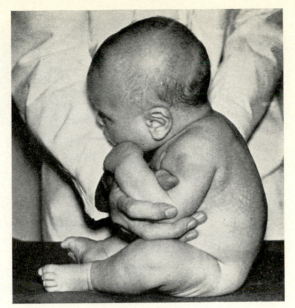

FIG. 102
8 weeks.
Back still rounded. Now raising head well.

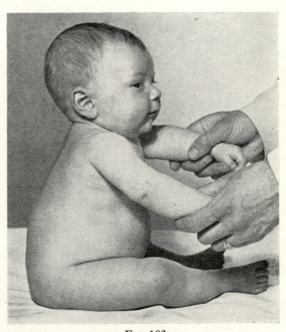

FIG. 103
16 weeks.
Back much straighter.

FIG. 104

26 weeks. Sitting with the hands forward for support.

FIG. 105

7 months onwards. Sitting without support.

FIG. 106

11 months. Pivoting—turning round to pick up a toy without overbalancing.

FIG. 104

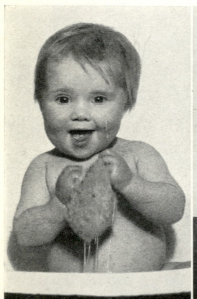

FIG. 105

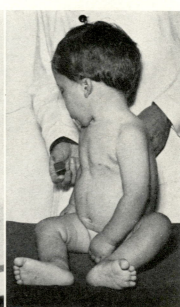

FIG. 106

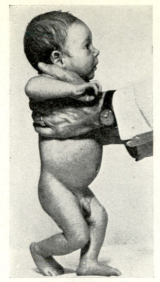

FIG. 107
About 12 weeks.
Bearing much weight.

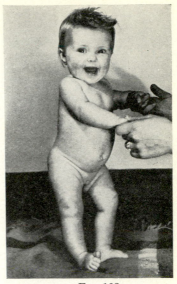

FIG. 108
24 weeks.
Bearing almost all weight.

FIG. 109
28 weeks.
Bears full weight.

FIG. 110
48 weeks.
Can stand holding on to furniture
and can walk holding on to it.
('Cruises'.)

FIG. 111
48 weeks.
Walks, 2 hands held.

FIG. 112
52 weeks.
Walks, 1 hand held.

FIG. 113
13 months.
Walks, no help. Arms abducted,
elbows flexed, Broad base. Steps
of varying length and direction.

FIG. 114
15 months.
Kneels without support

Pleasure and Displeasure

All babies express displeasure before they learn to show pleasure.

The first sign of pleasure shown by the baby is the quieting in the first few days when he is picked up. During his feeds he shows his pleasure by the splaying of his toes, and by their alternate flexion and extension. The smile at 6 weeks when he is spoken to is followed in 1 or 2 weeks by vocalising. At 3 months he squeals with delight. He then shows his pleasure by a massive response—the trunk, arms and legs move, and he pants with excitement. At 16 weeks he laughs aloud. He plays with the rattle placed in his hand. He smiles when pulled up to the sitting position.

After 5 or 6 months he takes great pleasure in newly acquired skills—sitting, standing, walking, feeding himself, and so on. He enjoys games from 6 months, and peep-bo and by 9 months likes to be read to, and enjoys nursery rhymes. He is ticklish by 4 or 5 months, and soon responds by a laugh when he sees a finger approaching to tickle him. He enjoys games and company more and more as he gets older.

Feeding and Dressing

The young baby cannot usually approximate his lips tightly round the areola of the breast or the teat of the bottle, so that milk leaks out at the corners of the mouth, and in addition he is likely to swallow air and so have 'wind'. As he matures he gets less wind, because of the complete approximation of his lips to the sucking surface.

In the first 4 months or so the baby's tongue tends to push food out if food is placed on the front of the tongue. Feeds, therefore, should be placed well back.

Babies can approximate their lips to the rim of a cup by 4 or 5 months, and cup-feeding at this time is likely to be quicker than bottle feeding.

The next milestone of importance is the beginning of chewing at 6 months, together with the ability to get hold of objects, enabling a child to feed himself with a biscuit. He also likes to hold his bottle.

At any time after 6 months the baby may begin to hold his spoon, and some babies can feed themselves fully with the spoon by 9 or 10 months, though the average age for this is about 15

13

months. In the early days of self feeding the fingers go into the food, and much is spilt, accidentally or deliberately.

When he is first allowed to use a cup, he lets it go when he has had what he wants. If he is given a chance to learn, however, he should be able to manage the cup fully by 15 months of age.

Children can manage a knife and fork by the age of $2\frac{1}{2}$ to 3 years.

The age at which children learn to dress themselves varies tremendously. Much depends on how much chance the mother gives the child to dress himself. A child of average intelligence can dress himself fully by the age of 3, provided that he is advised as to back and front, and as to the appropriate shoe for the foot. He will also need help with difficult buttons. He should be able to tie his shoelaces by 4 or 5 years, and so to be fully independent.

For a full description of the feeding behaviour of infants, the reader should refer to the book by Gesell and Ilg[1].

Summary

24 weeks	Drinks from cup when it is held to lips.
6 months	Chews. Eats biscuit.
15 months	Manages cup, picking it up, putting it down without much spilling.
	Rotates spoon near mouth.
	Feeds self fully, no help.
	Takes off shoes.
18 months	Takes off gloves, shoes, socks, unzips.
	No more rotation of spoon.
2 years	Puts on and takes off shoes, socks, pants.
3 years	Dress self fully apart from buttons behind.
	May put shoes on to wrong feet. Unbuttons front and side buttons.
5 years	Can tie shoe lace.

Opening of Mouth When the Nose is Obstructed

The young baby does not usually open his mouth spontaneously when his nose is obstructed until he is about four or five months old. This is of importance under various circumstances. For instance, the infant with choanal atresia gasps for breath and becomes cyanosed until he opens his mouth to cry or until an airway is inserted.

Speech

There have been several extensive studies on the speech of infants. A good simple review of the subject was provided by Lillywhite[11] and Sheridan.[16] The latter, in an excellent paper on the development of speech and on speech disorders, described the stages of preverbal and verbal communication. They are smiling, nestling, clinging, vigorous welcoming, frowning, resistive stiffening or pushing away, formless emotionally charged vocalisations, pulling the mother in his direction, pointing, taking the mother's hand and placing it near the object which he desires. Laughter, screaming and temper tantrums are other methods of communication.

Speech begins with the vocalisations of the 7 to 8 weeks old infant. Some infants vocalise sooner than this. The sounds are mostly vowels, but some consonants may be heard.

By 12 to 16 weeks the baby characteristically has long 'conversations' with his mother. Towards the latter end of this period he begins to use consonants m, k, g, p, and b. He laughs, gurgles, and coos. By 20 weeks he says 'Ah, goo' and makes syllables like 'Ba', 'da', and 'ka' at 28 weeks. When crying he makes sounds like 'mum'. There is much vocal play at this time, with razzing and much more intonation. A nasal tone may be heard and tongue-lip activity develops. At 32 weeks he combines syllables, like 'da-da', but does not say a word with meaning until he is 44 to 48 weeks old. At 32 weeks he adds d, t, and w. At 8 months, he makes noises to attract attention. At 10 months he comprehends 'no', and obeys orders. The average child can say 2 or 3 words with meaning by 1 year.

In the early weeks of speech he frequently omits the first or last part of a word—saying 'g' for 'dog'. Between 15 and 18 months the child jargons, speaking in an unintelligible but expressive language of his own, with modulations, phrasings and dramatic inflections but with only an occasional intelligible word in it. He may at this time repeat phrases such as 'Oh, dear', but the average child begins to join words together spontaneously by 21 to 24 months. Substitution of letters may occur, and some lisping, by protrusion of the tongue between the teeth when saying 's', is very common. By the age of 3 he is talking incessantly, but some substitution of letters and repetition of syllables is the usual thing rather than the exception.

Karelitz and Rosenfeld[10] have described a fascinating study of infants' vocalisations, a study which may well open up a new and valuable field of investigation. They took 1,300 recordings of the vocalisations of normal and 'brain damaged' infants in their first two years. They described the cry of the very young infant as short, staccato and repetitive. It builds up in a crescendo as the stimulus is applied. As he develops, the duration of the individual cry increases, and eventually becomes polysyllabic. The pitch becomes more varied and the inflections become more plaintive and meaningful at about six months of age. Later syllables (mumum) and real words and subsequently phrases can be heard as part of the cry.

Summary

8 weeks	Vocalises.
12 weeks	Squeals of pleasure. 'Talks' when spoken to.
16 weeks	Laughs aloud.
20 weeks	Razzing, 'Ah-goo'.
28 weeks	Syllables 'ba', 'da', 'ka'. 4 or more different sounds.
32 weeks	Combines syllables—'da-da', 'ba-ba'.
48 weeks	One word with meaning. Imitates sounds.
1 year	2 or 3 words with meaning. Imitates animals.
15 months	Jargon.
18 months	Jargon, but many intelligible words.
21–24 mnths.	2 or 3 words joined together (not in imitation). Repeats things said. Uses 'I', 'me', 'you'.
2-3 years	Lisping and some 'stuttering' common.
3 years	Normal speech.

Sphincter Control

In the newborn baby, micturition is a reflex act. It can be stimulated by handling the baby and other non-specific stimuli. Babies usually empty the bowel or bladder immediately after a meal. They can often be conditioned at any age (e.g. at a month or so) to empty the bladder when placed on the pottie, the bladder emptying when the buttocks come into contact with the rim of the pottie. Voluntary control does not begin until 15-18 months of age, when the baby first tells his mother that he has wet his pants. He then tells her just before he passes urine, but too late, and a little later he tells her in time. By about 16 to 18 months he may say 'No' if asked whether he wants to pass urine. There is great urgency at this time, so that as soon as he wants to pass urine he must be offered the pottie immediately, or it will be too late. As he matures, the urgency disappears—though in enuresis of the primary type diurnal urgency may continue for some years. By the age of two to two and a half years he can pull his pants down and climb on to the lavatory seat unaided. He is apt to forget to go to the lavatory when occupied with some new toy or play, but later can remember to look after his needs.

Most children are reasonably dry by day at 18 months. By two, 50 per cent. are dry at night: by three, 75 per cent., and by 5 some 90 per cent. are dry. This means that about one in ten at the age of five will still be wetting the bed at least *occasionally*.

Bowel control is usually acquired before control of the bladder.

Summary

15 months	Tells the mother that he wants to use the pottie. Indicates wet pants.
18 months	Dry by day, occasional accidents.
2 years	Dry by night if lifted out in evening.
2½ years	Attends to own toilet needs without help, except for wiping.

The Development of Handedness

Gesell and Ames[6] suggested that the first indication of handedness may be the direction of the asymmetrical tonic-neck reflex. In 19 children followed from infancy to 10 years, the direction of the tonic-neck reflex was predictive of handedness in 14. In 4 children left-handedness was correctly foretold in infancy by a persistently left tonic-neck reflex.

There are shifts from side to side in the first year. At 18 months a period of bilaterality is often found, followed by a definite use of the dominant hand at the age of 2 years. In many children, however, dominance is not fully established for 3 or 4 years later than this.

Development by Age

In the following section I have put together the main features of development at different ages. I have combined with these milestones a variety of simple developmental tests, mainly culled from Gesell.

THE AVERAGE LEVEL OF DEVELOPMENT AT DIFFERENT AGES

4 Weeks

GROSS MOTOR.

Ventral suspension—(held in prone position with hand under abdomen), head held up momentarily. Elbows flexed, hips partly extended, knees flexed.

Prone—pelvis high, knees drawn up largely under abdomen. Intermittent partial extension of hip and knee. Momentarily lifts chin off couch. Head predominantly to one side.

Pull to sit—almost complete head lag.

Held in sitting position—back uniformly rounded. May hold head up momentarily.

Supine—tonic-neck reflex seen when at rest.

Held standing—flops at knees and hips. May be residual walking reflex when sole of foot is pressed on flat surface.

HANDS.

Hands predominantly closed.

Grasp reflex.

GENERAL UNDERSTANDING.

Watches mother's face when she talks to him and he is not crying. Opens and closes mouth. Bobs head up and down.

VISION.

In supine—regards dangling object (*e.g.* ring on string) when brought into line of vision (3 feet away from the eyes), but not otherwise when in midline. Follows it less than 90 degrees.

SOUND.

Quiets when bell is rung.

6 Weeks

GROSS MOTOR.

Ventral suspension—head held up momentarily in same plane as rest of body. Some extension of hips and flexion of knees. Flexion of elbows.

Prone—pelvis high, but knees no longer under abdomen. Much intermittent extension of hips. Chin raised intermittently off couch. Head turned to one side.

Pull to sit—head lag considerable but not complete.

Held in sitting position—intermittently holds head up.

Held standing—no walking reflex. Head sags forward. May hold head up momentarily.

Supine—tonic-neck reflex at rest intermittently seen.

HANDS.

Often open. Grasp reflex may be lost.

GENERAL UNDERSTANDING.

Smiles at mother in response to overtures.

VISION.

Eyes fixate on objects. They follow moving persons.

In supine—looks at object held in midline, following it as it moves from the side to midline. (90 degrees).

8 Weeks

GROSS MOTOR.

Ventral suspension—can maintain head in same plane as rest of body.

Prone—head mostly in midline. Intermittently lifts chin off couch so that plane of face is at angle of 45 degrees to couch.

Pull to sit—less head lag.

Held in sitting position—less rounding of back. Head is held up but recurrently bobs forward.

Supine—head chiefly to side. Tonic-neck reflex seen intermittently at rest.

Held in standing position—able to hold head up more than momentarily.

HANDS.

Frequently open.   Only slight grasp reflex.

VOCALISATION.

Smiles and vocalises when talked to.

VISION.

Fixation, convergence and focusing. Follows moving person.
In supine—follows dangling toy from side to point beyond
midline.

12 Weeks

GROSS MOTOR.

Ventral suspension—head held up for prolonged period
beyond plane of rest of body.

Prone—pelvis flat on couch. Holds chin and shoulders off
couch for prolonged period, so that plane of face is at
angle of 45 degrees to 90 degrees from couch, weight
borne on forearms.

Pull to sit—only slight head lag.

Held in sitting position—head mostly held up, but still bobs
forward.

Supine—no more tonic-neck reflex.

HANDS.

No grasp reflex.

Hands loosely open.

When rattle is placed in hand, holds it for a minute or more.

Looks as if he would like to grasp object, but cannot without
it being placed in hand.

VOCALISATION.

Squeals of pleasure.

'Talks' a great deal when spoken to.

VISION.

Supine—characteristically watches movements of his own
hands. ('Hand regard').

Follows dangling toy from side to side. (180 degrees).

Promptly looks at object in midline.

HEARING.

Turns head to sound.

FIG. 115
Manipulation. 6 months. Transfers objects.

facing page 190

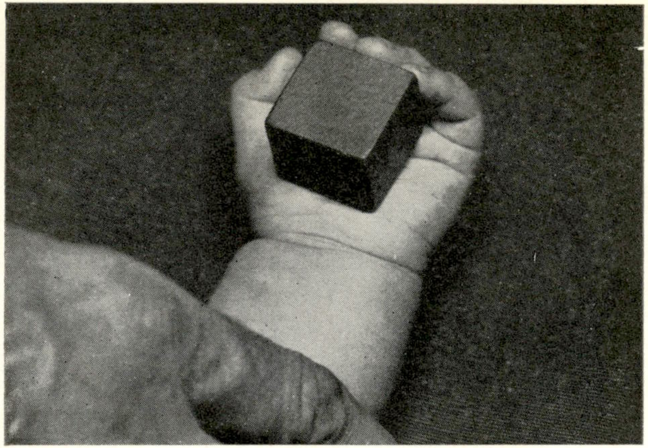

MANIPULATION

Fig. 116.—6 months. Immature palmar grasp of cube.
Fig. 117.—8 months. Grasp, intermediate stage.
Fig. 118.—1 year. Mature grasp of cube.

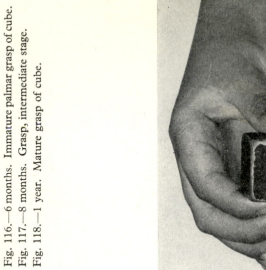

Fig. 118

Fig. 116

Fig. 117

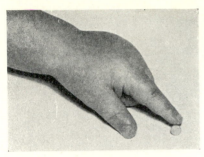

FIG. 119

40 weeks. Index finger approach to
object.

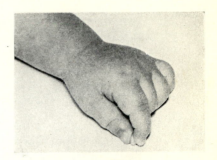

FIG. 120

40 weeks. Finger-thumb apposition,
enabling child to pick up pellet.

FIG. 121

40 weeks. Pokes clapper of bell
with index finger.

FIG. 122

10 month old child feeding himself.
Note the immature grasp.

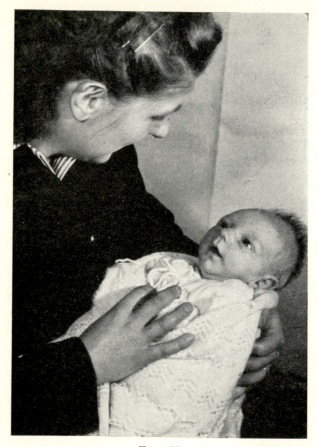

FIG. 123

4 weeks old baby, showing the baby's intent regard of his
mother as she speaks to him. Note his open mouth.

16 Weeks

GROSS MOTOR.

Prone—head and chest off couch so that plane of face is at angle of 90 degrees to couch.

'Swimming'—limbs stretched out in full extension.

Pull to sit—only slight head lag in beginning of movement.

Held in sitting position—head held up constantly.

Child looks actively around.

Head wobbles when examiner suddenly sways child, indicating that head control is incomplete.

Back now curved only in lumbar region.

Supine—head in midline.

HANDS.

Hands come together as he plays. Hand regard still present.

Pulls dress over face in play.

Tries to reach object with hands but overshoots it.

Plays with rattle placed in hand for long period and shakes it, but cannot pick it up if he drops it.

GENERAL UNDERSTANDING.

Excites when food prepared, toys seen, showing massive reaction, involving all 4 limbs and respirations.

Shows pleasure when pulled to sitting position. Likes to be propped up.

VOCALISATION.

Laughs aloud.

VISION.

Supine—immediate regard of dangling object.

20 Weeks

GROSS MOTOR.

Prone—weight on forearms.

Pull to sit—no head lag.

Held in sitting position—no head wobble when body swayed by examiner.

Back straight.

Supine—feet to mouth.

Held in standing position—bears most of weight.

HANDS.

Able to grasp objects voluntarily.
Plays with toes. Crumples paper.
Splashes in bath. Objects taken to mouth.

CUBE.

Grasps; bidextrous approach; takes it to mouth.

VOCALISATIONS.

Razzing; 'Ah-goo'.

GENERAL UNDERSTANDING.

Smiles at mirror image.
Pats bottle.

24 Weeks

GROSS MOTOR.

Prone—weight on hands, not forearms; chest and upper part
    of abdomen off couch.
When about to be pulled to sit, lifts head off couch.
Sits supported in high chair.
Held in standing position—almost full weight on legs.
Rolls prone to supine.
No more hand regard.

HANDS.

Holds bottle.
Grasps his feet.

CUBE.

Palmar grasp of cube.
Drops one cube when another is given.

FEEDING.

Drinks from cup when it is held to lips.

GENERAL UNDERSTANDING.

When he drops a toy he looks to see where it has gone to
    and tries to recover it.
May excite on hearing steps.
Mirror—smiles and vocalises at mirror image.

Stretches arms out to be taken.
Shows likes and dislikes.
May show fear of strangers and be 'coy'.
Displeasure at removal of toy.

PLAY.

Laughs when head is hidden in towel.

IMITATION.

Imitates cough or protrusion of tongue.

28 Weeks

GROSS MOTOR.

Prone—bears weight on one hand.
Sits with hands on couch for support.
Rolls from supine to prone.
Supine—spontaneously lifts head off couch.
Held standing—bounces with pleasure.

HANDS.

Feeds self with biscuit.
Likes to play with paper.
Unidextrous approach.

CUBES.

Bangs cube on table.
Transfers it from hand to hand.
If he has one cube in hand he retains it when second is offered.

FEEDING.

Chews.
Keeps lips closed when he is offered more food than he wants.

GENERAL UNDERSTANDING.

Imitates simple acts.
Pats image of self in mirror.
Responds to name.
Tries to establish contact with person by cough or other method.
Expectation in response to repetition of stimulus.

SPEECH.

Syllables—ba, da, ka.

32 Weeks

GROSS MOTOR.

> Sits momentarily on floor without support.
> Adjusts posture to reach object, *e.g.* leans forward to reach.
> Readily bears whole weight on legs when supported. May stand holding on.

GENERAL UNDERSTANDING.

> Reaches persistently for toys out of reach.
> Responds to 'No'.
> Looks for dropped toy.

IMITATION.

> Imitates sounds.

SPEECH.

> Combines syllables—da-da; ba-ba.

36 Weeks

GROSS MOTOR.

> Prone—in trying to crawl progresses backwards. [9 months]
> May progress by rolling.
> Sits steadily on floor for 10 minutes.
> Leans forward and recovers balance but cannot lean over sideways.
> Stands, holding on to furniture. Pulls self to stand.

HANDS.

> Can pick up object of size of currant between finger and thumb, or piece of string.

CUBES.

> Compares two cubes by bringing them together.

GENERAL UNDERSTANDING.

> Puts arms in front of face to prevent mother washing his face.

40 Weeks

GROSS MOTOR.

> Prone—crawl position, on abdomen.
> Crawls by pulling self forward with hands.

Sitting—can go over into prone, or change from prone to sitting.

Can pull self to sitting position.

Sits steadily with little risk of overbalancing.

Standing—can stand holding on to furniture. Collapses with a bump.

HANDS.

Goes for objects with index finger.

CUBES.

Beginning to let go of objects (release).

GENERAL UNDERSTANDING.

Looks round corner for object.

Responds to words, *e.g.* 'Where is daddy?'

Pulls clothes of another to attract attention. Holds object to examiner but won't release it.

Repeats performance laughed at.

IMITATION.

Waves bye-bye. Plays patacake.

44 Weeks

GROSS MOTOR.

Prone—creeps; abdomen off couch.

Standing—lifts foot.

CUBES.

Beginning to put objects in and out of containers.

DRESSING.

Holds arm out for sleeve or foot out for shoe.

GENERAL UNDERSTANDING.

Will not give object to examiner: holds it but will not release it.

Drops objects deliberately so that they will be picked up.

48 Weeks

GROSS MOTOR.

Prone—when creeping sole of foot may be flat on couch.
Sitting—pivots, twisting round to pick up object.
Walks, holding on to furniture.
Walks, 2 hands held.

GENERAL UNDERSTANDING.

Rolls ball to examiner.
Will now give toy to examiner, releasing it.
Anticipates body movements when nursery rhyme being said.
Shows interest in picture book.
Shakes head for 'No'.

PLAY.

Plays peep-bo, covering face.
Plays game—'Up, down'.

SPEECH.

One word with meaning.

1 Year

GROSS MOTOR.

Prone—walks on hands and feet like a bear.
Walks, 1 hand held.
May shuffle on buttock and hand.

HANDS.

Mouthing virtually stopped.
Beginning to throw objects to floor.

GENERAL UNDERSTANDING.

May understand meaning of phrases, 'Where is your shoe?'
May kiss on request.
Apt to be shy.

SPEECH.

Two or three words with meaning.
Knows meaning of more words.

SLOBBERING.
Virtually stopped.

15 Months

GROSS MOTOR.
Creeps up stairs. Kneels without support.
Walks without help (from 13 months).
Can get into standing position without support.
Falls by collapse.
Can't go round corners or stop suddenly.

HANDS.
Constantly throwing objects on to floor.

CUBES.
Builds tower of 2.
Holds 2 cubes in one hand.

BALL.
Can't throw without falling.

DRESSING.
Likes to take off shoes.

FEEDING.
Feeds self, picking up cup, drinking, putting it down.
Manages spoon, but rotates it near mouth.
Feeds self fully, no help.

PENCIL.
Imitates scribble, or scribbles spontaneously.

GENERAL UNDERSTANDING.
Asks for objects by pointing.
May kiss pictures of animal.
Beginning to imitate mother in domestic duties—sweeping,
    cleaning.

SPHINCTER CONTROL.
Begins to tell mother that he wants to use pottie.
Indicates wet pants.

SPEECH.
>Jargoning.
>Several intelligible words.

SIMPLE FORMBOARD.
>Inserts round block without being shown.

18 Months

GROSS MOTOR.
>Gets up and down stairs, holding rail, without help.
>Walks up stairs, one hand held.
>Walks, pulling toy or carrying doll.
>Seats self on chair.
>Beginning to jump (both feet).

CUBES.
>Tower of 3 or 4.

BALL.
>Throws ball without fall.

DRESSING.
>Takes off gloves, socks, unzips.

FEEDING.
>Manages spoon well, without rotation.

PENCIL.
>Spontaneous scribble.
>Makes stroke imitatively.

GENERAL UNDERSTANDING.
>'Domestic mimicry'.   Copies mother in dusting, washing, cleaning.

PARTS OF BODY.
>Points to 2 or 3 (nose, eye, hair, etc.).

SIMPLE ORDERS[1]
>Two.

[1] Take ball to mother, put it on chair, bring it to me, put it **on** table.

COMMON OBJECTS[2]
One.

PICTURE CARD.[3]
Points to one ('Where is the . . .?')

BOOK.
Turns pages, 2 or 3 at a time.
Points to picture of car or dog.
Shows sustained interest.

SPHINCTER CONTROL.
Dry by day; occasional accident.

SPEECH.
Jargon.   Many intelligible words.

SIMPLE FORMBOARD.
Piles 3 blocks.

2 Years

GROSS MOTOR.
Goes up and down stairs alone, 2 feet per step.   Walks backward in imitation (from 21 months).
Picks up object without falling.
Runs.   Kicks ball without overbalancing.

HANDS.
Turns door knob, unscrews lid.
Washes and dries hands.

CUBES.
Tower of 6 or 7.   (5 or 6 at 21 months).
Imitates train of cubes, without adding chimney.

BALL.
Kicks.

DRESSING.
Puts on shoes, socks, pants.
Takes off shoes and socks.

[2] Penny, shoe, pencil, knife, ball.
[3] Picture card. See Figure 130.

PENCIL.
 Imitates vertical and circular stroke.

GENERAL UNDERSTANDING.
 Pulls people to show them toys (from 21 months).

PARTS OF BODY.
 Points to 4.

SIMPLE ORDERS.[1]
 Obeys 4 (3 at 21 months).

COMMON OBJECTS.[2]
 Names 3 to 5.

PICTURE CARD.[3]
 Points to 5 ('Where is the . . .?')
 Names 3 ('What is this?')

BOOK.
 Turns pages singly.

SPHINCTER CONTROL
 Dry at night if lifted out in evening.

SPEECH.
 Asks for drink, toilet, food.
 Repeats things said (from 21 months).
 Uses 'I', 'me', 'you'.
 Joins 2 or 3 words in sentences (from 21-24 months), other
  than in imitation.
 Talks incessantly.

SIMPLE FORMBOARD.
 Places all. (Places 2 or 3 at 21 months). When formboard is
  rotated, places 3 in correctly, after 4 errors.

PLAY.
 Wraps up doll. Puts it to bed.
 Parallel play. Watches others play and plays near them,
  but not with them.

[1] Take ball to mother, put it on chair, bring it to me, put it on table.
[2] Penny, shoe, pencils, knife, ball.
[3] Picture card. See Figure 130.

2½ Years

GROSS MOTOR.

> Jumps with both feet.
> Walks on tiptoes when asked.

CUBES.

> Tower of 8.
> Imitates train, adding chimney.

PENCIL.

> Holds pencil in hand instead of fist.
> Imitates vertical and horizontal stroke.
> Two or more strokes for cross.

GENERAL UNDERSTANDING.

> Helps to put things away.
> Begins to notice sex differences.
> Knows full name.
> Knows sex.

COMMON OBJECTS.

> Names 5.

PICTURE CARDS.

> Points to 7: ('Where is the . . .?').
> Names 5: ('What is this . . .?').

DIGITS.

> Repeats 2 in 1 of 3 trials (*e.g.* say 'Eight five').

COLOURED FORMS.

> Places 1.

SPHINCTER CONTROL.

> Attends to toilet need without help, except for wiping.
> Climbs on to lavatory seat.

COLOUR SENSE.

> Names one colour.

SIMPLE FORMBOARD.

> Inserts all three, adapting after errors.

3 Years

GROSS MOTOR.

> Jumps off bottom step.
> Goes up stairs, one foot per step, and down stairs, two feet per step.
> Stands on one foot for seconds.
> Rides tricycle.

HANDS.

> Can help to set table, not dropping china.

CUBES.

> Tower of 9.
> Imitates building of bridge.

DRESSING.

> Dresses and undresses fully if helped with buttons, and advised about correct shoe, back and front.
> Unbuttons front and side buttons.

PENCILS.

> Copies circle (from a card).
> Imitates cross.
> Draws a man on request.

GENERAL UNDERSTANDING.

> Knows some nursery rhymes.
> May count up to 10.

PICTURE CARD.

> Names 8: ('What is this?').

DIGITS.

> Repeats 3: (1 of 3 trials).

COLOURED FORMS.

> Places 3.

UNCOLOURED GEOMETRIC FORMS.

> Places 4.

PREPOSITIONS[1].
 Obeys 2.

COLOUR.
 Names 1.

SIMPLE FORMBOARD.
 Adapts, no error, or immediate correction.

GESELL 'INCOMPLETE MAN'.
 Adds 1–2 parts.

SPEECH.
 Constantly asking questions. Uses pronoun.

PLAY.
 Dresses and undresses doll; speaks to it.
 Now joins in play.

3½ Years

CUBES. Copies bridge.

PICTURE CARD. Names 10.

DIGITS. Repeats 3: (2 of 3 trials).

PREPOSITIONS. Obeys 3.

UNCOLOURED GEOMETRIC FORMS. Places 6.

GODDARD FORMBOARD. 56 seconds (best of 3 trials).

PLAY. Imaginary companion.

4 Years

GROSS MOTOR.
 Goes down stairs, one foot per step.
 Skips on one foot.

HANDS.
 Can button clothes fully.

[1] Put the ball under the chair, at the side of the chair, behind the chair,
on the chair.

CUBES.
Imitates gate.

PENCIL.
Copies cross.

GENERAL UNDERSTANDING.
Questioning at its height. Says which is the larger of 2 lines. Tells tall stories.

DIGITS.
3 (3 of 3 trials).

COLOURED FORMS.
Places all.

UNCOLOURED FORMS.
Places 8.

PREPOSITIONS.
Obeys 4.

SPHINCTER CONTROL.
Attends to own toilet needs.

GODDARD FORMBOARD.
46 seconds: (best of 3 trials).

GOODENOUGH TEST.
4.

GESELL 'INCOMPLETE MAN'.
Adds 3 parts.

PLAY.
Imaginative play with doll (*e.g.* being **a nurse**).

4½ Years

CUBES. Copies gate.

PENCIL. Copies square.

DIGITS. 4: (1 of 3 trials).

UNCOLOURED GEOMETRIC FORMS. Places **9**.

GODDARD FORMBOARD. 40 seconds: (best of 3 trials).

GOODENOUGH TEST. 6.

GESELL 'INCOMPLETE MAN'.
Adds 6 parts.

5 Years

GROSS MOTOR.
Skips on both feet.

CUBES.
Cannot make steps.

DRESSING.
Can tie shoelaces.

PENCIL.
Copies triangle.

GENERAL UNDERSTANDING.
Gives age.
Distinguishes morning from afternoon.
Compares 2 weights.

UNCOLOURED GEOMETRIC FORMS.
All.

DIGITS.
Repeats 4: (2 of 3 trials).

GODDARD FORMBOARD.
35 seconds: (best of 3 trials).

GOODENOUGH TEST.
8.

GESELL 'INCOMPLETE MAN'.
Adds 6–7 parts.

COLOURS.
Names 4.

PREPOSITION (triple order).
> 'Put this on the chair, open the door, then give me that book'.

6 Years

PENCIL.
> Copies diamond.

DIGITS.
> Repeats 5.

GENERAL UNDERSTANDING.
> Knows number of fingers.   Names weekdays.
> Knows right from left.
> Counts 13 pennies, not in a row. Names 4 coins.

GODDARD FORMBOARD.
> 27 seconds: (best of 3 trials).

GOODENOUGH TEST.
> 12.

GESELL 'INCOMPLETE MAN'.
> Adds 7 parts.

REFERENCES

1. BERNARD, J., SONTAG, L. W. (1947) Foetal Hearing. *J. Genet. Psychol.*, **70,** 205.

2. BROWN, C. A. (1961) The Development of Visual Capacity in the Infant and Young Child. *Cerebral Palsy Bulletin.*, **3,** 364.

3. FREEDMAN, D. G. (1964) Smiling in Blind Infants and the Issue of innate VS acquired. *J. Child Psychol.*, **5,** 171.

4. GESELL, A., ILG, F. L. (1937) *Feeding Behaviour of Infants.* Philadelphia: Lippincott.

5. GESELL, A., AMES, L. B., (1943) Ontogenic Correspondences in the Supine and Prone Positions of the Human Infant. *Yale J. Biol. Med.*, **15,** 565.

6. GESELL, A., AMES, L. B. (1947) The Development of Handedness. *J. genet. Psychol.*, **70,** 155.

7. HALVERSON, H. M. (1931) An Experimental Study of Prehension in Infants by Means of Systematic Cinema Records. *Genet. Psychol. Monogr.*, **10,** 107.

8. HALVERSON, H. M. (1937) Studies of the Grasping Responses of Early Infancy. *J. genet. Psychol.*, **51** (Parts 1, 2, 3), 371-449.

9. ILLINGWORTH, R. S. (1958) Dissociation as a Guide to Developmental Assessment. *Arch. Dis. Childh.*, **33,** 118.

10. KARELITZ, S., KARELITZ, R. E., ROSENFELD, L. S. (1960) In Bowman, P. W., Mautner, H. V. *Mental Retardation.* New York: Grune and Stratton.

11. LILLYWHITE, H. (1958) Doctor's Manual of Speech Disorders. *J. Amer. med. Ass.*, **167,** 850.

12. McGRAW, M. B. (1940) Neuromuscular Mechanism of the Infant. *Amer. J. Dis. Child.*, **60,** 1031.

13. MURPHY, K. P. (1964) Learning Problems of the Cerebrally Palsied. Study Group. Oxford. London. Spastics Society.

14. MURPHY, K. P. (1962) Ascertainment of Deafness in Children. Panorama, Dec. 3rd.

15. PEIPER, A. (1963) *Cerebral Function in Infancy and Childhood.* London: Pitman.

16. SHERIDAN, M. (1964) Disorders of Communication in Young Children. *Mth. Bull. Minist. Hlth Lab. Serv.*, **23,** 20.

17. STIRNIMANN, E. (1940) Psychologie des Neugeborenen Kindes. Zurich and Leipzig.

CHAPTER 10

VARIATIONS IN INDIVIDUAL FIELDS OF DEVELOPMENT

'Whoever, said the old goat sheep, divided all living things into sheep and goats, was ignorant that we neutrals and nondescripts outnumber all the rest, and that your sheep and your goat are merely freak specimens of ourselves, chiefly remarkable for their rarity'.—*R. L. Stevenson*: *Fable of the Goat Sheep*.

In the study of the development of infants and children, it is absolutely essential to remember that all children are different. If they were all the same, the study of development would be easy. As they are all different, and different in a wide variety of ways, the study is one of great difficulty. We can all say what the average level of development is for a child of a given age, but none can say what the normal is, for it is impossible to draw the dividing line between normal and abnormal.

It is essential to realise that there are several different patterns of development. They are as follows:

1. Average.
2. Average, becoming superior.
3. Advanced in certain fields.
4. Advanced in all fields.
5. Average or superior, deteriorating, or slowing down in development.
6. Retarded in all fields.
7. Retarded in all fields, becoming average or superior.
8. Retarded in some fields.

The truly average child, the child who is average in everything, is a rarity. Some appear to be merely average at first, but later prove to be mentally superior; it may be that the early developmental tests were not able to detect the signs of superiority, or else full maturation was delayed. Some are advanced or retarded in certain fields of development—often because of a familial trait, or, in the case of retardation, because of a physical factor (such as deafness in the case of delayed speech). The course of development of some children slows down, as in mongols, while in others tragic deterioration occurs, because of severe emotional deprivation, poor education, degenerative diseases, psychosis, encephalitis, or metabolic diseases. Retardation in all fields usually signifies mental subnormality, but can occasionally be merely a feature of delayed maturation.

In this chapter the variations in the various fields of development, and the reasons for the variations will be discussed in detail.

Variations in Motor Activity

Irwin[43] studied the degree of activity shown by 73 infants in the first fortnight, with the help of a polygraph apparatus. All were full term normal babies. The most active infant was about 290 times more active than the least active one. Significant differences in the degree of activity appeared about the fourth or fifth day.

One knows that active wiry babies are liable to posset more than the fat placid, less active ones. Interesting correlations might have been found if Irwin's cases had been followed up for several years.

Variations in Gross Motor Development

There are considerable normal variations in the age of sitting, walking and other manifestations of gross motor development. In many children with delayed development there is no discoverable reason for the delay. In others there is a variety of factors, such as conditions affecting muscle tone, or mental retardation. It is probable that an important factor which governs the age of sitting and walking is myelination of the appropriate part of the nervous system.

ADVANCED MOTOR DEVELOPMENT. Some children learn to sit and walk at an unusually early age. One often finds that there is a family history of similarly advanced motor development. Advanced motor development can be detected very early, often as soon as the third or fourth week, and early sitting can be predicted by the sixth week with a good degree of accuracy. For the purpose of demonstrating this I took cinematograph records of infants with advanced motor development in the first 8 weeks, and showed the predictive value of the early tests by refilming the infants at later ages to show the unusually early development of sitting and walking.

Advanced motor development certainly does not give any indication of mental superiority.[18] Precocious puberty is not associated with advanced motor development.

I saw a boy who was able to creep actively at $4\frac{1}{2}$ months (not crawl), and to pull himself readily to the standing position at $5\frac{1}{2}$ months. I expressed the opinion at that time that his I.Q. was not better than the average. At the age of 6 months he could walk holding on to furniture, and at 8 months he could walk without support. At $4\frac{1}{2}$ years he could not dress himself fully, and could not draw anything or count. His I.Q. test score at 5 years was 88.

I saw another boy who could walk well without support at 8 months. His I.Q. score at the age of 6 years was 103.

There have been several studies of the motor development of negro children as compared with that of white children. Curti et al.[13] studied 29 negro children at 1 year, 21 at 2 years, and 26 at 3 years, using the Gesell schedules, and found that they were advanced in creeping, standing and walking, as compared with New Haven white children, but inferior in other fields of development. Pasamanick[65a] compared 53 negro children with 99 white children at New Haven, and found definite acceleration in gross motor development in the negroes. There was no difference in adaptive, fine motor, language or personal social development. In a subsequent paper[51] 44 of the negro children were re-examined. There was a decline in language development since the first examination, but motor development remained advanced. Geber and Dean[27, 28] studied 183 African negro children, aged 1 month to 6 years, supplemented by 113 newborn African infants, using the method of André-Thomas. They found remarkable precocity in motor development. They claimed that newborn African children behaved like European children of 3 to 4 weeks of age. Children were said to sit unsupported at 3 to 4 months for a few seconds, and for half an hour or more at 5 months. There was said to be finger-thumb apposition at 5 to 6 months. At 7 months they could stand without support, and they could walk alone at 9 months. Knobloch[53] cast doubt on this work, suggesting that the so-called precocity was due to improper testing and to undue reliance on motor items. Dr. Geber, who carried out the tests, was a highly trained worker, and there can be no doubt about the accuracy of the tests. The children examined were Bantu East Africans, and the origin of the American Negroes examined by Knobloch was completely different.[53]

The evidence for advanced development in African children is unsatisfactory. Biesheuvel[7a] found no general superiority of Bantu tribes over Europeans in Gesell tests.

The advanced motor development of Uganda infants was discussed by Mary Ainsworth.[2] She suggested that the precocious development was in some way related to close infant-mother relationship, and that social and cultural factors were responsible. Others have made similar suggestions.[52, 81] Yet in five longitudinal European studies, carried out in England, Belgium, France, Sweden and Switzerland, no social (or sex) differences were found in the age of walking.

Pavenstedt,[66] in her study of slum children, noted the relatively advanced motor development in children in grossly deprived homes, where protection from the usual hazards was minimal.

Confirmation of the work of Geber and Dean and others would be interesting. I have examined a number of children from the West Indies and a few from West Africa, and have found unusually advanced development in one child only. I saw him at 6 months, when he was actively creeping around the room. He was said to have begun to sit without support on the floor at 3 months, to creep at 4 months, and to pull himself up to a standing position at 5 months. From my own findings it seemed likely that these figures were correct. The boy subsequently walked without help at 7 months. Manipulation, however, was only average, and I did not think that in other fields of development he was unusual. It may be that there is advancement of motor development in certain races only.

Lateness in Gross Motor Development

The following are the usual factors related to delayed motor development.

1. *Familial Factors.* The age at which children learn to walk is often a familial feature. It probably depends on the familial rate of myelination of the spinal cord.

2. *Environmental Factors.* Children who are brought up in an institution from early infancy are likely to be late in motor development, as in other fields. This may be in part due to lack of practice. If mothers deliberately keep their infants off their

legs to prevent them developing rickets, knock-knee or bow legs, they weaken the child's legs and may retard walking.

Dennis[13] and others tried to teach children to walk earlier than usual, but failed, for the age of walking is governed in large part by maturation of the nervous system.

3. *Personality.* The personality of the child has some bearing on the age of walking, in that children with little confidence and much caution, or children who lose confidence as a result of falls, may be delayed in learning to walk. A child with extreme delay in learning to walk (4 years) had no mechanical difficulty and had a normal I.Q. She was able to walk with one finger held for a whole year before she eventually summoned up enough courage to walk alone. When a child like this eventually walks without support, it is at once obvious that the gait is a mature one, indicating that he could have walked long before, if his confidence had permitted. Slippery shoes in a child of 12 months may be enough to cause falls and delay in walking.

4. *Mental Subnormality.* Most mentally retarded children are late in learning to sit, but not all (Ch. 15).

Case Report.—This boy took no notice of his surroundings at all until 6 months of age, and did not smile until then. At 9 months he was able to sit without support and at 13 months he could walk without help. At 5 the I.Q. was well below 50.

Mongols are later in learning to walk than other mentally defective children of a comparable level of intelligence. The reason for this may be the hypotonia which characterises them.

As a general guide, one can say that a child with an I.Q. of less than 20 may learn to walk, as long as he has no cerebral palsy: a child with an I.Q. of 20 to 40, in the absence of cerebral palsy, can certainly be expected to learn to walk.

5. *Abnormalities of Muscle Tone.* If there is excessive muscle tone, as in cerebral palsy, walking will be delayed. Some children with cerebral palsy never walk. It would not be profitable to analyse the average age at which children with different forms of cerebral palsy learn to sit or walk, because there is an additional vital factor, the intelligence, which has a profound effect on motor development.

In the case of the spastic form of cerebral palsy, the child with hemiplegia is likely to learn to walk sooner than the child with diplegia or quadriplegia, especially if his I.Q. is satisfactory.

I have seen an occasional hemiplegic child with a good I.Q. who learned to sit and walk at the usual age. The child with diplegia with a normal I.Q. is not likely to be very late in sitting, but he will be considerably delayed in learning to walk. I do not know what factors, other than the I.Q., decide the age at which a child with diplegia will be able to sit unsupported. They may include the amount of spasm in the hamstrings and of the trunk muscles, the amount of extension thrust, and the presence and strength of an asymmetrical tonic neck reflex. I have seen several with quite severe diplegia who could sit at the usual age without support (7 months).

The usual story of diplegia with a good I.Q. is average or somewhat retarded sitting, with grossly delayed walking, but normal development in all other fields. Below is an example.

Case Report.—This girl was born prematurely, weighing 5 lbs. 2 ozs. She grasped a rattle voluntarily at 5 months, sat unsupported at 8 months, held and could manage a cup at 15 months. Slight general backwardness with diplegia was then diagnosed. She said single words at 20 months and put words together at 24 months. She walked alone at 6½ years, when her I.Q. score was 85.

I have, however, seen a child with a mild to moderate diplegia, but with a normal I.Q. who was able to walk without help at 18 months. The child with spastic quadriplegia is almost invariably retarded in both sitting and walking, and his I.Q. is usually lower than that of the child with hemiplegia or diplegia.

The child with athetosis is usually late in learning to sit and walk, but not always, provided that the I.Q. is normal.

The child with rigidity is virtually always severely mentally defective, and may never walk.

The child with ataxia or tremor is usually late in learning to walk.

The child with hypotonia is late in learning to sit or walk, and if the condition is severe he will never learn to do either. There are probably other related conditions. The child with benign congenital hypotonia will learn to sit and walk very late. I have seen several who were able to walk between the age of 4 and 6 years.

A child who develops hypotonia, as a result of severe illness, rickets, or acrodynia, will be delayed in gross motor development, but as the underlying disease improves, his motor development advances.

A child with meningomyelocele with involvement of the lower limbs will be unable to walk without a series of skilled orthopaedic procedures, including muscle transplants.

The following is an example of hypotonia, with a moderately low I.Q.

Case Report.—This girl was born at term, without asphyxia, but she was limp, and caused anxiety. The tendon jerks were normal. At 5 months there was complete head lag. At 13 months she showed mature transfer of objects, but the head control was that of a 10 week old baby. She was retarded in other fields. A diagnosis of benign congenital hypotonia with mental retardation was made. She was able to join words together at 27 months and to walk unaided at 5 years, when the I.Q. was 59.

The usual story in cases of benign congenital hypotonia is that of defective gross motor development, with normal development in other fields—normal age of smiling, chewing and manipulation, with late sitting and walking.

Another child was referred to me at the age of 8 months for confirmation of the diagnosis of mental defectiveness. The developmental history was not reliable. The head control was that of a 4 months old baby, but he was interested in test objects. His manipulative development was not less than that of an average 8 months old baby. He rapidly transferred objects from hand to hand, and his grasp was a mature one. He was seen to chew.

He was markedly hypotonic, and he showed the typical signs of acrodynia (erythroedema). He made an uninterrupted recovery, and on follow-up examination was normal in all respects.

6. *Neuromuscular Disease.* In the case below the only complaint was lateness in walking.

Case Report.—Delayed walking due to Werdnig-Hoffman's Disease.

This girl was referred to me when she was 12 months' old because she was not nearly able to walk. Her developmental history was average. She had begun to smile at 5 weeks, to grasp objects voluntarily and to chew at 5 months, to imitate at 6 months, to wave bye-bye and to hold her arm out for clothes at 9 months, and to say several words with meaning by 11 months. She was able to sit unsupported on the floor at 7 months, but the mother thought that she was not quite as steady when sitting 2 months ago as she was 3 months ago.

On examination she was an interested, alert girl with good concentration, vocalising well. The manipulation was normal, and there was a prompt finger-thumb apposition. She was able to sit steadily, but she bore virtually no weight on the legs. She was an obese girl, and there was doubtful slight hypotonia. Knee jerks could not be obtained, but tendon jerks elsewhere were normal. There was no congenital dermal sinus or other spinal abnormality. The gluteal and thigh creases were asymmetrical, but the X-ray of the hips was normal. No fibrillary twitching was seen, but the tentative diagnosis of Werdnig Hoffman's disease was made. She was observed for 5 months, during which time no change in her condition occurred. It was then decided that further investigation should be carried out, and the electrical reactions, muscle biopsy and electro-myogram confirmed the diagnosis of Werdnig-Hoffman's disease. The cerebrospinal fluid was normal.

In this case the developmental examination revealed the neurological disease.

7. *Shuffling.*   The peculiar mode of progression known as shuffling or hitching, on one hand and one buttock, may delay the onset of walking. The child learns to progress rapidly in this way. The retardation caused is not severe.

8. *Blindness.*   Blind children have to be taught to walk. In one study[25a] only two out of 12 children crawled before they learnt to walk. A blind child's motor development is apt to be retarded because he is not given the same chance to learn to walk as normal children. His parents may be so afraid that he will hurt himself that they do not let him practise walking.

9. *Cause Unknown.*   If gross motor development is considerably delayed, there is usually a good cause for it, but this is by no means always the case. I have seen 10 children with no physical or mental handicap, who were unable to walk without help until the second birthday or later. There was no discoverable cause for this in any of them. All were followed up, and were shown to be normal children.

Case 1.—This boy was delivered normally at term. He began to smile at 6 weeks, to vocalise at 8 weeks, to grasp objects voluntarily at 5 months, to transfer them from hand to hand at 6 months and to chew at that age. He began to release objects and to play patacake at 11 months. On the other hand he could not sit without support till 19 months, or walk without help until 30 months. At the age of 5 years his I.Q. test score was 104.

Case 2.—A girl who was delivered normally at term could grasp objects voluntarily at 4 months, manage a cup of milk without help at 10 months, and was speaking in sentences at 12 months. She sat without support at 9 months, but could not walk without help till 4 years. Her I.Q. at 5 years was in the region of 125. There was no physical disability.

Others walked without help at 24 months (I.Q. average), 24 months (with advanced speech in long sentences); 25 months (I.Q. just average), and 30 months (I.Q. 108).

Delayed walking is *not* due to congenital dislocation of the hip. It is *not* due to obesity. Norval[63] found that thin or tall babies tend to walk earlier than fat ones, but Peatman and Higgons[67] thought that this was an old wives' tale. I saw a grossly obese child, weighing 56 lbs. at 15 months, who walked without help at 10 months.

OTHER VARIATIONS IN MOTOR DEVELOPMENT. One of my colleagues at Sheffield[25a] has shown that the current tendency in the United States to place young babies in the prone position for sleep and play has apparently led to an alteration of the developmental pattern in the prone and supine positions. Babies managed in this way seem to be much more advanced in the prone position than do babies who are placed on their back for sleep and play. It was suggested that the relationship of posture to observed developmental variations might well repay further study.

For reasons unknown some children omit the stage of creeping.

Crawling and Walking Before Sitting

Below is a bizarre example of unusual motor development.

Case Report.—This girl, aged 19 months when first seen (birth weight 2 lbs. 6 ozs.) was referred because she could not sit, although she could crawl forwards and walk well with one hand held, or walk while holding on to furniture.

She had been able to go for objects and get them from 4 months. She had begun to say words with meaning at 9 months. She could pick up a cup, drink and put it down without help from one year, and she had begun to walk, holding on to furniture, at that date.

She was a bright, interested girl, talking and jargoning well. She was seen to walk well, holding on to the edge of the desk. When placed in the sitting position, although head control was full, the back was markedly rounded, but there was no spasm of the hamstrings. She repeatedly fell backwards. The grasp with each hand was normal. The knee jerks were normal and there was no ankle clonus. There was on shortening in either leg. Spinal muscles were normal and there was no evidence of vertebral or spinal anomalies.

The clinical diagnosis was either congenital shortening of the gluteus maximus or congenital shortening of the hamstrings.

Another child who was able to crawl before he was able to sit had suffered from emotional deprivation by being brought up in an institution. The explanation of the anomaly of development may have laid in the fact that he could crawl without help, but needed help to sit, and the staff had not time to give him that help.

Another child who showed this variation had congenital hypotonia.

Grasping and Manipulation

Voluntary grasping may begin as early as 3 months, but it is rare. It is most unusual for a normal full term child not to be able to grasp objects by 6 months.

The subsequent development of manipulation depends not only on intelligence, but on the child's aptitudes—some showing early manipulative ability greater than others of comparable intelligence.

Smiling

The earliest age at which I have personally seen a child smile in response to social overture was 3 days. From that day onwards smiling became rapidly more frequent. He was a uniformly advanced baby, holding and playing with a rattle, for instance, for several minutes at $2\frac{1}{2}$ weeks, and following an object for 180 degrees at 3 weeks. He proved to have a high I.Q. in later years.

Söderling[75] analysed the age of the first smile in 400 normal full term infants. The following are the figures:

First smile				Percentage
Before 2 weeks	–	–	–	0
2–3 weeks	–	–	–	11
3–4 weeks	–	–	–	49
4–5 weeks	–	–	–	21
5–6 weeks	–	–	–	19

Very few normal full term babies reach 8 weeks of age without having begun to smile. There is little latitude in this direction for normal babies. Nevertheless, I have seen an occasional full term baby who did not begin to smile until 8 to 10 weeks of age, without delay in other fields, and who subsequently turned out to be normal.

I had a child referred to me with a diagnosis of mental deficiency, the chief reason being a complete absence of smiling by the age of 1 year. She was an example of the Möbius syndrome of congenital facial diplegia, with an I.Q. score of about 75.

Delayed Visual Maturation

Delayed visual maturation may cause serious doubts as to whether a child is blind or not.[39]

I described a boy first seen by me at the age of just under four months, because he did not appear to see. He did not smile at his mother, or watch her face, or focus his eyes. He had begun to vocalise at seven weeks and to turn his head to sound at twelve weeks. On examination he was developmentally up to the average in all respects. On ophthalmoscopic examination (by me and by two ophthalmologists) no abnormality was found, and there was no nystagmus. The provisional diagnosis of delayed visual maturation was made, and the parents were informed that there were good grounds for optimism, though because of the rarity of the condition it was impossible to be sure.

He showed signs of seeing at five months, and by six months he was following a light and beginning to follow a dangling ring. He appeared to be normal in all respects at ten months. At the age of five years he was showing a better than average intelligence, at an ordinary preparatory school. He had a slight strabismus, for which glasses were worn, but the vision was normal.

I also saw a girl who apparently saw nothing for the first six months. She had spasmus nutans. No abnormality was noted in the eyes. She too was examined by an ophthalmologist, who found nothing abnormal. She began to show signs of seeing at six months, and by a year of age was normal. At school age she showed a better than average intelligence, with normal vision.

It is not possible to say whether these children were genuinely unable to see, or whether they were unable to interpret what they saw (visual agnosia).

The Blind Child

If blindness develops shortly after birth, the muscles round the eye—the orbicularis oculis, corrugator supercilii and frontalis muscles—are not involved in facial expression, remaining rigid and motionless. If the child becomes blind sometime after birth, the facial expression is normal.[68]

Blind children may show a variety of mannerisms,[80] such as eye-boring, pressing the finger into the eye—beginning in the first year and ending by the fifth or sixth year. The child may show rapid symmetrical flapping of the hands, hyperextension or flexion of the head, twirling massive to and fro body swaying, jumping backwards and forwards, or facial grimacing.

The assessment of the development of a blind child is difficult; the tests used and the problems of assessment were discussed by the Bakwins (1966). They wrote that over the age of three the Interim Hayes Bint Intelligence Test is favoured by many. Apparent backwardness may be due to unsatisfactory tests, restricted past experiences, inadequate opportunities for learning, and overprotection. The mean I.Q. of blind children is less than that of the normal population (see Chapter 5).

It would be expected that blindness would retard smiling.[26] Not only does he not receive the stimulus of seeing his mother's face, but he is 'at risk' of being mentally retarded—and therefore late in his milestones of development. The blind child is likely to smile at his mother's voice by about 8 weeks.

Blind children may show what Gesell termed 'hand regard'. This 'hand regard', seen in normal infants from 12 to 24 weeks of age, is presumably a developmental phenomenon and not related to vision.

Delayed Auditory Maturation

Some children, who are mentally normal, appear to be deaf for some weeks or months, and subsequently respond normally to sound. Ingram[40] has studied several examples of this. He suggests that it may be the result of damage to the auditory nerve or its central connections before birth, and that recovery then follows. He wrote that some infants with kernicterus do not begin to respond to sound until the age of 4 or 5 months. He considered that some children with brain damage appear to be deaf in the early weeks, but later are found to hear, though they may be later in distinguishing their parent's or sibling's voices, and late in learning to perceive or distinguish what is said. Others have difficulty in perceiving sounds and distinguishing them, and are late in acquiring speech. They are slow to react to sound, and slow to differentiate them or perceive their significance. He terms this developmental auditory imperception.

Sheridan[72] has seen children who appeared to be deaf for some weeks after an attack of meningitis, and were then found to hear normally.

Chewing

There is little variation in the age at which normal infants learn to chew. They may begin as early as 5 months, but nearly all full term infants can chew by the age of 7 months. The age of chewing is delayed if a sufficiently mature baby is given thickened feeds only, with nothing solid to bite on.

Feeding and Dressing

The age at which children learn to feed and dress themselves depends not only on their intelligence and manipulative ability, but on the opportunity to learn given by the parents. The age at which they do it also depends on their personality and desire for independence.

Sphincter Control

There are great individual variations in the age at which sphincter control is acquired. It is difficult to say how soon control can be acquired, because it is not easy to distinguish the early conditioning from voluntary control. I doubt whether voluntary control begins before the age of 12 months.

Many children do not acquire control of the bladder for several years. Thorough investigation reveals no abnormality, though some would disagree with this. Disagreement centres largely on the interpretation of micturating urethrograms and similar studies. When one sees a child who has never had a dry night, and has long passed the usual age for acquiring control of the bladder, there is usually a family history of the same complaint.

This is termed primary enuresis, and it is almost certainly due basically to delayed maturation of the nervous system. This cannot be the only factor, however, because there must be socioeconomic factors to explain the fact that primary enuresis is more common in the lower social classes than in the upper, and that the quality of home care is relevant. Many of these children retain the primitive urgency into school years. It is normal for an 18 to 24 month old child to have great urgency, so that he cannot wait to pass urine, but as he matures he loses this urgency; but the child with primary enuresis commonly retains this urgency for several years.

The Newcastle team[57] found that a low social class, emotional deprivation, deficient physical care, social dependence, marital instability, parental crime and corrective family supervision were strongly related to the incidence of enuresis. I agree with Miller's conclusion,[58] on the basis of the Newcastle work, that 'the social correlations were such that it is reasonable to think that most enuresis occurs in a child with a slow pattern of maturation when that child is in a family where he does not receive sufficient care to acquire proper conditioning. We doubt if the continuous type of enuresis is caused by major psychological difficulties at the onset, though we acknowledge that psychological difficulties can occur as an overlap'. 'Enuresis is not only a disturbance of development in an individual child, but also a reflection of family relationships and attitudes'.

When a child who has been dry at night begins to wet (secondary enuresis), the cause is almost always psychological, but may be due to the development of frequency of micturition or to polyuria, in either case particularly if he has only recently acquired control of the bladder. The cause usually lies in insecurity, separation from the parents, jealousy or other emotional trauma.

The acquisition of sphincter control can be delayed by over-enthusiastic 'training'—compelling the child to sit on the pottie when he is trying to get off, and punishment for failure to do what is expected of him, so that his normal negativism comes into play, and he may furthermore come to associate the pottie with unpleasantness, and become conditioned against it.

The Newcastle workers found that at least nine per cent at five were still wetting the bed habitually or frequently. This corresponds closely with White's figure[79] of 'nearly 10 per cent' for Croydon children.

Organic causes of delayed sphincter control are of great importance. Constant dribbling incontinence in a boy suggests urethral obstruction, and in a girl it suggests an ectopic ureter entering the vagina or urethra. In either sex the incontinence may be due to a meningomyelocele or other gross spinal abnormality. The surgical causes of enuresis were fully reviewed by Smith in Australia.[74]

Speech

The development of speech depends on a range of factors: genetic, auditory, environmental, intellectual and constitutional, one interacting with the other. As would be expected, therefore, there are wide variations in speech development in children. On the one hand, normal children may begin to say words with meaning by the age of 8 months, and even make sentences spontaneously before the first birthday: on the other hand many children of superior intelligence may not begin to speak at all until the third or fourth birthday and have defective speech by the age of 5.

In general girls learn to speak earlier than boys.

Morley,[61] in her sample of 114 children from the Newcastle-on-Tyne 1,000 family survey, found that 73 per cent. of the children were using words with meaning by the first birthday, with a range of 8 to 30 months, and 40 per cent. had begun to join words together, other than in imitation, by the age of 18 months. The range for this was 10 to 44 months. Eighty-nine per cent. had begun to join words by the age of 24 months. In 10 per cent. speech was not intelligible at the age of 4 years. Seventeen per cent. had defects of articulation of serious degree at 4 years, and 14 per cent. at 5 years. All these children had an I.Q. within the normal range. These figures, though based on a small sample in one city, give a good idea of the variations in speech development in normal children. In the same survey[57] it was found that speech defects such as stammering were more common in social classes 4 and 5, and in homes with poor maternal care.

Gesell *et al.*[29] wrote that a normal 2 year old may have a vocabulary of a few words or more than 2,000.

UNUSUALLY EARLY DEVELOPMENT OF SPEECH. There are several stories of unusually early speech. Some of these were described by Barlow.[6] Jean Cardiac, of France, was said to be able to repeat the alphabet at 3 months.

Delay in the Development of Speech and Aphasia

GENERAL ANALYSIS OF CAUSES

In any analysis of speech problems it is difficult to determine how selected the cases were. For instance, only a limited number of all children with delay in speech development are referred to a speech clinic. Morley[61] analysed a series of 280 children referred to her speech clinic at Newcastle-on-Tyne, and gave the following figures:

Hearing defects – – – – – –	110
Developmental expressive aphasia – – –	72
Mental retardation – – – – – –	71
Cerebral palsy – – – – – –	22
Psychogenic retardation – – – – –	3
Developmental receptive aphasia (congenital auditory imperception)– – – – –	2

Goodwin[31] analysed 454 cases of speech retardation in a mental centre. Their average age was 50 months. 277 were boys and 177 were girls. His figures were as follows:

	Percentage
Mental retardation alone. (I.Q. less than 70) –	35·7
Brain damage – – – – – –	26·4
Functional – – – – – –	11·7
Hearing loss – – – – – –	4·8
Deferred – – – – – –	21·4

If one includes the mentally retarded children with brain damage, the total percentage of children with mental retardation was 53.

Although I have not made a statistical analysis, I have no doubt that by far the commonest cause of delay in the development of speech as seen in an out-patient clinic is mental retardation. Only a few of these are referred to the speech therapy department.

Mental Retardation. There is a strong relationship between intelligence and speech, and mental retardation has a profound effect on speech development. Speech development, in fact, is relatively more retarded in mentally backward children than are other fields of development. The retarded child takes less notice of what is said to him, has poor concentration, is late in imitation, and is backward in the expression and comprehension of words.

Though defective articulation occurs in these children, probably to a greater degree than in children of average intelligence, the main problem is delay in the onset of speech and in its use as a means of expression. Common defects in older children include irrelevancy of ideas, echolalia (repetition of questions put instead of answering them), and perseveration—repeating phrases which have just been said.

It would be useful if one could predict the likelihood of speech development in severely retarded children. We know that the vast majority of mongols learn to speak in time. Karlin and Kennedy[47] found that of 32 children with an I.Q. of less than 20, seen between the age of 7 and 38, 20 had complete mutism and 10 had a 'jabber with an occasional intelligent word'. Of 32 children with an I.Q. of 20 to 50, seen between the age of 5 and 26, 7 had mutism, and 24 had defective speech. Of 249 children with an I.Q. of 50 to 70, none had mutism.

Brown[10] referred to an interesting finding in retarded children. He found that some children used single words by about 12 months, but only on infrequent occasions, and then not again for several months. Many parents have told me that their retarded child seemed to learn to say a few words and then to forget them, so that they were not heard again for many months.

Defects of Hearing. It is obvious that if there is a severe defect of hearing, the child will not learn to speak until special methods of teaching him are used. If the defect is less severe, he may learn to make sounds such as b, f, w, which he can see made, but not the g, l, and r. He substitutes for these, and is apt to say 'do' for go, 'yady' for lady, 'wed' for red.

When there is only high pitch deafness, involving those pitches which are used in human speech, *i.e.* between 512 and 2,048 double vibrations per second,[64] the child is late in learning to talk, or more commonly his speech is defective through the omission of certain high-pitched sounds such as the 's' and 'f' which the child does not hear in the speech of others. He tends to omit the final consonants in words. He does, however, respond to the low frequency whispers, clicks and clapping of the hands commonly used as hearing tests. He can hear the car passing and the door banging and the aeroplane, and will listen to the wireless, so that his parents and often the doctor do not consider the possibility of deafness.

If the defect of hearing develops after speech has been acquired, speech is not severely disturbed; but a relatively slight defect at an early stage of development will cause a serious defect of speech.

Delayed Maturation.   It is commonly thought that the development of speech depends on the maturation of the nervous system and probably on its myelination. It follows that no amount of practice can make a child speak before his nervous system is ready for it, and that speech therapy has only a limited place in the treatment of the mentally retarded child who is late in learning to speak.

In all normal children the understanding of the spoken word long precedes the ability to articulate. A patient of mine at the age of 15 months could only say 4 or 5 words with meaning, but he could readily point out 200 common objects in picture books, when asked, 'Where is the . . . ?' (drum, cup, soldier, etc.). I saw another child who at $2\frac{1}{2}$ could say 4 or 5 words only. His father and sister were late in speaking. Three weeks later he was speaking freely in 5 word sentences. Einstein gave his parents reason for anxiety about his mental development because of his retarded speech when he was 4. He lacked fluency of speech at 9.[24]

Familial Factors.   When a child is notably late in learning to speak, and has normal hearing with a normal level of intelligence, and has no mechanical disability such as cerebral palsy, it is common to find that there is a family history of the same problem —particularly in the mother or father. The reason may lie in a familial delay in the maturation of the appropriate part of the nervous system.

Association with Dyslexia.   Delay in speech development is commonly associated with later dyslexia and dysgraphia. This syndrome has been excellently reviewed by Ingram.[41, 42] Anyone interested should read this paper in detail. He drew attention to the frequency with which these three difficulties occur together, in varying degrees, although they can occur alone. The condition is familial. Most cases are inherited as a result of an autosomal mendelian dominant gene. It is much more common in boys than girls. In all cases there is weak lateralisation of handedness. In mild forms there is merely dyslalia. In moderate forms there is also delay in the acquisition of words and phrases. In severe forms the child is slow in learning to speak and slow in learning to comprehend speech. There may also be auditory imperception. All but the most severely affected children develop speech in time.

The Environment. It is customary to find in textbooks and papers the statement that over-protection is an important cause of retardation of speech. It is supposed to retard speech by making speech unnecessary, everything being done for the child before he asks for it. This statement is made, for instance, by Goertzen[30] in a rather uncritical review of speech problems, and by Ausubel[4] in an otherwise excellent discussion. I have never seen any evidence to this effect, neither have I ever seen a child in which there was anything to suggest that such 'overprotection' had any bearing on the child's development. If it were true, one would expect to find that speech would tend to be delayed in the first child of a family, in whom overprotection is more likely to occur than in subsequent children. There is no such evidence, and in fact the reverse is the case,[49] first born children tending to speak earlier than subsequent ones. Davis[14] wrote that 'only and over-valued children begin talking at an early age, because of the surfeit of adult attention, affection and stimulation they receive, and because of the increased availability of adult speech patterns'.

It is well known that language development is retarded in children who are brought up in an institution. It has been said that this retardation can be detected as early as the second month of life, by the variety and frequency of phonemes emitted.[6] These children tend to be late in acquiring speech and subsequently in sentence formation.

It must be exceptional for lack of stimulation to be so extreme in a private house that delay in speech development results.

Carrel and Bangs[11] wrote that 'lack of adequate stimulation as a cause for delayed language development requires only brief mention, although the notion that most speechless children do not talk because they don't have to, or because they are just lazy, is not only very common, but sometimes crops up where a more intelligent attitude might be expected'. Karlin[49] wrote that 'the concept that lack of stimulation will delay language development has been over-emphasised'.

Several workers have mentioned the relation of social class to speech development. In the upper social classes there is greater parent-child contact, there are better speech models in the home, and higher parental expectation regarding verbal accomplishment.[4]   In addition there is a higher mean level of intelligence. It is generally recognised that speech development occurs earlier in the upper social classes than the lower ones. Speech development and vocabulary are considerably retarded in slum children.

Eisenson[20] reviewed evidence that there was a tendency for parents of children with delayed speech to be unrealistic, rigid, perfectionist and overprotective.   The home environment was said to be characterised by confusion and lack of organisation. There was a tendency for the mothers to be maladjusted and neurotic. He suggested that parental rejection which takes the form of continuous disapproval and criticism of speech as well as of other forms of behaviour may cause the child to stop efforts to talk. Solomon[76] compared the background of a group of children with functional defects of articulation with that of normal controls. He found significant differences in overall adjustment and sleeping behaviour in the two groups. Affected children had less good relationships with their parents and more sleep problems, and tended to be passive, to internalise their responses, to be submissive, timid and needing approval.

It would certainly seem to be reasonable to suggest that severe rejection might cause at least partial mutism.

It is customary to say that delay in the acquisition of speech is due to jealousy. The new baby is blamed for a lot of things, but I have never seen any reason to blame him for this. It would indeed be difficult to prove that jealousy of a sibling has delayed speech, and I have never seen any attempt to supply evidence to that effect.

Many workers ascribe delay in speech to 'laziness'. It is argued that the child does not speak because he cannot be bothered to do so. I have never seen an example of this. I have certainly seen serious harm done by advice given to parents by a family doctor that the child should be made to express his needs, on the ground that his failure to speak is just 'laziness'. Really troublesome behaviour problems result from the consequent thwarting. In fact the reason why the children were not speaking was that they couldn't. I agree entirely with Morley[44] that laziness is rarely if ever the cause of delayed speech development.

In any consideration of psychological problems in relation to speech development, it must always be borne in mind that speech problems, including delay in the onset of speech and indistinctness of speech or stuttering, may themselves cause psychological problems, insecurity and withdrawal from the fellowship of others. It is easy to ascribe the speech problems to the psychological difficulties, when in fact the psychological difficulties are due to the speech problem.

For a good review of speech delay, the reader should refer to the book by Renfrew and Murphy.[70]

Psychosis. Delayed speech or absence of speech is a characteristic feature of infantile autism. Rutter[71] listed the principle features of autism as follows:–profound abnormality of language development, stereotyped mannerisms, ritualistic and compulsive phenomena, abnormal interpersonal relationships and aloofness, lack of interest in people, avoidance of eye gaze, little variation of facial expression, relative failure to exhibit feelings or appreciate humour, and lack of sympathy for others. The autistic infant commonly shows no desire to be picked up.

Mutism may be a manifestation of schizophrenia. I have seen one example of mutism due to hysteria.

Speech Delay in Twins and Triplets. It has long been recognised that speech tends to develop later in twins. Day[15] made a special study of the subject, investigating the development of speech in 80 pairs of twins, and comparing their speech with that of singletons of the same age, sex and socioeconomic status. He analysed the length of speech response to toys, the results of Piaget functional tests, the grammatical construction of sentences and the use of words. The twins were retarded in language development in each of the 4 tests. They learned to talk on an average a month later than their older siblings. The retardation increased with age. Twins of the upper social classes were superior in all tests to those of the lower classes. The twins were below average in intelligence tests, but the retardation in language was greater than that of the intelligence quotient. More than a fifth were left-handed.

The usual reason given for the delayed speech development in twins is exemplified by the statement of Jersild[45] that 'the type of companionship which twins provide each other means that there is less reason for using language to communicate with others'. Morley[61] pointed out, however, that the speech defect is rarely the same in both twins; that speech disorders may occur in one twin and not the other; and that twins may each have a speech disorder but of dissimilar type and degree. It would seem, therefore, that other factors are involved. It is likely that one cause is the fact that the mother of twins has not as much time to devote to the two children as she would have for a singleton: she reads to them less, and has less time to teach them the names of objects. Another cause may lie in the twin imitating the speech of his co-twin instead of that of an adult.

Russian psychologists have described an experiment on twins who were said (without satisfactory evidence) to be uniovular.[55] They had 5 older siblings, but their home environment was unsatisfactory. They were left to play with each other, without toys. They never heard a book read, were never told stories, and few spoke to them. Their mother and her brother were late in speaking. The twins were retarded in speech, but the I.Q. was not tested. There were indications, however, that the I.Q. may have been low. There appeared to be an element of receptive aphasia, but the question of high tone deafness was not mentioned. The authors thought that the retardation in speech was due to the fact that they did not need to speak to anyone else but each other. The psychologists therefore separated them, placing them in different kindergartens, and one in addition was given speech therapy. In each case the speech underwent rapid improvement, and they ascribed this to the separation of the twins. It was obvious, however, that other factors were involved—familial speech retardation, probably a low I.Q., some degree of receptive aphasia, and the absence of normal stimulation at home. The possibility that the children would have talked equally early if left as they were was not mentioned. Lulls in speech development, with subsequent rapid progress, are well known.

Lulls and Spurts. Many children go through phases in which the development of speech seems to come to a complete stop. Shirley[73] pointed out that when one skill is being actively learned another skill tends to go into abeyance. The child seems to make no progress for some months, and then suddenly, for no apparent reason, he makes rapid headway. These lulls cause considerable anxiety to parents. I have seen one child who at 15 months was well below the average in speech, being able to say only 4 or 5 words, while at 18 months he was much better than the average, speaking in long sentences. Another child at the age of 30 months was only able to say 4 or 5 single words.

Three weeks later he was speaking well in 5-word sentences. His father and sister had been late in learning to talk.

When a child is learning to speak, deterioration in the clarity of speech may occur when he has a respiratory infection, apart from the effect of nasal obstruction.

Lateral Dominance and Crossed Laterality. The relationship of lateral dominance and crossed laterality to speech problems has been discussed elsewhere (Ch. 4).

Cleft Palate. A cleft palate in itself causes only trivial retardation of speech development, though it causes indistinctness of speech if treatment is inadequate. I have shown elsewhere, however, that the intelligence of children with cleft palate tends to be on the average somewhat less than that of other children.[36] A low level of intelligence will affect speech development. Lillywhite[50] suggested that a cleft palate may also cause some retardation because consonant sounds p, b, t, d, k, g needed by the child to establish his early vocabulary are the ones most disturbed by the open palate, with the result that some prelanguage activity is omitted. It should be remembered that deafness commonly develops in children with cleft palate—usually, however, after speech has been acquired.

Other Defects. A submucous cleft or adenoids cause nasal speech. Rhinolalia may follow adenoidectomy, possibly as a result of decreased postoperative movement of the palate.

Malocclusion affects speech, especially if there is micrognathia or 'an open bite'.

There is a difference of opinion as to whether '*tongue-tie*' really affects speech or not. In general it would seem that the opinion of American speech therapists is against it. Some workers believe that the child with a short frenulum has difficulty in pronouncing the letters n, l, t, d, and th. It is certain that tongue-tie does not cause delay in the onset of speech.

Speech in Cerebral Palsy. Speech problems are very common in cerebral palsy. They include both delay in beginning to speak, receptive aphasia and dysarthria. Dunsdon[19] found speech defects in 70 per cent. of her cases, and Floyer[21] found a speech defect in 46 per cent. of the Liverpool school age children. The figure for the athetoid children was 88 per cent.

There are several causes for the speech problems of children with cerebral palsy. They include a low level of intelligence, hearing difficulties, inco-ordination or spasticity of the muscles of speech and respiration, the effect of prematurity and of multiple pregnancy, cortical defects and psychological factors. In addition, there is a high incidence of left-handedness in cerebral palsy. Fifty per cent. of children with cerebral palsy have an I.Q. of less than 70.[38] Defects of hearing are common, particularly in children with the athetoid form of cerebral palsy. Twenty per cent. or more have a significant defect of hearing. Inco-ordination of the muscles of the tongue, larynx and thorax interferes with articulation, especially in athetoid children. Thirty per cent. of all children with cerebral palsy were prematurely born and about 8 per cent. were products of multiple pregnancy—both factors related to speech delay. Psychological factors are important, for children with cerebral palsy may well lack normal stimulation and the contact of others. In addition there are probably other factors related to the cortical defect in cerebral palsy. Many factors, therefore, may operate to cause delays and difficulties in speech in these children.

Speech is not delayed by tongue tie, it is *not* delayed by laziness, it is *not* delayed by 'Everything being done for him'. A child does not speak because he cannot speak.

Aphasia

As in many other matters, it is impossible to draw the line between normal and abnormal. There are great variations in the age at which speech develops in normal children, and it is not at all clear at what stage of delay in development in relation to the I.Q. one should use the word aphasia.

One must try to distinguish the receptive form of aphasia (e.g. congenital auditory imperception) from the expressive form. Whereas the child with receptive aphasia cannot understand written or spoken language, the child with expressive aphasia can understand, but cannot use meaningful language. Karlin[48] thought that many children showed a combination of both forms.

Receptive aphasia is much commoner in boys than in girls. The child can hear what is said, but cannot understand the spoken word. There have been numerous papers on this condition. The term 'congenital auditory imperception' was suggested by Worster-Drought,[82] in a valuable article on the subject. He wrote that the essential feature is a failure to understand spoken language when it is spoken in his hearing but out of his sight. There is a striking difference between the child's ability to comprehend spoken language heard, from that seen. He added that in addition to failure to appreciate the significance of spoken words, there is also an inability to distinguish between less specialised sounds than those of spoken language. He therefore regarded 'congenital word deafness', a term used by others, as too limited. The child may cause confusion in diagnosis by repeating words said by another—but he fails to understand them. The condition may be familial. He advocated treatment as for deaf-mutism, with lip reading and the use of the kinaesthetic sense—the child feeling the shape of carved letters as they are spoken. He suggested that the defect may lie in aplasia of the post-temporal cortex on both sides.

The problem was reviewed by Forsius *et al.* in Finalnd.[22] I agree with their comment that it is very difficult to be sure that a child has purely motor or purely sensory aphasia.

Stuttering. Numerous famous men are said to have stuttered. They include Moses, Aristotle, Aesop, Demosthenes, Virgil, Charles I, Charles Lamb, and Charles Darwin. Hippocrates, Aristotle, Galen and Celsus discussed the causes of the problem.

According to Jenks[44] Dieffenbach in Berlin was one of the first to attempt the cure of stuttering by dividing the lingual muscles. He wrote that Mrs. Leigh and Dr. Yates of New York opened the New York institution for correcting impediments of speech in 1830. The stammerer had to press the tip of the tongue as hard as he could against the upper teeth, had to draw a deep breath every 6 minutes, and was instructed to keep perfectly silent for 3 days, during which period the deep respirations and tongue pressure had to be continued without interruption. During the night, small rolls of linen were placed under the tongue in order to give the tongue the right direction during sleep.

Other treatment included teaching the child to speak with pebbles in the mouth or with a cork between the teeth.

In the section below the words stutter and stammer are used as synonyms.

The onset of stuttering is usually between 2 and 4 years. It rarely begins after 7. About 1 to 2 per cent. of the school population stutter. It is 3 times commoner in young boys than girls, but much more common in older boys than girls—indicating that girls are more likely to recover from it than boys.

Morley[61] estimated that less than 3 per 1,000 of the population has a persistent stammer. There is no relationship between the incidence of stuttering and the intelligence quotient.

It is almost impossible to avoid over-simplification in writing a short section on stuttering. It is a complex problem with many facets and several aspects which are little understood. In the comments below I shall attempt to give what seem to me to be the most widely accepted views on the problem.

Many agree with Wendell Johnson[46] that a vital cause of stuttering is the diagnosis of stuttering. By this it is meant that parents or relatives fail to realise that normal children between 2 and 4 years of age frequently repeat words and stumble over them, particularly when they are excited. The parents, perhaps guided by a relative or neighbour, become alarmed about their child's speech and think that he is beginning to stutter. They thereupon tell the child to repeat himself, to speak clearly and distinctly, to 'take a big breath before he speaks', thus making the child self-conscious, and drawing his attention to his speech, so that true stuttering begins. Johnson wrote that, 'We simply could not escape the fact that, to all appearances, most of the parents of the young stutterers were applying the label "stuttering" to the same types of speech behaviour that other parents were labelling "normal speech".' Johnson advised that parents should 'do absolutely nothing at any time, by word or deed or posture, or facial expression, that would serve to call his attention to his interruptions in speech'. One is reminded of the centipede:

'The centipede was contented, quite
Until the toad one day in spite
Said, say, which foot comes after which?
This so wrought upon her mind
She lay distracted in a ditch,
Considering which came after which'.

It is probable that several other factors are involved. These are: (1) The familial factor. The significance of this is not understood. There is a possibility that imitation plays a part, or that a parent who stutters or has stuttered himself, shows undue anxiety about his own child's speech, and so causes him to stutter. (2) Lateral dominance and crossed laterality. Though most agree that there is a higher incidence of crossed laterality and ambidexterity in stutterers than there is in the normal population, its significance is not understood. It is commonly believed that stuttering which develops sometimes when a left-handed child is taught to use the right is due to tension created in trying to bring about the transfer of dominance, and that it is the method of teaching which is responsible rather than the fact of teaching him to use the opposite hand. (3) Insecurity. Though insecurity may be a factor in leading to stuttering, some psychological problems may be the result rather than the cause of the stuttering. Nevertheless, there is good evidence that insecurity is a factor, provided that it operates before speech is fully established. (4) Constitutional factors. Berry[7] compared the antecedents of 500 stutterers with those of 500 controls. He found that the stutterers were somewhat later in learning to walk than the controls. In the stuttering group there was more often retardation in the initiation of speech and the development of intelligible speech. (5) The personality of the child. It may well be that if the other factors operate as well, the more sensitive child by nature is more likely to stutter than the more placid child of even temperament.

Indistinctness of Speech. In this section I have included dysarthria, dyslalia, and nasal speech. Many children during the process of developing go through a stage of substituting consonants or other sounds (dyslalia), or of repeating certain sounds. They may omit consonants and make speech difficult to understand. The commonest form of dyslalia is the lisp, due usually to the protrusion of the tongue between the teeth on pronouncing an 's'.

The cause of dyslalia is obscure. Powers[69] wrote that 'although the etiology of functional articulation disorders remains unestablished, it is at least clear that it is complex'. She felt that it was likely to be related to an unsatisfactory parent-child relationship, leading to intellectual and emotional immaturity.

I find it difficult to know how much parents should be blamed for their children's dyslalia. One sees many examples of dyslalia in which the family background appears to be entirely satisfactory, and there are certainly vast numbers of families in which the background is unsatisfactory in a wide variety of ways and in which no child has dyslalia. Dyslalia seems to be due to immaturity in speech formation, but the explanation of that immaturity is not clear.

In all cases of delayed or indistinct speech, the hearing should be tested.

Ingram ([42]), in an excellent discussion of the problems of delayed speaking and reading, regarded many of the common speech difficulties as being grades of severity of one problem, rather than as separate and distinct problems. His four grades are as follows:

Mild—dyslalia.

Moderate—retarded acquisition of language with dyslalia, but normal comprehension of speech.

Severe—both comprehension and expression of speech defective. Congenital word blindness.

Very Severe—true auditory imperception. Defect of comprehension together with a failure to perceive the significance of sounds.

Perceptual and Allied Problems in Cerebral Palsy and Other Children

Only a brief note can be included here concerning certain sensory defects, especially spatial appreciation and body image, in certain children with cerebral palsy, especially in those with a lesion in the right hemisphere, and especially in young children who have been deprived of experience in the handling of toys and other objects because of their physical handicap.

Perceptual difficulties are by no means confined to children with cerebral palsy. They occur in normal children, perhaps as a result of genetic factors, or of delayed maturation, or of lack of the relevant experience in the early months. In this connection there is interesting work concerning perceptual difficulties in Africans.[78a] Bantus, for instance, have difficulty in understanding pictures. They cannot connect a drawing of a mechanical object with the object itself, nor can they see 'depth' in a picture.

Strauss and Lehtinen,[77] in their two-volume book on the *Brain Injured Child*, gave a comprehensive review of the difficulties experienced by these children. They emphasised that these problems are frequently found in children with no abnormal neurological signs at all, and they ascribe them to 'brain injury' in utero, in the broadest sense, implying that some noxious factor such as anoxia or toxaemia damaged the brain before birth.

The handicaps include particularly:

1. *Difficulty in Appreciating Space and Form*, so that an unduly poor score is achieved on formboards, and on pattern making and pattern copying, *e.g.* with bricks, or with strips of cardboard. Difficulty may be expected in the 'posting box' test.

2. *Defect of Body Image*. The child finds it difficult to reproduce movements of the lips, tongue, or other parts of the body. His drawings of the human figure (as in the Goodenough 'draw-a-man' test) are poor. If given the outline of a face and asked to insert cardboard models of the eyes, lips, nose, etc., he has difficulty in placing them in the appropriate position.

3. *Difficulty in Estimating Size, Depth, Distance, Time*. The child may find it difficult to estimate depth in walking down stairs, to estimate size in sorting out objects of different sizes, to estimate distance in jumping from one line to another on the floor, to estimate time in beating a rhythm. When older he may find it difficult to find his way round a page of print.

4. *Perseveration*. He finds it difficult to change from one task to another. When writing he may repeat the last letter. When counting cubes he fails to stop counting at the last brick in a row.

5. *Concentration*. Concentration tends to be unduly poor in relation to the I.Q. There is undue distractibility. There is a tendency for the child to be distracted by unimportant minutiae, such as the page number in a book, flaws in the paper, the teacher's dress. He is unduly distracted by sound or movement in the environment.

6. *Hyperkinesis and other Uninhibited Behaviour*.

The subject was also reviewed by Albitreccia in France,[3] Cruickshank,[12] Forward,[23] and Abercrombie.[1]

From the point of view of developmental assessment, the possibility of these sensory defects in children with cerebral palsy must be born in mind in testing, for they may lead to an unduly low score and to an underestimate of the child's ability. They also lead to an unduly poor performance in the nursery school and subsequent schools.

Reading Disability (Dyslexia) and Allied Disorders

Reading disability is more a problem in the child of school age than of the pre-school child; but it has its origin in pre-natal or other pre-school factors, and will therefore be discussed briefly here. Amongst many reviews of the subject are those of Monroe,[60] Hermann,[33] Keeney,[50] Natchez,[62] Vernon,[78] Ingram,[40,41] Mason,[56] Money[59] and Franklin.[25]

The usual causes of delayed reading are as follows:–

1. A low level of intelligence.

2. Emotional factors. Insecurity in its broadest sense may be one of the causes of delayed reading. Features commonly found in the home background are tense, critical, punitive parents, and a variety of behaviour problems in the child. The reading disability is often merely a small part of a much wider emotional difficulty. The child may become so convinced that he cannot learn to read that he stops trying; he is expected to fail and he does.

3. Other environmental problems. Factors commonly found in the history of affected children include a poor home, where there are no books and no suitable toys, where no-one reads to the child and where the vocabulary is poor. There is often a history of over-ambition, over-anxiety and over-protection, of failure to encourage curiosity and learning, and of failure to appreciate the importance of education. Poor teaching, including unsuitable teaching methods, is commonly found. The problem is much more common in large families and in the lower social classes.

4. Visual, auditory and spatial difficulties. Visuospatial difficulties include the transposition of letters. There may be poor auditory discrimination of speech sounds, so that common sounds are forgotten, or failure to synthesize into their correct words letters sounded correctly individually (e.g. C-L-O-C-K pronounced 'COCK'). According to Mason[56] delayed reading, always includes one or more visuospatial difficulties, poorly established laterality, clumsiness or poor writing, but these disappear except in children with 'pure' dyslexia.

5. Genetic. When the above causes of delayed reading have been eliminated, there remains the 'specific' dyslexia, which is genetic in origin, though emotional problems may well be superadded. It is more common in boys than in girls. Dr. John Hunter, famous British physician, could not read until he was 17, despite all efforts to teach him, and this occasioned great distress to his family.[65] It is probable that the problem in his case was of the

genetic variety. There is almost always a family history of the same complaint. Hermann[33] showed that if dyslexia occurs in one of uniovular twins, it occurs in the other too; the incidence in both of binovular twins is much less.

The problem is associated with easier than usual mirror reading, with reversal of letters (reading 'tub' for 'but'), with a tendency to read from right to left, and with ambidexterity or left handedness. A semi-colon may be interpreted as a question mark, an 'h' as 'y'. There is reversal of words, rotation of letters, confusion over letters of similar shape, a low reading speed, and misreading of words.

Gesell wrote[29] that reading difficulties may be anticipated by the following features:–

Scattering and inconsistency of the individual developmental examination.

Inconsistency of results on successive examinations.

Specific weakness in drawing tests.

Specific weakness in number tests (e.g. 'give me three blocks').

Strephosymbolia.

Family history of sinistrality.

Family history of reading disability.

Speech anomalies—delay in speech, dyslalia, stuttering.

Immature or excitable personality.

More recently a variety of other tests have been tried in order to predict reading failure.[16]   They include visual and auditory perceptual tests, language tests, including language comprehension, auditory memory span, tests for fine manual control (fitting pegs into a peg board, tying a knot, hand reference, pencil control, throwing, drawing a man), and the Bender Gestalt test.

It is known that reading difficulties are more common in children who were prematurely born than in those born at term.

Reading difficulty is a complex problem, due to a variety of causes, which are often closely intermingled. Expert psychological help is required to unravel them, and without such help the diagnosis of specific dyslexia should not be made.

Advanced reading ability may be a feature of an unusually high level of intelligence, in a child with a good home where the parents have read to him from an early age, shown him pictures, given him pre-reading toys, such as picture matching, jigsaws, picture dominoes, and cardboard or plastic shapes and forms; and where he is given the opportunity to practice visuospatial development.

Many famous persons were able to read fluently by the age of three or four years. We have described several of these in our book Lessons from Childhood, which discusses the features of the early childhood of famous men and women.

Multiple Factors Affecting Development

One often sees a combination of retarding factors, which make a developmental assessment extremely difficult. I found it almost impossible to determine the level of intelligence in an athetoid child who was blind and deaf. Retardation of walking in children with cerebral palsy is usually due to at least two factors—the mechanical disability due to the hypertonia, and the mental retardation. Institutional care and emotional deprivation is often a third factor.

The following case record illustrates the difficulty which multiple factors cause in developmental assessment:

Case Record.—This girl was referred at the age of 28 months on account of lateness in walking. She was born at term, weighing 8 lbs. The history of many of the previous milestones could not be obtained. It seemed that she had learnt to sit at 16 months, to play patacake, to hold her arms out for clothes, and to wave bye-bye at 22 months. She was only saying one word with meaning. She could only just manage a cup, and she had no sphincter control.

On examination she was a bright girl, interested in her surroundings, with moderate concentration, and co-operated well in developmental tests, in which her performance lay between that of an 18 and 24 month old child. The D.Q. was about 60. She had a mild degree of spastic diplegia. She was a very long way off learning to walk. Her siblings, who were otherwise normal, had only begun to speak at 3 and $3\frac{1}{2}$ years respectively.

In this case the spastic diplegia and mental retardation retarded the walking, and the mental retardation and probably the familial trait retarded the speech. One could not use the development of speech to assess the I.Q. because of the family history of late speech development.

Owing to the alertness and good concentration, I gave a guarded prognosis, saying that she would be educable, and that she might well fare better than appeared likely from her present level of development.

Summary and Conclusions

1. All children are different. They differ in the rate of development as a whole, and in the rate and pattern of development within each field.

2. Motor development may be advanced. In certain ethnic groups of negroes, children may show notable motor advancement. Gross motor development (sitting and walking) may be considerably delayed without any discoverable cause, some normal children being unable to walk until 2 to 4 years of age.

Known causes of delayed motor development are:
Familial factors.
Environmental factors; emotional deprivation, lack of opportunity to practice.
Personality—excessive timidity.
Mental subnormality.
Hypotonia or hypertonia; gross spinal defects.
Neuromuscular disorders.
Shuffling.
Blindness.

It is *not* due to congenital dislocation of the hip or to obesity.

3. There is much less variation in fine motor development (manipulation), except in association with mental retardation and cerebral palsy.

4. Delayed visual and auditory maturation may occur.

5. There is little variation in the age of chewing, except in association with mental retardation.

6. The age at which children learn to feed and dress themselves is affected by their intelligence, aptitudes, opportunities given to them to learn, and by mechanical difficulties.

7. Acquisition of sphincter control is delayed by:
Familial factors.
Psychosocial factors.
Overenthusiastic or neglectful training.
Organic disease.

8. Speech is delayed by:
Low intelligence.
Hearing defects.
Genetic factors.

Delayed maturation and familial factors.
Poor environment.
Twinning.
Psychoses.
Disturbance of lateral dominance.
Cerebral palsy.
Problems related to dyslexia and aphasia.

It is *not* delayed by tongue tie, by jealousy, or 'everything being done for him'.

The frequency of lulls in the development of speech is emphasised.

Stuttering is discussed briefly. The main known factors are:
(*a*) Parental efforts to make the child speak distinctly, together with their failure to recognise that the child's apparently hesitant speech is normal.
(*b*) Familial factors.
(*c*) Problems of laterality.
(*d*) Insecurity.
(*e*) Constitutional factors.
(*f*) The personality of the child.

It is probable that stuttering only develops when there is a combination of these factors in operation during the early months of speech development.

Known causes of indistinctness of speech include cleft palate, submucous cleft, malocclusion, adenoids, cerebral palsy and possibly tongue-tie.

9. The ability to read is delayed by:
Low intelligence.
Emotional factors.
Environmental factors.
Visual, auditory and spatial difficulties.
Genetic factors ('specific dyslexia').

10. The frequency with which there is a combination of retarding factors is emphasised.

REFERENCES

1. ABERCROMBIE, M. L. J. (1964) Perceptual and Visuomotor Disorders in Cerebral Palsy. *Clinics in Developmental Medicine.* No. 11. London. Heinemann.

2. AINSWORTH, M. (1967) *Infancy in Uganda.* Baltimore: John Hopkins Press.

3. ALBITRECCIA, S. I. (1958) Recognition and Treatment of Disturbances of the Body Image. *Cerebral Palsy Bull.* No. 4, p. 12.

4. AUSUBEL, D. P. (1958) *Theory and Problems of Child Development.* New York: Grune and Stratton.

5. BAKWIN, H., BAKWIN, R. M. (1966) *Clinical Management of Behaviour Disorders in Children.* Philadelphia: Saunders.

6. BARLOW, F. (1951) *Mental Prodigies.* London: Hutchinson.

7. BERRY, M. F. (1938) The Developmental History of Stuttering Children. *J. Pediat.*, **12,** 209.

7a BIESHEUVEL, S., quoted by VERNON, P. E. (1969) *Intelligence and Cultural Environment.* London: Methuen.

8. BRIT. MED. J. (1969) Leading Article. Still Bed-Wetting, **1,** 459.

9. BRODBECK, A. J., IRWIN, O. C. (1946) The Speech Behaviour of Infants without Families. *Child Develpm.*, **17,** 145.

10. BROWN, S. F. (1955) A Note on Speech Retardation in Mental Deficiency. *Pediatrics,* **16,** 272.

11. CARRELL, J. A., BANGS, J. L. (1951) Disorders of Speech Comprehension Associated with Idiopathic Language Retardation. *Nerv. Child,* **9,** 64.

12. CRUICKSHANK, W. M., BICE, H. V., WALLER, N. E. (1957) *Perception and Cerebral Palsy.* Syracuse Univ. Press.

13. CURTI, M. W., MARSHALL, F. B., STEGGERDA, M. (1935) The Gesell Schedules applied to One, Two and Three Year Old Negro Children of Jamaica. *J. comp. Psychol.*, **20,** 125.

14. DAVIS, E. A. (1937) The Mental and Linguistic Superiority of Only Girls. *Child Develpm.*, **8,** 139.

15. DAY, E. J. (1932) Development of Language in Twins. *Child Develpm.*, **3,** 179. 299.

16. DE HIRSCH, K., JANSKY, J. J., LANGFORD, W. W. (1966) *Predicting Reading Failure.* New York: Harper and Row.

17. DEAN, R. F. A. (1962) Personal Communication.

18. DENNIS, W. (1943) On the Possibility of Advancing and Retarding the Motor Development of Infants. *Psychol. Rev.*, **50,** 203.

19. DUNSDON, M. I. (1952). *The Educability of Cerebral Palsied Children.* London: Newnes Educational Co.

20. EISENSON, J. (1956) in Cruickshank, W. M., *Psychology of Exceptional Children and Youth* London: Staples Press.

21. FLOYER, E. B. (1955) *A Psychological Study of a City's Cerebral Palsied Children. Brit. Coun. Welf. of Spastics.*

22. FORSIUS, H., TORMA, S., VIITAMÄKI, R. O. (1949) *Ann. Paediat. Fenn.*, **5,** Suppl. 13.

23. FORWARD, G. E. (1959) The Treatment of Defective Children. *Occup. Ther.* July, p. 11.

24. FRANK, P. (1948) *Einstein*. London: Cape.

25. FRANKLIN, A. W. (1962) *Word Blindness or Specific Developmental Dyslexia*. London: Pitman.

26. FREEDMAN, D. G. (1964) Smiling in Blind Infants and the Issue of Innate VS Acquired. *J. Child Psychol.*, **5**, 171.

27. GEBER, M., DEAN, R. F. A. (1957) Gesell Tests in African Children. *Pediatrics*, **20**, 1055.

28. GEBER, M., DEAN, R. F. A. (1964) Le Developpement Psychomoteur et Somatique des Jeunes Enfants Africains en Ouganda. *Courrier*, **14**, 425.

29. GESELL, A., AMATRUDA, C. S., CASTNER, B. M., THOMPSON, H.   (1939) *Biographies of Child Development*. London: Hamish Hamilton.

30. GOERTZEN, S. M. (1957) Speech and the Mentally Retarded Child. *Amer. J. ment. Defic.*, **62**, 244.

31. GOODWIN, F. B. (1955) A Consideration of Etiologies in 454 Cases of Speech Retardation. *J. Speech Dis.*, **20**, 300

32. GORDON, N. (1968) Visual Agnosia in Childhood. *Develop. Med. Child. Neurol.*, **10**, 377.

33. HERMANN, K. (1959) *Reading Disability*. Copenhagen: Munksgaard.

34. HINDLEY, C. B., FILLIOZAT, A. M., KLACKENBERG, G., NICOLET-MEISTER, D., SAND, E. A. (1966) Differences in Age of Walking in Five European Longitudinal Samples. *Human Biology*, **38**, 364.

35. HOLT, K. S. (1960) Early Motor Development. Postural Induced Variations. *J. Pediat.*, **57**, 571.

36. ILLINGWORTH, R. S., BIRCH, L. B. (1956) The Intelligence of Children with Cleft Palate. *Arch. Dis. Childh.*, **31**, 300.

37. ILLINGWORTH, R. S., ILLINGWORTH, C. M. (1966) *Lessons from Childhood*. Edinburgh: Livingstone.

38. ILLINGWORTH, R. S. (1958) *Recent Advances in Cerebral Palsy*. London: Churchill.

39. ILLINGWORTH, R. S. (1961) Delayed Visual Maturation. *Arch. Dis. Childh.*, **36**, 407.

40. INGRAM, T. T. S. (1960) Personal Communication.

41. INGRAM, T. T. S. (1960) Paediatric Aspects of Specific Developmental Dysphasia, Dyslexia and Dysgraphia. *Cerebr. Palsy Bull.*, **2**, 254.

42. INGRAM, T. T. S. (1963) Delayed Development of Speech with Special Reference to Dyslexia. *Proc. R. Soc. Med.*, **56**, 199.

43. IRWIN, O. C. (1932) Amount of Motality of 73 Newborn Infants· *J. comp. Psychol.*, **14**, 415.

44. JENKS, W. F. (1953) *The Exceptional Child*. Washington: Catholic Univ. of America Press.

45. JERSILD, A. T. (1 94) *Child Psychology*. 4th ed. London: Staples.

46. JOHNSON, W. (1949) An Open Letter to the Mother of a Stuttering Child. *J. Speech Dis.*, **14**, 3.

47. KARLIN, I. W., KENNEDY, L. (1936) Delay in the Development of Speech. *Amer. J. Dis. Child.*, **51**, 1138.

48. KARLIN, I. W. (1954) Aphasias in Children. *Amer. J. Dis. Child.*, **87**, 752.

49. KARLIN, I. W.   (1958)   Speech and Language Handicapped Children. *Amer. J. Dis. Child.*, **95,** 370.

50. KEENEY, A. H., KEENEY, V. D. (1968) *Dyslexia. Diagnosis and Treatment of Reading Disorders.* St. Louis: C. V. Mosby.

51. KNOBLOCH, H., PASAMANICK, B.   (1953)   Further Observations on the Behavioural Development of Negro Children. *J. genet. Psychol.*, **83,** 137.

52. KNOBLOCH, H., PASAMANICK, B.   (1958)   The Relationship of Race and Socioeconomic Status to the Development of Motor Behavior Patterns in Infancy. *Psychiat. Res. Rep.* No. 10.

53. KNOBLOCH, H.   (1958)   Precocity of African Children. *Pediatrics,* **22,** 601.

54. LILLYWHITE, H.   (1958)   Doctor's   Manual   of   Speech   Disorders. *J. Amer. med. Ass.*, **167,** 850.

55. LURIA, A. R., YUDOVICH, I.   (1959)   *Speech and the Development of Mental Processes in the Child.* London: Staples.

56. MASON, A. W. (1967) Specific (Developmental) Dyslexia. *Develop. Med. Child. Neurol.,* **9,** 183.

57. MILLER, F. J. W., COURT, S. D. M., WALTON, W. S., KNOX, E. G. (1960) *Growing up in Newcastle-upon-Tyne.* London: Oxford University Press.

58. MILLER, F. J. W. (1966) Child Morbidity and Mortality in Newcastle Upon Tyne. *New Engl. J. Med.,* **275,** 683.

59. Money, J. (1962) *Reading Disability.* Baltimore: John Hopkins Press.

60. MONROE, M.   (1928)   Specific Reading Disability.   *Genet. Psychol. Monogr.,* **4,** 332.

61. MORLEY, M. E.   (1957)   *The Development and Disorders of Speech in Childhood.*   Edinburgh: Livingstone.

62. NATCHEZ, J. (1968) *Children with Reading Problems.* New York: Basic Books Inc.

63. NORVAL, M. A.   (1947)   Relationship of Weight and Length of Infants at Birth to the Age at which they Begin to Walk. *J. Pediat.,* **30,** 676.

64. ORTON, S. T.   (1939)   Delayed Development of Speech—some of its Causes, Diagnosis and Treatment. *J. Pediat.,* **15,** 453.

65. PAGET, S.   (1897)   *John Hunter.* London: Fisher Unwin.

65a PASAMANICK, B.   (1946)   A Comparative Study of the Behavioural Development of Negro Infants. *J. genet. Psychol.,* **69,** 3.

66. PAVENSTEDT, E. (1967) *The Drifters.   Children of Disorganised Lower Class Families.* Churchill: London.

67. PEATMAN, J. G., HIGGONS, R. A.   (1942)   Development of Sitting, Standing, and Walking of Children Reared with Optimal Pediatric Care. *Amer. J. Orthopsychiat.,* **10,** 88.

68. PEIPER, A. (1963) *Cerebral Function in Infancy and Childhood.* London. Pitman.

69. POWERS, M. H., in LIEBMAN, S.   (1958)   *Emotional Problems of Childhood.* Philadelphia: Lippincott.

70. RENFREW, C., MURPHY, K. (1964) The Child Who does not Talk. *Clinics in Developmental Medicine.* No. 13. London. Heinemann.

71. RUTTER, M. (1968) Concepts of Autism: A Review of Research. *J. Child Psychol. Psychiat.,* **9,** 1.

72. SHERIDAN, M. (1960) Personal Communication.

73. SHIRLEY, M. M. (1931) *The First Two Years of Life*. Minneapolis: Univ. of Minnesota Press.

74. SMITH, E. D. (1967) Diagnosis and Management of the Child with Wetting. *Australian Paediat. J.*, **3**, 193.

75. SÖDERLING, B. (1959) The First Smile. *Acta Paediat. (Uppsala)*, **48**, Suppl. 117. 78.

76. SOLOMON, A. L. (1961) Personality and Behaviour Patterns of Children with Functional Defects of Articulation. *Child Developm.*, **32**, 731.

77. STRAUSS, A. A., LEHTINEN, L. E. (1948) *Psychopathology and Education of the Brain Injured Child*. New York: Grune and Stratton.

78. VERNON, M. D. (1957) *Backwardness in Reading*. Cambridge: Cambridge Univ. Press.

78a VERNON, P. E. (1969) *Intelligence and Cultural Environment*. London: Methuen.

79. WHITE, M. (1968). A Thousand Consecutive Cases of Enuresis. *Medical Officer*, **120**, 151.

80. WILLIAMS, C. E. in O'GORMAN, G. (1968) *Modern Trends in Mental Health and Subnormality*.

81. WILLIAMS, J. R., SCOTT, R. B. (1953) Growth and Development of Negro Infants. IV. Motor Development and its Relationship to Child Rearing Practices in Two Groups of Negro Infants. *Child Develop.*, **24**, 103.

82. WORSTER-DROUGHT, C. (1943) Congenital Auditory Imperception (Congenital Word Deafness and its Relation to Idioglossia and Allied Speech Defects). *Med. Press*, **110**, 411.

CHAPTER 11

VARIATIONS IN THE GENERAL PATTERN OF DEVELOPMENT

In this chapter I have described variations in the general pattern of development, as distinct from variations in individual fields. It is obvious that the main factor related to development as a whole is the level of intelligence.

Variations in Intelligence

The lowest level of intelligence is so low that it is unscorable, and therefore there are no precise figures for the lowest levels. We have only limited information about I.Q. levels at the other extreme of the scale—at the very top.

Bakwin and Bakwin[2] gave the following range:

150 and over – – – – – –	0·1
130–149 – – – – – – –	1·0
120–129 – – – – – – –	5
110–119 – – – – – – –	14
100–109 – – – – – – –	30
90–99 – – – – – – –	30
80–89 – – – – – – –	14
70–79 – – – – – – –	5
Below 70 – – – – – – –	1

Asher and Schonell[1] gave the following figures:

130 and over – – – – – –	1
110–129 – – – – – – –	24
90–109 – – – – – – –	46
70–89 – – – – – – –	24
Below 70 – – – – – – –	3

Michal Smith[14] gave the following figures for the upper end of the scale:

Over 180 – – – – –	1 in 1,000,000
Over 170 – – – – –	1 in 100,000
Over 160 – – – – –	1 in 10,000
Over 150 – – – – –	1 in 1,000
Over 140 – – – – –	1 in 170
Over 136 – – – – –	1 in 100
Over 125 – – – – –	1 in 17

Apart from variations in the level of intelligence, there are many important variations in the pattern of development.

All those who are concerned with developmental diagnosis should read and re-read the book entitled *Biographies of Child Development*, by Arnold Gesell and his colleagues.[9]   This is a collection of biographical sketches to show the wide range of variations seen in human development.

In the sections to follow I shall describe some of the important variations in development as a whole.

Mental Superiority

It has proved difficult to detect mental superiority in infancy. Gesell[8] discussed the early signs of superiority in some detail. He emphasised the fact that superior endowment is not always manifested by quickened tempo of development, but the signs are there for careful observation.   He wrote that superiority 'manifests itself in dynamic excellence, in intensification and diversification of behaviour, rather than in conspicuous acceleration.   The maturity level is less affected than the vividness and vitality of reaction.   The young infant with superior promise is clinically distinguished not so much by an advance in developmental age, as by augmented alertness, perceptiveness and drive. The infant with superior equipment exploits his physical surroundings in a more varied manner, and is more sensitive and responsive to his social environment'.   He added that consistent language acceleration before 2 years is one of the most frequent signs of superior intelligence, while general motor ability and neuromuscular maturity, as revealed by drawing and co-ordinations tests, are not necessarily in advance.

Elsewhere Gesell and Amatruda wrote: 'The acceleration comes into clearer prominence in the second and third years, with the development of speech, comprehension and judgment. However, personal social adaption and attentional characteristics are usually excellent even in the early months.   The scorable end products may not be far in advance, but the manner of performance is superior'.   They added that the superior infant is emotionally sensitive to his environment, looks alertly, and displays an intelligent acceptance of novel situations.   He establishes rapport. He gives anticipatory action to test situations.   He shows initiative, independence, and imitativeness.   He gives a good performance

17

even if sleepy. He is poised, self-contained, discriminating, mature. The total output of behaviour for a day is more abundant, more complex, more subtle than that of a mediocre child. They described twins with an I.Q. of 180 who talked in sentences at 11 months. Terman (quoted by Hollingworth[7]), described a child who walked at 7 months, and knew the alphabet at 19 months. The I.Q. was 188.

Amongst many stories of prodigies, one of the best known is that of Christian Heineken, born in Lubeck.[5] It is said that at 14 months he knew the whole Bible: at $2\frac{1}{2}$ he was conversant with history, geography, anatomy and 800 Latin words, learning over 150 new ones weekly. He could read German and Latin, and spoke German, Latin and French fluently. When 3 years old he could add, subtract, and multiply, and in his fourth year he learned 220 songs, 80 psalms, and 1,500 verses and sentences of Latin writers. He died at 4 years and 4 months.

Many other stories of mental precocity in childhood have been described by me elsewhere.[13]

Hollingworth[11] wrote that nearly all superior children learned to read at about 3 years of age. Most of the children with an I.Q. of over 150 walked or talked or walked and talked earlier than usual. They ranked average in music and drawing. Stedman, in a discussion on the education of gifted children, found most of them friendly and co-operative, and not conceited, egotistical or vain. Hollingworth[11a] described 31 children with an I.Q. of over 180: 12 of them were children she had seen, and 19 were cases from the literature. They tended to read a great deal, to be tall and healthy, and to have a powerful imagination. Their problems included difficulty in 'learning to suffer fools gladly'; physical difficulties—their mental development having outstripped their physical development: a tendency to idleness: a tendency to be discouraged easily: and problems of immaturity. It was difficult for them to find enough interests at school, to avoid being negativistic toward authority, and to avoid becoming lonely, because of reduced contacts with others of their own age.

One feels that Michal-Smith[12] went a little too far with regard to the difficulties of children with a superior level of intelligence when he included a chapter on 'Mentally Gifted Children' in his book entitled *Management of the Handicapped Child*.

Terman and Oden,[17] in their unique study of 1,528 California children with an I.Q. of 135 or more, who were followed up to an average age of 35, found that compared with controls they had tended to walk and talk earlier: they had a better physique and fewer illnesses: they had been less boastful and more honest, and they were more stable emotionally: and they tended to have earlier puberty.   They had a wide range of interest, and they showed curiosity, sustained attention, and creative ability. Nearly half had learned to read before going to school. (The age of starting school is later in America than that in England.) Their greatest superiority was in reading, language usage, arithmetical reasoning, and information in science, literature and the arts. They were less good in arithmetical computation, spelling and factual information about history.   Their main interests were reading and collecting. There was no difference from controls in play interests.

The early indications of superior intelligence most often noted by parents were quicker understanding, insatiable curiosity, extensive information, retentive memory, large vocabulary, un-usual interest in number relations, atlases and encyclopedias.

When these children were followed up it was found that they suffered less insanity and alcoholism than the controls: the suicide rate and incidence of juvenile delinquency was less. The marriage rate was higher, and they tended to marry earlier. They had fewer children than the controls. They tended to choose a partner in marriage of higher intelligence than did the controls. The divorce rate was lower. Their income was greater. Six per cent. became minor clerical workers, policemen, firemen or semi-skilled craftsmen. One became a truck driver. Six per cent. became doctors. The mean I.Q. of the 384 offspring was 127·7 and the proportion of children with an I.Q. of 150 or more was 28 times that of the general population.

Uniformly Advanced Development

Subsequent high I.Q.

Below are two personally observed examples of uniformly advanced development, in which the early promise was fully maintained. The tests used were mainly those of Gesell.

Case 1:

    1st day   listened when spoken to and looked intently.

3rd day	smiled in response to overture. Virtually no grasp reflex.
9th day	advanced head control. Very interested in surroundings. Extremely interested in other children.
18 days	turned head repeatedly to sound. Holding rattle placed in hand almost indefinitely. Vocalising.
8 weeks	hand regard. 'Grasping with eyes' (Gesell).
11 weeks	smiling at self in mirror.
14 weeks	able to go for object and get it.
19 weeks	sitting on floor for seconds without support. Holds arms out to be pulled up. Laughs at peep-bo game. Rapid transfer of objects. Attention-seeking noises—*e.g.* cough.
23 weeks	chewing well. Feeding self with biscuits. Stands, holding on to furniture. Advanced vocalisation. Notably good concentration on toys.
29 weeks	progressing backwards in attempting to crawl.
35 weeks	laughs at familiar rhymes. Puts hands on feet and toes when hears 'This little pig went to market'. Bricks in and out of basket. Pulls self to stand. Casting. Crawling.
44 weeks	single words with meaning. Picks up doll on request.
48 weeks	standing and walking without support. Points to 2 objects in picture when asked, 'Where is the . . .?' 8 words with meaning.
13 months	knows numerous objects in books, and 7 parts of body. Carries out numerous errands on request. Feeds self with mythical fruit from pictures of fruit in books.
16 months	simple formboard—all 3 in without error. All pieces into Goddard formboard. Words together into sentences.
20 months	knows several rhymes. Answers questions intelligently, *e.g.* 'Where is your toothbrush?' Answer, 'Upstairs in the bathroom'. Spontaneously describes pictures shown to her. Counts 2 objects spontaneously. Speaking in 10 word sentences. Asks questions. Makes jokes—*e.g.* calling sibling a rogue and laughing.

24 months	'Reads' books in jargon, describing each page. Spontaneously changes name in a rhyme for sibling's name, and laughs.
26 months	geometric forms—9 correct. Goddard formboard, 76 seconds. Repeats 4 digits, 2–3 trials. Prepositions—4.
33 months	Goddard formboard, 44 seconds. Goodenough 'draw a man' test=51 months. Dressing self fully without help.
44 months	Goodenough 'draw a man' test=78 months. Repeats 5 digits, 3–3 trials. (6 not tried). Goddard formboard, 30 seconds. Able to read school books.
47 months	holds imaginative conversations with doll in 2 voices —*i.e.* replying in a different voice.
49 months	qualifies statements by, 'It depends on whether . . .' Showed memory of 18 months' span. Reading simple books very easily.
62 months	Goodenough 'draw a man' test=9 years. Repeats 7 digits easily.

Case 2:

3rd day	smile in response to social overture. Virtually no grasp reflex. Intent gaze when spoken to.
7th day	head well off couch in prone position.
3 weeks	followed moving object 180 degrees. Very good vocalisations.
9 weeks	'grasping with the eyes'. Advanced vocalisations, including 'Ah—goo'.
12 weeks	able to go for objects and get them. Ticklish.
14 weeks	smiles at mirror. Full weight on legs. Splashes in bath.
18 weeks	coughs to attract attention. Enjoys peep-bo game.
22 weeks	chew. Sitting without support on floor. Very good concentration.
24 weeks	stands, holding on to furniture.
30 weeks	laughs loud at 'This little piggie' game. Turns head to name. Pulls self to standing position. Matches cubes. Casting repeatedly.

35 weeks	great determination and concentration. Plays game of spilling milk from cup and laughing loudly.
40 weeks	hands a toy. Release. Patacake. Holds out foot for 'This little piggie' game.
44 weeks	knows meaning of numerous words. Will creep for object on request. Feeding self fully, managing cup without help. Obeys commands—get up, sit down. Creeping up stairs.
12 months	walks, no help. Moos or quacks when asked what cow, duck, says. Tries to take cardigan off on request.
13 months	tower of 6 cubes. Spontaneously 'picks cherries off pictures' and pretends to eat them.
16 months	carries out complicated commands, *e.g.* 'Go into the kitchen and put this into the toy cupboard'.
20 months	recognises colours. Knows what page in book has certain nursery rhymes on it. Advanced sentences.
21 months	Goddard formboard, 55 seconds. Geometric forms—all correct, immediately. Picture identification—all correct, immediately.
24 months	asks 'Why?' when told to do things.
30 months	repeats 5 digits easily, 3–3 trials. Asks 'What does this say?' when looking at books. Counts up to 25.
33 months	dressing self fully without help.
36 months	reading simple books readily.
39 months	Goddard formboard, 20 seconds. Goodenough 'draw a man' test=6 years. (The first man he had ever drawn). Cubes—made gate from model immediately, and made steps from 8 cubes.
50 months	able to do 78 piece jigsaw rapidly.
60 months	Goodenough 'draw a man' test=$7\frac{9}{12}$ years. Goddard formboard, 16 seconds (one attempt only). Repeats 4 digits backwards (*i.e.* say 8–4–3–6 backwards). Subsequent performance confirmed the early prediction of a very high I.Q.

COMMENT

The above are two examples of consistently advanced development. They are by no means typical of all children with a high level of intelligence, in whom development in most fields appears to be merely average in the first few months, though certain features, such as unusually good concentration, interest in surroundings and social responsiveness, may be seen by the discerning eye.

Delayed Maturation (*'Slow starters'*)

In the previous chapter I described children who were unaccountably late in acquiring certain individual skills, such as sitting, walking, talking and sphincter control, and have ascribed these, for want of anything better, to delayed maturation of the appropriate part of the nervous system.

One occasionally sees children who were very retarded in the first few weeks, not only in motor development, but in other fields as well, and who catch up to the 'normal', and are later shown to have an average level of intelligence without any mechanical or other disability. They can be termed 'slow starters'. One can only presume that it is due to widespread delay in maturation of the nervous system. These cases are rare, but important because of the ease with which mental deficiency could be wrongly diagnosed. Below are brief illustrative case histories:

Case 1.—This girl had a full term normal delivery, and was well in the newborn period. At 13 weeks, however, there was complete head lag when held in ventral suspension or when pulled to the sitting position. She did not follow with her eyes until 17 weeks or smile till 18 weeks. She appeared to 'waken up' at about 17 weeks, and then made rapid headway. At 25 weeks her head control was equivalent to that of a 16 weeks' old baby. She was able to sit like an average baby at $7\frac{1}{2}$ months, to stand holding on at 10 months, to walk with one hand held and to say 10 words with meaning at 1 year. At the age of 5 years there was no mechanical disability, and her I.Q. test score was 122.

Case 2.—This boy (birth weight, $7\frac{1}{2}$ lbs.) had a proved cerebral haemorrhage at birth, grade 3 asphyxia (using Flagg's classification), and severe neonatal convulsions. He was born at home, and the facts about the duration of apnoea are uncertain. He was seen in an apnoeic state approximately half an hour after birth, and was given oxygen.

Three hours after birth he made one spontaneous respiration each 30 seconds, and $3\frac{1}{2}$ hours after birth he made one each 20 seconds. Oxygen was continued until respirations were properly established 5 hours after birth. Blood was withdrawn under high pressure by lumbar puncture.

In the early weeks he showed gross retardation in development. At 4 weeks of age, for instance, his motor development corresponded to that of an average newborn baby.

At 27 weeks his motor development was that of a 4 month's old baby. At 1 year he was standing and walking without support, saying several words with meaning, had no mechanical disability, and was normal in all respects.

I have a cinematographic record of his progress from gross retardation to normality.

Case 3.—This girl had a normal full term delivery. There was no abnormality in the neonatal period.

She was able to grasp objects voluntarily at 6 months, but could not sit without support till 1 year or walk without help until 3 years. She was saying words with meaning at 1 year. She could not manage buttons until the age of 6 years. The diagnosis of 'minimal birth injury', as described by Gesell, was made, because there were minimal but non-specific neurological signs—if such a term can be used.

Her subsequent progress was good, but it was interesting to note that although she could run fast, ride a bicycle, play hockey and take a full part in sport, she had an unusual tendency to stumble in Physical Education Classes, her hand movements were slow, and she could only type 50 words per minute. She was top of her class at a technical school and passed her General Certificate of Education at 17.

Case 4.—This girl (birth weight, 8 lbs. 2 ozs.) had a proved cerebral haemorrhage on full term delivery, repeated lumbar punctures having to be performed on account of severe vomiting due to increased intracranial pressure. An intravenous drip had to be given on the fourth day with considerable reluctance, on account of dehydration resulting from the vomiting. Bloody cerebrospinal fluid, and later xanthochromic fluid, was repeatedly withdrawn by lumbar puncture.

There was gross retardation of motor development, but I was impressed by the fact that at 7 weeks she was beginning to take notice of her surroundings and she began to smile. At 9 weeks her head control corresponded to that of a newborn baby. At 16 weeks it corresponded to that of a 6 weeks old baby, and at 24 weeks to that of a 13 weeks baby. At 28 weeks she began to go for objects with her hands and get them, and her head control was that of a 24 weeks old baby. She was able to sit for a few seconds without support at 8 months, to pull herself to the standing position at 10 months, and to feed herself (with a cup) at 14 months. She walked without help at 18 months, and put words into sentences at 21 months. At 6 years her I.Q. was 100, and there was no mechanical disability. It is interesting to note that an epileptic fit occurred at the age of 8 years.

Case 5.—This girl was born normally 6 weeks before term, weighing 4 lbs. 5 ozs. She began to smile at 4 months, to grasp objects voluntarily at 6 months, to imitate noises at 8 months, and to cast objects at 11 months. At this age she could say one word with meaning. At one year she could say 3 words with meaning, but her head control was equivalent to that of an average $4\frac{1}{2}$ months old child. At 17 months she was examined by an expert in another city with a view to admission to a centre for cerebral palsy, but the diagnosis of simple mental deficiency was made. At 22 months she could stand holding on to furniture. I wrote that her I.Q. was 'only slightly below the average'. At 23 months she could sit without support, and at 25 months she began to walk, holding on to furniture. She began to walk without help at 4 years and two months.

Her I.Q. at the age of 8 was 118. She was running about well, but not really nimble on her feet.

Case 6.—After seeing an 18 month old boy on account of uniform backwardness in development, I wrote to the family doctor as follows:–

'I think that he is a normal boy, but I am not quite sure and will see him again in six months. The difficulty is that he has been backward in everything. He did not sit till a year. He is not walking or nearly walking. He was late in reaching out and getting things (nine months), in playing patacake (16 months), in waving bye bye (18 months), and in helping his mother to dress him (he has not started yet). Yet he is a bright little boy, alert and interested. He would not cooperate in tests, but I saw enough to know that he is certainly not less than 10 or 11 months in development of manipulation. His head is of normal size ($18\frac{7}{8}$ ins.). I think that he is merely a late starter. It is always a difficult diagnosis to make and time will tell whether we are right'.

At 2 years he began speaking in sentences; his performance on the simple formboard was like that of a three year old.

At 4 years he was well above average in developmental tests, and was entirely normal.

Case 7.—Below is another extract from a letter to a family doctor about a child referred to me at 22 months for uniform delay in development:–

'The immediate impression on seeing this girl was that she was normal mentally and showed normal concentration and interest in her surroundings. Yet she has been backward in all aspects of development. She is not walking or talking. She has no sphincter control. She can't feed herself. She has only recently started to hold her arm out for a coat. She can't point out any objects in pictures on request. When I gave her one inch cubes she cast the lot on to the floor like a child of 13 to 15 months. She is, therefore, uniformly retarded. Her head, however, is of normal circumference, and this together with her normal interest and the story of the sibling's lateness in walking and talking makes one extremely cautious about the prognosis. I told the mother that I cannot say whether she will catch up to the normal or not. Time alone will tell, but there are grounds for hoping that she will. I shall see her again in six months'.

She walked without help at 25 months, began to join words together into sentences at 33 months, and at that age her performance on the single formboard was that of a three year old. At 49 months she was entirely normal, with advanced speech, and could count up to 130. There was no disability.

Many workers have remarked about the unexpected improvement seen in some mentally retarded children. Gesell[8] wrote that 'developmental momentum may increase with age'. Spaulding[15] wrote that it was becoming increasingly evident that I.Q. increases may be considerable in young mentally defective children. Guertin[10] described 25 backward patients who showed a considerable rise in the test rating. Others have made similar observations.[3, 4, 6, 7]

In our follow-up of 135 infants at Sheffield who were thought to be mentally retarded in the first 2 years,[12] 4 proved to have a lower I.Q. than expected, while 16 fared better than expected. Unless deterioration occurs in association with epilepsy (especially infantile spasms), and unless there is a familial degenerative condition, or certain rare syndromes already described, deterioration is rare: but unexpected improvement is not uncommon.

More commonly one sees children who were grossly retarded in the early weeks, but who make rapid progress and reach a much higher level than expected, remaining, however, below the average. Below are some brief summaries of examples of these:

Case 1.—Clinical diagnosis: 'minimal birth injury'. Birth weight 6 lbs. 3 ozs. She had grade 2 asphyxia after a difficult forceps delivery. Breathing was established in 10 minutes. On the fifth day she became very lethargic, there was no Moro reflex, and she was severely hypotonic. Subdural taps were negative. Marked retardation was suspected. The subsequent course was as follows:

6 weeks	no head control, but smiling had begun.
8 weeks	no head control.
13 weeks	head control less than 6 weeks.
17 weeks	Tonic neck reflex and grasp reflex present. I wrote, 'I am still not sure whether she has mental retardation or cerebral palsy, but she is interested in objects'.
21 weeks	head control equivalent to 18 weeks.
6 months	grasping rattle.
7 months	roll, prone to supine.
8 months	sit, no support. Mature transfer. Diagnosis of minimal birth injury made, with good prognosis.
10 months	creep. 5 to 6 words.
16 months	walk, holding on. Managing cup. I.Q. thought to be normal.
18 months	walk, no help.
24 months	sentences.
5 years	I.Q. score 87. No disability.

Case 2.—This boy was born at term, weighing 7 lbs. 12 ozs. He was normal in the newborn period. Below is a brief summary of his development:

9 months	first smile. Grasp object voluntarily.
13 months	sit, no support. Onset of major convulsions.
18 months	no sphincter control. Unable to feed self. General level is that of 8 months old baby. Petit mal and grand mal epilepsy.
5 years	I.Q. score 77. No physical disability.

Case 3.—This boy was born at term, weighing 6 lbs. 12 ozs. He was well in the newborn period. Below is a summary of his development:

4 months	taking no notice of surroundings.
14 months	unable to pull self to standing position.
19 months	creep.
24 months	walk, no help.
35 months	5 words. Able to creep up stairs, but cannot get down stairs.
48 months	Unable to dress self, but tries to pull on trousers.
7 years	I.Q. score 92. No physical disability.

Case 4.—This boy was born at term. Below are some essential milestones:

3 months	smile.
12 months	sit, no help.
24 months	walk, no help.
29 months	able to manage cup. Dry by day.
33 months	odd words only.
6 years	I.Q. score. 87.

Case 5.—This boy was born at term, weighing 7 lbs. Below is a summary of the subsequent course:

2 days	major convulsions. Subdural tap negative.
3½ months	smile.
4 months	vocalise.
6 months	began to follow with eyes.
9 months	no voluntary grasp. No chew. Won't hold object in hand: just drops it. Very defective head control. General level that of 3 months baby. Still having major convulsions.
14 months	nearly able to grasp objects.
2½ years	words in sentences.
3 years	able to walk without help.
9 years	I.Q. test score 88. No disability.

Slow Maturation in Association with Cerebral Palsy: Unexpected Improvement

Below are some further examples of slow maturation, this time in association with cerebral palsy. In each case early development was grossly retarded, while the eventual level of intelligence reached was quite good. These cases indicate how easy it is to give an unduly bad prognosis when retardation is found in early infancy.

Case 1.—This girl, born at term, only began to smile at 6 months. She began to grasp objects voluntarily at 9 months, to acquire sphincter control and say single words at 23 m onths, to feed herself, walk unsupported, and to help to dress herself at 29 months. She put words together at 3 years. Her I.Q. at 5 years was 90. She had a mild cerebra'
palsy of the ataxic type.

Case 2.—This boy was born at term, weighing 6 lbs. 4 ozs. Below is a summary of his development:

1st 12 mnths.	took no notice of anything.
	Lay almost still. Did not kick. No response to overture.
1 year	began to take notice. Tried to reach objects.
26 months	major convulsions began.
39 months	single words only. Cerebral palsy of spastic type diagnosed.
7 years	I.Q. score 81. Diagnosis spastic quadriplegia. Interested, alert, occasional convulsions.

Case 3.—This boy was born by Caesarian section 9 weeks prematurely, weighing 2·0 lbs. The mother had toxaemia. Below is a summary of his development:

1st 8 months.	Just lay in pram, taking no notice of surroundings.
8 months	first smile.
35 months	words in sentences. Unable to sit.
	Good concentration. Athetosis diagnosed.
5 years	I.Q. score 75.

COMMENT

I have described these cases at some length because of their great importance.   It seems that on rare occasions one sees a child who is retarded in all fields of development in the early weeks, and who then reaches a normal level of intelligence.   It is possible that this picture may occur when there is a 'birth injury' using the term in its broadest sense, the brain having been previously normal, and that full functional recovery may then occur.   The picture may alternatively be due to delayed maturation of the nervous system for reasons unknown, perhaps familial.

Much more commonly one sees a child who is seriously retarded in all fields of development in the early weeks, but who makes an unexpected improvement, reaching a level of intelligence only slightly below the average.   These cases are relatively common, and have been mentioned by other workers.   The problem is discussed by Edith Taylor in her book on the appraisal of children with cerebral defects.[16]   She described an athetoid child who at 15 months was unable to sit, could hardly use the hands at all, could not chew, and had to have a semi-solid diet because of difficulty in swallowing and of regurgitation. The child had an expressionless face, but was said to be alert and observant. At the age of 12 years the I.Q. score was 103.

It follows that in developmental prediction the possibility of delayed maturation and unexpected improvement must always be borne in mind, and in all cases *the rate of development* must be observed and assessed. This is based partly on the history of previous development and partly on the findings on repeated examinations.

Unexplained Temporary Cessation of Development

Lulls in development of certain skills, such as speech, have already been described. Very occasionally one sees a much more general slowing down or cessation of development, without any apparent reason. The following are examples:

Case Report.—This girl was born at term by normal delivery. She developed normally until 8 weeks, having begun to smile at 5 weeks with good motor development. At 8 weeks she had a cold, and then became drowsy, inactive and disinterested in her surroundings. She was admitted at 10 weeks. She took no notice of her surroundings and was suspected of being blind. She was drowsy and apathetic. There were no other abnormal physical signs. A subdural tap and tests for toxoplasmosis were negative. An air encephalogram was thought to show cortical atrophy. The electroencephalogram was normal. The following letter was written to the family doctor: 'I am afraid that the outlook for this child is extremely poor; although she appeared to develop normally till the age of 8 weeks, she is now obviously mentally retarded; her mental retardation is likely to be of severe degree'. She was discharged, to be followed up as an outpatient.

At 14 weeks she was smiling and alert. At 7 months she was a normal happy smiling baby, vocalising well. At 3 years and 9 months in developmental tests she was above the average in all respects.

COMMENT

There is a possibility that the unexplained lull in development was due to encephalitis, but there were no neurological signs and there was no other evidence of that condition. In retrospect there seemed to be every reason to give a bad prognosis. The case shows the great need for caution.

Case 2.—This baby was born by breech delivery at term, weighing 7 lbs. Owing to a clerical error blood group incompatibility was not expected.   She developed mild haemolytic disease of the newborn, responding to 3 simple transfusions.   She began to smile at 6 weeks, and shortly after to vocalise.   She developed normally until the age of 3 months.   She then refused the breast, stopped playing with her toes, and just lay, with no interest in her surroundings for 4 months, without moving her arms or legs.   She then appeared to waken up, began to go for objects with her hands at 9 months, and to sit up without support, and to walk without support at 16 months, saying 2 words with meaning.   At 2 years she was well up to the average in all developmental tests, and was speaking in sentences.   At just under 7 years she was doing very well in an ordinary school.

COMMENT

These, too, are important cases, for they indicate further pitfalls in prognosis.   In both cases the period of non-development gave occasion to considerable parental alarm, and there was good reason for an expert to feel the same anxiety about the future of these children.

Severe Microcephaly with Initial Normal Development

I believe that sometimes a child with microcephaly may be relatively normal for the first few weeks, but that slowing down of development then occurs.   I have seen several examples of this. I have cinematographic records of 2 such children, giving permanent evidence of the normality of early development.

Case 1.—This girl (Fig. 154) was born at term, weighing 7 lbs. 7 ozs. There was gross microcephaly, and it was impossible to obtain a proper measurement of the head circumference: it was probably between 11 and 12 inches.   X-ray studies eliminated craniostenosis. I followed her up at frequent intervals, and recorded her progress by cinéphotography, because of the advanced development.   At 26 days her motor development was equivalent to that of an average 6 to 8 weeks old baby.   She was smiling and vocalising at 4 weeks.   The subsequent history was as follows:

10 weeks	laughs frequently. Tries to grasp objects.
6 months	sitting well without support. Chewing for a month.
8½ months	creeping. Imitating.
10 months	playing patacake; waving bye-bye.
11 months	pulls self to stand. Casting. Helping to dress.
	Very active, interested.
	Head circumferences $14\frac{7}{8}$ inches.

13 months	standing alone. Walking, holding on to furniture.
15 months	walking.
16 months	domestic mimicry. Head circumference 15¼ inches. Managing cup.
18 months	3 words with meaning.
33 months	head circumference 15½ inches. 5–6 words. D.Q. now 45.

The subsequent progress was one of gradual falling off in the rate of development.

A sibling was subsequently born with microcephaly. She showed a similar pattern of development. Both children at school age had an I.Q. score below 50.

Case 2.—This prematurely born boy was seen at the age of 6 months on account of the smallness of his head. At the age of 1 month it measured 12¼ inches in circumference, 12⅞ inches at 3 months, and 14 inches when seen by me. There was no radiological evidence of craniostenosis. He began to smile at 7 weeks. Ophthalmoscopic examination revealed a remarkable developmental anomaly of both eyes, with nystagmus and defective vision. An air encephalogram showed marked cerebral atrophy. Tests for toxoplasmosis were negative. At that time I wrote, 'The degree of microcephaly in surprising, in view of the relatively good head control and satisfactory development of manipulation. I do not suppose, however, that much further advancement will occur, and think that the developmental prognosis is thoroughly bad. It remains to be seen'.

The situation was reviewed when he was 13 months old. I wrote then that 'His level of development is exactly what one would have expected from previous tests. His D.Q. is about 75. I cannot help feeling, however, that in view of the marked microcephaly, it will be surprising if this relatively good level of development is maintained'.

The boy began to walk without help at 33 months, but when seen at 56 months he was grossly retarded. There was no sphincter control, poor concentration, poor speech, and a complete inability to dress or undress himself. He cast cubes and blocks of the formboard, like a child of 12 to 15 months. He was now well below the 'educable' level. At the age of six years his I.Q. score was 40.

Case 3.—Another child, 24 months old at the time of writing, was born weighing 7 lbs. 4 ozs., with a head circumference of 12⅛ inches. She began to smile at her mother at 7 weeks. She sat unsupported at eight months, her head circumference at this age being 14 inches, with a weight of 16 lbs. 7 ozs. She walked alone at 13 months; her weight was now 19 lbs. and the head circumference was 15 inches; she was saying two words with meaning. I wrote then that I expected her to be considerably retarded when older though she was then within normal limits. Domestic mimicry began at 13 months. She was able to manage a cup and drink from it without help at 15 months. At 24 months she was saying numerous words, and was beginning to join words into sentences (saying, for instance, 'Shut up' when her mother sang). She could get her pants and some other clothes on, and had bladder and bowel control by day. Her head circumference was now 15·4/8 inches. Time will tell what her eventual I.Q. will be.

Mental Deterioration

Slowing down in development, or worse still mental deterioration, occurs in a wide variety of conditions, of which the following are the chief examples and causes:–

Severe emotional deprivation: insecurity.

Bad home.

Bad education.

Personality problems.

Degenerative diseases of the nervous system.

Epilepsy (effect of drugs, effect of severe fits, underlying brain disease, emotional and educational problems).

Metabolic diseases (e.g. phenylketonuria, other abnormal aminoacidurias, lipoidoses, hypoglycaemia, thyroid deficiency).

Lead poisoning.

Meningitis, encephalitis.

Cerebral vascular disorders.

Severe head injury.

Normal development, followed by slowing and cessation of development, due to hypothyroidism. Rapid response to treatment.

Case Report.—This boy was interesting because of the slowing down and then cessation of development of motor control. He was born at term, and was followed by me from birth to the age of 8 years. At one month of age his head control was average: at 6 weeks I described it as almost average: at 11 weeks it was defective, corresponding to that of an average 6 weeks' old baby. I realised that he had probably developed hypothyroidism. His total serum lipoids were 1,100 mg. per cent., and the skeletal maturity was retarded. He was given thyroid extract. At 15 weeks his head control was greatly improved, corresponding to the 9 to 10 weeks' level. At 6 months he was normal in all respects. Subsequent progress was normal. At 13 months he was walking without support and saying more than a dozen words with meaning. He could manage a cup without any help.

At the age of 7 years his I.Q. score was just over 100.

COMMENT

The absence of the typical appearance of cretinism in children like this who develop thyroid deficiency after some weeks or months makes the diagnosis easy to miss.

Normal development for 4 months, followed by sudden mental deterioration with the development of infantile spasms.

Below is a summary of a typical case.

Case Report.—This child was born at term, after a normal delivery:

6 weeks	smile.
8 weeks	vocalising.
12 weeks	would hold rattle placed in hand for several minutes.
16 weeks	would hold bottle. Raising head spontaneously from supine.
20 weeks	began to look vacant and stopped showing interest in surroundings. A week later he had his first infantile spasm.
6 months	full head control. Able to sit like 6 months old baby. No interest in surroundings. No smile. All investigations negative except E.E.G. (hypsarrhythmia). Very bad prognosis given.
8 years	ineducable, in institution.

A similar picture is seen in some children who are moderately retarded from birth. Infantile spasms develop usually at about the age of 6 months, and there is then immediate and severe deterioration. The condition has been described in Chapter 5.

A bad prognosis was given because of the deterioration in social behaviour. When one first sees a child of this type the motor development may be up to the average, because he had previously developed normally, but there is a striking lack of interest in the surroundings, and the child has stopped smiling. I regard a history that smiling has stopped (in the absence of an obvious febrile illness) as a symptom of great importance and bad prognostic significance.

Normal Development, Followed by the So-called 'Acute Infantile Hemiplegia' and Mental Deficiency.

Another cause of normal initial development followed by mental deficiency is a cardiovascular accident.

Case Report.—This girl weighed 9½ lbs. at birth, and delivery was normal. She was normal in the neonatal period. Her development was normal. She began to smile at 5 weeks, to grasp objects voluntarily at 5 months, to chew at 6 months, and to sit without support at 7 months. At the age of 11 months she had a right-sided convulsion, followed immediately by status epilepticus which continued for 12 hours.

When we first saw her 9 days later she was in coma. There was a right hemiplegia. The fundi were normal. The cerebrospinal fluid was normal. An air-encephalogram showed excess of air over the left hemisphere, but no other gross abnormality. She was discharged home with a very bad prognosis, the diagnosis being acute infantile hemiplegia.

At the age of 6 years her I.Q. was too low to score. She was taking no interest in her surroundings. The hemiplegia was unchanged.

Severe mental deficiency may develop suddenly, usually in association with convulsions, during the course of gastroenteritis or dehydration for other reasons. It may be due to an electrolyte disturbance, such as hypernatraemia, or to a cerebral venous thrombosis.

I have already mentioned the way in which mongols slow down in development after the early weeks.

Conclusions and Summary

The case histories described indicate the importance of not only being thoroughly conversant with 'normal development' but with the variations which may occur. Knowledge of such cases is essential for one who assesses the development of infants. Unexpected slowing down of development, such as that described in several children, can never be anticipated. One must remember the fact that some children have unexpected lulls in development, followed by normal progress thereafter: and more important still, that even severe retardation in the early weeks may be followed by relatively normal or completely normal levels of intelligence later. Hence the importance of observing the rate of development —by taking a proper history and observing the child at intervals.

I have cited examples to illustrate the great danger of diagnosing mental retardation, when a child, though backward in all aspects of development, has a head of normal size, and is responsive, alert and interested in surrounding like a normal child should be—even though there is no helpful family history of delayed maturation.

REFERENCES

1. ASHER, P., SCHONELL, F. E. (1950) A Survey of 400 Cases of Cerebral Palsy in Childhood. *Arch. Dis. Childh.*, **25**, 360.
2. BAKWIN, H., BAKWIN, R. M. (1953) *Behaviour Disorders in Children.* Philadelphia: Saunders.
3. BENDER, L. (1958) Emerging Patterns in Child Psychiatry. *Bull. N.Y. Acad. Med.*, **34**, 794.
4. BENTON, A. L. (1956) Pseudofeeblemindedness. *Arch. Neurol.*, **75**, 379.
5. BRÜNING, H. (1921) quoted by STRAUCH, A. (1924) *Amer. J. Dis. Child.*, **27**, 163.
6. Child Adoption Research Committee. New York (1951) *A Follow-up Study of Adoptive Families.*
7. CLARKE, A. D. B., CLARKE, A. M. (1954-5) Pseudofeeblemindedness— Some Implications. *Amer. J. ment. Defic.*, **59**, 507.
8. GESELL, A., AMATRUDA, C. S. (1947) *Developmental Diagnosis.* New York: Hoeber.
9. GESELL, A., AMATRUDA, C. S., CASTNER, B. M., THOMPSON, H. (1939) *Biographies of Child Development.* London: Hamish Hamilton.
10. GUERTIN, W. H. (1949) Mental Growth in Pseudofeeblemindedness. *J. clin. Psychol.*, **5**, 414.
11. HOLLINGWORTH, L. S. (1929) *Gifted Children.* New York: Macmillan.
11a.HOLLINGWORTH, L. S. (1942) *Children above* 180 *I.Q.* New York: World Book Co.
12. ILLINGWORTH, R. S., BIRCH, L. B. (1959) The Diagnosis of Mental Retardation in Infancy. A Follow-up Study. *Arch. Dis. Childh.*, **34**, 269.
13. ILLINGWORTH, R. S., ILLINGWORTH, C. M. (1966) *Lessons from Childhood. Some Aspects of the Early Life of Unusual Men and Women.* Edinburgh: Livingstone.
14. MICHAL-SMITH, H. (1957) *Management of the Handicapped Child.* New York: Grune and Stratton.
15. SPAULDING, P. J. (1946-7) Retest Results on the Stanford L with Mental Defectives. *Amer. J. ment. Defic.*, **51**, 35.
16. TAYLOR, E. M. (1959) *Psychological Appraisal of Children with Cerebral Defects.* Cambridge Mass.: Harvard Univ. Press.
17. TERMAN, L. M., ODEN, M. H. (1947) *The Gifted Child Grows Up* Stanford: Stanford Univ. Press.

CHAPTER 12

HISTORY TAKING

I have already indicated that in my opinion the history is a vital part of the developmental diagnosis. Without a good history, which I have taken myself, I am most reluctant to give an opinion about a child's development. It is in this matter that I disagree most strongly with those psychologists who attempt to make their developmental diagnosis and predictions purely on one objective examination. In my opinion this attempt to be really scientific, by using nothing but objective methods, leads to considerable inaccuracy. They ignore vital information which has a profound bearing on the child's assessment.

It is of interest that in the books written by Bühler,[1] Cattell[2] and Griffiths[3] on developmental testing in infants, nothing or virtually nothing is said about history taking. In marked contrast to these is the excellent book by Hauessermann[4] concerning developmental testing in handicapped children. In that book there is a good account of the way in which the history should be taken.

The Importance of the History

The history is an essential part of the developmental diagnosis for the following reasons:

1. *A history of prenatal and perinatal factors may be relevant to the diagnosis.* With regard to prenatal factors, their importance must not be exaggerated. For instance, it must be constantly borne in mind that a history of mental retardation in parents, toxaemia, bleeding during pregnancy, premature delivery, anoxia on delivery, or genetic conditions such as phenylketonuria, do not imply that the child in question will be abnormal. It merely means that the risk that the child will be abnormal is greater than usual. This is particularly important in the case of the examination of babies for adoption, especially if one of the parents was known to be mentally retarded. It would be a tragedy if children born of such mothers were automatically excluded from adoption, for the great majority are mentally normal.

The history of prematurity is essential because of the allowance which must be made for premature delivery in assessing the early milestones.

A history of conditions known to be associated with kernicterus —hyperbilirubinaemia in the premature baby, excessive dosage of Vitamin K and improperly treated haemolytic disease, is important in developmental assessment. In the same way a history of severe anoxia at birth in a child subsequently found to be backward would make one particularly careful to look for athetoid movements.

Of all the prenatal and perinatal factors, one of the most important would be the history of perinatal convulsions in the baby. Even if that history is obtained, it will be remembered that the odds are that the child will be normal. It will be impossible to be sure, however, that epileptic fits will not develop subsequently.

With regard to hereditary neurological disorders, one needs to know the age at which those disorders manifested themselves in siblings.

2. *The environmental circumstances.* The importance of environmental circumstances in relation to a child's potentialities has been discussed in Chapter 4. Amongst other relevant factors are the social and educational status of the parents, and the opportunities which they are likely to give to the child.

With regard to the assessment of motor development, the opportunity given to the child to bear weight on the legs is important. Defective weight-bearing may be due merely to the mother's fear of allowing the baby to bear his weight.

In the case of the older infant, the mother's attitude has to be determined before an assessment of the baby can be made. If the mother leaves the 12 to 18 months old baby howling in the pram outside the house for most of the day, one would expect his developmental achievements to be less than those of a baby treated more imaginatively.

If a child has been brought up in an institution, the age at which he was placed in a foster home is relevant. The longer the period of institutional care, and the shorter the period in the foster home, the greater would be the retardation to be expected. A history of recent prolonged illness might well be relevant in assessing motor development.

With regard to skills such as feeding and dressing, the opportunities given to the child to attend to these needs himself must be assessed from the history. With regard to sphincter control, the parental management is relevant to the child's development in this field.

3. *The assessment of the rate of development.* This vital piece of information must be obtained from the mother at the time of the first interview. A careful history of the milestones of development gives one a good idea of the course of development. This history is particularly important in the case of those children who develop normally up to a point, and then deteriorate.

4. *An account of the rate and mode of development in siblings.* The importance of the familial factor in the age of walking, talking, and acquiring clean toilet habits, has already been discussed.

5. *Other family history.* A family history of sinistrality or ambi-dexterity, or of specific reading disability, is important.

6. *The history of achievements to supplement and confirm one's own observations.* The observant mother may observe many skills which one cannot necessarily see in a short examination oneself, particularly if the child is being unco-operative, on account of sleepiness or other factors. For instance, when showing a child a picture card, I usually ask a mother whether she thinks that her child would know the objects in question.

It is useful to determine whether the mother's account of the child's development tallies with one's own assessment. It does not always do so. One occasionally sees a child who, after careful questioning of the mother, is said to have been able to go for objects and grasp them for months, and yet who, on examination, has such an immature grasp that one does not believe the mother's story. On the other hand, one sometimes sees a child who is said to be unable to sit, yet who can sit steadily like an 8 or 9 months old child.

Essentials in History Taking

The first essential is that each should understand what the other means. The details of the child's development are asked in simple language, and the questions are put in a precise manner. The following are examples of questions which one puts, and of errors which can be made in taking a history.

1. When did he first begin to smile when you were talking to him? It is not enough to ask, 'When did he first smile?' Mothers

may interpret as a smile any facial movement in sleep, or wince of pain from wind or facial movement as a result of tickling the face with the finger. The early smile must be the result of social overture.

2. When did he first begin to hold for a minute or two toys placed in the hand? It is not enough to ask the mother when he first began to grasp. She may well be confused with the grasp reflex.

3. When did he first begin to go for a toy and get it without it being placed in the hand? It is useless to ask when he was first able to grasp objects. The mother will almost certainly refer to the age at which he was able to hold a toy if it was placed in the hand. The question should be put in words such as those above, and checked in different words when she has answered, in order to make sure that she is referring to a voluntary and deliberate grasp.

4. When did he first sit for a few seconds on the floor without rolling over? It is useless to ask, 'When did he sit?' A newborn baby can be held in the sitting position. An average baby can sit propped up in a pram at any age after 3 months or so. He can sit up 'unsupported' in the pram (with support, however, around the buttocks) several weeks before he can sit on a firm surface without support.

5. When did he first begin to chew? Mothers inevitably think of teeth when this question is asked. One wants to know the age at which chewing movements began. The mother must distinguish chewing from sucking, and this must be checked.

6. When did he first begin to roll? A clear distinction must be made between rolling from prone to supine and rolling from supine to prone (usually a month later). It is even more important to be sure that the mother refers to rolling completely over—not merely on to the side.

7. When did he first begin to creep, on hands and knees? The mother has to distinguish the crawl, the child pulling himself forward on his abdomen by his hands, the legs trailing behind.

8. When did he first say words, meaning something? It is useless merely to ask when he began to talk. It is surprising how often one sees this in papers on development. Mothers are likely to interpret the 6 months old baby's 'Mum-Mum' in crying as a word with meaning. When the child of about 7 months begins to

combine syllables such as 'dadada', these sounds are interpreted as words. In the case of the word 'dada', one wants to know whether the word is spoken only in the father's presence, or when he is not there. The only useful information concerns the use of words with meaning.

It is in fact difficult to know when a 'word' is a word. A child may say 'g' for dog, or 'og', before he can say the full word, but he is given the benefit of the doubt when he has obviously attempted to say the word.

9. When did he first walk for a few steps without support? A child of 9 months or so can walk with hands held. One wants to know when he could first walk without support at all.

10. When did he first begin to tell you that he wanted to use the pottie? It is no use asking, 'When was he first dry?' The mother will confuse voluntary control with early conditioning.

11. When could he first manage a cup, picking it up, drinking from it and putting it down? This is quite different from 'drinking from a cup'—which can be achieved by a newborn baby.

Other useful questions are as follows:

When did he begin to watch you intently when you spoke to him? (*i.e.* before the smile).

When did he begin to make little noises as well as smile when you talked to him?

Does he smile much? Is it only an occasional smile? This question is relevant in the case of defective children. Whereas a normal child who begins to smile at 4 weeks smiles a great deal by the age of 8 to 10 weeks, a defective child who begins to smile at 3 months, may smile only occasionally by 6 months.

How much does he sleep? This is relevant in mentally retarded infants, who are apt to sleep excessively.

Is he interested when he sees the feed being prepared?

When did he begin to pass an object from one hand to the other?

When could he pick up a small object like a currant between his thumb and forefinger?

When did he begin to put 2 or 3 words together into a sentence? This is quite different from imitating certain phrases such as 'Oh dear'. One wants to know when the child spontaneously began to join words together.

A particularly useless question is, 'When did he first begin to hold his head up?' Any answer means nothing. A baby can hold his head up momentarily in the sitting position when a few days old. He can spontaneously lift his head off the couch from the supine position when he is about 5 or 6 months old. It is obviously different for him to hold his head up if he is propped up at an angle of 45 degrees to the couch.

Does he imitate you in anything which you do—in making little noises, coughing, or putting the tongue out, for instance?

Does he try to draw your attention in any way, by a cough, squeak, or pulling at your clothes?

Will he play any games like peep-bo, patacake? When did he begin?

When did he begin to hand you a toy and give it to you? (as distinct from handing it and not letting it go).

When did he begin deliberately to throw bricks and other toys on to the floor?

When did he begin to wave bye-bye?

Does he show in any way that he understands or remembers nursery rhymes?

When was he able to feed himself with a biscuit?

How long will he play with one toy?

Does he help you when you are dressing him, by holding his arm out for a coat or foot out for a shoe? When did he begin?

After the first birthday, the following other questions are relevant:

1. Can he get up and down stairs alone? How does he do it? Does he creep up?
2. Does he imitate you in doing things about the house, such as sweeping, dusting, or washing up? When did he begin?
3. Would he know the meaning of words in a picture book? Would he be able to point out to you the horse, dog, baby, etc., if you asked him to do?
4. How much can he dress or undress himself?
5. When was he able to feed himself fully, without help?
6. When could he dress himself fully, without help, except with the back buttons?
7. When was he dry by day and dry by night?
8. How long does he play with any one toy?

It should be particularly noted that in all cases one **asks** *not only* 'Does he?' *but also* 'When did he begin to?'

In taking a history concerning a child in whom one suspects that there may be a defect of hearing, the following questions are useful:

Can he hear? Why do you think that he can hear?

Does he like squeaky toys?

Does he like being sung to?

Does he respond to music?

Has he favourite nursery rhymes?

Does he hear the telephone, aeroplane, father's footstep?

Will he come from another room when you call him without seeing you?

In addition to the above, it is often useful to ask a mother how the child in question compares with his siblings. If the child is referred to one on account of lateness in speech, one asks how the elder siblings compared with him at his present age in everything except speech, but especially in general understanding. One then asks how the siblings are faring at school, because there is the possibility that they might also be backward. I find that this comparison is a useful one to make.

The Reliability of the History

I disagree with those who consider that a mother's develop-mental history is totally unreliable. It is obvious that the further back one goes, the less reliable a history will be. It also happens that one does not usually need to go a long way back. When faced with a mentally defective boy of 10 years, minutiae of developmental history are irrelevant. One does want to know details, however, in a baby.

It is always the doctor's task to assess the reliability of a story about anything, whether an illness or otherwise. One has to form one's own opinion about a mother's memory. One has to form one's own conclusion as to whether she is obviously fabricating a reply, as to whether she is trying to make one believe that the child was 'normal' when he was not, and as to whether she is merely basing her replies on the age at which she thinks a child should achieve the skills in question.

In order to check a doubtful reply, one comes round to the question in a different way after an interval, in order to see if the answers tally.

One checks the answer about one milestone by that about

another. For instance, one can readily check the likelihood that a mother's reply about the age of smiling is correct by asking when he began to vocalise as well. If she said that the baby began to smile at 3 weeks, but did not begin to vocalise until 3 months, one will know that one or other answer is almost certainly incorrect. Babies usually begin to vocalise 1 or 2 weeks after they have begun to smile. One constantly checks one milestone against another, and one will also check the mother's story against one's own findings on objective examination.

Below is a reproduction of a duplicated sheet used at the Children's Hospital, Sheffield, as a guide to history taking.

DEVELOPMENTAL HISTORY

Reference No: ....   Date of Birth ....

NAME ....   Date of 1st examination.............. ..

Weight at Birth............................. .   Duration of gestation ....

Milestones	Average	Reported		
Smile in response –	6 w			
Vocalise with smile –	8 w			
Hold rattle for minutes when placed in hand	12 w			
Turn head to follow mother with eyes –	12 w			
Turn head to sound –	16 w			
Excite on preparation of feed – – –	16 w			
Go for and get object not placed in hand –	20 w			
Roll prone to supine –	24 w			
Transfer objects –	26 w			
Chew solids – –	26 w			
Roll supine to prone –	26 w			
Sit on floor for seconds, no support, no fall –	28 w			
Imitate noises, etc. –	28 w			
Stand holding on to playpen, chair –	36 w			
Crawl (*i.e.* on abdomen)	40 w			
Pull to stand, no help –	40 w			
Bye-bye – – –	40 w			
Patacake – – –	40 w			
Creep (*i.e.* on knees and hands) – – –	44 w			
Arms out for dress, coat, foot for shoe – –	44 w			
One word *with meaning*	44 w			
Cruise (walk, holding on to furniture) – –	48 w			

Milestones	Average	Reported		
Three words *with meaning* – – –	12 m			
Casting – – –	12–15 m			
Walk, no support –	13 m			
Pick up cup, drink, put down, no help –	15 m			
Ask M. for pottie –	15–18 m			
Domestic mimicry –	18 m			
Dry by day – –	18 m			
Words together (not imitation) – –	21–24 m			
Dry by night – –	2 yrs.			
Puts on shoes, socks, pants – – –	2 yrs.			
Dress fully apart from buttons – – –	3 yrs.			
Will come from another room when called, *i.e.* when out of sight –	–			
Concentrates well on toys: play long time with one – –	–			
How many objects would he be able to point out in pictures?	–			

The Minimum History

In all cases one must ask the history of prenatal, perinatal and postnatal factors which may have affected his development. e.g. Illness in pregnancy, mode of delivery, birth weight, duration of gestation, condition at birth, illnesses since birth. In addition one would always ask about the following at the ages stated, in all cases asking '*whether*' and '*when*'.

6 weeks—Smile (If not, ask whether he watches the mother intently as she speaks to him). Vocalisation.

6 months—Smile. Vocalisation. Turning head to sound. Reaching and getting without object being put in hand. Chewing. Copying (e.g. cough).

10 months—Smile. Reaching and getting etc. Chewing. Sitting (no support, on floor, seconds). Crawling. Creeping. Standing holding on. Pulling self to stand. Cruising. Steps, no support. Waving byebye. Playing patacake. Helping dress.

15 months—Words and understanding of words. Feeding self with cup, no help. Asking for pottie. Walking, no help. Domestic mimicry. Duration of play with one toy.

2 years—Feeding self, including cup. Sphincter control by day. Domestic mimicry. Walking. Dressing and undressing self—details. Words and sentences. Duration of play with one toy.

Summary

1. A full developmental and environmental history is an essential part of the developmental diagnosis. The history includes enquiry into prenatal and perinatal factors and the environment in which the child has been brought up. It includes a careful assessment of the child's previous rate of development, familial developmental features, and the mother's version of the child's present developmental status for comparison with one's own findings.

2. The essential point about history taking is the importance of ensuring that each understands what the other means. Questions must be precise and the mother's veracity must be assessed.

REFERENCES

1. BÜHLER, C. (1935) *From Birth to Maturity.* London: Kegan Paul.
2. CATTELL, P. (1947) *The Measurement of Intelligence of Infants and Young Children.* New York: The Psychological Corporation.
3. GRIFFITHS, R. (1954) *The Abilities of Babies.* London: Univ. of London Press.
4. HAUESSERMANN, E. (1958) *Developmental Potential of Pre-school Children.* London: Grune and Stratton.

CHAPTER 13

THE EXAMINATION OF THE OLDER INFANT AND CHILD

PART I.—THE DEVELOPMENTAL EXAMINATION

EQUIPMENT REQUIRED. The following equipment is required for developmental testing in the first 5 years:

10 one-inch cubes.

Hand bell.

Simple formboard.

Goddard formboard.

Coloured and uncoloured geometric forms.

Picture cards.

Scrap book.

Cards with circle, cross, square, triangle, diamond drawn on them. These can be made at the time of examination out of sight of the child.

Common objects (penny, pencil, knife, ball).

Patellar hammer.

Paper.

Pellets (8 mm). These can be made at the time of examination from cotton wool.

The relevant items are illustrated in figures.

The various structures made from the cubes are also illustrated (Figs. 132-136).

Examination after the Newborn Period

This section is based on the work of Arnold Gesell and has been modified for use in a busy paediatric out-patient clinic. It is obvious that the more one digresses from the exact technique of examination for developmental tests, the less valid is the statistical basis of one's tests. The modifications used here are, in my opinion, so small that they do not invalidate the result; and a follow-up study already described (Ch. 2) and many hundreds of other personally observed cases, has shown that the tests as described are of predictive value.

For further details of developmental tests the reader should refer to Arnold Gesell and his colleagues in *Developmental Diagnosis* and *The First Five Years of Life*, and books by Charlotte Buehler and Psyche Cattell. The latter's tests are based on those of Gesell.

For the purpose of the developmental examination, and to a lesser extent for the purpose of the physical examination, it is important to have the infant or small child in as good a temper as possible. In the Yale Clinic of Child Development, under Gesell, social workers visited the home in order to determine the baby's normal play time, and the developmental examination was arranged accordingly. Unfortunately the busy paediatrician cannot work under such ideal conditions, but he can at least see that the infant is not hungry at the time of examination. If he is sleepy, a note to that effect is made and he is re-examined before an opinion can be given.

I see no need for a special room for developmental examinations. Most paediatricians will, of necessity, have to examine infants and young children in the course of ordinary out-patient duties, in the usual room reserved for that purpose. I have not found the presence of students or post-graduates a disadvantage. The child should not be within sight of a window through which he can see objects and people passing. Irrelevant toys must be out of reach and sight. I always conduct my examination of the child in the mother's presence. This seems to be the normal and natural arrangement. Occasionally a mother is unable to resist trying to help a child to perform a test, but she can be asked to leave the test to the child. She is also apt to tell a child that he is making a mistake (in the formboard test, for instance), but she has to be asked not to do this. Sometimes the mother may help by asking the child to carry out a test, such as building a tower of cubes, when he shows no sign of doing it for the examiner. When one is not sure whether the child has really done his best, it is useful to ask the mother if she thinks that the child could do the test in question, or would be able to recognise the objects shown, so that one's findings can be confirmed.

The developmental examination of young children should always be performed before the physical examination, because the child may cry during the physical examination and he would then be unlikely to co-operate in developmental tests. It is

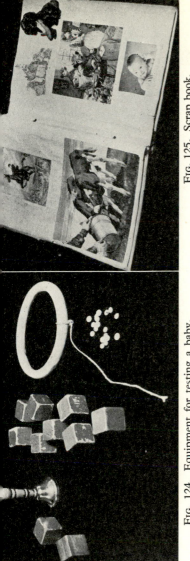

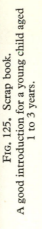

Fig. 124. Equipment for testing a baby.
(The cubes are used from 5 months to 6 years.) Pellets,
dangling ring, one-inch cubes, small bell.

Fig. 125. Scrap book.
A good introduction for a young child aged
1 to 3 years.

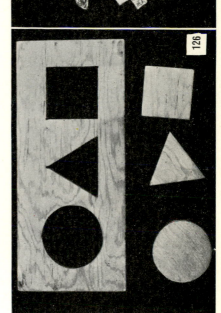

Fig. 126
Simple formboard. 14½ × 6¾ inches.

Fig. 127
Coloured geometric forms. Red card mounted on plain
cardboard, with corresponding cut-out pieces.

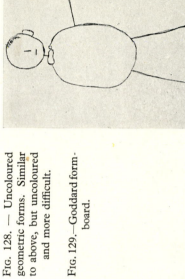

Fig. 128. — Uncoloured geometric forms. Similar to above, but uncoloured and more difficult.

Fig. 129.—Goddard form-board.

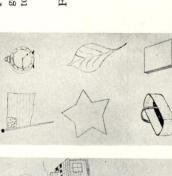

Fig. 130.—Pictures of common objects for picture identification.

Fig. 131.—Incomplete man.

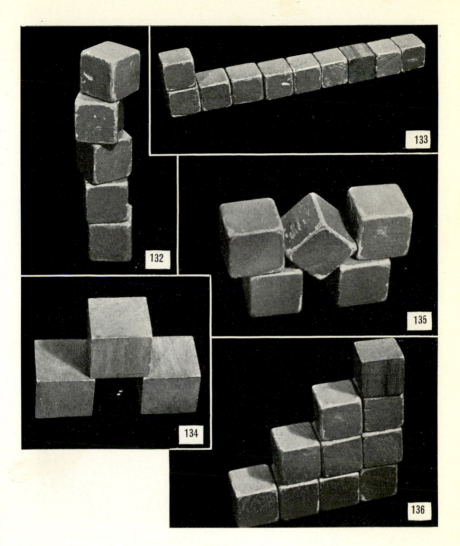

Fig. 132. Tower of cubes. Fig. 134. Bridge.
Fig. 133. Train of cubes Fig. 135. Gate.
    with chimney. Fig. 136. Step.

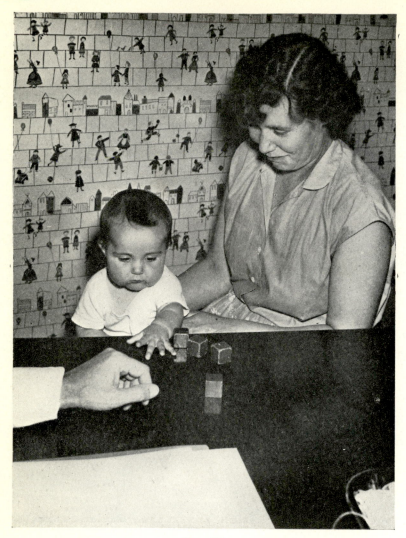

FIG. 137

Position for first stage of examination of young baby—before he is
undressed.

FIG. 138. 4 years 3 months.
FIG. 139. 4 years 3 months. (Girl with toy cupboard.)
FIG. 140.—5 years 3 months. (In colour.)
FIG. 141.—6 years 0 months.

FIG. 142

FIG. 143

FIG. 144

FIG. 142—7 years 5 months.

FIG. 143—8 years 11 months. (In colour.)

FIG. 144—9 years 9 months. (In colour.)

usually advisable to carry out the developmental examination before taking the history, for a young child, and particularly a retarded one, will soon become bored and restless and so co-operate less well.

In all tests one observes the child's interest, distractability, degree and duration of concentration, social responsiveness, alertness and rapidity of response. The child is watched intently throughout the examination. One particularly looks for abnormalities of movement (*e.g.* athetosis, ataxia, spasticity or tremor). One also listens and notes the vocalisations—their nature and frequency, and later the quality of speech.

All tests are carried out as quickly as possible, in order to preserve interest and co-operation. If a child does not seem to be interested in one test, another is substituted. In developmental testing of young or retarded children there is no place for long tests. I cannot agree with those who say that developmental testing in infancy is very time-consuming. It must not be.

Babies and young children readily begin to cry when undressed, and they are particularly liable to cry when placed in the prone or supine position. Accordingly one begins by acquiring as much information as possible as soon as the child comes into the room, when he is fully dressed. After that he is completely undressed for the rest of the examination and the nappy must be removed.

At the end of the discussion of each age period, I have provided a summary which is intended to serve as the minimum screening examination—unless, in the case of certain items, I have stated otherwise. In that case they are essential for assessment as distinct from mere screening.

The First Three Months

The mother sits at the side of the desk with her baby on her knees. The first item is to watch the baby as his mother speaks to him. He may open and close his mouth and bob his head up and down as she speaks. One also notices the intentness of the baby's regard, and his alertness. One notices the baby's smile, if any, and his interest in his surroundings. The shape and size of the head is noted and the head circumference is measured. The fontanelle is palpated, and if the head appears to be somewhat larger than usual, or of an unusual shape, one feels the sutures for undue separation (in the case of hydrocephalus), or for a thickened rim, indicating craniostenosis.

The next step is to hold the baby in ventral suspension—with the hand under the abdomen. One notices the degree to which the baby can hold his head up, and how long he can do this. One also notices the posture of the limbs. In a defective child the arms and legs often hang down lifelessly. In the normal child there is some extension of the hip and flexion of the knees, with flexion of the elbows.

The child is next placed in the prone position. One notices whether the head is turned to one side or maintained in the central position. One watches to see whether the baby lifts the chin off the couch, and how much he can do this. The posture of the pelvis and the degree of extension of the legs is observed.

The child is then placed in the supine position. The movements are noted. One watches to see whether they are normal or abnormal, as in athetosis. The tonic neck reflex is noted, if it occurs. The grasp reflex may be tested for by slipping one's finger into the palm of the hand. The extent to which the hands are kept open or closed is assessed. One then tests the baby's ability to follow a moving object, by bringing it into his line of vision and slowly moving it to the other side. The knee jerks are then tested, and if necessary one looks for ankle clonus. When the hips have been flexed to a right angle, they are rapidly abducted in order to elicit adductor spasm. Limited abduction of the hips might be due to congenital dislocation. The method of testing for subluxation of the hips is described on page 153.

It is not easy to test the hearing in this age period, but one can often demonstrate that in response to the sound of the bell or of the crinkling of paper on a level with the ear but out of sight, the child startles, cries, quietens or blinks; and at three months of age the baby may be beginning to turn the head to sound.

Although I do not personally test the hearing of each baby routinely in this age period, a small bell can be used for this purpose, care being taken to sound it behind the baby's head and out of sight. The younger baby quiets, his movements decreasing, while the older baby may turn his head to the sound.

Other tests are described by Buehler and Hetzer[3] and by Cattell.[4] They include (in the first month) turning the head when the cheek is touched, quieting when the baby is picked up, looking at a torch held one metre away, and a negative reaction to an unpleasant situation, such as a piece of cardboard over the nose. In the third month they include looking around when the baby is being carried.

Summary

1. Observe baby as mother speaks to him on her knee. Watch intentness of regard, smile, alertness. Listen for vocalisations.
2. Have the baby completely unclothed after observing his social responses.
3. Hold in ventral suspension. Observe head control and limb position.
4. Place in prone position. Observe head position, elevation of chin off couch, height of pelvis, extension of legs.
5. Place in supine position. Watch for tonic neck reflex. Test for grasp reflex. Observe whether hands are opened or closed. Pull into the sitting position. Return to supine position, and test eye-following with moving objects and perhaps response to unseen source of sound.
6. Measure the head circumference. Examine the hips for congenital subluxation, the back for a congenital dermal sinus or other abnormality, and the urine for phenylpyruvic acid.

Three to Six Months

The mother sits at the side of the desk, holding the baby on her knees. The baby's face, head and vocalisations are observed. The movements of both hands are watched. He may be seen to grasp his mother's brooch or clothes. His hearing is tested by the crumpling of tissue paper or a highpitched rattle, out of sight, on a level with the ear, and about 18 inches from it.

A one-inch cube or rattle is held in front of him, within easy reach. One observes whether he watches it as if he would like to get it, whether he excites and tries to get it, or reaches for it and grasps it. If it has to be placed in his hand, one observes whether he holds it and plays with it, or drops it. If he takes one cube, one watches for its transfer from hand to hand and one offers a second in order to determine whether he drops the first. By these simple operations one puts a date to his manipulative development. If, for instance, he cannot get hold of a rattle but will hold it for a few minutes when it is placed in his hand, and play with it, one can say that his manipulative development is not less than that of an average 3 months old baby, but not that of an average 5 months old baby. This gap is narrowed down by observing whether he merely shows a desire to get hold of it without reaching for it, like a 3 or 4 months old baby, or reaches for it without actually getting hold of it, like a 4 months old child. If he can get hold of the rattle or cube without it being placed in the hand, one can say that his level is not less than that of a 5 months baby. The next step is to determine whether he transfers it from hand to hand. If, after prolonged observation he fails to do so, one can say that he has reached the level (in manipulation) of a 5 months old baby, but not that of a 6 months one. One confirms this by watching for the maturity of grasp—the younger baby holding the cube in an insecure palmar grasp, dropping it promptly, the older one by a much more secure grasp, bringing the fingers more into play.

Having dated the manipulative development one assesses the gross motor development. He is placed in the supine position. If he spontaneously lifts his head off the couch, that immediately dates his gross motor development as not less than 6 months. It may be more than that, but it cannot be less. He may not have reached that point; he may merely lift his head up when he sees that he is about to be pulled up.

When in the supine position he is particularly watched for hand regard—a developmental trait which is seen in a narrow period of 12 to 24 weeks in a child of average development. The child lies, watching the movements of his hands. It is not a trait which is normally seen in older babies, but it is seen in mentally retarded ones. This dates his development—but, of course, one confirms this by other means.

One watches for efforts, successful or otherwise, to roll. He is then pulled to the sitting position in order to determine the presence or absence or degree of head lag. If there is any head lag, one can say immediately that in gross motor development he has not reached the level of the 5 months old baby. When he is in the sitting position, his body is swayed from side to side. There should be very little head wobble in a 5 months old baby. Once more, one dates the motor development, deciding that his development is not less than that of one age, but not as good as that of another age.

The child is then pulled to the standing position, in order to assess weight bearing, but one remembers that success in this depends to a large extent on the opportunity which he has been given by his mother to stand.

The baby is then placed in the prone position in order to determine how much he can hold his chin off the couch. The baby is watched throughout for his alertness, interest, and concentration on the toys.

Buehler included tests for imitation, the response to a cloth placed over the head, and a test for a defence reaction to the withdrawal of a toy.

Summary

1. Offer cube or rattle, placing it in hand if necessary. Watch for transfer. Offer second cube if he takes one.
2. Place in supine position. Watch for elevation of head. Watch for hand regard. Pull to sitting position and observe head lag; sway body to see if head control is complete. Pull to stand to observe weight bearing.
3. Place in prone.
4. Observe his interest, alertness, and concentration on toy.
5. In each test and position one 'dates' his development, deciding how far he has reached. One decides that he is not less than an average x months old baby in manipulation for example, but not as good as an average y months old baby in that skill. If one can pin-point the stage still further, one does. In each case one determines the maximum level of development which he has reached.
6. Note and record the degree of co-operation shown.
7. Test his hearing. Examine the urine for phenylpyruvic acid. Examine the hips for congenital subluxation.
8. Measure his head circumference.

Six to Twelve Months

The baby is offered a cube, and as soon as he takes it he is offered a second, and when he takes that a third is given. He is watched for 'matching' (the 9 months level), the baby bringing the 2 cubes together as if comparing them. One also watches for the 'index finger approach'—the average 9 to 10 months old baby characteristically going for objects with his index finger, whether the object is a cube, a pellet, or other toy. If he does show the index finger approach, one can immediately say that his manipulative development is not less than of an average 9 months old baby. In addition one confirms the apparent level reached by noting the maturity of grasp, the willingness to hand a cube to the examiner, and the ability to bring finger and thumb together to pick up an 8 mm pellet (conveniently made from a small piece of paper). If finger-thumb apposition is seen, and if he can pick up a pellet with them, one can immediately say that his development is not less than a 9 months old baby. If he achieves it promptly and easily, he is obviously better than that. If he cannot get hold of the pellet between finger and thumb, his development in this field is less than that of a 9 months baby. The hearing is tested, as before.

In the same way one dates the gross motor development by placing him in the sitting position, and assessing his stability, his ability to go forward into the prone and recover the sitting position, his ability to lean over to one side or to turn round to pick up an object behind him, without overbalancing.

He is placed in the prone position so that the maturity can be assessed. One looks particularly in the older baby for the placing of the sole of the foot flat on to the couch. He is then pulled to the standing position. One notices vocalisations and words.

Summary

1. Offer 3 cubes in succession, and then a small pellet of paper. Look for matching and for finger-thumb apposition. Offer him the bell, observing the maturity of the grasp. Watch for release and casting. Ask him to hand a toy.
2. Test the maturity of sitting.
3. Place in the prone position.
4. Test weight bearing in the standing position.
5. Watch for the interest, alertness, and concentration on toys, and the rapidity of his response.
6. Listen for vocalisations and words, and assess his speech.
7. Date the development in each field.

8. Test hearing and examine the hips. If the urine has not been tested for phenylpyruvic acid, the omission should be repaired.

9. Measure the head circumference.

One to Two Years

The motor development is assessed by watching his gait, if he is able to walk without help, and observing whether he can pick up objects from the floor, whether he can run, get up stairs, and so on. One remembers, however, that gross motor development is the least important field for the assessment of intelligence.

He is then handed 10 cubes. One watches the movement of both hands, to make sure that there is no sign of cerebral palsy. His ability to place cubes accurately, and to copy simple structures with the cubes, is then observed. If he does not build a tower, one places 1 on top of another, and asks him to continue. One observes how many he can place in a tower. One then makes a train of 9 cubes and places the tenth cube on top of the first to make a chimney. The child is asked to do the same, and one observes whether the train is made properly, or without the chimney. It must be emphasised that in all testing procedures, one must determine the maximum achievement. If, for instance, he achieves the building of a train with a chimney, one immediately asks him to copy a bridge. It would be futile, however, to ask him to proceed to the next stage if he cannot achieve the previous one.

The baby may then be shown a picture book. One notices the interest shown. He is asked to point out some common objects. One observes whether he turns pages singly, or several at once, thus dating the development in that test. His hearing is tested.

He may then be asked where his nose, eye, mouth or foot is.

He is given the simple formboard. The younger baby is offered the round block, and the older one is offered all 3. If he does not place the round block in, one shows him where to put it, and then leaves him to do it. If he succeeds, one slowly rotates the form-board, saying, 'Watch me carefully', and observes whether he can 'adapt', placing the blocks in the right place, with or without errors. The process is repeated 2 or 3 times, so that one can be sure that one's interpretation of what he is doing is correct. Mittler[21] wrote a critical review concerning the use of the formboards in developmental testing—rightly pointing out that they must not be used as a single test. They are only useful when employed in conjunction with other tests.

Once more, one seeks the maximum achievement. If he cannot get the round block in, it would be futile to offer him all 3. If he can get the round one in, one asks him to 'adapt' (rotating the board). If he achieves that, one offers him all 3 and determines whether he can 'adapt' with all 3 blocks.

He is given a pencil and paper. The younger infant merely scribbles. One then carries out a firm vertical stroke, and asks him to do the same. If he can, one asks him to imitate a horizontal stroke; if successful—a circle; if successful—a cross; if successful —a square, a triangle, and finally a diamond. Again, one determines the maximum skill achieved.

He is given simple orders (at about 18 months), being asked to take a ball to his mother, to put it on the chair, to bring it, and to put it on the table. He is asked the names of common objects— a penny, shoe, pencil, knife, and ball. He is shown the picture card, and asked to point to the right picture ('Where is the clock?').

The baby should no longer take objects to the mouth (at least after the first part of the period) and after about 15 months of age the 'casting' of toys on to the floor should cease. If mouthing or casting occur after these periods, they should be observed. They persist long after the normal time in retarded infants.

Throughout the examination the baby is watched intently. His interest, alertness, concentration, and words or jargon are noted and assessed. The tests must be given rapidly, before attention and interest flags.

Summary

1. Observe the gait.
2. Offer 10 cubes. Encourage to make a tower. Observe casting and relase; ask him if old enough to copy the making of a train.
3. Show the picture book. Watch page turning, and the interest shown.
4. Ask parts of the body.
5. Try simple formboard.
6. Give pencil and paper. Ask him to imitate vertical and circular strokes. (Not necessary for screening.)

7. Try simple orders, and names of common objects. (Not necessary for screening.)

8. Observe interest, alertness, rapidity of carrying out tests.

9. Date the development in each field.

10. Listen to his speech and assess it.

11. Note and record the degree of co-operation shown by him.

12. Test his hearing.

Age 2 to 5 Years

In the case of the younger child in this age group, or with a retarded older child, it is important to carry out the developmental tests as soon as the child comes into the consulting room, before he becomes bored with waiting while a long history is being taken.

There can be no rule as to the order in which tests are given. The essential thing is to maintain the child's interest, and to carry out each test quickly, changing to another if signs of boredom appear. If there is a complaint of clumsiness, or if a neurological abnormality is noticed, and he is over three years of age, he is asked to stand on one foot—without holding on to anything. (Normal age for standing for seconds on one foot — three years.) This is quite a sensitive test for a neurological abnormality such as a hemiplegia.

It is often convenient to begin with the cubes. Usually the child in this age group spontaneously begins to build a tower. One watches the hand movements, and tries to persuade the child to grasp with each hand, so that one can be sure that cerebral palsy is not present. The accuracy of release, assessed by the accuracy with which one cube is placed on another, is noted. The child is then asked to build a train, bridge, gate, or steps, according to one's rough assessment of the level he has reached, so that one can determine his maximum ability. In the case of the bridge, gate and steps, these are constructed behind a card or paper, so that the child cannot see the process of construction. He is then asked to copy the structure. It is easier for a child to imitate the building of a bridge (*i.e.* having watched a bridge being made) than to copy a bridge which he has not seen made. The score is slightly different for these two procedures.

The child may then be given a pencil and paper. He is asked to imitate a vertical stroke, horizontal stroke, circle, cross, square, triangle, or diamond, according to the level he is likely to have reached, being asked to draw these after the examiner, or he is asked to copy the above—from a paper on which they have been drawn, out of his sight. Again the score is different for imitation and copying.

Markham[20] found house-drawing a good technique for assessing the intelligence. Silver[30] discussed the value of drawing tests in intelligence testing.

The child may then be asked to name parts of the body, if that is not considered to be too easy for him, to carry out simple orders and to name common objects (as already described), and to identify pictures on the picture card ('Where is the clock?'), or to name them ('What is this?').

In the early part of the period he will be shown the simple form-board (as described above) and after about the third birthday, or before in a highly intelligent child, he is timed in his perform-ance on the Goddard formboard, the score being based on the best of 3 trials. If he can place the blocks correctly in the simple formboard, he should be tried with the coloured geometric forms, and if he is successful with these he is tried with the uncoloured forms. In each case he is asked where the shapes fit, being handed one after the other. On no account is he told that he has made a mistake. It is always my practice to give the child another chance with those which he has placed wrongly.

The child is then asked to repeat digits. For instance, he is asked, 'Say after me, nine, seven, eight', and he is given 3 trials. If he can repeat these, one tries 4 digits, and if he can repeat these, 5 digits, in each case giving 3 trials of different numbers. He is also asked to identify colours in a picture.

By the age of 3 or 4 years he is given a Goodenough 'draw a man' test. One gives the child pencil and paper, and asks him to draw a man. The scoring is described on page 291.

The older child in this age period is asked to execute a simple order. ('Put this on the chair, then open the door, and then give me that book'). He is asked which is his left and which is his right hand. He is asked to name the days of the week.

In each case the maximum achievement is obtained with each test. One determines the best he can achieve—*e.g.* how many digits he can repeat.

Throughout the test one observes his powers of concentration or his distractibility and his interest, and alertness, and one listens to and assesses his speech and notes the degree of co-operation in the tests and records it.

Summary

1. Watch his gait, note head shape, interest in surroundings and responsiveness.   If over three, get him to stand on one foot.

2. Offer the cubes and observe the hand movements, including tremor or ataxia.
   Ask him to build a tower (showing him how to do it), and observe how many bricks he can place on top of each other.
   For assessment of the older child—ask him to build a train, bridge, or steps, according to his likely ability.

3. Listen to his speech and assess it.

4. For assessment:–
   (a) Offer pencil.   According to probable level, ask him to imitate or copy a vertical, horizontal, or circular stroke, or to copy a cross, square, triangle, or diamond.
   (b) Ask him to name parts of the body, name common objects, identify or name pictures on the picture card and to carry out an order.
   (c) Give him the simple formboard or Goddard formboard, according to age, and the coloured or uncoloured geometric forms.
   (d) Ask him to repeat digits.
   (e) Ask him to draw a man.
   (f) In all cases ensure that the maximum achievement in each test has been obtained (not by repetition, except in the case of 3 trials in the Goddard formboard and in repeating digits).   In all cases observe his interest, alertness, powers of concentration and his distractibility. Determine a separate score for each item.
   (g) Listen to his speech and assess it.
   (h) Note the degree of co-operation shown by him and record it.

In the section to follow I have indicated the tests applied with the main test materials, with the average age at which success is achieved.

One Inch Cubes (Total needed—10)

16 weeks	Tries to reach cube, but overshoots and misses.
20 weeks	Able to grasp voluntarily. Bidextrous approach.
24 weeks	More mature grasp. Drops one cube when another is given.
28 weeks	Unidextrous approach. Bangs cube on table. Transfers. Retains 1 when another is given.
32 weeks	Reaches persistently for cube out of reach.
36 weeks	Matches cubes.
40 weeks	Index finger approach. Release beginning. Holds cube to examiner but will not release it.
44 weeks	Begins to put cubes in and out of container.
52 weeks	Beginning to cast objects on to floor.
15 months	Tower of 2. Holds 2 cubes in one hand.
18 months	Tower of 3 or 4.
2 years	Tower of 6 or 7.
	Imitates train; no chimney.
2½ years	Tower of 8.
	Imitates train, adding chimney.
3 years	Tower of 9. Imitates bridge.
3½ years	Copies bridge.
4 years	Imitates gate.
4½ years	Copies gate.
5 years	Cannot make steps.
6 years	May make steps.

Additional information is given by the cubes—the detection of mechanical disability in the hands, such as spasticity, athetosis, ataxia, tremor or rigidity.

Simple Orders. (Take ball to mother, put it on chair, bring it to me, put it on table.)

18 months	2.
2 years	4.

Common Objects. (Penny, shoe, pencil, knife, ball).

18 months	Names one.
2 years	Names 2-5.
2½ years	Names 5.

Picture Card.

18 months	Points to one ('Where is the . . .?').
2 years	Points to 5. Names 3 ('What is this?').
2½ years	Points to 7. Names 5.
3 years	Names 8.
3½ years	Names 10.

Colours

3 years	Names 1.
4 years	Names 2-3.
5 years	Names 4.

Drawing

15 months	Imitates scribble, or scribbles spontaneously.
18 months	Makes stroke imitatively.
2 years	Imitates vertical and circular stroke.
2½ years	Two or more strokes for cross. Imitates horizontal stroke.
3 years	Copies circle. Imitates cross. Draws a man.
4 years	Copies cross.
4½ years	Copies square.
5 years	Copies triangle.
6 years	Copies diamond.

The Goodenough 'Draw-a-Man' Test

The examiner asks the child to draw a man. He is urged to draw it carefully, in the best way he knows how and to take his time. The test is reasonably reliable, correlating well with the Binet tests. The test is most suitable for children between 3 and 10 years of age.

The child receives 1 point for each of the items which is present in his drawing. For each 4 points 1 year is added to the basal age which is 3 years. Thus if the child's drawing shows that 9 items are present in his drawing he scores 9 points and his mental age score is 3 plus $\frac{9}{4}$ —5¼ years.

Method of Scoring the Goodenough* 'Draw-a-Man' Test:[30]

1. Head present.
2. Legs present.

*From Goodenough, F. L. *Measurement of Intelligence by Drawings,* New York: World Book Company.

3. Arms present.
4. Trunk present.
5. Length of trunk greater than breadth.
6. Shoulders indicated.
7. Both arms and legs attached to trunk.
8. Legs attached to trunk; arms attached to trunk at correct point.
9. Neck present.
10. Neck outline continuous with head, trunk or both.
11. Eyes present.
12. Nose present.
13. Mouth present.
14. Nose and mouth in 2 dimensions; 2 lips shown.
15. Nostrils indicated.
16. Hair shown.
17. Hair non-transparent, over more than circumference.
18. Clothing present.
19. Two articles of clothing non-transparent.
20. No transparencies, both sleeves and trousers shown.
21. Four or more articles of clothing definitely indicated.
22. Costume complete, without incongruities.
23. Fingers shown.
24. Correct number of fingers shown.
25. Fingers in 2 dimensions, length greater than breadth, angle less than 180 degrees.
26. Opposition of thumb shown.
27. Hand shown distinct from fingers or arms.
28. Arm joint shown, elbow, shoulder or both.
29. Leg joint shown, knee, hip, or both.
30. Head in proportion.
31. Arms in proportion.
32. Legs in proportion.
33. Feet in proportion.
34. Both arms and legs in 2 dimensions.
35. Heel shown.
36. Firm lines without overlapping at junctions.
37. Firm lines with correct joining.
38. Head outline more than circle.
39. Trunk outline more than circle.

GOODENOUGH 'DRAW-A-MAN' TEST

Age shown is actual age of child at time of drawing.
The series illustrates the drawings of a man made by one child at different ages.

FIG. 145
1 year 6 months

FIG. 146
2 years 3 months.

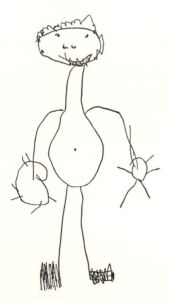

FIG. 147
2 years 11 months.

FIG. 148
3 years 4 months.

40. Outline of arms and legs without narrowing at junction with body.
41. Features symmetrical and in correct position.
42. Ears present.
43. Ears in correct position and proportion.
44. Eyebrows or lashes.
45. Pupil of eye.
46. Eye length greater than height.
47. Eye glance directed to front in profile.
48. Both chin and forehead shown.
49. Projection of chin shown.
50. Profile with not more than 1 error.
51. Correct profile.

It is said that the score tends to be unduly low in children who suffered anoxia in utero, and to be unduly high in children with schizophrenia.

Gesell 'Incomplete Man' Test

3 years	1-2 parts.	*5 years*	6-7 parts.
4 years	3 parts.	*6 years*	8 parts.
4½ years	6 parts.		

Simple Formboard

15 months	Inserts round block without being shown.
18 months	Piles 3 blocks, one on top of another.
2 years	Places all 3. Adapts after 4 errors.
2½ years	Inserts all 3, adapting after errors.
3 years	Adapts, no error, or immediate correction.

Goddard Formboard. (Best of 3 trials)

3½ years	56 seconds.	*6 years*	27 seconds.
4 years	46 seconds.	*7 years*	23 seconds.
4½ years	40 seconds.	*8 years*	20 seconds.
5 years	35 seconds.		

Coloured Geometric Forms

2½ years	Places 1.	*4 years*	Places all.
3 years	Places 3.		

Uncoloured Geometric Forms

3 years	Places 4.	*4½ years*	Places 9.
3½ years	Places 6.	*5 years*	Places all.
4 years	Places 8.		

Digits

$2\frac{1}{2}$ *years*	Repeats 2, 1 of 3 trials.
3 years	Repeats 3, 1 of 3 trials.
$3\frac{1}{2}$ *years*	Repeats 3, 2 of 3 trials.
4 years	Repeats 3, 3 of 3 trials.
$4\frac{1}{2}$ *years*	Repeats 4, 1 of 3 trials.
5 years	Repeats 4, 2 of 3 trials.
6 years	Repeats 5.
7 years	Repeats 3 backwards: ('Say these figures backwards').
8 years	Repeats 6 digits, 1 of 3 trials.

Simple Orders. (Put the ball under the chair, at the side of the chair, behind the chair, on the chair.)

3 years	Obeys 2.	*4 years*	Obeys 4.
$3\frac{1}{2}$ *years*	Obeys 3.		

Book

15 *months*	Interested.
18 *months*	Turns pages 2 or 3 at a time.
	Points to picture of car or dog.
2 *years*	Turns pages singly.

The Developmental Assessment in Handicapped Children

The assessment of the developmental potential of handicapped children can be a matter of great difficulty, but it is also a matter of great importance because of the necessity of selecting the right form of education for them. A comprehensive account of the method of testing children with cerebral palsy was given by Hauessermann.[17] The book by Edith Taylor[31] provides further valuable information. Some of the difficulties of testing were discussed by Schonell.[27] Parmelee *et al*.[25] found that Gesell tests were entirely suitable for testing blind infants.

It is obvious that tests have to be modified for children with mechanical and other handicaps, and that any departure from the exact method described by the authors of the tests must inevitably to some extent invalidate the results. This problem is covered in Hauessermann's book. That it is entirely feasible to form a reasonably reliable assessment of developmental potential in infants with cerebral palsy was shown by a study in Sheffield, to which reference has already been made (Chapter 2). In that

20

study we followed children with cerebral palsy who had been thought to be mentally retarded in infancy, and assessed the I.Q. at 5 years or later. Of 35 children in whom mental retardation was diagnosed in the first 6 months of life, 20 survived, and 19 proved to be mentally retarded later. Of 40 considered to be mentally retarded when seen at 6 to 12 months of age, 29 survived, and 26 were found on follow-up examination to be retarded; and of 59 considered to be retarded when seen between 12 and 24 months, 52 survived, and the diagnosis of retardation was confirmed in 51. I disagree, therefore, with the implication of Schonell's statement[27] that 'Most assessment scales, such as those of Gesell and Griffiths, especially designed for babies and very young children, are of the developmental type and hence are not suitable for those with cerebral palsy, many of whom, irrespective of intelligence, tend to be retarded in physical and social development'. I consider that the Gesell tests are entirely suitable for assessing these children, though of course the difficulties in prediction in severe cases can be very great.

It is obvious that with any handicap allowance must be made for the particular difficulty which the child has to face. Tests depending on vision, for instance, cannot be used for the blind child, and tests depending on hearing or speech cannot be used for the deaf child. In the same way, tests of manipulative development cannot be used for the child with severe spastic quadriplegia. In this case, however, one presents the test toy and observes the child's interest and desire to get hold of it. For instance, a 9 months old athetoid or spastic child with good intelligence will try really hard for a prolonged period to get hold of a brick or bell, and although he may fail to grasp it, he can be given a rough score for his determination to try to get it. In contrast a mentally defective child with cerebral palsy would show little or no interest in the object. One has to confine one's tests to those which are applicable to the child in question.

In examining children with cerebral palsy it is particularly important to remember the sensory and perceptual difficulties which some of these children experience. It should also be remembered that late maturation is more common in these children than in those with uncomplicated mental retardation, so that they may fare much better in the future than one would dare to expect when examining them in infancy. The difficulty of prediction, especially in athetoid children, is considerable, but our findings have shown that only occasional mistakes will be made, and one must be constantly aware that these mistakes *may* be made.

THE REMAINING PART OF THE PHYSICAL EXAMINATION AND INVESTIGATION

It is obvious that a full physical examination is always conducted when assessing a child's developmental level, and there is no need to describe the routine examination here. One is particularly interested in detecting any of those conditions which may be related directly or indirectly to the child's development.

As already stated, the examination must include the measurement of the head circumference, so that it can be assessed in relation to his weight, and examination of the hips for adductor spasm or subluxation. Other tests for muscle tone will be carried out if indicated.

The Reflexes

The plantar response can be difficult to determine in cases of athetosis, or in a struggling child. It should be remembered that the most sensitive site for eliciting the test is the distal half of the outer side of the foot.

Brain and Wilkinson[2] studied the plantar responses in 35 normal children ranging in age from 1 day to 27 months. They found that in children up to the age of 8 days, the plantar responses obtained were always extensor. They could often be elicited by stimulation as high as the third dorsal segment. The response was often limited to the side stimulated.

From the age of 5 to 20 weeks there was a bilateral response to stimulus applied to the sole or thigh. A bilateral response could usually be obtained from the abdomen and upper chest, but it was as likely to be flexor as extensor.

After 21 weeks the receptive field shrinks progressively from above downwards, probably as a result of myelination of the pyramidal tracts. After 20 weeks the extensor response became less definite or became a frank flexor, and after the age of 8 months it tended to be limited to the side stimulated, or to evoke only a weak response on the opposite side.

Even in the second year of life the plantar response was not invariably flexor when the sole was stimulated.

The area over which the reflex is obtained is greatly increased in disease of the pyramidal tract, and a convenient way of confirming a doubtful extensor response is to stroke very firmly with one's knuckle along the surface of the tibia (Oppenheim's sign). Flexion of the hip against resistance will elicit the response. In severely spastic children I have repeatedly demonstrated the extensor plantar response by stimulation anywhere on the trunk, and even below the ear.

In the older child, doubtful signs of disease of the pyramidal tract on one side can be detected by asking him to stand on one leg or to hop.

In testing the knee jerk (Fig. 16), the essential point to remember is the fact that in disease involving the pyramidal tract the area over which the knee jerk is obtained is greatly increased. It is always my practice to begin by tapping over the front of the ankle, and to tap at intervals up the leg until the patellar tendon is reached. The heel must be resting on the couch when the test is performed. A brisk response in front of the ankle is suggestive of disease of the pyramidal tract. Ankle clonus is frequently found in even the youngest infants with the spastic form of cerebral palsy, and is an invaluable sign when present, because it confirms one's impression that the knee jerk is abnormal. It is tested for with the hip abducted and the knee flexed, using one finger under the foot with a gentle but rapid movement of dorsiflexion. In spastic quadriplegia, the area over which the tendon jerks in the arms is also increased; a brisk biceps jerk may be obtained by tapping the upper arm near the shoulder.

The stretch reflex in the adductor muscles of the hip is tested for by flexing the hip to a right angle and *rapidly* abducting the hip. The stretch reflex is best detected by a rapid movement. (It is not essential to flex the hip to a right angle. I only recommend this in order that a valid comparison can be made between the degree of abduction in one child and that in another. In fact a more sensitive test for the stretch reflex is abduction of the hips with the legs in extension. Either method is satisfactory.)

Testing of Hearing

This section is modified from a section written by my colleague Dr. Holt in a previous edition of this book.

Before discussing methods of testing hearing, it is useful to consider the factors which increase the risk that a child will have a defect of hearing. The factors are as follows:–

Family History of Congenital Deafness.

Genetic conditions associated with deafness.

    Waardenburg's syndrome (White forelock, difference in the colour of the iris of the two eyes, deafness).

    Pendred's syndrome—goitre and deafness.

    Treacher Collins and First Arch Syndrome.

    Klippel-Feil syndrome.

    Congenital nephritis in males.

    Hyperprolinaemia.

    Retinitis pigmentosa.

    Syndrome of deafness and anomalies of cardiac rhythm.

Conditions in Pregnancy. Rubella in the first three months.

    Severe toxaemia. Administration of streptomycin to mother.

Severe anoxia or cerebral damage at birth.

Prematurity.

Hyperbilirubinaemia in newborn period.

Congenital syphilis.

Meningitis.

Recurrent otitis media.

Mental subnormality.

Cerebral palsy, especially athetosis and kernicterus.

Cleft palate.

Delayed or defective speech.

Effect of drugs—intrathecal dihydrostreptomycin, vancomycin, neomycin, kanamycin, gentomycin.

Deafness suspected by the parents.

Gesell and Amatruda[14] have described the early clinical signs of deafness in infants, listing the main features as follows:

1. *Hearing and Comprehension of Speech.*

    General indifference to sound.

    Lack of response to spoken word.

    Response to noises as opposed to voice.

2. *Vocalisation and Sound Production.*
> Monotonal quality.
> Indistinct.
> Lessened laughter.
> Meagre experimental sound play and squealing.
> Vocal play for vibratory sensation.
> Head banging, foot stamping for vibratory sensation.
> Yelling, screeching to express pleasure, annoyance or need.

3. *Visual Attention and Reciprocal Comprehension.*
> Augmented visual vigilance and attentiveness
> Alertness to gestures and movement.
> Marked imitativeness in play.
> Vehemence of gestures.

4. *Social Rapport and Adaptations.*
> Subnormal rapport in vocal nursery games.
> Intensified preoccupation with things rather than persons.
> Inquiring, sometimes surprised or thwarted facial expression.
> Suspicious alertness, alternating with co-operation.
> Markedly reactive to praise and affection.

5. *Emotional Behaviour.*
> Tantrums to call attention to self or need.
> Tensions, tantrums, resistance due to lack of comprehension.
> Frequent obstinacies, teasing tendencies.
> Irritability at not making self understood.
> Explosions due to self-vexation.
> Impulsive and avalanche initiatives.

Collins,[6] in a symposium on the deaf child, wrote that deaf babies gurgle and coo in a normal fashion, and that from 9 to 18 months they appear to be developing speech, saying 'mumum', 'dadada', but that no further progress in speech is then made. It is important to note this fact. Congenitally deaf babies do vocalise, and their vocalisation undergo changes leading up to spontaneous and playful sounds. This indicates the importance of maturation in speech development. Tape recordings of infants of congenitally deaf parents and of normal parents showed no differences. The vocalisations, cooing and crying were identical, and were regarded as developmental.[19]

Part of the routine examination of all babies certainly after the age of three months, includes a test of hearing. Sheridan[28] and Fisch[11, 12] have described simple screening tests. Other tests were described by Ewing. [8, 9, 10] Suitable test sounds include stiff toilet tissue, the spoken word (PS, Phth, 00), a plastic spoon in a plastic cup, or rattles of different pitches. I personally use soft paper, and the spoken sounds, for rough screening in the out-patient clinic. The sound is made on a level with the ear, about 18 inches away, and behind, so that he cannot see. It is essential to avoid blowing into the ear when making the sounds. Frequent repetition of the sounds will lead to habituation, so that he no longer responds. The baby must not be tested when he is tired or hungry, or when he is preoccupied with some other interest.

One notices not only whether he turns to sound, but the promptness with which he does so. When one tests the backward child at the age of six months or so, the response is likely to be slow and not easy to obtain.

In the case of a handicapped child, or a child after the first year, one needs an assistant to help in the examination.

Fisch[11, 12] made the following comments on hearing tests:

1. There is no single form of testing which will give a complete picture of the total hearing capacity of an individual.

2. Hearing tests are subjective tests requiring co-operation. There is no mechanical device which would enable us to test a child without gaining his confidence or co-operation. The handling of the child is decisive.

3. One should not draw any far-reaching conclusions or make final decisions on the basis of observations carried out on one single occasion.

4. A test should not be of such a nature that it would be associated with unpleasant or frightening experiences.

5. The child's obvious reaction to certain sounds or his understanding of familiar speech sounds in *tête-à-tête* conversation does not mean that the child could not have a hearing loss. When deafness is suspected, only a complete test is conclusive.

Wedenberg[32] described methods of testing the hearing of newborn babies. The hearing tests included a study of the sound required to cause blinking and to awaken a child from sleep, using a pure tone audiometer connected to a loudspeaker. One ear at a time was tested.

Sheridan's excellent paper[28] on simple clinical tests for use in very young or mentally retarded children should be read in detail. She felt that a clinical speech test should always be given, for audiometry cannot show how the child interprets what he hears. She described the appropriate tests for different ages from 6 months onwards, using the voice, noise-making objects such as toilet paper, rattles, squeaking dolls, a cup and spoon, and other toys and common household objects. She emphasised the importance of the examiner not being too far away from the child; he should be well to the side but outside the field of vision. When the baby is 6 months old the sound is made $1\frac{1}{2}$ feet from the ear, and on a level with the ear.

Hardy *et al.*[16] described their results of hearing test in infants. The method which they used was modified from the work of Ewing,[8, 9, 10] and the materials used were similar to those employed by Sheridan. The responses to sound included the Moro reflex, jumping or crying, eye blinking, grimacing, general muscular movements, immobilisation, disturbance of sleep, eye widening, eye turning, head turning, and cessation of crying. They showed that hearing can be readily tested in infants aged from 3 to 30 weeks.

For the older child the Peep-Show technique of Dix and Hallpike[7] may be used, in association with pure tone audiometry. Fisch's method[11, 12] depends largely on the establishment of conditioned reflexes—training the child to make a particular movement, such as putting a brick into a cup—when a sound is made. Full audiometry can be carried out from the age of three.

When it is found that the child can hear, it is then necessary to determine whether he can understand what he hears. He may suffer from congenital auditory imperception.

More recent tests include measurement of acoustic impedance, which test the activity of the ossicular chain, and evoked response audiometry. Psychogalvanic skin reactions have not proved to be reliable.

Vision Testing

Before considering methods of testing vision, it is as well to be

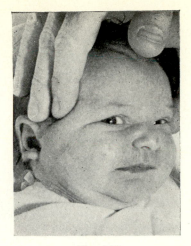

Fig. 149
The doll's eye phenomenon.

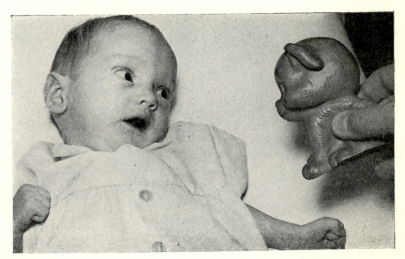

Fig. 150
Fixation and following with the eyes.

facing page 302

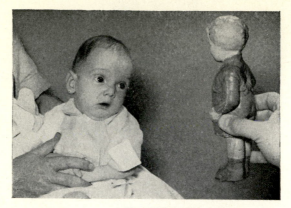

FIG. 151

"Grasping with the eyes".

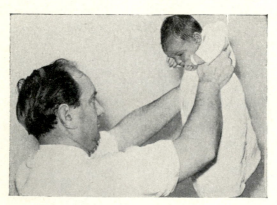

FIG. 152

Position for examining the eyes, e.g. for induction of
rotatory nystagmus.

Fig. 153
Test of visual acuity with small toys.

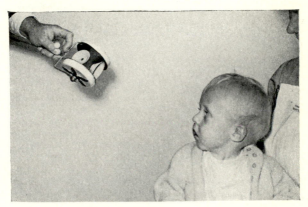

Fig. 154
Testing hearing responses in baby.

(after Murphy K.P.)

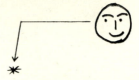

1. Lateral turning to side of sound.

2. Lateral turning followed by downward turning to source of sound. Appears about 5 months, well seen at 6 months.

3. Sweep to source of sound. Appears about 6 months, well seen at 7-8 months.

4. Direct diagonal localisation. Appears about 7 months but may not be well and consistently seen until 9-10 months.

FIG. 155

The maturation of sound localisation

aware of the factors which increase the risk that a child will have a defect of vision. The factors are as follows:–

Family history of blindness.
Prematurity (retrolental fibroplasia, myopia, cataract).
Rubella in first trimester of pregnancy.
Severe toxaemia in pregnancy. (Myopia in the child.)
Mental deficiency.
Cerebral palsy.
Hydrocephalus.
Craniostenosis.
Ophthalmia neonatorum.

In the older child the chief causes of blindness are trauma, rheumatoid arthritis, various causes of cataract formation, and the effect of drugs (such as chloroquin).

The method of inspecting the eye of the newborn baby has been discussed on page 155. Ophthalmoscopic examination is essential if a defect of vision is suspected, but the findings are not necessarily easy to interpret. When a baby is mentally defective, and therefore late in development of the usual responses, it can be extremely difficult to decide whether he can see or not. On ophthalmoscopy one sees the pale disc which is normal in the early weeks, and it is difficult to determine whether the pallor of the disc is within normal limits or not.

Dr. Mary Sheridan has described the method of screening young or handicapped children for vision,[29] and reference should be made to her papers. From the age of 21 to 36 months she tests with miniature toys, the child having one set and the examiner, having an identical set, holds one after another up at a fixed distance from the child, who is asked to match the examiner's toy with his own.

After six months of age a suspected squint can be tested for by the cover test. One eye is covered with a card while the infant is encouraged to fix upon a nearby object. The eye is then uncovered. If the eye has to move to fix upon the object, there is strabismus. Another test consists of directing a light onto the eyes from a distance of 12 to 14 inches. The light reflection should be centred in both pupils; if there is imbalance, one point of reflection may be off centre.

Testing for colour is a matter for the expert. According to

Peiper[26] colour blindness can be ruled out completely by the start of the third year. A useful screening device has been described by the Gallachers.[13] Their description is as follows:– "This simple brief evaluation employs the H.R.R. pseudoiso-chromatic plates which distinguish red green blindness, total colour blindness and blue yellow blindness. Graded colour symbols (triangle, circle, cross) with increasing saturation of the critical hues allow both a qualitative and quantitative evaluation of the defect; the child need only trace the symbol with a brush".

Handedness or Laterality

The child's lateral dominance can be tested in a variety of ways. Gordon[15] suggested that handedness can be diagnosed by asking the child to rub with a duster, draw, cut paper with scissors, pick an object up from the ground, wind a clock, grip a dynamometer, place counters in a tin, or hammer nails. The dominant foot is diagnosed by asking the child to kick a ball. The dominant ear is determined by asking the child to listen to a watch. The dominant eye is determined by asking the child to look at a distant object through a rolled piece of paper. The ability to mirror-read may be tested, because of the unusual facility with which some children with specific reading disability can achieve this.

Other Features

Other features of the physical examination include the palpation of the fontanelle in the young infant for bulging, the palpation of the sutures for undue separation, suggestive of hydrocephalus, or the rim over the suture line in craniostenosis, and the examination of the eyes for optic atrophy, choroidoretinitis or other lesions.

Congenital anomalies, such as cleft palate, congenital heart disease or skeletal anomalies, which are known to be associated with mental retardation, must be looked for.

The importance of a full physical examination in mentally retarded children is well shown by the following case history:

Case Report.—This boy was first seen by me at the age of $8\frac{1}{2}$ years on account of intracranial calcification seen in a radiograph, which had been taken on account of convulsions and mental retardation. His early motor development was said to have been normal. He was able to sit without support by 6 months and to walk unaided before his first birthday. Convulsions began at the age of 12 months. He did not say words with meaning until 2 years or put words together into sentences until 4 years. He went to school at 4½ years but was unmanageable. Intermittent fits occurred; they were of an unusual type and he would stare vacantly; they were followed by abdominal pain and a period of hyperkinesis. The E.E.G. showed a focus in the right temporal lobe and his I.Q. was 91. Behaviour at school continued to be difficult. On one occasion he absconded from school and was reported missing to the police. In school he would interfere with the work of other children and prevent them working. On one occasion he was missing at dinner time and was found lying down in a store cupboard. He was destructive and unco-operative.

At 7½ years his I.Q. had dropped to 57 and he was referred to a school for educationally subnormal children. Fits had become somewhat different in character. They started with abduction of the right arm, then he repeated certain words, striking the table at the same time, or else half way through a sentence he would repeat the last word over again.

At the age of 8 years the phenobarbitone which he had been receiving, was reduced on the chance that it was contributing to his bad behaviour. Occasional vomiting was noted at this time but it was infrequent. At this time an X-ray of the skull was carried out, and calcification was found. It seemed to outline the choroid plexus, and when I saw it I concluded that it was almost certainly due to toxoplasmosis. The dye test, however, was equivocal (1 in 9), and the complement fixation test was negative. The cerebrospinal fluid was normal and not under increased pressure. He was then referred to me, and to my surprise I found that instead of the expected choroidoretinitis he had bilateral papilloedema. There were no other abnormal physical signs. A right carotid angiogram showed a tumour in the parietal region and at operation a large very chronic partly calcified glioma was removed from the temperoparietal region.

There had been no recent change in the boy's behaviour. There had been no symptoms pointing to an intracranial tumour. It is a matter of speculation as to how long the tumour had been there and how much his apparent mental deterioration was due to the tumour.

Special Investigations

Investigations which may be needed include Kahn and Wassermann reaction, tests for toxoplasmosis, protein bound iodine and x-ray for skeletal maturation, examination of the urine for phenylpyruvic acid, galactose, abnormal amino acid excretion, metachromatic material and inclusion bodies. Examination of the blood of child and parent for evidence of haemolytic disease due to the rhesus and other factors, is indicated in appropriate cases.

Apart from these investigations in special cases, and certain other investigations for metabolic conditions (such as hypercalcaemia) it is surprising how infrequently special investigations are necessary in developmental diagnosis. The examination is essentially clinical.

With regard to electroencephalography, I have little personal experience of the value of this in developmental diagnosis, except in the case of infantile spasms and other forms of epilepsy. It may well be that the E.E.G., will be found to be of value in future.

Air encephalography is not often indicated in developmental diagnosis. It is easy to be misled by the findings. Amatruda[1] attempted to relate the findings in air encephalograms to the behaviour of 53 children. She wrote 'in the presence of normal behaviour development "cortical atrophy" does not necessarily cause a bad prognosis, and may, indeed, be almost without significance'. She added that 'behaviour is the final criterion of the functional integrity of the central nervous system'. Ostow[24] reviewed the literature concerning the relationship between the E.E.G. and intelligence, and found that there was little correlation between the two. Charash and Dunning[5] found a notable lack of correlation between 151 encephalograms and the mental state, but did find that the procedure was not free from risk, for there were 2 deaths and 9 serious complications. Knobloch et al.[18] described an interesting study on 50 patients. A radiologist and a neurosurgeon graded air encephalograms on the basis of ventricular dilatation and cortical markings. A paediatrician carried out Gesell tests and assessed the intellectual potential. There was no evidence of correlation between adaptive or gross motor development and the air encephalogram, or between the presence or absence of mental retardation and the degree of abnormality in the encephalogram. The severity of cerebral palsy was not related to the degree of abnormality in the X-ray.

I am always impressed by the frequency with which the cerebrospinal fluid has been examined in mentally defective children referred to me. It is an investigation which I hardly ever carry out in these children. It is only in a truly exceptional case that it will throw light on the problem, except, of course, in the diagnosis of certain neurological conditions not found in the ordinary mentally defective child.

REFERENCES

1. AMES, L. B. (1943) The Gesell Incomplete man Test as a Differential Indicator of Average or Superior Behaviour in Preschool Children. *J. genet. Psychol.*, **62**, 217.

2. BRAIN, R., WILKINSON, M. (1959) Observations on the Extensor Plantar Reflex and its Relationship to the Functions of the Pyramidal Tract. *Brain*, **82**, 297.

3. BUEHLER, C., HETZER, H. (1935) *Testing Children's Development from Birth to School Age.* London: Allen and Unwin.

4. CATTELL, P. (1947) *The Measurement of Intelligence of Infants and Young Children.* New York: The Psychological Corporation.

5. CHARASH, L. I., DUNNING, H. S. (1956) An Appraisal of Pneumoencephalography in Mental Retardation and Epilepsy. *Pediatrics*, **18**, 716.

6. COLLINS, V. L. (1954) The Early Recognition of Deafness in Childhood. *Med. J. Aust.*, **2**, 4.

7. DIX, M. R., HALLPIKE, C. S. (1947) The Peep-Show. *Brit. med. J.*, **2**, 719.

8. EWING, A. W. G. (1957) *Educational Guidance and the Deaf Child.* Manchester. Manchester University Press.

9. EWING, I. R., EWING, A. W. G. (1944) The Ascertainment of Deafness in Infancy and Early Childhood. *J. Laryng.*, **59**, 309.

10. EWING, I. R., EWING, A. W. G. (1947) *Opportunity and the Deaf Child.* London. University of London Press.

11. FISCH, L. (1964) Ed. *Research in Deafness in Children.* London. Blackwell.

12. FISCH, L. (1957) The Importance of Auditory Communication. *Arch. Dis. Childh.*, **32**, 230.

13. GALLACHER, J. R., GALLACHER, C. D. (1964) Colour Vision Screening of Preschool and First Grade Children. *Arch. Ophthalm*, **72**, 200.

14. GESELL, A., AMATRUDA, C. S. (1947) *Developmental Diagnosis.* New York: Hoeber.

15. GORDON, H. (1920) Left-handedness and Mirror Writing Especially Among Defective Children. *Brain*, **43**, 313.

16. HARDY, J. B., DOUGHERTY, A., HARDY, W. G. (1959) Hearing Responses and Audiologic Screening in Infants. *J. Pediat.*, **55**, 382.

17. HAUESSERMANN, E. (1958) *Developmental Potential of Preschool Children.* London: Grune and Stratton.

18. KNOBLOCH, H., SAYERS, M. P., HOWARD, W. H. R. (1958) The Relationship between Findings in Pneumoencephalograms and Clinical Behaviour. *Pediatrics*, **22**, 13.

19. LENNEBERG, E. H., REBELSKY, F. G., NICHOLS, I. A. (1965) The Vocalisations of Infants Born Deaf. *Human Development*, **8**, 23.

20. MARKHAM, S.   (1954)   An Item Analysis of Children's Drawings of a House. *J. clin. Psychol.*, **10**, 185.

21. MITTLER, P.   (1964)   The Use of Formboards in Developmental Assess-ment. *Develop. Med. child Neurol.*, **6**, 510.

22. MURPHY, K. P.   (1962)   Ascertainment of Deafness in Children. 'Panorama'. December 3.

23. MURPHY, K. P.   (1964)   *Learning Problems of the Cerebrally Palsied. Study Group. Oxford.* London: Spastics Society.

24. OSTOW, M.   (1950)   Psychic Function and the E.E.G.   *Arch. Neurol. Psychiat.*, **64**, 385.

25. PARMELEE, A. H., FISKE, C. E., WRIGHT, R. H.   (1959)   The Develop-ment of Ten Children with Blindness as a Result of Retrolental Fibroplasia. *Amer. J. Dis. Child.*, **98**, 198.

26. PEIPER, A.   (1963)   *Cerebral Function in Infancy and Childhood.* London: Pitman.

27. SCHONELL, F. E., in ILLINGWORTH, R. S.   (1958)   *Recent Advances in Cerebral Palsy.* London: Churchill.

28. SHERIDAN, M. D.   (1958)   Simple Clinical Hearing Tests for Very Young or Mentally Retarded Children. *Brit. med. J.*, **2**, 999.

29. SHERIDAN, M. D.   (1960)   Vision Screening of Very Young or Handicapped Children. *Brit. med. J.*, **2**, 453.

30. SILVER, A. A.   (1950)   Diagnostic Value of Three Drawing Tests for Children.   *J. Pediat.*, **37**, 129.

31. TAYLOR, E. M.   (1959)   *Psychological Appraisal of Children with Cerebral Defects.* Cambridge Mass.: Harvard Univ. Press.

32. WEDENBERG, E.   (1956)   Auditory Tests in Newborn Infants. *Acta otolaryng. (Stockh.)*, **46**, 446.

CHAPTER 14

INTERPRETATION

In developmental assessment it is essential to realise that much more importance must be placed on some aspects of development than on others. In this chapter I have attempted to describe my view of the relative importance of the different fields of development.

Gross Motor Development

It is unfortunate that the aspect of development which is the most easily assessed and scored is the least valuable for the overall assessment of a child's development and capability. It would be quite wrong to suggest that gross motor development is useless as part of the developmental examination. It is of great value, but its limitations have to be recognised. It is true that defective motor development, as determined by head control in ventral suspension and the prone position, is commonly the first sign of abnormality in a child who is mentally retarded from birth or before birth. It is true that the majority of mentally retarded children are late in learning to sit and to walk, but the exceptions are so frequent that one can hardly deny that the age of sitting and walking is only of limited value in assessing intelligence.

In Table 6 I have analysed the age at which mentally retarded children, seen by me at the Children's Hospital, Sheffield, learnt to sit for a few seconds without support, and to walk a few steps without support. None had cerebral palsy or other mechanical disability. None had any degenerative disease, so that there was no deterioration in these children. Mongols are kept separate from the others. The gradings 'seriously subnormal' and 'educationally subnormal' were based on I.Q. tests at school age.

It will be seen that the age at which unsupported sitting began was average (6 to 7 months) in 8·3 per cent. of the ineducable children, in 6·7 per cent. of the mongols, and in 10·7 per cent. of

TABLE 6

Age of Sitting Unsupported

Age in months	Seriously subnormal Total 48 Percentage	Educationally subnormal Total 28 Percentage	Mongols Total 45 Percentage
6 to 7	8·3	10·7	6·7
8 to 9	14·5	39·3	31·1
10 to 11	2·1	7·2	26·6
12 to 17	35·4	39·3	22·0
18 to 23	15·0	3·6	} 13·4
24+	22·9	0	

Age of Walking Unsupported

Age in months	Seriously subnormal Total 59 Percentage	Educationally subnormal Total 42 Percentage	Mongols Total 37 Percentage
Under 12 months	0	4·7	0
12 to 14	5·1	9·5	0
15 to 17	10·1	14·3	0
18 to 23	18·6	19·0	24·3
24 to 35	37·2	40·5	51·4
36 to 47	13·5	4·7	10·7
48 to 59	10·1	2·4	} 13·5
60+	5·1	4·7	

those who were educationally subnormal. On the other hand the skill was not acquired until after the first birthday in 73·3 per cent. of the ineducable children other than mongols, 35·4 per cent. of the mongols, and 42·9 per cent. of the educationally subnormal children.

The age of walking without support was average (12 to 17 months) in 15·2 per cent. of the ineducable children other than mongols, and in 29·5 per cent. of the educationally subnormal ones. No mongols walked as soon as this. On the other hand the skill was not acquired until the second birthday or after in 65·9 per cent. of the ineducable children, 75·6 per cent. of the mongols and 52·3 per cent. of the educationally subnormal ones.

It has already been mentioned that there are great variations in the age of sitting and walking in normal children, some learning to walk without support by the age of 8 months, and some not until the age of 3 or 4 years. Early locomotion does not in any way indicate a high level of intelligence. On page 210 I described a boy who had uniformly advanced gross motor development, but his I.Q. score subsequently was only 88. All that one can say about unusually early motor development is that it at least excludes mental deficiency.

There is only a measure of truth in the view expressed by Abt et al.[1] that there is a positive relationship between the age of walking and intelligence. Their figures indicate that the reason for the correlation is the fact that most retarded children are late in learning to walk. Hurlock[6] wrote that, 'Babies who are slow in sitting up, standing up or walking generally prove, as time goes on, to be backward in intellectual development. On the other hand, those who are precocious in motor development prove to be, for the most part, intellectually precocious'. I think that the latter part of the statement is doubtful. One agrees with Shirley[8] who wrote that 'Locomotor precocity, such as walking at an early age, certainly should not be used as a single criterion for predicting superior intelligence'. Terman,[11] however, wrote that the average age of walking was 1 month earlier in gifted children than average children; yet an occasional child in his gifted group did not walk before the age of 2 years.

I would feel that the main clinical importance of delayed locomotion lies in the fact that it should make one extremely careful to look for signs of cerebral palsy, though delayed locomotion may occur without discoverable cause. The main importance of unusually early locomotion is that it virtually excludes mental deficiency and cerebral palsy.

Fine Motor Development (Manipulation)

Though I have no figures with which to prove it, I feel that the development of manipulation is a better guide to the level of intelligence than is gross motor development. I have not seen notable delay in manipulative development in normal children. The only children in whom I have seen unusually early development of manipulation have proved to have a high I.Q. later. It is obvious that some children have certain aptitudes, irrespective of intelligence, and that some children are better than others in the use of their hands. I believe that this may be detected in the latter part of the first year in some children.

I have already said that if one sees good finger-thumb apposition and a definite index finger approach at 10 months, one is fairly safe in saying that the child is not mentally defective. I have not seen a mentally defective child with average manipulative ability, provided that he was defective from birth or before, and has therefore not acquired normal manipulation before the development of mental deficiency. I believe that the relationship of fine motor development to subsequent intelligence would repay further study.

Speech

The words speech and language are often used as synonyms, whereas they should really be distinguished from each other. By speech one denotes the use of words, but by language one means the expression of thought in words. The assessment of language from the developmental point of view is difficult, but the use of 'speech' as an indication of developmental level is relatively easy, the two chief milestones, as already stated, being the age at which words are first used with meaning, and the age at which words are first joined together spontaneously.

It is the experience of many workers that the early development of speech is a most important sign of a good level of intelligence. Terman[11] wrote that 'Earliness of onset of speech is one of the most striking developmental characteristics of intellectually gifted children'. Abt et al.[1] wrote that 'The development of speech and intelligence go hand in hand'. Anderson[2] wrote that 'Early language development appears to be more closely related to later intelligence test scores than any other grouping of tests. A tentative conclusion may be drawn, namely, that the best indication of intelligence at 18 and 24 months of age is development in the use and understanding of language'. Spiker and Irwin[10] found a good correlation between speech sounds and the level of intelligence, and between subsequent speech and the I.Q. Catalano and McCarthy[5] described work by Fisichelli, who made a phonemic analysis of tape recordings of the vocalisations of 23 infants in an institution, at the mean age of 13·3 months. They followed these children up and conducted Stanford-Binet tests on them at the mean age of 44·8 months. There was a strongly positive correlation between the infant sounds and the subsequent Stanford-Binet tests, especially with regard to consonant types, the frequency of consonant sounds, the number of different kinds of consonant sounds, and the consonant-vowel frequency and type ratio. The correlation between the I.Q. and the number of different kinds of consonants gave a coefficient of ·45 with the Stanford-Binet tests.

Ausubel[3] wrote that 'intelligence is perhaps the most important determinant of precocity in speech, since it affects both the ability to mimic and to understand the meaning of verbal symbols'.

In my opinion the greatest importance should be attached to speech development as an index of intelligence. It has already been stated that the development of speech may be delayed in children of average or superior intelligence, so that it follows that delayed speech in itself can never be used as an indication of mental retardation. Advanced speech, however, is in my experience always an indication of superior intelligence. I should be most surprised, for instance, if I heard a child speaking well in sentences at 15 months, and subsequently found that his I.Q. was 100 (unless there was subsequent emotional deprivation, or other retarding factor).

It must be mentioned again that the understanding of words far outstrips the ability to articulate them. I should be just as impressed with a child who was able to point to a large number of objects in a picture book as an indication that he understood the meaning of words. I believe that there is a need for a new developmental test for children aged 12 to 18 months, based entirely on their understanding of the meaning of words.

Just as advanced speech can be regarded as a sign of superior intelligence, average speech can be regarded as a sign of at least average intelligence, though a child of 12 to 24 months with average speech may also prove to be of superior intelligence. The above opinion is important, because one sees children with delayed motor development, with or without some mechanical disability, in whom an assessment of intelligence is required. The presence of average speech immediately tells one that his intelligence is normal, even though he is also retarded in another field, such as sphincter control.

In the same way speech is important in the assessment of retarded children, and especially those with a physical handicap such as cerebral palsy. If, for instance, a child were severely retarded in all fields but speech, in which retardation was only slight, I should give a good prognosis with regard to his intelligence, because I would think that his I.Q. would be only slightly below the average. I have only once seen a possible exception to this.

Smiling and Social Behaviour

The age at which a baby begins to smile is of considerable importance in the assessment of a child. The mentally retarded child almost invariably begins to smile long after the age of 4 to 6 weeks, the average age for this. The mean age of smiling in a consecutive series of 62 mongols seen by me was 4·1 months. It is vital, of course, to make due allowance for prematurity in these early milestones.

I do not know whether unusually early smiling presages superior intelligence, or whether it is affected by the child's personality. I suspect that it usually presages superior intelligence.

There is some disagreement as to what the baby's early smiles signify. Bowlby[4] regarded the smile as a 'built-in species specific pattern'—a view with which I agree. Bowlby implies that the smile is not merely a learned conditioned response, as has been suggested by some. It has been shown that the essential stimulus for the early smile is the face.

Whatever the psychological explanation of the smile, the age at which the baby begins to smile at his mother in response to her overtures is an important and valuable milestone of development, in that this is bound up with the child's maturity and therefore with his mental development. I agree with Soderling[9] that smiling is in some way dependent on maturation, though environment must play a part.

It is important to note the age at which babies begin to laugh, to play games, to imitate, to draw the attention of their parents (*e.g.* by a cough), and their general social responsiveness. More important still are those features like the alertness, the power of concentration, the degree of determination of a baby (*e.g.* to obtain a toy out of reach, or to grasp a pellet when he is not quite mature enough). 'The child speaks with his eyes'. It is very difficult to convert many of these into scores: but they can be observed, and used in a child's assessment. They are far more important than the readily scored sensorimotor items, which have been the basis of most of the tests used by those psychologists who found that developmental tests have no predictive value.

Sphincter Control

This is of relatively little value for the assessment of a child. Mentally retarded children are usually late in acquiring control of the bladder, but not always, while many children of superior intelligence are late in acquiring control. Apart from constitutional and anatomical factors, the parental management has considerable bearing on the age at which control is learnt, and this is irrelevant in the assessment of a child's intelligence.

Chewing

I find that the age at which a child begins to chew is of considerable value in assessing a child. Mentally retarded children are always late in learning to chew. It is my impression that babies who begin to chew unusually early (the earliest being about $4\frac{1}{2}$ months), are bright children, but I have no figures to support this.

It has already been said that an extraneous factor has to be considered (and eliminated by the history) and that is failure of the parents to give the child solid foods to chew. This would delay the development of chewing—or at least the age at which it is observed.

The Relationship of One Field of Development to Another: Dissociation

In the assessment of the value of the history for diagnosis and prediction, it is important to balance one field of development against another. In the great majority of children the development in one field approximates fairly closely to the development in another. For instance, most children at the age of 6 to 7 months are nearly able to sit on the floor without support: they are able to grasp objects easily and they have recently learnt to transfer them from hand to hand: they have recently learnt to chew: they have just begun to imitate: they are making certain characteristic sounds when vocalising. In assessing any child, one automatically assesses his development in each field. Gesell remarked that the developmental quotient can be specifically ascertained for each separate field of behaviour and for individual behaviour traits.

In some children, however, the development in one field is out of step with that in other fields. It has already been explained that there are great individual variations in various fields of development, children learning some skills much sooner or later than others, though they are just average in other fields. For instance, some children are late in single fields, such as speech or walking, and yet are average in other aspects of development. I have termed this 'Dissociation'.[7] It is important for enabling one to determine the likelihood that the mother's story is correct, and it draws one's attention to variations in development, such as lateness in one field, which require investigation. The following case history may be cited as an example:

Case Report.—This girl, born at term, reached important stages of development at the times below:

6 weeks	Smile.
5 months	Grasp objects voluntarily.
6 months	Chew.
1 year	Casting. Saying 3 words. Good concentration and interest. Very defective weight bearing; equivalent to that of average 3 months' old baby. Knee jerks normal. Marked general hypotonia.
Diagnosis	Benign congenital hypotonia.

She walked without help at 5 years. Her I.Q. was 100.

Whenever one finds that a child is notably retarded in one field as compared with his development in others, a search should be made for the cause. In many, as has already been said, no cause will be found, but the cause will be found in others. Below is an example of dissociation.

Case Record.—Diplegia in an Infant with Minimal Neurological signs.

This boy was referred to me at the age of $5\frac{1}{2}$ months for assessment of suitability for adoption. He had been a full term baby. He began to smile at 7 weeks and to vocalise 2 weeks later. It was uncertain when he had begun to grasp objects. He had not begun to chew. It was said that he was very interested when his feed was being prepared.

On examination he did not grasp an object. The head control was not full, being that of a 4 months' old baby. He bore very little weight on his legs—being no better in weight bearing than an average 2 months old baby, though it was said that he had been given a chance to do so. I thought that the knee jerks were normal. The baby seemed alert. I advised the foster parents to let me see the boy in three months, and not to clinch the adoption until I had done so.

I saw him at 9½ months. He had begun to chew and to sit without support at 6 months. At that age he had begun to cough to attract attention, and to shake his head when his mother said 'No'. He could not nearly grasp the pellet between finger and thumb, but his grasp of a cube (with each hand) was average for the age. He was alert, vocalising well and sitting securely. He had begun to play patacake. Yet his weight bearing was seriously defective. I now realised that both knee jerks were definitely exaggerated and there was bilateral ankle clonus. The knee jerk was more brisk on the left than on the right. When I discussed this with the foster parents they remarked that he had always kicked more with the right leg than the left. The diagnosis was spastic diplegia, with a normal level of intelligence. The full implications were explained to the parents, who unhesitatingly decided to adopt him in spite of his physical handicap.

This case was interesting because of the minimal signs of spastic diplegia, discovered on routine developmental examination. There were no suggestive symptoms, and the only developmental sign pointing to the diagnosis was defective weight bearing. It may be that the inability to grasp the pellet was the only sign of truly minimal involvement of the upper limbs, for judging from his developmental level in other fields, he should have acquired finger-thumb apposition.

Below is another case report which illustrates the importance of balancing one field of development against another.

Case Report.—Mental Retardation with Anomalous Features.

This girl was referred to me at the age of 14 months because the parents were unable to accept the gloomy prognosis given to them by a paediatrician in another city.

She was born a month after term by Caesarian section as a result of signs of foetal distress. The birth weight was 9 lbs. 9 ozs. Pregnancy had been normal throughout. There were no other children. She was asphyxiated at birth and had 'several' convulsions in the first 3 weeks. She was kept in an oxygen tent for 5 days. The condition in the newborn period was such that the parents were given a bad prognosis with regard to her future development.

The subsequent history was somewhat confusing. She had never picked any object up. Both parents were uncertain whether she could see. She had been examined on that account by an ophthalmologist when she was under an anaesthetic, and no abnormality was found in the eyes. She was said to turn her head to sound at 3 months. She had begun to smile at 4 or 5 months, and to vocalise at 6 or 7 months. She was said to laugh heartily now. At 6 months she had begun to hold a rattle placed in her hand. She had begun to imitate sounds (a laugh, a song) at 8 months and to imitate the rhythm of songs. She said 'dadada' from 8 months. She had just begun to play with her hands, watching them in front of her face (hand regard). She had begun to chew at 11 to 12 months, and at that age would eat a biscuit.

On examination she was a microcephalic girl with a head circumference of $16\frac{7}{8}$ inches, which was very small when her weight at birth was considered. The fontanelle was closed. She was very obese, weighing 32 lbs. and tall for her age. She showed no interest whatsoever in test toys, but was seen to smile at her mother when she talked to her. She was heard to make vocalisations (complex sounds with 'ch' and 'dada') such as one would expect to hear at 10 months. The grasp of a cube placed in the hands was immature. Her head control was that of a 3 months old baby. In the prone position her face was held at an angle of 45 degrees to the couch. There was head lag when she was pulled to the sitting position, with considerable head wobble when she was swayed from side to side. There were asymmetrical creases in the thighs. She played for a prolonged period with a rattle placed in the hand, but would not go for any object. She bore virtually no weight on her legs. It was difficult to assess muscle tone owing to the obesity, but the impression was one of hypotonia rather than hypertonia; and abduction of the hips was greater than usual. The knee jerks were normal, but there was bilateral unsustained ankle clonus. The optic fundi were normal. The X-ray of the hips was normal, and the X-ray of the skull showed normal sutures. The urine did not contain phenylpyruvic acid.

There were difficulties about giving a confident prognosis here, and these difficulties were explained to the parents, who were intelligent. The developmental history and examination indicated dissociation. She was severely retarded in manipulation and motor development, and there was no evidence that she could see—though it is difficult to be sure whether a severely retarded baby can see or not until he is old enough. On the other hand, in chewing, imitation, and vocalisation she was only moderately retarded and her I.Q. in these respects would indicate that she should fall into the educable range later. This strongly suggested a mechanical disability, and the unsustained ankle clonus suggested that she might prove to have the spastic form of cerebral palsy. Subsequent athetosis, however, could not be excluded. The relatively good development in speech and imitation suggested that the I.Q. would not be as bad as it appeared on the surface.

The second difficulty was the question of blindness. I was unable to say whether the child could see or not. Blindness would explain some of the features of the history and examination, and in particular the complete lack of interest in surroundings was out of keeping with the fact that the girl turned her head to sound from about 3 months.

The third difficulty was the history of convulsions. There was a considerable possibility that convulsions would occur later, possibly with mental deterioration.

I gave my opinion that the prognosis was bad, and that she would probably prove ineducable, but said that in view of the difficulties mentioned above she might prove better than expected—though possibly with the complication of cerebral palsy and perhaps with blindness. I arranged to see her in a year.

The significance of the development of speech in relation to other fields has been mentioned. In general the finding that speech development is relatively more advanced than motor development would make one look particularly carefully for a mechanical disability, such as hypertonia or hypotonia, though the occasional late walker has also been discussed.

The Calculation of a Score

Though it is very much a matter of opinion, I think that it is unwise to calculate a single figure for the D.Q. or I.Q. in the pre-school child—at least in many cases. The reason is that some fields of development are so much more important than others, that a single figure is apt to be fallacious. Ruth Griffiths used an interesting method. She used the term G.Q., meaning the General-intelligence Quotient, and to obtain this she worked out the quotient for each of 5 fields of development (the Q.A., loco-motor quotient; Q.B., personal social; Q.C., speech; Q.D., hand and eye quotient; Q.E., performance quotient—which includes the ability to reason, or to manipulate material intelligently). She then added up all five quotients, divided by 5, and termed this

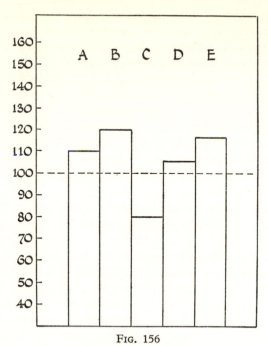

FIG. 156
A developmental profile.
(*After Ruth Griffiths*).
A to E represent five different fields of development.

the G.Q. I consider that the method of working out the quotient in each field separately and showing a 'Profile' (Fig. 156) is excellent; but I disagree entirely with the idea of obtaining a G.Q. from the product of these 5 quotients, because that would imply that all fields of development are of equal importance. They are not.

Such a scoring method fails to take into account physical, mechanical or even environmental causes for retardation in individual fields—factors which have no bearing on the child's intelligence.

If one were to calculate one overall score for a child with paralysed legs due to meningomyelocele, his score would be lowered by the fact that he could not walk.

Below is an example of the difficulty of assessing a child on the basis of one overall score.

I saw the girl for the first time at the age of three years five months. The following are extracts from the letter which I wrote to the family doctor:–

'There are several difficulties about giving a confident prognosis here. One is that there is a family history of late walking in both mother and father, and it would not be surprising if the children were to take after them.

There was delayed motor development. She began to sit without help at 14 months and walk without help at 22 months. I have seen quite a few normal children who were unable to walk until after the second birthday. On the other hand her speech was good. She was saying single words under a year, and sentences at 18 months. I have never met a mentally subnormal child who could do that. Furthermore sphincter control began at 12 months. She has, however, been late in learning to manage a cup, and she has only just begun to do so, and she is not very good at dressing herself, but I am not sure whether the parents have given her a chance to learn these things. This is a difficult age at which to carry out developmental testing, but I have come to the conclusion that in one or two tests she was average, but in others she was retarded. There is, therefore, considerable scatter in her perform-ance which makes a confident opinion about the future impossible. She looks normal. She concentrated well on a doll's house when I was talking to the mother. Her head is of normal size. Her gait is normal. I explained that when a child has learned to walk as late as this, you must expect her to be unsteady in walking for quite a long time afterwards.

On the whole I think that Mary will prove to be normal, and not below the average, but one cannot by sure at this stage. I shall be seeing her again in about a year in order to re-assess progress.'

I followed her progress with interest. By the age of four years she was reading well, and at five years she was assessed as having a reading age of $9\frac{1}{2}$ years. Her manipulative, creative and physical ability were described by her teacher as excellent.

I would certainly decry the conversion of any scores into one figure to denote the I.Q., because that would imply that the I.Q. is a static figure, which the child will always have. It has been amply shown that it is far from static, and that it may be pro-foundly affected by a wide variety of factors.

Gesell's term 'The Developmental Quotient' seems to be as good as any: it indicates how far the child has developed in relation to the average level of development at that age: and no implication is made that it will not alter as future years go by. By observing the rate of development and changes in the D.Q., one can form a good conclusion as to how far the child is likely to develop, given good environmental circumstances. One assesses, in other words, his developmental potential.

I personally prefer to say in my letters to family doctors that a child has developed as far as an average child of x months: but I always qualify that by commenting on the individual fields of development, emphasising where relevant, that one is particularly concerned with his interest, powers of concentration, alertness, and speech, and much less concerned with his gross motor development. I might say, for instance, that a 36 months old boy has in general only developed as far as an average 24 months old boy but the fact that his speech is very much better than the 24 months old level, even though he appears to be below the 24 months old level in other fields, indicates that there is real hope that he is well above the 24 months level in potential growth, and that he may well do much better than superficially appears likely at present.

In some cases the difficulties of assessment are such that it is quite impossible to forecast the child's future without further observation. It is impossible, for instance, to predict the child's future development if there had been adverse environmental factors, such as prolonged institutional care or some serious debilitating disease, in an infant who is found to be uniformly retarded. A period of observation after the correction of these adverse factors is essential before any opinion is expressed about his developmental potential.

I was asked to assess the mental development of a 21 months old child with nephrogenic diabetes insipidus. He had not thrived, weighing only 15 lbs. at the time. He had had repeated admissions to hospital. His general level of development was that of a 12 months old baby with little scatter in different fields, though he showed good and normal interest in his surroundings and in toys—an important observation suggesting that he might well prove to have a normal level of intelligence. It was impossible to assess this child's developmental potential without serial observations of his rate of development.

The experienced paediatrician will resist the temptation to

attempt to give an accurate figure for the child's developmental quotient. He is merely deceiving himself if he thinks that he can distinguish a developmental quotient of 70 from one of 71. He can and should be able to place the child into an approximate position in the developmental range. Any attempt to be more accurate will only lead to inaccuracy.

Summary

Some fields of development are much more important than others for the purposes of developmental assessment.

Gross motor development, which is the easiest field of development to assess, and which was the field used more than any other in many studies, is the least useful for the purposes of prediction. Quite severely retarded children may learn to walk at the average age. Advanced motor development in no way presages a high I.Q.

Manipulative development and the age of chewing are useful for predictive purposes.

The most valuable of all fields for prediction is speech (and pre-speech vocalisation), provided that it is recognised that retardation in speech development does not in itself portend a low I.Q.

The age of beginning to smile, and social behaviour, are valuable fields for study. The age of acquiring clean toilet habits is of only slight value for prediction.

More important than any of the above are the baby's alertness, interest in surroundings, powers of concentration, and determination—all items which are difficult to translate into scores.

In all cases the development in one field should be compared and contrasted with that in another. If a child is notably out of step in one field of development ('dissociation') the cause should be looked for.

Because of the relatively greater importance of some fields of development than of others, it is usually unwise to express the whole of a baby's development in one score.

REFERENCES

1. ABT, I. A., ADLER, H. M., BARTELME, P. (1929) The Relationship between the Onset of Speech and Intelligence. *J. Amer. med. Ass.*, **93**, 1351.
2. ANDERSON, L. D. (1939) The Predictive Efficiency of Infancy Tests in Relation to Intelligence at 5 Years. *Child Develpm.*, **10**, 203.

3. AUSUBEL, D. P. (1958) *Theory and Problems of Child Development.* New York: Grune and Stratton.
4. BOWLBY, J. (1957) Symposium on the Contribution of Current Theories to an Understanding of Child Development. *Brit. J. med. Psychol.*, **30**, 230.
5. CATALANO, F. L., McCARTHY, D. (1954) Infant Speech as a Possible Predictor of Later Intelligence. *J. Psychol.*, **38**, 203.
6. HURLOCK, E. B. (1956) *Child Development.* London: McGraw Hill.
7. ILLINGWORTH, R. S. (1958) Dissociation as a Guide to Developmental Assessment. *Arch. Dis. Childh.*, **33**, 118.
8. SHIRLEY, H. F. (1931) *The First 2 Years.* Minneapolis: Univ. of Minnesota Press.
9. SÖDERLING, B. (1959) The First Smile. *Acta Paediat. (Uppsala)*, **48**, Suppl. 117. 78.
10. SPIKER, C. C., IRWIN, O. C. (1949) The Relationship between I.Q. and Indices of Infant Speech Sound Development. *J. Speech Dis.*, **14**, 335.
11. TERMAN, L. M. (1926) *Genetic Studies of Genius.* London. Harrap.

CHAPTER 15

MENTAL RETARDATION

This is only a brief chapter, because the diagnosis of mental retardation has been mentioned directly or indirectly in almost every preceding chapter.

In the sections below, however, I shall bring together the main points about the early diagnosis of mental retardation, and add something about the prognosis.

The Child at Risk

As implied in previous chapters, the following conditions place a child at greater risk of being mentally subnormal than others.

Prenatal—Family history of mental deficiency.

Low birth weight in relation to the duration of gestation.

Prematurity, especially when extreme.

Multiple pregnancy.

Relative infertility before the birth.

Maternal toxaemia, antepartum haemorrhage.

Maternal infections in early pregnancy, especially rubella.

Severe congenital deformities and the many conditions described in Chapter 5.

Cretinism.

Cerebral Palsy.

Natal—Convulsions, severe anoxia, cerebral haemorrhage, hyperbilirubinaemia, cerebral palsy.

Postnatal—Retrolental fibroplasia.

Meningitis, encephalitis.

Severe hypoglycaemia.

Head injury.

Lead poisoning.

Epilepsy (really prenatal).

Emotional deprivation.

Clinical Features

The essential principle in the early diagnosis of mental retardation is the fact that the mentally retarded child who is retarded from birth or before birth is backward in all fields of development, except occasionally in gross motor development and rarely in sphincter control. He is relatively less retarded in gross motor development than in other fields unless there is a superimposed mechanical difficulty, such as cerebral palsy; he is relatively more retarded in speech, and in the amount of interest which he shows in his surroundings, in concentration, alertness, and promptness of response.

The situation is different in the case of a child who develops normally for a time, and then develops a degenerative disease, or infantile spasms with mental deficiency. In the case of the latter condition, for instance, one may see a child of 7 months who has learnt to grasp and to sit and who therefore appears to be up to the average in motor development, but who is totally disinterested in his surroundings and has stopped smiling and who, in fact, has a grave degree of mental deficiency.

As in the case of any developmental assessment, one takes the history of prenatal factors which may be relevant, and of the perinatal history. One also takes a history of mental defectiveness in the family. As with any other developmental assessment, however, one remembers that most children born with this background or who have such conditions as anoxia in the perinatal period, prove to be perfectly normal in intelligence.

As in any other assessment, one must note the history of any possible extenuating factors, such as illness or adverse environmental circumstances, which may have affected his development.

The Early Weeks

As the mentally retarded child is retarded in all fields of development except occasionally gross motor development, it follows that the mentally retarded child at birth is in many ways in a similar position to the premature baby who has a normal level of intelligence. He is apt to sleep excessively, and to have feeding difficulties such as failure to demand feeds, drowsiness, difficulty in sucking and easy regurgitation. The excessive tendency to sleep may persist for several months. Below are some comments by mothers about their severely defective children in the early weeks:

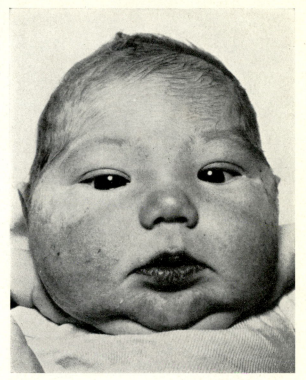

FIG. 157
Child with severe microcephaly.

facing page 326

1. He didn't move much when a baby. He didn't seem to live until he was 8 months old.
2. She was a good baby. She never cried.
3. She seemed to live in a world of her own.
4. She was good all the time. She never cried. She just lay.
5. He was a marvellous baby. He was very good. He lay without crying.
6. He just lay in his pram. We didn't know we had him.
7. He just lay in his pram without moving for 6 months. He used to sleep nearly all the time.
8. He was like a cabbage for the first 2 years. He would just sit in his pram.
9. He was a very good baby, and no trouble at all; his brother was a lot more trouble. (The older brother was normal).

The developmental history after birth is nearly always one of lateness in everything, except occasionally in learning to sit and to walk. There is no need to recapitulate the various milestones here except to mention certain special points.

1. The first obvious sign of mental retardation is likely to be lateness in smiling and taking notice, with delayed motor development, as seen in the ventral suspension, supine and prone position. One can detect many cases of mental retardation in the first 6 to 8 weeks if one is in the habit of performing rough developmental tests in all babies in a well baby clinic.

2. The lateness in following with the eyes is apt to lead to an erroneous diagnosis of blindness. The child appears to take no notice of his surroundings, so that blindness can be readily suspected.

3. The lateness in responding to sound is apt to lead to a mistaken diagnosis of deafness.

4. The lateness in learning to chew leads to feeding difficulties. If the retarded child is given solid foods (as distinct from thickened feeds) before he can chew, he is apt to vomit.

5. The reciprocal kick, which disappears normally when a child is beginning to walk, persists in a retarded child until he can walk. One may see this, therefore, in a retarded child 2 or 3 years of age.

6. The persistence of hand regard. The normal baby between 12 and 24 weeks of age can frequently be seen lying on his

back watching the movements of his hands. This can frequently be seen in retarded children much older than 24 weeks of age.

7. Mouthing—the taking of all objects to the mouth, characteristic of the 6 to 12 months old child, persists in retarded children. It normally stops when the child has become proficient in manipulation. One sees, therefore, a 2 or 3 years old retarded child taking cubes and toys to the mouth.

8. Slobbering normally stops by the age of about a year, but it persists in defective children.

9. Lack of interest and concentration. Of all features of the retarded child, these are the most important. There is a notable lack of interest in surroundings. There is a fleeting interest in toys, or else he does not seem to notice them at all. If given a toy, he will not do anything constructive with it. It does not hold his attention. If he drops it he makes no effort to recover it. If it is out of reach he makes little or no effort to obtain it. He lacks an alert expression. He is usually less responsive than a normal child. He is slower at responding to test situations.

I have repeatedly seen children who were average in motor development, but whose defective interest and concentration indicated marked deficiency. For instance, a full term child learnt to sit without support at 8 months and to walk without support at 17 months. She was dry by day at 18 months and dry by night at 2 years. At 1 year her interest and concentration were defective. She began to say single words at 3 years and sentences at 5 years. At the age of 9 years her I.Q. was 20. There had been no deterioration.

10. Aimless over-activity. Many children who were sleeping excessively and 'so good' as babies undergo a remarkable transition as they grow older, to aimless over-activity, concentrating on nothing.

11. Toothgrinding (Bruxism). Toothgrinding when awake is almost (but not entirely) confined to quite severely mentally defective children.

12. Microcephaly.

13. Altered Vocalisations. Karelitz and Rosenfeld,[8] in their study of infant vocalisations, found that there were striking differences between the cry of the abnormal baby and that of

the normal one. In the abnormal child there was a much longer latent period between the application of the stimulus and the cry. He needed repeated or almost constant stimulation to elicit the cry. The voice quality was different in the abnormal child, and was often guttural, in some it was piercing and shriek-like, and in some high pitched, weak or thin. The normal increasing variety of sounds found in the developing normal infant was greatly delayed in the abnormal one.

As with all developmental assessments, the diagnosis is only made after a careful consideration of the history, the clinical and developmental examination, and a judicious consideration of the evidence, taking full account of any possible extenuating factors which may have caused retardation, and of any glimmer of hope in the way of better than expected vocalisation or interest or concentration.

Below are two typical case histories of children followed up from birth, in whom a very early diagnosis of mental retardation was made.

Early Diagnosis of Mental Retardation: Confirmation on Follow-up

Case 1.—This full term child was admitted to hospital at the age of 3 months on account of laryngotracheobronchitis. She showed no interest in her surroundings. She would not hold a toy placed in her hand. Head control was defective. A diagnosis of mental retardation was made.

At the age of 15 months she learned to sit without support and to chew. At 30 months she began to walk without support and to say odd words. She could not manage a cup. She could build a tower of four cubes. Concentration was poor. At 5 years and 8 months the I.Q. was 60.

Case 2.—This boy was prematurely born, weighing 4 lb. The mother had toxaemia of pregnancy. Delivery was normal. He had two convulsions on the second day and had head retraction. On the third, fourth and fifth days he had a series of cyanotic attacks. A diagnosis of cerebral oedema was made. The lower limbs were thought to be flaccid. The subsequent history in the follow-up clinic was as follows:

6 months	Hand regard seen.
9½ months	Began to chew.
11 months	One word with meaning. Able to grasp objects.
1·0 year	Sit without help. Beginning to transfer objects.

22 months	Walks, no help.
24 months	D.Q. 70.
3 years	Sentences.
6 years	I.Q. 61.

The Prognosis of Mental Defectiveness

The unexpected improvement seen in some mentally retarded children has already been described. I think that this improvement is chiefly confined to the first years of life. I have not, for instance, seen a mentally defective child of 5 years improve rapidly and reach a near-normal level of intelligence.

As for the ultimate prognosis in mentally retarded children, it is roughly true to say that a child with an I.Q. of over 50 is likely to be able to earn his living, unless there are associated handicaps.

Fox[7] followed 116 males and 98 females who had been certified in childhood as feeble-minded, re-examining them at 20 and 25 years. Forty-six of the males and 19 of the females were wholly self-supporting and 42 of the males and 25 of the females were partially self-supporting.

In Fairbank's well known study[5] 122 subnormal children were followed up for 17 years, 95 were self-supporting, two-thirds of them in manual labour. Compared with normal controls there was more juvenile delinquency, a higher marriage rate, more children and more divorces.

Ferguson and Kerr[6] followed 400 boys and girls from special schools in Glasgow for mentally handicapped children and re-examined them in the early twenties. Seventy-five per cent of the girls with an I.Q. of over 50 had at least 5 years' continuous employment. Only 8 boys were unemployed. Thirteen of the 162 boys were skilled craftsmen. Half the girls and a fifth of the boys were in semi-skilled jobs. By the age of 22, 30 per cent had one or more convictions in law.

In a follow up study of 1,000 boys for a 10 year period, 75·8 per cent. of those with an I.Q. score of more than 60 were self-supporting.[10]

Clarke and Hermelin[4] described the work which adult male imbeciles could perform, with an I.Q. of 20 to 49. They were able to fold cardboard boxes in a workshop at an average rate of 30,000 to 40,000 per 35 hour week. Supervision was minimal. Elsewhere the Clarkes[3] reviewed their own work on the 'ability and trainability' of imbeciles. They wrote that 'the belief that the best that can be done for the imbecile is merely to keep him happily occupied is clearly incorrect and he is capable of doing useful and remunerative work under sheltered conditions'. They felt that there was a need to change occupational centres to sheltered workshops.

Some mentally defective adults have acquired remarkable facility in certain skills, such as arithmetic. Several stories about these so-called 'idiots-savants' are told in Tredgold's book.[13] McGrath[11] described a certified man with megalencephaly, whose head circumference was $27\frac{3}{4}$ inches, who at the age of 32 had a mental age of 5 years and 11 months. He could not read, write, or tell the time, but he had a remarkable talent for calculating dates—such as the day of the week for any date mentioned. Others have shown remarkable talents in music and feats of memory.[1]

In attempting to give a prognosis, we must remember not only the possibility of unexpected improvement, which has already been mentioned, but the possibility of deterioration, especially if epilepsy develops.

Much depends not just on the level of intelligence, but on his behaviour. If he is a hyperkinetic, destructive type he is less likely to achieve much than a quiet, easily managed child of the same level of intelligence. He is likely to achieve more if brought up at home, than if he is placed in an institution.

A child may have to be graded ineducable even though his I.Q. is well over 50. I saw one child with an I.Q. of 77 who was so intensely hyperkinetic that he could not be managed in a special school and he had to be certified as ineducable. A child with cerebral palsy may have to be certified as ineducable on account of his physical handicap, even though his I.Q. score is well over 50.

Differential Diagnosis

It is a tragedy to diagnose mental subnormality when the child is normal, for the mistake will cause untold anxiety and suffering. On the other hand it is important for many reasons already outlined not to miss the diagnosis.

Many of the sources of confusion in the diagnosis have been discussed by writers under the heading of pseudofeeblemindedness. I share the dislike of Clarke and Clarke[4a] for this term. They suggested that the term, if it is to be used at all, 'should be applied merely to cases in which it appears that the erroneous diagnosis of mental deficiency was the result of insufficient examination by the clinician. The term is quite inappropriate when applied to those who show (by reliable criteria) accelerated mental growth, for it obscures the factor of real chance, which is no different essentially from long term increment or decrement higher in the intellectual scale'. They suggested that when an apparently average child subsequently shows that he has superior ability, one might as well term him 'pseudoaverage'. They thought that except in the case of an adverse environment, it is rare for development to alter.

The following are the main conditions which have to be distinguished from mental subnormality.

1. DELAYED MATURATION. This has been discussed in Chapter 10. It was stated there that an occasional child is backward in the first weeks and subsequently catches up and becomes normal. If there is definite microcephaly, such a course of events is unlikely to occur: but if the head circumference is of normal size, one should be particularly cautious in giving a definite prognosis without follow-up study.

2. CEREBRAL PALSY. It is easy to confuse some forms of cerebral palsy with mental deficiency. The two conditions are commonly combined. A child with athetosis, particularly before the athetoid movements become obvious, can easily be thought to have simple mental deficiency, whereas in fact his I.Q. level is normal. (See also Chapter 16.)

3. SENSORY DEFECTS. Failure to recognise a visual defect, or a defect of hearing, may well lead to an erroneous diagnosis of mental subnormality. In an older child, the specific problems of dysphasia, dyslexia, difficulties of spatial appreciation, and allied conditions, are important pitfalls.

4. THE EFFECTS OF EMOTIONAL DEPRIVATION. The retardation which can result from severe emotional deprivation was described in Chapter 4. It is especially important to remember in assessing children for suitability for adoption when they have been in an institution, or have been moved from one foster home to another.

When retardation in such a child is found, one must never suggest that there should be a further period of institutional care, so that his progress can be assessed, for a further period would retard his development still further. The correct procedure is to place him in a good foster home, and then observe his development after a period of say 3 months in that home. Sometimes a retarded child has had such an unfavourable environment that it is most unwise to express an opinion about his potentialities at all. One must always be prepared to postpone judgment if in doubt, or to withhold one altogether.

5. SCHIZOPHRENIA AND INFANTILE AUTISM. Striking features of the autistic child include a preference for toys instead of persons, refusal to look a person in the eyes, total lack of response to affection, retarded or absent speech, with a normal shaped head and intelligent appearance. Words spoken may be well formed, but they bear no relation to the person listening to them, and no apparent relation to the existing situation.

I was asked to see a boy of 4 with a diagnosis of mental retardation. My immediate impression when he walked into the room was that the diagnosis was correct, for he took no notice of anyone in the room. I gave him a Goddard formboard to keep him occupied for a few minutes, and was immediately impressed by the way in which he rapidly fitted the blocks in their correct places. I knew immediately that he was a case of autism.

It can be very difficult to distinguish schizophrenia from mental subnormality. The lack of response, delayed or absent speech, and peculiar behaviour, can readily lead to errors in diagnosis. It is commoner in boys than girls. There is a family history of schizophrenia in 40 per cent of cases.[2] The differential diagnosis was discussed by Schachter et al.[12] on the basis of the history, psychological tests, play observation and response to therapy.

A working party in London suggested the following criteria for the diagnosis of schizophrenia.[14]

> Gross and sustained impairment of emotional relationships with people: including aloofness, impersonal attitude to them, difficulty in mixing with other children.
> Apparent unawareness of his own personal identity to a degree inappropriate to his age. Abnormal posturing, scrutiny of parts of the body. The confusion of personal pronouns.
> Pathological preoccupation with particular objects or certain characteristics of them without regard to their accepted functions.
> Sustained resistance to change in the environment and a striving to maintain or restore sameness.

Abnormal perceptual experience (in the absence of discernible organic abnormality) is implied by excessive, diminished or unpredictable response to sensory stimulants—for example visual and auditory avoidance, insensibility to pain and temptation.

Acute excessive and seemingly illogical anxiety.

Speech may have been lost or never acquired or may have failed to develop beyond a level appropriate to an earlier stage. There may be confusion of personal pronouns, or mannerisms of use and diction. Though words or phrases may be uttered they may convey no sense of communication.

Distortion in mobility patterns—excess (hyperkinesis), immobility (katatonia) or bizarre patterns, or ritualistic mannerisms such as rocking or spinning.

A background of serious retardation in which islets of normal, near normal or exceptional intellectual function or skill may appear.

Sometimes psychoses are superimposed on mental deficiency and this increases the difficulty of assessment.

Summary

The mentally retarded child, who is retarded from birth or before birth, is backward in *all* fields of development, except occasionally in gross motor development and less often in sphincter control: he is relatively more retarded in speech, alertness, concentration and interest in surroundings than in other fields, and relatively less retarded in motor development.

There may be unexpected improvement in some mentally retarded children, though there were no undesirable environmental factors.

As a rough guide, one can say that a child with an I.Q. of over 50 is likely to be able to earn his own living, unless he has a severe physical handicap.

REFERENCES

1. ANASTASI, A., LEVEE, R. F. (1960) Intellectual Defect and Music Talent. *Amer. J. ment. Defic.*, **64,** 695.
2. BENDER, L. (1960) Diagnostic and Therapeutic Aspects of Childhood Schizophrenia. In Bowman, P. W., Mautner, H. V. *Mental Retardation.* New York: Grune & Stratton.
3. CLARKE, A. D. B., CLARKE, A. M. (1958) *Mental Deficiency. The Changing Outlook.* London: Methuen.
4. CLARKE, A. D. B., HERMELIN, B. F. (1955) Adult Imbeciles. Their Ability and Trainability. *Lancet*, **2,** 337.
4a.CLARKE, A. D. B., CLARKE, A. M. (1954-5) Pseudofeeblemindedness— some Implications. *Amer. J. ment. Defic.*, **59,** 507.
5. FAIRBANK, R. E. (1933) The Subnormal Child 17 Years After. *J. ment. Hyg.*, **17,** 177.
6. FERGUSON, T., KERR, A. W. (1958) After Histories of Boys Educated in Special Schools for Mentally Handicapped Children. *Scot. med. J.*, **3,** 31.
7. FOX, J. W. (1929) Careers of the Feeble Minded. *Med. Offr.*, **41,** 251.
8. KARELITZ, S., KARELITZ, R. E., ROSENFELD, L. S. (1960) In Bowman, P. W., Mautner, H. V., *Mental Retardation.* New York: Grune & Stratton.
9. KATTER, F. E. (1959) The Pseudomental Deficiency Syndrome. *J. ment. Sci.*, **105,** 406.
10. McINTOSH, W. J. (1949) Follow up Study of 1,000 Non-academic Boys. *J. except. Child.*, **15,** 166.
11. McGRATH, W. M. (1935) A Case of Megalencephaly showing an Unusual Talent for Calculating Dates. *Brit. med. J.*, **1,** 699.
12. SCHACHTER, F. F., MEYER, L. R., LOOMIS, E. A. (1962) Childhood Schizophrenia and Mental Retardation: Differential Diagnosis before and after One Year of Psychotherapy. *Amer. J. Orthopsychiat.*, **32,** 584.
13. TREDGOLD, R. F., SODDY, K. (1956) *Textbook of Mental Deficiency.* 9th ed. London: Bailliere, Tindall and Cox.
14. WORKING PARTY. (1961) Schizophrenia Syndrome in Childhood. *Brit. med. J.*, **2,** 890.

CHAPTER 16

THE DIAGNOSIS OF CEREBRAL PALSY

The Difficulties

The diagnosis of cerebral palsy in the first year is regarded by some as a matter of great difficulty. For instance, Skatvedt[11] wrote that 'spasticity in the usual sense, as demonstrated in spastic stretch reflex, is not seen in the infant', and, 'In the course of the second year of life, the diagnosis of cerebral palsy should be possible for the experienced physician'. In fact cerebral palsy of the spastic type, except in mild cases, can be readily diagnosed in the first few days of life. I have seen an obvious case on the second day of life, and filmed and followed up cases diagnosed on the fourth and fifth days of life. The rigid form can be readily diagnosed in the earliest infancy. The athetoid form cannot usually be diagnosed early, because one cannot be sure of the diagnosis until athetoid movements develop, which may not be for one or two years after birth. Congenital cerebellar ataxia cannot be diagnosed until about 6 months, because it is dependent on certain purposive movements not found before then: but tremor can be diagnosed early, certainly by the time the baby is able to sit.

It would be profitable to begin by enumerating the main difficulties in early diagnosis.

1. There are all grades of severity of cerebral palsy, from the severe form diagnosed readily in the newborn period, to the mildest form, which is first brought to the doctor's attention at 9 or 10 years.

There is no doubt that it can be extremely difficult to diagnose mild degrees of spasticity in early infancy. Signs may be equivocal for several months before it finally becomes clear that disease is present. For instance, brisk knee jerks may be thought to be within normal limits. With the passage of time it becomes clear that they are in fact pathological. It is always difficult to draw the line between normal and abnormal, and to say, for instance, whether brisk tendon jerks, or slight hypertonia, is normal or otherwise. In some cases one has to be prepared to wait and see—

in order to determine whether a child is affected or not. In the majority of cases, however, the diagnosis is obvious in the early weeks or days of life.

2. There are several types of cerebral palsy, each with its own features. Using the American Academy of Cerebral Palsy classification these are the spastic form, athetosis, rigidity, ataxia, tremor, atonic form and mixed types.

3. The diagnosis is greatly complicated by the wide range of levels of intelligence, and particularly by the frequency with which mental retardation is found. Mental retardation alone has a profound effect on the developmental pattern.

4. The delayed appearance of signs of cerebral palsy, particularly signs of athetosis. As babies grow older, certain signs become more obvious. André-Thomas referred to the delayed development of signs of cerebral palsy.

5. The occasional disappearance of signs of cerebral palsy. One sometimes detects signs of the spastic form of cerebral palsy in early infancy and finds that these signs gradually disappear. Perlstein and Barnett[8] described these transient forms. They wrote that 'all the signs and symptoms of spasticity may be present at the age of 2 or 3 months, and may disappear completely by the age of 1 year'. A colleague,[4] saw a boy who was born after precipitate delivery at term, weighing 7 lbs., and who was well in the newborn period. He began to smile and to watch his mother at 2 weeks. The mother noticed right-sided ankle clonus at the age of 2 weeks, and an experienced doctor confirmed its presence. It could be triggered by just touching the feet in the direction of dorsiflexion. The presence of ankle clonus was confirmed. When the boy was 5 weeks of age, clonus disappeared, and the baby walked alone without help at $8\frac{1}{2}$ months, being entirely normal. I have several times found exaggeration of tendon jerks and defective motor development in the early weeks, and found that the signs disappeared as the child grew older. Some of these fall into the category termed by Gesell 'minimal birth injury'.

I have been able to follow an example of this condition from birth to the age of 14 years. In the newborn period and subsequently in the first year of life the boy had an obvious left hemiplegia. The left upper limb was not used at all for the first few months. The arm improved as he grew older, and by the age of

5 or 6 years the sole remaining sign of cerebral palsy was a left extensor plantar response. There was no spasticity of the leg. The hand was entirely normal. There were no other abnormal signs.

André-Thomas[1a] described several examples of the disappearance of signs of cortical injury, especially hemiplegia, and emphasised that on that account prognosis must always be guarded and that examinations must always be repeated.

In France Minkowski,[7] using the André Thomas method of examination, divided 74 newborn babies into three groups, (a) normal (25 infants), (b) minor neurological abnormalities (43 infants), (c) gross neurological abnormalities (6 infants). On re-examination 2 years or more later, of the 25 who were normal in the newborn period, 19 were normal subsequently and 6 had minor but temporary problems (such as ocular defects and delayed walking): of 43 in Group B (showing minor neurological signs in the newborn period), 22 were normal subsequently: 18 had minor neurological handicaps, but three had serious sequelae. Of 6 who showed serious neurological signs in the newborn period, three continued to show severe sequelae on follow-up, while the remainder showed trivial and temporary neurological signs.

Solomons, Holden and Denhoff[9] described 12 infants who showed abnormal neurological signs in the first year, and who had been followed for a period of one to three years, during which time all abnormal signs disappeared.

In general, one pays much less attention to single signs than to a combination of signs. For instance, one would pay little attention to some degree of hypertonia alone, but one would pay much more attention to a combination of hypertonia and delayed motor development, or an usually small head circumference. One pays much less attention to delayed motor development alone than one does to delayed motor development combined with delayed social responsiveness (late smiling), or a small head circumference.

The difficulties in the early diagnosis, the impossibility of drawing the line between normal and abnormal in some cases (with particular reference to the knee jerks and abduction of the hip), and especially the occasional disappearance of signs of cerebral palsy, make it essential not to tell the mother about one's suspicions until one is quite

certain about the diagnosis and the permanence of the condition. Continued observation is essential in all but the severe cases.

The Child at Risk

Certain prenatal and natal conditions place a child 'at risk' of cerebral palsy. They include:

Family history of cerebral palsy.

Prematurity, especially extreme.

Multiple pregnancy.

Low birth weight in relation to the duration of gestation.

Mental subnormality.

Relative infertility.

Antepartum haemorrhage, toxaemia.

Severe anoxia, convulsions, hyperbilirubinaemia, cerebral haemorrhage, meningitis.

Retrolental fibroplasia.

Dissociation in development.

Diagnosis of Any Form of Cerebral Palsy

The diagnosis must be made, as always, on the basis of the history, the examination, and the interpretation of one's findings.

The history includes the 'risk factors'. The mother may herself have noticed that the baby feels stiff, or is stiff on one side, or keeps one hand clenched when the other is open, or does not kick the legs properly. The baby may kick both legs together, instead of reciprocal kicking. The mother may have noticed that when the baby creeps, one leg trails after the other. She may notice that the child consistently refuses to use one hand. She may give a clear history of 'dissociation'—meaning in this context that there is severe retardation in gross motor development, such as sitting, while the baby is much more advanced in other fields of development. For instance, she may say that the child can readily pick up a currant between the tip of the forefinger and the tip of the thumb, but cannot nearly sit unsupported. This would immediately suggest an abnormality of muscle tone—hypotonia or hypertonia. There is likely to be a history of delay in reaching other milestones of development, because of the commonly associated mental retardation.

The next step is to observe the child—his head size and shape, his facial expression, alertness and interest in his surroundings. If he is a newborn baby one notices the quantity and quality of his limb movements, for the spastic infant is relatively immobile. One notes in particular the symmetry of movement. The spastic newborn may lie in an abnormal posture, with his legs unduly extended. After about three months, his hands should be predominantly loosely open; a hemiplegic child may have one hand tightly closed while the other is open. One may notice shortening of the arm and leg.

The other important signs are as follows:-

1. Abnormal extension of hip and knees when the child is held up with one's hand under the axillae. The legs extend and may cross.

2. Delayed motor development—as shown in the case of the young baby in ventral suspension, the prone position, the pull to the sit movement, and later in sitting and walking.

There is nearly always undue head lag when the child is pulled to the sitting position, or when he is held in ventral suspension. This is commonly and wrongly ascribed to hypotonia. There may perhaps be hypotonia in the neck muscles, but there is hypertonia elsewhere.

3. Increased muscle tone (Ch. 8), as seen especially by reduced dosiflexion of the ankle, reduced abduction of the hip, the limb shaking test, and the increased resistance to passive movement.

4. Exaggerated knee and biceps jerks; sustained ankle clonus: extensor plantar response.

5. Persistence of the Moro reflex, grasp reflex, and asymmetrical tonic neck reflexes (amongst others), long after the child should have lost these.

6. After five months, the typical spastic approach to an object when he is trying to grasp it. There is a slow characteristic dorsiflexion of the wrist with splaying out of the fingers as he reaches out (Fig. 166). It is quite different from the approach by the athetoid or ataxic child.

7. Sometimes excessive extensor tone (Fig. 54). In ventral suspension and in the prone position, the child may appear to show advanced motor development; but when he is pulled to the sitting position, there is gross head lag.

8. When he is pulled to the sitting position, he may tend to rise on to his legs instead of sitting, because of excessive extensor tone.

9. A tendency to fall backwards in the sitting position, because of spasm of the glutei, erector spinae and hamstrings. Normal babies tend to fall forwards rather than backwards, and a persistent tendency to fall backwards should make one suspect cerebral palsy.

When the baby is pulled to the sitting position, his knees flex. I have one hand under the popliteal space in this manoeuvre, so that I can feel the spasm of the hamstrings.

10. Slight wasting and slight or moderate shortening of the affected limbs of a hemiplegic child. The affected limbs are cold to the touch as compared with the normal side.

11. General retardation in development, except in the unusual spastic child who has normal mental development.

12. A tendency to toe walking in the case of the older spastic infant or child.

13. Difficulty in standing on one foot (in the case of the older spastic child, after the age of three).

14. In the case of the mildest cerebral palsy, mere clumsiness in building a tower of bricks (readily noticed if the child has a mild hemiplegia), poor performance on a timed bead threading test, and slight general clumsiness in his gait.

These are the basic signs of the spastic form of cerebral palsy. In a busy clinic, it would take perhaps two or three minutes to carry out the tests described.

The following is a typical case history of a mentally retarded child with cerebral palsy of the spastic type:

Case Report.—Typical Course of Mental Retardation with Mild Cerebral Palsy, 4 Weeks to $5\frac{1}{2}$ Years.

This boy was born at term by normal delivery, and was well in the newborn period. The subsequent course can be summarised as follows:

4 weeks	I wrote, 'Note the immature prone position. Suggestion of spasticity in lower limbs, but hands loosely open'.
6 weeks	'Very primitive in prone position. Poor head control'.
9 weeks	Smiles.
14 weeks	Vocalising. Following with eyes.
6 months	Grasping voluntarily.

15 months	Sitting, no support.
18 months	Single words beginning.
2 years	Walk, no help—no sphincter control. Cannot feed self. Concentration defective. Would do nothing with cubes.
3 years	Words together.
5½ years	I.Q. 47.
	Very mild right hemiplegia.

Athetosis

It is virtually impossible to make a definite diagnosis of athetosis until the athetoid movements are seen, and these may be delayed for some years, though I have seen them in the first week. The condition may be suspected because of one of the conditions known in some cases to be followed by athetosis—in particular, severe anoxia at birth, haemolytic disease of the newborn, or neonatal hyperbilirubinaemia. Athetosis can certainly be expected to develop if there was kernicterus in the neonatal period.

Observation of the development of babies with kernicterus has provided us with useful information concerning its natural history.

Polani[10] described 73 cases. The kernicterus was due either to haemolytic disease or to the hyperbilirubinaemia of prematurity. The early signs of kernicterus which appear not later than the sixth day in a full term baby, or the tenth day in a premature baby, were opisthotonos, rolling of the eyes, high-pitched cry, loss of the Moro reflex and of the mouth reflexes, jaundice, refusal of feeds, drowsiness or irritability, hypertonia, respiratory difficulties, cyanotic attacks and sometimes fever. These usually disappear by the end of the second week. He then described a silent period from the second week to the end of the first or second month, though feeding and sucking difficulties or stridor were common at this time. After the second month, neurological disturbances were obvious in 9 out of 10 babies. In 8, the only abnormality was delay in development. The infant often characteristically extends the elbows and pronates the wrist (Fig. 168). In 37 there were attacks of opisthotonos following stimulation or distress. These attacks became more frequent with the passage of time, and then developed spontaneously. They began to decrease in severity by the age of 9 to 11 months. Between the attacks the

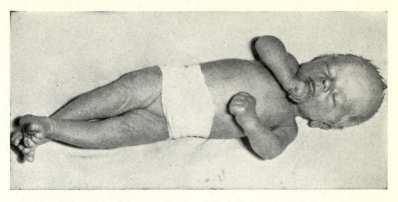

FIG. 158

Abnormal appearance of child aged 8 days. Hands very tightly closed.
The legs tend to cross and they are unusually extended. Knee jerks normal.
Cerebral haemorrhage. Severe convulsions age 3 days. (The development
was entirely average at 6 weeks.)

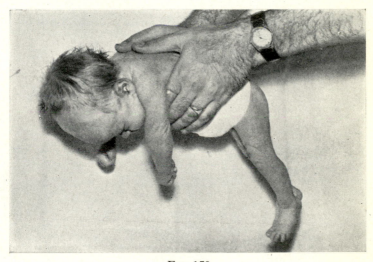

FIG. 159
Same child as Figure 158.
Head held up quite well, but arms and legs not flexed.

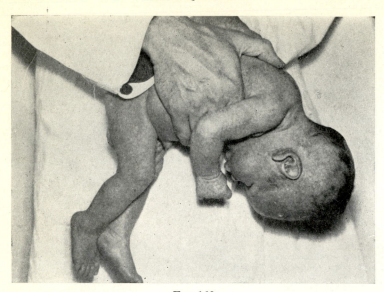

FIG. 160

A case of proved cerebral palsy at 6 weeks. (This boy is now a severely mentally defective case of spastic quadriplegia.)

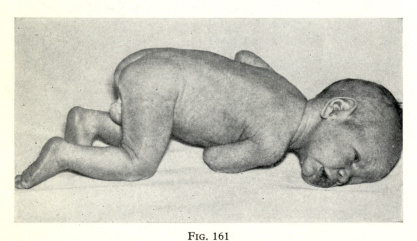

FIG. 161

Defective head control. Inadequate extension of hips and flexion of knees. Same boy as Figure 157. Pelvis rather high for the age.

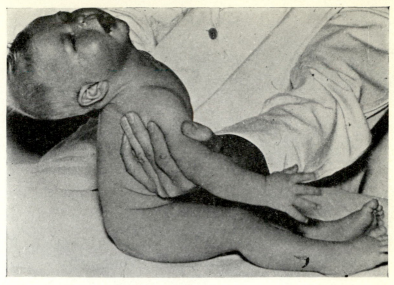

FIG. 162

Severely mentally defective child with spastic quadriplegia, aged 6 months, showing severe head lag on being pulled to the sitting position.

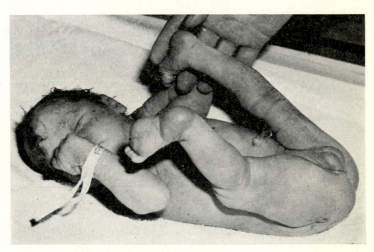

FIG. 163

Breech with extended legs. Age 10 days. Note the posture.

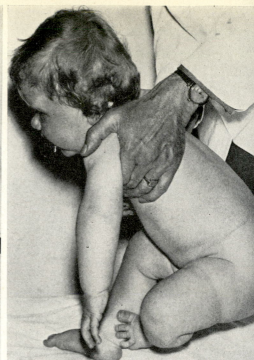

FIG. 164.   Shows ordinary sitting posture.

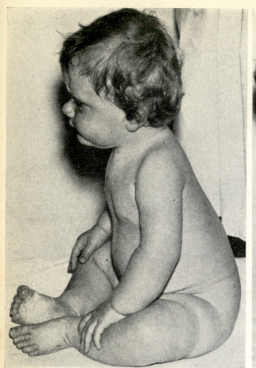

FIG. 165.   Shows defective weight bearing.

Fig. 164 and Fig. 165.—Child referred for assessment for adoption (aged 8 months).   Defective weight-bearing found. Pathologically exaggerated knee jerks and ankle clonus found. Diagnosis spastic paraplegia in a child with normal intelligence.

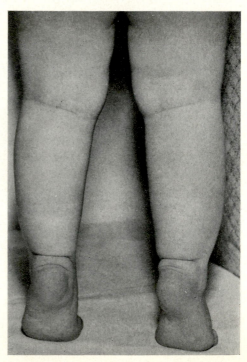

FIG. 166

Toe walking due to congenital shortening of the Tendo Achillis.
There is also a constriction band.

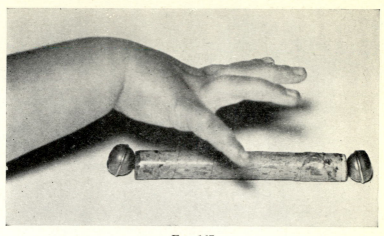

FIG. 167
Typical spastic approach to object, with splaying out of fingers.
(Mild hemiplegia.)

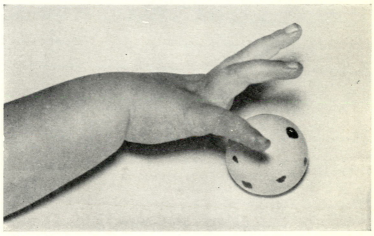

FIG. 168
The same.

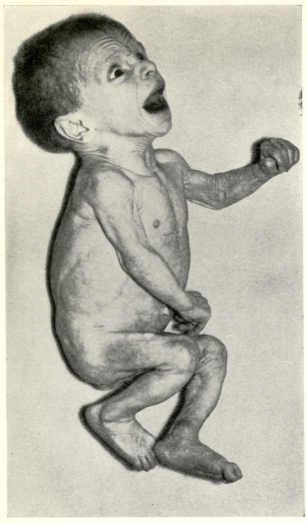

FIG. 169
Kernicterus, aged 2 weeks.

children tended to be hypotonic. In half the children this phase was followed by hypotonia; in the other half it was followed by athetoid movements. In 25 children hypertonia developed after the second month, with relaxation in sleep. In 21 the phase of hypertonia was followed by athetoid movements. In 4 children hypotonia and developmental retardation appeared after the second month.

At the end of the first year 55 children were surveyed. There was marked hypotonia in 23, hypertonia in 11, mere developmental retardation in 19, and athetoid movements in 2.

The age of onset of athetoid movements was studied in 56 children. In 39 the onset was before $2\frac{1}{2}$, and in 17 it was between 3 and $3\frac{1}{2}$ years.

Polani's paper is a useful one, and has supplied us with valuable information. I am sceptical, however, of any studies of the age of onset of athetoid movements because I know from experience how easy it is to miss them in the early months. I believe that careful examination will reveal signs of athetosis much sooner than is commonly thought. One of the earliest signs is ataxia in carrying out voluntary movements, such as grasping a cube. I have made the mistake of diagnosing cerebellar ataxia, only to alter it later to athetosis.

I would emphasise the rhythmical tongue thrusting commonly seen in babies who will subsequently prove to have athetosis. I think that this may occur in other babies, but when I see it I regard athetosis as the most likely condition.

The Moro and asymmetrical tonic neck reflexes persist longer than usual. As the infant grows older, retardation in motor development becomes more obvious. After 12 months or so the typical tetrad of athetosis, will be found. This consists of difficulty in vertical gaze (present in 90 per cent), enamel hypoplasia of the deciduous teeth, high tone deafness (found in the majority), and athetoid movements.

Not all athetosis is due to kernicterus. In those cases in which kernicterus was not a factor, the signs are usually delayed motor development, often rhythmical tongue thrusting, and then ataxia, followed by typical athetoid movements.

The knee jerks and biceps jerks are normal in athetoids, and the plantar responses are flexor.

The athetoid child is by no means always late in development, provided that the I.Q. is average. The following is an example:

A child with known haemolytic disease of the newborn, which had been improperly treated, was followed up particularly carefully because of the possibility of the development of signs of athetosis. At 4 months, the motor development was thought to be better than average. At 6 months he began to sit without support. At 11 months he began to walk, holding on to furniture, and he could pull himself up to the standing position. He was saying 2 words with meaning at 16 months. He walked without help at 20 months, and at this time athetoid movements became obvious. The I.Q. at 6 was 86.

I have seen other athetoid children who were able to sit unsupported by 6 or 7 months and to walk without help by the first birthday.

Rigidity

The rigid form is diagnosed by the extreme rigidity of all limbs, in the absence of signs of disease of the pyramidal tract, such as increased tendon jerks, ankle clonus, positive stretch reflex, and extensor plantar response in the older child. It is almost always associated with a severe degree of mental deficiency.

Ataxia

The ataxic form is diagnosed by the ataxia in the child's approach to an object, and ataxia in sitting and walking.

Hypotonic Form of Cerebral Palsy

This is a rare form of cerebral palsy which can readily be confused with the hypotonias. Almost all infants with this condition are mentally defective.[6] The circumference of the skull is likely to be small. There is an increased range of movements. Fits occur in a third. The plantar responses are extensor, and the knee jerks are exaggerated, so that benign congenital hypotonia, Werdnig-Hoffman disease and myopathies can be readily excluded.

The Clumsy Child

There are all gradations between the normal and the abnormal, and it is impossible to draw the line between the two. Not all clumsy children should be included in the section on cerebral palsy, but it is likely that many clumsy children are examples of that condition.

Clumsy children are usually regarded as normal for several years, and then they begin to get into trouble at school, or worry their parents because of their awkwardness. Mothers commonly say that the child 'falls a lot', 'always has bruises on his legs', is 'awkward with his hands', 'cannot pedal a cycle', and say that the teacher complains that 'his writing is bad', or that 'he doesn't seem to hold his pencil properly'.

Ford,[2] in his book, used the term 'congenital maladroitness'. Annell[1] used the term 'Motorial Infantilism'. Arnold Gesell[3] used the term 'Minimal Birth Injury'—an undesirable term, because it implies knowledge of the causation. Others have called these children 'motor morons'.

They are awkward at tying shoe laces or at buttoning their clothes. They tend to misjudge distances, as when passing through a doorway; they break objects more than others; they cannot thread a needle, or throw a ball well, or jump like normal children of their age. They cannot stand on one foot as well as their contemporaries, though they walk normally. On building a tower of cubes slight unsteadiness or tremor is usually noted. In a few there are minimal signs of athetosis, or of disease of the pyramidal tract in the way of an extensor plantar response. Timed tests of manual dexterity—such as the pegboard, reveal that the child is a long way behind in these for his age. The intelligence quotient may be average or superior, though it is probably more common to find that it is below average.

Clumsiness may be due to hypotonia, congenital myopathy, muscular dystrophy, familial dysautonomia, the Klippel-Feil syndrome, agenesis of the corpus callosum, and other organic causes. Older children may be clumsy because of drugs—such as the antiepileptic drugs, imipramine, meprobamate, or chlordiazepoxide. Clumsiness is often associated with overactivity. There may be a history of severe maternal toxaemia, or anoxia at birth, of excessive irritability or inactivity at birth, of being small for dates.

One begins by asking the child to build a tower of one inch cubes. One may notice tremor or ataxia in the hands as he builds. When he is older he is likely to have difficulty in standing on one foot, in walking along a ledge, in the timed bead-threading test, in the Goodenough draw-a-man test, in the Goddard formboard test, and in right left discrimination. He achieves a better score on the Wechsler verbal scale than on the performance scale.

From the point of view of developmental assessment, the condition is important because of the frequency with which these children are wrongly thought to be mentally subnormal. As always, one has to assess a child not on the question of whether he can do a given test, but on the way in which he does it.

Differential Diagnosis

1. MENTAL RETARDATION. By far the greatest difficulty in diagnosis lies in the differentiation of cerebral palsy in association with mental retardation, from mental retardation alone. The two conditions are frequently associated. It follows that when signs of mental retardation are found, a thorough search for signs of cerebral palsy should always be made.

2. ISOLATED MOTOR RETARDATION. It is very easy to confuse mild diplegia with isolated motor retardation. I have myself made this mistake.

Case Report.—I was asked, by a paediatrician, Dr. R. Gordon, to see a child of 10 months of age on account of defective head control and suspected cerebral palsy. There was no retardation in other fields. Diplegia was suspected, but although the knee jerks were brisk, I mistakenly decided that they were within normal limits. There was no adductor spasm in the thigh muscles. He learned to sit without support at 14 months, to feed himself with a cup at 18 months, and to join words together at 23 months. I saw him at intervals, but it was not until he was over 3 three years old that it became obvious that the plantar responses were extensor. He had no deformity.

3. VOLUNTARY RESISTANCE TO PASSIVE MOVEMENT. The child may be thought to be spastic, whereas in fact he is merely resisting passive movement.

4. ABNORMALITY OF JOINTS. Abduction of hips may appear to be limited, so suggesting adductor spasm, when in fact the child is voluntarily resisting the movement. Limited abduction of hips may be due to congenital dislocation of hips. I have myself made the mistake of diagnosing spasticity in a newborn baby who had notable limitation of movements of the joints due to punctate epiphyseal dysplasia. The limited movement of joints in arthrogryposis multiplex congenita might be confused with spasticity.

5. UNSTEADINESS OF GAIT. I have often been asked to see a toddler on account of unsteadiness of gait, with a view to diagnosing cerebral palsy. In all cases the children had been late in learning to walk, and it was not realised that such a child is also later than others in walking steadily. For example, a child who walks without help at 12 months will probably be walking quite steadily with relatively few falls by 18 months. But a child who does not learn to walk without help until 21 months will probably be 30 months old before he can walk as steadily as the earlier walker.

6. NORMAL MOVEMENTS. It is easy to confuse the normal movements of the arms and legs of a baby with those of athetosis, if he has had some condition such as severe jaundice, which leads one to look carefully for athetoid movements.

7. CONGENITAL SHORTENING OF THE TENDO ACHILLES. This may cause confusion by causing the child to walk on his toes, like a child with a spastic lower limb. The tendon jerks, however, are normal and the plantar responses are flexor.

8. CONGENITAL SHORTENING OF THE GLUTEUS MAXIMUS or of the hamstrings. This makes it difficult for the child to sit, and delays sitting. The tendon jerks in these conditions are normal, thus eliminating the spastic form of cerebral palsy.

9. WEAKNESS OF MUSCLES DUE TO MYOPATHY, HYPOTONIA OR ERB'S PALSY. In all these cases, weakness rather than stiffness would be detected. Erb's palsy rarely persists, and in the older child the characteristic grasp of the spastic hand, with the slow splaying out of the fingers, is quite different from the grasp of the child with Erb's palsy.

10. OTHER CAUSES OF INVOLUNTARY MOVEMENTS. These include tremor, torsion spasm, spasmus nutans, chorea and tics. It is easy to confuse athetosis with ataxia, particularly in the infant, in whom the first sign of athetosis is in fact ataxia, before the characteristic involuntary movements begin.

In torsion spasm the first sign is often hypertonicity of the calf muscles, leading to plantar flexion and inversion with adduction of the foot. Later torticollis develops, followed later by the typical torsion spasm.

Spasmus mutans can be confused with tremor, but the characteristic head nodding or twitching, with the peculiar habit of looking out of the corner of the eyes, should establish the diagnosis. The movements are often inhibited by looking fixedly at an object.

Athetosis should not be confused with the more irregular movements of Sydenham's or Huntington's chorea.

11. DEGENERATIVE CONDITIONS OF THE NERVOUS SYSTEM. It is easy to diagnose these on the grounds that no abnormality had been previously noted, when in fact there were neurological abnormalities which had not been looked for or recognised. The conditions at issue include the lipoidoses, and leucoencephalopathies. Schilder's disease (encephalitis periaxalis) and multiple sclerosis may be confused with cerebral palsy of prenatal origin. Toxoplasmosis may cause convulsions and spasticity, the real cause being missed. Phenylketonuria rarely but occasionally causes spasticity.

12. ABNORMALITIES OF THE SPINAL CORD. These include diastematomyelia, syringomyelia and spinal dysraphism. Holman et al.[5] reviewed the conditions known as diastomatomyelia. It is a congenital anomaly in which a spicule of bone transfixes the spinal cord, and leads to progressive paresis of the lower limbs. In about half of all cases a tuft of hair or congenital dermal sinus reveals the condition.

Syringomyelia may occur in later childhood. There is likely to be muscular atrophy, arthropathy, weakness or spacticity and dissociated anaesthesia.

Paraplegia may be due to a purely spinal lesion. Congenital absence of the sacrum causes weakness of the legs with absence of sphincter control.

13. TOE WALKING. Toe walking may be normal. Occasional children walk on their toes for a while when learning to walk. It may also be due to muscular dystrophy, congenital shortening of the Tendo Achilles (Fig. 165) or to early infantile autism. It is seen temporarily in the prematurely born baby when he is held in the standing position. Cerebral palsy of the spastic type cannot be diagnosed on this sign alone.

Cleidocranial Dysostosis

This familial condition is characterised by absence of the middle third of the clavicle, allowing the shoulder to be approximated in the midline anteriorly. There may be mental deficiency and spasticity.

Platybasia and anomalies of the base of the skull.

Spillane *et al.*[12] fully reviewed these conditions. There may be ataxia or hypotonia, often in association with shortness of the neck. The diagnosis is established by X-ray examination.

REFERENCES

1. ANNELL, A. L. (1952) *Disorders of Motor Function in Schoolchildren. The Affective Contact.* p. 367. Amsterdam: Strengholt.

1a. ANDRÉ-THOMAS, DARGASSIES SAINTE-ANNE (1952) *Études Neurologiques sur le Nouveau-né et le Jeune Nourrisson.* Paris: Masson and Perrin.

2. FORD, F. R. (1960) *Diseases of the Nervous System in Infancy and Childhood and Adolescence.* Oxford: Blackwell.

3. GESELL, A., AMATRUDA, C. S. (1947) *Developmental Diagnosis.* New York: Hoeber.

4. HARVEY, C. C. (1959) Personal Communication.

5. HOLMAN, C. P., SVIEN, H. J., BICKEL, W. H., KEITH, H. M. (1955) Diastematomyelia. *Pediatrics,* **15,** 191.

6. LESNY, I. (1960) The Hypotonic Forms of Cerebral Palsy. *Cereb. Palsy Bull.,* **2,** 158.

7. MINKOWSKI, A. (1960) Personal Communication.

8. PERLSTEIN, M. A., BARNETT, H. S. (1952) Nature and Recognition of Cerebral Palsy in Infancy. *J. Amer. med. Ass.,* **148,** 1389.

9. SOLOMONS, G., HOLDEN, R. H., DENHOFF, E. (1963) The Changing Pattern of Cerebral Dysfunction in Early Childhood. *J. Pediat.,* **63,** 113.

10. POLANI, P. E. (1959) The Natural Clinical History of Choreoathetoid Cerebral Palsy. *Guy's Hosp. Rep.,* **108,** 32.

11. SKATVEDT, M. (1958) Cerebral Palsy. *Acta Paedia. (Uppsala),* **46.** Suppl. 111.

12. SPILLANE, J. D., PALLIS, C., JONES, A. M. (1957) Developmental Anomalies in the Region of the Foramen Magnum. *Brain,* **80,** 11.

CHAPTER 17

ASSESSMENT OF SUITABILITY
FOR ADOPTION

When assessing a child's suitability for adoption, it must be constantly remembered that the interests of the child are the primary consideration. Nevertheless, the interests of the adopting parents have also to be considered, for they have a considerable bearing on those of the child. For instance, one has to try to prevent a mentally defective child being unwittingly adopted, in order to protect the adopting parents from a tragic disappointment, and to protect the adopted child from possible rejection by the adopting parents. An important aim of the doctor is therefore the detection of a severe mental or physical handicap. It may also be argued that one should attempt to match the child's developmental potential with that of the intelligence and social status of the adopting parents, as was done in Arnold Gesell's clinic in New Haven. This is a debatable aim, (see Ch. 4), but it is difficult to deny that a child who is thought to be of slightly below average developmental potential would fit in better in the home of a manual labourer than in the home of professional parents. In this connection my constantly reiterated warnings about the difficulties and fallacies of developmental prediction should be remembered.

It is a tragedy, on the one hand, if a doctor wrongly diagnoses mental subnormality or cerebral palsy, so that the baby cannot be adopted; and it is most unfortunate if he passes a baby as normal, when in fact he is a microcephalic spastic idiot. I have seen a good many examples of both mistakes.

The Limitations of Developmental Assessment

It is important that a doctor who is attempting to assess a baby should be conversant with the limitations of developmental assessment. He should know that by proper assessment one can diagnose mental subnormality, and one can detect cerebral palsy of moderate or severe degree.

The assessment is made, as always, on the basis of the history, the examination and the interpretation.

The History

The importance of a full history, prior to any developmental examination, has already been described. It would be wrong to agree to any child being adopted without a proper history concerning the real parents, the pregnancy, birth weight, duration of gestation, the delivery and the condition of the child in the newborn period. One must know whether there is a family history of hereditary diseases, and particularly of degenerative diseases of the nervous system, or of psychosis. One must know whether there is a history of illnesses during pregnancy, such as toxaemia or antepartum haemorrhage, which increase the risk of abnormality in the child. One must know about any factor making the child 'at risk', or more likely than others, to be abnormal. It is essential, however, that none of these factors should be given an exaggerated importance. For instance, a history of mental subnormality in a parent should certainly not be regarded as contraindicating the adoption of the child. A history of epilepsy in a mother should not prevent a child being adopted. I find a constant tendency to exaggerate the importance of these factors. The doctor who assesses the baby should note the factors carefully, and keep them in proper perspective. He should then concentrate on assessing the child, and except in the case of degenerative diseases of the nervous system and psychoses, be careful not to give the 'risk' factors more importance than they merit. For example, if the doctor is asked to assess a 6 months old baby whose mother was mentally defective, it would be quite wrong for him promptly to conclude that the baby was unsuitable for adoption. He should assess the baby, as he would any other, and if he found that he was in all respects up to the average, or above average, he would pass the baby as suitable. If, however, the baby were a little below average, he would certainly take the family history into account, and postpone a decision until say 10 months, when he would reassess the baby, and take into account the rate of development in the intervening period.

As in the case of any assessment, one must obtain a history of previous milestones, in order that one can estimate the rate of development, and of factors which might have affected the development, such as illnesses.

The Examination

Grossly defective infants, such as mongols, and those with severe microcephaly, will already have been sifted out, and are not likely to reach the doctor who is assessing babies for adoption.

The age at which the assessment for adoption is made is of the greatest importance. It has already been stated that we are not able as yet to assess a baby seriously before he is about four weeks of age (and at a similar corrected age in the case of premature babies). In my opinion the earliest age at which one should attempt to assess a full term baby is six weeks. This is because it is relatively easy to assess the motor development at this age, and normal full term babies have begun to smile at the mother's overtures, and probably to vocalise. They will watch her intently as she speaks to them. It is the normal practice in this country to place an infant at the age of one or two weeks in a foster home in which the foster parents are likely to adopt; and the age of six weeks would be a convenient one for assessment, giving the foster parents a little time in which to become acquainted with the baby. If one is doubtful about the development at this age, he should be reassessed at six months, but not sooner.

I have no doubt that it is much easier and safer to assess a baby at the age of six months, if this can be arranged. The difficulty lies in the foster parents' natural desire to clinch the adoption, and the fear that the real mother may change her mind and demand the return of the baby. At the age of six months one can readily assess the gross motor development, particularly in the sitting position; the child has begun (at four or five months) to reach out and grasp objects without their being put into the hand, and the maturity of the grasp can be assessed at six months. He begins to transfer objects from one hand to the other at this age. He begins to chew. He may have begun to imitate (e.g. a cough or other noise). His interest in his surroundings and determination can be observed. The maturity of his response to sound can be determined. For instance, he should immediately turn his head to sound.

If one is doubtful about the baby's development at six months, the best time to see him again is at ten months. By this age he should be able to stand holding on to the furniture, and perhaps to walk, holding on to it; he may be able to creep; but much more important than this is the index finger approach to objects and finger thumb apposition. He should be able to wave bye bye and play patacake, and he should be helping his mother to dress him by holding his arm out for a coat or his foot out for a shoe.

In the first year the most difficult age for assessment is two to four months, and the next most difficult age is eight to nine months. This is because there are so few significant new milestones at these times. It is easy to make a mistake at two to four months in the assessment of motor development, and there are no useful new developments in manipulation or social behaviour. The same applies to some extent to the age of eight to nine months.

There is much to be said for a doctor assessing adoption babies at the same age—so that he becomes really conversant with the developmental features of that age. There is not usually any difficulty about arranging this.

The disadvantage of placing a child at two to three weeks in a foster home in which adoption is desired is the possibility that he will turn out to be defective. The great advantage, however, is that the infant does not suffer emotional trauma by being changed from one home to another. If the child should turn out to be defective, the foster parents will be bitterly disappointed; but one must remember that if they adopt earlier and he subsequently turns out to be defective, the parents will suffer a great deal more. It is certainly wrong to keep him in an institution for a long period, such as six months. In that case he will suffer emotional deprivation, which apart from anything else will retard his development and make assessment much more difficult.

It must be remembered that in this country a period of three months must elapse between the institution of adoption proceedings and their finalisation.

If the final verdict is that the child is backward, one has to try to assess the degree of backwardness. It is certainly important to try to predict whether he will be educable in an ordinary school or a school for educationally subnormal children, and still more important to predict that he will not be suitable for education at school. Such predictions are fraught with great difficulties, and one must take the head circumference into full account. The additional finding of cerebral palsy may simplify matters, if it is severe, or make it more difficult, if it is less severe. In all cases one has to state the position to the parents, making it clear, if one thinks it to be the case, that the child may make an unexpected improvement and even turn out to be entirely normal. Again, this will depend in large part on the head size.

Many foster parents, on being told that the child is thought to be backward, state unhesitatingly that they will adopt in any case. In one way this is desirable, because it would be a tragedy for the child if he were not adopted. In that case prolonged stay in the foster home is the best substitute for adoption. On the other hand, it is impossible for parents who have never had a mentally subnormal child to know all the implications of adopting such a child. They cannot possibly know all that it involves. They cannot know what it is like to have a mentally defective child in the home, who has to be watched all the time for his own safety. They cannot really know the physical, social, emotional and financial stresses to which they will be exposed. At least they will not feel the guilt, disappointment and other attitudes which real parents feel when they find that their own child is defective. They will have no sense of shame when their neighbours and relatives see the child. They may be respected for their courage for knowingly adopting such a child. They will not expect too much of him, and yet they may always hope for some improvement. It is reasonable to suppose that a couple would not deliberately adopt a defective child unless they were the sort of people who would be likely to be able to cope with him.

If a child is of normal intelligence, and yet is found to be handicapped, there is no objection to the child being adopted, provided that the parents understand the implications, as far as possible. Again, it would be a tragedy for the child if he were not adopted.

Jonathan Gould[6] in his book on 'Stress in Children' wrote that ideally it would be most desirable to match the abilities and temperament of the child to those of the adoptive parents. I am not sure that it would. I am not sure that it would be better for a neurotic mother to adopt a neurotic child. Knowing the importance of environmental factors in schizophrenia, it might well be better to try to place a child of a schizophrenic parent in a particularly calm and stable home.

I am not sure that we are right in saying that a baby who is thought to have a rather low developmental potential should be placed in the home of a manual labourer rather than in a professional home. A child a little below the average at six months might well prove to be above average if placed in a good loving stimulating home; if placed in a less good home, he may become further retarded. In the same way a mentally superior baby might not be expected to achieve his best if placed in a poor home. Admittedly, it is not the function of the paediatrician to chose the home for a baby; but in deciding whether a baby is suitable for adoption, he may be influenced in his decision by observing the sort of foster parent who wants to adopt.

The doctor who assesses the suitability of a baby for adoption frequently has to give genetic advice. Only an expert should do this. The common problems are as follows:–

1. Incest. This is said now to be more common than cousin marriages. The risk of abnormalities in the child is given as somewhere between 33 and 66 per cent.

2. Schizophrenia. The genetic factor probably acts by predisposing to schizophrenia under the influence of additional environmental factors. There is probably a 10 per cent risk of the child developing it if a parent had it. The difficulty is that if the grandparent had schizophrenia, the mother may not be old enough for one to know whether she has developed it. I have met a similar problem in the case of Huntington's chorea.

3. Manic depressive psychoses. The risk of the child developing it is 10 to 15 per cent. Again, the mother may not develop it until the age of 40 or 50.

4. Epilepsy. The genetic factor is only a small one. The risk of the child being affected is about 2·5 per cent.

5. Degenerative diseases of the nervous system. The opinion to be given must depend on the exact diagnosis in the parent.

6. Mental deficiency.

7. Neurosis or alcoholism. These are probably in the main environmental in origin, and so there is no added risk of the child developing it.

In conclusion, there are many difficulties in assessing a child for adoption. The assessment should on no account be made by a doctor who has no interest or special experience in such work. The difficulties are considerable, and experience can only be obtained by examining a large number of babies, and by following them all up in order that one can learn from mistakes. In my opinion all children assessed should be followed up at school age.

One must do one's best to prevent foster parents unknowingly adopting a defective child. However careful one is, some children, for reasons stated, will turn out to be defective when they were thought to be normal at the time of assessment. Yet one must remember that parents having their own children have no certainty at all that their children will not be defective, and unlike adopting parents, they cannot even choose the child's sex. There will always be some risk in adoption. Unless adopting parents are willing to take some risk, they should not adopt at all.

REFERENCES

1. BAKWIN, R. M., BAKWIN, H. (1952) Adoption. *J. Pediat.*, **40,** 130.
2. BLACK, J. A., STONE, F. H. (1958) Medical Aspects of Adoption. *Lancet,* **2,** 1272.
3. BRIT. MED. J. (1953) Adoption. I Supplement P. 240.
4. EDWARDS, G. (1954) Adoption. *Proc. Roy. Soc. Med.,* **47,** 1044.
5. ELLISON, M. (1958) *The Adopted Child.* London: Gollancz.
6. GOULD, F. (1968) *Stress in Children.* London: Churchill.
7. KARELITZ, S. (1957) Adoption. *Pediatrics,* **20,** 366.
8. KARELITZ, S. (1958). Adoption. *Ann. Ped. Fenn.,* **4,** 1.
9. KORNITZER, M. (1959) *Adoption.* London: Putnam.
10. KORNITZER, M. (1968) *Adoption and Family Life.* London: Putnam.
11. NORMAN, A. P. (1960). The Problem of Adoption. *Practitioner,* **185,** 175.
12. ROWE, J. (1966) *Parents, Children and Adoption.* London: Routledge and Kegan Paul.
13. WITTENBORN, J. R. (1957) *The Placement of Adoptive Children.* Springfield: Charles Thomas.

CHAPTER 18

MISTAKES AND PITFALLS IN
DEVELOPMENTAL DIAGNOSIS

Although it may be felt that I have said enough about the difficulties of developmental diagnosis, I feel that the matter is of such importance that it would be profitable to summarise what has been said by putting together the common mistakes and pitfalls in developmental prediction. In doing so one will bear in mind the many warnings of Arnold Gesell. He wrote: 'So utterly unforeseen are the vicissitudes of life that our common-sense will deter us from attempting to forecast too precisely the developmental career even of a mediocre child'.[4] 'Diagnostic prudence is required at every turn'.[5] He quoted a saying of William James, that 'Biographies will never be written in advance'.

The main mistakes and pitfalls are as follows:

1. Failure to Take a Proper History

In view of the importance of prenatal factors and perinatal events, such as convulsions, for the development of the child, a careful history of these is important. One must certainly know about hereditary conditions, such as mental deficiency, degenerative diseases and psychoses. One should ascertain whether there are any particular developmental patterns in the family, such as delayed speech.

Failure to take a history of the milestones of development makes it impossible to assess the previous rate of development. This is vital, for the history may suggest that although the child was backward at first, he is showing signs of catching up to the average. Conversely the history may show that the child's development is slowing down, or that he is actually deteriorating. Apart from this, the developmental history serves as a useful check against one's own objective findings. One always compares one's own findings with the mother's statements about the child's abilities.

Of particular importance is the effect of emotional deprivation. It is especially important in the assessment of suitability for

357

adoption, when the child in question has been in an institution, or has been moved from one foster home to another. When retardation in such a child is found, one must never suggest that there should be a further period of institutional care, so that his progress can be assessed, for a further period would retard his development still further. The correct procedure is to place him in a good foster home, and then observe his development after a period of say 3 months in that home. Sometimes a retarded child has had such an unfavourable environment that it is most unwise to express an opinion about his potentialities at all. One must always be prepared to postpone judgment if in doubt, or to withhold one altogether.

Failure to take a proper history may lead to the regrettable mistake of considering that retardation is due to inborn factors, when in fact it is environmental in origin. Insufficient attention may be paid to a history of severe illness, emotional deprivation, institutional care, or lack of opportunity to practise. For instance, the age at which a child bears weight on the legs, chews, feeds himself, dresses himself or attends to his own toilet needs, depends on the domestic environment.

In the case of mentally retarded children, there is particularly liable to be an unsatisfactory environment, so that they may function at a level lower than that of which they are really capable. If the environment is improved, they make an unexpected advance in their level of functioning.

2. Undue Reliance on the History

I have sometimes felt that when children are being examined for the purposes of adoption, too much reliance is sometimes placed on the history. With this in mind I have emphasised in preceding chapters that although certain adverse prenatal factors, such as bleeding during pregnancy, maternal toxaemia, hydramnios or premature delivery, are associated with a somewhat high incidence of abnormalities in the foetus, the vast majority of babies born of mothers with these conditions are perfectly normal. The same applies to perinatal morbidity in the baby: although perinatal anoxia, cerebral irritability and even convulsions are associated with a higher incidence of abnormalities in the baby, the great majority of children who survived these adverse conditions in the newborn period grow up to be perfectly normal. In the same way undue attention should not be paid to the fact that one of the parents was mentally backward, or that one of the siblings had some anomaly of the central nervous system. In the former case, the great majority of children will be normal. In the latter case, the incidence of anomalies in the child depends on the disease in question. I have seen it suggested that adoption should be postponed if any of the above adverse factors are found in the history. This, I am sure, would be wrong.

3. Failure to Allow for Prematurity

A disastrous mistake in the assessment of a young baby is a failure to allow for premature birth. One is occasionally in a real difficulty in the case of babies who are being examined for adoption, if the maturity at birth is unknown. One fairly often comes across another difficulty, that of a child whose birth weight was 4 or 5 lbs., but who was stated by the mother to have been born at term. It can be difficult to know whether to accept the mother's dates or not. A study of the weight chart in the newborn period may give some clue as to the right course. A rapid weight gain, unlike that of the usual premature baby of comparable birth weight, would help one to decide. The difficulty is increased by the fact, already mentioned, that follow-up studies have shown more low I.Q. test scores in children who were small babies born at or near term, than in those who were comparably small, but born prematurely.

In Chapter 7 we have discussed the findings in the newborn period which distinguish a premature baby from a baby of the same birth weight born at term. Unfortunately we do not usually have such information when we are faced with a six months baby who weighed 4 lbs. at birth and who may or may not have been born prematurely.

Some allowance should be made for postmaturity, but this is not now likely to be of significant degree.

4. Errors in the Timing of the Examination

The timing of the examination in relation to the child's normal play time has been described in Chapter 13.

Mistakes can readily be made in the case of epilepsy. One should never attempt to assess an epileptic child who has had a fit on that day, or who is still in a confused state after a fit even a few days previously, or who is having frequent petit mal attacks.

24

In the same way one must not examine him when he has toxic symptoms from drug therapy, which may make him drowsy, ataxic or irritable and unco-operative.

The ideal age at which a developmental examination should be made, if one can choose the age, is of importance. For the purposes of adoption I would feel that the age of 6 weeks or 6 months is ideal for the purpose. In some ways I would rather give an opinion about a child when he is 6 to 8 weeks of age than I would when he is 3 or 4 months old. There are several readily assessable features of development at the age of 6 to 8 weeks, and at 6 months, but not at 3 or 4 months. At 3 or 4 months there is little apart from gross motor development which lends itself to assessment; while at 6 months, apart from gross motor development there are other important features, manipulation (ability to grasp, the maturity of the grasp, and transferring); chewing; imitation; concentration (in trying to get a toy out of reach); and syllables in vocalisation. This has been the experience of others, including Cattell.[2]

The age of 10 months is a good one at which to assess a baby, and if I am in doubt about the development of a baby at 6 months, I try to see him again at 10 months. At ten months one has available various new milestones of development—the index finger approach to objects, the finger thumb apposition, the child's co-operation in dressing (holding an arm out for a sleeve, a foot out for a shoe, transferring an object from a hand which is about to be put into a sleeve), the creep, the ability of the child to pull himself to the standing position, and to cruise (walking, when holding on to the furniture). There is the imitation of the mother (byebye, 'patacake', 'so big',) and the possibility of words with meaning. The age of ten months is an excellent one for assessing a baby. By the age of 12 to 24 or more months, children are apt to be coy and non co-operative, and very difficult to test.

Wherever possible, I would avoid testing a child between 8 and 16 weeks of age, and between 8 and 9 months of age.

5. Errors in Choice of Test

Binet Simon tests indicated that 60 per cent. of canal boat children were mentally defective, while other tests gave a figure of 7 per cent. The modification of tests for children with cerebral palsy has been very well discussed by Haeussermann.[7]

In my opinion some of Ruth Griffith's tests are unsatisfactory.

Most of her tests are modified Gesell items, but some are not, and some are in my opinion seriously misleading. For instance, the score for the personal social quotient in the first 3 months consists of the following 8 items: smiling: regarding persons momentarily: enjoying his bath: quieting if crying by being picked up: vocalising when talked to: recognising mother visually: returning examiner's glance with smiling back or cooing: following many persons, especially the mother, with his eyes. It is impossible to bunch these items together in this fashion. In the first place, the item 'enjoys his bath' is hardly a good sign of intelligence. Many intelligent babies scream violently when bathed. Secondly, quieting on being picked up is hardly a sign of intelligence. A newborn baby responds in this way. An average baby begins to smile at 6 weeks and to vocalise at about 8 weeks, and one certainly cannot score them together. The important thing is not *whether* a child smiles, but *when* he began to smile in response to his mother's overtures, and with what degree of maturity he does it: *i.e.* how readily and frequently he smiles. If a full term child had only just begun to smile at 3 months, I should say that he is almost certainly mentally defective; but on the Griffiths' scale he scores his point. The whole scale is far too coarse at this age. One must remember that a performance of a 3 month baby at a 2 month level may mean that at 10 years he will be in the educationally subnormal class. Small variations from the average are important, and really coarse methods of assess- ment add greatly to the inaccuracy of infant testing.

One may criticise many other of her items. For instance, she included the grasp reflex as a sign of motor maturity at 1 month, but the grasp reflex is not a sign of intelligence. The loss of the grasp reflex may be a sign of maturation, but that is the opposite of what she appears to mean. Other items which I would feel are unsuitable include: friendliness to strangers (fourth month): stopping crying when talked to (fifth month): holding on to spoon (fifth month): drinking from a cup (seventh month): being able to be left sitting on floor.

The first two of these do not require comment. As for the third 'he holds on to a spoon' one has to assess, as before, not just the occurrence of the act, but the maturity of the act. As for drinking from a cup, newborn babies have been known to do this. As for the item 'can be left sitting on the floor', this is far too coarse for a test: there is much more to the assessment of the maturity of sitting than the fact that he can be left sitting on the floor.

6. Errors in the Performance of the Tests

It is wrong, as stated in Chapter 13, to conduct the physical examination of the infant before carrying out the developmental tests. He is likely to be much more co-operative if given test objects before he is undressed for his physical examination.

It is usually a mistake to examine the child in the absence of the mother.

I was reminded of the importance of having the mother present during the test when I nearly made a mistake in assessment. I was testing the child's ability to copy strokes made with a pencil. He had successfully imitated a vertical, horizontal and circular stroke, and I made a cross, asking him to do the same. He made a circle close to the cross. I assumed that he could not make the cross, but the mother said, 'He is playing noughts and crosses; he likes it'.

Slowness in presenting the tests, or failure to modify the sequence of testing if a child is showing signs of boredom, will lead to errors. The importance of carrying out the testing before a long history is taken in a young child has been mentioned in Chapter 13.

7. Errors in Respect of the Physical Examination

The vital importance of the measurement of the head circumference has been mentioned in Chapter 8.

Even though a head is smaller than usual, a normal rate of growth should prevent one making the mistake of diagnosing mental subnormality on the basis of smallness of the head. On the other hand an abnormal rate of growth of the head circumference, especially the slowing down in the growth, would make one strongly suspicious of mental subnormality.

It is vital not to forget the fact that the head size must be related to the size of the baby. A little baby can be expected to have a little head, and a big baby a big one.

No child should ever be suspected of mental subnormality merely on account of physical features such as a small or large head, or even because of gross abnormalities such as hypertelorism or craniostenosis. The developmental diagnosis can never be presumed: it must be made on a full developmental examination.

One must not be misled by the facial appearance.

Amongst famous people of history who were renowned for their ugliness were Socrates, Mirabeau, Napoleon Bonaparte, and Leo Tolstoy. Napoleon, on account of the ugly shape of his head, was thought to be the least likely in his family to achieve much. Mirabeau was regarded as the ugly duckling of the family, and had a disproportionately large head. Bakwin stated that Dr. Abraham Jacobi, the first professor of pediatrics in America, had a very large head, and he was quoted as having said that 'a little hydrocephalus stimulates mental functioning'! Lord Byron and H. G. Wells had particularly small heads.

Hydrocephalus is not necessarily incompatable with a good level of intelligence. In the first place, it may be arrested at birth. I well remember seeing a seriously disturbed mother who had been told that her baby had hydrocephalus and would be spastic and mentally defective. The diagnosis was undoubtedly correct, but I told the mother that the prediction given, though likely, was by no means necessarily correct. In fact, within a month it was obvious that the hydrocephalus was arrested, and the child proved to be perfectly normal.

Bakwin described the dreadful tragedy which resulted from a wrong diagnosis of mental deficiency in a child with hydrocephalus and spina bifida. The father was given a bad prognosis, and was given the extraordinary advice that he should tell his wife that the baby had died. The girl was then transferred to an institution, but as she grew older it became clear that her intelligence was within normal limits. The father was then advised to tell his wife that the girl was in fact alive, but he would not do so. The mother was then told by another person.

Hydrocephalus may cause difficulty in two ways. In the first place, the process may become arrested at any stage, so that development may be normal. In the second place, it is difficult to assess head control, when the sheer weight of a large head may cause undue head lag.

8. Failure to Diagnose Sensory Defects

Sensory defects, such as visual or auditory ones, are obvious factors which profoundly affect development. Visual defects, for instance, will affect the age of smiling, following with the eyes, and manipulation. In the older child, specific reading disability or congenital auditory imperception may be missed.

The fact that sensory defects, such as visual or auditory impairment, may also lead to emotional deprivation and reduced manipulative and other experiences, should not be forgotten: one defect may lead to another, so that development is retarded by a combination of factors. The combination of retarding factors in cerebral palsy has been described elsewhere.

A failure to detect mechanical factors, such as hypotonia or cerebral palsy, will cause gross errors in assessment.

9. Failure to detect Other Signs of Organic Disease

Minimal neurological signs may be missed, so that the organic reason for a child's lateness in motor development may not be recognised. There may be an organic basis for the child's lateness in feeding himself, dressing himself, or acquiring sphincter control.

It would clearly be foolish to attempt a developmental assessment of a child who has a physical illness which would reduce the level of his performance.

CEREBRAL PALSY. Cerebral palsy and so-called 'birth injury' interfere with the assessment of a child for a variety of reasons. Cerebral palsy causes mechanical difficulties, which interfere with the use of the hands and with gross motor development; it is frequently associated with visual and auditory defects, with mental retardation, with poor attention span even in the absence of mental retardation, with emotional problems, with perceptional difficulties, such as defects of body image, space appreciation, and form perception, so that tests with formboards are misleading; and there may be other defects arising from cortical damage. Speech, in addition, is usually defective. The child's environment has not been conducive to a good level of achievement in tests commonly employed;[1] he may have been kept indoors, and had little contact with other children, and be unable to speak. Haeussermann[7] emphasised the fact that brain lesions 'penalise' a child. She wrote that: 'While the actual ability to comprehend and reason may be well within the normal range, in some cases the level of adaptation may be disproportionately lower'. 'Children with cerebral palsy will be more readily understood and their attempts to communicate more alertly observed and accepted by an examiner to whom it has become evident that while a child may be non-speaking, he may be far from non-communicating'.

Of all forms of cerebral palsy in which mistakes can be made in the assessment of intelligence, I would think that athetosis has the pride of place. Perlstein[9] has made the same comment, when referring to kernicterus. I have myself made such a mistake. The following is a brief case history:

Case Report.—This boy was born at term, by a difficult forceps delivery, weighing 8 lbs. 8 ozs. There was a severe degree of asphyxia, but he was well in the neonatal period. I saw him at 1 year, because of lateness in sitting and walking. The milestones were confusing. He had learnt to chew at 8½ months, and to roll from supine to prone at 6½ months. He had begun to say single words just before I saw him. He was interested, and laughing at the antics of his sibling. There was no sign of the spastic form of cerebral palsy. The grasp was a little ataxic, like that of a 5 month old baby. There were no abnormal movements. In my letter to the consultant who referred him to me, I wrote, 'I find it difficult to reconcile the fact that in the development of speech and chewing he is at the level of an 8 month old child, while in the use of hands and of sitting he is only at the level of a 5 month old child. This would suggest a mechanical difficulty. There is no doubt at all that he is quite considerably mentally retarded, apart altogether from his mechanical difficulty. Further observation is essential over a period of some months, in order to see how he develops'. (In retrospect, the diagnosis of mental retardation was obviously wrong, because of the normal speech development).

At 18 months I wrote: 'There is a mechanical difficulty, which is not spasticity. The point I made before about the lack of correlation between his locomotor development and speech is particularly obvious now, for he can say a lot of words and still cannot sit. This must represent a mechanical difficulty, and not mere mental retardation, for no child who is unable to sit on account of severe mental retardation is nevertheless able to talk'.

He began to put words together and to walk a few steps at 2 years. At 4 years athetoid movements became obvious. His I.Q. at 5 years was 100.

Another difficulty in the assessment of infants with cerebral palsy is the delayed maturation which is sometimes seen, and to which reference has already been made.

10. Undue Attention to the Results of Special Investigations, such as Air Encephalograms

The relative lack of correlation between these and performance has already been described.

Case Report.—I saw a child at the age of 2 months, who was admitted to hospital with a history of frequent convulsions in the previous 3 weeks. He was found to be backward in development. He had been born at term, but had only begun to smile at his mother at 8 weeks. On examination there was complete head lag in ventral suspension and when pulled to the sitting position. A subdural tap was negative, but an air encephalogram showed a large amount of air on the surface of the brain, indicating cortical atrophy. He was discharged in 2 weeks, with a diagnosis of epilepsy and mental retardation. On follow-up examination he was soon found to be making rapid progress. His head control was full at 5½ months, he grasped objects voluntarily at 7 months, and began to transfer them at 8 months. At 10 months he was considered to be mentally normal. His I.Q. score at 9 years was 122, and there was no physical disability.

11. Errors in Interpretation caused by the Child's Failure to Co-operate

It is easy to diagnose mental subnormality in a child who is behaving badly and who will not co-operate. His behaviour may be due to fatigue, hunger, shyness or other reasons. If a child arrives tired and will not co-operate, he must be given a rest before he is examined or the opinion must be withheld altogether until he can be examined under more favourable circumstances.

One can make the mistake of considering lack of co-operation or interest to be a sign of low intelligence, when in fact it is merely a feature of the child's personality. One must also avoid the mistake of confusing the obsessional perseveration of the mentally defective child—who not uncommonly plays with one toy for hours on end—with true good concentration, such as one sees in an intelligent child.

12. The Difficulty of the Sleepy Baby

Errors in the assessment of motor development in the young baby are readily made if a child is sleepy or asleep. The sleeping 6 weeks old baby, for instance, often assumes the foetal position in the prone, with his knees drawn high up under the abdomen; in the wakeful state his pelvis is lower and the legs often extended.

13. The Interpretation of Prone Development

It is easy to underestimate a young baby's development in the prone position, particularly between 2 and 8 months of age. He is apt to lie without attempting to raise his head from the couch, when if he tries he can raise it to a considerable extent.

14. Examiner Regard

The 5 or 6 month old baby may look at the examiner so closely that one makes the mistake of thinking that he shows no interest in the test objects.

The child may be so interested in other objects around the room that one wrongly thinks that he has poor concentration.

15. Errors in Assessment of Maturity of Responses

Though the rapidity with which a baby drops a cube gives some indication of the maturity of the grasp, it is obvious that a child may drop the brick accidentally.

One must distinguish the accidental dropping of a cube from true casting—a feature which usually commences at about 12 months of age.

In the older child one may fail to observe the maturity with which an act is performed. For instance, a child who has only learnt to walk 2 or 3 days before the examination may show a mature gait, indicating that he could have walked alone weeks earlier if he had had the desire or confidence.

In the case of speech, when a child is said not to be able to talk at all, one may fail to observe the vital fact that he knows the meaning of numerous words.

The excessive head lag due to the mere size of the head in hydrocephalus can lead to errors in assessment.

In several of the studies on child development, the score is based on an all or none achievement: for instance, a 7 months old baby can either sit without support or he cannot. In one case he obtains a mark, and in the other he does not. This completely ignores the maturity of the act; one child who can sit without support may sit like an average 7 months old baby, and another like a 9 months old baby. The score should obviously be different.

16. Errors due to the Attractive Appearance of an Infant

The absence of shyness, the presence of good looks, a pleasant personality and charm, may lead to an erroneous diagnosis of mental superiority. It is easy to make the mistake of giving a higher assessment to a bouncing active baby than to a sleepy placid one, without any good justification. The facile behaviour and talkativeness of older children with hydrocephalus is apt to give an exaggerated idea of their intelligence.

Some of the features of a child's behaviour, good or bad, may be related purely to his personality, and not to his intelligence. The facile behaviour of the hydrocephalic child, with his talkativeness, is apt to give a wrong idea of the level of his intelligence.

17. Failure to Realise that some Aspects of Development are Vastly More Important for Assessment than Others

Some have placed far too much reliance on motor items of development, because thay are readily scorable, and far too little on the more important features of a child's behaviour—the alertness, the rapidity of response, the interest in surroundings, the degree of determination, persistence and concentration. Gesell called these 'Insurance factors' and paid great attention to them.

A child may have average motor ability and yet show grossly defective concentration, indicating mental subnormality. Aimless overactivity or defective concentration in a child who appears to be normal in other respects should make one suspect mental retardation and follow up closely for confirmation of that suspicion.

18. Ascribing Retardation to Laziness

I am frequently told that a child's general retardation or delay in speech or sphincter control is due to mere laziness. This diagnosis is always wrong.

19. Failure to Assess the Rate of Development

A common mistake is to fail to assess the rate of development—by taking the developmental history, and seeing the child again, repeatedly if necessary, before a conclusion as to his developmental potential is reached. I regard this as of the utmost importance. For instance, in the case of assessment of suitability for adoption, the over-confident and inexperienced doctor will make a practice of assessing babies on a single examination. In many cases one can do this: in many others it is impossible, and the child must be seen again before a confident opinion can be given.

20. Failure to remember the Different Patterns of Development

Lulls in development cause confusion. A child's apparent failure to progress in speech development may cause anxiety if the frequency of this in normal children is forgotten.

21. Difficulties with Regard to Deterioration

It has already been noted that mongols and children with untreated phenylketonuria slow down in development. I have several times heard that an unusually good intelligence level had been predicted for a mongol on account of good early development. This feature, however, should not be termed deterioration: it represents a slowing down of the process of development.

True deterioration may occur as a result of readily diagnosable conditions, such as lead poisoning, hypoglycaemia, head injury, meningitis or encephalitis. These cannot usually be anticipated: in the absence of a family history of a degenerative disease it is almost impossible to predict most other forms of deterioration. The deterioration associated with epilepsy has been described in Chapter 5. I am always particularly mindful of the possibility of deterioration in a retarded child who is having uncontrollable fits. It is well known that deterioration may occur in severe forms of cerebral palsy.

Quite marked deterioration can be expected when a mentally defective child is placed in an institution.

One cannot expect to predict an unusual course of development, whether due to known extraneous circumstances or not. There may be unexpected and unexplained deterioration, or merely failure to fulfil early promise: or more commonly there may be unexpected improvement.

The improvement sometimes found in retarded infants has been described in Chapter 11. One is much more likely to underestimate a child's potentiality than to over-estimate it. The possibility of unexpected improvement will always be borne in mind, but the likelihood of such improvement must not be over-estimated. In my opinion unexpected improvement is rare.

I have referred in Chapter 5 to conditions in which mental deterioration occurs, and in Chapter 8 to the falling D.Q. in mongols as they grow older.

22. Failure to Assess the Child as a Whole

As described in Chapter 14 one balances the development in one field with that in other fields. When there is 'dissociation' one must look for the cause—which is often organic disease.

The whole child has to be assessed with regard to prenatal and perinatal conditions, environment, physical abnormalities, the rate of development, and the developmental examination. A proper assessment cannot be made on the basis of purely objective tests.

Hallowell[8] wrote of the importance of considering all available data on the physical condition, emotional problems, family background and environmental factors.

Safian and Harms[11] in a discussion of 4 cases of mistaken diagnosis of mental retardation wrote: 'We hope that in the future we shall become somewhat less dependent on these testing methods and shall rely more and more on a totalitarian aspect on the one hand, and on the other, the individualisation study of any child whose fate is given into our hands'. Charles[3] wrote: 'The overall impression one gains from the literature on diagnosis is that the soundest approach depends upon clinical judgment reinforced by social data and test results interpreted in the light of all the evidence'.

23. Confusion by Schizophrenia and Autism

These are described on Page 228.

It must be remembered that psychoses can be superimposed on mental deficiency.

24. Failure to Withhold Judgment in Case of Doubt

In some children, owing to the presence of confusing factors, prediction is impossible without further prolonged observations. The following is an example of a combination of difficulties of this nature.

Case Report.—Unusual Skull, Developmental Retardation and Difficulties in Prediction.

I was asked to see this boy at 11 weeks because of suspected hydrocephalus. The circumference of the head at birth was $14\frac{3}{4}$ inches, his weight then being 8 lbs. 6 ozs. On examination at 11 weeks the circumference was $16\frac{6}{8}$ inches, but the fontanelle and sutures felt normal. There was a slight antimongoloid slant of the eyes, and there was a prominent forehead, but I thought that the head could be within normal limits. The head was unlike that of either parent.

The boy was said to have begun to smile at 7 weeks and to vocalise at 8 weeks. The head control was that of a 6 weeks old baby. There were no other abnormal physical signs.

He was seen at intervals. He was said to hold a rattle placed in the hands at 3 months. At 4 months the head control was that of a 3 months old baby.

At one year the head circumference was 19½ inches. I thought that the clinical picture was that of megalencephaly. He showed hand regard. The head control was that of a 3½ months old baby. He was unable to grasp objects, though he 'grasped with the eye'; he did not hold on to an object placed in the hand. I wrote that 'In no way can I see development beyond the 4 month level'. I thought that his development had slowed down.

At this stage a full investigation was carried out with a view to possible operation for the hydrocephalus by insertion of a valve. Ventricular studies and an air encephalogram showed that there was no hydrocephalus, and the appearance was consistent with a diagnosis of megalencephaly. The E.E.G. was normal. The interpupillary distance was large—55 mm. While in hospital he was able to sit like a 7 month baby (at the age of 13 months), and he was seen to wave bye-bye. This had just begun. He bore virtually no weight on the legs. Voluntary grasping began at 14 months.

At 20 months the head measured 20 inches. I was immediately impressed by his incessant jargoning, and his responsiveness to his parents. He had begun to jargon at 18 months. He said 8 or 9 words clearly. He was unable to crawl or roll, but he could bear almost all his weight on his legs momentarily. He could not stand holding on to furniture. He was said to play only a short time with individual toys, usually merely throwing them to the ground. He would not grasp cubes or other test objects. His mother said that he would be unable to point out objects in pictures. He would not feed himself at all with a biscuit or spoon, and there was no sphincter control. He held his arms out for clothes from 18 months and played patacake at the same age. I thought that in view of the speech he had developed as far as a child of 14 or 18 months, though in all other respects he was much more retarded. I gave as my opinion that his I.Q. would be not less than 60 or 70, and that it might well turn out to be well up to the average.

The family developmental history was interesting. An older child had been a 'slow-starter'. I had seen him at 2 years, when he had just begun to walk a few steps. He was then very advanced in speech, speaking in long mature sentences. In all respects he was a normal child of advanced intelligence. The parents thought that the youngest child (with the megalencephaly) had throughout compared well with his older sibling in speech and all other aspects of development.

I have described this case at some length to show the difficulties which are sometimes encountered. Firstly, he had a peculiar head. Secondly, his development appeared to slow down and he took less interest in his surroundings. Thirdly (at 20 months), his speech had made remarkable progress, and was far in advance of all other fields of development. (No physical disability, such as spasticity, had ever been found). One rarely sees a child with uniform retardation except in speech, in which retardation was only slight. Fourthly, there was the family history of severe motor retardation in a sibling, who was now normal and of superior intelligence.

In such a case a prognosis must be guarded, and only prolonged observation could give one a clear picture of the developmental potential. At the time of writing (when he was 20 months old) he was still under observation. The parents, who were highly intelligent, had been given a full explanation of my difficulties in assessment, and I gave them hope that the child would be normal. I promised that he would not be severely defective (unless he developed some unforeseen complication like encephalitis).

One must always be prepared to withhold a prognosis altogether, sometimes, even for 2 or 3 years, in particularly difficult cases.

25. The Problem of the Possible Effect of Future Environment or Illness

It is quite impossible to predict certain variables which may affect the child's development in future, even though one has assessed his developmental potential. One cannot predict changes in environment which will profoundly affect the child's progress: one cannot predict illness, epilepsy or degenerative diseases of the nervous system, or other conditions which will affect his development.

26. Difficulties with Regard to the Prognosis of Infantile Spasms

Case Report.—A boy of 8 months was seen with the recent onset of the clinical picture of infantile spasms. He showed no interest in one-inch cubes or other test objects. Air studies and an electroencephalogram were carried out.

Two months later he was taking a little more interest in his surroundings, but he was sleeping nearly all the twenty-four hours every day. At 13 months he was still making no attempt to reach out for objects or to chew. I thought that he was severely mentally defective.

Two months later he had begun to hold his arm out for clothes and to wave byebye. He walked without help at 19 months, joined words together at three years, but had no sphincter control. At 43 months he had reached the level of a 24-month child.

At 69 months he had reached the level of a 60-month boy, and at seven his I.Q. score was 100.

COMMENT

It is not easy to give a confident prediction of the future in cases of infantile spasms in which there is no obvious cause, such as tuberous sclerosis, severe hypoglycaemia, or phenylketonuria. The great majority do badly, and remain defective, though some degree of improvement is usual. Occasional children, however, make an almost complete recovery. One child with this condition later had an I.Q. score of 100, but had troublesome visuospatial difficulties.

27. The Difficulty of Assessing the Effect of Acute Infections or other Disease of the Nervous System

It is impossible to predict the outcome of encephalitis, or severe meningitis, until sufficient time has elapsed to observe the rate of improvement.

The following is a remarkable case history which well illustrates the error which can be made in assessment of such a child.

Case Report.—Unexpected Recovery from State of Decerebrate Rigidity in Tuberculous Meningitis.

This girl was admitted to the Children's Hospital, Sheffield, at the age of 2 years and 5 months. The clinical and bacteriological diagnosis was tuberculous meningitis. She was drowsy and irritable on admission, and in spite of full intrathecal and intramuscular antibiotic treatment, she deteriorated progressively, until she became more and more deeply unconscious. 3 months after admission she was in deep coma, and in a state of decerebrate rigidity. There was no evidence that she could see or hear. She had bizarre movements of the limbs, bruxism, and extreme spasticity, with opisthotonos and severe emaciation. An air encephalogram showed a moderate degree of hydrocephalus. After consultation with the parents, treatment was abandoned and she went home.

She unexpectedly made remarkable improvement at home, so that 5 months after discharge it was decided to resume treatment in order to ensure that she did not relapse. She made a complete recovery, both physically and mentally.

At the age of 7½ years she weighed 84 lbs., and was 51 inches high. Her fundi, vision and hearing were normal, and there were no neurological signs. The X-ray of her skull showed calcification above the sella. Her school progress was excellent, and her I.Q. was 101. The E.E.G. remained abnormal.

COMMENT

There was every reason to give an extremely bad prognosis here, and yet she made a complete recovery. This is a perfect example of the extreme caution needed in predicting development in the early days after an attack of meningitis or encephalitis, even though at the time the future seems as black as it could be.

I gave a bad prognosis in the case described below:

Case Report.—Cerebral Venous Thrombosis with Recovery.

This boy, born at term, developed normally until 4 months, having begun to smile at 4 weeks. He then developed an upper respiratory tract infection, perspired profusely and became severely dehydrated, developing keratitis and bronchopneumonia. He was admitted with diarrhoea, vomiting and major convulsions. He passed into coma and had several further convulsions. When he emerged from coma he was spastic, with grossly exaggerated knee jerks, tightly clenched hands and opisthotonos, and took no notice of his surroundings. The cerebrospinal fluid was normal and all virus studies were negative. A diagnosis of cerebral venous thrombosis was made.

At 13 months, the boy was a bright, normal boy without any abnormality. He was walking without support, helping his mother to dress him, and saying words with meaning.

COMMENT

It was easy to give an extremely bad prognosis with regard to his subsequent development.

Case Report.—A girl aged 22 months was admitted with advanced tuberculous meningitis after unsuccessful treatment of some weeks' duration in another hospital. She was deeply unconscious, with left sided spastic hemiplegia, bilateral optic atrophy and convulsive movements on the right side of her body.

She was treated with intrathecal streptomycin, isoniazid, prednisolone and pyridoxine. She recovered consciousness, but was found to be blind. Her eyesight after two months began slowly to recover, and at the age of 4 years the vision on the right was 6/12 and on the left 6/60. A year later the vision was 6/9 on each side. The left disc remained pale, but the right disc was almost normal.

COMMENT

It is easy to give a bad prognosis in such a case, particularly with regard to eyesight. Caution should be used at all times in giving a prognosis.

28. Failure to Recognise the Difficulty of Diagnosing Mental Superiority in Infancy, and still more, the Impossibility of Predicting Future Eminence

I have said enough to indicate that the developmental quotient merely indicates how far the child has progressed in his environment, under the circumstances of his health, good or bad, and that on the basis of his D.Q., in the light of all possible factors which might have affected it or might be going to affect it, and in the light of the evidence concerning his rate of development, one makes a judicious guess as to the potentialities which he has for the future.

I am not competent to enter the numerous arguments amongst educationalists and psychologists concerning the meaning or definition of intelligence, and the significance of the intelligence quotient, particularly in relation to backwardness at school. As Stoddard[12] wrote, I.Q. tests show what the child knows, but they do not show how far he can go in pursuit of ideas, or determine his originality or ability to concentrate on his tasks.

Pidgeon and Yates[10] warned against the idea that a score on an intelligence test provides an indication of a child's inmost intellectual capacity and therefore sets a limit to the level of attainment that he can be expected to reach. They wrote: 'We can say that the child's level of attainment is likely to fall within a specified range of scores above or below the level of his intelligence test performance'.

29. Failure to Learn from Mistakes, because of Failure to Keep Proper Records, to which Reference can be and is Constantly Made

Developmental diagnosis is fraught with difficulties, and he who is over-confident, makes 'spot-diagnoses', and fails to follow up the children whom he has assessed, will inevitably make unnecessary mistakes. A really careful follow-up system is essential for anyone hoping to become proficient in this field. Mistakes made must be examined in detail, the reasons for the mistakes being determined, so that the mistake can be avoided in future.

If children are assessed for the purposes of adoption, they should be re-examined (preferably by a different person) when they are of school age, so that the accuracy and usefulness of one's assessments can be determined. If mental retardation or cerebral palsy is diagnosed in other infants, they should be followed up so that one's opinion can be confirmed or disproved. A punch card system, which enables one to determine in a moment the names of children who are due for follow-up examination, is invaluable. I also find that repeated cinematographic records of infants with suspected abnormality is useful not only for self-instruction, but for the teaching of others.

If one is to learn from mistakes, and become reasonably proficient in developmental assessment, a really adequate follow-up scheme is absolutely essential.

30. Failure to recognise the Difficulties of Developmental Prediction, and its Limitations: The Idea that Developmental Diagnosis is Easy

This is a suitable note on which to end this book. The more one learns about the subject, the more one realises what the difficulties are and how great they can be. He who thinks that developmental diagnosis is easy is making a serious mistake. Developmental diagnosis can only be made on the basis of a careful detailed history, a full developmental, neurological and physical examination, and interpretation of the results in the light of one's own experience and particularly in the light of the experience of others who have warned everyone that developmental diagnosis demands the greatest diagnostic acumen, commonsense and caution.

I was once asked to see a boy because of behaviour problems. These turned out to be due to dyslexia and allied difficulties. Two psychiatrists who had seen the boy on previous occasions had assessed his I.Q. score as 79 and 79·1 respectively.

In a clinical meeting I saw a demonstration of the treatment and results of treatment of phenylketonuria. I read the following 'The Intelligence Quotient on the . . . scale at the age of 5 weeks was 89'.

Perhaps one day such accuracy will be possible. I doubt it.

REFERENCES

1. BERKO, M. J. (1955) The Measurement of Intelligence in Children with Cerebral Palsy. The Columbia Mental Maturity Scale. *J. Pediat.*, **47**, 253.
2. CATTELL, P. (1947) *The Measurement of Intelligence of Infants and Young Children*. New York: The Psychological Corporation.
3. CHARLES, D. C. (1953) Ability and Accomplishment of Persons Earlier Judged Mentally Deficient. *Genet. Psychol. Monogr.*, **47**, 3.
4. GESELL, A., AMATRUDA, C. S., CASTNER, B. M., THOMPSON, H. (1939) *Biographies of Child Development*. London: Hamish Hamilton.
5. GESELL, A., THOMPSON, H. (1938) *The Psychology of Early Growth*. New York: Macmillan.
6. GRIFFITHS, R. (1954) *The Abilities of Babies*. London: Univ. of London Press.
7. HAEUSSERMANN, E. (1958) *Developmental Potential of Preschool Children*. London: Grune and Stratton.
8. HALLOWELL, D. K. (1941) Validity of Mental Tests for Young Children. *J. genet. Psychol.*, **58**, 265.
9. PERLSTEIN, M. (1950) Neurologic Sequelae of Erythroblastosis Fetalis. *Amer. J. Dis. Child.*, **79**, 605.
10. PIDGEON, D. A., YATES, A. (1957) Ability and Attainment. *Bull. Nat. Found. Educ. Res.* No. 10. 22.
11. SAFIAN, D., HARMS, E. (1948) Social and Educational Impairment Wrongly Diagnosed. *Nerv. Child*, **7**, 416.
12. STODDARD, A. D. S. (1943) *The Meaning of Intelligence*. New York: Macmillan.

INDEX